the discovery of the source of the Nile

JOHN HANNING SPEKE

WHITE STAR
PUBLISHERS

Graphic Design
PATRIZIA BALOCCO LOVISETTI

Via Candido Sassone, 22/24
13100 Vercelli, Italia
www.whitestar.it

ISBN 88-544-0177-3

Printed by G. Canale & C., Torino, Italy

Excerpts from John Hanning Speke, *Journal of the Discovery of the Source of the Nile*, William Blackwood and Sons, Edinburgh and London 1864

Artworks drawn from
Grant e Speke, *Viaggio alle sorgenti del Nilo,*
Serafino Muggiani e Comp., Milan 1878;
John Hanning Speke, *Journal of the Discovery of the Source of the Nile*,
William Blackwood and Sons, Edinburgh and London 1864

The explorers Speke and Grant.

4

CONTENTS

In the following pages I have endeavoured to describe all that appeared to me most important and interesting among the events and the scenes that came under my notice during my sojourn in the interior of Africa. If my account should not entirely harmonise with preconceived notions as to primitive races, I cannot help it. I profess accurately to describe native Africa – Africa in those places where it has not received the slightest impulse, whether for good or evil, from European civilisation. If the picture be a dark one, we should, when contemplating these sons of Noah, try and carry our mind back to that time when our poor elder brother Ham was cursed by his father, and condemned to be the slave of both Shem and Japheth; for as they were then, so they appear to be now – a strikingly existing proof of the Holy Scriptures. But one thing must be remembered: Whilst the people of Europe and Asia were blessed by communion with God through the medium of His prophets, and obtained divine laws to regulate their ways and keep them in mind of Him who made them, the Africans were excluded from this dispensation, and consequently have no idea of an overruling Providence or a future state; they therefore trust to luck and to charms, and think only of self-preservation in this world. Whatever, then, may be said against them for being too avaricious or too destitute of fellow-feeling, should rather reflect on our-selves, who have been so much better favoured, yet have neglected to teach them, than on those who, whilst they are sinning, know not what they are doing. To say a negro is incapable of instruction, is a mere absurdity; for those few boys who have been educated in our schools have proved themselves even quicker than our own at learning; whilst, amongst themselves, the deepness of their cunning and their power of repartee are quite surprising, and are especially shown in their proficiency for telling lies most appropriately in preference to truth, and with an off-handed manner that makes them most amusing.

With these remarks, I now give, as an appropriate introduction to my narrative – (1.) An account of the general geographical features of the countries we are about to travel in, leaving the details to be treated under each as we successively pass through them; (2.) A general view of the atmospheric agents which wear down and so continually help to reduce the continent, yet at the same time assist to clothe it with vegetation; (3.) A general view of the Flora; and, lastly, that which consumes it, (4.) Its Fauna; ending with a few special remarks on the Wanguana, or men freed from slavery.

Geography

The continent of Africa is something like a dish turned upside down, having a high and flat central plateau, with a higher rim of hills surrounding it, from below which, exterially, it suddenly slopes down to the flat strip of land bordering on the sea. A dish, however, is generally uniform in shape – Africa is not. For instance, we find in its centre a high group of hills surrounding the head of the Tanganyika Lake, composed chiefly of argillaceous sandstones which I suppose to be the Lunae Montes of Ptolemy, or the Soma Giri of the ancient Hindus. Further, instead of a rim at the northern end, the country shelves down from the equator to the Mediterranean Sea; and on the general surface of the interior plateau there are basins full of water (lakes), from which, when rains overflow them, rivers are formed, that, cutting through the flanking rim of hills, find their way to the sea.

Atmospheric Agents

On the east coast, near Zanzibar, we find the rains following the track of the sun, and lasting not more than forty days on any part that the sun crosses; whilst the winds blow from southwest or north-east, towards the regions heated by its vertical position. But in the centre of the continent, within 5° of the equator, we find the rains much more lasting. For instance, at 5° south latitude, for the whole six months that the sun is in the south, rain continues to fall, and I have heard that the same takes place at 5° north; whilst on the equator, or rather a trifle to northward of it, it rains more or less the whole year round, but most at the equinoxes, as shown in the table on the following page. The winds, though somewhat less steady, are still very determinable. With an easterly tending, they deflect north and south, following the sun. In the drier season they blow so cold that the sun's heat is not distressing; and in consequence of this, at the average altitude of the plateau, which is 3000 feet, the general temperature of the atmosphere is very pleasant, as I found from experience, for I walked every inch of the journey

11

dressed in thick woollen clothes, and slept every night between blankets.

The number of days on which rain fell (more or less) during the march of the East African Expedition from Zanzibar to Gondokoro:

Days on which rain fell

1860			1861		1862	
***	***	January	19	January	14
***	***	February	21	February[1]	12
***	***	March	17	March	21
***	***	April	17	April	27
***	***	May	3	May	26
***	***	June	0	June	20
***	***	July	1	July	22
***	***	August	1	August	20
***	***	September	9	September	18
October	2	October	11	October	27
November	0	November	17	November	20
December	20	December	16	December	6

Flora

From what has been said regarding the condition of the atmosphere, it may readily be imagined that Africa, in those parts, after all, is not so bad as people supposed it was; for, when so much moisture falls under a vertical sun, all vegetable life must grow up almost spontaneously. It does so on the equator in the most profuse manner; but down at 5° south, where there are six months' drought, the case is somewhat different; and the people would be subject to famines if they did not take advantage of their rainy season to lay in sufficient stores for the fine: and here we touch on the misfortune of the country; for the negro is too lazy to do so effectively, owing chiefly, as we shall see presently, to want of a strong protecting government. One substantial fact has been established, owing to our having crossed over ten degrees of latitude in the centre of the continent, or from 5° south to 5° north latitude, which is this: There exists a regular gradation of fertility, surprisingly rich on the equator, but decreasing systematically from it; and the reason why this great fertile zone is confined to the equatorial regions, is the same as that which has constituted it the great focus of water or lake supply, whence issue the principal rivers of Africa. On the equator lie the rain-bearing influences of the Mountains of the Moon. The equatorial line is, in fact, the centre of atmospheric motion.

Fauna

In treating of this branch of natural history, we will first take man – the true curly-head, flab-nosed, pouch-mouthed negro – not the Wahuma.[2] They are well distributed all over these latitudes, but are not found anywhere in dense communities. Their system of government is mostly of the patriarchal character. Some are pastorals, but most are agriculturalists; and this difference, I believe, originates solely from want of a stable government, to enable them to reap what they produce; for where the negro can save his cattle, which is his wealth, by eating grain, he will do it. In the same way as all animals, whether wild or tame, require a guide to lead their flocks, so do the negroes find it necessary to have chiefs over their villages and little com-

13

munities, who are their referees on all domestic or political questions. They have both their district and their village chiefs, but, in the countries we are about to travel over, no kings such as we shall find that the Wahuma have. The district chief is absolute, though guided in great measure by his "grey-beards," who constantly attend his residence, and talk over their affairs of state. These commonly concern petty internal matters; for they are too selfish and too narrow-minded to care for anything but their own private concerns. The grey-beards circulate the orders of the chief amongst the village chiefs, who are fined when they do not comply with them; and hence all orders are pretty well obeyed.

One thing only tends to disorganise the country, and that is war, caused, in the first instance, by polygamy, producing a family of half-brothers, who, all aspiring to succeed their father, fight continually with one another, and make their chief aim slaves and cattle; whilst, in the second instance, slavery keeps them ever fighting and reducing their numbers. The government revenues are levied, on a very small scale, exclusively for the benefit of the chief and his grey-beards. For instance, as a sort of land-tax, the chief has a right to drink free from the village brews of pombe (a kind of beer made by fermentation), which are made in turn by all the villagers successively. In case of an elephant being killed, he also takes a share of the meat, and claims one of its tusks as his right; further, all leopard, lion, or zebra skins are his by right. On merchandise brought into the country by traders, he has a general right to make any exactions he thinks he has the power of enforcing, without any regard to justice or a regulated tariff. This right is called Hongo, in the plural Mahongo. Another source of revenue is in the effects of all people condemned for sorcery, who are either burnt, or speared and cast into the jungles, and their property seized by the grey-beards for their chief.

As to punishments, all irreclaimable thieves or murderers are killed and disposed of in the same manner as these sorcerers; whilst on minor thieves a penalty equivalent to the extent of the depredation is levied. Illicit intercourse being treated as petty larceny, a value is fixed according to the value of the woman – for it must be remembered all women are property. Indeed, marriages are considered a very profitable speculation, the girl's hand being in the father's gift, who marries her to any one who will pay her price. This arrangement, however, is not considered a simple matter of buying and selling, but delights in the high-sounding title of "dowry." Slaves, cows, goats, fowls, brass wire, or beads, are the usual things given for this species of dowry. The marriage-knot, however, is never irretrievably tied; for if the wife finds a defect in her husband, she can return to her father by refunding the dowry; whilst the husband, if he objects to his wife, can claim half-price on sending her home again, which is considered fair, because as a second-hand article her future value would be diminished by half. By this system, it must be observed, polygamy is a source of wealth, since a man's means are measured by the number of his progeny; but it has other advantages besides the dowry, for the women work more than the men do, both in and out of doors; and, in addition to the females, the sons work for the household until they marry, and in after life take care of their parents in the same way as in the first instance the parents took care of them.

Twins are usually hailed with delight, because they swell the power of the family, though in some instances they are put to death. Albinos are valued, though their colour is not admired. If death occurs in a natural manner, the body is usually either buried in the village or outside. A large portion of the negro races affect nudity, despising clothing as effeminate; but these are chiefly the more boisterous roving pastorals, who are too lazy either to grow cotton or strip the trees of their bark. Their young women go naked; but the mothers suspend a little tail both before and behind. As the hair of the negro will not grow long, a barber might be dispensed with, were it not that they delight in odd fashions, and are therefore continually either shaving it off altogether, or else fashioning it after the most whimsical designs. No people in the world are so proud and headstrong as the negroes, whether they be pastoral or agriculturalists. With them, as with the rest of the world, "familiarity breeds contempt"; hospitality lives only one day; for though proud of a rich or white visitor – and they implore him to stop, that they may keep feeding their eyes on his curiosities – they seldom give more than a cow or a goat, though professing to supply a whole camp with provisions.

Taking the negroes as a whole, one does not find very marked or much difference in them. Each tribe has its characteristics, it is true. For instance, one cuts his teeth or tattoos his face in a different manner from the others; but by the constant intermarriage with slaves, much of this effect is lost, and it is further lost sight of owing to the prevalence of migrations caused by wars and the division of governments. As with the tribal marks so with their weapons; those most commonly in use are the spear, assage, shield, bow and arrow. It is true some affect one, some the other; but in no way do we see that the courage of tribes can be determined by the use of any particular weapon: for the bravest use the arrow, which is the more dreaded; while the weakest confine themselves to the spear. Lines of traffic are the worst tracks (there are no roads in the districts here referred to) for a traveller to go upon, not only because the hospitality of the people has been damped by frequent communication with travellers, but, by intercourse with the semi-civilised merchant, their natural honour and honesty are corrupted, their cupidity is increased, and the show of firearms ceases to frighten them.

Of paramount consideration is the power held by the magician (Mganga), who rules the minds of the kings as did the old popes of Europe. They, indeed, are a curse to the traveller; for if it suits their inclinations to keep him out of the country, they have merely to prognosticate all sorts of calamities – as droughts, famines, or wars – in the event of his setting eyes on the soil, and the chiefs, people, and all, would believe them; for, as may be imagined, with men unenlightened, supernatural and imaginary predictions work with more force than substantial reasons. Their implement of divination, simple as it may appear, is a cow's or antelope's horn (Uganga), which they stuff with magic powder, also called Uganga. Stuck into the ground in front of the village, it is supposed to have sufficient power to ward off the attacks of an enemy.

By simply holding it in the hand, the magician pretends he can discover anything that has been stolen or lost; and instances have been told of its dragging four men after it with irresistible impetus up to a thief, when it be-laboured the culprit and drove him out of his senses. So imbued are the natives' minds with belief in the power of charms, that they pay the magician for sticks, stones, or mud, which he has doctored for them. They believe certain flowers held in the hand will conduct them to anything lost; as also that the voice of certain wild animals, birds, or beasts, will insure them good-luck, or warn them of danger. With the utmost complacency our sable brother builds a dwarf hut in his fields, and places some grain on it to propitiate the evil spirit, and suffer him to reap the fruits of his labour, and this too they call Uganga or church.

These are a few of the more innocent alternatives the poor negroes resort to in place of a "Saviour." They have also many other and more horrible devices. For instance, in times of tribulation, the magician, if he ascertains a war is projected by inspecting the blood and bones of a fowl which he has flayed for that purpose, flays a young child, and having laid it lengthwise on a path, directs all the warriors, on proceeding to battle, to step over his sacrifice and insure themselves victory. Another of these extra barbarous devices takes place when a chief wishes to make war on his neighbour by his calling in a magician to discover a propitious time for commencing. The doctor places a large earthen vessel, half full of water, over a fire, and over its mouth a grating of sticks, whereon he lays a small child and a fowl side by side, and covers them over with a second large earthen vessel, just like the first, only inverted, to keep the steam in, when he sets fire below, cooks for a certain period of time, and then looks to see if his victims are still living or dead – when, should they be dead, the war must be deferred, but, otherwise commenced at once.

These extremes, however, are not often resorted to, for the natives are usually content with simpler means, such as flaying a goat, instead of a child, to be walked over; while, to prevent any evil approaching their dwellings, a squashed frog, or any other such absurdity, when place on the track, is considered a specific.

How the negro has lived so many ages without advancing, seems marvellous, when all the countries surrounding Africa are so forward in comparison; and judging from the progressive state of the world, one is led to suppose that the African must soon either step out from his darkness, or be superseded by a being superior to himself. Could a government be formed for them like ours in India, they would be saved; but without it, I fear there is very little chance; for at present the African neither can help himself nor will he be helped about by others, because his country is in such a constant state of turmoil he has too much anxiety on hand looking out for his food to think of anything else. As his fathers ever did, so does he. He works his wife, sells his children, enslaves all he can lay hands upon, and, unless when fighting for the property of others, contents himself with drinking, singing, and dancing like a baboon to drive dull care away. A few only make cotton cloth, or work in wood, iron, copper, or salt; their rule being to do as little as possible, and to store up nothing beyond the necessities of the next season, lest their chiefs or neighbours should covet and take it from them.

Slavery, I may add, is one great cause of laziness, for the masters become too proud to work, lest they should be thought slaves themselves. In consequence of this, the women look after the household work – such as brewing, cooking, grinding corn, making pottery and baskets, and taking care of the house and the children, besides helping the slaves whilst cultivating, or even tending the cattle sometimes.

Now, descending to the inferior order of creation, I shall commence with the domestic animals first, to show what the traveller may expect to find for his usual support. Cows, after leaving the low lands near the coast, are found to be plentiful everywhere, and to produce milk in small quantities, from which butter is made. Goats are common all over Africa; but sheep are not so plentiful, nor do they show such good breeding – being generally lanky, with long fat tails. Fowls, much like those in India, are abundant everywhere. A few Muscovy ducks are imported, also pigeons and cats. Dogs, like the Indian pariah, are very plentiful, only much smaller; and a few donkeys are found in certain localities. Now, considering this good supply of meat, whilst all tropical plants will grow just as well in central equatorial Africa as they do in India, it surprises the traveller there should be any famines; yet such is too often the case, and the negro, with these bounties within his reach, is sometimes found eating dogs, cats, rats, porcupines, snakes, lizards, tortoises, locusts, and white ants, or is forced to seek the seeds of wild grasses, or to pluck wild herbs, fruits, and roots; whilst at the proper seasons they hunt the wild elephant, buffalo, giraffe, zebra, pigs, and antelopes; or, going out with their arrows, have battues against the guinea-fowls and small birds.

The frequency with which collections of villages are found all over the countries we are alluding to, leaves but very little scope for the runs of wild animals, which are found only in dense jungles, open forests, or praires generally speaking, where hills can protect them, and near rivers whose marshes produce a thick growth of vegetation to conceal them from their most dreaded enemy – man. The prowling, restless elephant, for instance, though rarely seen, leaves indications of his nocturnal excursions in every wilderness, by wantonly knocking down the forest-trees. The morose rhinoceros, though less numerous, are found in every thick jungle. So is the savage buffalo, especially delighting in dark places, where he can wallow in the mud and slake his thirst without much trouble; and here also we find the wild pig.

The gruff hippopotamus is as widespread as any, being found wherever there is water to float him; whilst the shy giraffe and zebra affect all open forests and plains where the grass is not too long; and antelopes, of great variety in species and habits, are found wherever man will let them alone and they can find water. The lion is, however, rarely heard – much more seldom seen. Hyenas are numerous, and thievishly inclined. Leopards, less common, are the terror of the villagers. Foxes are not numerous, but frighten the black traveller by their ill-omened bark. Hares, about half the size of English ones – there are no rabbits – are widely spread, but not numerous; porcupines the same. Wild cats, and animals of the ferret kind, destroy game. Monkeys of various kinds and squirrels harbour in the trees, but are rarely seen. Tortoises and snakes, in great variety, crawl over the ground, mostly after the rains. Rats and lizards – there are but few mice – are very abundant, and feed both in the fields and on the stores of the men.

The wily ostrich, bustard, and florikan affect all open places. The guinea-fowl is the most numerous of all game-birds. Par-

21

tridges come next, but do not afford good sport; and quails are rare. Ducks and snipe appear to love Africa less than any other country; and geese and storks are only found where water most abounds. Vultures are uncommon; hawks and crows much abound, as in all other countries; but little birds, of every colour and note, are discoverable in great quantities near water and by the villages. Huge snails and small ones, as well as fresh-water shells, are very abundant, though the conchologist would find but little variety to repay his labours; and insects, though innumerable, are best sought for after the rains have set in.[3] The Wanguana (Wa-n-guana) or Freed Men, as their name implies, are men freed from slavery; and as it is to these singular negroes acting as hired servants that I have been chiefly indebted for opening this large section of Africa, a few general remarks on their character cannot be out of place here.

Of course, having been born in Africa, and associated in childhood with the untainted negroes, they retain all the superstitious notions of the true aborigines, though somewhat modified, and even corrupted, by that acquaintance with the outer world which sharpens their wits.

Most of these men were doubtless caught in wars, as may be seen every day in Africa, made slaves of and sold to the Arabs for a few yards of common cloth, brass wire, or beads. They would then be taken to the Zanzibar market, resold like horses to the highest bidder, and then kept in bondage by their new masters, more like children of his family than anything else. In this new position they were circumcised to make Mussulmans of them, that their hands might be "clean" to slaughter their master's cattle, and extend his creed; for the Arabs believe the day must come when the tenets of Mohammed will be accepted by all men.

The slave in this new position finds himself much better off than he ever was in his life before, with this exception, that as a slave he feels himself much degraded in the social scale of society, and his family ties are all cut off from him – probably his relations have all been killed in the war in which he was captured. Still, after the first qualms have worn off, we find him much attached to his master, who feeds him and finds him in clothes in return for the menial services which he performs. In a few years after capture, or when confidence has been gained by the attachment shown by the slave, if the master is a trader in ivory, he will intrust him with the charge of his stores, and send him all over the interior of the continent to purchase for him both slaves and ivory; but should the master die, according to the Mohammedan creed the slaves ought to be freed. In Arabia this would be the case; but at Zanzibar it more generally happens that the slave is willed to his successor.

The whole system of slaveholding by the Arabs in Africa, or rather on the coast or at Zanzibar, is exceedingly strange; for the slaves, both in individual physical strength and in numbers, are so superior to the Arab foreigners, that if they chose to rebel, they might send the Arabs flying out of the land. It happens, however, that they are spell-bound, not knowing their strength any more than domestic animals, and they even seem to consider that they would be dishonest if they ran away after being purchased, and so brought pecuniary loss on their owners.

There are many positions into which the slave may get by the course of events, and I shall give here, as a specimen, the ordinary case of one who has been freed by the death of his master, that master having been a trader in ivory and slaves in the interior. In such a case, the slave so freed in all probability would commence life afresh by taking service as a porter with other merchants, and in the end would raise sufficient capital to commence trading himself – first in slaves, because they are the most easily got, and then in ivory. All his accumulations would then go to the Zanzibar market, or else to slavers looking out off the coast. Slavery begets slavery. To catch slaves is the first thought of every chief in the interior; hence fights and slavery impoverish the land, and that is the reason both why Africa does not improve, and why we find men of all tribes and tongues on the coast. The ethnologist need only go to Zanzibar to become acquainted with all the different tribes to the centre of the continent on that side, or to Congo to find the other half south of the equator there.

Some few freed slaves take service in vessels, of which they are especially fond; but most return to Africa to trade in slaves and ivory. All slaves learn the coast language, called at Zanzibar Kisuahili; and therefore the traveller, if judicious in his selections, could find there interpreters to carry him throughout the eastern half of South Africa. To the north of the equator the system of language entirely changes.

Laziness is inherent in these men, for which reason, although extremely powerful, they will not work unless compelled to do so.

Having no God, in the Christian sense of the term, to fear or worship, they have no love for truth, honour, or honesty.

Controlled by no government, nor yet by home ties, they have no reason to think of or look to the future. Any venture attracts them when hard-up for food; and the more roving it is, the better they like it. The life of the sailor is most particularly attractive to the freed slave; for he thinks, in his conceit, that he is on an equality with all men when once on the muster-rolls, and then he calls all his fellow-Africans "savages." Still the African's peculiarity sticks to him: he has gained no permanent good. The association of white men and the glitter of money merely dazzle him. He apes like a monkey the jolly Jack Tar, and spends his wages accordingly. If chance brings him back again to Zanzibar, he calls his old Arab master his father, and goes into slavery with as much zest as ever.

I have spoken of these freed men as if they had no religion. This is practically true, though theoretically not so; for the Arabs, on circumcising them, teach them to repeat the words Allah and Mohammed, and perhaps a few others; but not one in ten knows what a soul means, nor do they expect to meet with either reward or punishment in the next world, though they are taught to regard animals as clean and unclean, and some go through the form of a pilgrimage to Mecca. Indeed the whole of their spiritual education goes into oaths and ejaculations – Allah and Mohammed being as common in their mouths as damn and blast are with our soldiers and sailors. The long and short of this story is, that the freed men generally turn out a loose, roving, reckless set of beings, quick-witted as the Yankee, from the simple fact that they imagine all political matters affect them, and therefore they must have a word in every debate. Nevertheless they are seldom wise; and lying being more familiar to their constitution than truth-saying, they are for ever concocting dodges with the view, which they glory in, of successfully cheating people. Sometimes they will show great kindness, even bravery amounting to heroism, and proportionate affection; at another time, without any cause, they will desert and be treacherous to their sworn friends in the most dastardly manner. Whatever the freak of the moment is, that they adopt in the most thoughtless manner, even though they may have calculated on advantages beforehand in the opposite direction. In fact, no one can rely upon them even for a moment. Dog wit, or any silly remarks, will set them giggling. Any toy will amuse them. Highly conceited of their personal appearance, they are for ever cutting their hair in different fashions, to surprise a friend; or if a rag be thrown away, they will all in turn fight for it to bind on their heads, then on their loins or spears, peacocking about with it before their admiring comrades. Even strange feathers or skins are treated by them in the same way.

Should one happen to have anything specially to communicate to his master in camp, he will enter giggling, sidle up to the pole of a hut, commence scratching his back with it, then stretch and yawn, and gradually, in bursts of loud laughter, slip down to the ground on his stern, when he drums with his hands on the top of a box until summoned to know what he has at heart, when he delivers himself in a peculiar manner, laughs and yawns again, and, saying it is time to go, walks off in the same way as he came. At other times when he is called, he will come sucking away at the spout of a tea-pot, or, scratching his naked arm-pits with a table-knife, or, perhaps, polishing the plates for dinner with his dirty loin-cloth. If sent to market to purchase a fowl, he comes back with a cock tied by the legs to the end of a stick, swinging and squalling in the most piteous manner. Then, arrived at the cook-shop, he throws the bird down on the ground, holds its head between his toes, plucks the feathers to bare its throat, and then, raising a prayer, cuts its head off.

But enough of the freed man in camp; on the march he is no better. If you give him a gun and some ammunition to protect him in case of emergencies, he will promise to save it, but forthwith expends it by firing it off in the air, and demands more, else he will fear to venture amongst the "savages." Suppose you give him a box of bottles to carry, or a desk, or anything else that requires great care, and you caution him of its contents, the first thing he does is to commence swinging it round and round, or putting it topsy-turvy on the top of his head, when he will run off at a jog-trot, singing and laughing in the most provoking manner, and thinking no more about it than if it were an old stone; even if rain were falling, he would put it in the best place to get wet through. Economy, care, or forethought never enters his head; the first thing to hand is the right thing for him; and rather then take the trouble even to look for his own rope to tie up his bundle, he would cut off his master's tent-ropes or steal his comrade's. His greatest delight is in the fair sex, and when he can't get them, next comes beer, song, and a dance.

Now, this is a mild specimen of the "rowdy" negro, who has contributed more to open Africa to enterprise and civilisation than any one else. Possessed of a wonderful amount of loquacity, great risibility, but no stability – a creature of impulse – a grown child, in short – at first sight it seems wonderful how he can be trained to work; for there is no law, no home to bind him – he could run away at any moment; and presuming on this, he sins, expecting to be forgiven. Great forbearance, occasionally tinctured with a little fatherly severity, is I believe, the best dose for him; for he says to his master, in the most childish manner, after sinning, "You ought to forgive and to forget; for are you not a big man who should be above harbouring spite, though for a moment you may be angry? Flog me if you like, but don't keep count against me, else I shall run away; and what will you do then?" The language of this people is just as strange as they are themselves. It is based on euphony, from which cause it is very complex, the more especially so as it requires one to be possessed of a negro's turn of mind to appreciate the system, and unravel the secret of its euphonic concord. A Kisuahili grammar, written by Dr. Krapf, will exemplify what I mean. There is one peculiarity, however, to which I would direct the attention of the reader most particularly, which is, that Wa prefixed to the essential word of a country, means men or people; M prefixed, means man or individual; U, in the same way, means place or locality; and Ki prefixed indicates the language. Example: – Wagogo, is the people of Gogo; Mgogo, is a Gogo man; Ugogo, is the country of Gogo; and Kigogo, the language of Gogo.

The only direction here necessary as regards pronunciation of native words refers to the *u*, which represents a sound corresponding to that of the *oo* in *woo*.

1) The equator was crossed on the 8th February 1862.

2) The Wahuma are treated of in Chapter IX.

3) The list of my fauna collection will be found in an early number of the "Proceedings of the Zoological Society of London."

CHAPTER 1

LONDON TO ZANZIBAR, 1859

The Design – The Preparations – Departure – The Cape – The Zulu Kafirs – Turtle-Turning – Capture of a Slaver – Arrive at Zanzibar – Local Politics and News Since Last Visit – Organisation of the Expedition.

My third expedition in Africa, which was avowedly for the purpose of establishing the truth of my assertion that the Victoria N'yanza, which I discovered on the 30th July 1858, would eventually prove to be the source of the Nile, may be said to have commenced on the 9th May 1859, the first day after my return to England from my second expedition, when, at the invitation of Sir R. I. Murchison, I called at his house to show him my map for the information of the Royal Geographical Society. Sir Roderick, I need only say, at once accepted my views; and, knowing my ardent desire to prove to the world, by actual inspection of the exit, that the Victoria N'yanza was the source of the Nile, seized the enlightened view, that such a discovery should not be lost to the glory of England and the Society of which he was President; and said to me, "Speke, we must send you there again." I was then officially directed, much against my own inclination, to lecture at the Royal Geographical Society on the geography of Africa, which I had, as the sole surveyor of the second expedition, laid down on our maps.[1] A council of the Geographical Society was now convened to ascertain what projects I had in view for making good my discovery by connecting the lake with the Nile, as also what assistance I should want for that purpose.

Some thought my best plan would be to go up the Nile, which seemed to them the natural course to pursue, especially as the Nile was said, though nobody believed it, to have been navigated by expeditions sent out by Mehemet Ali, Viceroy of Egypt, up to 3° 22' north latitude. To this I objected, as so many had tried it and failed, from reasons which had not transpired; and, at the same time, I said that if they would give me $5,000 down at once, I would return to Zanzibar at the end of the year, March to Kaze again, and make the necessary investigations of the Victoria lake. Although, in addition to the journey to the source of the river, I also proposed spending three years in the country, looking up tributaries, inspecting watersheds, navigating the lake, and making collections on all branches of natural history, yet $5,000 was thought by the Geographical Society too large a sum to expect from the Government; so I accepted the half, saying that, whatever the expedition might cost, I would make good the rest, as, under any circumstances, I would complete what I had begun, or die in the attempt.

My motive for deferring the journey a year was the hope that I might, in the meanwhile, send on fifty men, carrying beads and brass wire, under charge of Arab ivory-traders, to Karague, and fifty men more, in the same way, to Kaze; whilst I, arriving in the best season for travelling (May, June, or July), would be able to push on expeditiously to my depots so formed, and thus escape the great disadvantages of travelling with a large caravan in a country where no laws prevail to protect one against desertions and theft. Moreover, I knew that the negroes who would have to go with me, as long as they believed I had property in advance, would work up to it willingly, as they would be the gainers by doing so; whilst, with nothing before them, they would be always endeavouring to thwart my advance, to save them from a trouble which their natural laziness would prompt them to escape from.

This beautiful project, I am sorry to say, was doomed from the first; for I did not get the $2,500 grant of money or appointment to the command until fully nine months had elapsed, when I wrote to Colonel Rigby, our Consul at Zanzibar, to send on the first instalment of property towards the interior.

As time then advanced, the Indian branch of the Government very graciously gave me fifty artillery carbines, with belts and sword-bayonets attached, and 20,000 rounds of ball ammunition.

They lent me as many surveying instruments as I wanted; and, through Sir George Clerk, put at my disposal some rich presents, in gold watches, for the chief Arabs who had so generously assisted us in the last expedition. Captain Grant, hearing that I was bound on this journey, being an old friend and brother sportsman in India, asked me to take him with me, and his appointment was settled by Colonel Sykes, then chairman of a committee of the Royal Geographical Society, who said it would only be "a matter of charity" to allow me a companion.

Much at the same time, Mr. Petherick, an ivory merchant, who had spent many years on the Nile, arrived in England, and

31

gratuitously offered, as it would not interfere with his trade, to place boats at Gondokoro, and send a party of men up the White River to collect ivory in the meanwhile, and eventually to assist me in coming down. Mr. Petherick, I may add, showed great zeal for geographical exploits, so, as I could not get money enough to do all that I wished to accomplish myself, I drew out a project for him to ascend the stream now known as the Usua river (reported to be the larger branch of the Nile), and, if possible, ascertain what connection it had with my lake. This being agreed to, I did my best, through the medium of Earl de Grey (then President of the Royal Geographical Society), to advance him money to carry out this desirable object.

The last difficulty I had now before me was to obtain a passage to Zanzibar. The Indian Government had promised me a vessel of war to convey me from Aden to Zanzibar, provided it did not interfere with the public interests. This doubtful proviso induced me to apply to Captain Playfair, Assistant-Political at Aden, to know what Government vessel would be available; and should there be none, to get for me a passage by some American trader. The China war, he assured me, had taken up all the Government vessels, and there appeared no hope left for me that season, as the last American trader was just then leaving for Zanzibar. In this dilemma it appeared that I must inevitably lose the travelling season, and come in for the droughts and famines. The tide, however, turned in my favour a little; for I obtained, by permission of the Admiralty, a passage in the British screw steam-frigate *Forte*, under orders to convey Admiral Sir H. Keppel to his command at the Cape; and Sir Charles Wood most obligingly made a request that I should be forwarded thence to Zanzibar in one of our slaver-hunting cruisers by the earliest opportunity.

On the 27th April, Captain Grant and I embarked on board the new steam-frigate *Forte*, commanded by Captain E. W. Turnour, at Portsmouth; and after a long voyage, touching at Madeira and Rio de Janeiro, we arrived at the Cape of Good Hope on the 4th July.

Here Sir George Grey, the Governor of the colony, who took a warm and enlightened interest in the cause of the expedition, invited both Grant and myself to reside at his house. Sir George had been an old explorer himself – was once wounded by savages in Australia, much in the same manner as I had been in the Somali country – and, with a spirit of sympathy, he called me his son, and said he hoped I would succeed. Then, thinking how best he could serve me, he induced the Cape Parliament to advance to the expedition a sum of $300, for the purpose of buying baggage-mules; and induced Lieut.-General Wynyard, the Commander-in-Chief, to detach ten volunteers from the Cape Mounted Rifle Corps to accompany me. When this addition was made to my force, of twelve mules and ten Hottentots, the Admiral of the station placed the screw steam-corvette *Brisk* at my disposal, and we all sailed for Zanzibar on the 16th July, under the command of Captain A. F. de Horsey – the Admiral himself accompanying us, on one of his annual inspections to visit the east coast of Africa and the Mauritius. In five days more we touched at East London, and, thence proceeding north, made a short stay at Delagoa Bay, where I first became acquainted with the Zulu Kafirs, a naked set of negroes, whose national costume principally consists in having their hair trussed up like a hoop on the top of the head, and an appendage like a thimble, to which they attach a mysterious importance. They wear additional ornaments, charms, &c., of birds' claws, hoofs and horns of wild animals tied on with strings, and sometimes an article like a kilt, made of loose strips of skin, or the entire skins of vermin strung close together. These things I have merely noticed in passing, because I shall hereafter have occasion to allude to a migratory people, the Watuta, who dressing much in the same manner, extend from Lake N'yassa to Uzinza, and may originally have been a part of this same Kafir race, who are themselves supposed to have migrated from the regions at present occupied by the Gallas. Next day (the 28th) we went on to Europa, a small island of coralline, covered with salsolacious shrubs, and tenanted only by sea-birds, owls, finches, rats, and turtles. Of the last we succeeded in turning three, the average weight of each being 360 lb., and we took large numbers of their eggs.

We then went to Mozambique, and visited the Portuguese Governor, John Travers de Almeida, who showed considerable interest in the prospects of the expedition, and regretted that, as it cost so much money to visit the interior from that place, his officers were unable to go there. One experimental trip only had been accomplished by Mr. Soares, who was forced to pay the Makua chiefs $120 footing, to reach a small hill in view of the sea, about twenty-five miles off.

Leaving Mozambique on the 9th August, bound for Johanna, we came the next day, at 11:30 A.M., in sight of a slaver, ship-rigged, bearing on us full sail, but so distant from us that her mast-tops were only just visible. As quick as ourselves, she saw who we were and tried to escape by retreating. This manoeuvre left no doubt what she was, and the *Brisk*, all full of excitement, gave chase at full speed, and in four hours more drew abreast of her. A great commotion ensued on board the slaver. The sea-pirates threw overboard their colours, bags, and numerous boxes, but would not heave-to, although repeatedly challenged, until a gun was fired across her bows. Our boats were then lowered, and in a few minutes more the "prize" was taken, by her crew being exchanged for some of our men, and we learnt all about her from accurate reports furnished by Mr. Frere, the Cape Slave Commissioner. Cleared from Havannah as the *Sunny South*, professing to be destined for Hong-Kong, she changed her name to the *Manuela*, and came slave-hunting in these regions. The slaver's crew consisted of a captain, doctor, and several sailors, mostly Spaniards. The vessel was well stored with provisions and medicines; but there was scarcely enough room in her, though she was said to be only half freighted, for the 544 creatures they were transporting. The next morning, as we entered Pamoni harbour by an intricate approach to the rich little island hill Johanna, the slaver, as she followed us, stranded, and for a while caused considerable alarm to everybody but her late captain. He thought his luck very bad, after escaping so often, to be taken thus; for his vessel's power of sailing were so good, that, had she had the wind in her favour, the *Brisk*, even with the assistance of steam, could not have come up with her. On going on board her, I found the slaves to be mostly Wahiyow. A few of them were old women, but all the rest children. They had been captured during wars in their own country, and sold to Arabs, who brought them to the coast, and kept them half-

35

starved until the slaver arrived, when they were shipped in dhows and brought off to the slaver, where, for nearly a week, whilst the bargains were in progress, they were kept entirely without food. It was no wonder then, every man of the *Brisk* who first looked upon them did so with a feeling of loathing and abhorrence of such a trade. All over the vessel, but more especially below, old women, stark naked, were dying in the most disgusting "ferret-box" atmosphere; while all those who had sufficient strength were pulling up the hatches, and tearing at the salt fish they found below, like dogs in a kennel.

On the 15th the *Manuela* was sent to the Mauritius, and we, after passing the Comoro Islands, arrived at our destination, Zanzibar – called Lunguja by the aborigines, the Wakhadim – and Unguja by the present Wasuahili.

On the 17th, after the anchor was cast, without a moment's delay I went off to the British Consulate to see my old friend Colonel Rigby. He was delighted to see us; and, in anticipation of our arrival, had prepared rooms for our reception, that both Captain Grant and myself might enjoy his hospitality until arrangements could be made for our final start into the interior. The town, which I had left in so different a condition sixteen months before, was in a state of great tranquillity, brought about by the energy of the Bombay Government on the Muscat side, and Colonel Rigby's exertions on this side, in preventing an insurrection Sultan Majid's brothers had created with a view of usurping his government.

The news of the place was as follows: In addition to the formerly constituted consulates – English, French, and American – a fourth one, representing Hamburg, had been created. Dr.

Roscher, who during my absence had made a successful journey to the N'yinyezi N'yassa, or Star Lake, was afterwards murdered by some natives in Uhiyow; and Lieutentant-Colonel Baron van der Decken, another enterprising German, was organising an expedition with a view to search for the relics of his countryman, and, if possible, complete the project poor Roscher had commenced.

Slavery had received a severe blow by the sharp measures Colonel Rigby had taken in giving tickets of emancipation to all those slaves whom our Indian subjects the Banyans had been secretly keeping, and by fining the masters and giving the money to the men to set them up in life. The interior of the continent had been greatly disturbed, owing to constant war between the natives and Arab ivory merchants. Mguru Mfupi (or "Short-legs"), the chief of Khoko in Ugogo, for instance, had been shot, and Manua Sera ("the Tippler"), who succeeded the old Sultan Fundi Kira, of Unyanyembe, on his death, shortly after the late expedition left Kaze, was out in the field fighting the

A tembe, or Arab house, in Kaseh.

Arabs. Recent letters from the Arabs in the interior, however, gave hopes of peace being shortly restored. Finally, in compliance with my request – and this was the most important item of news to myself – Colonel Rigby had sent on, thirteen days previously, fifty-six loads of cloth and beads, in charge of two of Ramji's men, consigned to Musa at Kaze.

To call on the Sultan, of course, was our first duty. He received us in his usually affable manner; made many trite remarks concerning our plans; was surprised, if my only object in view was to see the great river running out of the lake, that I did not go by the more direct route across the Masai country and Usoga; and then, finding I wished to see Karague, as well as to settle many other great points of interest, he offered to assist me with all the means in his power.

The Hottentots, the mules, and the baggage having been landed, our preparatory work began in earnest. It consisted in proving the sextants; rating the watches; examining the compasses and boiling thermometers; making tents and packsaddles; ordering supplies of beads, cloth, and brass wire; and collecting servants and porters.

Sheikh Said bin Salem, our late Cafila Bashi, or caravan captain, was appointed to that post again, as he wished to prove his character for honour and honesty; and it now transpired that he had been ordered not to go with me when I discovered the Victoria N'yanza. Bombay and his brother Mabruki were bound to me of old, and the first to greet me on my arrival here; while my old friends the Beluchs begged me to take them again. The Hottentots, however, had usurped their place. I was afterwards sorry for this, though, if I ever travel again, I shall trust to none but natives, as the climate of Africa is too trying to foreigners. Colonel Rigby, who had at heart as much as anybody the success of the expedition, materially assisted me in accomplishing my object – that men accustomed to discipline and a knowledge of English honour and honesty should be enlisted, to give confidence to the rest of the men; and he allowed me to select from his boat's crew any men I could find who had served as men-of-war, and had seen active service in India.

For this purpose my factotum, Bombay, prevailed on Baraka, Frij, and Rahan – all of them old sailors, who, like himself, knew Hindustani – to go with me. With this nucleus to start with, I gave orders that they should look out for as many Wanguana (freed men – i.e., men emancipated from slavery) as they could enlist, to carry loads, or do any other work required of them, and to follow men in Africa wherever I wished, until our arrival in Egypt, when I would send them back to Zanzibar. Each was to receive one year's pay in advance, and the remainder when their work was completed.

While this enlistment was going on here, Ladha Damji, the customs' master, was appointed to collect a hundred pagazis (Wanyamuezi porters) to carry each a load of cloth, beads, or brass wire to Kaze, as they do for the ivory merchants. Meanwhile, at the invitation of the Admiral, and to show him some sport in hippopotamus-shooting, I went with him in a dhow over to Kusiki, near which there is a tidal lagoon, which at high tide is filled with water, but at low water exposes sand islets covered with mangrove shrub. In these islets we sought for the animals, knowing they were keen to lie wallowing in the mire, and we bagged two. On my return to Zanzibar, the *Brisk* sailed for the Mauritius, but fortune sent Grant and myself on a different cruise. Sultan Majid, having heard that a slaver was lying at Pangani, and being anxious to show his good faith with the English, begged me to take command of one his vessels of war and run it down. Accordingly, embarking at noon, as soon as the vessel could be got ready, we lay-to that night at Tombat, with a view of surprising the slaver next morning; but next day, on our arrival at Pangani, we heard that she had merely put in to provision there three days before, and had let immediately afterwards. As I had come so far, I thought we might go ashore and look at the town, which was found greatly improved since I last saw it, by the addition of several coralline houses and a dockyard. The natives were building a dhow with Lindi and Madagascar timber. On going ashore, I might add, we were stranded on the sands, and, coming off again, nearly swamped by the increasing surf on the bar of the river; but this was a trifle; all we thought of was to return to Zanzibar, and hurry on our preparations there. This, however, was not so easy: the sea current was running north, and the wind was too light to propel our vessel against it; so, after trying in vain to make way in her, Grant and I, leaving her to follow, took to a boat, after giving the captain, who said we would get drowned, a letter, to say we left the vessel against his advice.

We had a brave crew of young negroes to pull us; but, pull as they would, the current was so strong that we feared, if we persisted, we should be drawn into the broad Indian Ocean; so, changing our line, we bore into the little coralline island, Maziwa, where, after riding over some ugly coral surfs, we put in for the night. There we found, to our relief, some fisher-

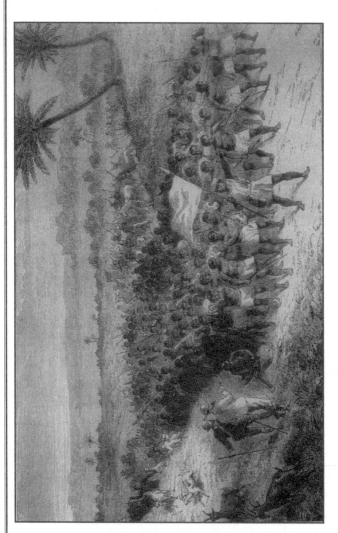

The departure.

man, who gave us fish for our dinner, and directions how to proceed.

Next morning, before daylight, we trusted to the boat and our good luck. After passing, without landmarks to guide us, by an intricate channel, through foaming surfs, we arrived at Zanzibar in the night, and found that the vessel had got in before us.

Colonel Rigby now gave me a most interesting paper, with a map attached to it, about the Nile and the Mountains of the Moon. It was written by Lieutenant Wilford, from the "Purans" of the Ancient Hindus. As it exemplifies, to a certain extent, the supposition I formerly arrived at concerning the Mountains of the Moon being associated with the country of the Moon, I would fain draw the attention of the reader of my travels to the volume of the "Asiatic Researches" in which it was published.[2] It is remarkable that the Hindus have christened the source of the Nile Amara, which is the name of a country at the north-east corner of the Victoria N'yanza. This, I think, shows clearly that the ancient Hindus must have had some kind of communication with both the northern and southern ends of the Victoria N'yanza.

Having gone to work again, I found that Sheikh Said had brought ten men, four of whom were purchased for one hundred dollars, which I had to pay; Bombay, Baraka, Frij, and Rahan had brought twenty-six more, all freed men; while the Sultan Majid, at the suggestion of Colonel Rigby, gave me thirty-four men more, who were all raw labourers taken from his gardens. It was my intention to have taken one hundred of this description of men throughout the whole journey; but as so many could not be found in Zanzibar, I still hoped to fill up the complement in Unyamuezi, the land of the Moon, from the large establishments of the Arab merchants residing there. The payment of these men's wages for the first year, as well as the terms of the agreement made with them, by the kind consent of Colonel Rigby were now entered in the Consular Office books, as a security to both parties, and a precaution against disputes on the way. Any one who saw the grateful avidity with which they took the money, and the warmth with which they pledged themselves to serve me faithfully through all dangers and difficulties, would, had he had no dealings with such men before, have thought that I had a first-rate set of followers. I lastly gave Sheikh Said a double-barrelled rifle by Blissett, and distributed fifty carbines among the seniors of the expedition, with the condition that they would forfeit them to others more worthy if they did not behave well, but would retain possession of them for ever if they carried them through the journey to my satisfaction.

On the 21st, as everything was ready on the island, I sent Sheikh Said and all the men, along with the Hottentots, mules, and baggage, off in dhows to Bagamoyo, on the opposite mainland. Colonel Rigby, with Captain Grant and myself, then called on the Sultan, to bid him adieu, when he graciously offered me, as a guard of honour to escort me through Uzaramo, one jemadar and twenty-five Beluch soldiers. These I accepted, more as a government security in that country against the tricks of the natives, than for any accession they made to our strength. His highness then places his 22-gun corvette, *Secundra Shah*, at our disposal, and we went all three over to Bagamoyo, arriving on the 25th. Immediately on landing, Ladha and Sheikh Said showed us into a hut prepared for us, and all things looked pretty well. Ladha's hundred loads of beads, cloths, and brass wire were all tied up for the march, and seventy-five pagazis (porters from the Moon country) had received their hire to carry these loads to Kaze in the land of the Moon. Competition, I found, had raised these men's wages, for I had to pay, to go even as far as Kaze, nine and a quarter dollars a-head! – as Masudi and some other merchants were bound on the same line as myself, and all were equally in a hurry to be off and avoid as much as possible the famine we knew we should have to fight through at this late season. Little troubles, of course, must always be expected, else these blacks would not be true negroes. Sheikh Said now reported it quite impossible to buy anything at a moderate rate; for, as I was a "big man," I ought to "pay a big price"; and my men had all been obliged to fight in the bazaar before they could get even tobacco at the same rate as other men, because they were the servants of the big man, who could afford to give higher wages than any one else. The Hottentots, too, began to fall sick, which my Wanguana laughingly attributed to want of grog to keep their spirits up, as these little creatures, the "Tots," had frequently at Zanzibar, after heavy potations, boasted to the more sober free men, that they "were strong, because they could stand plenty drink." The first step now taken was to pitch camp under large shady mango-trees, and to instruct every man in his particular duty. At the same time, the Wanguana, who had carbines, were obliged to be drilled in their use and formed into companies, with captains of ten, headed by General Baraka, who was made commander-in-chief.

On the 30th September, as things were looking more orderly, I sent forward half of the property, and all the men I had then collected, to Ugeni, a shamba, or garden, two miles off; and on the 2nd October, after settling with Ladha for my "African money," as my pagazis were completed to a hundred and one, we wished Rigby adieu, and all assembled together at Ugeni, which resembles the richest parts of Bengal.

1) Captain Burton, on receiving his gold medal at the hands of Sir Roderick I. Murchison, said, "You have alluded, sir, to the success of the last expedition. Justice compels me to state the circumstances under which it attained that success. To Captain Speke are due those geographical results to which you have alluded in such flattering terms. Whilst I undertook the history and ethnography, the languages, and the peculiarity of the people, to Captain Speke fell the arduous task of delineating an exact topography, and of laying down our positions by astronomical observations – a labour to which, at times, even the undaunted Livingstone found himself unequal."

2) Vol. III. of A.D. 1801.

CHAPTER 2

UZARAMO

The Nature of the Country – The Order of March – The Beginning of Our Taxation – Sultan Lion's Claw, and Sultan Monkey's Tail – The Kingani – Jealousies and Difficulties in the Camp – The Murderer of M. Maizan.

We were now in U-za-Ramo, which may mean the country of Ramo, though I have never found any natives who could enlighten me on the derivation of this obviously triple word. The extent of the country, roughly speaking, stretches from the coast to the junction or bifurcation of the Kingani and its upper branch the Mgeta river, westwards; and from the Kingani, north, to the Lufigi river, south; though in the southern portions several subtribes have encroached upon the lands. There are no hills in Uzaramo; but the land in the central line, formed like a ridge between the two rivers, furrow fashion, consists of slightly elevated flats and terraces, which, in the rainy season, throw off their surplus waters to the north and south by nullahs into these rivers. The country is uniformly well covered with trees and large grasses, which, in the rainy season, are too thick, tall, and green to be pleasant; though in the dry season, after the grasses have been burnt, it is agreeable enough, though not pretty, owing to the flatness of the land. The villages are not large or numerous, but widely spread, consisting generally of conical grass huts, while others are gable-ended, after the coast-fashion – a small collection of ten or twenty comprising one village. Over these villages certain headmen, titled Phanze, hold jurisdiction, who take black-mail from travellers with high presumption when they can. Generally speaking, they live upon the coast, and call themselves Diwans, headsmen, and subjects of the Sultan Majid; but they no sooner hear of the march of a caravan than they transpose their position, become sultans in their own right, and levy taxes accordingly.

The Wazaramo are strictly agriculturists; they have no cows, and but few goats. They are of low stature and thick set and their nature tends to the boisterous. Expert slavehunters, they mostly clothe themselves by the sale of their victims on the coast, though they do business by the sale of goats and grain as well. Nowhere in the interior are natives so well clad as these creatures. In dressing up their hair, and otherwise smearing their bodies with ochreish clay, they are great dandies. They always keep their bows and arrows, which form their national arm, in excellent order, the latter well poisoned, and carried in quivers nicely carved. To intimidate a caravan and extort a hongo or tax, I have seen them drawn out in line as if prepared for battle; but a few soft words were found sufficient to make them all withdraw and settle the matter at issue by arbitration in some appointed place. A few men without property can cross their lands fearlessly, though a single individual with property would stand no chance, for they are insatiable thieves. But little is seen of these people on the journey, as the chiefs take their taxes by deputy, partly out of pride, and partly because they think they can extort more by keeping in the mysterious distance. At the same time, the caravan prefers camping in the jungles beyond the villages to mingling with the inhabitants, where rows might be engendered. We sometimes noticed Albinos, with greyish-blue eyes and light straw-coloured hair. Not unfrequently we would pass on the track side small heaps of white ashes, with a calcined bone or two among them. These, we were told, were the relics of burnt witches. The caravan track we had now to travel on leads along the right bank of the Kingani valley, over-looking Uzegura, which, corresponding with Uzaramo, only on the other side of the Kigani, extends northwards to the Pangani river, and is intersected in the centre by the Wami river, of which more hereafter.

Starting on a march with a large mixed caravan, consisting of 1 corporal and 9 privates, Hottentots – 1 jemadar and 25 privates, Beluchs – 1 Arab Cafila Bashi and 75 freed slaves – 1 kirangozi, or leader, and 100 negro porters – 12 mules untrained, 3 donkeys, and 22 goats – one could hardly expect to find everybody in his place at the proper time for breaking ground; but, at the same time, it could hardly be expected that ten men, who had actually received their bounty-money, and had sworn fidelity, should give one the slip the very first day. Such, how-ever, was the case. Ten out of the thirty-six given by the Sultan ran away, because they feared that the white men, whom they believed to be cannibals, were only taking them into the interi-or to eat them; and one pagazi, more honest than the freed men, deposited his pay upon the ground, and ran away too. Go we must, however; for one desertion is sure to lead to more; and go we did. Our procession was in this fashion: The kirangozi, with a load on his shoulder, led the way, flag in hand, followed by the pagazis carrying spears and bows and arrows in their hands, and bearing their share of the baggage in the shape either of bolster-shaped loads of cloth and beads covered with matting, each tied into the fork of a three-pronged stick, or else coils of brass or copper wire tied in even weights to each end of sticks which they laid on the shoulder; then helter-skelter came the Wanguana, carrying carbines in their hands, and boxes, bundles, tents, cooking-pots – all the miscellaneous property – on their heads; next the Hottentots, dragging the refractory mules laden with ammunition-boxes, but very lightly, to save the animals for the future; and, finally, Sheikh Said and the Beluch escort; while the goats, sick women, and stragglers, brought up the rear. From first to last, some of the sick Hottentots rode the hospital donkeys, allowing the negroes to tug their animals; for the smallest ailment threw them broadcast on their backs. In a little while we cleared from the rich gardens, mango clumps, and cocoa-nut trees, which characterise the fertile coast-line. After traversing fields of grass well clothed with green trees, we arrived at the little settlement of Bomani, where camp was formed, and everybody fairly appointed to his place. The process of camp-forming would be thus: Sheikh Said, with Bombay under him, issues cloths to the men for rations at the rate of one-fourth load a-day (about 15 lb.) amongst 165; the Hottentots cook our dinners and their own, or else lie rolling on the ground overcome with fatigue; the Beluchs are supposed to guard the camp, but prefer gossip and brightening their arms. Some men are told off to look after the mules, donkeys, and goats, whilst out grazing; the rest have to pack the kit, pitch our tents, cut boughs for huts, and for fencing in the camp – a thing rarely done, by-the-by. After cooking, when the night has set it, the everlasting dance begins, attended with clapping of hands and jingling small bells strapped to the legs – the whole being accompanied by a constant repetition of senseless words, which stand in place of the song to the negroes; for song they have none, being mentally incapacitated for musical composition, though as timists they are not to be surpassed.

What remains to be told is the daily occupation of Captain Grant, myself, and our private servants. Beginning at the foot: Rahan, a very peppery little negro, who had served in a British man-of-war at the taking of Rangoon, was my valet; and Baraka, who had been trained much in the same manner, but had seen engagements at Multan, was Captain Grant's. They both knew Hindustani; but while Rahan's services at sea had been short, Baraka had served nearly all his life with Englishmen – was the smartest and most intelligent negro I ever saw – was invaluable to Colonel Rigby as a detector of slave-traders, and enjoyed his confidence completely – so much so, that he said, on parting with him, that he did not know where he should be able to find another man to fill his post. These two men had now charge of our tents and personal kit, while Baraka was considered the general of the Wanguana forces, and Rahan a captain of ten.

My first occupation was to map the country. This is done by timing the rate of march with a watch, taking compass-bearings along the road, or on any conspicuous marks – as, for instance, hills off it – and by noting the watershed – in short, all topographical objects. On arrival in camp every day came the ascertaining, by boiling a thermometer, of the altitude of the station above the sea-level; of the latitude of the station by the meridian altitude of the star taken with a sextant; and of the compass variation by azimuth. Occasionally there was the fixing of certain crucial stations, at intervals of sixty miles or so, by lunar observations, or distances of the moon either from the sun or from certain given stars, for determining the longitude, by which the original-timed course can be drawn out with certainty on the map by proportion. Should a date be lost, you can always discover it by taking a lunar distance and comparing it with the Nautical Almanac, by noting the time when a star passes the meridian if your watch is right, or by observing the phases of the moon, or her rising or setting, as compared with the Nautical Almanac. The rest of my work, besides sketching and keeping a diary, which was the most troublesome of all, consisted in making geological and zoological collections.

With Captain Grant rested the botanical collections and thermometrical registers. He also boiled one of the thermometers, kept the rain-gauge, and undertook the photography; but after a time I sent the instruments back, considering this work too severe for the climate, and he tried instead sketching with watercolours – the results of which form the chief part of the illustrations in this book. The rest of our day went in breakfasting after the march was over – a pipe, to prepare us for rummaging the fields and villages to discover their contents for scientific purposes – dinner close to sunset, and tea and pipe before turning in at night.

A short stage brought us to Ikamburu, included in the district of Nzasa, where there is another small village presided over by Phanze Khombe la Simba, meaning Claw of Lion. He, immediately after our arrival, sent us a present of a basket of rice, value one dollar, of course expecting a return – for absolute generosity is a thing unknown to the negro. Not being aware of the value of the offering, I simply requested the Sheikh to give him four yards of American sheeting, and thought no more about the matter, until presently I found the cloth returned. The "Sultan" could not think of receiving such a paltry present from me, when on the former journey he got so much; if he showed this cloth at home, nobody would believe him, but would say he took much more and concealed it from his family, wishing to keep all his goods to himself. I answered that my footing in the country had been paid for on the last journey, and unless he would accept me as any other common traveller, he had better walk away; but the little Sheikh, a timid, though very gentlemanly creature, knowing the man, and dreading the consequences of too high a tone, pleaded for him, and proposed as a fitting hongo, one dubuani, one sahari, and eight yards merikani, as the American sheeting is called here. This was pressed by the jemadar, and acceded to by myself, as the very utmost I could afford. Lion's Claw, however, would not accept it; it was too far below the mark of what he got last time. He therefore returned the cloths to the Sheikh, as he could get no hearing from myself, and retreated in high dudgeon, threatening the caravan with a view of his terrible presence on the morrow. Meanwhile the little Sheikh, who always carried a sword fully two-thirds the length of himself, commenced casting bullets for his double-barrelled rifle, ordered the Wanguana to load their guns, and came wheedling up to me for one more cloth, as it was no use hazarding the expedition's safety for four yards of cloth. This is a fair specimen of tax-gathering, within twelve miles of the coast, by a native who claims the protection of Zanzibar. We shall soon see what they are further on. The result of experience is, that, ardent as the traveller is to see the interior of Africa, no sooner has he dealings with the natives, than his whole thoughts tend to discovering some road where he won't be molested, or a short cut, but long march, to get over the ground.

Quite undisturbed, we packed and marched as usual, and soon passed Nzasa close to the river, which is only indicated by a line of trees running through a rich alluvial valley. We camped at the little settlement of Kizoto, inhospitably presided over by Phanze Mukia ya Nyani or Monkey's Tail, who no sooner heard of our arrival than he sent a demand for his "rights." One dubani was issued, with orders that no one need approach me again, unless he wanted to smell my powder. Two taxes in five miles was a thing unheard of; and I heard no more about the matter, until Bombay in the evening told me how Sheikh Said, fearing awkward consequences, had settled to give two dubuani, one being taken from his own store. Lion's Claw also turned up again, getting his cloths of yesterday – one more being added from the Sheikh's stores – and he was then advised to go off quietly, as I was a fire-eater whom nobody dared approach after my orders had been issued. This was our third march in Uzaramo; we had scarcely seen a man of the country, and had no excessive desire to do so.

Deflecting from the serpentine course of the Kingani a little, we crossed a small bitter rivulet, and entered on the elevated cultivation of Kiranga Ranga, under Phanze Mkungu-pare, a very mild man, who, wishing to give no offence, begged for a trifling present. He came in person, and his manner having pleased us, I have him one sahari, four yards merikani, and eight yards kiniki, which pleased our friend so much that he begged us to consider his estate our own, even to the extent of administering his justice, should any Mzaramo be detected stealing from us. Our target-practice, whilst instructing the men, astonished him not a little, and produced an exclamation that, with so many guns, we need fear nothing, go where we would. From this place a good view is obtained of Uzegura. Beyond the flat alluvial valley of the Kingani, seven to eight miles broad, the land rises suddenly to a table-land of no great height, on which trees grow in profusion. In fact it appeared, as far as the eye could reach, the very counterpart of that where we stood, with the exception of a small hill, very distant, called Phongue.

A very welcome packet of quinine and other medicines reached us here from Rigby, who, hearing our complaints that the Hottentots could only be kept alive by daily potions of brandy and quinine, feared our supplies were not enough, and sent us more.

We could not get the Sultan's men to chum with the Wanguana proper; they were shy, like wild animals – built their huts by themselves – and ate and talked by themselves, for they felt themselves inferiors; and I had to nominate one of their number to be their chief, answerable for the actions of the whole. Being in the position of "boots" to the camp, the tending of goats fell to their lot. Three goats were missing this evening, which the goatherds could not account for, nor any of their men. Suspecting that they were hidden for a private feast, I told their chief to inquire farther, and report. The upshot was, that the man was thrashed for intermeddling, and came back only with his scars. This was a nice sort of insubordination, which of course could not be endured. The goatherd was pinioned and brought to trial, for the double offence of losing the goats and rough-handling his chief. The tricking scoundrel – on quietly saying he could not be answerable for other men's actions if they stole goats, and he could not recognise a man as his chief whom the Sheikh, merely by a whim of his own, thought proper to appoint – was condemned to be tied up for the night with the prospect of a flogging in the morning. Seeing his fate, the cunning vagabond said, "Now I do see it was by your orders the chief was appointed, and not by a whim of Sheikh Said's; I will obey him for the future"; and these words were hardly pronounced than the three missing goats rushed like magic into camp, nobody of course knowing where they came from.

Skirting along the margin of the rising ground overlooking the river, through thick woods, cleared in places for cultivation, we arrived at Thumba Lhere. The chief here took a hongo of three yards merikani and two yards kiniki without much fuss, for he had no power. The pagazis struck, and said they would not move from this unless I gave them one fundo or ten necklaces of beads each daily, in lieu of rations, as they were promised by Ladha on the coast that I would do so as soon as they had made four marches. This was an obvious invention, concocted to try my generosity, for I had given the kirangozi a goat, which is customary, to "make the journey prosperous" –

had suspended a dollar to his neck in recognition of his office, and given him four yards merikani, that he might have a grand feast with his brothers; while neither the Sheikh, myself, nor any one else in the camp, had heard of such a compact. With high words the matter dropped, African fashion.

The pagazis would not start at the appointed time, hoping to enforce their demands of last night; so we took the lead and started, followed by the Wanguana. Seeing this, the pagazis cried out with one accord: "The master is gone, leaving the responsibility of his property in our hands; let us follow, let us follow, for verily he is our father"; and all came hurrying after us. Here the river, again making a bend, is lost to sight, and we marched through large woods and cultivated fields to Muhugue, observing, as we passed long, the ochreish colour of the earth, and numerous pits which the copal-diggers had made searching for their much-valued gum. A large coast-bound caravan, carrying ivory tusks with double-toned bells suspended to them, ting-tonging as they moved along, was met on the way; and as some of the pagazis composing it were men who had formerly taken me to the Victoria N'yanza, warm recognitions passed between us. The water found here turned our brandy and tea as black as ink. The chief, being a man of small pretensions, took only one sahari and four yards merikani.

Instead of going on to the next village we halted in this jungly place for the day, that I might comply with the desire of the Royal Geographical Society to inspect Muhonyera, and report if there were really any indications of a "raised sea-beach" there, such as their maps indicate. An inspection brought me to the conclusion that no mind but one prone to discovering sea-beaches in the most unlikely places could have supposed for a moment that one existed here. The form and appearance of the land are the same as we have seen everywhere since leaving Bomani – a low plateau subtended by a bank cut down by the Kingani river, and nothing more. There are no pebbles; the soil is rich reddish loam, well covered with trees, bush, and grass, in which some pigs and antelopes are found. From the top of this enbankment we gain the first sight of the East Coast Range, due west of us, represented by the high elephant's-back hill, Mkambaku, in Usagara, which, joining Uraguru, stretches northwards across the Pangani river to Usumbara and the Kilimandjaro, and southwards, with a westerly deflection, across the Lufiji to Southern N'yassa. What course the range takes beyond those two extremes, the rest of the world knows as well as I. Another conspicuous landmark here is Kidunda (the little hill), which is the southernmost point of a low chain of hills, also tending northwards, and representing an advance-guard to the higher East Coast Range in its rear. At night, as we had no local "sultans" to torment us, eight more men of Sultan Majid's donation ran away, and, adding injury to injury, took with them all our goats, fifteen in number. This was a sad loss. We could keep ourselves on guinea-fowls or green pigeons, doves, etc.; but the Hottentots wanted nourishment much more than ourselves, and as their dinner always consisted of what we left, "short-commons" was the fate in store for them. The Wanguana, instead of regarding these poor creatures as soldiers, treated them like children; and once, as a diminutive Tot – the common name they go by – was exerting himself to lift his pack and place it on his mule, a fine Herculean Mguana stepped up behind, grasped Tot, pack and all, in his muscular arms, lifted the whole over his head, paraded the Tot about, struggling for release, and put him down amidst the laughter of the camp, then saddled his mule and patted him on the back.

After sending a party of Beluch to track down the deserters and goats, in which they were not successful, we passed through the village of Sagesera, and camped one mile beyond, close to the river. Phanze Kirongo (which means Mr. Pit) here paid us his respects, with a presentation of rice. In return he received four yards merikani and one dubuani, which Bombay settled, as the little Sheikh, ever done by the sultans, pleaded indisposition, to avoid the double fire he was always subjected to on these occasions, by the sultans grasping on the one side, and my resisting on the other; for I relied on my strength, and thought it very inadvisable to be generous with my cloth to the prejudice of future travellers, by decreasing the value of merchandise, and increasing proportionately the expectations of these negro chiefs. From the top of the bank bordering on the valley, a good view was obtainable of the Uraguru hills, and the top of a very distant cone to its northward; but I could see no signs of any river joining the Kingani on its left, though on the former expedition I heard that the Mukondokua river, which was met with in Usagara, joined the Kingani close to Sagesera, and actually formed its largest head branch. Neither could Mr. Pit inform me what became of the Mukondokua, as the Wazaramo are not given to travelling. He had heard of it from the traders, but only knew himself of one river beside the Kingani. It was called Wami in Uegura, and mouths at Utondue, between the ports of Whindi and Saadani. To try and check the desertions of Sultan Majid's men, I advised

59

– ordering was of no use – that their camp should be broken up, and they should be amalgamated with the Wanguana; but it was found that the two would not mix. In fact, the whole native camp consisted of so many clubs of two, four, six, or ten men, who originally belonged to one village or one master, or were united by some other family tie which they preferred keeping intact; so they cooked together, ate together, slept together, and sometimes mutinied together. The amalgamation having failed, I wrote some emanicipation tickets, called the Sultan's men all up together, selected the best, gave them these tickets, announced that their pay and all rewards would be placed for the future on the same conditions as those of the Wanguana, and as soon as I saw any signs of improvement in the rest, they would all be treated in the same manner; but should they desert, they would find my arm long enough to arrest them on the coast and put them into prison.

During this march we crossed three deep nullahs which drain the Uzaramo plateau, and arrived at the Makutaniro, or junction of this line with those of Mboamaji and Konduchi, which traverse central Uzaramo, and which, on my former return journey, I went down. The gum-copal diggings here cease. The Dum palm is left behind; the large rich green-leaved trees of the low plateau give place to the mimosa; and now, having ascended the greater decline of the Kingani river, instead of being confined by a bank, we found ourselves on flat open-park land, where antelopes roam at large, buffalo and zebra are sometimes met with, and guinea-fowl are numerous. The water for the camp is found in the river, but supplies of grain come from the village of Kipora farther on.

The Sultan of Zanzibar.

A march through the park took us to a camp by a pond, from which, by crossing the Kingani, rice and provisions for the men were obtained on the opposite bank. One can seldom afford to follow wild animals on the line of march, otherwise we might have bagged some antelopes to-day, which, scared by the interminable singing, shouting, bell-jingling, horn-blowing, and other such merry noises of the moving caravan, could be seen disappearing in the distance.

Leaving the park, we now entered the richest part of Uzaramo, affording crops as fine as any part of India. Here it was, in the district of Dege la Mhora, that the first expedition to this country, guided by a Frenchman, M. Maizan, came to a fatal termination, that gentleman having been barbarously murdered by the sub-chief Hembe. The cause of the affair was distinctly explained to me by Hembe himself, who, with his cousin Darunga, came to call upon me, presuming, as he was not maltreated by the last expedition, that the matter would now be forgotten. The two men were very great friends of the little Sheikh, and as a present was expected, which I should have to pay, we all talked cheerfully and confidentially, bringing in the fate of Maizan for no other reason than to satisfy curiosity. Hembe, who lives in the centre of an almost impenetrable thicket, confessed that he was the murderer, but said the fault did not rest with him, as he merely carried out the instructions of his father, Mzungera, who, a Diwan on the coast, sent him a letter directing his actions. Thus it is proved that the plot against Maizan was concocted on the coast by the Arab merchants – most likely from the same motive which has induced one rival merchant to kill another as the best means of checking rivalry or competition. When Arabs – and they are the only class of people who would do such a deed – found a European going into the very middle of their secret trading-places, where such large profits were to be obtained, they would never suppose that the scientific Maizan went for any other purpose than to pry into their ivory stores, bring others into the field after him, and destroy their monopoly. The Sultan of Zanzibar, in those days, was our old ally Said Said, commonly called the Emam of Muscat; and our Consul, Colonel Hamerton, had been M. Maizan's host as long as he lived upon the coast. Both the Emam and Consul were desirous of seeing the country surveyed, and did everything in their power to assist Maizan, the former even appointing the Indian Musa to conduct him safely as far as Unyamuezi; but their power was not found sufficient to damp the raging fire of jealousy in the ivory-trader's heart. Musa commenced the journey with Maizan, and they travelled together a march or two, when one of Maizan's domestic establishment fell sick and stopped his progress. Musa remained with him eight or ten days, to his own loss in trade and expense in keeping up a large establishment, and then they parted by mutual consent, Maizan thinking himself quite strong enough to take care of himself. This separation was, I believe, poor Maizan's death-blow. His power, on the Emam's side, went with Musa's going, and left the Arabs free to carry out their wicked wills.

The presents I had to give here were one sahari and eight yards merikani to Hembe, and the same to Darunga, for which they gave a return in grain. Still following close to the river – which, unfortunately, is so enshrouded with thick bush that we could seldom see it – a few of the last villages in Uzaramo were passed.

Here antelopes reappear amongst the tall mimosa, but we let them alone in prosecution of the survey, and finally encamped opposite the little hill of Kidunda, which lying on the left bank of the Kingani, stretches north, a little east, into Uzegura. The hill crops out through pisolitic limestone, in which marine fossils were observable. It would be interesting to ascertain whether this lime formation extends down the east coast of Africa from the Somali country, where also, on my first expedition, I found marine shells in the limestone, especially as a vast continuous band of limestone is known to extend from the Tagus, through Egypt and the Somali country, to the Burrumputra. To obtain food it was necessary here to ferry the river and purchase from the Wazaramo, who, from fear of the passing caravans, had left their own bank and formed a settlement immediately under this pretty little hill – rendered all the more enchanting to our eyes, as it was the first we had met since leaving the sea-coast. The Diwan, or head man, was a very civil creature; he presented us freely with two fine goats – a thing at that time we were very much in want of – and took, in return, without any comments, one dubani and eight yards merikani.

The next day, as we had no further need of our Beluch escort, a halt was made to enable me to draw up a "Progress Report," and pack all the specimens of natural history collected on the way, for the Royal Geographical Society. Captain Grant, taking advantage of the spare time, killed for the larder two buck antelopes, and the Tots brought in, in high excited triumph, a famous pig.

This march, which declines from the Kingani a little, leads through rolling, jungly ground, full of game, to the tributary stream Mgeta. It is fordable in the dry season, but has to be bridged by throwing a tree across it in the wet one. Rising in the Usagara hills to the west of the hog-backed Mkambaku, this branch intersects the province of Ukhutu in the centre, and circles round until it unites with the Kingani about four miles north of the ford. Where the Kingani itself rises, I never could find out; though I have heard that its source lies in a gurgling spring on the eastern face of the Mkambaku, by which account the Mgeta is made the longer branch of the two.

CHAPTER 3

USAGARA

Nature of the Country – Resumption of the March – A Hunt – Bombay and Baraka – The Slave-Hunters – The Ivory-Merchants – Collection of Natural-History Specimens – A Frightened Village – Tracking a Mule.

Under U-Sagara, or, as it might be interpreted, U-sa-Gara – country of Gara – is included all the country lying between the bifurcation of the Kingani and Mgeta rivers east, and Ugogo, the first country on the interior plateau west – a distance of a hundred miles. On the north it is bounded by the Mukondokua, or upper course of the Wami river and on the south by the Ruaha, or northern great branch of the Lufiji river. It forms a link of the great East Coast Range; but though it is generally comprehended under the single name Usagara, many subtribes occupy and apply their own names to portions of it; as, for instance, the people on whose ground we now stood at the foot of the hills, are Wa-Khutu, and their possessions consequently are U-Khutu, which is by far the best producing land hitherto alluded to since leaving the sea-coast line. Our ascent by the river, though quite imperceptible to the eye, has been 500 feet. From this level the range before us rises in some places to 5,000 to 6,000 feet, not as one grand mountain, but in two detached lines, lying at an angle of 45 degrees from N.E. to S.W., and separated one from the other by elevated valleys, tables, and crab-claw spurs of hill which incline towards the flanking rivers. The whole having been thrown up by volcanic action, is based on a strong foundation of granite and other igneous rocks, which are exposed in many places in the shape of massive blocks; otherwise the hill-range is covered in the upper part with sandstone, and in the bottoms with alluvial clay. This is the superficial configuration of the land as it strikes the eye; but, knowing the elevation of the interior plateau to be only 2,500 feet above the sea immediately on the western flank of these hills, whilst the breath of the chain is 100 miles, the mean slope of incline of the basal surface must be on a gradual rise of twenty feet per mile. The hill tops and sides, where not cultivated, are well covered with bush and small trees, amongst which the bamboo is conspicuous; whilst the bottoms, having a soil deeper and richer, produce fine large fig-trees of exceeding beauty, the huge calabash, and a variety of other trees. Here, in certain places where water is obtainable throughout the year, and wars, or slave-hunts more properly speaking, do not disturb the industry of the people, cultivation thrives surprisingly; but such a boon is rarely granted them. It is in consequence of these constantly-recurring troubles that the majority of the Wasagara villages are built on hill-spurs, where the people can the better resist attack, or, failing, disperse and hide effectually. The normal habitation is the small conical hut of grass. These compose villages, varying in number according to the influence of their head men. There are, however, a few mud villages on the table-lands, each built in a large irregular square of chambers with a hollow yard in the centre, known as tembe.

As to the people of these uplands, poor, meagre-looking wretches, they contrast unfavourably with the lowlanders on both sides of them. Dingy in colour, spiritless, shy, and timid, they invite attack in a country where every human being has a market value, and are little seen by the passing caravan. In habits they are semi-pastoral agriculturalists, and would be useful members of society were they left alone to cultivate their own possessions, rich and beautiful by nature, but poor and desolate by force of circumstance. Some of the men can afford a cloth, but the greater part wear an article which I can only describe as a grass kilt. In one or two places throughout the passage of these hills a caravan may be taxed, but if so, only to a small amount; the villagers more frequently fly to the hill-tops as soon as the noise of the advancing caravan is heard, and no persuasions will bring them down again, so much ground have they, from previous experience, to fear treachery. It is such sad sights, and the obvious want of peace and prosperity, that weary the traveller, and make him every think of pushing on to his journey's end from the instant he enters Africa until he quits the country.

Knowing by old experience that the beautiful green park in the fork of these rivers abounded in game of great variety and in vast herds, where no men are ever seen except some savage hunters sitting in the trees with poisoned arrows, or watching their snares and pitfalls, I had all along determined on a hunt myself, to feed and cheer the men, and also to collect some specimens for the home museums. In the first object we succeeded well, as "the bags" we made counted two brindled gnu, four water-boc, one pallah-boc, and one pig – enough to feed abundantly the whole camp round. The feast was all the better relished as the men knew well that no Arab master would have given them what he could sell; for if a slave shot game, the animals would be the master's, to be sold bit by bit among the porters, and compensated from the proceeds of their pay. In the variety and number of our game we were disappointed, partly because so many wounded got away, and partly because we could not find what we knew the park to contain, in addition to what we killed – namely, elephants, rhinoceros, giraffes, buffaloes, zebra, and many varieties of antelopes, besides lions and hyenas. In fact, "the park," as well as all the adjacent land at the foot of the hills, is worth thinking of, with a view to a sporting tour as well as scientific investigation.

A circumstance arose here, which, insignificant though it appeared, is worth noting, to show how careful one must be in understanding and dealing with negro servants. Quite unaccountably to myself, the general of my Wanguana, Baraka, after showing much discontent with his position as head of Captain Grant's establishment, became so insolent, that it was necessary to displace him, and leave him nothing to do but look after the men. This promoted Frij, who enjoyed his rise as much as Baraka, if his profession was to be believed, enjoyed his removal from that office. Though he spoke in this manner, still I knew that there was something rankling in his mind which depressed his spirits as long as he remained with us, though what it was I could not comprehend, nor did I fully understand it till months afterwards. It was ambition, which was fast making a fiend of him;

View of the mountains to the west of Zungomero.

and had I known it, he would, and with great advantage too, have been dismissed upon the spot. The facts were these: He was exceedingly clever, and he knew it. His command over men was surprising. At Zanzibar he was the Consul's right-hand man: he ranked above Bombay in the consular boat's crew, and became a terror even to the Banyans who kept slaves. He seemed, in fact, in his own opinion, to have imbibed all the power of the British Consul who had instructed him. Such a man was an element of discord in our peaceful caravan. He was far too big-minded for the sphere which he occupied; and my surprise now is that he ever took service, knowing what he should, at the time of enlistment, have expected, that no man would be degraded to make room for him. But this was evidently what he had expected, though he dared not say it. He was jealous of Bombay, because he thought his position over the money department was superior to his own over the men; and he had seen Bombay, on one occasion, pay a tax in Uzaramo – a transaction which would give him consequence with the native chiefs. Of Sheikh Said he was equally jealous, for a like reason; and his jealousy increased the more that I found it necessary to censure the timidity of this otherwise worthy little man. Baraka thought, in his conceit, that he could have done all things better, and gained signal fame, had he been created chief. Perhaps he thought he had gained the first step towards this exalted rank, and hence his appearing very happy for this time. I could not see through so deep a scheme and only hoped that he would shortly forget, in the changes of the marching life, those beautiful wives he had left behind him, which Bombay in his generosity tried to persuade me was the cause of his mental distraction.

Our halt at the ford here was cut short by the increasing sickness of the Hottentots, and the painful fact that Captain Grant was seized with fever.[6] We had to change camp to the little village of Kiruru, where, as rice was grown – an article not to be procured again on this side of Unyamuezi – we stopped a day to lay in supplies of this most valuable of all travelling food. Here I obtained the most consistent accounts of the river system which, within five days' journey, trends through Uzegura; and I concluded, from what I heard, that there is no doubt of the Mukondokua and Wami rivers being one and the same stream. My informants were the natives of the settlement, and they all concurred in saying that the Kingani above the junction is called the Rufu, meaning the parent stream. Beyond it, following under the line of the hills, at one day's journey distant, there is a smaller river called Msonge. At an equal distance beyond it, another of the same size is known as Lungerengeri; and a fourth river is the Wami, which mouths in the sea at Utondue, between the ports of Whindi and Saadami. In former years, the ivory-merchants, ever seeking for an easy road for their trade, and knowing they would have no hills to climb if they could only gain a clear passage by this river from the interior plateau to the sea, made friends with the native chiefs of Uzegura, and succeeded in establishing it as a thoroughfare. Avarice, however, that fatal enemy to the negro chiefs, made them overreach themselves by exorbitant demands of taxes. Then followed contests for the right of appropriating the taxes, and the whole ended in the closing of the road, which both parties were equally anxious to keep open for their mutual gain. This foolish disruption having at first only lasted for a while, the road was again opened and again closed, for the merchants wanted an easy passage, and the native chiefs desired cloths. But it was shut again; and now we heard of its being for a third time opened, with what success the future only can determine – for experience WILL not teach the negro, who thinks only for the moment. Had they only sense to see, and patience to wait, the whole trade of the interior would inevitably pass through their country instead of Uzaramo; and instead of being poor in cloths, they would be rich and well dressed like their neighbours. But the curse of Noah sticks to these his grandchildren by Ham, and no remedy that has yet been found will relieve them. They require a government like ours in India; and without it, the slave trade will wipe them off the face of the earth.

Now leaving the open parks of pretty acacias, we followed up the Mgazi branch of the Mgeta, traversed large tree-jungles, where the tall palm is conspicuous, and drew up under the lumpy Mkambaku, to find a residence for the day. Here an Arab merchant, Khamis, bound for Zanzibar, obliged us by agreeing for a few dollars to convey our recent spoils in natural history to the coast.

My plans for the present were to reach Zungomero as soon as possible, as a few days' halt would be required there to fix the longitude of the eastern flank of the East Coast Range by astronomical observation; but on ordering the morning's march, the porters – too well fed and lazy – thought our marching-rate much too severe, and resolutely refused to move. They ought to have made ten miles a-day, but preferred doing five. Argument was useless, and I was reluctant to apply the stick, as the Arabs would have done when they saw their porters trifling with their pockets. Determining, however, not to be frustrated in this puerile manner, I ordered the bugler to sound the march, and started with the mules and coast-men, trusting to Sheikh and Baraka to bring on the Wanyamuezi as soon as they could move them. The same day we crossed the Mgazi where we found several Wakhutu spearing fish in the muddy hovers of its banks.

We slept under a tree, and this morning found a comfortable residence under the eaves of a capacious hut. The Wanyamuezi porters next came in at their own time, and proved to us how little worth are orders in a land where every man, in his own opinion, is a lord, and no laws prevail. Zungomero, bisected by the Mgeta, lies on flat ground, in a very pretty amphitheatre of hills, S. lat. 7° 26' 53", and E. long. 37° 36' 45". It is extremely fertile, and very populous, affording everything that man can wish, even to the cocoa and papwa fruits; but the slave-trade has almost depopulated it, and turned its once flourishing gardens into jungles. As I have already said, the people who possess these lands are cowardly by nature, and that is the reason why they are so much oppressed. The Wasuahili, taking advantage of their timidity, flock here in numbers to live upon the fruits of their labours. The merchants on the coast, too, though prohibited by their Sultan from interfering with the natural course of trade, send their hungry slaves, as touters, to entice all approaching caravans to trade with their particular ports, authorising the touters to pay such premiums as may be necessary for the purpose. Where they came from we could not ascertain; but during our residence, a large party of the Wasuahili marched past, bound for the coast, with one hundred head of cattle, fifty slaves in chains, and as many goats. Halts always end disastrously in Africa, giving men time for mischief; and here was an example of it. During the target-practice, which was always instituted on such occasions to give confidence to our men, the little pepper-box Rahan, my head valet, challenged a comrade to a duel with carbines. Being stopped by those around him, he vented his wrath in terrible oaths, and swung about his arms, until his gun accidentally went off, and blew his middle finger off.

Baraka next, with a kind of natural influence of affinity when a row is commenced, made himself so offensive to Bombay, as to send him running to me so agitated with excitement that I thought him drunk. He seized my hands, cried, and implored me to turn him off. What could this mean? I could not divine; neither could he explain, further than that he had come to a determination that I must send either him or Baraka to the right-about; and his first idea was that he, and not Baraka, should be the victim. Baraka's jealousy about his position had not struck me yet. I called them both together and asked what quarrel they had, but could not extract the truth. Baraka protested that he had never given, either by word or deed, the slightest cause of rupture; he only desired the prosperity of the march, and that peace should reign throughout the camp; but Bombay was suspicious of him, and malignantly abused him, for what reason Baraka could not tell. When I spoke of this to Bombay, like a bird fascinated by the eye of a viper, he shrank before the slippery tongue of his opponent, and could only say, "No, Sahib – oh no, that is not it; you had better turn me off, for his tongue is so long, and mine so short, you never will believe me." I tried to make them friends, hoping it was merely a passing ill-wind which would soon blow over; but before long the two disputants were tonguing it again, and I distinctly heard Bombay ordering Baraka out of camp as he could not keep from intermeddling, saying, which was true, he had invited him to join the expedition, that his knowledge of Hindustani might be useful to us; he was not wanted for any other purpose, and unless he was satisfied with doing that alone, we would get on much better without him. To this provocation Baraka mildly made the retort, "Pray don't put yourself in a passion, nobody is hurting you, it is all in your own heart, which is full of suspicions and jealousy without the slightest cause." This complicated matters more than ever. I knew Bombay to be a generous, honest man, entitled by his former services to be in the position he was now holding as fundi, or supervisor in the camp. Baraka, who never would have joined the expedition excepting through his invitation, was indebted to him for the rank he now enjoyed – a command over seventy men, a duty in which he might have distinguished himself as a most useful accessory to the camp. Again I called the two together, and begged them to act in harmony like brothers, noticing that there was no cause for entertaining jealousy on either side, as every order rested with myself to reward for merit or to punish. The relative position in the camp was like that of the senior officers in India, Bombay representing the Mulki lord, or Governor-General, and Baraka the Jungi lord, or Commander-in-Chief. To the influence of this distinguished comparison they both gave way, acknowledging myself their judge, and both protesting that they wished to serve in peace and quietness for the benefit of the march.

Zungomero is a terminus or junction of two roads leading to the interior – one, the northern, crossing over the Goma Pass, and trenching on the Mukondokua river, and the other crossing over the Mabruki Pass, and edging on the Ruaha river. They both unite again at Ugogi, the western terminus on the present great Unyamuezi line. On the former expedition I went by the northern line and returned by the southern, finding both equally easy, and, indeed, neither is worthy of special and permanent preference. In fact, every season makes a difference in the supply of water and provisions; and with every year, owing to incessant wars, or rather slave-hunts, the habitations of the wretched inhabitants become constantly changed – generally speaking, for the worse. Our first and last object, therefore, as might be supposed, from knowing these circumstances, was to ascertain, before mounting the hill-range, which route would afford us the best facilities for a speedy march now. No one, however, could or would advise us. The whole country on ahead, especially Ugogo, was oppressed by drought and famine. To avoid this latter country, then, we selected the southern route, as by doing so it was hoped we might follow the course of the Ruaha river from Maroro to Usenga and Usanga, and thence strike across to Unyanyembe, sweeping clear of Ugogo.

With this determination, after despatching a third set of specimens, consisting of large game animals, birds, snakes, insects, land and freshwater shells, and a few rock specimens, of which one was fossiliferous, we turned southwards, penetrating the forests which lie between the greater range and the little outlying one. At the foot of this is the Maji ya Wheta, a hot, deep-seated spring of fresh water, which bubbles up through many apertures in a large dome-shaped heap of soft lime – an accumulation obviously thrown up by the force of the spring, as the rocks on either side of it are of igneous character. We arrived at the deserted village of Kirengue. This was not an easy go-ahead march, for the halt had disaffected both men and mules. Three of the former bolted, leaving their loads upon the ground; and on the line of march, one of the mules, a full-conditioned animal, gave up the ghost after an eighteen hours' sickness. What his disease was I never could ascertain; but as all the remaining animals died afterwards much in the same manner, I may state for once and for all, that these attacks commenced with general swelling, at first on the face, then down the neck, along the belly and down the legs. It proved so obstinate that fire had no effect upon it; and although we cut off the tails of some to relieve them by bleeding, still they died.

In former days Kirengue was inhabited, and we reasonably hoped to find some supplies for the jungly march before us. But we had calculated without our host, for the slave-hunters had driven every vestige of humanity away; and now, as we were delayed by our three loads behind, there was nothing left but to send back and purchase more grain. Such was one of the many days frittered away in do-nothingness.

This day, all together again, we rose the first spurs of the well-wooded Usagara hills, amongst which the familiar bamboo was plentiful, and at night we bivouacked in the jungle.

Rising betimes in the morning, and starting with a good will, we soon reached the first settlements of Mbuiga, from which could be seen a curious blue mountain, standing up like a giant overlooking all the rest of the hills. The scenery here formed a strong and very pleasing contrast to any we had seen since leaving the coast. Emigrant Waziraha, who had been driven from their homes across the Kingani river by the slave-hunters, had taken possession of the place, and disposed their little conical-hut villages on the heights of the hill-spurs in such a picturesque manner, that one could not help hoping they would here at least be allowed to rest in peace and quietness. The valleys, watered by little brooks, are far richer, and even prettier, than the high lands above, being lined with fine trees and evergreen shrubs; while the general state of prosperity was such that the people could afford, even at this late season of the year, to turn their corn into malt to brew beer for sale; and goats and fowls were plentiful in the market.

Passing by the old village of Mbuiga, which I occupied on my former expedition, we entered some huts on the western flank of the Mbuiga district; and here, finding a coast-man, a great friend of the little sheikh's, willing to take back to Zanzibar anything we might give him, a halt was made, and I drew up my reports. I then consigned to his charge three of the most sickly of the Hottentots in a deplorable condition – one of the mules, that they might ride by turns – and all the specimens that had been collected. With regret I also sent back the camera; because I saw, had I allowed my companion to keep working it, the heat he was subjected to in the little tent whilst preparing and fixing his plates would very soon have killed him. The number of guinea-fowl seen here was most surprising.

A little lighter and much more comfortable for the good riddance of those grumbling "Tots," we worked up to and soon breasted the stiff ascent of the Mabruki Pass, which we surmounted without much difficulty. This concluded the first range of these Usagara hills; and once over, we dropped down to the elevated valley of Makata, where we halted two days to shoot. As a travelling Arab informed me that the whole of the Maroro district had been laid waste by the marauding Wahehe, I changed our plans again, and directed our attention to a middle and entirely new line, which in the end would lead us to Ugogi. The first and only giraffe killed upon the journey was here shot by Grant, with a little 40-gauge Lancaster rifle, at 200 yards' distance. Some smaller animals were killed; but I wasted all my time in fruitlessly stalking some wounded striped eland – magnificent animals, as large as Delhi oxen – and some other animals, of which I wounded three, about the size of hartebeest, and much their shape, only cream-coloured, with a conspicuous black spot in the centre of each flank. The eland may probably be the animal first mentioned by Livingstone, but the other animal is not known.

Though reluctant to leave a place where such rare animals were to be found, the fear of remaining longer on the road induced us to leave Kikobogo, and at a good stride we crossed the flat valley of Makata, and ascended the higher lands beyond, where we no sooner arrived than we met the last down trader from Unyamuezi, well known to all my men as the great Mamba or Crocodile. Mamba, dressed in a dirty Arab gown, with coronet of lion's nails decorating a thread-bare cutch cap, greeted us with all the dignity of a savage potentate surrounded by his staff of half-naked officials. As usual, he had been the last to leave the Unyamuezi, and so purchased all his stock of ivory at a cheap rate, there being no competitors left to raise the value of that commodity; but his journey had been a very trying one. With a party, at his own estimate, of two thousand souls – we did not see anything like that number – he had come from Ugogo to this, by his own confession, living on the products of the jungle, and by boiling down the skin aprons of his porters occasionally for a soup. Famines were raging throughout the land, and the Arabs preceding him had so harried the country, that every village was deserted. On hearing our intention to march upon the direct line, he frankly said he thought we should never get through for my men could not travel as he had done, and therefore he advised our deflecting northwards from New Mbumi to join the track leading from Rumuma to Ugogi. This was a sad disappointment; but, rather than risk a failure, I resolved to follow his advice.

After reaching the elevated ground, we marched over rolling tops, covered with small trees and a rich variety of pretty bulbs, and reached the habitations of Muhanda, where we no sooner appeared than the poor villagers, accustomed only to rough handling, immediately dispersed in the jungles. By dint of persuasion, however, we induced them to sell us provisions, though at a monstrous rate, such as no merchant could have afforded; and having spent the night quietly, we proceeded on to the upper courses of the M'yombo river, which trends its way northwards to the Mukondokua river. The scenery was most interesting, with every variety of hill, roll, plateau, and ravine, wild and prettily wooded; but we saw nothing of the people. Like frightened rats, as soon as they caught the sound of our advancing march, they buried themselves in the jungles, carrying off their grain with them. Foraging parties, of necessity, were sent out as soon as the camp was pitched, with cloth for purchases, and strict orders not to use force; the upshot of which was, that my people got nothing but a few arrows fired at them by the lurking villagers, and I was abused for my squeamishness. Moreover, the villagers, emboldened by my lenity, vauntingly declared they would attack the camp by night, as they could only recognise in us such men as plunder their houses and steal their children. This caused a certain amount of alarm among my men, which induced them to run up a stiff bush-fence round the camp, and kept them talking all night.

This morning we marched on as usual, with one of the Hottentots lashed on a donkey; for the wretched creature, after lying in the sun asleep, became so sickly that he could not move or do anything for himself, and nobody would do anything for him. The march was a long one, but under ordinary circumstances would have been very interesting, for we passed an immense lagoon, where hippopotami were snorting as if they invited an attack. In the larger tree-jungles the traces of elephants, buffaloes, rhinoceros, and antelopes were very numerous; while a rich variety of small birds, as often happened, made me wish I had come on a shooting rather than on a long exploring expedition. Towards sunset we arrived at New Mbimi, a very pretty and fertile place, lying at the foot of a cluster of steep hills, and pitched camp for three days to lay in supplies for ten, as this was reported to be the only place where we could buy corn until we reached Ugogo, a span of 140 miles. Mr. Mbumi, the chief of the place, a very affable negro, at once took us by the hand, and said he would do anything we desired, for he had often been to Zanzibar. He knew that the English were the ruling power in that land, and that they were opposed to slavery, the terrible effects of which had led to his abandoning Old Mbumi, on the banks of the Mukondokua river, and rising here.

The sick Hottentot died here, and we buried him with Christian honours. As his comrades said, he died because he had determined to die – an instance of that obstinate fatalism in their mulish temperament which no kind words or threats can cure. This terrible catastrophe made me wish to send all the remaining Hottentots back to Zanzibar; but as they all preferred serving with me to returning to duty at the Cape, I selected two of the MOST sickly, put them under Tabib, one of Rigby's old servants, and told him to remain with them at Mbumi until such time as he might find some party proceeding to the coasts; and, in the meanwhile, for board and lodgings I have Mbumi beads and cloth. The prices of provisions here being a good specimen of what one has to pay at this season of the year, I give a short list of them: sixteen rations corn, two yards cloth; three fowls, two yards cloth; one goat, twenty yards cloth; one cow, forty yards cloth, the cloth being common American sheeting. Before we left Mbumi, a party of forty men and women of the Waquiva tribe, pressed by famine, were driven there to purchase food. The same tribe had, however, killed many of Mbumi's subjects not long since, and therefore, in African revenge, the chief seized them all, saying he would send them off for sale to Zanzibar market unless they could give a legitimate reason for the cruelty they had committed. These Waquiva, I was given to understand, occupied the steep hills surrounding this place. They were a squalid-looking set, like the generality of the inhabitants of this mountainous region.

This march led us over a high hill to the Mdunhwi river, another tributary to the Mukondokua. It is all clad in the upper regions with the slender pole-trees which characterise these hills, intermingled with bamboo; but the bottoms are characterised by a fine growth of fig-trees of great variety along with high grasses; whilst near the villages were found good gardens of plantains, and numerous Palmyra trees. The rainy season being not far off, the villagers were busy in burning rubble and breaking their ground. Within their reach everywhere is the sarsaparilla vine, but growing as a weed, for they know nothing of its value.

Rising up from the deep valley of Mdunhwi we had to cross another high ridge before descending to the also deep valley of Chongue, as picturesque a country as the middle heights of the Himalayas, dotted on the ridges and spur-slopes by numerous small conical-hut villages; but all so poor that we could not, had we wanted it, have purchased provisions for a day's consumption.

Leaving this valley, we rose to the table of Manyovi, overhung with much higher hills, looking, according to the accounts of our Hottentots, as they eyed the fine herds of cattle grazing on the slopes, so like the range in Kafraria, that they formed their expectations accordingly, and appeared, for the first time since leaving the coast, happy at the prospect before them, little dreaming that such rich places were seldom to be met with. The Wanyamuezi porters even thought they had found a paradise, and forthwith threw down their loads as the villagers came to offer them grain for sale; so that, had I not had the Wanguana a little under control, we should not have completed our distance that day, and so reached Manyonge, which reminded me, by its ugliness, of the sterile Somali land. Proceeding through the semi-desert rolling table-land – in one place occupied by men who build their villages in large open squares of flat-topped mud huts, which, when I have occasion to refer to them in future, I shall call by their native name tembe – we could see on the right hand the massive mountains overhanging the Mukondokua river, to the front the western chain of these hills, and to the left the high crab-claw shaped ridge, which, extending from the western chain, circles round conspicuously above the swelling knolls which lie between the two main rocky ridges. Contorted green thorn-trees, "elephant-foot" stumps, and aloes, seem to thrive best here, by their very nature indicating what the country is, a poor stony land. Our camp was pitched by the river Rumuma, where, sheltered from the winds, and enriched by alluvial soil, there ought to have been no scarcity; but still the villagers had nothing to sell.

On we went again to Marenga Mkhaili, the "Salt Water," to breakfast, and camped in the crooked green thorns by night, carrying water on for our supper. This kind of travelling – forced marches – hard as it may appear, was what we liked best, for we felt that we were shortening the journey, and in doing so, shortening the risks of failure by disease, by war, by famine, and by mutiny. We had here no grasping chiefs to detain us for presents, nor had our men time to become irritable and truculent, concoct devices for stopping the way, or fight amongst themselves.

On again, and at last we arrived at the foot of the western chain; but not all together. Some porters, overcome by heat and thirst, lay scattered along the road, while the corporal of the Hottentots allowed his mule to stray from him, never dreaming the animal would travel far from his comrades, and, in following after him, was led such a long way into the bush, that my men became alarmed for his safety, knowing as they did that the "savages" were out living like monkeys on the calabash fruit, and looking out for any windfalls, such as stragglers worth plundering, that might come in their way. At first the Wanguana attempted to track down the corporal; but finding he would not answer their repeated shots, and fearful for their own safety, they came into camp and reported the case. Losing no time, I ordered twenty men, armed with carbines, to carry water for the distressed porters, and bring the corporal back as soon as possible. They all marched off, as they always do on such exploits, in high good-humour with themselves for the valour which they intended to show; and in the evening came in, firing their guns in the most reckless manner, beaming with delight; for they had the corporal in tow, two men and two women captives, and a spear as a trophy. Then in high impatience, all in a breath, they began a recital of the great day's work. The corporal had followed on the spoor of the mule, occasionally finding some of his things that had been torn from the beast's back by the thorns, and, picking up these one by one, had become so burdened with the weight of them, that he could follow no farther. In this fix the twenty men came up with him, but not until they had had a scrimmage with the "savages," had secured four, and taken the spear which had been thrown at them. Of the mule's position no one could give an opinion, save that they imagined, in consequence of the thickness of the bush, he would soon become irretrievably entangled in the thicket, where the savages would find him, and bring him in as a ransom for the prisoners.

What with the diminution of our supplies, the famished state of the country, and the difficulties which frowned upon us in advance, together with unwillingness to give up so good a mule, with all its gear and ammunition, I must say I felt doubtful as to what had better be done, until the corporal, who felt confident he would find the beast, begged so hard that I sent him in command of another expedition of sixteen men, ordering him to take one of the prisoners with him to proclaim to his brethren that we would give up the rest if they returned us the mule. The corporal then led off his band to the spot where he last saw traces of the animal, and tracked on till sundown; while Grant and myself went out pot-hunting and brought home a bag consisting of one striped eland, one saltiana antelope, four guinea-fowl, four ringdoves, and one partridge – a welcome supply, considering we were quite out of flesh.

Next day, as there were no signs of the trackers, I went again to the place of the elands, wounded a fine male, but gave up the chase, as I heard the unmistakable gun-firing return of the party, and straightway proceeded to camp. Sure enough, there they were; they had tracked the animal back to Marenga Mkhali, through jungle – for he had not taken to the footpath. Then finding he had gone on, they returned quite tired and famished. To make the most of a bad job, I now sent Grant on to the Robe-ho (or windy) Pass, on the top of the western chain, with the mules and heavy baggage, and directions to proceed thence across the brow of the hill the following morning, while I re-

One of Speke and Grant's camps.

mained behind with the tired men, promising to join him by breakfast-time. I next released the prisoners, much to their disgust, for they had not known such good feeding before, and dreaded being turned adrift again in the jungles to live on calabash seeds; and then, after shooting six guinea-fowl, turned in for the night.

Betimes in the morning we were off, mounting the Robeho, a good stiff ascent, covered with trees and large blocks of granite, excepting only where cleared for villages; and on we went rapidly, until at noon the advance party was reached, located in a village overlooking the great interior plateau – a picture, as it were, of the common type of African scenery. Here, taking a hasty meal, we resumed the march all together, descended the great western chain, and, as night set in, camped in a ravine at the foot of it, not far from the great junction-station Ugogi, where terminate the hills of Usagara.

---

1) It was such an attack as I had on my former journey; but while mine ceased to trouble me after the first year, his kept recurring every fortnight until the journey ended.

CHAPTER 4

UGOGO, AND THE WILDERNESS
OF MGUNDA MKHALI

The Lie of the Country – Rhinoceros-Stalking – Scuffle of Villagers Over a Carcass – Chief "Short-legs" and His Successors – Buffalo-Shooting – Getting Lost – A Troublesome Sultan – Desertions from the Camp – Getting Plundered – Wilderness March – Diplomatic Relations with the Local Powers – Manua Sera's Story – Christmas – The Relief from Kaze.

This day's work led us from the hilly Usagara range into the more level lands of the interior. Making a double march of it, we first stopped to breakfast at the quiet little settlement of Inenge, where cattle were abundant, but grain so scarce that the villagers were living on calabash seeds. Proceeding thence across fields delightfully checkered with fine calabash and fig trees, we marched, carrying water through thorny jungles, until dark, when we bivouacked for the night, only to rest and push on again next morning, arriving at Marenga Mkhali (the saline water) to breakfast. Here a good view of the Usagara hills is obtained. Carrying water with us, we next marched half-way to the first settlement of Ugogo, and bivouacked again, to eat the last of our store of Mbumi grain.

At length the greater famine lands had been spanned; but we were not in lands of plenty – for the Wagogo we found, like their neighbours Wasagara, eating the seed of the calabash, to save their small stores of grain.

The East Coast Range having been passed, no more hills had to be crossed, for the land we next entered on is a plateau of rolling ground, sloping southward to the Ruaha river, which forms a great drain running from west to east, carrying off all the rainwaters that fall in its neighbourhood through the East Coast Range to the sea. To the northward can be seen some low hills, which are occupied by Wahumba, a subtribe of the war-like Masai; and on the west is the large forest-wilderness of Mgunda Mkhali. Ugogo, lying under the lee side of the Usagara hills, is comparatively sterile. Small outcrops of granite here and there poke through the surface, which, like the rest of the rolling land, being covered with bush, principally acacias, have a pleasing appearance after the rains have set in, but are too brown and desert-looking during the rest of the year. Large prairies of grass also are exposed in many places, and the villagers have laid much ground bare for agricultural purposes.

Altogether, Ugogo has a very wild aspect, well in keeping with the natives who occupy it, who, more like the Wazaramo than the Wasagara, carry arms, intended for use rather than show. The men, indeed, are never seen without their usual arms – the spear, the shield, and the assage. They live in flat-topped, square, tembe villages, wherever springs of water are found, keep cattle in plenty, and farm enough generally to supply not only their own wants, but those of the thousands who annually pass in caravans.

They are extremely fond of ornaments, the most common of which is an ugly tube of the gourd thrust through the lower lobe of the ear. Their colour is a soft ruddy brown, with a slight infusion of black, not unlike that of a rich plum. Impulsive by nature, and exceedingly avaricious, they pester travellers beyond all conception, by thronging the road, jeering, quizzing, and pointing at them; and in camp, by intrusively forcing their way into the midst of the kit, and even into the stranger's tent. Caravans, in consequence, never enter their villages, but camp outside, generally under the big "gouty-limbed" trees – encircling their entire camp sometimes with a ring-fence of thorns to prevent any sudden attack.

To resume the thread of the journey: we found, on arrival in Ugogo, very little more food than in Usagara for the Wagogo were mixing their small stores of grain with the monkey-bread seeds of the gouty-limbed tree. Water was so scarce in the wells at this season that we had to buy it at the normal price of country beer; and, as may be imagined where such distress in food was existing, cows, goats, sheep, and fowls were also selling at high rates.

Our mules here gave us the slip again, and walked all the way back to Marenga Mkhali, where they were found and brought back by some Wagogo, who took four yards of merikani in advance, with a promise of four more on return, for the job – their chief being security for their fidelity. This business detained us two days, during which time I shot a new variety of florikan, peculiar in having a light blue band stretching from the nose over the eye to the occiput. Each day, while we resided here, cries were raised by the villagers that the Wahumba were coming, and then all the cattle out in the plains, both far and near, were driven into the village for protection.

At last, on the 26th, as the mules were brought it, I paid a hongo or tax of four barsati and four yards of chintz to the chief, and departed, but not until one of my porters, a Mhehe, obtained a fat dog for his dinner; he had set his heart on it, and would not move until he had killed it, and tied it on to his load for the evening's repast. Passing through the next villages – a collection called Kifukuro – we had to pay another small tax of two barsati and four yards of chintz to the chief. There we breakfasted, and pushed on, carrying water to a bivouac in the jungles, as the famine precluded our taking the march more easily.

Pushing on again, we cleared out of the woods, and arrived at the eastern border of the largest clearance of Ugogo, Kanyenye. Here we were forced to halt a day, as the mules were done up, and eight of the Wanyamuezi porters absconded, carrying with them the best part of their loads. There was also another inducement for stopping here; for, after stacking the loads, as we usually did on arriving in camp, against a large gouty-limbed tree, a hungry Mgogo, on eyeing our guns, offered his services to show us some bicornis rhinoceros, which, he said paid nightly visits to certain bitter pools that lay in the nullah bottoms not far off. This exciting intelligence made me inquire if it was not possible to find them at once; but, being assured that they lived very far off, and that the best chance was the night, I gave way, and settled on starting at ten, to arrive at the ground before the full moon should rise.

I set forth with the guide and two of the sheikh's boys, each carrying a single rifle, and ensconced myself in the nullah, to hide until our expected visitors should arrive, and there remained until midnight. When the hitherto noisy villagers turned into bed, the silvery moon shed her light on the desolate scene, and the Mgogo guide, taking fright, bolted. He had not, however, gone long, when, looming above us, coming over the horizon line, was the very animal we wanted.

In a fidgety manner the beast then descended, as if he expected some danger in store – and he was not wrong; for, attaching a bit of white paper to the fly-sight of my Blissett, I approached him, crawling under cover of the banks until within eighty yards of him, when, finding that the moon shone full on his flank, I raised myself upright and planted a bullet behind his left shoulder. Thus died my first rhinoceros.

To make the most of the night, as I wanted meat for my men to cook, as well as a stock to carry with them, or barter with the villagers for grain, I now retired to my old position, and waited again.

After two hours had elapsed, two more rhinoceros approached me in the same stealthy, fidgety way as the first one. They came even closer than the first, but, the moon having passed beyond their meridian, I could not obtain so clear a mark. Still they were big marks, and I determined on doing my best before they had time to wind us; so stepping out, with the sheikh's boys behind me carrying the second rifle to meet all emergencies, I planted a ball in the larger one, and brought him round with a roar and whooh-whooh, exactly to the best position I could wish for receiving a second shot; but, alas! on turning sharply round for the spare rifle, I had the mortification to see that both the black boys had made off, and were scrambling like monkeys up a tree. At the same time the rhinoceros, fortunately for me, on second consideration turned to the right-about, and shuffled away, leaving, as is usually the case when conical bullets are used, no traces of blood.

Thus ended the night's work. We now went home by dawn to apprise all the porters that we had flesh in store for them, when the two boys who had so shamelessly deserted me, instead of hiding their heads, described all the night's scenes with such capital mimicry as to set the whole camp in a roar. We had all now to hurry back to the carcass before the Wagogo could find it; but though this precaution was quickly taken, still, before the tough skin of the beast could be cut through, the Wagogo began assembling like vultures, and fighting with my men. A more savage, filthy, disgusting, but at the same time grotesque, scene than that which followed cannot be conceived. All fell to work armed with swords, spears, knives, and hatchets – cutting and slashing, thumping and bawling, fighting and tearing, tumbling and wrestling up to their knees in filth and blood in the middle of the carcass. When a tempting morsel fell to the possession of any one, a stronger neighbour would seize and bear off the prize in triumph. All right was now a matter or pure might, and lucky it was that it did not end in a fight between our men and the villagers. These might be afterwards seen, one by one, covered with blood, scampering home each with his spoil – a piece of tripe, or liver, or lights, or whatever else it might have been his fortune to get off with.

We were still in great want of men; but rather than stop a day, as all delays only lead to more difficulties, I pushed on to Magomba's palace with the assistance of some Wagogo carrying our baggage, each taking one cloth as his hire.

I *Richard Francis Burton (1821-90), top, and James Augustus Grant (1827-87), bottom.*
(© The Bridgeman Art Library)

II *This map, drawn by Speke, shows the water system of the African Great Lakes area.*
(© Royal Geographic Society)

III top *A work by H. W. Phillips depicting Speke and Grant with a native of the*
Upper Nile region.
(© Private Collection/National Potrait Gallery, London)

III bottom *One of Speke's maps showing the area of the Nile's exit from Lake Victoria.*
(© Royal Geographic Society)

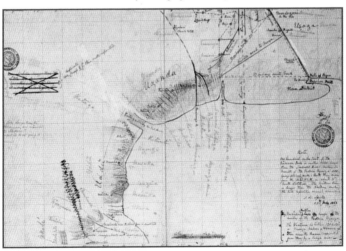

IV top *Grant presents King Rumanika of the Karagwe with a rhinoceros that he has killed.*

IV bottom *Grant during an elephant hunt, accompanied by a native guide.*

V top and V bottom *Nineteenth-century explorers like Speke, shown here shooting a buffalo, were often also skilled hunters. Hunting was necessary to provide fresh meat for the many members of their expeditions.*
(all from John Hanning Speke's, *Journal of the Discovery of the Nile*, London, 1863
© Private collection/Archivio White Star)

VI top *Grant caught up in the celebrations organized by Rumanika in his honor.*

VI bottom *At the court of the Ugandan king, Mtesa, ceremonies were held each day and British guests invited. This picture shows the king watching a parade of warriors.*

VII top *Speke and Grant sitting in the presence of Mtesa, while some of the king's subjects prostrate themselves.*

VII bottom *Mtesa lets himself be treated by Speke, who depicted him nude in his notebook.* (all from John Hanning Speke, *Journal of the Discovery of the Nile*, London, 1863 © Private collection/Archivio White Star)

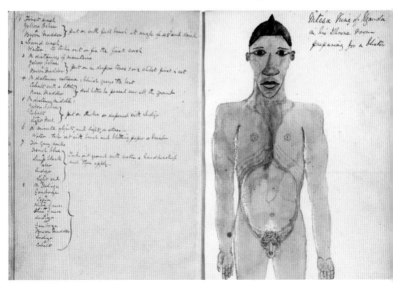

VIII top *Mtesa's "palace" was a complex of huts built on a hill.*

VIII bottom *Speke named the rapids formed by the Nile as it exits Lake Victoria the Ripon Falls.*
(all from John Hanning Speke, *Journal of the Discovery of the Nile*, London, 1863 © Private collection)

The chief wazir at once come out to meet me on the way, and in an apparently affable manner, as an old friend, begged that I would live in the palace – a bait which I did not take, as I knew my friend by experience a little too well. He then, in the politest possible manner, told me that a great dearth of food was oppressing the land – so much so, that pretty cloths only would purchase grain. I now wished to settle my hongo, but the great chief could not hear of such indecent haste.

The next day, too, the chief was too drunk to listen to any one, and I must have patience. I took out this time in the jungles very profitably, killing a fine buck and doe antelope, of a species unknown. These animals are much about the same size and shape as the common Indian antelope, and, like them, roam about in large herds. The only marked difference between the two is in the shape of their horns, as may be seen by the woodcut; and in their colour, in which, in both sexes, the Ugogo antelopes resemble the picticandata gazelle of Tibet, except that the former have dark markings on the face.

At last, after thousands of difficulties much like those I encountered in Uzaramo, the hongo was settled by a payment of one kisutu, one dubani, four yards bendera, four yards kiniki, and three yards merikani. The wazir then thought he would do some business on his own account, and commenced work by presenting me with a pot of ghee and flour, saying at the same time "empty words did not show true love," and hoping that I would prove mine by making some slight return. To get rid of the animal I gave him the full value of his present in cloth, which he no sooner pocketed than he had the audacity to accuse Grant of sacrilege for having shot a lizard on a holy stone, and demanded four cloths to pay atonement for this offence against the "church." As yet, he said, the chief was not aware of the damage done, and it was well he was not; for he would himself, if I only paid him the four cloths, settle matters quietly, otherwise there would be no knowing what demands might be made on my cloth. It was necessary to get up hot temper, else there was no knowing how far he would go; so I returned him his presents, and told the sheikh, instead of giving four, to fling six cloths in his face, and tell him that the holy-stone story was merely a humbug, and I would take care no more white men ever came to see him again.

Some Wanyamuezi porters, who had been left sick here by former caravans, now wished to take service with me as far as Kaze; but the Wagogo, hearing of their desire, frightened them off it. A report also at this time was brought to us, that a caravan had just arrived at our last ground, having come up from Whindi, direct by the line of the Wami river, in its upper course called Mukondokua, without crossing a single hill all the way; I therefore sent three men to see if they had any porters to spare, as it was said they had; but the three men, although they left their bows and arrows behind, never came back.

Another mule died to-day. This was perplexing indeed, but to stop longer was useless; so we pushed forward as best we could to a pond at the western end of the district where we found a party of Makua sportsmen who had just killed an elephant. They had lived in Ugogo one year and a half, and had killed in all seventeen elephants; half the tusks of which, as well as some portion of the flesh, they gave to Magomba for the privilege of residing there. There were many antelopes there, some of which both Grant and I shot for the good of the pot, and he also killed a crocute hyena. From the pond we went on to the middle of a large jungle, and bivouacked for the night in a shower of rain, the second of the season.

During a fierce downpour of rain, the porters all quivering and quaking with cold, we at length emerged from the jungle, and entered the prettiest spot in Ugogo – the populous district of Usekhe – where little hills and huge columns of granite crop out. Here we halted.

Next day came the hongo business, which was settled by paying one dubani, one kitambi, one msutu, four yards merikani, and two yards kiniki; but whilst we were doing it eight porters ran away, and four fresh ones were engaged (Wanyamuezi) who had run away from Kanyenye.

With one more march from this we reached the last district in Ugogo, Khoko. Here the whole of the inhabitants turned out to oppose us, imagining we had come there to revenge the Arab, Mohinna, because the Wagogo attacked him a year ago, plundered his camp, and drove him back to Kaze, for having shot their old chief "Short-legs." They, however, no sooner found out who we were than they allowed us to pass on, and encamp in the outskirts of the Mgunda Mkhali wilderness. To this position in the bush I strongly objected, on the plea that guns could be best used against arrows in the open; but none would go out in the field, maintaining that the Wagogo would fear to attack us so far from their villages, as we now were, lest we might cut them off in their retreat.

Hori Hori was now chief in Short-leg's stead, and affected to be much pleased that we were English, and not Arabs. He told us we might, he thought, be able to recruit all the men that we were in want of, as many Wanyanuezi who had been left there sick wished to go to their homes; and I would only, in addition to their wages, have to pay their "hotel bills" to the Wagogo. This, of course, I was ready to do, though I knew the Wanyamuezi had paid for themselves, as is usual, by their work in the fields of their hosts. Still, as I should be depriving these of hands, I could scarcely expect to get off for less than the value of a slave for each, and told Sheikh said to look out for some men at once, whilst at the same time he laid in provisions of grain to last us eight days in the wilderness, and settle the hongo.

For this triple business, I allowed three days, during which time, always eager to shoot something, either for science or the pot, I killed a bicornis rhinoceros, at a distance of five paces only, with my small 40-gauge Lancaster, as the beast stood quietly feeding in the bush; and I also shot a bitch fox of the genus Octocyon lalandii, whose ill-omened cry often alarms the natives by forewarning them of danger. This was rather tame sport; but next day I had better fun.

Starting in the early morning, accompanied by two of Sheikh Said's boys, Suliman and Faraj, each carrying a rifle, while I carried a shot-gun, we followed a footpath to the westward in the wilderness of Mgunda Mkhali. There, after walking a short while in the bush, as I heard the grunt of a buffalo close on my left, I took "Blissett" in hand, and walked to where I soon espied a large herd quietly feeding. They were quite unconscious of my approach, so I took a shot at a cow, and wounded her; then, after reloading, put a ball in a bull and staggered him also. This caused great confusion among them; but as none of the animals knew where the shots came from, they simply shifted about in a fidgety manner, allowing me to kill the first cow, and even fire a fourth shot, which sickened the great bull, and induced him to walk off, leaving the herd to their fate, who, considerably puzzled, began moving off also.

I now called up the boys, and determined on following the herd down before either skinning the dead cow or following the bull, who I knew could not go far. Their footprints being well defined in the moist sandy soil, we soon found the herd again; but as they now knew they were pursued, they kept moving on in short runs at a time, when, occasionally gaining glimpses of their large dark bodies as they forced through the bush, I repeated my shots and struck a good number, some more and some less severely. This was very provoking; for all of them being stern shots were not likely to kill, and the jungle was so thick I could not get a front view of them. Presently, however, one with her hind leg broken pulled up on a white-ant hill, and, tossing her horns, came down with a charge the instant I showed myself close to her. One crack of the rifle rolled her over, and gave me free scope to improve the bag, which was very soon done; for on following the spoors, the traces of blood led us up to another one as lame as the last. He then got a second bullet in the flank, and, after hobbling a little, evaded our sight and threw himself into a bush, where we not sooner arrived than he plunged headlong at us from his ambush, just, and only just, giving me time to present my small 40-gauge Lancaster.

It was a most ridiculous scene. Suliman by my side, with the instinct of a monkey, made a violent spring and swung himself by a bough immediately over the beast, whilst Faraj bolted away and left me single-gunned to polish him off. There was only one course to pursue, for in one instant more he would have been into me; so, quick as thought, I fired the gun, and, as luck would have it, my bullet, after passing through the edge of one of his horns, stuck in the spine of his neck, and rolled him over at my feet as dead as a rabbit. Now, having cut the beast's throat to make him "hilal," according to Mussulman usage, and thinking we had done enough if I could only return to the first wounded bull and settle him too, we commenced retracing our steps, and by accident came on Grant. He was passing by from another quarter, and became amused by the glowing description of my boys, who never omitted to narrate their own cowardice as an excellent tale. He begged us to go on in our course, whilst he would go back and send us some porters to carry home the game.

Now, tracking back again to the first point of attack, we followed the blood of the first bull, till at length I found him standing like a stuck pig in some bushes, looking as if he would like to be put out of his miseries. Taking compassion, I levelled my Blissett; but, as bad luck would have it, a bough intercepted the flight of the bullet, and it went "pinging" into the air, whilst the big bull went off at a gallop. To follow on was no difficulty, the spoor was so good; and in ten minutes more, as I opened on a small clearance, Blissett in hand, the great beast, from the thicket on the opposite side, charged down like a mad bull, full of ferocity – as ugly an antagonist as ever I saw, for the front of his head was all shielded with horn. A small mound fortunately stood between us, and as he rounded it, I jumped to one side and let fly at his flank, but without the effect of stopping him; for, as quick as thought, the huge monster was at my feet, battling with the impalpable smoke of my gun, which fortunately hung so thick on the ground at the height of his head that he could not see me, though I was so close that I might, had I been possessed of a hatchet, have chopped off his head. This was a predicament which looked very ugly, for my boys had both bolted, taking with them my guns; but suddenly the beast, evidently regarding the smoke as a phantom which could not be mastered, turned round in a bustle, to my intense relief, and galloped off at full speed, as if scared by some terrible apparition.

O what would I not then have given for a gun, the chance was such a good one! Still, angry though I was, I could not help laughing as the dastardly boys came into the clearance full of their mimicry, and joked over the scene they had witnessed in security, whilst my life was in jeopardy because they were too frightened to give me my gun. But now came the worst part of the day; for, though rain was falling, I had not the heart to relinquish my game. Tracking on through the bush, I thought every minute I should come up with the brute; but his wounds ceased to bleed, and in the confusion of the numerous tracks which scored all the forest we lost our own.

Much disappointed at this, I now proposed to make for the track we came by in the morning, and follow it down into camp; but this luxury was not destined to be our lot that night, for the rain had obliterated all our footprints of the morning, and we passed the track, mistaking it for the run of wild beasts. It struck me we had done so; but say what I would, the boys thought they knew better; and the consequence was that, after wandering for hours no one knew where – for there was no sun to guide us – I pulled up, and swore I would wait for the stars, else it might be our fate to be lost in the wilderness, which I did not much relish. We were all at this time "hungry as hunters," and beginning to feel very miserable from being wet through. What little ammunition I had left I fired off as signals, or made tinder of to get up a fire, but the wood would not burn. In this hapless condition the black boys began murmuring, wishing to go on, pretending, though both held opposite views, that each knew the way; for they thought nothing could be worse than their present state of discomfort.

Night with its gloom was then drawing on, heightened by thunder and lightning, which set in all around us. At times we thought we heard musketry in camp, knowing that Grant would be sure to fire signals for us; and doubtless we did so, but its sound and the thunder so much resembled one another that we distrusted our ears. At any rate, the boys mistook the west for the east; and as I thought they had done so, I stood firm to one spot, and finally lay down with them to sleep upon the cold wet ground, where we slept pretty well, being only disturbed occasionally by some animals sniffing at our feet. As the clouds broke towards morning, my obstinate boys still swore that west was east, and would hardly follow me when tracking down Venus; next up rose the moon and then followed the sun, when, as good luck would have it, we struck on the track, and walked straight into camp.

Here every one was in a great state of excitement: Grant had been making the men fire volleys. The little sheikh was warmly congratulatory as he spoke of the numbers who had strayed away and had been lost in that wilderness; whilst Bombay admitted he thought we should turn up again if I did not listen to the advice of the boys, which was his only fear. Nothing as yet, I now found, had been done to further our march. The hongo, the sheikh said, had to precede everything; yet that had not been settled, because the chief deferred it the day of our arrival, on the plea that it was the anniversary of Short-legs's death; and he also said that till then all the Wagogo had been in mourning by ceasing to wear all their brass bracelets and other ornaments, and they now wished to solemnise the occasion by feasting and renewing their finery. This being granted, the next day another pretext for delay was found, by the Wahumba having made a raid on their cattle, which necessitated the chief and all his men turning out to drive them away; and to-day nothing could be attended to, as a party of fugitive Wanyamuezi had arrived and put them all in a fright. These Wanyamuezi, it then transpired, were soldiers of Manua Sera, the "Tippler," who was at war with the Arabs. He had been defeated at Mguru, a district in Unyamuezi, by the Arabs, and had sent these men to cut off the caravan route, as the best way of retaliation that lay in his power.

At last the tax having been settled by the payment of one dubani, two barsati, one sahari, six yards merikani, and three yards kiniki (not, however, until I had our tents struck, and threatened to march away if the chief would not take it), I proposed going on with the journey, for our provisions were stored. But when the loads were being lifted, I found ten more men were missing; and as nothing now could be done but throw ten loads away, which seemed too great a sacrifice to be made in a hurry, I simply changed ground to show we were ready to march, and sent my men about, either to try to induce the fugitive Wanyamuezi to take service with me or else to buy donkeys, as the chief said he had some to sell.

We had already been here too long. A report was now spread that a lion had killed one of the chief's cows; and the Wagogo, suspecting that our being here was the cause of this ill luck, threatened to attack us. This no sooner got noised over the camp than all my Wanyamuezi porters, who had friends in Ugogo, left to live with them, and would not come back again even when the "storm had blown over," because they did not like the incessant rains that half deluged the camp. The chief, too, said he would not sell us his donkeys, lest we should give them back to Mohinna, from whom they were taken during his fight here. Intrigues of all sorts I could see were brewing, possibly at the instigation of the fugitive Wanyamuezi, who suspected we were bound to side with the Arabs – possibly from some other cause, I could not tell what; so, to clear out of this pandemonium as soon as possible I issued cloths to buy double rations, intending to cross the wilderness by successive relays in double the ordinary number of days. I determined at the same time to send forward two freed men to Kaze to ask Musa and the Arabs to send me out some provisions and men to meet us half-way.

Matters grew worse and worse. The sultan, now finding me unable to move, sent a message to say if I would not give him some better cloths to make his hongo more respectable, he would attack my camp; and advised all the Wanyamuezi who regarded their lives not to go near me if I resisted. This was by no means pleasant; for the porters showed their uneasiness by extracting their own cloths from my bundles, under the pretext that they wished to make some purchases of their own. I ought, perhaps, to have stopped this; but I thought the best plan was to show total indifference; so, at the same time that they were allowed to take their cloths, I refused to comply with the chief's request, and begged them to have no fear so long as they saw I could hold my own ground with my guns.

The Wanyamuezi, however, were panic-stricken, and half of them bolted, with the kirangozi at their head, carrying off all the double-ration cloths as well as their own. At this time, the sultan, having changed tactics, as he saw us all ready to stand on the defensive, sent back his hongo; but, instead of using threats, said he would oblige us with donkeys or anything else if we would only give him a few more pretty cloths. With this cringing, perfidious appeal I refused to comply, until the sheikh, still more cringing, implored me to give way else not a single man would remain with me. I then told him to settle with the chief himself, and give me the account, which amounted to three barsati, two sahari, and three yards merikani; but the donkeys were never alluded to.

With half my men gone, I still ordered the march, though strongly opposed to the advice of one of old Mamba's men, who was then passing by on his way to the coast, in command of his master's rear detachment. He thought it impossible for us to pull through the wilderness, with its jungle grasses and roots, depending for food only on Grant's gun and my own; still we made half-way to the Mdaburu nullah, taking some of Mamba's out to camp with us, as he promised to take letters and specimens down to the coast for us, provided I paid him some cloths as ready money down, and promised some more to be paid at Zanzibar. These letters eventually reached home, but not the specimens.

The rains were so heavy that the whole country was now flooded, but we pushed on to the nullah by relays, and pitched on its left bank. In the confusion of the march, however, we lost many more porters, who at the same time relieved us of their loads, by slipping off stealthily into the bush.

The fifteenth was a forced halt, as the stream was so deep and so violent we could not cross it. To make the best of this very unfortunate interruption, I now sent on two men to Kaze, with letters to Musa and Sheikh Snay, both old friends on the former expedition, begging them to send me sixty men, each carrying thirty rations of grain, and some country tobacco. The tobacco was to gratify my men, who said of all things they most wanted to cheer them was something to smoke. At the same time I sent back some other men to Khoko, with cloth to buy grain for present consumption, as some of my porters were already reduced to living on wild herbs and white ants. I then sent all the remaining men, under the directions of Bombay and Baraka, to fell a tall tree with hatchets, on the banks of the nullah, with a view to bridging it; but the tree dropped to the wrong side, and thwarted the plan. The rain ceased on the 17th, just as we put the rain-gauge out, which was at once interpreted to be our Uganga, or religious charm, and therefore the cause of its ceasing. It was the first fine day for a fortnight, so we were only too glad to put all our things out to dry, and rejoiced to think of the stream's subsiding. My men who went back to Khoko for grain having returned with next to nothing – though, of course, they had spent all the cloths – I sent back another batch with pretty cloths, as it was confidently stated that grain was so scarce there, nothing but the best fabrics would but it. This also proved a dead failure; but although animals were very scarce, Grant relieved our anxiety by shooting a zebra and an antelope.

After five halts, we forded the stream, middle deep, and pushed forwards again, doing short stages of four or five miles a-day, in the greatest possible confusion; for, whilst Grant and I were compelled to go out shooting all day for the pot, the sheikh and Bombay went on with the first half of the property and then, keeping guard over it sent the men back again to Baraka, who kept rear-guard, to have the rest brought on. Order there was none: the men hated this "double work"; all the Wanyamuezi but three deserted, with the connivance of the coast-men, carrying off their loads with them, under a mutual understanding, as I found out afterwards, that the coast-men were to go shares in the plunder as soon as we reached Unyamuezi. The next great obstacle in this tug-and-pull wilderness-march presented itself on the 24th, when, after the first half of the property had crossed the Mabunguru nullah, it rose in flood and cut off the rear half. It soon, however, subsided; and the next day we reached "the Springs," where we killed a pig and two rhinoceros. Not content, however, with this fare – notwithstanding the whole camp had been living liberally on zebra's and antelope's flesh every day previously – some of my coast-men bolted on to the little settlement of Jiwa la Mkoa, contrary to orders, to purchase some grain; and in doing so, increased our transport difficulties.

Pulling on in the same way again – when not actually engaged in shooting, scolding and storming at the men, to keep them up to the mark, and prevent them from shirking their work, which they were for every trying to do – we arrived on the 28th at the "Boss," a huge granite block, from the top of which the green foliage of the forest-trees looked like an interminable cloud, soft and waving, fit for fairies to dwell upon. Here the patience of my men fairly gave way, for the village of Jiwa la Mkoa was only one long march distance from us; and they, in consequence, smelt food on in advance much sweeter than the wild game and wild grasses they had been living on; and many more of them could not resist deserting us, though they might, had we all pulled together, have gone more comfortably in, as soon as the rear property arrived next day with Baraka.

All the men who deserted on the 25th, save Johur and Mutwana, now came into camp, and told us they had heard from travellers that those men who had been sent on for reliefs to Kaze were bringing us a large detachment of slaves to help us on. My men had brought no food either for us or their friends, as the cloths they took with them, "which were their own," were scarcely sufficient to purchase a meal – famines being as bad where they had been as in Ugogo. To try and get all the men together again, I now sent off a party loaded with cloths to see what they could get for us; but they returned on the 30th grinning and joking, with nothing but a small fragment of goat-flesh, telling lies by the dozens. Johur then came into camp, unconscious that Baraka by my orders had, during his absence, been inspecting his kit, where he found concealed

Captain Speke hunting buffalo.

seventy-three yards of cloth, which could only have been my property, as Johur had brought no akaba or reserve fund from the coast.

The theft having been proved to the satisfaction of every one, I ordered Baraka to strip him of everything and give him three dozen lashes; but after twenty-one had been given, the rest were remitted on his promising to turn Queen's evidence, when it transpired that Mutwana had done as much as himself. Johur, it turned out, was a murderer, having obtained his freedom by killing his master. He was otherwise a notoriously bad character; so, wishing to make an example, as I knew all my men were robbing me daily, though I could not detect them, I had him turned out of camp. Baraka was a splendid detective, and could do everything well when he wished it, so I sent him off now with cloths to see what he could to at Jiwa la Mkoa, and next day he returned triumphantly driving in cows and goats. Three Wanyamuezi, also, who heard we were given to shooting wild animals continually, came with him to offer their services as porters.

As nearly all the men had now returned, Grant and I spent New Year's Day with the first detachment at Jiwa la Mkoa, or Round Rock – a single tembe village occupied by a few Wakimbu settlers, who, by their presence and domestic habits, made us feel as though we were well out of the wood. So indeed we found it; for although this wilderness was formerly an entire forest of trees and wild animals, numerous Wakimbu, who formerly occupied the banks of the Ruaha to the southward, had been driven to migrate here, wherever they could find springs of water, by the boisterous naked pastorals the Warori.

At night three slaves belonging to Sheikh Salem bin Saif stole into our camp, and said they had been sent by their master to seek for porters at Kaze, as all the Wanyamuezi porters of four large caravans had deserted in Ugogo, and they could not move. I was rather pleased by this news, and thought it served the merchants right, knowing, as I well did, that the Wanyamuezi, being naturally honest, had they not been defrauded by foreigners on the down march to the coast, would have been honest still. Some provisions were now obtained by sending men out to distant villages; but we still supplied the camp with our guns, killing rhinoceros, wild boar, antelope, and zebras. The last of our property did not come up till the 5th, when another thief being caught, got fifty lashes, under the superintendence of Baraka, to show that punishment was only inflicted to prevent further crime.

The next day my men came from Kaze with letters from Sheikh Snay and Musa. They had been detained there some days after arrival, as those merchants' slaves had gone to Utambara to settle some quarrel there; but as soon as they returned, Musa ordered them to go and assist us, giving them beads to find rations for themselves on the way, as the whole country about Kaze had been half-starved by famines, though he did send a little rice and tobacco for me. The whole party left Kaze together; but on arrival at Tura the slaves said they had not enough beads and would return for some more, when they would follow my men. This bit of news was the worst that could have befallen us; my men were broken-hearted enough before, and this drove the last spark of spirit out of them. To make the best of a bad job, I now sent Bombay with two other men off to Musa to see what he could do, and ordered my other men to hire Wakimbu from village to village. On the 7th, a nervous excitement was produced in the camp by some of my men running in and calling all to arm, as the fugitive chief Manua Sera was coming, with thirty armed followers carrying muskets. Such was the case: and by the time my men were all under arms, with their sword-bayonets fixed, drawn up by my tent, the veritable "Tippler" arrived; but, not liking the look of such a formidable array as my men presented, he passed on a short way, and then sent back a deputation to make known his desire of calling on me, which was no sooner complied with than he came in person, attended by a body-guard. On my requesting him to draw near and sit, his wooden stool was placed for him. He began the conversation by telling me he had heard of my distress from want of porters, and then offered to assist me with some, provided I would take him to Kaze, and mediate between him and the Arabs; for, through their unjustifiable interference in his government affairs, a war had ensued, which terminated with the Arabs driving him from his possessions a vagabond. Manua Sera, I must say, was as fine a young man as ever I looked upon. He was very handsome, and looked as I now saw him the very picture of a captain of the banditti of the romances. I begged him to tell me his tale, and, in compliance, he gave me the following narrative: "Shortly after you left Kaze for England, my old father, the late chief Fundi Kira, died, and by his desire I became lawful chief; for, though the son of a slave girl, and not of Fundi Kira's wife, such is the law of inheritance – a constitutional policy established to prevent any chance of intrigues between the sons born in legitimate wedlock. Well, after assuming the title of chief, I gave presents of ivory to all the Arabs with a liberal hand, but most so to Musa, which caused great jealousy amongst the other merchants. Then after this I established a property tax on all merchandise that entered my country. Fundi Kira had never done so, but I did not think that any reason why I should not, especially as the Arabs were the only people who lived in my country exempt from taxation. This measure, however, exasperated the Arabs, and induced them to send me hostile messages, to

Ugogo antelopes.

115

the effect that, if I ever meddled with them, they would dethrone me, and place Mkisiwa, another illegitimate son, on the throne in my stead. This," Manua Sera continued, "I could not stand; the merchants were living on sufferance only in my country. I told them so, and defied them to interfere with my orders, for I was not a 'woman,' to be treated with contempt; and this got up a quarrel. Mkisiwa, seizing at the opportunity of the prize held out to him by the Arabs as his supporters, then commenced a system of bribery. Words led to blows; we had a long and tough fight; I killed many of their number, and they killed mine. Eventually they drove me from my palace, and placed Mkisiwa there as chief in my stead. My faithful followers however, never deserted me; so I went to Rubuga, and put up with old Maula there. The Arabs followed – drove me to Nguru, and tried to kill Maula for having fostered me. He, however, escaped them; but they destroyed his country, and then followed me down to Nguru. There we fought for many months, until all provisions were exhausted, when I defied them to catch me, and forced my way through their ranks. It is needless to say I have been a wanderer since; and though I wish to make friends, they will not allow it, but do all they can to hunt me to death. Now, as you were a friend of my father, I do hope you will patch up this war for me, which you must think is unjust." I told Manua Sera I felt very much for him, and I would do my best if he would follow me to Kaze; but I knew that nothing could ever be done unless he returned to the free-trade principles of his father. He then said he had never taken a single tax from the Arabs, and would gladly relinquish his intention to do so. The whole affair was commenced in too great a hurry; but whatever happened he would gladly forgive all if I would use my influence to reinstate him, for by no other means could he ever get his crown back again. I then assured him that I would do what I could to restore the ruined trade of his country, observing that, as all the ivory that went out of his country, came to ours, and all imports were productions of our country also, this war injured us as well as himself. Manua Sera seemed highly delighted, and said he had a little business to transact in Ugogo at present, but he would overtake me in a few days. He then sent me one of my runaway porters, whom he had caught in the woods making off with a load of my beads. We then separated; and Baraka, by my orders, gave the thief fifty lashes for his double offence of theft and desertion.

On the 9th, having bought two donkeys and engaged several men, we left Jiwa la Mkoa, with half our traps, and marched to Garaeswi, where, to my surprise, there were as many as twenty tembes – a recently-formed settlement of Wokimbu. Here we halted a day for the rear convoy, and then went on again by detachments to Zimbo, where, to our intense delight, Bombay returned to us on the 13th, triumphantly firing guns, with seventy slaves accompanying him, and with letters from Snay and Musa, in which they said they hoped, if I met with Manua Sera, that I would either put a bullet through his head, or else bring him in a prisoner, that they might do for him, for the scoundrel had destroyed all their trade by cutting off caravans. Their fights with him commenced by his levying taxes in opposition to their treaties with his father, Fundi Kira, and then preventing his subjects selling them grain.

Once more the whole caravan moved on; but as I had to pay each of the seventy slaves sixteen yards of cloth, by order of their masters, in the simple matter of expenditure it would have been better had I thrown ten loads away at Ugogo, where my difficulties first commenced. On arrival at Mgongo Thembo – the Elephant's Back – called so in consequence of a large granitic rock, which resembles the back of that animal, protruding through the ground – we found a clearance in the forest, of two miles in extent, under cultivation. Here the first man to meet me was the fugitive chief of Rubuga, Maula. This poor old man – one of the honestest chiefs in the country – had been to the former expedition a host and good friend. He now gave me a cow as a present, and said he would give me ten more if I would assist him in making friends with the Arabs, who had driven him out of his country, and had destroyed all his belongings, even putting a slave to reign in his stead, though he had committed no fault of intentional injury towards them. It was true Manua Sera, their enemy, had taken refuge in his palace, but that was not his fault; for, anticipating the difficulties that would arise, he did his best to keep Manua Sera out of it, but Manua Sera being too strong for him, forced his way in. I need not say I tried to console this unfortunate victim of circumstances as best I could, inviting him to go with me to Kaze, and promising to protect him with my life if he feared the Arabs; but the old man, being too feeble to travel himself, said he would send his son with me.

Next day we pushed on a double march through the forest, and reached a nullah. As it crosses the track in a southerly direction, this might either be the head of the Kululu mongo or river, which, passing through the district of Kiwele, drains westward into the Malagarazi river, and thence into the Tanganyika, or else the most westerly tributary to the Ruaha river, draining eastward into the sea. The plateau, however, is apparently so flat here, that nothing but a minute survey, or rather following the watercourse, could determine the matter. Then emerging from the wilderness, we came into the open cultivated district of Tura, or "put down" – called so by the natives because it was, only a few years ago, the first cleared space in the wilderness, and served as a good halting-station, after the normal ten day's march in the jungles, where we had now been struggling more than a month.

The whole place, once so fertile, was now almost depopulated and in a sad state of ruin, showing plainly the savage ravages of war; for the Arabs and their slaves, when they take the field, think more of plunder and slavery than the object they started on – each man of the force looking out for himself. The incentives, too, are so great; – a young woman might be caught (the greatest treasure of earth), or a boy or a girl, a cow or a goat – all of the fortunes, of themselves too irresistible to be overlooked when the future is doubtful. Here Sheikh Said broke down in health of a complaint which he formerly had suffered from, and from which I at once saw he would never recover sufficiently well to be ever effective again. It was a sad misfortune, as the men had great confidence in him, being the representative of their Zanzibar government: still it could not be helped; for, as a sick man is, after all, the greatest possible impediment to a march, it was better to be rid of him than have the trouble of dragging him; so I made up my mind, as soon as we reached

Kaze, I would drop him there with the Arabs. He could not be moved on the 16th, so I marched across the plain and put up in some villages on its western side. Whilst waiting for the sheikh's arrival, some villagers at night stole several loads of beads, and ran off with them; but my men, finding the theft out in time, hunted them down, and recovered all but one load – for the thieves had thrown their loads down as soon as they found they were hotly pursued.

Early this morning I called all the head men of the village together, and demanded the beads to be restored to me; for, as I was living with them, they were responsible, according to the laws of the country. They acknowledged the truth and force of my demand, and said they would each give me a cow as an earnest, until their chief, who was absent, arrived. This, of course, was objected to, as the chief, in his absence, must have deputed some one to govern for him, and I expected him to settle at once, that I might proceed with the march. Then selecting five of my head men to conduct the case, with five of their elders, it was considered my losses were equivalent to thirty head of cattle. As I remitted the penalty to fifteen head, these were made over to me, and we went on with the march – all feeling delighted with the issue but the Hottentots, who, not liking the loss of the second fifteen cows, said that in Kafirland, where the laws of the country are the same as here, the whole would have been taken, and, as it was, they thought I was depriving them of their rights to beef.

By a double march, the sheikh riding in a hammock slung on a pole, we now made Kuale, or "Partridge" nullah, which, crossing the road to the northward, drains these lands to the Malagarazi river, and thence into the Tanganyika lake. Thence, having spent the night in the jungle, we next morning pushed into the cultivated district of Rubuga, and put up in some half-deserted tembes, where the ravages of war were even more disgusting to witness than at Tura. The chief, as I have said, was a slave, placed there by the Arabs on the condition that he would allow all traders and travellers to help themselves without payment as long as they chose to reside there. In consequence of this wicked arrangement, I found it impossible to keep my men from picking and stealing. They looked upon plunder as their fortune and right, and my interference as unjustifiable.

By making another morning and evening march, we then reached the western extremity of this cultivated opening; where, after sleeping the night, we threaded through another forest to the little clearance of Kigue, and in one more march through forest arrived in the large and fertile district of Unyanyembe, the centre of Unyamuezi – the Land of the Moon – within five miles of Kaze, which is the name of a well in the village of Tbora, now constituted the great central slave and ivory merchants' depot.

My losses up to this date (23d) were as follows: One Hottentot dead and five returned; one freeman sent back with the Hottentots, and one flogged and turned off; twenty-five of Sultan Majid's gardeners deserted; ninety-eight of the original Wanyamuezi porters deserted; twelve mules and three donkeys dead. Besides which, more than half of my property had been stolen; whilst the travelling expenses had been unprecedented, in consequence of the severity of the famine throughout the whole length of the march.

CHAPTER 5

UNYAMUEZI

The Country and People of U-n-ya-muezi – Kaze, the Capital – Old Musa – The Naked Wakidi – The N'yanza, and the Question of the River Running In or Out – The Contest between Mohinna and "Short-legs" – Famine – The Arabs and Local Wars – The Sultana of Unyambewa – Ungurue "The Pig" – Pillage.

U-n-ya-muezi – Country of Moon – must have been one of the largest kingdoms in Africa. It is little inferior in size to England, and of much the same shape, though now, instead of being united, it is cut up into petty states. In its northern extremities it is known by the appellation U-sukuma – country north; and in the southern, U-takama – country south. There are no historical traditions known to the people; neither was anything ever written concerning their country, as far as we know, until the Hindus, who traded with the east coast of Africa, opened commercial dealings with its people in salves and ivory, possibly some time prior to the birth of our Saviour, when, associated with their name, Men of the Moon, sprang into existence the Mountains of the Moon. These Men of the Moon are hereditarily the greatest traders in Africa, and are the only people who, for love of barter and change, will leave their own country as porters and go to the coast, and they do so with as much zest as our country-folk go to a fair. As far back as we can trace they have done this, and they still do it as heretofore. The whole of their country ranges from 3,000 to 4,000 feet above the sea-level – a high plateau, studded with little outcropping hills of granite, between which, in the valleys, there are numerous fertilising springs of fresh water, and rich iron ore is found in sandstone. Generally industrious – much more so than most other negroes – they cultivate extensively, make cloths of cotton in their own looms, smelt iron and work it up very expertly, build tembes to live in over a large portion of their country, but otherwise live in grass huts, and keep flocks and herds of considerable extent.

The Wanyamuezi, however, are not a very well-favoured people in physical appearance, and are much darker than either the Wazaramo or the Wagogo, though many of their men are handsome and their women pretty; neither are they well dressed or well armed, being wanting in pluck and gallantry. Their women, generally, are better dressed than the men. Cloths fastened round under the arms are their national costume, along with a necklace of beads, large brass or copper wire armlets, and a profusion of thin circles, called sambo, made of the giraffe's tail-hairs bound round by the thinnest iron or copper wire; whilst the men at home wear loin-cloths, but in the field, or whilst travelling, simply hang a goat-skin over their shoulders, exposing at least three-fourths of their body in a rather indecorous manner. In all other respects they ornament themselves like the women, only, instead of a long coil of wire wound up the arm, they content themselves with having massive rings of copper or brass on the wrist; and they carry for arms a spear and bow and arrows. All extract more or less their lower incisors, and cut a [upside-down V shape] between their two upper incisors. The whole tribe are desperate smokers, and greatly given to drink.

On the 24th, we all, as many as were left of us, marched into the merchant's depot, S. lat. 5° 0' 52", and E. long. 33° 1' 34",[1] escorted by Musa, who advanced to meet us, and guided us into his tembe, where he begged we would reside with him until we could find men to carry our property on to Karague. He added that he would accompany us; for he was on the point of going there when my first instalment of property arrived, but deferred his intention out of respect to myself. He had been detained at Kaze ever since I last left it in consequence of the Arabs having provoked a war with Manua Sera, to which he was adverse. For a long time also he had been a chained prisoner; as the Arabs, jealous of the favour Manua Sera had shown to him in preference to themselves, basely accused him of supplying Manua Sera with gunpowder, and bound him hand and foot "like a slave." It was delightful to see old Musa's face again, and the supremely hospitable, kind, and courteous manner in which he looked after us, constantly bringing in all kind of small delicacies, and seeing that nothing was wanting to make us happy. All the property I had sent on in advance he had stored away; or rather, I should say, as much as had reached him, for the road expenses had eaten a great hole in it.

Once settled down into position, Sheikh Snay and the whole conclave of Arab merchants came to call on me. They said they had an army of four hundred slaves armed with muskets ready to take the field at once to hunt down Manua Sera, who was

125

cutting their caravan road to pieces, and had just seized, by their latest reports, a whole convoy of their ammunition. I begged them strongly to listen to reason, and accept my advice as an old soldier, not to carry on their guerilla warfare in such a headlong hurry, else they would be led a dance by Manua Sera, as we had been by Tantia Topee in India. I advised them to allow me to mediate between them, after telling them what a favourable interview I had had with Manua Sera and Maula, whose son was at that moment concealed in Musa's tembe. My advice, however, was not wanted. Snay knew better than any one how to deal with savages, and determined on setting out as soon as his army had "eaten their beef-feast of war." On my questioning him about the Nile, Snay still thought the N'yanza was the source of the Jub river[2] as he did in our former journey, but gave way when I told him that vessels frequented the Nile, as this also coincided with his knowledge of navigators in vessels appearing on some waters to the northward of Unyoro. In a great hurry he then bade me good-bye; when, as he thought it would be final, I gave him, in consideration of his former good services to the last expedition, one of the gold watches given me by the Indian Government. I saw him no more, though he and all the other Arabs sent me presents of cows, goats, and rice, with a notice that they should have gone on their war-oath before, only, hearing of my arrival, out of due respect to my greatness they waited to welcome me in. Further, after doing for Manua Sera, they were determined to go on to Ugogo to assist Salem bin Saif and the other merchants on, during which, at the same time, they would fight all the Wagogo who persisted in taking taxes and in harassing caravans. At the advice of Musa, I sent Maula's son off at night to tell the old chief how sorry I was to find the Arabs so hot-headed I could not even effect an arrangement with them. It was a great pity; for Manua Sera was so much liked by the Wanyamuezi, they would, had they been able, have done anything to restore him.

Next day the non-belligerent Arabs left in charge of the station, headed by my old friends Abdulla and Mohinna, came to pay their respects again, recognising in me, as they said, a "personification of their sultan," and therefore considering what they were doing only due to my rank. They regretted with myself that Snay was so hot-headed; for they themselves thought a treaty of peace would have been the best thing for them, for they were more than half-ruined already, and saw no hope for the future. Then, turning to geography, I told Abdulla all I had

The water system in the mountains west of Nyanza.

written and lectured in England concerning his stories about navigators on the N'yanza, which I explained must be the Nile, and wished to know if I should alter it in any way: but he said, "Do not; you may depend it will all turn out right"; to which Musa added, all the people in the north told him that when the N'yanza rose, the stream rushed with such violence it tore up islands and floated them away.

I was puzzled at this announcement, not then knowing that both the lake and the Nile, as well as all ponds, were called N'yanza: but we shall see afterwards that he was right; and it was in consequence of this confusion in the treatment of distinctly different geographical features under one common name by these people, that in my former journey I could not determine where the lake had ended and the Nile began. Abdulla again – he had done so on the former journey – spoke to me of a wonderful mountain to the northward of Karague, so high and steep no one could ascend it. It was, he said, seldom visible, being up in the clouds, where white matter, snow or hail, often fell. Musa said this hill was in Ruanda, a much larger country than Urundi; and further, both men said, as they had said before, that the lands of Usoga and Unyoro were islands, being surrounded by water; and a salt lake, which was called N'yanza, though not the great Victoria N'yanza lay on the other side of the Unyoro, from which direction Rumanika, king of Karague, sometimes got beads forwarded to him by Kamrasi, king of Unyoro, of a different sort from any brought from Zanzibar. Moreover, these beads were said to have been plundered from white men by the Wakidi – a stark-naked people who live up in trees – have small stools fixed on behind, always ready for sitting – wear their hair hanging down as far as the rump, all covered with cowrie-shells – suspend beads from wire attached to their ears and their lower lips – and wear strong iron collars and bracelets.

This people, I was told, are so fierce in war that no other tribe can stand against them, though they only fight with short spears.

When this discourse was ended, ever perplexed about the Tanganyika being a still lake, I enquired of Mohinna and other old friends what they thought about the Marungu river: did it run into or out of the lake? And they all still adhered to its running into the lake – which, after all, in my mind, is the most conclusive argument that it does run out of the lake, making it one of a chain of lakes leading to the N'yanza, and through it by the Zambezi into the sea; for all the Arabs on the former journey said the Rusizi river ran out of the Tanganyika, as also the Kitangule ran out of the N'yanza, and the Nile ran into it, even though Snay said he thought the Jub river drained the N'yanza. All these statements were, when literally translated into English, the reverse of what the speakers, using a peculiar Arab idiom, meant to say; for all the statements made as to the flow of rivers by the negroes – who apparently give the same meaning to "out" and "in" as we do – contradicted the Arabs in their descriptions of the direction of the flow of these rivers.

Mohinna now gave us a very graphic description of his fight with Short-legs, the late chief of Khoko. About a year ago, as he was making his way down to the coast with his ivory merchandise, on arrival at Khoko, and before his camp was fortified with a ring-fence of thorns, some of his men went to drink at a well, where they no sooner arrived than the natives began to bean them with sticks, claiming the well as their property. This commenced a row, which brought out a large body of men, who demanded a bullock at the point of their spears. Mohinna hearing this, also came to the well, and said he would not listen to their demand, but would drink as he wished, for the water was the gift of God. Words then changed to blows. All Mohinna's pagazis bolted, and his merchandise fell into the hands of the Wagogo. Had his camp been fortified, he think he would have been too much for his enemies; but, as it was, he retaliated by shooting Short-legs in the head, and at once bolted back to Kaze with a few slaves as followers, and his three wives.

The change that had taken place in Unyanyembe since I last left it was quite surprising. Instead of the Arabs appearing merchants, as they did formerly, they looked more like great farmers, with huge stalls of cattle attached to their houses; whilst the native villages were all in ruins – so much so that, to obtain corn for my men, I had to send out into the district several days' journey off, and even then had to pay the most severe famine prices for what I got. The Wanyamuezi, I was assured, were dying of starvation in all directions; for, in addition to the war, the last rainy season had been so light, all their crops had failed.

27th and 28th. – I now gave all my men presents for the severe trials they had experienced in the wilderness, forgetting, as I told them, the merciless manner in which they had plundered me; but as I gave a trifle more in proportion to the three sole remaining pagazis, because they had not finished their work, my men were all discontented, and wished to throw back their presents, saying I did not love them, although they were "perminents," as much as the "temperaries." They, however, gave in, after some hours of futile arguments, on my making them understand, through Baraka, that what they saw me give to the pagazis would, if they reflected, only tend to prove to them that I was not a bad master who forgot his obligations when he could get no more out of his servants.

I then went into a long inquiry with Musa about our journey northward to Karague; and as he said there were no men to be found in or near Unyanyembe, for they were either all killed or engaged in the war, it was settled he should send some of his head men on to Rungua, where he had formerly resided, trading for some years, and was a great favourite with the chief of the place, by name Kiringuana. He also settled that I might take out of his establishment of slaves as many men as I could induce to go with me, for he thought them more trouble than profit, hired porters being more safe; moreover, he said the plan would be of great advantage to him, as I offered to pay, both man and master, each the same monthly stipend as I gave my present men. This was paying double, and all the heavier a burden, as the number I should require to complete my establishment to one hundred armed men would be sixty. He, however, very generously advised me not to take them, as they would give so much trouble; but finally gave way when I told him I felt I could not advance beyond Karague unless I was quite independent of the natives there – a view in which he concurred.

29th and 30th. – Jafu, another Indian merchant here, and co-partner of Musa, came in from a ten days' search after grain, and described the whole country to be in the most dreadful state of famine. Wanyamuezi were lying about dead from starvation in all directions, and he did not think we should ever get through Usui, as Suwarora, the chief, was so extortionate he would "tear us to pieces"; but advised our waiting until the war was settled, when all the Arabs would combine and go with us. Musa even showed fear, but arranged, at my suggestion, that he should send some men to Rumanika, informing him of our intention to visit him, and begging, at the same time, he would use his influence in preventing our being detained in Usui.

I may here explain that the country Uzinza was once a large kingdom, governed by a king named Ruma, of Wahuma blood. At his death, which took place in Dagara's time (the present Rumanika's father), the kingdom was contested by his two sons, Rohinda and Suwarora, but, at the intercession of Dagara, was divided – Rohinda taking the eastern, called Ukhanga, and Suwarora the western half of the country, called Usui. This measure made Usui feudatory to Karague, so that much of the produce of the extortions committed in Usui went to Karague, and therefore they were recognised, though the odium always rested on Suwarora, "the savage extortioner," rather than on the mild-disposed king of Karague, who kept up the most amicable relations with every one who visited him.

Musa, I must say, was most loud in his praises of Rumanika; and on the other hand, as Musa, eight years ago, had saved Rumanika's throne for him against an insurrection got up by his younger brother Rogero, Rumanika, always regarding Musa as his saviour, never lost an opportunity to show his gratitude, and would have done anything that Musa might have asked him. Of this matter, however, more in Karague.

132

31st. – To-day, Jafu, who had lost many ivories at Khoko when Mohinna was attacked there, prepared 100 slaves, with Said bin Osman, Mohinna's brother, with a view to follow down Snay, and, combining forces, attack Hori Hori, hoping to recover their losses; for it appeared to them the time had now come when their only hope left in carrying their trade to a successful issue, lay in force of arms. They would therefore not rest satisfied until they had reduced Khoko and Usekhe both, by actual force, to acknowledge their superiority, "feeding on them" until the Ramazan, when they would return with all the merchants detained in Ugogo, and, again combining their forces, they would fall on Usui, to reduce that country also.

When these men had gone, a lunatic set the whole place in commotion. He was a slave of Musa's, who had wounded some men previously in his wild excesses, and had been tied up; but now, breaking loose again, he swore he would not be satisfied until he killed some "big man." His strength was so great no one could confine him, though they hunted him into a hut, where, having seized a gun and some arrows, he defied any one to put hands on him. Here, however, he was at last reduced to submission and a better state of his senses by starvation: for I must add, the African is much given to such mental fits of aberration at certain periods; these are generally harmless, but sometimes not; but they come and they go again without any visible cause.

1st. – Musa's men now started for Rungua, and promised to bring all the porters we wanted by the first day of the next moon. We found that this would be early enough, for all the members of the expedition, excepting myself, were suffering from the effects of the wilderness life – some with fever, some with scurvy, and some with ophthalmia – which made it desirable they should all have rest. Little now was done besides counting out my property, and making Sheikh Said, who became worse and worse, deliver his charge of Cafila Bashi over to Bombay for good. When it was found so much had been stolen, especially of the best articles, I was obliged to purchase many things from Musa, paying 400 per cent, which he said was their value here, over the market price of Zanzibar. I also got him to have all my coils of brass and copper wire made into bracelet, as is customary, to please the northern people.

7th. – To-day information was brought here that whilst Manua Sera was on his way from Ugogo to keep his appointment with me, Sheikh Snay's army came on him at Tura, where he was ensconced in a tembe. Hearing this, Snay, instead of attacking the village at once, commenced negotiations with the chief of the place by demanding him to set free his guest, otherwise they, the Arabs, would storm the tembe. The chief, unfortunately, did not comply at once, but begged grace for one night, saying that if Manua Sera was found there in the morning they might do as they liked. Of course Manua bolted; and the Arabs, seeing the Tura people all under arms ready to defend themselves the next morning, set at them in earnest, and shot, murdered, or plundered the whole of the district. Then, whilst Arabs were sending in their captures of women, children, and cattle, Manua Sera made off to a district called Dara, where he formed an alliance with its chief, Kifunja, and boasted he would attack Kaze as soon as the travelling season commenced, when the place would be weakened by the dispersion of the Arabs on their ivory excursions.

The startling news set the place in a blaze, and brought all the Arabs again to seek my advice for they condemned what Snay had done in not listening to me before, and wished to know if I could not now treat for them with Manua Sera, which they thought could be easily managed, as Manua Sera himself was not only the first to propose mediation, but was actually on his way here for the purpose when Snay opposed him. I said nothing could give me greater pleasure than mediating for them, to put a stop to these horrors, but it struck me the case had now gone too far. Snay, in opposition to my advice, was bent on fighting; he could not be recalled and unless all the Arabs were of one mind, I ran the risk of committing myself to a position I could not maintain. To this they replied that the majority were still at Kaze, all wishing for peace at any price, and that whatever terms I might wish to dictate they would agree to. Then I said, "What would you do with Mkisiwa? You have made him chief, and cannot throw him over." "Oh, that," they said, "can be easily managed; for formerly, when we confronted Manua Sera at Nguru, we offered to give him as much territory as his father governed, though not exactly in the same place; but he treated our message with disdain, not knowing then what a fix he was in. Now, however, as he has seen more, and wishes for peace himself, there can be no difficulty." I then ordered two of my men to go with two of Musa's to acquaint Manua Sera with what we were about, and to know his views on the subject; but these men returned to say Manua Sera could not be found, for he was driven from "pillar to post" by the different native chiefs, as, wherever he went, his army ate up their stores, and brought nothing but calamities with them. Thus died this second attempted treaty. Musa then told me it was well it turned out so; for Manua Sera would never believe the Arabs, as they had broken faith so often before, even after exchanging blood by cutting incisions in one another's legs – the most sacred bond or oath the natives know of.

As nothing more of importance was done, I set out with Grant to have a week's shooting in the district, under the guidance of an old friend, Fundi Sangoro, Musa's "head gamekeeper," who assured me that the sable antelope and blanc boc, specimens of which I had not yet seen, inhabited some low swampy place called N'yama, or "Meat," not far distant, on the left bank of the Wale nullah. My companion unfortunately got fever here, and was prevented from going out, and I did little better; for although I waded up to my middle every day, and wounded several blanc boc, I only bagged one, and should not have got even him, had it not happened that some lions in the night pulled him down close to our camp, and roared so violently that they told us the story. The first thing in the morning I wished to have at them; but they took the hint of daybreak to make off, and left me only the half of the animal. I saw only one sable antelope. We all went back to Kaze, arriving there on the 24th.

25th to 13th. – Days rolled on, and nothing was done in particular – beyond increasing my stock of knowledge of distant places and people, enlarging my zoological collection, and taking long series of astronomical observations – until the 13th, when the whole of Kaze was depressed by a sad scene of mourning and tears. Some slaves came in that night – having made their way through the woods from Ugogo, avoiding the track to save themselves from detection – and gave information that Snay, Jafu, and five other Arabs, had been killed, as well as a great number of slaves. The expedition, they said, had been defeated, and the positions were so complicated nobody knew what to do. At first the Arabs achieved two brilliant successes, having succeeded in killing Hori Hori of Khoko, when they recovered their ivory, made slaves of all they could find, and took a vast number of cattle; then attacking Usekhe they reduced that place to submission by forcing a ransom out of its people. At this period, however, they heard that a whole caravan, carrying 5,000 dollars' worth of property, had been cut up by the people of Mzanza, a small district ten miles north of Usekhe; so, instead of going on to Kanyenye to relieve the caravans which were waiting there for them, they foolishly divided their forces into three parts. Of these they sent one to take their loot back to Kaze, another to form a reserve force at Mdaburu, on the east flank of the wilderness, and a third, headed by Snay and Jafu, to attack Mzanza. At the first onset Snay and Jafu carried everything before them, and became so excited over the amount of their loot that they lost all feelings of care or precaution.

In this high exuberance of spirits, a sudden surprise turned their momentary triumph into a total defeat; for some Wahumba, having heard the cries of the Wagogo, joined in their cause, and both together fell on the Arab force with such impetuosity that the former victors were now scattered in all directions. Those who could run fast enough were saved – the rest were speared to death by the natives. Nobody knew how Jafu fell; but Snay, after running a short distance, called one of his slaves, and begged him to take his gun, saying, "I am too old to keep up with you; keep this gun for my sake, for I will lie down here and take my chance." He never was seen again. But this was not all their misfortunes; for the slaves who brought in this information had met the first detachment, sent with the Khoko loot, at Kigua, where, they said, the detachment had been surprised by Manua Sera, who, having fortified a village with four hundred men, expecting this sort of thing, rushed out upon them, and cut them all up.

The Arabs, after the first burst of their grief was over, came to me again in a body, and begged me to assist them, for they were utterly undone. Manua Sera prevented their direct communication with their detachment at Mdaburu, and that again was cut off from their caravans at Kanyenye by the Mzanza people, and in fact all the Wagogo; so they hoped at least I would not forsake them, which they heard I was going to do, as Manua Sera had also threatened to attack Kaze. I then told them, finally that their proposals were now beyond my power, for I had a duty to perform as well as themselves, and in a day or two I should be off.

14th to 17th. – On the 14th thirty-nine porters were brought in from Rungua by Musa's men, who said they had collected one hundred and twenty, and brought them to within ten miles of this, when some travellers frightened all but thirty-nine away, by telling them, "Are you such fools as to venture into Kaze now? All the Arabs have been killed, or were being cut up and pursued by Manua Sera." This sad disappointment threw me on my "beam-ends." For some reason or other none of Musa's slaves would take service, and the Arabs prevented theirs from leaving the place, as it was already too short of hands. To do the best under these circumstances, I determined on going to Rungua with what kit could be carried, leaving Bombay behind with Musa until such time as I should arrive there, and, finding more men, could send them back for the rest. I then gave Musa the last of the gold watches the Indian Government had given me;[3] and, bidding Sheikh Said take all our letters and specimens back to the coast as soon as the road was found practicable, set out on the march northwards with Grant and Baraka, and all the rest of my men who were well enough to carry loads, as well as some of Musa's head men, who knew where to get porters.

After passing Masange and Zimbili, we put up a night in the village of Iviri, on the northern border of Unyanyembe, and found several officers there, sent by Mkisiwa, to enforce a levy of soldiers to take the field with the Arabs at Kaze against Manua Sera; to effect which, they walked about ringing bells, and bawling out that if a certain percentage of all the inhabitants did not muster, the village chief would be seized, and their plantations confiscated. My men all mutinied here for increase of ration allowances. To find themselves food with, I had given them all one necklace of beads each per diem since leaving Kaze, in lieu of cloth, which hitherto had been served out for that purpose. It was a very liberal allowance, because the Arabs never gave more than one necklace to every three men, and that, too, of inferior quality to what I served. I brought them to at last by starvation, and then we went on. Dipping down into a valley between two clusters of granitic hills, beautifully clothed with trees and grass, studded here and there with rich plantations, we entered the district of Usagari, and on the second day forded the Gombe nullah again – in its upper course, called Kuale.

Rising again up to the main level of the plantation, we walked into the boma of the chief of Unyambewa, Singinya, whose wife was my old friend the late sultana Ungugu's lady's-maid. Immediately on our entering her palace, she came forward to meet me with the most affable air of a princess, begged I would always come to her as I did then, and sought to make every one happy and comfortable. Her old mistress, she said, died well stricken in years; and, as she had succeeded her, the people of her country invited Singinya to marry her, because feuds had arisen about the rights of succession; and it was better a prince, whom they thought best suited by birth and good qualities, should head their warriors, and keep all in order. At that moment Singinya was out in the field fighting his enemies; and she was sure, when he heard I was here, that he would be very sorry he had missed seeing me.

We next went on to the district of Ukumbi, and put up in a village there, on approaching which all the villagers turned out to resist us, supposing we were an old enemy of theirs. They flew about brandishing their spears, and pulling their bows in the most grotesque attitudes, alarming some of my porters so much that they threw down their loads and bolted. All the country is richly cultivated, though Indian corn at that time was the only grain ripe. The square, flat-topped tembes had now been left behind, and instead the villagers lived in small collections of grass huts, surrounded by palisades of tall poles.

Proceeding on we put up at the small settlement of Usenda, the proprietor of which was a semi-negro Arab merchant called

Sangoro. He had a large collection of women here, but had himself gone north with a view to trade in Karague. Report, however, assured us that he was then detained in Usui by Suwarora, its chief, on the plea of requiring his force of musketeers to prevent the Watuta from pillaging his country, for these Watuta lived entirely on plunder of other people's cattle.

With one move, by alternately crossing strips of forest and cultivation, studded here and there with small hills of granite, we forded the Qaunde nullah – a tributary to the Gombe – and entered the rich flat district of Mininga, where the gingerbread-palm grows abundantly. The greatest man we found here was a broken-down ivory merchant called Sirboko, who gave us a good hut to live in. Next morning, I believe at the suggestion of my Wanguana, with Baraka at their head, he induced me to stop there; for he said Rungua had been very recently destroyed by the Watuta, and this place could afford porters better than it. To all appearance this was the case, for this district was better cultivated than any place I had seen. I also felt a certain inclination to stop, as I was dragging on sick men, sorely against my feelings; and I also thought I had better not go farther away from my rear property; but, afraid of doing wrong in not acting up to Musa's directions, I called up his head men who were with me, and asked them what they thought of the matter, as they had lately come from Rungua. On their confirming Sirboki's story, and advising my stopping, I acceded to their recommendation, and immediately gave Musa's men orders to look out for porters.

Hearing this, all my Wanguana danced with delight; and I, fearing there was some treachery, called Musa's men again, saying I had changed my mind, and wished to go on in the afternoon; but when the time came, not one of our porters could be seen. There was now no help for it; so, taking it coolly, I gave Musa's men presents, begged them to look sharp in getting the men up, and trusted all would end well in the longrun. Sirboko's attentions were most warm and affecting. He gave us cows, rice, and milk, with the best place he had to live in, and looked after us as constantly and tenderly as if he had been our father. It seemed quite unjust to harbour any suspicion against him.

He gave the following account of himself: He used to trade in ivory, on account of some Arabs at Zanzibar. On crossing Usui, he once had a fight with one of the chiefs of the country and killed him; but he got through all right, because the natives, after two or three of their number had been killed, dispersed, and feared to come near his musket again. He visited Uganda when the late king Sunna was living, and even traded Usoga; but as he was coming down from these northern countries he lost all his property by a fire breaking out in a village he stopped in, which drove him down here a ruined man. As it happened, however, he put up with the chief of this district, Ugali – Mr. Paste – at a time when the Watuta attacked the place and drove all the inhabitants away. The chief, too, was on the point of bolting, when Sirboko prevented him by saying, "If you will only have courage to stand by me, the Watuta shall not come near – at any rate, if they do, let us both die together." The Watuta at that time surrounded the district, crowning all the little hills overlooking it; but fearing the Arabs' guns might be many, they soon walked away, and left them in peace. In return for this magnanimity, and feeling a great security in firearms, Ugali then built the large enclosure, with huts for Sirboko, we were now living in. Sirboko, afraid to return to the coast lest he should be apprehended for debt, has resided here ever since, doing odd jobs for other traders, increasing his family, and planting extensively. His agricultural operations are confined chiefly to rice, because the natives do not like it enough to be tempted to steal it.

25th to 2d. – I now set to work, collecting, stuffing, and drawing, until the 2d, when Musa's men came in with three hundred men, whom I sent on to Kaze at once with my specimens and letters, directing Musa and Bombay to come on and join us immediately. Whilst waiting for these men's return, one of Sirboko's slaves, chained up by him, in the most piteous manner cried out to me: "Hai Bana wangi, Bana wangi (Oh, my lord, my lord), take pity on me! When I was a free man I saw you at Uvira, on the Tanganyika lake, when you were there; but since then the Watuta, in a fight at Ujiji, speared me all over and left me for dead, when I was seized by the people, sold to the Arabs, and have been in chains ever since. Oh, I saw, Bana wangi, if you would only liberate me I would never run away, but would serve you faithfully all my life." This touching appeal was too strong for my heart to withstand, so I called up Sirboko, and told him, if he would liberate this one man to please me he should be no loser; and the release was effected. He was then christened Farham (Joy), and was enrolled in my service with the rest of my freed men. I then inquired if it was true the Wabembe were cannibals, and also circumcised. In one of their slaves the latter statement was easily confirmed. I was assure that he was not a cannibal; for the whole tribe of Wabembe, when they cannot get human flesh otherwise, give a goat to their neighbours for a sick or dying child, regarding such flesh as the best of all. No other cannibals, however, were known of; but the Masai, and their cognates, the Wahumba, Wataturu, Wakasange, Wanyaramba, and even the Wagogo and Wakimbu, circumcise.

On the 15th I was surprised to find Bombay come in with all my rear property and a great quantity of Musa's, but with out the old man. By a letter from Sheikh Said I then found that, since my leaving Kaze, the Arabs had, along with Mkisiwa, invested the position of Manua Sera at Kigue, and forced him to take flight again. Afterwards the Arabs, returning to Kaze, found Musa preparing to leave. Angry at this attempt to desert them, they persuaded him to give up his journey north for the present; so that at the time Bombay left, Musa was engaged as public auctioneer in selling the effects of Snay, Jafu, and others, but privately said he would follow me on to Karague as soon as his rice was cut. Adding a little advice of his own, Sheikh Said pressed me to go on with the journey as fast as possible, because all the Arabs had accused me of conspiring with Manua Sera, and would turn against me unless I soon got away.

2d to 30th. – Disgusted with Musa's vacillatory conduct, on the 22d I sent him a letter containing a bit of my mind. I had given him, as a present, sufficient cloth to pay for his porters, as well as a watch and a good sum of money, and advised his coming on at once, for the porters who had just brought in my rear property would not take pay to go on to Karague; and so I was detained again, waiting whilst his head man went to Rungua to look for more. Five days after this, a party of Sangoro's arrived from Karague, saying they had been detained three months in Usui by Suwarora, who had robbed them of an enormous quantity of property, and oppressed them so that all their porters ran away. Now, slight as this little affair might appear, it was of vital importance to me, as I found all my men shaking their heads and predicting what might happen to us when we got there; so, as a forlorn hope, I sent Baraka with another letter to Musa, offering to pay as much money for fifty men carrying muskets as would buy fifty slaves, and, in addition to that, I offered to pay them what my men were receiving as servants. Next day (23d) the chief Ugali came to pay his respects to us. He was a fine-looking young man, about thirty years old, the husband of thirty wives, but he had only three children. Much surprised at the various articles composing our kit, he remarked that our "sleeping-clothes" – blankets – were much better than his royal robes; but of all things that amused him most were our picture-books, especially some birds drawn by Wolf.

Everything still seemed going against me; for on the following day (24th) Musa's men came in from Rungua to say the Watuta were "out." They had just seized fifty head of cattle from Rungua, and the people were in such a state of alarm they dared not leave their homes and families. I knew not what to do, for there was no hope left but in what Baraka might bring; and as that even would be insufficient, I sent Musa's men into Kaze, to increase the original number by thirty men more.

Patience, thank God, I had a good stock of, so I waited quietly until the 30th, when I was fairly upset by the arrival of a letter from Kaze, stating that Baraka had arrived, and had been very insolent both to Musa and to Sheikh Said. The bearer of the letter was at once to go and search for porters at Rungua, but not a word was said about the armed men I had ordered. At the same time reports from the other side came in, to the effect that the Arabs at Kaze and Msene had bribed the Watuta to join them, and overrun the whole country from Ugogo to Usui; and, in consequence of this, all the natives on the line I should have to take were in such dread of that terrible wandering race of savages, who had laid waste in turn all the lands from N'yassa to Usui on their west flank, that not a soul dared leave his home. I could now only suppose that this foolish and hasty determination of the Arabs, who, quite unprepared to carry out their wicked alliance to fight, still had set every one against their own interests as well as mine, had not reached Musa, so I made up my mind at once to return to Kaze, and settle all matters I had in my heart with himself and the Arabs in person.

This settled, I next, in this terrible embarrassment, determined on sending back the last of the Hottentots, as all four of them, though still wishing to go on with me, distinctly said they had not the power to continue the march, for they had never ceased suffering from fever and jaundice, which had made them all yellow as guineas, save one, who was too black to change colour. It felt to me as if I were selling my children, having once undertaken to lead them through the journey; but if I did not send them back then, I never could afterwards, and therefore I allowed the more substantial feelings of humanity to overcome these compunctions.

Next morning, then, after giving the Tots over in charge of some men to escort them on to Kaze quietly, I set our myself with a dozen men, and the following evening I put up with Musa, who told me Baraka had just left without one man – all his slaves having become afraid to go, since the news of the Arab alliance had reached Kaze. Suwarora had ordered his subjects to run up a line of bomas to protect his frontier, and had proclaimed his intention to kill every coast-man who dared attempt to enter Usui. My heart was ready to sink as I turned into bed, and I was driven to think of abandoning everybody who was not strong enough to go on with me carrying a load.

3d to 13th. – Baraka, hearing I had arrived, then came back to me, and confirmed Musa's words. The Arabs, too, came flocking in to beg, nay implore, me to help them out of their difficulties. Many of them were absolutely ruined, they said; others had their houses full of stores unemployed. At Ugogo those who wished to join them were unable to do so, for their porters, what few were left, were all dying of starvation; and at that moment Manua Sera was hovering about, shooting, both night and day, all the poor villagers in the district, or driving them away. Would to God, they said, I would mediate for them with Manua Sera – they were sure I would be successful – and then they would give me as many armed men as I liked. Their folly in all their actions, I said, proved to me that anything I might attempt to do would be futile, for their alliance with the Watuta, when they were not prepared to act, at once damned them in my eyes as fools. This they in their terror acknowledged, but said it was not past remedy, if I would join them, to counteract what had been done in that matter. Suffice it now to say, after a long conversation, arguing all the pros and cons over, I settled I would write out all the articles of a treaty of peace, by which they should be liable to have all their property forfeited on the coast if they afterwards broke faith; and I begged them to call the next day and sign it.

They were no sooner gone, however, than Musa assured me they had killed old Maula of Rubuga in the most treacherous manner, as follows: Khamis, who is an Arab of most gentlemanly aspect, on returning from Ugogo attended by slaves, having heard that Maula was desirous of adjusting a peace, invited him with his son to do so. When old Maula came as desired, bringing his son with him, and a suitable offering of ivory and cattle, the Arab induced them both to kneel down and exchange blood with him, when, by a previously concerted arrangement, Khamis had them shot down by his slaves. This disgusting story made me quite sorry, when next day the Arabs arrived, expecting that I should attempt to help them; but as the matter had gone so far, I asked them, in the first place, how they could hope Manua Sera would have any faith in them when they were so treacherous, or trust to my help, since they had killed Maula, who was my protege? They all replied in a breath, "Oh, let the past be forgotten, and assist us now! For in you alone we can look for a preserver." At length an armistice was agreed to; but as no one dared go to negotiated it but my men, I allowed them to take pay from the Arabs, which was settled on the 4th by ten men taking four yards of cloth each, with a promise of a feast on sweetmeats when they returned. Ex-Mrs. Musa, who had been put aside by her husband because she was too fat for her lord's taste, then gave me three men of her private establishment, and abused Musa for being wanting in "brains." She had repeatedly advised him to leave this place and go with me, lest the Arabs, who were all in debt to him, should put him to death; but he still hung on to recover his remaining debts, a portion having been realised by the sale of Snay's and Jafu's effects; for everything in the shape of commodities had been sold at the enormous price of 500 per cent – the male slaves even fetching 100 dollars per head, though the females went for less. The Hottentots now arrived, with many more of my men, who, seeing their old "flames," Snay's women, sold off by auction, begged me to advance them money to purchase them with, for they could not bear to see these women, who were their own when they formerly stayed here, go off like cattle no one knew where. Compliance, of course, was impossible, as it would have crowded the caravan with women. Indeed, to prevent my men every thinking of matrimony on the march, as well as to incite them on through the journey, I promised, as soon as we reached Egypt, to give them all wives and gardens at Zanzibar, provided they did not contract marriages on the road.

On the 6th, the deputation, headed by Baraka, returned triumphantly into Kaze, leading in two of Manua Sera's ministers – one of them a man with one eye, whom I called Cyclops – and two others, ministers of a chief called Kitambi, or Little Blue Cloth. After going a day's journey, they said they came to where Manua Sera was residing with Kitambi, and met with a most cheerful and kind reception from both potentates, who, on hearing of my proposition, warmly acceded to it, issued orders at once that hostilities should cease, and, with one voice, said they were convinced that, unless through my instrumentality, Manua Sera would never regain his possessions. Kitambi was quite beside himself, and wished my men to stop one night to enjoy his hospitality. Manua Sera, after reflecting seriously about the treacherous murder of old Maula, hesitated, but gave way when it had been explained away by my men, and said, "No; they shall go at once, for my kingdom depends on the issue, and Bana Mzungu (the White Lord) may get anxious if they do not return promptly." One thing, however, he insisted on, and that was, the only place he would meet the Arabs in was Unyanyembe, as it would be beneath his dignity to settle matters anywhere else. And further, he specified that he wished all the transactions to take place in Musa's house.

Next day, 7th, I assembled all the Arabs at Musa's "court," with all my men and the two chiefs, four men attending, when Baraka, "on his legs," told them all I proposed for the treaty of peace. The Arabs gave their assent to it; and Cyclops, for Manua Sera, after giving a full narrative of the whole history of the war, in such a rapid and eloquent manner as would have done justice to our Prime Minister, said his chief was only embittered against Snay, and now Snay was killed, he wished to make friends with them. To which the Arabs made a suitable answer, adding, that all they found fault with was an insolent remark which, in his wrath, Manua Sera had given utterance to, that their quarrel with him was owing chiefly to a scurvy jest which he had passed on them, and on the characteristic personal ceremony of initiation to their Mussulman faith. Now, however, as Manua Sera wished to make friends, they would abide by anything that I might propose. Here the knotty question arose again, what territory they, the Arabs, would give to Manua Sera? I thought he would not be content unless he got the old place again; but as Cyclops said no, that was not in his opinion absolutely necessary, as the lands of Unyanyembe had once before been divided, the matter was settled on the condition that another conference should be held with Manua Sera himself on the subject.

I now (8th and 9th) sent these men all off again, inviting Manua Sera to come over and settle matters at once, if he would, otherwise I should go on with my journey, for I could not afford to wait longer here. Then, as soon as they left, I made Musa order some of his men off to Rungua, requesting the chief of the place to send porters to Mininga to remove all our baggage over to his palace; at the same time I begged him not to fear the Watuta's threat to attack him, as Musa would come as soon as the treaty was concluded, in company with me, to build a boma alongside his palace, as he did in former years, to be nearer his trade with Karague. I should have mentioned, by the way, that Musa had now made up his mind not to go further than the borders of Usui with me, lest I should be "torn to pieces," and he would be "held responsible on the coast." Musa's men, however, whom he selected for this business, were then engaged making Mussulmans of all the Arab slave boys, and said they would not go until they had finished, although I offered to pay the "doctor's bill," or allowance they expected to get. The ceremony, at the same time that it helps to extend their religion, as christening does ours, also stamps the converts with a mark effective enough to prevent desertion; because, after it has been performed, their own tribe would not receive them again. At last, when they did go, Musa, who was suffering from a sharp illness, to prove to me that he was bent on leaving Kaze the same time as myself, began eating what he called his training pills – small dried buds of roses with alternate bits of sugar-candy. Ten of these buds, he said, eaten dry, were sufficient for ordinary cases, and he gave a very formidable description of the effect likely to follow the use of the same number boiled in rice-water or milk.

Fearful stories of losses and distress came constantly in from Ugogo by small bodies of men, who stole their way through the jungles. To-day a tremendous commotion took place in Musa's tembe amongst all the women, as one had been delivered of still-born twins. They went about in procession, painted and adorned in the most grotesque fashion, bewailing and screech-ing, singing and dancing, throwing their arms and legs about as if they were drunk, until the evening set in, when they gathered a huge bundle of bulrushes, and, covering it with a cloth, car-ried it up to the door of the bereaved on their shoulders, as though it had been a coffin. Then setting it down on the ground, they planted some of the rushes on either side of the entrance, and all kneeling together, set to bewailing, shrieking, and howling incessantly for hours together.

After this (10th to 12th), to my great relief, quite unexpect-edly, a man arrived from Usui conveying a present of some ivories from a great mganga or magician, named Dr. K'yengo, who had sent them to Musa as a recollection from an old friend, begging at the same time for some pretty cloths, as he said he was then engaged as mtongi or caravan director, collecting to-gether all the native caravans desirous of making a grand march to Uganda. This seemed to me a heaven-born opportunity of making friends with one who could help me so materially, and I begged Musa to seal it by sending him something on my account, as I had nothing by me; but Musa objected, thinking it better simply to say I was coming, and if he, K'yengo, would assist me in Usui, I would then give him some cloths as he wanted; otherwise, Musa said, the man who had to convey it would in all probability make away with it, and then do his best to prevent my seeing K'yengo. As soon as this was settled, against my wish and opinion, a special messenger arrived from Suwarora, to inquire of Musa what truth there was in the story of the Arabs having allied themselves to the Watuta. He had full faith in Musa, and hoped, if the Arabs had no hostile intentions towards him, he, Musa, would send him two of theirs; further, Suwarora wished Musa would send him a cat. A black cat was then given to the messenger for Suwarora, and Musa sent an account of all that I had done towards effecting a peace, saying that the Arabs had accepted my views, and if he would have patience until I arrived in Usui, the four men required would be sent with me.

In the evening my men returned again with Cyclops, who said, for his master, that Manua Sera desired nothing more than peace, and to make friends with the Arabs; but as nothing was settled about deposing Mkisiwa, he could not come over here. Could the Arabs, was Manua Sera's rejoinder, suppose for a moment that he would voluntarily divide his dominion with one whom he regarded as his slave! Death would be preferable; and although he would trust his life in the Mzungu's hands if he called him again, he must know it was his intention to hunt Mkisiwa down like a wild animal, and would never rest satisfied until he was dead. The treaty thus broke down; for the same night Cyclops decamped like a thief, after brandishing an arrow which Manua Sera had given him to throw down as a gauntlet of defiance to fight Mkisiwa to death. After this the Arabs were too much ashamed of themselves to come near me, though invited by letter, and Musa became so ill he would not take my advice and ride in a hammock, the best possible cure for his complaint; so, after being humbugged so many times by his procrastinations, I gave Sheikh Said more letters and specimens, with orders to take the Tots down to the coast as soon as practicable, and started once more for the north, expecting very shortly to hear of Musa's death, though he promised to follow me the very next day or die in the attempt, and he also said he would bring on the four men required by Suwarora; for I was fully satisfied in my mind that he would have marched with me then had he had the resolution to do so at all.

Before I had left the district I heard that Manua Sera had collected a mixed force of Warori, Wagogo, and Wasakuma, and had gone off to Kigue again, whilst the Arabs and Mkisiwa were feeding their men on beef before setting out to fight him. Manua Sera, it was said, had vast resources. His father, Fundi Kira, was a very rich man, and had buried vast stores of property, which no one knew of but Manua Sera, his heir. The Wanyamuezi all inwardly loved him for his great generosity, and all alike thought him protected by a halo of charm-power so effective against the arms of the Arabs that he could play with them just as he liked.

On crossing Unyambewa (14th), when I a third time put up with my old friend the sultana, her chief sent word to say he hoped I would visit him at his fighting boma to eat a cow which he had in store for me, as he could not go home and enjoy the society of his wife whilst the war was going on; since, by so doing, it was considered he "would lose strength." On arriving at Mininga, I was rejoiced to see Grant greatly recovered. Three villagers had been attacked by two lions during my absence. Two of the people escaped, but the third was seized as he was plunging into his hut, and was dragged off and devoured by the animals. A theft also had taken place, by which both Grant and Sirboko lost property; and the thieves had been traced over the borders of the next district. No fear, however, was entertained about the things being recovered, for Sirboko had warned Ugali the chief, and he had promised to send his Waganga, or magicians, out to track them down, unless the neighbouring chief chose to give them up. After waiting two days, as no men came from Rungua, I begged Grant to push ahead on to Ukani, just opposite Rungua, with all my coast-men, whilst I remained behind for the arrival of Musa's men and porters to carry on the rest of the kit – for I had now twenty-two in addition to men permanently enlisted, who took service on the same rate of pay as my original coast-men; though, as usual, when the order for marching was issued, a great number were found to be either sick or malingering.

Two days afterwards, Musa's men came in with porters, who would not hire themselves for more than two marches, having been forbidden to do so by their chief on account of the supposed Watuta invasion; and for these two marches they required a quarter of the whole customary hire to Karague. Musa's traps, too, I found, were not to be moved, so I saw at once Musa had not kept faith with me, and there would be a fresh set of difficulties; but as every step onwards was of the greatest importance – for my men were consuming my stores at a fearful pace – I paid down the beads they demanded, and next day joined Grant at Mbisu, a village of Ukuni held by a small chief called Mchimeka, who had just concluded a war of two years' standing with the great chief Ukulima (the Digger), of Nunda (the Hump). During the whole of the two years' warfare the loss was only three men on each side. Meanwhile Musa's men bolted like thieves one night, on a report coming that the chief of Unyambewa, after concluding the war, whilst amusing himself with his wife, had been wounded on the foot by an arrow that fell from her hand. The injury had at once taken a mortal turn, and the chief sent for his magicians, who said it was not the fault of the wife – somebody else must have charmed the arrow to cause such a deadly result. They then seized hold of the magic horn, primed for the purpose, and allowed it to drag them to where the culprits dwelt. Four poor men, who were convicted in this way, were at once put to death, and the chief from that moment began to recover.

After a great many perplexities, I succeeded in getting a kirangozi, or leader, by name Ungurue (the Pig). He had several times taken caravans to Karague, and knew all the languages well, but unfortunately he afterwards proved to be what his name implied. That, however, I could not foresee, so, trusting to him and good-luck, I commenced making fresh enlistments of porters; but they came and went in the most tantalising manner, notwithstanding I offered three times the hire that any merchant could afford to give. Every day seemed to be worse and worse. Some of Musa's men came to get palm-toddy for him, as he was too weak to stand, and was so cold nothing would warm him. There was, however, no message brought for myself; and as the deputation did not come to me, I could only infer that I was quite forgotten, of that Musa, after all, had only been humbugging me. I scarcely knew what to do. Everybody advised me to stop where I was until the harvest was over, as no porters could be found on ahead, for Ukuni was the last of the fertile lands on this side of Usui.

Stopping, however, seemed endless; not so my supplies, I therefore tried advancing in detachments again, sending the free men off under Grant to Ukulima's, whilst I waited behind keeping ourselves divided in the hopes of inducing all hands to see the advisability of exerting themselves for the general good – as my men, whilst we were all together, showed they did not care how long they were kept doing no more fatiguing work than chaffing each other, and feeding at my expense.

In the meanwhile the villagers were very merry, brewing and drinking their pombe (beer) by turns, one house after the other providing the treat. On these occasions the chief – who always drank freely, and more than any other – heading the public gatherings of men and women, saw the large earthen pots placed all in a row, and the company taking long draughts from bowls made of plaited straw, laughing as they drank, until, half-screwed, they would begin bawling and shouting. To increase the merriment, one or two jackanapes, with zebras' manes tied over their heads, would advance with long tubes like monster bassoons, blowing with all their might, contorting their faces and bodies, and going through the most obscene and ridiculous motions to captivate their simple admirers. This, however, was only the feast; the ball then began, for the pots were no sooner emptied than five drums at once, of different sizes and tones, suspended in a line from a long horizontal bar, were beaten with fury, and all the men, women, and children, singing and clapping their hands in time, danced for hours together.

A report reached me, by some of Sirboko's men, whom he had sent to convey to us a small present of rice, that an Arab, who was crossing Msalala to our northward, had been treacherously robbed of all his arms and guns by a small district chief, whose only excuse was that the Wanyamuezi had always traded very well by themselves until the Arabs came into the country; but now, as they were robbed of their property, on account of the disturbances caused by these Arabs, they intended for the future to take all they could get, and challenged the Arabs to do the same.

My patience was beginning to suffer again, for I could not help thinking that the chiefs of the place were preventing their village men going with me in order that my presence here might ward of the Watuta; so I called up the kirangozi, who had thirteen "Watoto," as they are called, or children of his own, wishing to go, and asked him if he knew why no other men could be got. As he could not tell me, saying some excused themselves on the plea they were cutting their corn, and others that they feared the Watuta, I resolved at once to move over to Nunda; and if that place also failed to furnish men, I would go on to Usui or Karague with what men I had, and send back for the rest of my property; for though I could bear the idea of separating from Grant, still the interests of old England were at stake, and demanded it.

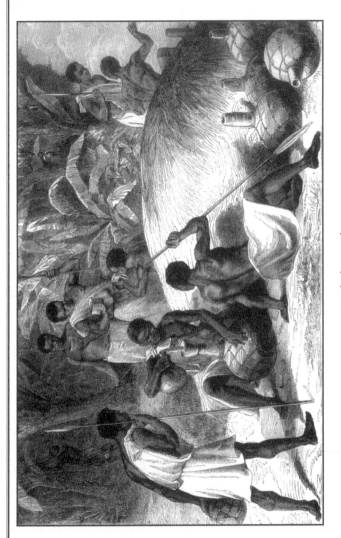

Natives drinking pombe.

This resolve being strengthened by the kirangozi's assurance that the row in Msalala had shaken the few men who had half dreaded to go with me, I marched over to Hunda, and put up with Grant in Ukulima's boma, when Grant informed me that the chief had required four yards of cloth from him for having walked round a dead lioness, as he had thus destroyed a charm that protected his people against any more of these animals coming, although, fortunately, the charm could be restored again by paying four yards of cloth. Ukulima, however, was a very kind and good man, though he did stick the hands and heads of his victims on the poles of his boma as a warning to others. He kept five wives, of whom the rest paid such respect to the elder one, it was quite pleasing to see them. A man of considerable age, he did everything the state or his great establishment required himself. All the men of his district clapped their hands together as a courteous salutation to him, and the women curtsied as well as they do at our court – a proof that they respected him as a great potentate – a homage rarely bestowed on the chiefs of other small states. Ukulima was also hospitable; for on one occasion, when another chief came to visit him, he received his guest and retainers with considerable ceremony, making all the men of the village get up a dance; which they did, beating the drums and firing off guns, like a lot of black devils let loose.

We were not the only travellers in misfortune here, for Masudi, with several other Arabs, all formed in one large caravan, had arrived at Mchimeka's, and could not advance for want of men. They told me it was the first time they had come on this line, and they deeply regretted it, for they had lost 5,000 dollar's worth of beads by their porters running away with their loads, and now they did not know how to proceed. Indeed, they left the coast and arrived at Kaze immediately in rear of us, and had, like ourselves, found it as much as they could do even to reach this, and now they were at a standstill for want of porters.

As all hopes of being able to get any more men were given up, I called on Bombay and Baraka to make arrangements for my going ahead with the best of my property as I had devised. They both shook their heads, and advised me to remain until the times improved, when the Arabs, being freed from the pressure of war, would come along and form with us a "sufari ku" or grand march, as Ukulima and every one else had said we should be torn to pieces in Usui if we tried to cross that district with so few men. I then told them again and again of the messages I had sent on to Rumanika in Karague, and to Suwarora in Usui, and begged them to listen to me, instancing as an example of what could be done by perseverance the success of Columbus, who, opposed by his sailors' misgivings, still went on and triumphed, creating for himself immortal renown.

They gave way at last; so, after selecting all the best of my property, I formed camp at Phunze, left Bombay with Grant behind, as I thought Bombay the best and most honest man I had got, from his having had so much experience, and then went ahead by myself, with the Pig as my guide and interpreter, and Baraka as my factotum. The Waguana then all mutinied for a cloth apiece, saying they would not lift a load unless I gave it. Of course a severe contest followed; I said, as I had given them so much before, they could not want it, and ought to be ashamed of themselves. They urged, however, they were doing double work, and would not consent to carry loads as they had done at Mgunda Mkhali again.

Arguments were useless, for, simply because they were tired of going on, they WOULD not see that as they were receiving pay every day, they therefore ought to work every day. However, as they yielded at last, by some few leaning to my side, I gave what they asked for, and went to the next village, still inefficient in men, as all the Pig's Watoto could not be collected together. This second move brought us into a small village, of which Ghiya, a young man, was chief.

He was very civil to me, and offered to sell me a most charming young woman, quite the belle of the country; but as he could not bring me to terms, he looked over my picture-books with the greatest delight, and afterwards went into a discourse on geography with considerable perspicacity; seeming fully to comprehend that if I got down the Nile it would afterwards result in making the shores of the N'yanza like that of the coast at Zanzibar, where the products of his country could be exchanged, without much difficulty, for cloths, beads, and brass wire. I gave him a present; then a letter was brought to me from Sheikh Said, announcing Musa's death, and the fact that Manua Sera was still holding out at Kigue; in answer to which I desired the sheikh to send me as many of Musa's slaves as would take service with me, for they ought now, by the laws of the Koran, to be all free.

On packing up to leave Ghiya's, all the men of the village shut the bars of the entrance, wishing to extract some cloths from me, as I had not given enough, they said, to their chief. They soon, however, saw that we, being inside their own fort, had the best of it, and they gave way. We then pushed on to Ungurue's, another chief of the same district. Here the men and women of the place came crowding to see me, the fair sex all playfully offering themselves for wives, and wishing to know which I admired most. They were so importunate, after a time, that I was not sorry to hear an attack was made on their cattle because a man of the village would not pay his dowry-money to his father-in-law, and this set everybody flying out to the scene of action.

After this, as Bombay brought up the last of my skulking men, I bade him good-bye again, and made an afternoon-march on to Takina, in the district of Msalala, which we no sooner approached than all the inhabitants turned out and fired their arrows at us. They did no harm, however, excepting to create a slight alarm, which some neighbouring villagers took advantage of to run off with two of my cows. To be returned to them, but called in vain, as the scoundrels said, "Findings are keepings, by the laws of our country; and as we found your cows, so we will keep them." For my part I was glad they were gone, as the Wanguana never yet kept anything I put under their charge; so, instead of allowing them to make a fuss the next morning, I marched straight on for M'ynoga's, the chief of the district, who was famed for his infamy and great extortions, having pushed his exactions so far as to close the road.

On nearing his palace, we heard war-drums beat in every surrounding village, and the kirangozi would go no farther until permission was obtained from M'yonga. This did not take long, as the chief said he was most desirous to see a white man, never having been to the coast, though his father-in-law had, and had told him that the Wazungu were even greater people than the sultan reigning there. On our drawing near the palace,

163

a small, newly-constructed boma was shown for my residence; but as I did not wish to stop there, knowing how anxious Grant would be to have his relief, I would not enter it, but instead sent Baraka to pay the hongo as quickly as possible, that we might move on again; at the same time ordering him to describe the position both Grant and myself were in, and explain that what I paid now was to frank both of us, as the whole of the property was my own. Should he make any remarks about the two cows that were stolen, I said he must know that I could not wait for them, as my brother would die of suspense if we did not finish the journey and send back for him quickly. Off went Baraka with a party of men, stopping hours, of course, and firing volleys of ammunition away. He did not return again until the evening, when the palace-drums announced that the hongo had been settled for one barsati, one lugoi, and six yards merikani. Baraka approached me triumphantly, saying how well he had managed the business. M'yonga did not wish to see me, because he did not know the coast language. He was immensely pleased with the present I had given him, and said he was much and very unjustly abused by the Arabs, who never came this way, saying he was a bad man. He should be very glad to see Grant, and would take nothing from him; and, though he did not see me in person, he would feel much affronted if I did not stop the night there. In the meanwhile he would have the cows brought in, for he could not allow any one to leave his country abused in any way.

My men had greatly amused him by firing their guns off and showing him the use of their sword-bayonets. I knew, as a matter of course, that if I stopped any longer I should be teased for more cloths, and gave orders to my men to march the same instant, saying, if they did not – for I saw them hesitate – I would give the cows to the villagers, since I knew that was the thing that weighed on their minds. This raised a mutiny. No one would go forward with the two cows behind; besides which, the day was far spent, and there was nothing but jungle, they said, beyond. The kirangozi would not show the way, nor would any man lift a load. A great confusion ensued. I knew they were telling lies, and would not enter the village, but shot the cows when they arrived, for the villagers to eat, to show them I cared for nothing but making headway, and remained out in the open all night. Next morning, sure enough, before we could get under way, M'yonga sent his prime minister to say that the king's sisters and other members of his family had been crying and tormenting him all night for having let me off so cheaply – they had got nothing to cover their nakedness, and I must pay something more. This provoked fresh squabbles. The drums had beaten and the tax was settled; I could not pay more. The kirangozi, however, said he would not move a peg unless I gave something more, else he would be seized on his way back. His "children" all said the same; and as I thought Grant would only be worsted if I did not keep friends with the scoundrel, I gave four yards more merikani, and then went on my way.

For the first few miles there were villagers, but after that a long tract of jungle, inhabited chiefly by antelopes and rhinoceros. It was wilder in appearance than most parts of Unyamuezi. In this jungle a tributary nullah to the Gombe, called Nurhungure, is the boundary-line between the great Country of the Moon and the kingdom of Uzinza.

1) It may be as well to remark here, that the figures both in latitude and longitude, representing the position of Kaze, computed by Mr. Dunkin, accord with what appeared in Blackwood's Magazine, computed by myself, and in the R. G. S. Journal Map, computed by Captain George. This applies also to the position of Ujiji; at any rate, the practical differences are so trifling that it would require a microscope to detect them on the map.

2) The Jub is the largest river known to the Zanzibar Arabs. It debouches on the east coast north of Zanzibar, close under the equator.

3) The two first gold watches were given away at Zanzibar.

CHAPTER 6

UZINZA

The Politics of Uzinza – The Wahuma – "The Pig's" Trick – First Taste of Usui Taxation – Pillaged by Mfumbi – Pillaged by Makaka – Pillaged by Lumeresi – Grant Stripped by M'Yonga – Stripped Again by Ruhe – Terrors and Defections in the Camp – Driven Back to Kaze with New Tribulations and Impediments.

Uzinza, which we now entered, is ruled by two Wahuma chieftains of foreign blood, descended from the Abyssinian stock, of whom we saw specimens scattered all over Unyamuezi, and who extended even down south as far as Fipa. Travellers see very little, however, of these Wahuma, because, being pastorals, they roam about with their flocks and build huts as far away as they can from cultivation. Most of the small district chiefs, too, are the descendants of those who ruled in the same places before the country was invaded, and with them travellers put up and have their dealings. The dress of the Wahuma is very simple, composed chiefly of cow-hide tanned black – a few magic ornaments and charms, brass or copper bracelets, and immense number of sambo for stockings, which looked very awkward on their long legs. They smear themselves with rancid butter instead of macassar, and are, in consequence, very offensive to all but the negro, who seems, rather than otherwise, to enjoy a good sharp nose tickler. For arms they carry both bow and spear; more generally the latter. The Wazinza in the southern parts are so much like the Wanyamuezi, as not to require any especial notice; but in the north, where the country is more hilly, they are much more energetic and actively built. All alike live in grass-hut villages, fenced round by bomas in the south, but open in the north. Their country rises in high rolls, increasing in altitude as it approaches the Mountains of the Moon, and is generally well cultivated, being subjected to more of the periodical rains than the regions we have left, though springs are not so abundant, I believe, as they are in the Land of the Moon, where they ooze out by the flanks of the little granitic hills.

After tracking through several miles of low bush-jungle, we came to the sites of some old bomas that had been destroyed by the Watuta not long since. Farther on, as we wished to enter a newly-constructed boma, the chief of which was Mafumbu Wantu (a Mr. Balls), we felt the effects of those ruthless marauders; for the villagers, thinking us Watuta in disguise, would not let us in; for those savages, they said, had once tricked them by entering their village, pretending to be traders carrying ivory and merchandise, whilst they were actually spies. This was fortunate for me, however, as Mr. Balls, like M'yonga, was noted for his extortions on travellers. We then went on and put up in the first village of Bogue, where I wished to get porters and return for Grant, as the place seemed to be populous. Finding, however, that I could not get a sufficient number for that purpose, I directed those who wished for employment to go off at once and take service with Grant.

I found many people assembled here from all parts of the district, for the purpose of fighting M'yonga; but the chief Ruhe, having heard of my arrival, called me to his palace, which, he said, was on my way, that he might see me, for he never in all his life had a white man for his guest, and was so glad to hear of my arrival that he would give orders for the dispersing of his forces. I wished to push past him, as I might be subjected to such calls every day; but Ungurue, in the most piggish manner – for he was related to Ruhe – insisted that neither himself nor any of his children would advance one step farther with me unless I complied with their wish, which was a simple conformity with the laws of their country, and therefore absolute. At length giving in, I entered Ruhe's boma, the poles of which were decked with the skulls of his enemies stuck upon them. Instead, however, of seeing him myself, as he feared my evil eye, I conducted the arrangements for the hongo through Baraka, in the same way as I did at M'yonga's, directing that it should be limited to the small sum of one barsati and four yards kiniki.

The drum was beaten, as the public intimation of the payment of the hongo, and consequently of our release, and we went on to Mihambo, on the west border of the eastern division of Uzinza, which is called Ukhanga. It overlooks the small district of Sorombo, belonging to the great western division, known as Usui, and is presided over by a Sorombo chief, named Makaka, whose extortions had been so notorious that no Arabs now ever went near him. I did not wish to do so either, though his palace lay in the direct route. It was therefore agreed we should skirt round by the east of this district, and I even promised the Pig I would give him ten necklaces a-day in addition to his wages, if he would avoid all the chiefs, and march steadily ten miles every day. By doing so, we should have avoided the wandering Watuta, whose depredations had laid waste nearly all of this country; but the designing blackguard, in opposition to my wishes, to accomplish some object of his own, chose to mislead us all, and quietly took us straight into Sorombo to Kague, the boma of a sub-chief, called Mfumbi, where we no sooner arrived than the inhospitable brute forbade any one of his subjects to sell us food until the hongo was paid, for he was not sure that we were not allied with the Watuta to rob his country. After receiving what he called his dues – one barsati, two yards merikani, and two yards kiniki – the drums beat, and all was settled with him; but I was told the head chief Makaka, who lived ten miles to the west, and so much out of my road, had sent expressly to invite me to see him. He said it was his right I should go to him as the principal chief of the district. Moreover he longed for a sight of a white man; for though he had travelled all across Uganda and Usoga into Masawa, or the Masai country, as well as to the coast, where he had seen both Arabs and Indians, he had never yet seen an Englishman. If I would oblige him, he said he would give me guides to Suwarora, who was his mkama or king. Of course I knew well what all this meant; and at the same time that I said I could not comply, I promised to send him a present of friendship by the hands of Baraka.

This caused a halt. Makaka would not hear of such an arrangement. A present, he said, was due to him of course, but of more importance than the present was his wish to see me.

Baraka and all the men begged I would give in, as they were sure he must be a good man to send such a kind message. I strove in vain, for no one would lift a load unless I complied; so, perforce, I went there, in company, however, with Mfumbi, who now pretended to be great friends; but what was the result? On entering the palace we were shown into a cowyard without a tree in it, or any shade; and no one was allowed to sell us food until a present of friendship was paid, after which the hongo would be discussed.

The price of friendship was not settled that day, however, and my men had to go supperless to bed. Baraka offered him one common cloth, and then another – all of which he rejected with such impetuosity that Baraka said his head was all on a whirl. Makaka insisted he would have a deole, or nothing at all. I protested I had no deoles I could give him; for all the expensive cloths which I had brought from the coast had been stolen in Mgunda Mkhali. I had three, however, concealed at the time – which I had bought from Musa, at forty dollars each – intended for the kings of Karague and Uganda.

Incessant badgering went on for hours and hours, until at last Baraka, clean done with the incessant worry of this hot-headed young chief, told him, most unfortunately, he would see again if he could find a deole, as he had one of his own. Baraka then brought one to my tent, and told me of his having bought it for eight dollars at the coast; and as I now saw I was let in for it, I told him to give it. It was given, but Makaka no sooner saw it than he said he must have another one; for it was all nonsense saying a white man had no rich cloths. Whenever he met Arabs, they all said they were poor men, who obtained all their merchandise from the white men on credit, which they refunded afterwards, by levying a heavy percentage on the sale of their ivory.

I would not give way that night; but next day, after fearful battling, the present of friendship was paid by Baraka's giving first a dubuani, then one sahari, then one barsati, then one kisutu, and then eight yards of merikani – all of which were contested in the most sickening manner – when Baraka, fairly done up, was relieved by Makaka's saying, "That will do for friendship; if you had given the deole quietly, all this trouble would have been saved; for I am not a bad man, as you will see." My men then had their first dinner here, after which the hongo had to be paid. This for the time was, however, more easily settled; because Makaki at once said he would never be satisfied until he had received, if I had really not got a deole, exactly double in equivalents of all I had given him. This was a fearful drain on my store; but the Pig, seeing my concern, merely laughed at it, and said, "Oh, these savage chiefs are all alike here; you will have one of these taxes to pay every stage to Uyofu, and then the heavy work will begin; for all these men, although they assume the dignity of chief to themselves, are mere officers, who have to pay tribute to Suwarora, and he would be angry if they were shortcoming." The drums as yet had not beaten, for Makaka said he would not be satisfied until we had exchanged presents, to prove that we were the best of friends. To do this last act properly, I was to get ready whatever I wished to give him, whilst he would come and visit me with a bullock; but I was to give him a royal salute, or the drums would not beat. I never felt so degraded as when I complied, and gave orders to my men to fire a volley as he approached my tent; but I ate the dirt with a good grace, and met the young chief as if nothing had happened. My men, however, could not fire the salute fast enough for him; for he was one of those excitable impulsive creatures who expect others to do everything in as great a hurry as their minds wander. The moment the first volley was fired, he said, "Now, fire again, fire again; be quick, be quick! What's the use of those things?" (meaning the guns). "We could spear you all whilst you are loading: be quick, be quick, I tell you." But Baraka, to give himself law, said: "No; I must ask Bana (master) first, as we do everything by order; this is not fighting at all." The men being ready, file-firing was ordered, and then the young chief came into my tent. I motioned him to take my chair, which, after he sat down upon it, I was very sorry for, as he stained the seat all black with the running colour of one of the new barsati cloths he had got from me, which, to improve its appearance, he had saturated with stinking butter, and had tied round his loins. A fine-looking man of about thirty, he wore the butt-end of a large sea-shell cut in a circle, and tied on his forehead, for a coronet, and sundry small saltiana antelope horns, stuffed with magic powder, to keep off the evil eye. His attendants all fawned on him, and snapped their fingers whenever he sneezed. After passing the first compliment, I gave him a barsati, as my token of friendship, and asked him what he saw when he went to the Masai country. He assured me "that there were two lakes, and not one"; for, on going from Usoga to the Masai country, he crossed over a broad strait, which connected the big N'yanza with another one at its north-east corner. Fearfully impetuous, as soon as this answer was given, he said, "Now I have replied to your questions, do you show me all the things you have got, for I want to see everything, and be very good friends. I did not see you the first day, because you being a stranger, it was necessary I should first look into the magic horn to see if all was right and safe; and now I can assure you that, whilst I saw I was safe, I also saw that your road would be prosperous. I am indeed delighted to see you, for neither my father, nor any of my forefathers, ever were honoured with the company of a white man in all their lives." My guns, clothes, and everything were then inspected, and begged for in the most importunate manner. He asked for the picture-books, examined the birds with intense delight – even trying to insert under their feathers his long royal fingernails, which are grown like a Chinaman's by these chiefs, to show they have a privilege to live on meat. Then turning to the animals, he roared over each one in turn as he examined them, and called out their names. My bull's-eye lantern he coveted so much, I had to pretend exceeding anger to stop his further importunities. He then began again begging for lucifers, which charmed him so intensely I thought I should never get rid of him. He would have one box of them. I swore I could not part with them. He continued to beg, and I to resist. I offered a knife instead, but this he would not have, because the lucifers would be so valuable for his magical observances. On went the storm, till at last I drove him off with a pair of my slippers, which he had stuck his dirty feet into without my leave. I then refused to take his bullock, because he had annoyed me. On his part he was resolved not to beat the drum; but he graciously said he would think about it if I paid another lot of cloth equal to the second deole I ought to have given him.

I began seriously to consider whether I should have this chief shot, as a reward for his oppressive treachery, and a warning to others; but the Pig said it was just what the Arabs were subjected to in Ubena, and they found it best to pay down at once, and do all they were ordered. If I acted rightly, I would take the bullock, and then give the cloth; whilst Baraka said, "We will shoot him if you give the order, only remember Grant is behind, and if you commence a row you will have to fight the whole way, for every chief in the country will oppose you." I then told the Pig and Baraka to settle at once. They no sooner did so than the drums beat, and Makaka, in the best humour possible, came over to say I had permission to go when I liked, but he hoped I would give him a gun and a box of lucifers. This was too provoking. The perpetual worry had given Baraka a fever, and had made me feel quite sick; so I said, if he ever mentioned a gun or lucifers again, I would fight the matter out with him, for I had not come there to be bullied. He then gave way, and begged I would allow my men to fire a volley outside his boma, as the Watuta were living behind a small line of granitic hills flanking the west of his district, and he wished to show them what a powerful force he had got with him. This was permitted; but his wisdom in showing off was turned into ridicule; for the same evening the Watuta made and attack on his villages and killed three of his subjects, but were deterred from committing further damage by coming in contact with my men, who, as soon as they saw the Watuta fighting, fired their muskets off in the air and drove them away, they themselves at the same time bolting into my camp, and as usual vaunting their prowess.

I then ordered a march for the next morning, and went out in the fields to take my regular observations for latitude. Whilst engaged in this operation, Baraka, accompanied by Wadimoyo (Heart's-stream), another of my freeman, approached me in great consternation, whispering to themselves. They said they had some fearful news to communicate, which, when I heard it, they knew would deter our progress: it was of such great moment and magnitude, they thought they could not deliver it then. I said, "What nonsense! Out with it at once. Are we such chickens that we cannot speak about matters like men? Out with it at once." Then Baraka said, "I have just heard from Makaka, that a man who arrived from Usui only a few minutes ago has said Suwarora is so angry with the Arabs that he has detained one caravan of theirs in his country, and, separating the whole of their men, has placed each of them in different bomas, with orders to his village officers that, in case the Watuta came into his country, without further ceremony they were to be all put to death." I said, "Oh, Baraka, how can you be such a fool? Do you not see through this humbug? Makaka only wishes to keep us here to frighten away the Watuta; for Godsake be a man, and don't be alarmed at such phantoms as these. You always are nagging at me that Bombay is the 'big' and you are the 'small' man. Bombay would never be frightened in this silly way. Now, do you reflect that I have selected you for this journey, as it would, if you succeed with me in carrying out our object, stamp you for ever as a man of great fame. Pray, don't give way, but do your best to encourage the men, and let us march in the morning." On this, as on other occasions of the same kind, I tried to impart confidence, by explaining, in allusion to Petherick's expedition, that I had arranged to meet white men coming up from the north. Baraka at last said, "All right – I am not afraid; I will do as you desire." But as the two were walking off, I heard Wadimoyo say to Baraka, "Is he not afraid now? Won't he go back?" – which, if anything, alarmed me more than the first intelligence; for I began to think that they, and not Makaka, had got up the story.

All night Makaka's men patrolled the village, drumming and shouting to keep off the Watuta, and the next morning, instead of a march, after striking my tent I found that the whole of my porters, the Pig's children, were not to be found. They had gone off and hidden themselves, saying that they were not such fools as to go any farther, as the Watuta were out, and would cut us up on the road. This was sickening indeed.

I knew the porters had not gone far, so I told the Pig to bring them to me, that we might talk the matter over; but say what I would, they all swore they would not advance a step farther. Most of them were formerly men of Utambara. The Watuta had invaded their country and totally destroyed it, killing all their wives and children, and despoiling everything they held dear to them. They did not wish to rob me, and would give up their hire, but not one step more would they advance. Makaka then came forward and said, "Just stop here with me until this ill wind blows over"; but Baraka, more in a fright at Makaka than at any one else, said, No – he would do anything rather than that; for Makaka's bullying had made him quite ill. I then said to my men, "If nothing else will suit you, the best plan I can think of is to return to Mihambo in Bogue, and there form a depot, where, having stored my property, I shall give the Pig a whole load, or 63 lb., of Mzizima beads if he will take Baraka in disguise on to Suwarora, and ask him to send me eighty men, whilst I go back to Unyanyembe to see what men I can get from the late Musa's establishment, and then we might bring on Grant, and move in a body together." At first Baraka said, "Do you wish to have us killed? Do you think if we went to Suwarora's you would ever see us back again? You would wait and wait for us, but we should never return." To which I replied, "Oh, Baraka, do not think so! Bombay, if he were here, would go in a minute. Suwarora by this time knows I am coming, and you may depend on it he will be just as anxious to have us in Usui as Makaka is to keep us here, and he cannot hurt us, as Rumanika is over him, and also expects us." Baraka then, in the most doleful manner, said he would go if the Pig would. The Pig, however, did not like it either, but said the matter was so important he would look into the magic horn all night, and give his answer next morning as soon as we arrived at Mihambo.

On arrival at Mihambo next day, all the porters brought their pay to me, and said they would not go, for nothing would induce them to advance a step farther. I said nothing; but, with "my heart in my shoes," I gave what I thought their due for coming so far, and motioned them to be off; then calling on the Pig for his decision, I tried to argue again, though I saw it was no use, for there was not one of my own men who wished to go on. They were unanimous in saying Usui was a "fire," and I had no right to sacrifice them. The Pig then finally refused, saying three loads even would not tempt him, for all were opposed to it. Of what value, he observed, would the beads be to him if his life was lost? This was crushing; the whole camp was unanimous in opposing me. I then made Baraka place all my kit in the middle of the boma, which was a very strong one, keeping out only such beads as I wished him to use for the men's rations daily, and ordered him to select a few men who would return with me to Kaze; when I said, if I could not get all the men I wanted, I would try and induce some one, who would not fear, to go on to Usui; failing which, I would even walk back to Zanzibar for men, as nothing in the world would ever induce me to give up the journey.

This appeal did not move him; but, without a reply, he sullenly commenced collecting some men to accompany me back to Kaze. At first no one would go; they then mutinied for more beads, announcing all sorts of grievances, which they said they were always talking over to themselves, though I did not hear them.

The greatest, however, that they could get up was, that I always paid the Wanyamuezi "temporaries" more than they got, though "permanents." "They were the flesh, and I was the knife"; I cut and did with them just as I liked, and they could not stand it any longer. However, they had to stand it; and next day, when I had brought them to reason, I gave over the charge of my tent and property to Baraka, and commenced the return with a bad hitching cough, caused by those cold easterly winds that blow over the plateau during the six dry months of the years, and which are, I suppose, the Harmattan peculiar to Africa.

Next day I joined Grant once more, and found he had collected a few Sorombo men, hoping to follow after me. I then told him all my mishaps in Sorombo, as well as of the "blue-devil" frights that had seized all my men. I felt greatly alarmed about the prospects of the expedition, scarcely knowing what I should do. I resolved at last, if everything else failed, to make up a raft at the southern end of the N'yanza, and try to go up to the Nile in that way. My cough daily grew worse. I could not lie or sleep on either side. Still my mind was so excited and anxious that, after remaining one day here to enjoy Grant's society, I pushed ahead again, taking Bombay with me, and had breakfast at Mchimeka's.

There I found the Pig, who now said he wished he had taken my offer of beads, for he had spoken with his chief, and saw that I was right. Baraka and the Wanguana were humbugs, and had they not opposed his going, he would have gone then; even now, he said, he wished I would take him again with Bombay. Though half inclined to accept his offer, which would have saved a long trudge to Kaze, yet as he had tricked me so often, I felt there would be no security unless I could get some coast interpreters, who would not side with the chiefs against me as he had done.

From this I went on to Sirboko's, and spent the next day with him talking over my plans. The rafting up the lake he thought a good scheme; but he did not think I should ever get through Usui until all the Kaze merchants went north in a body, for it was no use trying to force my men against their inclinations; and if I did not take care how I handled them, he thought they would all desert.

My cough still grew worse, and became so bad that, whilst mounting a hill on entering Ungugu's the second day after, I blew and grunted like a broken-winded horse, and it became so distressing I had to halt a day. In two more marches, however, I reached Kaze, and put up with Musa's eldest son, Abdalla, on the 2nd July, who now was transformed from a drunken slovenly boy into the appearance of a grand swell, squatting all day as his old father used to do. The house, however, did not feel the same – no men respected him as they had done his father. Sheikh Said was his clerk and constant companion, and the Tots were well fed on his goats – at my expense, however. On hearing my fix, Abdalla said I should have men; and, what's more, he would go with me as his father had promised to do; but he had a large caravan detained in Ugogo, and for that he must wait.

At that moment Manua Sera was in a boma at Kigue, in alliance with the chief of that place; but there was no hope for him now, as all the Arabs had allied themselves with the surrounding chiefs, including Kitambi; and had invested his position by forming a line, in concentric circles, four deep, cutting off his supplies of water within it, so that they daily expected to hear of his surrendering. The last news that had reached them brought intelligence of one man killed and two Arabs wounded; whilst, on the other side, Manua Sera had lost many men, and was put to such straits that he had called out if it was the Arabs' determination to kill him he would bolt again; to which the Arabs replied it was all the same; if he ran up to the top of the highest mountain or down into hell, they would follow after and put him to death.

3d. – After much bother and many disappointments, as I was assured I could get no men to help me until after the war was over, and the Arabs had been to Ugogo, and had brought up their property, which was still lying there, I accepted two men as guides – one named Bui, a very small creature, with very high pretensions, who was given me by Abdalla – the other, a steady old traveller, named Nasib (or Fortune), who was given me by Fundi Sangoro. These two slaves, both of whom knew all the chiefs and languages up to and including Uganda, promised me faithfully they would go with Bombay on to Usui, and bring back porters in sufficient number for Grant and myself to go on together. They laughed at the stories I told them of the terror that had seized Baraka and all the Wanguana, and told me, as old Musa had often done before, that those men, especially Baraka, had from their first leaving Kaze made up their minds they would not enter Usui, or go anywhere very far north.

I placed those men on the same pay as Bombay, and then tried to buy some beads from the Arabs, as I saw it was absolutely necessary I should increase my fast-ebbing store if I ever hoped to reach Gondokoro. The attempt failed, as the Arabs would not sell at a rate under 2,000 per cent; and I wrote a letter to Colonel Rigby, ordering up fifty armed men laden with beads and pretty cloths – which would, I knew, cost me $1,000 at the least – and left once more for the north on the 5th.

Marching slowly, as my men kept falling sick, I did not reach Grant again until the 11th. His health had greatly improved, and he had been dancing with Ukulima, as may be seen by the accompanying woodcut. So, as I was obliged to wait for a short time to get a native guide for Bui, Nasib and Bombay, who would show them a jungle-path to Usui, we enjoyed our leisure hours in shooting guinea-fowls for the pot. A report then came to us that Suwarora had heard with displeasure that I had been endeavouring to see him, but was deterred because evil reports concerning him had been spread. This unexpected good news delighted me exceedingly; confirmed my belief that Baraka, after all, was a coward, and induced me to recommend Bombay to make his cowardice more indisputable by going on and doing what he had feared to do.

To which Bombay replied, "Of course I will. It is all folly pulling up for every ill wind that blows, because, until one actually SEES there is something in it, you never can tell amongst these savages – 'shaves' are so common in Africa. Besides, a man has but one life, and God is the director of everything." "Bravo!" said I, "we will get on as long as you keep to that way of thinking." At length a guide was obtained, and with him came some of those men of the Pig's who returned before; for they had a great desire to go with me, but had been deterred, they said, by Baraka and the rest of my men. Seeing all this, I changed my plans again, intending, on arrival at Baraka's camp, to prevail on the whole of the party to go with me direct, which I thought they could not now refuse, since Suwarora had sent us an invitation. Moreover, I did not like the idea of remaining still whilst the three men went forwards, as it would be losing time.

These separations from Grant were most annoying, but they could not be helped; so, when all was settled here, I bade him adieu – both of us saying we would do our best – and set out on my journey, thinking what a terrible thing it was I could not prevail on my men to view things as I did. Neither my experience with native chiefs, nor my money and guns, were of any use to me, simply because my men were such incomprehensible fools, though many of them who had travelled before ought to have known better.

More reports came to us about Suwarora, all of the most inviting nature; but nothing else worth mentioning occurred until we reached the border of Msalala, where an officer of M'yonga's, who said he was a bigger man than his chief, demanded a tax, which I refused, and the dispute ended in his snatching Nasib's gun out of his hands. I thought little of this affair myself, beyond regretting the delay which it might occasion, as M'yonga, I knew, would not permit such usage, if I chose to go round by his palace and make a complaint. Both Bui and Nasib, however, were so greatly alarmed, that before I could say a word they got the gun back again by paying four yards merikani. We had continued bickering again, for Bui had taken such fright at this kind of rough handling, and the "push-ahead" manner in which I persisted "riding over the lords of the soil," that I could hardly drag the party along.

However, on the 18th, after breakfasting at Ruhe's, we walked into Mihambo, and took all the camp by surprise. I found the Union Jack hoisted upon a flag-staff, high above all the trees, in the boma. Baraka said he had done this to show the Watuta that the place was occupied by men with guns – a necessary precaution, as all the villages in the neighbourhood had, since my departure, been visited and plundered by them.

Lumeresi, the chief of the district, who lived ten miles to the eastward, had been constantly pressing him to leave this post and come to his palace, as he felt greatly affronted at our having shunned him and put up with Ruhe. He did not want property, he said, but he could not bear that the strangers had lived with his mtoto, or child, which Ruhe was, and yet would not live with him. He thought Baraka's determined obstinacy on this could only be caused by the influence of the head man of the village, and threatened that if Baraka did not come to visit him at once, he would have the head man beheaded. Then, shifting round a bit, he thought of ordering his subjects to starve the visitors into submission, and said he must have a hongo equal to Ruhe's. To all this Baraka replied, that he was merely a servant, and as he had orders to stop where he was, he could not leave it until I came; but to show there was no ill-feeling towards him, he sent the chief a cloth.

These first explanations over, I entered my tent, in which Baraka had been living, and there I found a lot of my brass wires on the ground, lying scattered about. I did not like the look of this, so ordered Bombay to resume his position of factotum, and count over the kit. Whilst this was going on, a villager came to me with a wire, and asked me to change it for a cloth. I saw at once what the game was; so I asked my friend where he got it, on which he at once pointed to Baraka. I then heard the men who were standing round us say one to another in under-tones, giggling with the fun of it, "Oh, what a shame of him! Did you hear what Bana said, and that fool's reply to it? What a shame of him to tell in that way." Without appearing to know, or rather to hear, the by-play that was going on, I now said to Baraka, "How is it this man has got one of my wires, for I told you not to touch or unpack them during my absence?" To which he coolly replied, in face of such evidence, "It is not one of your wires; I never gave away one of yours; there are lots more wires besides yours in the country. The man tells a falsehood; he had the wire before, but now, seeing your cloth open, wants to exchange it." "If that is the case," I said, taking things easy, "how is it you have opened my loads and scattered the wires about in the tent?" "Oh, that was to take care of them; for I thought, if they were left outside all night with the rest of the property, some one would steal them, and I should get the blame of it." Further parley was useless; for, though both my wires and cloths were short, still it was better not to kick up a row, when I had so much to do to keep all my men in good temper for the journey.

Baraka then, wishing to beguile me, as he thought he could do, into believing him a wonderful man for both pluck and honesty, said he had had many battles to fight with the men since I had been gone to Kaze, for there were two strong parties in the camp; those who, during the late rebellion at Zanzibar, had belonged to the Arabs that sided with Sultan Majid, and were royalists, and those who, having belonged to the rebellious Arabs, were on the opposite side. The battle commenced, he stated, by the one side abusing the other for their deeds during that rebellion, the rebels in this sort of contest proving themselves the stronger. But he, heading the royalist party, soon reduced them to order, though only for a short while, as from that point they turned round to open mutiny for more rations; and some of the rebels tried to kill him, which, he said, they would have done had he not settled the matter by buying some cows for them. It was on this account he had been obliged to open my loads. And now he had told me the case, he hoped I would forgive him if he had done wrong. Now, the real facts of the case were these – though I did not find them out at the time: Baraka had bought some slaves with my effects, and he had had a fight with some of my men because they tampered with his temporary wife – a princess he had picked up in Phunze. To obtain her hand he had given ten necklaces of MY beads to her mother, and had agreed to the condition that he should keep the girl during the journey; and after it was over, and he took her home, he would, if his wife pleased him, give her mother ten necklaces more.

Next day Baraka told me his heart shrank to the dimensions of a very small berry when he saw whom I had brought with me yesterday – meaning Bombay, and the same porters whom he had prevented going on with me before. I said, "Pooh, nonsense; have done with such excuses, and let us get away out of this as fast as we can. Now, like a good man, just use your influence with the chief of the village, and try and get from him five or six men to complete the number we want, and then we will work round the east of Sorombo up to Usui, for Suwarora has invited us to him." This, however, was not so easy; for Lumeresi, having heard of my arrival, sent his Wanyapara, or grey-beards, to beg I would visit him. He had never seen a white man in all his life, neither had his father, nor any of his forefathers, although he had often been down to the coast; I must come and see him, as I had seen his mtoto Ruhe. He did not want property; it was only the pleasure of my company that he wanted, to enable him to tell all his friends what a great man had lived in his house.

This was terrible: I saw at once that all my difficulties in Sorombo would have to be gone through again if I went there, and groaned when I thought what a trick the Pig had played me when I first of all came to this place; for if I had gone on then, as I wished, I should have slipped past Lumeresi without his knowing it.

I had to get up a storm at the grey-beards, and said I could not stand going out of my road to see any one now, for I had already lost so much time by Makaka's trickery in Sorombo. Bui then, quaking with fright at my obstinacy, said, "You must – indeed you must – give in and do with these savage chiefs as the Arabs when they travel, for I will not be a party to riding rough-shod over them." Still I stuck out, and the grey-beards departed to tell their chief of it. Next morning he sent them back to say he would not be cheated out of his rights as the chief of the district. Still I would not give in, and the whole day kept "jawing" without effect, for I could get no man to go with me until the chief gave his sanction. I then tried to send Bombay off with Bui, Nasib, and their guide, by night; but though Bombay was willing, the other two hung back on the old plea. In this state of perplexity, Bui begged I would allow him to go over to Lumeresi and see what he could do with a present. Bui really now was my only stand-by, so I sent him off, and next had the mortification to find that he had been humbugged by honeyed words, as Baraka had been with Makaka, into believing that Lumeresi was a good man, who really had no other desire at heart than the love of seeing me. His boma, he said, did not lie much out of my line, and he did not wish a stitch of my cloth. So far from detaining me, he would give me as many men as I wanted; and, as an earnest of his good intentions, he sent his copper hatchet, the badge of office as chief of the district, as a guarantee for me.

To wait there any longer after this, I knew, would be a mere waste of time, so I ordered my men to pack up that moment, and we all marched over at once to Lumeresi's, when we put up in his boma. Lumeresi was not in then, but, on his arrival at night, he beat all his drums to celebrate the event, and fired a musket, in reply to which I fired three shots. The same night, whilst sitting out to make astronomical observations, I became deadly cold – so much so, that the instant I had taken the star, to fix my position, I turned into bed, but could not get up again; for the cough that had stuck to me for a month then became so violent, heightened by fever succeeding the cold fit, that before the next morning I was so reduced that I could not stand. For the last month, too, I had not been able to sleep on either side, as interior pressure, caused by doing so, provoked the cough; but now I had, in addition, to be propped in position to get any repose whatever. The symptoms, altogether, were rather alarming, for the heart felt inflamed and ready to burst, pricking and twingeing with every breath, which was exceedingly aggravated by constant coughing, when streams of phlegm and bile were ejected. The left arm felt half-paralysed, the left nostril was choked with mucus, and on the centre of the left shoulder blade I felt a pain as if some one was branding me with a hot iron. All this was constant; and, in addition, I repeatedly felt severe pains – rather paroxysms of fearful twinges – in the spleen, liver, and lungs; whilst during my sleep I had all sorts of absurd dreams: for instance – I planned a march across Africa with Sir Roderick Murchison; and I fancied some curious creatures, half-men and half-monkeys, came into my camp to inform me that Petherick was waiting in boats at the south-west corner of the N'yanza, etc., etc.

Though my mind was so weak and excited when I woke up from these trances, I thought of nothing but the march, and how I could get out of Lumeresi's hands. He, with the most benign countenance, came in to see me, the very first thing in the morning, as he said, to inquire after my health; when, to please him as much as I could, I had a guard of honour drawn up at the tent door to fire a salute as he entered; then giving him my iron camp-chair to sit upon, which tickled him much – for he was very corpulent, and he thought its legs would break down with his weight – we had a long talk, though it was as much as I could do to remember anything, my brain was so excited and weak. Kind as he looked and spoke, he forgot all his promises about coveting my property, and scarcely got over the first salutation before he began begging for many things that he saw, and more especially for a deole, in order that he might wear it on all great occasions, to show his contemporaries what a magnanimous man his white visitor was. I soon lost my temper whilst striving to settle the hongo. Lumeresi would have a deole, and I would not admit that I had one.

23d to 31st. – Next morning I was too weak to speak moderately, and roared more like a madman than a rational being, as, breaking his faith, he persisted in bullying me. The day after, I took pills and blistered my chest all over, still Lumeresi would not let me alone, nor come to any kind of terms until the 25th, when he said he would take a certain number of pretty common cloths for his children if I would throw in a red blanket for himself. I jumped at this concession with the greatest eagerness, paid down my cloths on the spot; and, thinking I was free at last, ordered a hammock to be slung on a pole, that I might leave the next day. Next morning, however, on seeing me actually preparing to start, Lumeresi found he could not let me go until I increased the tax by three more cloths, as some of his family complained that they had got nothing. After some badgering, I paid what he asked for, and ordered the men to carry me out of the palace before anything else was done, for I would not sleep another night where I was. Lumeresi then stood in my way, and said he would never allow a man of his country to give me any assistance until I was well, for he could not bear the idea of hearing it said that, after taking so many cloths from me, he had allowed me to die in the jungles – and dissuaded my men from obeying my orders.

In vain I appealed to his mercy, declaring that the only chance left me of saving my life would be from the change of air in the hammock as I marched along. He would not listen, professing humanity, whilst he meant plunder; and I now found that he was determined not to beat the drum until I had paid him some more, which he was to think over and settle next day. When the next day came, he would not come near me, as he said I must possess a deole, otherwise I would not venture on to Karague; for nobody ever yet "saw" Rumanika without one. This suspension of business was worse than the rows; I felt very miserable, and became worse. At last, on my offering him anything that he might consider an equivalent for the deole if he would but beat the drums of satisfaction, he said I might consider myself his prisoner instead of his guest if I persisted in my obstinacy in not giving him Rumanika's deole; and then again peremptorily ordered all of his subjects not to assist me in moving a load. After this, veering round for a moment on the generous tack, he offered me a cow, which I declined.

1st to 4th. – Still I rejected the offered cow, until the 2nd, when, finding him as dogged as ever, at the advice of my men I accepted it, hoping thus to please him; but it was no use, for he now said he must have two deoles, or he would never allow me to leave his palace. Every day matters got worse and worse. Mfumbi, the small chief of Sorombo, came over, in an Oily-Gammon kind of manner, to say Makaka had sent him over to present his compliments to me, and express his sorrow on hearing that I had fallen sick here. He further informed me that the road was closed between this and Usui, for he had just been fighting there, and had killed the chief Gomba, burnt down all his villages, and dispersed all the men in the jungle, where they now resided, plundering every man who passed that way. This gratuitous, wicked, humbugging terrifier helped to cause another defeat. It was all nonsense, I knew, but both Bui and Nasib, taking fright, begged for their discharges. In fearful alarm and anxiety, I begged them to have patience and see the hongo settled first, for there was no necessity, at any rate, for immediate hurry; I wished them to go on ahead with Bombay, as in four days they could reach Suwarora's. But they said they could not hear of it--they would not go a step beyond this. All the chiefs on ahead would do the same as Lumeresi; the whole country was roused. I had not even half enough cloths to satisfy the Wasui; and my faithful followers would never consent to be witness to my being "torn to pieces."

5th and 6th. – The whole day and half of the next went in discussions. At last, able for the first time to sit up a little, I succeeded in prevailing on Bui to promise he would go to Usui as soon as the hongo was settled, provided, as he said, I took on myself all responsibilities of the result. This cheered me so greatly, I had my chair placed under a tree and smoked my first pipe. On seeing this, all my men struck up a dance, to the sound of the drums, which they carried on throughout the whole night, never ceasing until the evening of the next day. These protracted caperings were to be considered as their con-

Sultan Lumeresi's palace.

gratulation for my improvement in health; for, until I got into my chair, they always thought I was going to die. They then told me, with great mirth and good mimicry, of many absurd scenes which, owing to the inflamed state of my brain, had taken place during my interviews with Lumeresi. Bombay at this time very foolishly told Lumeresi, if he "really wanted a deole," he must send to Grant for one. This set the chief raving. He knew there was one in my box, he said, and unless I gave it, the one with Grant must be brought; for under no circumstances would he allow of my proceeding northwards until that was given him. Bui and Nasib then gave me the slip, and slept that night in a neighbouring boma without my knowledge.

7th to 9th. – As things had now gone so far, I gave Lumeresi the deole I had stored away for Rumanika, telling him, at the same time as he took it, that he was robbing Rumanika, and not myself; but I hoped, now I had given it, he would beat the drums. The scoundrel only laughed as he wrapped my beautiful silk over his great broad shoulders, and said, "Yes, this will complete our present of friendship; now then for the hongo – I must have exactly double of all you have given." This Sorombo trick I attributed to the instigation of Makaka, for these savages never fail to take their revenge when they can. I had doubled back from his country, and now he was cutting me off in front. I expected as much when the oily blackguard Mfumbi came over from his chief to ask after my health; so, judging from my experience with Makaka, I told Lumeresi at once to tell me what he considered his due, for this fearful haggling was killing me by inches. I had no more deoles, but would make that up in brass wire. He then fixed the hongo at fifteen masango or brass wire bracelets, sixteen cloths of sorts, and a hundred necklaces of samisami or red coral beads, which was to pay for Grant as well as myself. I paid it down on the spot; the drums beat the "satisfaction," and I ordered the march with the greatest relief of mind possible.

But Bui and Nasib were not to be found; they had bolted. The shock nearly killed me. I had walked all the way to Kaze and back again for these men, to show mine a good example – had given them pay and treble rations, the same as Bombay and Baraka – and yet they chose to desert. I knew not what to do, for it appeared to me that, do what I would, we would never succeed; and in my weakness of body and mind I actually cried like a child over the whole affair. I would rather have died than have failed in my journey, and yet failure seemed at this juncture inevitable.

8th. – As I had no interpreters, and could not go forward myself, I made up my mind at once to send back all my men with Bombay, to Grant; after joining whom, Bombay would go back to Kaze again for other interpreters, and on his return would pick up Grant, and bring him on here. This sudden decision set all my men up in a flame; they swore it was no use my trying to go on to Karague; they would not go with me; they did not come here to be killed. If I chose to lose my life, it was no business of theirs, but they would not be witness to it. They all wanted their discharge at once; they would not run away, but must have a letter of satisfaction, and then they would go back to their homes at Zanzibar. But when they found they lost all their arguments and could not move me, they said they would go back for Grant, but when they had done that duty, then they would take their leave.

10th to 15th. – This business being at last settled, I wrote to Grant on the subject, and sent all the men off who were not sick.

Thinking then how I could best cure the disease that was keeping me down, as I found the blister of no use, I tried to stick a packing needle, used as a seton, into my side; but finding it was not sharp enough, in such weak hands a mine, to go through my skin, I got Baraka to try; and he failing too, I then made him fire me, for the coughing was so incessant I could get no sleep at night. I had now nothing whatever to think of but making dodges for lying easy, and for relieving my pains, or else for cooking strong broths to give me strength, for my legs were reduced to the appearance of pipe-sticks, until the 15th, when Baraka, in the same doleful manner as in Sorombo, came to me and said he had something to communicate, which was so terrible, if I heard it I should give up the march. Lumeresi was his authority, but he would not tell it until Grant arrive. I said to him, "Let us wait till Grant arrives; we shall then have some one with us who won't shrink from whispers" – meaning Bombay; and so I let the matter drop for the time being. But when Grant came, we had it out of him, and found this terrible mystery all hung on Lumeresi's prognostications that we never should get through Usui with so little cloth.

16th to 19th. – At night, I had such a terrible air-catching fit, and made such a noise whilst trying to fill my lungs, that it alarmed all the camp, so much so that my men rushed into my tent to see if I was dying. Lumeresi, in the morning, then went on a visiting excursion into the district, but no sooner left than the chief of Isamiro, whose place lies close to the N'yanza, came here to visit him (17th); but after waiting a day to make friends with me, he departed (18th), as I heard afterwards, to tell his great Mhuma chief, Rohinda, the ruler of Ukhanga, to which district this state of Bogue belongs, what sort of presents I had given to Lumeresi. He was, in fact, a spy whom Rohinda had sent to ascertain what exactions had been made from me, as he, being the great chief, was entitled to the most of them himself. On Lumeresi's return, all the men of the village, as well as mine, set up a dance, beating the drums all day and all night.

20th to 21st. – Next night they had to beat their drums for a very different purpose, as the Watuta, after lifting all of Maka-ka's cattle in Sorombo, came hovering about, and declared they would never cease fighting until they had lifted all those that Lumeresi harboured round his boma; for it so happened that Lumeresi allowed a large party of Watosi, alias Wahuma, to keep their cattle in large stalls all round his boma, and these the Watuta had now set their hearts upon. After a little reflec-tion, however, they thought better of it, as they were afraid to come in at once on account of my guns.

Most gladdening news this day came in to cheer me. A large mixed caravan of Arabs and coast-men, arriving from Karague, announced that both Rumanika and Suwarora were anxiously looking out for us, wondering why we did not come. So great, indeed, was Suwarora's desire to see us, that he had sent four men to invite us, and they would have been here now, only that one of them fell sick on the way, and the rest had to stop for him. I cannot say what pleasure this gave me; my fortune, I thought, was made; and so I told Baraka, and pretended he did not believe the news to be true. Without loss of time I wrote off to Grant, and got these men to carry the letter.

Next day (22d) the Wasui from Suwarora arrived. They were a very gentle, nice-dispositioned-looking set of men – small, but well knit together. They advanced to my tent with much seeming grace; then knelt at my feet, and began clapping their hands together, saying, at the same time, "My great chief, my great chief, I hope you are well; for Suwarora, having heard of your detention here, has sent us over to assure you that all those reports that have been circulated regarding his ill-treatment of caravans are without foundation; he is sorry for what has happened to deter your march, and hopes you will at once come to visit him." I then told them all that had happened – how Grant and myself were situated – and begged them to assist me by going off to Grant's camp to inspire all the men there with confidence, and bring my rear property to me – saying, as they agreed to do so, "Here are some cloths and some beads for your expenses, and when you return I will give you more." Baraka at once, seeing this, told me they were not trustworthy, for at Mihambo an old man had come there and tried to inveigle him in the same manner, but he kicked him out of the camp, because he knew he was a touter, who wished merely to allure him with sweet words to fleece him afterwards. I then wrote to Grant another letter to be delivered by these men.

Lumeresi no sooner heard of the presents I had given them, than he flew into a passion, called them imposters, abused them for not speaking to him before they came to me, and said he would not allow them to go. High words then ensued. I said the business was mine, and not his; he had no right to inter-fere, and they should go. Still Lumeresi was obstinate, and de-termined they should not, for I was his guest; he would not al-low any one to defraud me. It was a great insult to himself, if true, that Suwarora should attempt to snatch me out of his house; and he could not bear to see me take these strangers by the hand, when, as we have seen, it took him so long to entice me to his den, and he could not prevail over me until he actu-ally sent his copper hatchet.

When this breeze blew over, by Lumeresi's walking away, I told the Wasui not to mind him, but to do just as I bid them. They said they had their orders to bring me, and if Lumeresi would not allow them to go for Grant, they would stop where they were, for they knew that if Suwarora found them delaying long, he would send more men to look after them. There was no peace yet, however; for Lumeresi, finding them quietly set-tled down eating with my men, ordered them out of his dis-trict, threatening force if they did not comply at once. I tried my best for them, but the Wasui, fearing to stop any longer, said they would take leave to see Suwarora, and in eight days more they would come back again, bringing something with them, the sight of which would make Lumeresi quake. Further words were now useless, so I gave them more cloth to keep them up to the mark, and sent them off. Baraka, who seemed to think this generosity a bit of insanity, grumbled that if I had cloths to throw away it would have been better had I disposed of them to my own men.

Next day (26th), as I was still unwell, I sent four men to Grant with inquiries how he was getting on, and a request for medicines. The messengers took four days to bring back the information that Bombay had not returned from Kaze, but that Grant, having got assistance, hoped to break ground about the 5th of next month. They brought me at the same time information that the Watuta had invested Ruhe's, after clearing off all the cattle in the surrounding villages, and had proclaimed their intention of serving out Lumeresi next. In consequence of this, Lumeresi daily assembled his grey-beards and had councils of war in his drum-house; but though his subjects sent to him constantly for troops, he would not assist them.

Another caravan then arrived (31st) from Karague, in which I found an old friend, of half Arab breed, called Saim, who whilst I was residing with Sheikh Snay at Kaze on my former expedition, taught me the way to make plantain-wine. He, like the rest of the porters in the caravan, wore a shirt of fig-tree bark called mbugu. As I shall have frequently to use this word in the course of the Journal, I may here give an explanation of its meaning. The porter here mentioned told me that the people about the equator all wore this kind of covering, and made it up of numerous pieces of bark sewn together, which they stripped from the trees after cutting once round the trunk above and below, and then once more down the tree from the upper to the lower circular cutting. This operation did not kill the trees, because, if they covered the wound, whilst it was fresh, well over with plantain-leaves, shoots grew down from above, and a new bark came all over it. The way they softened the bark, to make it like cloth, was by immersion in water, and a good strong application of a mill-headed mallet, which ribbed it like corduroy. [1] Saim told me he had lived ten years in Uganda, had crossed the Nile, and had traded eastward as far as the Masai country. He thought the N'yanza was the sources of the Ruvuma river; as the river which drained the N'yanza, after passing between Uganda and Usoga, went through Unyoro, and then all round the Tanganyika lake into the Indian Ocean, south of Zanzibar. Kiganda, he also said, he knew as well as his own tongue; and as I wanted an interpreter, he would gladly take service with me. This was just what I wanted – a heaven-born stroke of luck. I seized at his offer with avidity, gave him a new suit of clothes, which made him look quite a gentleman, and arranged to send him next day with a letter to Grant.

1st and 2d. – A great hubbub and confusion now seized all the place, for the Watuta were out, and had killed a woman of the place who had formerly been seized by them in war, but had since escaped and resided here. To avenge this, Lumeresi headed his host, and was accompanied by my men; but they succeeded in nothing save in frightening off their enemies, and regaining possession of the body of the dead woman. Then another hubbub arose, for it was discovered that three Wahuma women were missing (2d); and, as they did not turn up again, Lumeresi suspected the men of the caravan, which left with Saim, must have taken them off as slaves. He sent for the chief of the caravan, and had him brought back to account for this business. Of course the man swore he knew nothing about the matter, whilst Lumeresi swore he should stop there a prisoner until the women were freed, as it was not the first time his women had been stolen in this manner. About the same time a man of this place, who had been to Sorombo to purchase cows, came in with a herd, and was at once seized by Lumeresi; for, during his absence, one of Lumeresi's daughters had been discovered to be with child, and she, on being asked who was the cause of it, pointed out that man. To compensate for damage done to himself, as his daughter by this means had become reduced to half her market-value, Lumeresi seized all the cattle this man had brought with him.

3d to 10th. – When two days had elapsed, one of the three missing Wahuma women was discovered in a village close by. As she said she had absconded because her husband had illtreated her, she was flogged, to teach her better conduct. It was reported they had been seen in M'yonga's establishment; and I was at the same time informed that the husbands who were out in search of them would return, as M'yonga was likely to demand a price for them if they were claimed, in virtue of their being his rightful property under the acknowledged law of buni, or findings-keepings.

For the next four days nothing but wars and rumours of wars could be heard. The Watuta were out in all directions plundering cattle and burning villages, and the Wahuma of this place had taken such fright, they made a stealthy march with all their herds to a neighbouring chief, to whom it happened that one of Lumeresi's grey-beards was on a visit. They thus caught a Tartar; for the grey-beard no sooner saw them than he went and flogged them all back again, rebuking them on the way for their ingratitude to their chief, who had taken them in when they sought his shelter, and was now deserted by them on the first alarm of war.

10th. – Wishing now to gain further intelligence of Grant, I ordered some of my men to carry a letter to him; but they all feared the Watuta meeting them on the way, and would not. Just then a report came in that one of Lumeresi's sons, who had gone near the capital of Ukhanga to purchase cows, was seized by Rohinda in consequence of the Isamiro chief telling him that Lumeresi had taken untold wealth from me, and he was to be detained there a prisoner until Lumeresi either disgorged, or sent me on to be fleeced again. Lumeresi, of course, was greatly perplexed at this, and sought my advice, but could get nothing out of me, for I laughed in my sleeve, and told him such was the consequence of his having been too greedy.

11th to 15th. – Masudi with his caravan arrived from Mchimeka – Ungurue "the Pig," who had led me astray, was, by the way, his kirangozi or caravan-leader. Masudi told us he had suffered most severely from losses by his men running away, one after the other, as soon as they received their pay. He thought Grant would soon join me, as, the harvest being all in, the men about Rungua would naturally be anxious for service. He had had fearful work with M'yonga, having paid him a gun, some gunpowder, and a great quantity of cloth; and he had to give the same to Ruhe, with the addition of twenty brass wires, one load of mzizima, and one load of red coral beads. This was startling, and induced me to send all the men I could prudently spare off to Grant at once, cautioning him to avoid Ruhe's, as Lumeresi had promised me he would not allow one other thing to be taken from me. Lumeresi by this time was improving, from lessons on the policy of moderation which I had been teaching him; for when he tried to squeeze as much more out of Masudi as Ruhe had taken, he gave way, and let him off cheaply at my intercession. He had seen enough to be persuaded that this unlimited taxation or plunder system would turn out a losing game, such as Unyamyembe and Ugogo were at that time suffering from. Moreover, he was rather put to shame by my saying, "Pray, who now is biggest – Ruhe or yourself? For any one entering this country would suspect that he was, as he levies the first tax, and gives people to understand that, by their paying it, the whole district will be free to them; such at any rate he told me, and so it appears he told Masudi. If you are the sultan, and will take my advice, I would strongly recommend your teaching Ruhe a lesson, by taking from him what the Arabs paid, and giving it back to Masudi.

At midnight (16th) I was startled in my sleep by the hurried tramp of several men, who rushed in to say they were Grant's porters – Bogue men who had deserted him. Grant, they said, in incoherent, short, rapid, and excited sentences, was left by them standing under a tree, with nothing but his gun in his hand. All the Wanguana had been either killed or driven away by M'yonga's men, who all turned out and fell upon the caravan, shooting, spearing, and plundering, until nothing was left. The porters then, seeing Grant all alone, unable to help him, bolted off to inform me and Lumeresi, as the best thing they could do. Though disbelieving the story in all its minutiae, I felt that something serious must have happened; so, without a moment's delay, I sent off the last of my men strong enough to walk to succour Grant, carrying with them a bag of beads. Baraka then stepped outside my tent, and said in a loud voice, purposely for my edification, "There, now, what is the use of thinking any more about going to Karague? I said all along it was impossible"; upon hearing which I had him up before all the remaining men, and gave him a lecture, saying, happen what would, I must die or go on with the journey, for shame would not allow me to give way as Baraka was doing. Baraka replied, he was not afraid – he only meant to imply that men could not act against impossibilities. "Impossibilities!" I said; "what is impossible? Could I not go on as a servant with the first caravan, or buy up a whole caravan if I liked? What is impossible? For Godsake don't try any more to frighten my men, for you have nearly killed me already in doing so."

Next day (17th) I received a letter from Grant, narrating the whole of his catastrophes:

In the Jungles, near M'yonga's, 16th Sept. 1861.

My dear Speke, – The caravan was attacked, plundered, and the men driven to the winds, while marching this morning into M'yonga's country.

Awaking at cock-crow, I roused the camp, all anxious to rejoin you; and while the loads were being packed, my attention was drawn to an angry discussion between the head men and seven or eight armed fellows sent by Sultan M'yonga, to insist upon my putting up for the day in his village. They were summarily told that as YOU had already made him a present, he need not expect a visit from ME. Adhering, I doubt not, to their master's instructions, they officiously constituted themselves our guides till we chose to strike off their path, when, quickly heading our party, they stopped the way, planted their spears, and DARED our advance!

This menace made us firmer in our determination, and we swept past the spears. After we had marched unmolested for some seven miles, a loud yelping from the woods excited our attention, and a sudden rush was made upon us by, say two hundred men, who came down seemingly in great glee. In an instant, at the caravan's centre, they fastened upon the poor porters. The struggle was short; and with the threat of an arrow or spear at their breasts, men were robbed of their cloths and ornaments, loads were yielded and run away with before resistance could be organised; only three men of a hundred stood by me, the others, whose only thought was their lives, fled into the woods, where I went shouting for them. One man, little Rahan – rip as he is – stood with cocked gun, defending his load, against five savages with uplifted spears. No one else could be seen. Two or three were reported killed; some were wounded. Beads, boxes, cloths, etc., lay strewed about the woods. In fact, I felt wrecked. My attempt to go and demand redress from the sultan was resisted, and, in utter despair, I seated myself among a mass of rascals jeering round me, and insolent after the success of the day.

Several were dressed in the very cloths, etc., they had stolen from my men.

In the afternoon, about fifteen men and loads were brought me, with a message from the sultan, that the attack had been a mistake of his subjects – that one man had had a hand cut off for it, and that all the property would be restored!

Yours sincerely, J. W. Grant

Now, judging from the message sent to Grant by M'yonga, it appeared to me that his men had mistaken their chief's orders, and had gone one step beyond his intentions. It was obvious that the chief merely intended to prevent Grant from passing through or evading his district without paying a hongo, else he would not have sent his men to invite him to his palace, doubtless with instructions, if necessary, to use force. This appears the more evident from the fact of his subsequent contrition, and finding it necessary to send excuses when the property was in his hands; for these chiefs, grasping as they are, know they must conform to some kind of system, to save themselves from a general war, or the avoidance of their territories by all travellers in future. To assist Grant, I begged Lumeresi to send him some aid in men at once; but he refused, on the plea that M'yonga was at war with him, and would kill them if they went. This was all the more provoking, as Grant, in a letter next evening, told me he could not get all his men together again, and wished to know what should be done. He had recovered all the property except six loads of beads, eighty yards of American sheeting, and many minor articles, besides what had been rifled more or less from every load. In the same letter he asked me to deliver up a Mhuma woman to a man who came with the bearers of his missive, as she had made love to Saim at Ukulima's, and had bolted with my men to escape from her husband.

On inquiring into this matter, she told me her face had been her misfortune, for the man who now claimed her stole her from her parents at Ujiji, and forcibly made her his wife, but ever since had ill-treated her, often thrashing her, and never giving her proper food or clothing. It was on this account she fell in love with Saim; for he, taking compassion on her doleful stories, had promised to keep her as long as he travelled with me, and in the end to send her back to her parents at Ujiji. She was a beautiful woman, with gazelle eyes, oval face, high thin nose, and fine lips, and would have made a good match for Saim, who had a good deal of Arab blood in him, and was therefore, in my opinion, much of the same mixed Shem-Hamitic breed. But as I did not want more women in my camp, I have her some beads, and sent her off with the messenger who claimed her, much against my own feelings. I had proposed to Grant that, as Lumeresi's territories extended to within eight miles of M'yonga's, he should try to move over the Msalala border by relays, when I would send some Bogue men to meet him; for though Lumeresi would not risk sending his men into the clutches of M'yonga, he was most anxious to have another white visitor.

20th and 21st. – I again urged Lumeresi to help on Grant, saying it was incumbent on him to call M'yonga to account for maltreating Grant's porters, who were his own subjects, else the road would be shut up – he would lose all the hongos he laid on caravans – and he would not be able to send his own ivory down to the coast. This appeal had its effect: he called on his men to volunteer, and twelve porters came forward, who no sooner left, than in came another letter from Grant, informing me that he had collected almost enough men to march with, and that M'yonga had returned on of the six missing loads, and promised to right him in everything.

Next day, however, I had from Grant two very opposite accounts – one, in the morning, full of exultation, in which he said he hoped to reach Ruhe's this very day, as his complement of porters was then completed; while by the other, which came in the evening, I was shocked to hear that M'yonga, after returning all the loads, much reduced by rifling, had demanded as a hongo two guns, two boxed ammunition, forty brass wires, and 160 yards of American sheeting, in default of which he, Grant, must lend M'yonga ten Wanguana to build a boma on the west of his district, to enable him to fight some Wasona who were invading his territory, otherwise he would not allow Grant to move from his palace. Grant knew not what to do. He dared not part with the guns, because he knew it was against my principle, and therefore deferred the answer until he heard from me, although all his already collected porters were getting fidgety, and two had bolted. In this fearful fix I sent Baraka off with strict orders to bring Grant away at any price, except the threatened sacrifice of men, guns, and ammunition, which I would not listen to, as one more day's delay might end in further exactions; at the same time, I cautioned him to save my property as far as he could, for it was to him that M'yonga had formerly said that what I paid him should do for all.

Some of M'yonga's men who had plundered Grant now "caught a Tartar." After rifling his loads of a kilyndo, or bark box of beads, they, it appeared, received orders from M'yonga to sell a lot of female slaves, amongst whom were the two Wahuma women who had absconded from this. The men in charge, not knowing their history, brought them for sale into this district, where they were instantly recognised by some of Lumeresi's men, and brought in to him. The case was not examined at once, Lumeresi happening to be absent; so, to make good their time, the men in charge brought their beads to me to be exchanged for something else, not knowing that both camps were mine, and that they held my beads and not Grant's.

Of course I took them from them, but did not give them a flogging, as I knew if I did so they would at once retaliate upon Grant. The poor Wahuma women, as soon as Lumeresi arrived, were put to death by their husbands, because, by becoming slaves, they had broken the laws of their race.

22d to 24th. – At last I began to recover. All this exciting news, with the prospect of soon seeing Grant, did me a world of good – so much so, that I began shooting small birds for specimens – watching the blacksmiths as they made tools, spears, ad bracelets – and doctoring some of the Wahuma women who came to be treated for ophthalmia, in return for which they gave me milk. The milk, however, I could not boil excepting in secrecy, else they would have stopped their donations on the plea that this process would be an incantation or bewitchment, from which their cattle would fall sick and dry up. I now succeeded in getting Lumeresi to send his Wanyapara to go and threaten M'yonga, that if he did not release Grant at once, we would combine to force him to do so. They, however, left too late, for the hongo had been settled, as I was informed by a letter from Grant next day, brought to my by Bombay, who had just returned from Kaze after six weeks' absence. He brought with him old Nasib and another man, and told me both Bui and Nasib had hidden themselves in a boma close to Lumeresi's the day when my hongo was settled; but they bolted the instant the drums beat, and my men fired guns to celebrate the event, supposing that the noise was occasioned by our fighting with Lumeresi. These cowards then made straight for Kaze, when Fundi Sangoro gave Nasib a flogging for deserting me, and made him so ashamed of his conduct that he said he would never do it again. Bui also was flogged, but, admitting himself to be a coward, was set to the "right-about." With him Bombay also brought three new deoles, for which I had to pay 160 dollars, and news that the war with Manua Sera was not then over. He had effected his escape in the usual manner, and was leading the Arabs another long march after him.

Expecting to meet Grant this morning (25th), I strolled as far as my strength and wind would allow me towards Ruhe's; but I was sold, for Ruhe had detained him for a hongo. Lumeresi also having heard of it, tried to interpose, according to a plan arranged between us in case of such a thing happening, by sending his officers to Ruhe, with an order not to check my "brother's" march, as I had settled accounts for all. Later in the day, however, I heard from Grant that Ruhe would not let him go until he had paid sixteen pretty cloths, six wires, one gun, one box of ammunition, and one load of mzizima beads, coolly saying that I had only given him a trifle, under the condition that, when the big caravan arrived, Grant would make good the rest. I immediately read this letter to Lumeresi, and asked him how I should answer it, as Grant refused to pay anything until I gave the order.

To which Lumeresi replied, Ruhe, "my child," could not dare to interfere with Grant after his officers arrived, and advised me to wait until the evening. At all events, if there were any further impediments, he himself would go over there with a force and release Grant. In the evening another messenger arrived from Grant, giving a list of his losses and expenses at M'yonga's.

They amounted to an equivalent of eight loads, and were as follows: 100 yards cloth, and 4,600 necklaces of beads (these had been set aside as the wages paid to the porters, but being in my custody, I had to make them good); 300 necklaces of beads stolen from the loads; one brass wire stolen; one sword-bayonet stolen; Grant's looking-glass stolen; one saw stolen; one box ammunition stolen. Then paid in hongo, 160 yards cloth; 150 necklaces; one scarlet blanket, double; one case ammunition; ten brass wires. Lastly, there was one donkey beaten to death by the savages. This was the worst of all; for this poor brute carried me on the former journey to the southern end of the N'yanza, and in consequence was a great pet.

As nothing further transpired, and I was all in the dark (26th), I wrote to Grant telling him of my interviews with Lumeresi, and requesting him to pay nothing; but it was too late, for Grant, to my inexpressible delight, was the next person I saw; he walked into camp, and then he was a good laugh over all our misfortunes.

Poor Grant, he had indeed had a most troublesome time of it. The scoundrel Ruhe, who only laughed at Lumeresi's orders, had stopped his getting supplies of food for himself and his men; told him it was lucky that he came direct to the palace, for full preparations had been made for stopping him had he attempted to avoid it; would not listen to any reference being made to avoid myself; badgered and bullied over every article that he extracted; and, finally, when he found compliance with his extortionate requests was not readily granted, he beat the wardrums to frighten the porters, and ordered the caravan out of his palace, to where he said they would find his men ready to fight it out with them. It happened that Grant had just given Ruhe a gun when my note arrived, on which they made an agreement, that it was to be restored, provided that, after the full knowledge of all these transactions had reached us, it was both Lumeresi's and my desire that it should be so.

I called Lumeresi (27th), and begged he would show whether he was the chief or not, by requiring Ruhe to disgorge the property he had taken from me. His Wanyapara had been despised, and I had been most unjustly treated. Upon this the old chief hung down his head, and said it touched his heart more than words could tell to hear my complaint, for until I came that way no one had come, and I had paid him handsomely. He fully appreciated the good service I had done to him and his country by opening a road which all caravans for the future would follow if property dealt with. Having two heads in a country was a most dangerous thing, but it could not be helped for the present, as his hands were too completely occupied already. There were Rohinda, the Watuta, and M'yonga, whom he must settle with before he could attend to Ruhe; but when he was free, then Ruhe should know who was the chief. To bring the matter to a climax, Mrs. Lumeresi then said she ought to have something, because Ruhe was her son, whilst Lumeresi was only her second husband and consort, for Ruhe was born to her by her former husband. She therefore was queen.

Difficulties now commenced again (28th). All the Wanguana struck, and said they would go no further. I argued – they argued; they wanted more pay – I would not give more. Bombay, who appeared the only one of my men anxious to go on with Grant and myself, advised me to give in, else they would all run away, he said. I still stuck out, saying that if they did go, they should be seized on the coast and cast into jail for desertion. I had sent for fifty more men on the same terms as themselves, and nothing in the world would make me alter what had been established at the British Consulate. There all their engagements were written down in the office-book, and the Consul was our judge.

29th to 4th. – This shut them up, but at night two of them deserted; the Wanyamuezi porters also deserted, and I had to find more. Whilst this was going on, I wrote letters and packed up my specimens, and sent them back by my late valet, Rahan, who also got orders to direct Sheikh Said to seize the two men who deserted, and take them down chained to the coast when he went there. On the 4th, Lumeresi was again greatly perplexed by his sovereign Rohinda calling on him for some cloths; he must have thirty at least, else he would not give up Lumeresi's son. Further, he commanded in a bullying tone that all the Wahuma who were with Lumeresi should be sent to him at once, adding, at the same time, if his royal mandate was not complied with as soon as he expected, he would at once send a force to seize Lumeresi, and place another man in his stead to rule over the district.

Lumeresi, on hearing this, first consulted me, saying his chief was displeased with him, accusing him of being too proud, in having at once two such distinguished guests, and meant by these acts only to humble him. I replied, if that was the case, the sooner he allowed us to go, the better it would be for him; and, reminding him of his original promise to give me assistance on to Usui, said he could do so now with a very good grace.

Quite approving himself of this suggestion, Lumeresi then gave me one of his officers to be my guide – his name was Sangizo. This man no sooner received his orders than, proud of his office as the guide of such a distinguished caravan, he set to work to find us porters. Meanwhile my Wasui friends, who left on the 25th of August, returned, bearing what might be called Suwarora's mace – a long rod of brass bound up in stick charms, and called Kaquenzingiriri, "the commander of all things." This they said was their chief's invitation to see us, and sent this Kaquenzingiriri, to command us respect wherever we went.

5th. – Without seeing us again, Lumeresi, evidently ashamed of the power held over him by this rod of Suwarora's, walked off in the night, leaving word that he was on his way to Ruhe's, to get back my gun and all the other things that had been taken from Grant.

The same night a large herd of cattle was stolen from the boma without any one knowing it; so next morning, when the loss was discovered, all the Wahuma set off on the spoor to track them down; but with what effect I never knew.

As I had now men enough to remove half our property, I made a start of it, leaving Grant to bring up the rest. I believe I was a most miserable spectre in appearance, puffing and blowing at each step I took, with shoulder drooping, and left arm hanging like a dead leg, which I was unable ever to swing. Grant, remarking this, told me then, although from a friendly delicacy he had abstained from saying so earlier, that my condition, when he first saw me on rejoining, gave him a sickening shock. Next day (7th) he came up with the rest of the property, carried by men who had taken service for that one march only.

Before us now lay a wilderness of five marches' duration, as the few villages that once lined it had all been depopulated by the Sorombo people and the Watuta. We therefore had to lay in rations for those days, and as no men could be found who would take service to Karague, we filled up our complement with men at exorbitant wages to carry our things on to Usui. At this place, to our intense joy, three of Sheikh Said's boys came to us with a letter from Rigby; but, on opening it, our spirits at once fell far below zero, for it only informed us that he had sent us all kinds of nice things, and letters from home, which were packed up in boxes, and despatched from the coast on the 30th October 1860.

The boys then told me that a merchant, nickname Msopora, had left the boxes in Ugogo, in charge of some of those Arabs who were detained there, whilst he went rapidly round by the south, following up the Ruaha river to Usanga and Usenga, whence he struck across to Kaze. Sheikh Said, they said, sent his particular respects to me; he had heard of Grant's disasters with great alarm. If he could be of service, he would readily come to me; but he had dreamed three times that he saw me marching into Cairo, which, as three times were lucky, he was sure would prove good, and he begged I would still keep my nose well to the front, and push boldly on. Manua Sera was still in the field, and all was uncertain. Bombay then told me – he had forgotten to do so before – that when he was last at Kaze, Sheikh said told him he was sure we would succeed if both he and myself pulled together, although it was well known no one else of my party wished to go northwards.

With at last a sufficiency of porters, we all set out together, walking over a new style of country. Instead of the constantly-recurring outcrops of granite, as in Unyamuezi, with valleys between, there were only two lines of little hills visible, one right and one left of us, a good way off; whilst the ground over which we were travelling, instead of being confined like a valley, rose in long high swells of sandstone formation, covered with small forest-trees, among which flowers like primroses, only very much larger, and mostly of a pink colour, were frequently met with. Indeed, we ought all to have been happy together, for all my men were paid and rationed trebly – far better than they would have been if they had been travelling with any one else; but I had not paid all, as they thought, proportionably, and therefore there were constant heartburnings, with strikes and rows every day. It was useless to tell them that they were all paid according to their own agreements – that all short-service men had a right to expect more in proportion to their work than long-service ones; they called it all love and partiality, and in their envy would think themselves ill-used.

At night the kirangozi would harangue the camp, cautioning all hands to keep together on the line of march, as the Watuta were constantly hovering about, and the men should not squabble and fight with their master, else no more white men would come this way again. On the 11th we were out of Bogue, in the district of Ugomba, and next march brought us into Ugombe (12th), where we crossed the Ukongo nullah, draining westwards to the Malagarai river. Here some of the porters, attempting to bolt, were intercepted by my coast-men and had a fight of it, for they fired arrows, and in return the coast-men cut their bows. The whole camp, of course, was in a blaze at this; their tribe was insulted, and they would not stand it, until Bombay put down their pride with a few strings of beads, as the best means of restoring peace in the camp.

At this place we were visited by the chief of the district, Pongo (Bush-boc), who had left his palace to see us and invite us his way, for he feared we might give him the slip by going west into Uyofu. He sent us a cow, and said he should like some return; for Masudi, who had gone ahead, only gave him a trifle, professing to be our vanguard, and telling him that as soon as we came with the large caravan we would satisfy him to his heart's content. We wished for an interview, but he would not see us, as he was engaged looking into his magic horn, with an endeavour to see what sort of men we were, as none of our sort had ever come that way before.

The old sort of thing occurred again. I sent him one kitambi and eight yards kiniki, explaining how fearfully I was reduced from theft and desertions, and begging he would have mercy; but instead of doing so he sent the things back in a huff, after a whole day's delay, and said he required, besides, one sahari, one kitambi, and eight yards kiniki. In a moment I sent them over, and begged he would beat the drums; but no, he thought he was entitled to ten brass wires, in addition, and would accept them at his palace the next day, as he could not think of allowing us to leave his country until we had done him that honour, else all the surrounding chiefs would call him inhospitable.

Too knowing now to be caught with such chaff, I told him, through Bombay, if he would consider the ten brass wires final, I would give them, and then go to his palace, not otherwise. He acceded to this, but no sooner got them, than he broke his faith, and said he must either have more pretty cloths, or five more brass wires, and then, without doubt, he would beat the drums. A long badgering bargain ensued, at which I made all my men be present as witnesses, and we finally concluded the hongo with four more brass wires.

The drums then no sooner beat the satisfaction, than the Wasui mace-bearers, in the most feeling and good-mannered possible manner, dropped down on their knees before me, and congratulated me on the cessation of this tormenting business. Feeling much freer, we now went over and put up in Pong's palace, for we had to halt there a day to collect more porters, as half my men had just bolted. This was by no means an easy job, for all my American sheeting was out, and so was the kini-ki. Pongo then for the first time showed himself, sneaking about with an escort, hiding his head in a cloth lest our "evil eyes" might bewitch him. Still he did us a good turn; for on the 16th he persuaded his men to take service with us at the enormous hire of ten necklaces of beads per man for every day's march – nearly ten times what an Arab pays. Fowls were as plentiful here as elsewhere, though the people only kept them to sell to travellers, or else for cutting them open for diving purposes, by inspection of their blood and bones.

From the frying pan we went into the fire in crossing from Ugombe into the district of Wanga, where we beat up the chief, N'yaruwamba, and at once went into the hongo business. He offered a cow to commence with, which I would not accept until the tax was paid, and then I made my offering of two wires, one kitambi, and one kisutu. Badgering then commenced: I must add two wires, and six makete or necklaces of mzizima beads, the latter being due to the chief for negotiating the tax. When this addition was paid, we should be freed by beat of drum.

I complied at once, by way of offering a special mark of respect and friendship, and on the reliance that he would keep his word.

The scoundrel, however, no sooner got the articles, than he said a man had just come there to inform him that I gave Pongo ten wires and ten cloths; he, therefore, could not be satisfied until I added one more wire, when, without fail, he would beat the drums. It was given, after many angry words; but it was the old story over again – he would have one more wire and a cloth, or else he would not allow us to proceed on the morrow. My men, this time really provoked, said they would fight it out – a king breaking his word in that way! But in the end the demand had to be paid; and at last, at 9 P.M., the drums beat the satisfaction.

From this we went on to the north end of Wanga, in front of which was a wilderness, separating the possessions of Rohinda from those of Suwarora. We put up in a boma, but were not long ensconced there when the villagers got up a pretext for a quarrel, thinking they could plunder us of all our goods, and began pitching into my men. We, however, proved more than a match for them. Our show of guns frightened them all out of the place; my men then gave chase, firing off in the air, which sent them flying over the fields, and left us to do there as we liked until night, when a few of the villagers came back and took up their abode with us quietly. Next, after dark, the little village was on the alert again. The Watuta were out marching, and it was rumoured that they were bound for M'yaruwamba's. The porters who were engaged at Pongo's now gave us the slip: we were consequently detained here next day (19th), when, after engaging a fresh set, we crossed the wilderness, and in Usui put up with Suwarora's border officer of this post, N'yamanira.

Here we were again brought to a standstill.

·

---

1) If one asked the name of a tree, and it happened to be the kind from which this cloth was made, the answer would be "mbugu." If, again, the question was as to the bark, the same answer; and the same if one saw the shirt, and asked what it was. Hence I could not determine whether the word had been originally the name of the tree, of its bark, or of the article made from the bark, though I am inclined to think it is the bark, as there are many varieties of these trees, which, being besides being called mbugu, had their own particular names.

CHAPTER 7

USUI

Taxation Recommenced – A Great Doctor – Suwarora Pillaging –
The Arabs – Conference with an Ambassador from Uganda – Dis-
putes in Camp – Rivalry of Bombay and Baraka – Departure from
the Inhospitable Districts.

We were now in Usui, and so the mace-bearers, being on
their own ground forgot their manners, and peremptorily demanded their pay before they would allow us to move one step
farther. At first I tried to stave the matter off, promising great rewards if they took us quickly on to Suwarora; but they would
take no alternative – their rights were four wires each. I could
not afford such a sum, and tried to beat them down, but without effect; for they said, they had it in their power to detain us
here a whole month, and they could get us bullied at every stage
by the officers of the stations. No threats of reporting them to
their chief had any effect, so, knowing that treachery in these
countries was a powerful enemy, I ordered them to be paid.
N'yamanira, the Mkungu, then gave us a goat and two pots of
pombe, begging, at the same time, for four wires, which I paid,
hoping thus to get on in the morning.

I then made friends with him, and found he was a great doctor as well as an officer. In front of his hut he had his church or

uganga – a tree, in which was fixed a blaue boc's horn charged with magic powder, and a zebra's hoof, suspended by a string over a pot of water sunk in the earth below it. His badges of office he had tied on his head; the butt of a shell, representing the officer's badge, being fixed on the forehead, whilst a small sheep's horn, fixed jauntily over the temple, denoted that he was a magician. Wishing to try my powers in magical arts, as I laughed at his church, he begged me to produce an everlasting spring of water by simply scratching the ground. He, however, drew short up, to the intense delight of my men, on my promising that I would do so if he made one first.

At night, 22d, a steel scabbard and some cloths were extracted from our camp, so I begged my friend the great doctor would show us the use of his horn. This was promised, but never performed. I then wished to leave, as the Wasui guides, on receiving their pay, promised we should; but they deferred, on the plea that one of them must see their chief first, and get him to frank us through, else, they said, we should be torn to pieces. I said I thought the Kaquenzingiriri could do this; but they said, "No; Suwarora must be told first of your arrival, to prepare him properly for your coming; so stop here for three days with two of us, whilst the third one goes to the palace and returns again; for you know the chiefs of these countries do not feel safe until they have a look at the uganga." One of them then went away, but no sooner had left than a man named Makinga arrived to invite us on, as he said, at his adopted brother K'yengo's request. Makinga then told us that Suwarora, on first hearing that we were coming, became greatly afraid, and said he would not let us set eyes on his country, as he was sure we were king-dethroners; but, referring for opinion to Dr. K'yengo, his fears were overcome by the doctor assuring him that he had seen hosts of our sort at Zanzibar; and he knew, moreover, that some years ago we had been to Ujiji and to Ukerewe without having done any harm in those places; and, further, since Musa had sent word that I had done my best to subdue the war at Unyanyembe, and had promised to do my best here, he, Suwarora, had been anxiously watching our movements, and longed for our arrival. This looked famous, and it was agreed we should move the next morning. Just then a new light broke in on my defeat at Sorombo, for with Makinga I recognised one of my former porters, who I had supposed was a "child" of the Pig's. This man now said before all my men, Baraka included, that he wished to accept the load of mzizima I had offered the Pig if he would go forward with Baraka and tell Suwarora I wanted some porters to help me to reach him. He was not a "child" of the Pig's, but a "child" of K'yengo's; and as Baraka would not allow him to accept the load of mzizima, he went on to K'yengo by himself, and told all that had happened. It was now quite clear what motives induced Suwarora to send out the three Wasui; but how I blessed Baraka for this in my heart, though I said nothing about it to him, for fear of his playing some more treacherous tricks. Grant then told me Baraka had been frightened at Mininga, by a blackguard Mganga to whom he would not give a present, into the belief that our journey would encounter some terrible mishap; for, when the M'yonga catastrophe happened, he thought that a fulfillment of the Mganga's prophecy.

I wished to move in the morning (23d), and had all hands ready, but was told by Makinga he must be settled with first. His dues for the present were four brass wires, and as many more when we reached the palace. I could not stand this: we were literally, as Musa said we should be, being "torn to pieces"; so I appealed to the mace-bearers, protested that Makinga could have no claims on me, as he was not a man of Usui, but a native of Utambara, and brought on a row. On the other hand, as he could not refute this, Makinga swore the mace was all a pretence, and set a-fighting with the Wasui and all the men in turn.

To put a stop to this, I ordered a halt, and called on the district officer to assist us, on which he said he would escort us on to Suwarora's if we would stop till next morning. This was agreed to; but in the night we were robbed of three goats, which he said he could not allow to be passed over, lest Suwarora might hear of it, and he would get into a scrape. He pressed us strongly to stop another day whilst he sought for them, but I told him I would not, as his magic powder was weak, else he would have found the scabbard we lost long before this.

At last we got under way, and, after winding through a long forest, we emerged on the first of the populous parts of Usui, a most convulsed-looking country, of well-rounded hills composed of sandstone. In all the parts not under cultivation they were covered with brushwood. Here the little grass-hut villages were not fenced by a boma, but were hidden in large fields of plantains. Cattle were numerous, kept by the Wahuma, who could not sell their milk to us because we ate fowls and a bean called maharague.

Happily no one tried to pillage us here, so on we went to Vikora's, another officer, living at N'yakasenye, under a sandstone hill, faced with a dyke of white quartz, over which leaped a small stream of water – a seventy-feet drop – which, it is said, Suwarora sometimes paid homage to when the land was oppressed by drought. Vikora's father it was whom Sirboko of Mininga shot. Usually he was very severe with merchants in consequence of that act; but he did not molest us, as the messenger who went on to Suwarora returned here just as we arrived, to say we must come on at once, as Suwarora was anxious to see us, and had ordered his Wakungu not to molest us. Thieves that night entered our ringfence of thorns, and stole a cloth from off one of my men while he was sleeping.

We set down Suwarora, after this very polite message, "a regular trump," and walked up the hill of N'yakasenye with considerable mirth, singing his praises; but we no sooner planted ourselves on the summit than we sang a very different tune. We were ordered to stop by a huge body of men, and to pay toll.

Suwarora, on second thoughts, had changed his mind, or else he had been overruled by two of his officers – Kariwami, who lived here, and Virembo, who lived two stages back, but were then with their chief. There was no help for it, so I ordered the camp to be formed, and sent Nasib and the mace-bearers at once off to the palace to express to his highness how insulted I felt as his guest, being stopped in this manner, even when I had his Kaquenzingiriri with me as his authority that I was invited there as a guest. I was not a merchant who carried merchandise, but a prince like himself, come on a friendly mission to see him and Rumanika. I was waiting at night for the return of the messengers, and sitting out with my sextant observing the stars, to fix my position, when some daring thieves, in the dark bushes close by, accosted two of the women of the camp, pretending a desire to know what I was doing. They were no sooner told by the unsuspecting women, than they whipped off their cloths and ran away with them, allowing their victims to pass me in a state of absolute nudity. I could stand this thieving no longer. My goats and other things had been taken away without causing me much distress of mind, but now, after this shocking event, I ordered my men to shoot at any thieves that came near them.

This night one was shot, without any mistake about it; for the next morning we tracked him by his blood, and afterwards heard he had died of his wound. The Wasui elders, contrary to my expectation, then came and congratulated us on our success. They thought us most wonderful men, and possessed of supernatural powers; for the thief in question was a magician, who until now was thought to be invulnerable. Indeed, they said Arabs with enormous caravans had often been plundered by these people; but though they had so many more guns than ourselves, they never succeeded in killing one.

Nasib then returned to inform us that the king had heard our complaint, and was sorry for it, but said he could not interfere with the rights of his officers. He did not wish himself to take anything from us, and hoped we would come on to him as soon as we had satisfied his officers with the trifle they wanted. Virembo then sent us some pombe by his officers, and begged us to have patience, for he was then fleecing Masudi at the en-camping-ground near the palace. This place was alive with thieves. During the day they lured my men into their huts by inviting them to dinner; but when they got them they stripped them stark-naked and let them go again; whilst at night they stone our camp. After this, one more was shot dead and two others wounded.

I knew that Suwarora's message was all humbug, and that his officers merely kept about one per cent of what they took from travellers, paying the balance into the royal coffers. Thinking I was now well in for a good fleecing myself, I sent Bombay off to Masudi's camp, to tell Insangez, who was travelling with him on a mission of his master's, old Musa's son, that I would reward him handsomely if he would, on arrival at Karague, get Rumanika to send us his mace here in the same way as Suwarora had done to help us out of Bogue, as he knew Musa at one time said he would go with us to Karague in person. When Bombay was gone, Virembo then deputed Kariwami to take the hongo for both at once, mildly requiring 40 wires, 80 cloths, and 400 necklaces of every kind of bead we possessed. This was, indeed, too much of a joke. I complained of all the losses I had suffered, and begged for mercy; but all he said, after waiting the whole day, was, "Do not stick at trifles; for, after settling with us, you will have to give as much more to Vikora, who lives down below." Next morning, as I said I could not by any means pay such an exorbitant tax as was demanded, Kariwami begged me to make an offer which I did by sending him four wires. These, of course, were rejected with scorn; so, in addition, I sent an old box.

That, too, was thrown back on me, as nothing short of 20 wires, 40 cloths, and 200 necklaces of all sorts of beads, would satisfy him; and this I ought to be contented to pay, as he had been so moderate because I was the king's guest, and had been so reduced by robbery. I now sent six wires more, and said this was the last I could give – they were worth so many goats to me – and now by giving them away, I should have to live on grain like a poor man, though I was a prince in my own country, just like Suwarora. Surely Suwarora could not permit this if he knew it; and if they would not suffice, I should have to stop here until called again by Suwarora. The ruffian, on hearing this, allowed the wires to lie in his hut, and said he was going away, but hoped, when he returned, I should have, as I had got no cloths, 20 wires, and 1,000 necklaces of extra length, strung and all ready for him.

Just then Bombay returned flushed with the excitement of a great success. He had been in Masudi's camp, and had delivered my message to Insangez. Asudi, he said, had been there a fortnight unable to settle his hongo, for the great Mkama had not deigned to see him, though the Arab had been daily to his palace requesting an interview. "Well," I said, "that is all very interesting, but what next? – will the big king see us?" "O no; by the very best good fortune in the world, on going into the palace I saw Suwarora, and spoke to him at once; but he was so tremendously drunk, he could not understand me." "What luck was there in that?" I asked. On which Bombay said, "Oh, everybody in the place congratulated me on my success in having obtained an interview with that great monarch the very first day, when Arabs had seldom that privilege under one full month of squatting; even Masudi had not yet seen him." To which Nasib also added, "Ah, yes – indeed it is so – a monstrous success; there is great ceremony as well as business at these courts; you will better see what I mean when you get to Uganda. These Wahuma kings are not like those you ever saw in Unyamuezi or anywhere else; they have officers and soldiers like Said Majid, the Sultan at Zanzibar." "Well," said I to Bombay, "what was Suwarora like?" "Oh, he is a very fine man – just as tall, and in the face very like Grant; in fact, if Grant were black you would not know the difference." "And were his officers drunk too?" "O yes, they were all drunk together; men were bringing in pombe all day." "And did you get drunk?" "O yes," said Bombay, grinning, and showing his whole row of sharp-pointed teeth, "they WOULD make me drink; and then they showed me the place they assigned for your camp when you come over there. It was not in the palace, but outside, without a tree near it; anything but a nice-looking residence." I then sent Bombay to work at the hongo business; but, after haggling till night with Kariwami, he was told he must bring fourteen brass wires, two cloths, and five mukhnai of kanyera, or white porcelain beads – which, reduced, amounted to three hundred necklaces; else he said I might stop there for a month.

At last I settled this confounded hongo, by paying seven additional wires in lieu of the cloth; and, delighted at the termination of this tedious affair, I ordered a march. Like magic, however, Vikora turned up, and said we must wait until he was settled with. His rank was the same as the others, and one bead less than I had given them he would not take. I fought all the day out, but the next morning, as he deputed his officers to take nine wires, these were given, and then we went on with the journey.

Tripping along over the hill, we descended to a deep miry watercourse, full of bulrushes, then over another hill, from the heights of which we saw Suwarora's palace, lying down in the

Uthungu valley, behind which again rose another hill of sandstone, faced on the top with a dyke of white quartz. The scene was very striking, for the palace enclosures, of great extent, were well laid out to give effect. Three circles of milk bush, one within the other, formed the boma, or ring-fence. The chief's hut (I do not think him worthy of the name of king, since the kingdom is divided in two) was three times as large as any of the others, and stood by itself at the farther end; whilst the smaller huts, containing his officers and domestics, were arranged in little groups within a circle, at certain distances apart from one another, sufficient to allow of their stalling their cattle at night.

On descending into the Uthungu valley, Grant, who was preceding the men, found Makinga opposed to the progress of the caravan until his dues were paid. He was a stranger like ourselves, and was consequently treated with scorn, until he tried to maintain what he called his right, by pulling the loads off my men's shoulders, whereupon Grant cowed him into submission, and all went on again – not to the palace, as we had supposed, but, by the direction of the mace-bearers, to the huts of Suwarora's commander-in-chief, two miles from the palace; and here we found Masudi's camp also. We had no sooner formed camp for ourselves and arranged all our loads, than the eternal Vikora, whom I thought we had settled with before we started, made a claim for some more wire, cloth, and beads, as he had not received as much as Kariwani and Virembo. Of course I would not listen to this, as I had paid what his men asked for, and that was enough for me. Just then Masudi, with the other Arabs who were travelling with him, came over to pay us a visit, and in-

Camp in the Uthungu Valley:
the natives are bringing provisions.

quire what we thought of the Usui taxes. He had just concluded his hongo to Suwarora by paying 80 wires, 120 yards of cloth, and 130 lb. of beads, whilst he had also paid to every officer from 20 to 40 wires, as well as cloths and beads. On hearing of my transactions, he gave it as his opinion that I had got off surprisingly well.

Next morning, (1st) Masudi and his party started for Karague.

They had been more than a year between this and Kaze, trying all the time to get along. Provisions here were abundant – hawked about by the people, who wore a very neat skin kilt strapped round the waist, but otherwise were decorated like the Wanyamuezi. It was difficult to say who were of true breed here, for the intercourse of the natives with the Wahuma and the Wanyamuezi produced a great variety of facial features amongst the people. Nowhere did I ever see so many men and women with hazel eyes as at this place.

In the evening, an Uganda man, by name N'yamgundu, came to pay his respects to us. He was dressed in a large skin wrapper, made up of a number of very small antelope skins: it was as soft as kid, and just as well sewn as our gloves. To our surprise the manners of the man were quite in keeping with his becoming dress. I was enchanted with his appearance, and so were my men, though no one could speak to him but Nasib, who told us he knew him before. He was the brother of the dowager queen of Uganda, and, along with a proper body of officers, he had been sent by Mtesa, the present king of Uganda, to demand the daughter of Suwarora, as reports had reached his king that she was surprisingly beautiful. They had been here more than a year, during which time this beautiful virgin had died; and now Suwarora, fearful of the great king's wrath, consequent on his procrastinations, was endeavouring to make amends for it, by sending, instead of his daughter, a suitable tribute in wires. I thought it not wonderful that we should be fleeced.

Next day (2d) Sirhid paid us a visit, and said he was the first man in the state. He certainly was a nice-looking young man, with a good deal of the Wahuma blood in him. Flashily dressed in coloured cloths and a turban, he sat down in one of our chairs as if he had been accustomed to such a seat all his life, and spoke with great suavity. I explained our difficulties as those of great men in misfortune; and, after listening to our tale, he said he would tell Suwarora of the way we had been plundered, and impress upon him to deal lightly with us. I said I had brought with me a few articles of European manufacture for Suwarora, which I hoped would be accepted if I presented them, for they were such things as only great men like his chief every possessed. One was a five-barrelled pistol, another a large block-in box, and so fourth; but after looking at them, and seeing the pistol fired, he said; "No; you must not show these things at first, or the Mkama might get frightened, thinking them magic. I might lose my head for presuming to offer them, and then there is no knowing what might happen afterwards."

"Then can I not see him at once and pay my respects, for I have come a great way to obtain that pleasure?"

"No," said Sirhid, "I will see him first; for he is not a man like myself, but requires to be well assured before he sees anybody."

"Then why did he invite me here!"

"He heard that Makaka, and afterwards Lumeresi, had stopped your progress; and as he wished to see what you were like, he ordered me to send some men to you, which, as you know, I did twice. He wishes to see you, but does not like doing things in a hurry. Superstition, you know, preys on these men's minds who have not seen the world like you and myself."

Sirhid then said he would ask Suwarora to grant us an interview as soon as possible; then, whilst leaving, he begged for the iron chair he had sat upon; but hearing we did not know how to sit on the ground, and therefore could not spare it, he withdrew without any more words about it.

Virembo then said (3d) he must have some more wire and beads, as his proxy Kariwami had been satisfied with too little. I drove him off in a huff, but he soon came back again with half the hongo I had paid to Kariwami, and said he must have some cloths or he would not have anything. As fortune decreed it, just then Sirhid dropped in, and stopped his importunity for the time by saying that if we had possessed cloths his men must have known it, for they had been travelling with us. No sooner, however, did Virembo turn tail than the Sirhid gave us a broad hint that he usually received a trifle from the Arabs before he made an attempt at arranging the hongo with Suwarora. Any trifle would do but he preferred cloth.

This was rather perplexing. Sirhid knew very well that I had a small reserve of pretty cloths, though all the common ones had been expended; so, to keep in good terms with him who was to be our intercessor, I said I would give him the last I had got if he would not tell Suwarora or any one else what I had done. Of course he was quite ready to undertake the condition,

236

Uganda: Tools and ornaments.
1. Warrior. 2. Ivory leg rings. 3. King's leg ornaments.
4 and 5. Men's head ornaments, diadems and garlands.
6 and 15. Shield and spears. 7, 8 and 10. Necklaces. 9. King's bracelet-amulet.
11. Woman's dagger. 12, 13 and 14. Amulets.
16. Snakeskin rope knot.

so I gave him two pretty cloths, and he in return gave me two goats. But when this little business had been transacted, to my surprise he said: "I have orders from Suwarora to be absent five days to doctor a sick relation of his, for there is no man in the country so skilled in medicines as myself; but whilst I am gone I will leave Karambule, my brother, to officiate in my stead about taking your hongo; but the work will not commence until to-morrow, for I must see Suwarora on the subject myself first." Irungu, a very fine-looking man of Uganda, now called on me and begged for beads. He said his king had heard of our approach, and was most anxious to see us. Hearing this I begged him to wait here until my hongo was paid, that we might travel on to Uganda together. He said, No, he could not wait, for he had been detained here a whole year already; but, if I liked, he would leave some of his children behind with me, as their presence would intimidate Suwarora, and incite him to let us off quickly.

I then begged him to convey a Colt's six-chamber revolving rifle to his king, Mtesa, as an earnest that I was a prince most desirous of seeing him. No one, I said, but myself could tell what dangers and difficulties I had encountered to come thus far for the purpose, and all was owing to his great fame, as the king of kings, having reached me even as far off as Zanzibar. The ambassador would not take the rifle, lest his master, who had never seen such a wonderful weapon before, should think he had brought him a malign charm, and he would be in danger of losing his head. I then tried to prevail on him to take a knife and some other pretty things, but he feared them all; so, as a last chance – for I wished to send some token, by way of card or letter, for announcing my approach and securing the road – I gave him a red six-penny pocket-handkerchief, which he accepted; and he then told me he was surprised I had come all this way round to Uganda, when the road by the Masai country was so much shorter. He told me how, shortly after the late king of Uganda, Sunna, died, and before Mtesa had been selected by the officers of the country to be their king, an Arab caravan came across the Masai as far as Usoga, and begged for permission to enter Uganda; but as the country was disturbed by the elections, the officers of the state advised the Arabs to wait, or come again when the king was elected. I told him I had heard of this before, but also heard that those Arabs had met with great disasters, owing to the turbulence of the Masai. To which he replied: "That is true; there were great difficulties in those times, but now the Masai country was in better order; and as Mtesa was most anxious to open that line, he would give me as many men as I liked if I wished to go home that way." This was pleasant information, but not quite new, for the Arabs had told me Mtesa was so anxious to open that route, he had frequently offered to aid them in it himself. Still it was most gratifying to myself as I had written to the Geographical Society, on leaving Bogue, that if I found Petherick in Uganda, or on the northern end of the N'yanza, so that the Nile question was settled, I would endeavour to reach Zanzibar via the Masai country. In former days, I knew, the kings of Uganda were in the habit of sending men to Karague when they heard that Arabs wished to visit them – even as many as two hundred at a time – to carry their kit; so I now begged Irungu to tell Mtesa that I should want at least sixty men; and then, on his promising that he would be my commissioner, I gave him the beads he had begged for himself.

4th to 6th. – Karambule now told us to string our beads on the fibre of the Mwale tree, which was sold here by the Wasui, as he intended to live in the palace for a couple of days, arranging with Suwarora what tax we should have to pay, after which he would come and take it from us; but we must mind and be ready, for whatever Suwarora said, it must be done instantly. There was no such thing as haggling with him; you must pay and be off at once, failing which you might be detained a whole month before there would be an opportunity to speak on the subject again. Beads were then served out to all my men to be strung, a certain quantity to every kambi or mess, and our work was progressing; but next day we heard that Karambule was sick or feigning to be so, and therefore had never gone to the palace at all. On the 6th, provoked at last by the shameful manner in which we were treated, I send word to him to say, if he did not go at once I would go myself, and force my way in with my guns, for I could not submit to being treated like a slave, stuck out here in the jungle with nothing to do but shoot for specimens, or make collections of rocks, etc. This brought on another row; for he said both Virembo and Vikora had returned their hongos, and until their tongues were quieted he could not speak to Suwarora.

To expedite matters (7th), as our daily consumption in camp was a tax of itself, I gave these tormenting creatures one wire, one pretty cloth, and five hundred necklaces of white beads, which were no sooner accepted than Karambule, in the same way as Sirhid had done, said it would be greatly to my advantage if I gave him something worth having before he saw the Mkama. Only too glad to being work I gave him a red blanket, called joho, and five strings of mzizima beads, which were equal to fifty of the common white.

8th and 9th. – All this time nothing but confusion reigned in camp, khambi fighting against khambi. Both men and women got drunk, whilst from outside we were tormented by the Wasui, both men and women pertinaciously pressing into our hut, watching us eat, and begging in the most shameless manner. They did not know the word bakhshish, or present; but, as bad as the Egyptians, they held our their hands, patted their bellies, and said Kaniwani (my friend) until we were sick of the sound of that word. Still it was impossible to dislike these simple creatures altogether, they were such perfect children. If we threw water at them to drive them away, they came back again, thinking it fun.

Ten days now had elapsed since we came here, still nothing was done (10th), as Karambule said, because Suwarora had been so fully occupied collecting an army to punish an officer who had refused to pay his taxes, had ignored his authority, and had set himself us as king of the district he was appointed to superintend. After this, at midnight, Karambule, in an excited manner, said he had seen Suwarora, and it then was appointed that, not he, but Virembo should take the royal hongo, as well as the Wahinda, or princes' shares, the next morning – after which we might go as fast as we liked, for Suwarora was so full occupied with his army he could not see us this time. Before, however, the hongo could be paid, I must give the Sirhid and himself twenty brass wires, three joho, three barsati, twenty strings of mzizima, and one thousand strings of white beads. They were given.

A fearful row now broke out between Bombay and Baraka (11th).

Many of my men had by this time been married, notwithstanding my prohibition. Baraka, for instance, had with him the daughter of Ungurue, chief of Phunze; Wadimoyo, a woman called Manamaka; Sangizo, his wife and sister; but Bombay had not got one, and mourned for a girl he had set his eyes on, unfortunately for himself letting Baraka into his confidence. This set Baraka on the qui vive to catch Bombay tripping; for Baraka knew he could not get her without paying a good price for her, and therefore watched his opportunity to lay a complaint against him of purloining my property, by which scheme he would, he thought, get Bombay's place as storekeeper himself. In a sly manner Bombay employed some of my other men to take five wires, a red blanket, and 500 strings of beads, to his would-be father-in-law, which, by a previously-concocted arrangement, was to be her dowry price.

These men did as they were bid; but the father-in-law returned things, saying he must have one more wire. That being also supplied, the scoundrel wanted more, and made so much fuss about it, that Baraka became conversant with all that was going on, and told me of it.

This set the whole camp in a flame, for Bombay and Baraka were both very drunk, as well as most of the other men, so that it was with great difficulty I could get hold of the rights of their stories. Bombay acknowledged he had tried to get the girl, for they had been sentimentalising together for several days, and both alike wished to be married. Baraka, he said, was allowed to keep a wife, and his position, demanded that he should have one also; but the wires were his own property, and not mine, for he was given them by the chiefs as a perquisite when I paid their hongo through him. He thought it most unjust and unfair of Baraka to call him to account in that way, but he was not surprised at it, as Baraka, from the beginning of the journey to the present moment, had always been backbiting him, to try and usurp his position. Baraka, at this, somewhat taken aback, said there were no such things as perquisites on a journey like this; for whatever could be saved from the chiefs was for the common good of all, and all alike ought to share in it – repeating words I had often expressed. Then Bombay retorted trembling and foaming in his liquor: "I know I shall get the worst of it, for whilst Baraka's tongue is a yard long, mine is only an inch; but I would not have spent any wires of master's to purchase slaves with (alluding to what Baraka had done at Mihambo); nor would I, for any purpose of making myself richer; but when it comes to a wife, that's a different thing." In my heart I liked Bombay all the more for this confession, but thought it necessary to extol Baraka for his quickness in finding him out, which drove Bombay nearly wild. He wished me to degrade him, if I thought him dishonest; threw himself on the ground, and kissed my feet. I might thrash him, turn him into a porter, or do anything else that I liked with him, as long as I did not bring a charge of dishonesty against him. He could not explain himself with Baraka's long tongue opposed to him, but there were many deficiencies in my wires before he took overcharge at Bogue, which he must leave for settlement till the journey was over, and then, the whole question having been sifted at Zanzibar, we would see who was the most honest. I then counted all the wires over, at Bombay's request, and found them complete in numbers, without those he had set aside from the dowry money. Still there was a doubt, for the wires might have been cut by him without detection, as from the commencement they were of different lengths. However, I tried to make them friends, claimed all the wires myself, and cautioned every man in the camp again, that they were all losers when anything was misappropriated; for I brought this property to pay our way with and whatever balance was over at the end of the journey I would divide amongst the whole of them.

12th and 13th. – When more sober, Bombay again came to crave a thousand pardons for what he had done, threw himself down at my feet, then at Grant's, kissed our toes, swore I was his Ma Pap (father and mother); he had no father or mother to teach him better; he owed all his prosperity to me; men must err sometimes; oh, if I would only forgive him – and so forth. Then being assured that I knew he never would have done as he had if a woman's attractions had not led him astray, he went to his work again like a man, and consoled himself by taking Sangizo's sister to wife on credit instead of the old love, promising to pay the needful out of his pay, and to return her to her brother when the journey was over.

In the evening Virembo and Karambule came to receive the hongo for their chief, demanding 60 wires, 160 yards merikani, 300 strings of mzizima, and 5,000 strings of white beads; but they allowed themselves to be beaten down to 50 wires, 20 pretty cloths, 100 strings mzizima, and 4,000 kutuamnazi, or cocoa-nut-leaf coloured beads, my white being all done. It was too late, however, to count all the things out, so they came the next day and took them. They then said we might go as soon as we had settled with the Wahinda or Wanawami (the king's children), for Suwarora could not see us this time, as he was so engaged with his army; but he hoped to see us and pay us more respect when we returned from Uganda, little thinking that I had sworn in my mind never to see him, or return that way again. I said to those men, I thought he was ashamed to see us, as he had robbed us so after inviting us into the country, else he was too superstitious, for he ought at least to have given us a place in his palace. They both rebutted the insinuation; and, to change the subject, commenced levying the remaining dues to the princes, which ended by my giving thirty-four wires and six pretty cloths in a lump.

Early in the morning we were on foot again, only too thankful to have got off so cheaply. Then men were appointed as guides and protectors, to look after us as far as the border. What an honour! We had come into the country drawn there by a combination of pride and avarice and now we were leaving it in hot haste under the guidance of an escort of officers, who were in reality appointed to watch us as dangerous wizards and objects of terror. It was all the same to us, as we now only thought of the prospect of relief before us, and laughed at what we had gone through.

Rising out of the Uthungu valley, we walked over rolling ground, drained in the dips by miry rush rivulets. The population was thinly scattered in small groups of grass huts, where the scrub jungle had been cleared away. On the road we passed cairns, to which every passer-by contributed a stone. Of the origin of the cairns I could not gain any information, though it struck me as curious I should find them in the first country we had entered governed by the Wahuma, as I formerly saw the same thing in the Somali country, which doubtless, in earlier days, was governed by a branch of the Abyssinians. Arrived at our camping, we were immediately pounced upon by a deputation of officers, who said they had been sent by Semamba, the officer of this district. He lived ten miles from the road; but hearing of our approach, he had sent these men to take his dues. At first I objected to pay, lest he should afterwards treat me as Virembo had done; but I gave way in the end, and paid nine wires, two chintz and two bindera cloths, as the guides said they would stand my security against any further molestation.

Rattling on again as merry as larks, over the same red sandstone formation, we entered a fine forest, and trended on through it as a stiff pace until we arrived at the head of a deep valley called Lohuati, which was so beautiful we instinctively pulled up to admire it. Deep down its well-wooded side below us was a stream, of most inviting aspect for a trout-fisher, flowing towards the N'yanza. Just beyond it the valley was clothed with fine trees and luxuriant vegetation of all descriptions, amongst which was conspicuous the pretty pandana palm, and rich gardens of plantains; whilst thistles of extraordinary size and wild indigo were the more common weeds. The land beyond that again rolled back in high undulations, over which, in the far distance, we could see a line of cones, red and bare on their tops, guttered down with white streaks, looking for all the world like recent volcanoes; and in the far background, rising higher than all, were the rich grassy hills of Karague and Kishakka.

Uthungu Valley.

On resuming our march, a bird, called *khongota*, flew across our path; seeing which, old Nasib, beaming with joy, in his superstitious belief cried out with delight, "Ah, look at that good omen! – Now our journey will be sure to be prosperous." After fording the stream, we sat down to rest, and were visited by all the inhabitants, who were more naked than any people we had yet seen. All the maidens, even at the age of puberty, did not hesitate to stand boldly in front of us – for evil thoughts were not in their minds. From this we rose over a stony hill to the settlement of Vihembe, which, being the last on the Usui frontier, induced me to give our guides three wires each, and four yards of bindera, which Nasib said was their proper fee. Here Bombay's would-be, but disappointed, father-in-law sent after us to say that he required a hongo; Suwarora had never given his sanction to our quitting his country; his hongo even was not settled. He wished, moreover, particularly to see us; and if we did not return in a friendly manner, an army would arrest our march immediately.

CHAPTER 8

KARAGUE

Relief from Protectors and Pillagers – The Scenery and Geology – Meeting with the Friendly King Rumanika – His Hospitalities and Attention – His Services to the Expedition – Philosophical and Theological Inquiries – The Royal Family of Karague – The M-Fumbiro Mountain – Navigation of "The Little Windermere" – The New-Moon Levee – Rhinoceros and Hippopotamus Hunting – Measurement of a Fattened Queen – Political Polygamy – Christmas – Rumours of Petherick's Expedition – Arrangements to Meet It – March to Uganda.

This was a day of relief and happiness. A load was removed from us in seeing the Wasui "protectors" depart, with the truly cheering information that we now had nothing but wild animals to contend with before reaching Karague. This land is "neutral," by which is meant that it is untenanted by human beings; and we might now hope to bid adieu for a time to the scourging system of taxation to which we had been subjected.

Gradually descending from the spur which separates the Lohugati valley from the bed of the Lueru lo Urigi, or Lake of Urigi, the track led us first through a meadow of much pleasing beauty, and then through a passage between the "saddle-back" domes we had seen from the heights above Lohugati, where a new geological formation especially attracted my notice. From the green slopes of the hills, set up at a slant, as if the central line of pressure on the dome top had weighed on the inside plates, protruded soft slabs of argillaceous sandstone, whose laminae presented a beef-sandwich appearance, puce or purple alternating with creamy-white. Quartz and other igneous rocks were also scattered about, lying like superficial accumulations in the dips at the foot of the hills, and red sandstone conglomerates clearly indicated the presence of iron. The soil itself looked rich and red, not unlike our own fine country of Devon.

On arriving in camp we pitched under some trees, and at once were greeted by an officer sent by Rumanika to help us out of Usui. This was Kachuchu, an old friend of Nasib's, who no sooner saw him than, beaming with delight, he said to us, "Now, was I not right when I told you the birds flying about on Lohugati hill were a good omen? Look here what this man says: Rumanika has ordered him to bring you on to his palace at once, and wherever you stop a day, the village officers are instructed to supply you with food at the king's expenses, for there are no taxes gathered from strangers in the kingdom of Karague. Presents may be exchanged, but the name of tax is ignored." Grant here shot a rhinoceros, which came well into play to mix with the day's flour we had carried on from Vihembe.

Deluded yesterday by the sight of the broad waters of the Lueru lo Urigi, espied in the distance from the top of a hill, into the belief that we were in view of the N'yanza itself, we walked triumphantly along, thinking how well the Arabs at Kaze had described this to be a creek of the great lake; but on arrival in camp we heard from the village officer that we had been misinformed, and that it was a detached lake, but connected with the Victoria N'yanza by a passage in the hills and the Kitangule river. Formerly, he said, the Urigi valley was covered with water, extending up to Uhha, when all the low lands we had crossed from Usui had to be ferried, and the saddleback hills were a mere chain of islands in the water. But the country had dried up, and the lake of Urigi became a small swamp. He further informed us, that even in the late king Dagara's time it was a large sheet of water; but the instant he ceased to exist, the lake shrank to what we now saw.

Our day's march had been novel and very amusing. The hilly country surrounding us, together with the valley, brought back to recollection many happy days I had once spent with the Tartars in the Thibetian valley of the Indus – only this was more picturesque; for though both countries are wild, and very thinly inhabited, this was greened over with grass, and dotted here and there on the higher slopes with thick bush of acacias, the haunts of rhinoceros, both white and black; whilst in the flat of the valley, herds of hartebeests and fine cattle roamed about like the kiyang and tame yak of Thibet. Then, to enhance all these pleasure, so different from our former experiences, we were treated like guests by the chief of the place, who, obeying the orders of his king, Rumanika, brought me presents, as soon as we arrived, of sheep, fowls, and sweet potatoes, and was very thankful for a few yards of red blanketing as a return, without begging for more.

The farther we went in this country the better we liked it, as the people were all kept in good order; and the village chiefs were so civil, that we could do as we liked. After following down the left side of the valley and entering the village, the customary presents and returns were made. Wishing then to obtain a better view of the country, I strolled over the nearest hills, and found the less exposed slopes well covered with trees. Small antelopes occasionally sprang up from the grass. I shot a florikan for the pot; and as I had never before seen white rhinoceros, killed one now; though, as no one would eat him, I felt sorry rather than otherwise for what I had done. When I returned in the evening, small boys brought me sparrows for sale; and then I remembered the stories I had heard from Musa Mzuri – that in the whole of Karague the small birds were so numerous, the people, to save themselves from starvation were obliged to grow a bitter corn which the birds disliked; and so I found it. At night, whilst observing for latitude, I was struck by surprise to see a long noisy procession pass by where I sat, led by some men who carried on their shoulders a woman covered up in a blackened skin. On inquiry, however, I heard she was being taken to the hut of her espoused, where, "bundling fashion," she would be put in bed; but it was only with virgins they took so much trouble.

A strange but characteristic story now reached my ears. Masudi, the merchant who took up Insangez, had been trying his best to deter Rumanika from allowing us to enter his country, by saying we were addicted to sorcery; and had it not been for Insangez's remonstrances, who said we were sent up by Musa, our fate would have been doubtful. Rumanika, it appeared, as I always had heard, considered old Musa his saviour, for having eight years before quelled a rebellion, when his younger broth-

Karagwe native.

er, Rogero, aspired to the throne; whilst Musa's honour and honesty were quite unimpeachable. But more of this hereafter.

Khonze, the next place, lying in the bending concave of this swamp lake, and facing Hangiro, was commanded by a fine elderly man called Muzegi, who was chief officer during Dagara's time. He told me with the greatest possible gravity, that he remembered well the time when a boat could have gone from this to Vigura; as also when fish and crocodiles came up from the Kitangule; but the old king no sooner died than the waters dried up; which showed as plainly as words could tell, that the king had designed it, to make men remember him with sorrow in all future ages. Our presents after this having been exchanged, the good old man, at my desire, explained the position of all the surrounding countries, in his own peculiar manner, by laying a long stick on the ground pointing due north and south, to which he attached shorter ones pointing to the centre of each distant country. He thus assisted me in the protractions of the map, to the countries which lie east and west of the route.

Shortly after starting this morning, we were summoned by the last officer on the Urigi to take breakfast with him, as he could not allow us to pass by without paying his respects to the king's guests. He was a man of most affable manners, and loth we should part company without one night's entertainment at least; but as it was a matter of necessity, he gave us provisions to eat on the way, adding, at the same time, he was sorry he could not give more, as a famine was then oppressing the land. We parted with reiterated compliments on both sides; and shortly after, diving into the old bed of the Urigi, were constantly amused with the variety of game which met our view. On several occasions the rhinoceros were so numerous and impudent as to contest the right of the road with us, and the greatest sport was occasioned by our bold Wanguana going at them in parties of threes and fours, when, taking good care of themselves at considerable distances, they fired their carbines all together, and whilst the rhinoceros ran one way, they ran the other. Whilst we were pitching our tents after sunset by some pools on the plain, Dr. K'yengo arrived with the hongo of brass and copper wires sent by Suwarora for the great king Mtesa, in lieu of his daughter who died; so next morning we all marched together on to Uthenga.

Rising out of the bed of the Urigi, we passed over a low spur of beef-sandwich clay sandstones, and descended into the close, rich valley of Uthenga, bound in by steep hills hanging over us more than a thousand feet high, as prettily clothed as the mountains of Scotland; whilst in the valley there were not only magnificent trees of extraordinary height, but also a surprising amount of the richest cultivation, amongst which the banana may be said to prevail. Notwithstanding this apparent richness in the land, the Wanyambo, living in their small squalid huts, seem poor. The tobacco they smoke is imported from the coffee-growing country of Uhaiya. After arrival in the village, who should we see but the Uganda officer, Irungu! The scoundrel, instead of going on to Uganda, as he had promised to do, conveying my present to Mtesa, had stopped here plundering the Wanyambo, and getting drunk on their pombe, called, in their language, marwa – a delicious kind of wine made from the banana. He, or course, begged for more beads; but, not able to trick me again, set his drummers and fifers at work, in hopes that he would get over our feelings in that way.

Henceforth, as we marched, Irungu's drummers and fifers kept us alive on the way. This we heard was a privilege that Uganda Wakungu enjoyed both at home and abroad, although in all other countries the sound of the drum is considered a notice of war, unless where it happens to accompany a dance or festival. Leaving the valley of Uthenga, we rose over the spur of N'yamwara, where we found we had attained the delightful altitude of 5,000 odd feet. Oh, how we enjoyed it! Every one feeling so happy at the prospect of meeting so soon the good king Rumanika. Tripping down the greensward, we now worked our way to the Rozoka valley, and pitched our tents in the village.

Kachuchu here told us he had orders to precede us, and prepare Rumanika for our coming, as his king wished to know what place we would prefer to live at – the Arab depot at kufro, on the direct line to Uganda, in his palace with himself, or outside his enclosures. Such politeness rather took us aback; so, giving our friend a coil of copper wire to keep him in good spirits, I said all our pleasure rested in seeing the king; whatever honours he liked to confer on us we should take with good grace, but one thing he must understand, we came not to trade, but to see him and great kings and therefore the Arabs had no relations with us. This little point settled, off started Kachuchu in his usual merry manner, whilst I took a look at the hills, to see their geological formation, and found them much as before, based on streaky clay sandstones, with the slight addition of pure blue shales, and above sections of quartzose sandstone lying in flags, as well as other metamorphic and igneous rocks scattered about.

Moving on the next morning over hill and dale, we came to the junction of two roads, where Irungu, with his drummers, fifers and amazon followers, took one way to Kufro, followed by the men carrying Suwarora's hongo, and we led off on the other, directed to the palace. The hill-tops in many places were breasted with dykes of pure white quartz, just as we had seen in Usui, only that here their direction tended more to the north. It was most curious to contemplate, seeing that the chief substance of the hills was a pure blue, or otherwise streaky clay sandstone, which must have been formed when the land was low, but has now been elevated, making these hills the axis of the centre of the continent, and therefore probably the oldest of all.

When within a few miles of the palace we were ordered to stop and wait for Kachuchu's return; but no sooner put up in a plaintain grove, where pombe was brewing, and our men were all taking a suck at it, than the worthy arrived to call us on the same instant, as the king was most anxious to see us. The love of good beer of course made our men all too tired to march again; so I sent off Bombay with Nasib to make our excuses, and in the evening found them returning with a huge pot of pombe and some royal tobacco, which Rumanika sent with a notice that he intended it exclusively for our own use, for though there was abundance for my men, there was nothing so good as what came from the palace; the royal tobacco was as sweet and strong as honey-dew, and the beer so strong it required a strong man to drink it.

After breakfast next morning, we crossed the hill-spur called Waeranhanje, the grassy tops of which were 5,500 feet above the sea. Descending a little, we came suddenly in view of what appeared to us a rich clump of trees, in S. lat. 1° 42' 42", and E. long. 31° 1' 49"; and, 500 feet below it, we saw a beautiful sheet of water lying snugly within the folds of the hills. We were not altogether unprepared for it, as Musa of old had described it, and Bombay, on his return yesterday, told us he had seen a great pond. The clump, indeed, was the palace enclosure. As to the lake, for want of a native name, I christened it the Little Winderemere, because Grant thought it so like our own English lake of that name. It was one of many others which, like that of Urigi, drains the moisture of the overhanging hills, and gets drained into the Victoria N'yanza through the Kitangule river.

To do royal honours to the king of this charming land, I ordered my men to put down their loads and fire a volley. This was no sooner done than, as we went to the palace gate, we received an invitation to come in at once, for the king wished to see us before attending to anything else. Now, leaving our traps outside, both Grant and myself, attended by Bombay and a few of the seniors of my Wanguana, entered the vestibule, and, walking through extensive enclosures studded with huts of kingly dimensions, were escorted to a pent-roofed baraza, which the Arabs had built as a sort of government office where the king might conduct his state affairs.

Here, as we entered, we saw sitting cross-legged on the ground Rumanika the king, and his brother Nnanaji, both of them men of noble appearance and size. The king was plainly dressed in an Arab's black choga, and wore, for ornament, dress-stockings of rich-coloured beads, and neatly-worked wristlets of copper.

Nnanaji, being a doctor of very high pretensions, in addition to a check cloth wrapped round him, was covered with charms. At their sides lay huge pipes of black clay. In their rear, squatting quiet as mice, were all the king's sons, some six or seven lads, who wore leather middle-coverings, and little dream-charms tied under their chins. The first greetings of the king, delivered in good Kisuahili, were warm and affecting, and in an instant we both felt and saw we were in the company of men who were as unlike as they could be to the common order of the natives of the surrounding districts. They had fine oval faces, large eyes, and high noses, denoting the best blood of Abyssinia. Having shaken hands in true English style, which is the peculiar custom of the men of this country, the ever-smiling Rumanika begged us to be seated on the ground opposite to him, and at once wished to know what we thought of Karague, for it had struck him his mountains were the finest in the world; and the lake, too, did we not admire it? Then laughing, he inquired – for he knew all the story – what we thought of Suwarora, and the reception we had met with in Usui. When this was explained to him, I showed him that it was for the interest of his own kingdom to keep a check on Suwarora, whose exorbitant taxations prevented the Arabs from coming to see him and bringing things from all parts of the world. He made inquiries for the purpose of knowing how we found our way all over the world; for on the former expedition a letter had come to him for Musa, who no sooner read it than he said I had called him and he must leave, as I was bound for Ujiji.

This of course led to a long story, describing the world, the proportions of land and water, and the power of ships, which conveyed even elephants and rhinoceros – in fact, all the animals in the world – to fill our menageries at home, etc., etc.; as well as the strange announcement that we lived to the northward, and had only come this way because his friend Musa had assured me without doubt that he would give us the road on through Uganda. Time flew like magic, the king's mind was so quick and enquiring; but as the day was wasting away, he generously gave us our option to choose a place for our residence in or out of his palace, and allowed us time to select one. We found the view overlooking the lake to be so charming, that we preferred camping outside, and set our men at once to work cutting sticks and long grass to erect themselves sheds.

One of the young princes – for the king ordered them all to be constantly in attendance on us – happening to see me sit on an iron chair, rushed back to his father and told him about it. This set all the royals in the palace in a state of high wonder, and ended by my getting a summons to show off the white man sitting on his throne; for of course I could only be, as all of them called me, a king of great dignity, to indulge in such state. Rather reluctantly I did as I was bid, and allowed myself once more to be dragged into court. Rumanika, as gentle as ever, then burst into a fresh fit of merriment, and after making sundry enlightened remarks of enquire, which of course were responded to with the greatest satisfaction, finished off by saying, with a very expressive shake of the head, "Oh, these Wazungu, these Wazungu! They know and do everything." I then put in a word for myself. Since we had entered Karague we never could get one drop of milk either for love or for money, and I wished to know what motive the Wahuma had for with-

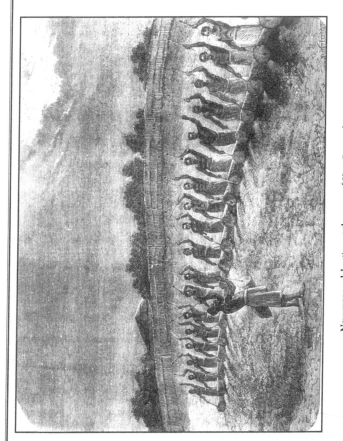

New moon celebration at the court of King Rumanika.

holding it. We had heard they held superstitious dreads; that any one who ate the flesh of pigs, fish, or fowls, or the bean called *maharague*, if he tasted the products of their cows, would destroy their cattle – and I hoped he did not labour under any such absurd delusions. To which he replied, It was only the poor who thought so; and as he now saw we were in want, he would set apart one of his cows expressly for our use. On bidding adieu, the usual formalities of handshaking were gone through; and on entering camp, I found the good thoughtful king had sent us some more of his excellent beer.

The Wanguana were now all in the highest of good-honour; for time after time goats and fowls were brought into camp by the officers of the king, who had received orders from all parts of the country to bring in supplies for his guests; and this kind of treatment went on for a month, though it did not diminish my daily expenditures of beads, as grain and plantains were not enough thought of. The cold winds, however, made the coastmen all shiver, and suspect, in their ignorance, we must be drawing close to England, the only cold place they had heard of.

16th. – Hearing it would be considered indecent haste to present my tributary offering at once, I paid my morning's visit, only taking my revolving-pistol, as I knew Rumanika had expressed a strong wish to see it. The impression it made was surprising – he had never seen such a thing in his life; so, in return for his great generosity, as well as to show I placed no value on property, not being a merchant, I begged him to accept it. We then adjourned to his private hut, which rather surprised me by the neatness with which it was kept. The roof was supported by numerous clean poles, to which he had fastened a large assortment of spears – brass-headed with iron handles, and iron-headed with wooden ones – of excellent workmanship. A large standing-screen, of fine straw-plait work, in elegant devices, partitioned off one part of the room; and on the opposite side, as mere ornaments, were placed a number of brass grapnels and small models of cows, made in iron for his amusement by the Arabs at Kufro. A little later in the day, as soon as we had done breakfast, both Rumanika and Nnanaji came over to pay us a visit; for they thought, as we could find our way all over the world, so we should not find much difficulty in prescribing some magic charms to kill his brother, Rogero, who lived on a hill overlooking the Kitangule. Seating them both on our chairs, which amused them intensely, I asked Rumanika, although I had heard before the whole facts of the case, what motives now induced him to wish the committal of such a terrible act, and brought out the whole story afresh.

Before their old father Dagara died, he had unwittingly said to the mother of Rogero, although he was the youngest born, what a fine king he would make; and the mother, in consequence, tutored her son to expect the command of the country, although the law of the land in the royal family is the primogeniture system, extending, however, only to those sons who are born after the accession of the king to the throne.

As soon, therefore, as Dagara died, leaving the three sons alluded to, all by different mothers, a contest took place with the brothers, which, as Nnanaji held by Rumanika, ended in the two elder driving Rogero away. It happened, however, that half the men of the country, either from fear or love, attached themselves to Rogero. Feeling his power, he raised an army and attempted to fight for the crown, which it is generally admitted would have succeeded, had not Musa, with unparalleled magnanimity, employed all the ivory merchandise at his command to engage the services of all the Arabs' slaves residing at Kufro, to bring muskets against him. Rogero was thus frightened away; but he went away swearing that he would carry out his intentions at some future date, when the Arabs had withdrawn from the country.

Magic charms, of course, we had none; but the king would not believe it, and, to wheedle some out of us, said they would not kill their brother even if they caught him – for fratricide was considered an unnatural crime in their country – but they would merely gouge out his eyes and set him at large again; for without the power of sight he could do them no harm.

I then recommended, as the best advice I could give him for the time being, to take some strong measures against Suwarora and the system of taxation carried on in Usui. These would have the effect of bringing men with superior knowledge into the country – for it was only through the power of knowledge that good government could be obtained. Suwarora at present stopped eight-tenths of the ivory-merchants who might be inclined to trade here from coming into the country, by the foolish system of excessive taxation he had established. Next I told him, if he would give me one or two of his children, I would have them instructed in England; for I admired his race, and believed them to have sprung from our old friends the Abyssinians, whose king, Sahela Selassie, had received rich presents from our Queen. They were Christians like ourselves, and had the Wahuma not lost their knowledge of God they would be so

The residence of Ugandan king.

also. A long theological and historical discussion ensued, which so pleased the king, that he said he would be delighted if I would take two of his sons to England, that they might bring him a knowledge of everything. Then turning again to the old point, his utter amazement that we should spend so much property in travelling, he wished to know what we did it for; when men had such means they would surely sit down and enjoy it. "Oh no," was the reply; "we have had our fill of the luxuries of life; eating, drinking, or sleeping have no charms for us now; we are above trade, therefore require no profits, and seek for enjoyment the run of the world. To observe and admire the beauties of creation are worth much more than beads to us. But what led us this way we have told you before; it was to see your majesty in particular, and the great kings of Africa – and at the same time to open another road to the north, whereby the best manufactures of Europe would find their way to Karague, and you would get so many more guests." In the highest good-humour the king said, "As you have come to see me and see sights, I will order some boats and show you over the lake, with musicians to play before you, or anything else that you like." Then, after looking over our pictures with intensest delight, and admiring our beds, boxes, and outfit in general, he left for the day.

In the afternoon, as I had heard from Musa that the wives of the king and princes were fattened to such an extent that they could not stand upright, I paid my respects to Wazezeru, the king's eldest brother – who, having been born before his father ascended the throne, did not come in the line of succession – with the hope of being able to see for myself the truth of the story. There was no mistake about it. On entering the hut I found the old man and his chief wife sitting side by side on a bench of earth strewed over with grass, and partitioned like stalls for sleeping apartments, whilst in front of them were placed numerous wooden pots of milk, and hanging from the poles that supported the beehive-shaped hut, a large collection of bows six feet in length, whilst below them were tied an even larger collection of spears, intermixed with a goodly assortment of heavy-headed assages. I was struck with no small surprise at the way he received me, as well as with the extraordinary dimensions, yet pleasing beauty, of the immoderately fat fair one his wife. She could not rise; and so large were her arms that, between the joints, the flesh hung down like large, loose-stuffed puddings. Then in came their children, all models of the Abyssinian type of beauty, and as polite in their manners as thorough-bred gentlemen. They had heard of my picture-books from the king, and all wished to see them; which they no sooner did, to their infinite delight, especially when they recognised any of the animals, then the subject was turned by my inquiring what they did with so many milk-pots. This was easily explained by Wazezeru himself, who, pointing to his wife, said, "This is all the product of those pots: from early youth upwards we keep those pots to their mouths, as it is the fashion at court to have very fat wives."

27th. – Ever anxious to push on with the journey, as I felt every day's delay only tended to diminish my means – that is, my beads and copper wire – I instructed Bombay to take the under-mentioned articles to Rumanika as a small sample of the products of my country;[1] to say I felt quite ashamed of their being so few and so poor, but I hoped he would forgive my shortcomings, as he knew I had been so often robbed on the way to him; and I trusted, in recollection of Musa, he would give me leave to go on to Uganda, for every day's delay was consuming my supplies. Nnanaji, however, it was said, should get something; so, in addition to the king's present, I apportioned one out for him, and Bombay took both up to the palace.[2] Everybody, I was pleased to hear, was surprised with both the quantity and quality of what I had been able to find for them; for, after the plundering in Ugogo, the immense consumption caused by such long delays on the road, the fearful prices I had had to pay for my porters' wages, the enormous taxes I had been forced to give both in Msalala and Uzinza, besides the constant thievings in camp, all of which was made public by the constantly-recurring tales of my men, nobody thought I had got anything left.

Rumanika, above all, was as delighted as if he had come in for a fortune, and sent to say the Raglan coat was a marvel, and the scarlet broadcloth the finest thing he had ever seen. Nobody but Musa had ever given him such beautiful beads before, and none ever gave with such free liberality. Whatever I wanted I should have in return for it, as it was evident to him I had really done him a great honour in visiting him. Neither his father nor any of his forefathers had had such a great favour shown them. He was alarmed, he confessed, when he heard we were coming to visit him, thinking we might prove some fearful monsters that were not quite human, but now he was delighted beyond all measure with what he saw of us. A messenger should be sent at once to the king of Uganda to inform him of our intention to visit him, with his own favourable report of us. This was necessary according to the etiquette of the country. Without such a recommendation our progress would be stopped by the people, whilst with one word from him all would go straight; for was he not the gatekeeper, enjoying the full confidence of Uganda? A month, however, must elapse, as the distance to the palace of Uganda was great; but, in the meantime, he would give me leave to go about in his country to do and see what I liked, Nnanaji and his sons escorting me everywhere. Moreover, when the time came for my going on to Uganda, if I had not enough presents to give the king, he would fill up the complement from his own stores, and either go with me himself, or send Nnanaji to conduct me as far as the boundary of Uganda, in order that Rogero might not molest us on the way. In the evening, Masudi, with Sangoro and several other merchants, came up from Kufro to pay us a visit of respect.

28th and 29th. – A gentle hint having come to us that the king's brother, Wazezeru, expected a trifle in virtue of his rank, I sent him a blanket and seventy-five blue egg-beads. These were accepted with the usual good grace of these people. The king then, ever attentive to our position as guests, sent his royal musicians to give us a tune. The men composing the band were a mixture of Waganda and Wanyambo, who played on reed instruments made telescope fashion, marking time by hand-drums. At first they marched up and down, playing tunes exactly like the regimental bands of the Turks, and then commenced dancing a species of "hornpipe," blowing furiously all the while. When dismissed with some beads, Nnanaji dropped in and invited me to accompany him out shooting on the slopes of the hills overlooking the lake. He had in attendance all the king's sons, as well as a large number of beaters, with three or four dogs. Tripping down the greensward of the hills together, these tall, athletic princes every now and then stopped to see who could shoot furthest, and I must say I never witnessed better feats in my life. With powerful six-feet-long bows they pulled their arrows' heads up to the wood, and made wonderful shots in the distance. They then placed me in position, and arranging the field, drove the covers like men well accustomed to sport – indeed, it struck me they indulged too much in that pleasure, for we saw nothing but two or three montana and some diminutive antelopes, about the size of mouse deer, and so exceedingly shy that not one was bagged.

Returning home to the tents as the evening sky was illumined with the red glare of the sun, my attention was attracted by observing in the distance some bold sky-scraping cones situated in the country Ruanda, which at once brought back to recollection the ill-defined story I had heard from the Arabs of a wonderful hill always covered with clouds, on which snow or hail was constantly falling. This was a valuable discovery, for I found these hills to be the great turn-point of the Central African watershed. Without loss of time I set to work, and, gathering all the travellers I could in the country, protracted, from their descriptions, all the distance topographical features set down in the map, as far north as 3° of north latitude, as far east as 36°, and as far west as 26° of east longitude; only afterwards slightly corrected, as I was better able to connect and clear up some trifling but doubtful points.

Indeed, I was not only surprised at the amount of information about distant places I was enabled to get here from these men, but also at the correctness of their vast and varied knowledge, as I afterwards tested it by observation and the statements of others. I rely so far on the geographical information I thus received, that I would advise no one to doubt the accuracy of these protractions until he has been on the spot to test them by actual inspection. About the size only of the minor lakes do I feel doubtful, more especially the Little Luta Nzige, which on the former journey I heard was a salt lake, because salt was found on its shores and in one of its islands. Now, without going into any lengthy details, and giving Rumanika due credit for everything – for had he not ordered his men to give me every information that lay in their power, they would not have done so – I will merely say for the present that, whilst they conceived the Victoria N'yanza would take a whole month for a canoe to cross it, they thought the Little Luta Nzige might be crossed in a week. The Mfumbiro cones in Ruanda, which I believe reach 10,000 feet, are said to be the highest of the "Mountains of the Moon." At their base are both salt and copper mines, as well as hot springs. There are also hot springs in Mpororo, and one in Karague near where Rogero lived.

30th. – The important business of announcing our approach to Uganda was completed by Rumanika appointing Kachuchu to go to king Mtesa as quickly as possible, to say we were coming to visit him. He was told that we were very great men, who only travelled to see great kings and great countries; and, as such, Rumanika trusted we should be received with courteous respect, and allowed to roam all over the country wherever we liked, he holding himself responsible for our actions for the time being. In the end, however, we were to be restored to him, as he considered himself our father, and therefore must see that no accident befell us.

To put the royal message in proper shape, I was now requested to send some trifle by way of a letter or visiting card; but, on taking out a Colt's revolving rifle for the purpose, Rumanika advised me not to send it, as Mtesa might take fright, and, considering it a charm of evil quality, reject us as bad magicians, and close his gates on us. Three bits of cotton cloth were then selected as the best thing for the purpose; and, relying implicitly on the advice of Rumanika, who declared his only object was to further our views, I arranged accordingly, and off went Kachuchu.

To keep my friend in good-humour, and show him how well the English can appreciate a kindness, I presented him with a hammer, a sailor's knife, a Rodger's three-bladed penknife, a gilt letter-slip with paper and envelopes, some gilt pens, an ivory holder, and a variety of other small articles. Of each of these he asked the use, and then in high glee put it into the big block-tin box, in which he kept his other curiosities, and which I think he felt more proud of than any other possession. After this, on adjourning to his baraza, Ungurue the Pig, who had floored my march in Sorombo, and Makinga, our persecutor in Usui, came in to report that the Watuta had been fighting in Usui, and taken six bomas, upon which Rumanika asked me what I thought of it, and if I knew where the Watuta came from. I said I was not surprised to hear Usui had attracted the Watuta's cupidity, for every one knew of the plundering propensities of the inhabitants, and as they became rich by their robberies, they must in turn expect to be robbed. Where the Watuta came

*Speke presenting his hunting trophies
to HM Rumanika.*

from, nobody could tell; they were dressed something like the Zulu Kaffirs of the South, but appeared to be now gradually migrating from the regions of N'yazza. To this Dr. K'yengo, who was now living with Rumanika as his head magician, added that, whilst he was living in Utambara, the Watuta invested his boma six months; and finally, when all their cows and stores were exhausted, they killed all the inhabitants but himself, and he only escaped by the power of the charms which he carried about him. These were so powerful, that although he lay on the ground, and the Watuta struck at him with their spears, not one could penetrate his body.

In the evening after this, as the king wished to see all my scientific instruments, we walked down to the camp; and as he did not beg for anything, I gave him some gold and mother-of-pearl shirt studs to swell up his trinket-box. The same evening I made up my mind, if possible, to purchase a stock of beads from the Arabs, and sent Baraka off to Kufro, to see what kind of a bargain he could make with them; for, whilst I trembled to think what those "blood-suckers" would have the impudence to demand when they found me at their mercy, I felt that the beads must be bought, or the expedition would certainly come to grief.

1st and 2d. – Two days after this the merchants came in a body to see me, and said their worst beads would stand me 80 dollars per frasala, as they would realise that value in ivory on arrival at the coast. Of course no business was done, for the thing was preposterous by all calculation, being close on 2,500 per cent above Zanzibar valuation. I was "game" to give 50 dollars, but as they would not take this, I thought of dealing with

Rumanika instead. I then gave Nnanaji, who had been constantly throwing out hints that I ought to give him a gun as he was a great sportsman, a lappet of beadwork to keep his tongue quiet, and he in return sent me a bullock and sundry pots of pombe, which, in addition to the daily allowance sent by Rumanika, made all my people drunk, and so affected Baraka that one of the women – also drunk – having given him some sharp abuse, he beat her in so violent a manner that the whole drunken camp set upon him, and turned the place into a pandemonium. A row amongst the negroes means a general rising of arms, legs, and voices; all are in a state of the greatest excitement; and each individual thinks he is doing the best to mend matters, but is actually doing his best to create confusion.

By dint of perseverance, I now succeeded in having Baraka separated from the crowd and dragged before me for justice. I found that the woman, who fully understood the jealous hatred which existed in Baraka's heart against Bombay, flirted with both of them; and, pretending to show a preference for Bombay, set Baraka against her, when from high words they came to blows, and set the place in a blaze. It was useless to remonstrate – Baraka insisted he would beat the woman if she abused him, no matter whether I thought it cowardly or not; he did not come with me expecting to be bullied in this way – the whole fault lay with Bombay – I did not do him justice – when he proved Bombay a thief at Usui, I did not turn him off, but now, instead, I showed the preference to Bombay by always taking him when I went to Rumanika. It was useless to argue with such a passionate man, so I told him to go away and cool himself before morning.

When he was gone, Bombay said there was not one man in the camp, besides his own set, who wished to go on to Egypt – for they had constant arguments amongst themselves about it; and whilst Bombay always said he would follow me wherever I led, Baraka and those who held by him abused him and his set for having tricked them away from Zanzibar, under the false hopes that the road was quite safe. Bombay said his arguments were, that Bana knew better than anybody else what he was about, and he would follow him, trusting to luck, as God was the disposer of all things, and men could die but once. Whilst Baraka's arguments all rested the other way – that no one could tell what was ahead of him – Bana had sold himself to luck and the devil – but though he did not care for his own safety, he ought not to sacrifice the lives of others – Bombay and his lot were fools for their pains in trusting to him.

3d. – At daybreak Rumanika sent us word he was off to Mo-ga-Namarinzi, a spur of a hill beyond "the Little Windermere," overlooking the Ingezi Kagera, or river which separates Kishak-ka from Karague, to show me how the Kiangule river was fed by small lakes and marshes, in accordance with my expressed wish to have a better comprehension of the drainage system of the Mountains of the Moon. He hoped we would follow him, not by the land route he intended to take, but in canoes which he had ordered at the ferry below. Starting off shortly afterwards, I made for the lake, and found the canoes all ready, but so small that, besides two paddlers, only two men could sit down in each. After pushing through the tall reeds with which the end of the lake is covered, we emerged in the clear open, and skirt-ed the further side of the water until a small strait was gained, which led us into another lake, drained at the northern end with a vast swampy plain, covered entirely with tall rushes, excepting only in a few places where bald patches expose the surface of the water, or where the main streams of the Ingezi and Luchoro valleys cut a clear drain for themselves.

The whole scenery was most beautiful. Green and fresh, the slopes of the hills were covered with grass, with small clumps of soft cloudy-looking acacias growing at a few feet only above the water, and above them, facing over the hills, fine detached trees, and here and there the gigantic medicinal aloe. Arrived near the end of the Moga-Namirinzi hill in the second lake, the paddlers splashed into shore, where a large concourse of people, headed by Nnanaji, were drawn up to receive me. I landed with all the dignity of a prince, when the royal band struck up a march, and we all moved on to Rumanika's frontier palace, talking away in a very complimentary manner, not unlike the very polite and flowery fashion of educated Orientals.

Rumanika we found sitting dressed in a wrapper made of an nzoe antelope's skin, smiling blandly as we approached him. In the warmest manner possible he pressed me to sit by his side, asked how I had enjoyed myself, what I thought of his country, and if I did not feel hungry; when a picnic dinner was spread, and we all set to at cooked plantains and pombe, ending with a pipe of his best tobacco. Bit by bit Rumanika became more interested in geography, and seemed highly ambitious of gaining a world-wide reputation through the medium of my pen. At his invitation we now crossed over the spur to the Ingezi Kagera side, when, to surprise me, the canoes I had come up the lake in appeared before us. They had gone out of the lake at its northern end, paddled into, and then up the Kagera to where we stood, showing, by actual navigation, the connection of these highland lakes with the rivers which drain the various spurs of the Mountains of the Moon. The Kagera was deep and dark, of itself a very fine stream, and, considering it was only one – and that, too, a minor one – of the various affluents which drain the mountain valleys into the Victoria N'yanza through the medium of the Kitangule river, I saw at once there must be water sufficient to make the Kitangule a very powerful tributary to the lake.

On leaving this interesting place, with the widespread information of all the surrounding countries I had gained, my mind was so impressed with the topographical features of all this part of Africa, that in my heart I resolved I would make Rumanika as happy as he had made me, and asked K'yengo his doctor, of all things I possessed what the king would like best. To my surprise I then learnt that Rumanika had set his heart on the revolving rifle I had brought for Mtesa – the one, in fact, which he had prevented my sending on to Uganda in the hands of Kachuchu, and he would have begged me for it before had his high-minded dignity, and the principle he had established of never begging for anything, not interfered. I then said he should certainly have it; for as strongly as I had withheld from giving anything to those begging scoundrels who wished to rob me of all I possessed in the lower countries, so strongly now did I feel inclined to be generous with this exceptional man Rumanika. We then had another picnic together, and whilst I went home to join Grant, Rumanika spent the night doing homage and sacrificing a bullock at the tomb of his father Dagara.

Instead of paddling all down the lake again, I walked over the hill, and, on crossing at its northern end, whished to shoot ducks; but the superstitious boatmen put a stop to my intended amusement by imploring me not to do so, lest the spirit of the lake should be roused to dry up the waters.

4th. – Rumanika returned in the morning, walking up the hill, followed by a long train of his officers, and a party of men carrying on their shoulders his state carriage, which consisted of a large open basket laid on the top of two very long poles.

After entering his palace, I immediately called on him to thank him for the great treat he had given me, and presented him, as an earnest of what I thought, with the Colt's revolving rifle and a fair allowance of ammunition. His delight knew no bounds on becoming the proprietor of such an extraordinary weapon, and induced him to dwell on his advantages over his brother Rogero, whose antipathy to him was ever preying on his mind. He urged me again to devise some plan for overcoming him; and, becoming more and more confidential, favoured me with the following narrative, by way of evidence how the spirits were inclined to show all the world that he was the rightful successor to the throne: When Dagara died, and he, Nnanaji, and Rogero, were the only three sons left in line of succession to the crown, a small mystic drum of diminutive size was placed before them by the officers of state. It was only feather weight in reality, but, being loaded with charms, became so heavy to those who were not entitled to the crown, that no one could lift it but the one person whom the spirits were inclined towards as the rightful successor. Now, of all the three brothers, he, Rumanika, alone could raise it from the ground; and whilst his brothers laboured hard, in vain attempting to move it, he with his little finger held it up without any exertion.

This little disclosure in the history of Karague led us on to further particulars of Dagara's death and burial, when it transpired that the old king's body, after the fashion of his predecessors, was sewn up in a cow-skin, and placed in a boat floating on the lake, where it remained for three days, until decomposition set in and maggots were engendered, of which three were taken into the palace and given in charge to the heir-elect; but instead of remaining as they were, one worm was transformed into a lion, another into a leopard, and the third into a stick. After this the body of the king was taken up and deposited on the hill Moga-Namirinzi, where, instead of putting him underground, the people erected a hut over him, and, thrusting in five maidens and fifty cows, enclosed the doorway in such a manner that the whole of them subsequently died from starvation.

This, as may naturally be supposed, led into further genealogical disclosures of a similar nature, and I was told by Rumanika that his grandfather was a most wonderful man; indeed, Karague was blessed with more supernatural agencies than any other country. Rohinda the Sixth, who was his grandfather, numbered so many years that people thought he would never die; and he even became so concerned himself about it, reflecting that his son Dagara would never enjoy the benefit of his position as successor to the crown of Karague, that he took some magic powders and charmed away his life. His remains were then taken to Moga-Namirinzi, in the same manner as were those of Dagara; but, as an improvement on the maggot story, a young lion emerged from the heart of the corpse and kept guard over the hill, from whom other lions came into existence, until the whole place has become infested by them, and has since made Karague a power and dread to all other nations; for these lions became subject to the will of Dagara, who, when attacked by the countries to the northward, instead of assembling an army of men, assembled his lion force, and so swept all before him.

Another test was then advanced at the instigation of K'yengo, who thought Rumanika not quite impressive enough of his right to the throne; and this was, that each heir in succession, even after the drum dodge, was required to sit on the ground in a certain place of the country, where, if he had courage to plant himself, the land would gradually rise up, telescope fashion, until it reached the skies, when, if the aspirant was considered by the spirits the proper person to inherit Karague, he would gradually be lowered again without any harm happening; but, otherwise, the elastic hill would suddenly collapse, and he would be dashed to pieces. Now, Rumanika, by his own confession, had gone through this ordeal with marked success; so I asked him if he found the atmosphere cold when so far up aloft, and as he said he did so, laughing at the quaintness of the question, I told him I saw he had learnt a good practical lesson on the structure of the universe, which I wished he would explain to me. In a state of perplexity, K'yengo and the rest, on seeing me laughing, thought something was wrong; so, turning about, they thought again, and said, "No, it must have been hot, because the higher one ascended the nearer he got to the sun." This led on to one argument after another, on geology, geography, and all the natural sciences, and ended by Rumanika showing me an iron much the shape and size of a carrot. This he said was found by one of his villagers whilst tilling the ground, buried some way down below the surface; but dig as he would, he could not remove it, and therefore called some men to his help. Still the whole of them united could not lift the iron, which induced them, considering there must be some magic in it, to inform the king. "Now," says Rumanika, "I no sooner went there and saw the iron, and brought it here as you see it. What can such a sign mean?" "Of course that you are the rightful king," said his flatterers. "Then," said Rumanika, in exuberant spirits, "during Dagara's time, as the king was sitting with many other men outside his hut, a fearful storm of thunder and lightning arose, and a thunderbolt struck the ground in the midst of them, which dispersed all the men but Dagara, who calmly took up the thunderbolt and placed it in the palace. I, however, no sooner came into possession, and Rogero began to contend with me, than the thunderbolt vanished. How would you account for this?" The flatterers said, "It is as clear as possible; God gave the thunderbolt to Dagaro as a sign he was pleased with him and his rule; but when he found two brothers contending, he withdrew it to show their conduct was wicked."

5th. – Rumanika in the morning sent me a young male nzoe (water-boc) [3] which his canoe-men had caught in the high rushes at the head of the lake, by the king's order, to please me; for I had heard this peculiar animal described in such strange ways at Kaze, both by Musa and the Arabs, I was desirous of having a look at one. It proved to be closely allied to a water-boc found by Livingstone on the Ngami Lake; but, instead of being striped, was very faintly spotted, and so long were its toes, it could hardly walk on the dry ground; whilst its coat, also well adapted to the moist element it lived in, was long, and of such excellent quality that the natives prize it for wearing almost more than any other of the antelope tribe. The only food it would eat were the tops of the tall papyrus rushes; but though it ate and drank freely, and lay down very quietly, it always charged with ferocity any person who went near it.

In the afternoon Rumanika invited both Grant and myself to witness his New Moon Levee, a ceremony which takes place every month with a view of ascertaining how many of his subjects are loyal. On entering his palace enclosure, the first thing we saw was a blaue boc's horn stuffed full of magic powder, with very imposing effect, by K'yengo, and stuck in the ground, with its mouth pointing in the direction of Rogero. In the second court, we found thirty-five drums ranged on the ground, with as many drummers standing behind them, and a knot of young princes and officers of high dignity waiting to escort us into the third enclosure, where, in his principal hut, we found Rumanika squatting on the ground, half-concealed by the portal, but showing his smiling face to welcome us in. His head was got up with a tiara of beads, from the centre of which, directly over the forehead, stood a plume of red feathers, and encircling the lower face with a fine large white beard set in a stock or band of beads. We were beckoned to squat alongside Nnanaji, the master of ceremonies, and a large group of high officials outside the porch. Then the thirty-five drums all struck up together in very good harmony; and when their deafening noise was over, a smaller band of hand-drums and reed instruments was ordered in to amuse us.

This second performance over, from want of breath only, district officers, one by one, came advancing on tip-toe, then pausing, contorting and quivering their bodies, advancing again with a springing gait and outspread arms, which they moved as if they wished to force them out of their joints, in all of which actions they held drum-sticks or twigs in their hands, swore with a maniacal voice an oath of their loyalty and devotion to their king, backed by the expression of a hope that he would cut off their heads if they ever turned from his enemies, and then, kneeling before him, they held out their sticks that he might touch them. With a constant reiteration of these scenes – the saluting at one time, the music at another – interrupted only once by a number of girls dancing something like a good rough Highland fling whilst the little band played, the day's ceremonies ended.

6th and 7th. – During the next two days, as my men had all worn out their clothes, I gave them each thirty necklaces of beads to purchase a suit of the bark cloth called mbugu, already described. Finding the flour of the country too bitter to eat by itself, we sweetened it with ripe plantains, and made a good cake of it. The king now, finding me disinclined to fight his brother Rogero, either with guns or magic horns, asked me to give him a "doctor" or charm to create longevity and to promote the increase of his family, as his was not large enough to maintain the dignity of so great a man as himself. I gave him a blister, and, changing the subject, told him the history of the creation of man. After listening to it attentively, he asked what thing in creation I considered the greatest of all things in the world; for whilst a man at most could only live one hundred years, a tree lived many; but the earth ought to be biggest, for it never died.

I then told him again I wished one of his sons would accompany me to England, that he might learn the history of Moses, wherein he would find that men had souls which live for ever, but that the earth would come to an end in the fullness of time. This conversation, diversified by numerous shrewd remarks on the part of Rumanika, led to his asking how I could account for the decline of countries, instancing the dismemberment of the Wahuma in Kittara, and remarking that formerly Karague included Urundi, Ruanda, and Kishakka, which collectively were known as the kingdom of Meru, governed by one man. Christian principles, I said, made us what we are, and feeling a sympathy for him made me desirous of taking one of his children to learn in the same school with us, who, on returning to him, could impart what he knew, and, extending the same by course of instruction, would doubtless end by elevating his country to a higher position than it ever knew before, etc., etc. The policy and government of the vast possessions of Great Britain were then duly discussed, and Rumanika acknowledged that the pen was superior to that of the sword, and the electric telegraph and steam engine the most wonderful powers he had ever heard of.

Before breaking up, Rumanika wished to give me any number of ivories I might like to mention, even three or four hundred, as a lasting remembrance that I had done him the honour of visiting Karague in his lifetime, for though Dagara had given to coloured merchants, he would be the first who had given to a white man. Of course this royal offer was declined with politeness; he must understand that it was not the custom of big men in my country to accept presents of value when we made visits of pleasure. I had enjoyed my residence in Karague, his intellectual conversations and his kind hospitality, all of which I should record in my books to hand down to posterity; but if he would give me a cow's horn, I would keep it as a trophy of the happy days I had spent in his country. He gave me one, measuring 3 feet 5 inches in length, and 18 3/4 inches in circumference at the base. He then offered me a large sheet, made up of a patchwork of very small N'yera antelope skins, most exquisitely cured and sewn. This I rejected, as he told me it had been given to himself, explaining that we prided ourselves on never parting with the gifts of a friend; and this speech tickled his fancy so much, that he said he never would part with anything I gave him.

8th and 9th. – The 8th went off much in the usual way, by my calling on the king, when I gave him a pack of playing-cards, which he put into his curiosity-box. He explained to me, at my request, what sort of things he would like any future visitors to bring him – a piece of gold and silver embroidery; but, before anything else, I found he would like to have toys – such as Yankee clocks with the face in a man's stomach, to wind up behind, his eyes rolling with every beat of the pendulum; or a china-cow milk-pot, a jack-in-the-box, models of men, carriages, and horses – all animals in fact, and railways in particular.

On the 9th I went out shooting, as Rumanika, with his usual politeness, on hearing my desire to kill some rhinoceros, ordered his sons to conduct the filed for me. Off we started by sunrise to the bottom of the hills overlooking the head of the Little Windermere lake. On arrival at the scene of action – a thicket or acacia shrubs – all the men in the neighbourhood were assembled to beat. Taking post myself, by direction, in the most likely place to catch a sight of the animals, the day's work began by the beaters driving the covers in my direction. In a very short time, a fine male was discovered making towards me, but not exactly knowing where he should bolt to. While he was in this perplexity, I stole along between the bushes, and caught sight of him standing as if anchored by the side of a tree and gave him a broadsider with Blissett, which, too much for his constitution to stand, sent him off trotting, till exhausted by bleeding he lay down to die, and allowed me to give him a settler.

In a minute or two afterwards, the good young princes, attracted by the sound of the gun, came to see what was done. Their surprise knew no bounds; they could scarcely believe what they saw; and then, on recovering, with the spirit of true gentlemen, they seized both my hands, congratulating me on the magnitude of my success, and pointed out, as an example of it, a bystander who showed fearful scars, both on his abdomen and at the blade of his shoulder, who they declared had been run through by one of these animals. It was, therefore, wonderful to them, they observed, with what calmness I went up to such formidable beasts.

Just at this time a distant cry was heard that another rhinoceros was concealed in a thicket, and off we set to pursue her. Arriving at the place mentioned, I settled at once I would enter with only two spare men carrying guns, for the acacia thorns were so thick that the only tracks into the thicket were runs made by these animals. Leading myself, bending down to steal in, I tracked up a run till half-way through cover, when suddenly before me, like a pig from a hole, a large female, with her young one behind her, came straight down whoof-whoofing upon me. In this awkward fix I forced myself to one side, though pricked all over with thorns in doing so, and gave her one on the head which knocked her out of my path, and induced her for safety to make for the open, where I followed her down and gave her another. She then took to the hills and crossed over a spur, when, following after her, in another dense thicket, near the head of a glen, I came upon three, who no sooner sighted me, than all in line they charged down my way. Fortunately at the time my gun-bearers were with me; so, jumping to one side, I struck them all three in turn. One of them dropped dead a little way on; but the others only pulled up when they arrived at the bottom. To please myself now I had done quite enough; but as the princes would have it, I went on with the chase. As one of the two, I could see, had one of his fore-legs broken, I went at the sounder one, and gave him another shot, which simply induced him to walk over the lower end of the hill. Then turning to the last one, which could not escape, I asked the Wanyambo to polish him off with their spears and arrows, that I might see their mode of sport. As we moved up to the animal, he kept charging with such impetuous fury, they could not go into him; so I gave him a second ball, which brought him to anchor. In this helpless state the men set at him in earnest, and a more barbarous finale I never did witness. Every man sent his spear, assage, or arrow, into his sides, until, completely exhausted, he sank like a porcupine covered with quills. The day's sport was now ended, so I went home to breakfast, leaving instructions that the heads should be cut off and sent to the king as a trophy of what the white man could do.

10th and 11th. – The next day, when I called on Rumanika, the spoils were brought into court, and in utter astonishment he said, "Well, this must have been done with something more potent than powder, for neither the Arabs nor Nnanaji, although they talk of their shooting powers, could have accomplished such a great feat as this. It is no wonder the English are the greatest men in the world." Neither the Wanyambo nor the Wahuma would eat the rhinoceros, so I was not sorry to find all the Wanyamuezi porters of the Arabs at Kufro, on hearing of the sport, come over and carry away all the flesh. They passed by our camp half borne down with their burdens of sliced flesh, suspended from poles which they carried on their shoulders; but the following day I was disgusted by hearing that their masters had forbidden their eating "the carrion," as the throats of the animals had not been cut; and, moreover, had thrashed them soundly because they complained they were half starved, which was perfectly true, by the poor food that they got as their pay.

12th. – On visiting Rumanika again, and going through my geographical lessons, he told me, in confirmation of Musa's old stories, that in Ruanda there existed pigmies who lived in trees, but occasionally came down at night, and, listening at the hut doors of the men, would wait until they heard the name of one of its inmates, when they would call him out, and, firing an arrow into his heart, disappear again in the same way as they came. But, more formidable even than these little men, there were monsters who could not converse with me, and never showed themselves unless they saw women pass by; then, in voluptuous excitement, they squeezed them to death. Many other similar stories were then told, when I, wishing to go, was asked if I could kill hippopotami. Having answered that I could, the king graciously said he would order some canoes for me the next morning; and as I declined because Grant could not accompany me, as a terrible disease had broken out in his leg, he ordered a pig-shooting party. Agreeably with this, the next day I went out with his sons, numerously attended; but although we beat the covers all day, the rain was so frequent that the pigs would not bolt.

14th. – After a long and amusing conversation with Rumanika in the morning, I called on one of his sisters-in-law, married to an elder brother who was born before Dagara ascended the throne. She was another of those wonders of obesity, unable to stand excepting on all fours. I was desirous to obtain a good view of her, and actually to measure her, and induced her to give me facilities for doing so, by offering in return to show her a bit of my naked legs and arms. The bait took as I wished it, and after getting her to sidle and wriggle into the middle of the hut, I did as I promised, and then took her dimensions as noted below.[4] All of these are exact except the height, and I believe I could have obtained this more accurately if I could have her laid on the floor. Not knowing what difficulties I should have to contend with in such a piece of engineering, I tried to get her height by raising her up. This, after infinite exertions on the part of us both, was accomplished, when she sank down again, fainting, for her blood had rushed to her head. Meanwhile, the daughter, a lass of sixteen, sat stark-naked before us, sucking at a milk-pot, on which the father kept her at work by holding a rod in his hand, for as fattening is the first duty of fashionable female life, it must be duly enforced by the rod if necessary. I got up a bit of flirtation with missy, and induced her to rise and shake hands with me. Her features were lovely, but her body was as round as a ball.

In the evening we had another row with my head men – Baraka having accused Bombay of trying to kill him with magic. Bombay, who was so incessantly bullied by Baraka's officious attempts to form party cliques opposed to the interests of the journey, and get him turned out of the camp, indiscreetly went to one of K'yengo's men, and asked him if he knew of any medicine that would affect the hearts of the Wanguana so as to incline them towards him; and on the sub-doctor saying Yes, Bombay gave him some beads, and bought the medicine required, which, put into a pot of pombe, was placed by Baraka's side. Baraka in the meanwhile got wind of the matter through K'yengo, who, misunderstanding the true facts of the case, said it was a charm to deprive Baraka of his life. A court of inquiry having been convened, with all the parties concerned in attendance, K'yengo's mistake was discovered, and Bombay was lectured for his folly, as he had a thousand times before abjured his belief in such magical follies; moreover, to punish him for the future, I took Baraka, whenever I could, with me to visit the king, which, little as it may appear to others, was of the greatest consequence to the hostile parties.

15th and 16th. – When I next called on Rumanika I gave him a Vautier's binocular and prismatic compass; on which he politely remarked he was afraid he was robbing me of everything. More compliments went round, and then he asked if it was true we could open a man's skull, look at his brains, and close it up again; also if it was true we sailed all round the world into regions where there was no difference between night and day, and how, when he ploughed the seas in such enormous vessels as would carry at once 20,000 men, we could explain to the sailors what they ought to do; for, although he had heard of these things, no one was able to explain them to him.

After all the explanations were given, he promised me a boat-hunt after the nzoe in the morning; but when the time came, as difficulties were raised, I asked him to allow us to anticipate the arrival of Kachuchu, and march on to Kitangule. He answered, with his usual courtesy, that he would be very glad to oblige us in any way that we liked; but he feared that, as the Waganda were such superstitious people, some difficulties would arise, and he must decline to comply with our request. "You must not," he added, "expect ever to find again a reasonable man like myself." I then gave him a book on "Kafir laws," which he said he would keep for my sake, with all the rest of the presents, which he was determined never to give away, though it was usual for him to send novelties of this sort to Mtesa, king of Uganda, and Kamrasi, king of Unyoro, as a friendly recognition of their superior positions in the world of great monarchies.

17th. – Rumanika next introduced me to an old woman who came from the island of Gasi, situated in the little Luta Nzige. Both her upper and lower incisors had been extracted, and her upper lip perforated by a number of small holes, extending in an arch from one corner to the other. This interesting but ugly old lady narrated the circumstances by which she had been enslaved, and then sent by Kamrasi as a curiosity to Rumanika, who had ever since kept her as a servant in his palace. A man from Ruanda then told us of the Wilyanwantu (men-eaters), who disdained all food but human flesh; and Rumanika confirmed the statement. Though I felt very sceptical about it, I could not help thinking it a curious coincidence that the position they were said to occupy agreed with Petherick's Nyam Nyams (men-eaters).

Of far more interest were the results of a conversation which I had with another of Kamrasi's servants, a man of Amara, as it threw some light upon certain statements made by Mr. Leon of the people of Amara being Christians. He said they bore single holes in the centres both of their upper and lower lips, as well as in the lobes of both of their ears, in which they wear small brass rings. They live near the N'yanza – where it is connected by a strait with a salt lake, and drained by a river to the northward – in comfortable houses, built like the tembes of Unyamuezi. When killing a cow, they kneel down in an attitude of prayer, with both hands together, held palm upwards, and utter Zu, a word the meaning of which he did not know. I questioned him to try if the word had any trace of a Christian meaning – for instance, a corruption of Jesu – but without success. Circumcision is not known amongst them, neither have they any knowledge of God or a soul. A tribe called Wakuavi, who are white, and described as not unlike myself, often came over the water and made raids on their cattle, using the double-edged sime as their chief weapon of war. These attacks were as often resented, and sometimes led the Wamara in pursuit a long way into their enemy's country, where, at a place called Kisiguisi, they found men robed in red cloths. Beads were imported, he thought, both from the east and from Ukidi. Associated with the countries Masau or Masai, and Usamburu, which he knew, there was a large mountain, the exact position of which he could not describe.

I took down many words of his language, and found they corresponded with the North African dialects, as spoken by the people of Kidi, Gani, and Madi. The southerners, speaking of these, would call them Wakidi, Wagani, and Wamadi, but among themselves the syllable was is not prefixed, as in the southern dialects, to signify people. Rumanika, who appeared immensely delighted as he assisted me in putting the questions I wanted, and saw me note them down in my book, was more confirmed than ever in the truth of my stories that I came from the north, and thought as the beads came to Amara, so should I be able to open the road and bring him more visitors. This he knew was his only chance of ever seeing me more, for I swore I would never go back through Usui, so greatly did I feel the indignities imposed on me by Suwarora.

18th. – To keep the king in good-humour, I now took a table-knife, spoon, and fork to the palace, which, after their several uses were explained, were consigned to his curiosity-box. Still Rumanika could not understand how it was I spent so much and travelled so far, or how it happened such a great country as ours could be ruled by a woman. He asked the Queen's name, how many children she had, and the mode of succession; then, when fully satisfied, led the way to show me what his father Dagara had done when wishing to know of

The banks of the Kitangule River.

what the centre of the earth was composed. At the back of the palace a deep ditch was cut, several yards long, the end of which was carried by a subterranean passage into the palace, where it was ended off with a cavern led into by a very small aperture. It then appeared that Dagara, having failed, in his own opinion, to arrive any nearer to the object in view, gave the excavating up as a bad job, and turned the cave into a mysterious abode, where it was confidently asserted he spent many days without eating or drinking, and turned sometimes into a young man, and then an old one, alternately, as the humour seized him.

19th to 22d. – On the 19th I went fishing, but without success, for they said the fish would not take in the lake; and on the following day, as Grant's recovery seemed hopeless, for a long time at least, I went with all the young princes to ses what I could do with the hippopotami in the lake, said to inhabit the small island of Conty. The part was an exceedingly merry one. We went off to the island in several canoes, and at once found an immense number of crocodiles basking in the sun, but not a single hippopotamus was in sight. The princes then, thinking me "green" at this kind of sport, said the place was enchanted, but I need not fear, for they would bring them out to my feet by simply calling out certain names, and this was no sooner done than four old and one young one came immediately in font of us. It seemed quite a sin to touch them, they looked all so innocent; but as the king wanted to try me again, I gave one a ball on the head which sent him under, never again to be seen, for on the 22nd, by which time I supposed he ought to have risen inflated with gases, the king sent out his men to look out for him; but they returned to say, that whilst all the rest were in the old place, that one, in particular, could not be found.

On this K'yengo, who happened to be present whilst our interview lasted, explained that the demons of the deep were annoyed with me for intruding on their preserves, without having the courtesy to commemorate the event by the sacrifice of a goat or a cow. Rumanika then, at my suggestions, gave Nnanaji the revolving pistol I first gave him, but not without a sharp rebuke for his having had the audacity to beg a gun of me in consideration of his being a sportsman. We then went into a discourse on astrology, when the intelligent Rumanika asked me if the same sun we saw one day appeared again, or whether fresh suns came every day, and whether or not the moon made different faces, to laugh at us mortals on earth.

23d and 24th. – This day was spent by the king introducing me to his five fat wives, to show with what esteem he was held by all the different kings of the countries surrounding. From Mpororo – which, by the by, is a republic – he was wedded to Kaogez, the daughter of Kahaya, who is the greatest chief in the country; from Unyoro he received Kauyangi, Kamrasi's daughter; from Nkole, Kambiri, the late Kasiyonga's daughter; from Utumbi, Kirangu, the late Kiteimbua's daughter; and lastly, the daughter of Chiuarungi, his head cook.

After presenting Rumanika with an india-rubber band – which, as usual, amused him immensely – for the honour he had done me in showing me his wives, a party of Waziwa, who had brought some ivory from Kidi, came to pay their respects to him. On being questioned by me, they said that they once saw some men like my Wanguana there; they had come from the north to trade, but, though they carried firearms, they were all killed by the people of Kidi. This was famous; it corroborated what I knew, but could not convince others of – that traders could find their way up to Kidi by the Nile. It in a manner explained also how it was that Kamrasi, some years before, had obtained some pink beads, of a variety the Zanzibar merchants had never thought of bringing into the country. Bombay was now quite convinced, and we all became transported with joy, until Rumanika, reflecting on the sad state of Grant's leg, turned that joy into grief by saying that the rules of Uganda are so strict, that no one who is sick could enter the country. "To show," he said, "how absurd they are, your donkey would not be permitted because he has no trousers; and you even will have to put on a gown, as your unmentionables will be considered indecorous." I now asked Rumanika if he would assist me in replenishing my fast-ebbing store of beads, by selling tusks to the Arabs at Kufro, when for every 35lb. weight I would give him 50 dollars by orders on Zanzibar, and would insure him from being cheated, by sending a letter of advice to our Consul residing there.

At first he demurred, on the high-toned principle that he could not have any commercial dealings with myself; but, at the instigation of Bombay and Baraka, who viewed it in its true character, as tending merely to assist my journey in the best manner he could, without any sacrifice to dignity, he eventually yielded, and, to prove his earnestness, sent me a large tusk, with a notice that his ivory was not kept in the palace, but with his officers, and as soon as they could collect it, so soon I should get it.

Rumanika, on hearing that it was our custom to celebrate the birth of our Saviour with a good feast of beef, sent us an ox. I immediately paid him a visit to offer the compliments of the season, and at the same time regretted, much to his amusement, that he, as one of the old stock of Abyssinians, who are the oldest Christians on record, should have forgotten this rite; but I hoped the time would come when, by making it known that his tribe had lapsed into a state of heathenism, white teachers would be induced to set it all to rights again. At this time some Wahaiya traders (who had been invited at my request by Rumanika) arrived. Like the Waziwa, they had traded with Kidi, and they not only confirmed what the Waziwa had said, but added that, when trading in those distant parts, they heard of Wanguana coming in vessels to trade to the north of Unyoro; but the natives there were so savage, they only fought with these foreign traders. A man of Ruanda now informed us that the cowrie-shells, so plentiful in that country, come there from the other or western side, but he could not tell whence they were originally obtained. Rumanika then told me Suwarora had been so frightened by the Watuta, and their boastful threats to demolish Usui bit by bit, reserving him only as a tit-bit for the end, that he wanted a plot of ground in Karague to preserve his property in.

26th, 27th, and 28th. – Some other travellers from the north again informed us that they had heard of Wanguana who attempted to trade in Gani and Chopi, but were killed by the natives. I now assured Rumanika that in two or three years he would have a greater trade with Egypt than he ever could have with Zanzibar; for when I opened the road, all those men he heard of would swarm up here to visit him. He, however, only laughed at my folly in proposing to go to a place of which all I heard was merely that every stranger who went there was killed. He began to show a disinclination to allow my going there, and though from the most friendly intention, this view was alarming, for one word from him could have ruined my projects. As it was, I feared my followers might take fright and refuse to advance with me. I thought it good policy to talk of there being many roads leading through Africa, so that Rumanika might see he had not got, as he thought, the sole key to the interior. I told him again of certain views I once held of coming to see him from the north up the Nile, and from the east through the Masai. He observed that, "To open either of those routes, you would require at least two hundred guns." He would, however, do something when we returned from Uganda; for as Mtesa followed his advice in everything, so did Kamrasi, for both held the highest opinion of him.

The conversation then turning on London, and the way men and carriages moved up the streets like strings of ants on their migrations, Rumanika said the villages in Ruanda were of enormous extent, and the people great sportsmen, for they turned out in multitudes, with small dogs on whose necks were tied bells, and blowing horns themselves, to hunt leopards. They were, however, highly superstitious, and would not allow any strangers to enter their country; for some years ago, when Arabs went there, a great drought and famine set in, which they attributed to evil influences brought by them, and, turning them out of their country, said they would never admit any of their like amongst them again. I said, in return, I thought his

Wanyambo just as superstitious, for I observed, whilst walking one day, that they had placed a gourd on the path, and on inquiry found they had done so to gain the sympathy of all passers-by to their crop close at hand, which was blighted, imagining that the voice of the sympathiser heard by the spirits would induce them to relent, and restore a healthy tone to the crop.

During this time an interesting case was brought before us for judgment. Two men having married one woman, laid claim to her child, which, as it was a male one, belonged to the father. Baraka was appointed the umpire, and immediately comparing the infant's face with those of its claimants, gave a decision which all approved of but the loser. It was pronounced amidst peals of laughter from my men; for whenever any little excitement is going forward, the Wanguana all rush to the scene of action to give their opinions, and joke over it afterwards.

29th and 30th. – On telling Rumanika this story next morning, he said, "Many funny things happen in Karague"; and related some domestic incidents, concluding with the moral that "Marriage in Karague was a mere matter of money." Cows, sheep, and slaves have to be given to the father for the value of his daughter; but if she finds she has made a mistake, she can return the dowry-money, and gain her release. The Wahuma, although they keep slaves and marry with pure negroes, do not allow their daughters to taint their blood by marrying out of their clan. In warfare it is the rule that the Wahinda, or princes, head their own soldiers, and set them the example of courage, when, after firing a few arrows, they throw their bows away, and close at once with their spears and assages. Life is never taken in Karague, either for murder or cowardice, as they value so much their Wahuma breed; but, for all offences, fines of cows are exacted according to the extent of the crime.

31st. – Ever proud of his history since I had traced his descent from Abyssinia and King David, whose hair was as straight as my own, Rumanika dwelt on my theological disclosures with the greatest delight, and wished to know what difference existed between the Arabs and ourselves; to which Baraka replied, as the best means of making him understand, that whilst the Arabs had only one Book, we had two; to which I added, Yes, that is true in a sense; but the real merits lie in the fact that we have got the better BOOK, as may be inferred from the obvious fact that we are more prosperous, and their superiors in all things, as I would prove to him if he would allow me to take one of his sons home to learn that BOOK; for then he would find his tribe, after a while, better off than the Arabs are. Much delighted, he said he would be very glad to give me two boys for that purpose.

Then, changing the subject, I pressed Rumanika, as he said he had no idea of a God or future state, to tell me what advantage he expected from sacrificing a cow yearly at his father's grave. He laughingly replied he did not know, but he hoped he might be favoured with better crops if he did so. He also place pombe and grain, he said, for the same reason, before a large stone on the hillside, although it could not eat, or make any use of it; but the coast-men were of the same belief as himself, and so were all the natives.

No one in Africa, as far as he knew, doubted the power of magic and spells; and if a fox barked when he was leading an army to battle, he would retire at once, knowing that this prognosticated evil. There were many other animals, and lucky and unlucky birds, which all believed in.

I then told him it was fortunate he had no disbelievers like us to contend with in battle, for we, instead of trusting to luck and such omens, put our faith only in skill and pluck, which Baraka elucidated from his military experience in the wars in British India. Lastly, I explained to him how England formerly was as unenlightened as Africa, and believing in the same sort of superstitions, and the inhabitants were all as naked as his skin-wearing Wanyambo; but now, since they had grown wiser, and saw through such impostures, they were the greatest men in the world.

He said, for the future he would disregard what the Arabs said, and trust to my doctrines, for without doubt he had never seen such a wise man as myself; and the Arabs themselves confirmed this when they told him that all their beads and cloths came from the land of the Wazungu, or white men.

1st, 2d, and 3d. – The new year was ushered in by the most exciting intelligence, which drove us half wild with delight, for we fully believed Mr. Petherick was indeed on his road up the Nile, endeavouring to meet us. It was this: An officer of Rumanika's, who had been sent four years before on a mission to Kamrasi, had just then returned with a party of Kamrasi's who brought ivory for sale to the Arabs at Kufro; along with a vaunting commission to inform Rumanika that Kamrasi had foreign visitors as well as himself.

They had not actually come into Unyoro, but were in his dependency, the country of Gani, coming up the Nile in vessels.

They had been attacked by the Gani people, and driven back with considerable loss both of men and property, although they were in sailing vessels, and fired guns which even broke down the trees on the banks. Some of their property had been brought to him, and he in return had ordered his subjects not to molest them, but allow them to come on to him. Rumanika enjoyed this news as much as myself, especially when I told him of Petherick's promise to meet us, just as these men said he was trying to do; and more especially so, when I told him that if he would assist me in trying to communicate with Petherick, the latter would either come here himself, or send one of his men, conveying a suitable present, whilst I was away in Uganda; and then in the end we would all go off to Kamrasi's together.

4th. – Entering warmly into the spirit of this important intelligence, Rumanika inquired into its truth; and, finding no reason to doubt it, said he would send some men back with Kamrasi's men, if I could have patience until they were ready to go. There would be no danger, as Kamrasi was his brother-in-law, and would do all that he told him.

I now proposed to send Baraka, who, ashamed to cry off, said he would go with Rumanika's officers if I allowed him a companion of his own choosing, who would take care of him if he got sick on the way, otherwise he should be afraid they would leave him to die, like a dog, in the jungles. We consoled him by assenting to the companion he wished, and making Rumanika responsible that no harm should come to him from any of the risks which his imagination conjured up. Rumanika then gave him and Uledi, his selected companion, some sheets of mbugu, in order that they might disguise themselves as his officers whilst crossing the territories of the king of Uganda. On inquiring as to the reason of this, it transpired that, to reach Unyoro, the party would have to cross a portion of Uddu, which the late king Sunna, on annexing that country to Uganda, had divided, not in halves, but by alternate bands running transversely from Nkole to the Victoria N'yanza.

5th and 6th. – To keep Rumanika up to the mark, I introduced to him Saidi, one of my men, who was formerly a slave, captured in Walamo, on the borders of Abyssinia, to show him, by his similarity to the Wahuma, how it was I had come to the conclusion that he was of the same race. Saidi told him his tribe kept cattle with the same stupendous horns as those of the Wahuma; and also that, in the same manner, they all mixed blood and milk for their dinners, which, to his mind, confirmed my statement. At night, as there was a partial eclipse of the moon, all the Wanguana marched up and down from Rumanika's to Nnanaji's huts, singing and beating our tin cooking-pots to frighten off the spirit of the sun from consuming entirely the chief object of reverence, the moon.

7th. – Our spirits were now further raised by the arrival of a semi-Hindu-Suahili, named Juma, who had just returned from a visit to the king of Uganda, bringing back with him a large present of ivory and slaves; for he said he had heard from the king of our intention to visit him, and that he had despatched officers to call us immediately. This intelligence delighted Rumanika as much as it did us, and he no sooner heard it than he said, with ecstasies, "I will open Africa, since the white men desire it; for did not Dagara command us to show deference to strangers?" Then, turning to me, he added, "My only regret is, you will not take something as a return for the great expenses you have been put to in coming to visit me." The expense was admitted, for I had now been obliged to purchase from the Arabs upwards of $400 worth of beads, to keep such a store in reserve for my return from Uganda as would enable me to push on to Gondokoro. I thought this necessary, as every report that arrived from Unyamuezi only told us of further disasters with the merchants in that country. Sheikh Said was there even then, with my poor Hottentots, unable to convey my post to the coast.

8th to 10th. – At last we heard the familiar sound of the Uganda drum. Maula, a royal officer, with a large escort of smartly-dressed men, women, and boys, leading their dogs and playing their reeds, announced to our straining ears the welcome intelligence that their king had sent them to call us. N'yamgundu, who had seen us in Usui, had marched on to inform the king of our advance and desire to see him; and he, intensely delighted at the prospect of having white men for his guests, desired no time should be lost in our coming on. Maula told us that his officers had orders to supply us with everything we wanted whilst passing through his country, and that there would be nothing to pay.

One thing only now embarrassed me – Grant was worse, without hope of recovery for at least one or two months. This large body of Waganda could not be kept waiting. To get on as fast as possible was the only chance of ever bringing the journey to a successful issue; so, unable to help myself, with great remorse at another separation, on the following day I consigned my companion, with several Wanguana, to the care of my friend Rumanika. I then separated ten loads of beads and thirty copper wires for my expenses in Uganda; wrote a letter to Petherick, which I gave to Baraka; and gave him and his companion beads to last as money for six months, and also a present both for Kamrasi and the Gani chief. To Nsangez I gave charge of my collections in natural history, and the reports of my progress, addressed to the Geographical Society, which he was to convey to Sheikh Said at Kaze, for conveyance as far as Zanzibar.

This business concluded in camp, I started my men and went to the palace to bid adieu to Rumanika, who appointed Rozaro, one of his officers, to accompany me wherever I went in Uganda, and to bring me back safely again. At Rumanika's request I then gave Mtesa's pages some ammunition to hurry on with to the great king of Uganda, as his majesty had ordered them to bring him, as quickly as possible, some strengthening powder, and also some powder for his gun.

Then, finally, to Maula, also under Rumanika's instructions, I gave two copper wires and five bundles of beads; and, when all was completed, set out on the march, perfectly sure in my mind that before very long I should settle the great Nile problem for ever; and, with this consciousness, only hoping that Grant would be able to join me before I should have to return again, for it was never supposed for a moment that it was possible I ever could go north from Uganda. Rumanika was the most resolute in this belief, as the kings of Uganda, ever since that country was detached from Unyoro, had been making constant raids, seizing cattle and slaves from the surrounding communities.

1) Rumanika's present. – One block-tin box, one Raglan coat, five yards scarlet broadcloth, two coils copper wire, a hundred large blue egg-beads, five bundles best variegated beads, three bundles minute beads – pink, blue, and white.

2) Nnanaji's present. – One deole or gold-embroidered silk, two coils copper wire, fifty large blue egg-beads, five bundles best variegated beads, three bundles minute beads – pink, blue and white.

3) Since named by Dr. P. L. Sclater "Tragelaphus Spekii." These nzoe have been drawn by Mr. Wolf, from specimens brought home by myself.

4) Round arm, 1 ft. 11 in.; chest, 4 ft. 4 in.; thigh, 2 ft. 7 in.; calf, 1 ft. 8 in.; height, 5 ft. 8 in.

CHAPTER 9

HISTORY OF THE WAHUMA

The Abyssinians and Gallas – Theory of Conquest of Inferior by Superior Races – The Wahuma and the Kingdom of Kittara – Legendary History of the Kingdom of Uganda – Its Constitution, and the Ceremonials of the Court.

The reader has now had my experience of several of the minor states, and has presently to be introduced to Uganda, the most powerful state in the ancient but now divided great kingdom of Kittara. I shall have to record a residence of considerable duration at the court there; and, before entering on it, I propose to state my theory of the ethnology of that part of Africa inhabited by the people collectively styled Wahuma – otherwise Gallas or Abyssinians. My theory is founded on the traditions of the several nations, as checked by my own observations of what I saw when passing through them. It appears impossible to believe, judging from the physical appearance of the Wahuma, that they can be of any other race than the semi-Shem-Hamitic of Ethiopia. The traditions of the imperial government of Abyssinia go as far back as the scriptural age of King David, from whom the late reigning king of Abyssinia, Sahela Selassie, traced his descent.

Most people appear to regard the Abyssinians as a different

race from the Gallas, but, I believe, without foundation. Both alike are Christians of the greatest antiquity. It is true that, whilst the aboriginal Abyssinians in Abyssinia proper are more commonly agriculturists, the Gallas are chiefly a pastoral people; but I conceive that the two may have had the same relations with each other which I found the Wahuma kings and Wahuma herdsmen holding with the agricultural Wazinza in Uzinza, the Wanyambo in Karague, the Waganda in Uganda, and the Wanyoro in Unyoro.

In these countries the government is in the hands of foreigners, who had invaded and taken possession of them, leaving the agricultural aborigines to till the ground, whilst the junior members of the usurping clans herded cattle – just as in Abyssinia, or wherever the Abyssinians or Gallas have shown themselves. There a pastoral clan from the Asiatic side took the government of Abyssinia from its people and have ruled over them ever since, changing, by intermarriage with the Africans, the texture of their hair and colour to a certain extent, but still maintaining a high stamp of Asiatic feature, of which a market characteristic is a bridged instead of bridgeless nose.

It may be presumed that there once existed a foreign but compact government in Abyssinia, which, becoming great and powerful, sent out armies on all sides of it, especially to the south, south-east, and west, slave-hunting and devastating wherever they went, and in process of time becoming too great for one ruler to control. Junior members of the royal family then, pushing their fortunes, dismembered themselves from the parent stock, created separate governments, and, for reasons which cannot be traced, changed their names. In this manner we may suppose that the Gallas separated from the Abyssinians, and located themselves to the south of their native land.

Other Abyssinians, or possibly Gallas – it matters not which they were or what we call them – likewise detaching themselves, fought in the Somali country, subjugated that land, were defeated to a certain extent by the Arabs from the opposite continent, and tried their hands south as far as the Jub river, where they also left many of their numbers behind. Again they attacked Omwita (the present Mombas), were repulsed, were lost sight of in the interior of the continent, and, crossing the Nile close to its source, discovered the rich pasture-lands of Unyoro, and founded the great kingdom of Kittara, where they lost their religion, forgot their language, extracted their lower incisors like the natives, changed their national name to Wahuma, and no longer remembered the names of Hubshi or Galla – though even the present reigning kings retain a singular traditional account of their having once been half white and half black, with hair on the white side straight, and on the black side frizzly. It was a curious indication of the prevailing idea still entertained by them of their foreign extraction, that it was surmised in Unyoro that the approach of us white men into their country from both sides at once, augured an intention on our part to take back the country from them. Believing, as they do, that Africa formerly belonged to Europeans, from whom it was taken by negroes with whom they had allied themselves, the Wahuma make themselves a small residue of the original European stock driven from the land – an idea which seems natural enough when we consider that the Wahuma are, in numbers, quite insignificant compared with the natives.

Again, the princes of Unyoro are called Wawitu, and point to the north when asked where their country Uwitu is situated, doubtfully saying, when questioned about its distance, "How can we tell circumstances which took place in our forefathers' times? We only think it is somewhere near your country." Although, however, this very interesting people, the Wahuma, delight in supposing themselves to be of European origin, they are forced to confess, on closer examination, that although they came in the first instance from the doubtful north, they came latterly from the east, as part of a powerful Wahuma tribe, beyond Kidi, who excel in arms, and are so fierce no Kidi people, terrible in war as these too are described to be, can stand against them. This points, if our maps are true, to the Gallas – for all pastorals in these people's minds are Wahuma; and if we could only reconcile ourselves to the belief that the Wawitu derived their name from Omwita, the last place they attacked on the east coast of Africa, then all would be clear: for it must be noticed the Wakama, or kings, when asked to what race they owe their origin, invariably reply, in the first place, from princes – giving, for instance, the titles Wawitu in Unyoro, and Wahinda in Karague – which is most likely caused by their never having been asked such a close question before, whilst the idiom of the language generally induces them to call themselves after the name applied to their country.

So much for ethnological conjecture. Let us now deal with the Wahuma since they crossed the Nile and founded the kingdom of Kittara, a large tract of land bounded by the Victoria N'yanza and Kitangule Kagera or River on the south, the Nile on the east, the Little Luta-Nzige Lake[1] on the north, and the kingdoms of Utubi and Nkole on the west.

The general name Kittara is gradually becoming extinct, and is seldom applied to any but the western portions; whilst the north-eastern, in which the capital is situated, is called Unyoro, and the other, Uddu apart from Uganda, as we shall presently see.

Nobody has been able to inform us how many generations old the Wahuma government of Unyoro is. The last three kings are Chiawambi, N'yawongo, and the present king Kamrasi. In very early times dissensions amongst the royal family, probably contending for the crown, such as we presume must have occurred in Abyssinia, separated the parent stock, and drove the weaker to find refuge in Nkole, where a second and independent government of Wahuma was established. Since then, twenty generations ago, it is said the Wahuma government of Karague was established in the same manner. The conspirator Rohinda fled from Kittara to Karague with a large party of Wahuma; sought the protection of Nono, who, a Myambo, was king over the Wanyambo of that country; ingratiated himself and his followers with the Wanyambo; and, finally, designing a crown for himself, gave a feast, treacherously killed King Nono in his cups, and set himself on the throne, the first mkama or king who ruled in Karague. Rohinda was succeeded by Ntare, then Rohinda II., then Ntare II., which order only changed with the eleventh reign, when Rusatira ascended the throne, and was succeeded by Mehinga, then Kalimera, then Ntare VII., then Rohinda VI., then Dagara, and now Rumanika. During this time the Wahuma were well south of the equator, and still destined to spread. Brothers again contended for the crown of their father, and the weaker took refuge in Uzinza, where the fourth

Wahuma government was created, and so remained under one king until the last generation, when King Ruma died, and his two sons, Rohinda, the eldest, and Suwarora, contended for the crown, but divided the country between them, Rohinda taking the eastern half, and Suwarora the western, at the instigation of the late King Dagara of Karague.

This is the most southerly kingdom of the Wahuma, though not the farthest spread of its people, for we find the Watusi, who are emigrants from Karague of the same stock, overlooking the Tanganyika Lake from the hills of Uhha, and tending their cattle all over Unyamuezi under the protection of the native negro chiefs; and we also hear that the Wapoka of Fipa, south of the Rukwa Lake are the same. How or when their name became changed from Wahuma to Watusi no one is able to explain; but, again deducing the past from the present, we cannot help suspecting that, in the same way as this change has taken place, the name Galla may have been changed from Hubshi, and Wahuma from Gallas. But though in these southern regions the name of the clan has been changed, the princes still retain the title of Wahinda as in Karague, instead of Wawitu as in Unyoro, and are considered of such noble breed that many of the pure negro chiefs delight in saying, I am a Mhinda, or prince, to the confusion of travellers, which confusion is increased by the Wahuma habits of conforming to the regulations of the different countries they adopt. For instance, the Wahuma of Uganda and Karague, though so close to Unyoro, do not extract their lower incisors; and though the Wanyoro only use the spear in war, the Wahuma in Karague are the most expert archers in Africa. We are thus left only the one very distinguishing mark, the physical appearance of this remarkable race, partaking even more of the phlegmatic nature of the Shemitic father than the nervous boisterous temperament of the Hamitic mother, as a certain clue to their Shem-Hamitic origin.

It remains to speak of the separation of Uddu from Unyoro, the present kingdom of Uganda – which, to say the least of it, is extremely interesting, inasmuch as the government there is as different from the other surrounding countries as those of Europe are compared to Asia.

In the earliest times the Wahuma of Unyoro regarded all their lands bordering on the Victoria Lake as their garden, owing to its exceeding fertility, and imposed the epithet of Wiru, or slaves, upon its people, because they had to supply the imperial government with food and clothing. Coffee was conveyed to the capital by the Wiru, also mbugu (bark-cloaks), from an inexhaustible fig-tree; in short, the lands of the Wiru were famous for their rich productions.

Now Wiru in the northern dialect changes to Waddu in the southern; hence Uddu, the land of the slaves, which remained in one connected line from the Nile to the Kitangule Kagera until eight generations back, when, according to tradition, a sportsman from Unyoro, by name Uganda, came with a pack of dogs, a woman, a spear, and a shield, hunting on the left bank of Katonga valley, not far from the lake. He was but a poor man, though so successful in hunting that vast numbers of the Wiru flocked to him for flesh, and became so fond of him as to invite him to be their king, saying, "Of what avail to us is our present king, living so far away that when we sent him a cow as a tributary offering, that cow on the journey gave a calf, and the calf became a cow and gave another calf, and so on, and yet the present has not reached its destination?" At first Uganda hesitated, on the plea that they had a king already, but on being farther pressed consented; when the people hearing his name said, "Well, let it be so; and for the future let this country between the Nile and Katonga be called Uganda, and let your name be Kimera, the first king of Uganda." The same night Kimera stood upon a stone with a spear in his hand, and a woman and dog sitting by his side; and to this day people assert that his footprints and the mark left by his spear-end, as well as the seats of the woman and dog, are visible. The report of these circumstances soon reached the great king of Unyoro, who, in his magnificence, merely said, "The poor creature must be starving; allow him to feed there if he likes." The kings who have succeeded Kimera are: 1. Mahanda; 2. Katereza; 3. Chabago; 4. Simakokiro; 5. Kamanya; 6. Sunna; 7. Mtesa, not yet crowned.

These kings have all carried on the same system of government as that commenced by Kimera, and proved themselves a perfect terror to Unyoro, as we shall see in the sequel. Kimera, suddenly risen to eminence, grew proud and headstrong – formed a strong clan around him, whom he appointed to be his Wakunga, or officers – rewarded well, punished severely, and soon became magnificent. Nothing short of the grandest palace, a throne to sit upon, the largest harem, the smartest officers, the best dressed people, even a menagerie for pleasure – in fact, only the best of everything – would content him. Fleets of boats, not canoes, were built for war, and armies formed, that the glory of the king might never decrease. In short, the system of government, according to barbarous ideas was perfect. Highways were cut from one extremity of the country to the other, and all rivers bridged. No house could be built without its necessary appendages for cleanliness; no person, however poor, could expose his person; and to disobey these laws was death.

After the death of Kimera, the prosperity of Uganda never decreased, but rather improved. The clan of officers formed by him were as proud of their emancipation from slavery, as the king they had created was of his dominion over them. They buried Kimera with state honours, giving charge of the body to the late king's most favourite consort, whose duty it was to dry the corpse by placing it on a board resting on the mouth of an earthen open pot heated by fire from below. When this drying process was completed, at the expiration of three months, the lower jaw was cut out and neatly worked over with beads; the umbilical cord, which had been preserved from birth, was also worked with beads. These were kept apart, but the body was consigned to a tomb, and guarded ever after by this officer and a certain number of the king's next most favourite women, all of whom planted gardens for their maintenance, and were restricted from seeing the succeeding king.

By his large establishment of wives, Kimera left a number of princes or Warangira, and as many princesses. From the Warangira the Wakunga now chose as their king the one whom they thought best suited for the government of the country – not of too high rank by the mother's side, lest their selection in his pride should kill them all, but one of low birth. The rest were placed with wives in a suite of huts, under charge of a keeper, to prevent any chance of intrigues and dissensions. They were to enjoy life until the prince-elect should arrive at the age of discretion and be crowned, when all but two of the princes would be burnt to death, the two being reserved in case of accident as long as the king wanted brother companions, when one would be banished to Unyoro, and the other pensioned with suitable possessions in Uganda. The mother of the king by this measure became queen-dowager, or N'yamasore. She halved with her son all the wives of the deceased king not stationed at his grave, taking second choice; kept up a palace only little inferior to her son's with large estates, guided the prince-elect in the government of the country, and remained until the end of his minority the virtual ruler of the land; at any rate, no radical political changes could take place without her sanction. The princesses became the wives of the king; no one else could marry them.

Both mother and son had their Ktikiros or commander-in-chief, also titled Kamraviona, as well as other officers of high rank.

Amongst them in due order of gradation are the Ilmas, a woman who had the good fortune to have cut the umbilical cord at the king's birth; the Sawaganzi, queen's sister and king's barber; Kaggao, Polino, Sakibobo, Kitunzi, and others, governors of provinces; Jumab, admiral of the fleet; Kasugu, guardian of the king's sister; Mkuenda, factor; Kunsa and Usungu, first and second class executioners; Mgemma, commissioner in charge of tombs; Seruti, brewer; Mfumbiro, cook; numerous pages to run messages and look after the women, and minor Wakungu in hundreds. One Mkungu is always over the palace, in command of the Wanagalali, or guards which are changed monthly; another is ever in attendance as seizer of refractory persons. There are also in the palace almost constantly the Wanangalavi, or drummers; Nsase, pea-gourd rattlers; Milele, flute-players; Mukonderi, clarionet-players; also players on wooden harmonicons and lap-harps, to which the players sing accompaniments; and, lastly, men who whistle on their fingers – for music is half the amusement of these courts. Everybody in Uganda is expected to keep spears, shields and dogs, the Uganda arms and cognisance; whilst the Wakungu are entitled to drums. There is also a Neptune Mgussa, or spirit, who lives in the depths of the N'yanza, communicates through the medium of his temporal Mkungu, and guides to a certain extent the naval destiny of the king.

It is the duty of all officers, generally speaking, to attend at court as constantly as possible; should they fail, they forfeit their lands, wives, and all belongings. These will be seized and given to others more worthy of them; as it is presumed that either insolence or disaffection can be the only motive which would induce any person to absent himself for any length of time from the pleasure of seeing his sovereign. Tidiness in dress is imperatively necessary, and for any neglect of this rule the head may be the forfeit. The punishment for such offences, however, may be commuted by fines of cattle, goats, fowls, or brass wire. All acts of the king are counted benefits, for which he must be thanked; and so every deed done to his subjects is a gift received by them, though it should assume the shape of flogging or fine; for are not these, which make better men of them, as necessary as anything? The thanks are rendered by gravelling on the ground, floundering about and whining after the manner of happy dogs, after which they rise up suddenly, take up sticks – spears are not allowed to be carried in court – make as if charging the king, jabbering as fast as tongues can rattle, and so they swear fidelity for all their lives.

This is the greater salutation; the lesser one is performed kneeling in an attitude of prayer, continually throwing open the hands, and repeating sundry words. Among them the word "n'yanzig" is the most frequent and conspicuous; and hence these gesticulations receive the general designation n'yanzig – a term which will be frequently met with, and which I have found it necessary to use like an English verb. In consequence of these salutations, there is more ceremony in court than business, though the king, ever having an eye to his treasury, continually finds some trifling fault, condemns the head of the culprit, takes his liquidation-present, if he has anything to pay, and thus keeps up his revenue.

No one dare stand before the king whilst he is either standing still or sitting, but must approach him with downcast eyes and bended knees, and kneel or sit when arrived. To touch the king's throne or clothes, even by accident, or to look upon his women is certain death. When sitting in court holding a levee, the king invariably has in attendance several women, Wabandwa, evil-eye averters or sorcerers. They talk in feigned voices raised to a shrillness almost amounting to a scream. They wear dried lizards on their heads, small goat-skin aprons trimmed with little bells, diminutive shields and spears set off with cock-hackles – their functions in attendance being to administer cups of marwa (plantain wine). To complete the picture of the court, one must imagine a crowd of pages to run royal messages; they dare not walk for such deficiency in zeal to their master might cost their life. A further feature of the court consists in the national symbols already referred to – a dog, two spears, and shield.

With the company squatting in large half-circle or three sides of a square many deep before him, in the hollow of which are drummers and other musicians, the king, sitting on his throne in high dignity, issues his orders for the day much to the following effect: "Cattle, women, and children are short in Uganda; an army must be formed of one to two thousand strong, to plunder Unyoro. The Wasoga have been insulting his subjects, and must be reduced to subjection: for this emergency another army must be formed, of equal strength, to act by land in conjunction with the fleet. The Wahaiya have paid no tribute to his greatness lately and must be taxed." For all these matters the commander-in-chief tells off the divisional officers, who are approved by the king, and the matter is ended in court. The divisional officers then find subordinate officers, who find men, and the army proceeds with its march. Should any fail with their mission, reinforcements are sent, and the runaways, called women, are drilled with a red-hot iron until they are men no longer, and die for their cowardice. All heroism, however, ensures promotion. The king receives his army of officers with great ceremony, listens to their exploits, and gives as rewards, women, cattle, and command over men – the greatest elements of wealth in Uganda – with a liberal hand.

As to the minor business transacted in court, culprits are brought in bound by officers, and reported. At once the sentence is given, perhaps awarding the most torturous, lingering death – probably without trial or investigation, and, for all the king knows, at the instigation of some one influenced by wicked spite. If the accused endeavour to plead his defence, his voice is at once drowned, and the miserable victim dragged off in the roughest manner possible by those officers who love their king, and delight in promptly carrying out his orders. Young virgins, the daughters of Wakungu, stark naked, and smeared with grease, but holding, for decency's sake, a small square of mbugu at the upper corners in both hands before them, are presented by their fathers in propitiation for some offence, and to fill the harem. Seizing-officers receive orders to hunt down Wakungu who have committed some indiscretions, and to confiscate their lands, wives, children, and property. An officer observed to salute informally is ordered for execution, when everybody near him rises in an instant, the drums beat, drowning his cries, and the victim of carelessness is dragged off, bound by cords, by a dozen men at once. Another man, perhaps, exposes an inch of naked leg whilst squatting, or has his mbugu tied contrary to regulations, and is condemned to the same fate.

Fines of cows, goats, and fowls are brought in and presented; they are smoothed down by the offender's hands, and then applied to his face, to show there is no evil spirit lurking in the gift; then thanks are proferred for the leniency of the king in letting the presenter off so cheaply, and the pardoned man retires, full of smiles, to the ranks of the squatters. Thousands of cattle, and strings of women and children, sometimes the result of a victorious plundering hunt, or else the accumulated seizures from refractory Wakungu, are brought in; for there is no more common or acceptable offering to appease the king's wrath towards any refractory or blundering officer than a present of a few young beauties, who may perhaps be afterwards given as the reward of good service to other officers.

Stick-charms, being pieces of wood of all shapes, supposed to have supernatural virtues, and coloured earths, endowed with similar qualities, are produced by the royal magicians. The master of the hunt exposes his spoils – such as antelopes, cats, porcupines, curious rats, etc., all caught in nets, and placed in baskets – zebra, lion, and buffalo skins being added. The fishermen bring their spoils; also the gardeners. The cutlers show knives and forks made of iron inlaid with brass and copper; the furriers, most beautifully-sewn patchwork of antelopes' skins; the habit-maker, sheets of mbugu barkcloth; the blacksmith, spears; the maker of shields, his productions – and so forth; but nothing is ever given without rubbing it down, then rubbing the face, and going through a long form of salutation for the gracious favour the king has shown in accepting it.

When tired of business, the king rises, spear in hand, and, leading his dog, walked off without word or comment leaving his company, like dogs, to take care of themselves.

Strict as the discipline of the exterior court is, that of the interior is not less severe. The pages all wear turbans of cord made from aloe fibres. Should a wife commit any trifling indiscretion, either by word or deed, she is condemned to execution on the spot, bound by the pages and dragged out. Notwithstanding the stringent laws for the preservation of decorum by all male attendants, stark-naked full-grown women are the valets.

On the first appearance of the new moon every month, the king shuts himself up, contemplating and arranging his magic horns – the horns of wild animals stuffed with charm-powder – for two or three days. These may be counted his Sundays or church festivals, which he dedicates to devotion. On other days he takes his women, some hundreds, to bathe or sport in ponds; or, when tired of that, takes long walks, his women running after him, when all the musicians fall in, take precedence of the party, followed by the Wakungu and pages, with the king in the centre of the procession, separating the male company from the fair sex. On these excursions no common man dare look upon the royal procession. Should anybody by chance happen to be seen, he is at once hunted down by the pages, robbed of everything he possessed, and may count himself very lucky if nothing worse happens. Pilgrimages are not uncommon, and sometimes the king spends a fortnight yachting; but whatever he does, or wherever he goes, the same ceremonies prevail – his musicians, Wakungu, pages, and the wives take part in all.

But the greatest of all ceremonies takes place at the time of the coronation. The prince-elect then first seeks favour from the kings of all the surrounding countries, demanding in his might and power one of each of their daughters in marriage, or else recognition in some other way, when the Ilmas makes a pilgrimage to the deceased king's tomb, to observe, by the growth an other signs of certain trees, and plants, what destiny awaits the king. According to the prognostics, they report that he will either have to live a life of peace, or after coronation take the field at the head of an army to fight either east, west, or both ways, when usually the first march is on Kittara, and the second on Usoga. The Mgussa's voice is also heard, but in what manner

I do not know, as all communication on state matters is forbidden in Uganda. These preliminaries being arranged, the actual coronation takes place, when the king ceases to hold any farther communion with his mother. The brothers are burnt to death, and the king, we shall suppose, takes the field at the head of his army.

It is as the result of these expeditions that one-half Usogo and the remaining half of Uddu have been annexed to Uganda.

---

1) I.e. Dead Locust Lake – Luta, dead – Nzige, locust.

CHAPTER 10

KARAGUE AND UGANDA

Escape from Protectors – Cross the Kitangule, the First Affluent of the Nile – Enter Uddu – Uganda – A Rich Country – Driving Away the Devil – A Conflict in the Camp – A Pretending Prince – Three Pages with a Diplomatic Message from the King of Uganda – Crime in Uganda.

Crossing back over the Weranhanje spur, I put up with the Arabs at Kufro. Here, for the first time in this part of the world, I found good English peas growing. Next day (11th), crossing over a succession of forks, supporters to the main spur, we encamped at Luandalo. Here we were overtaken by Rozaro, who had remained behind, as I now found, to collect a large number of Wanyambo, whom he called his children, to share with him the gratuitous living these creatures always look out for on a march of this nature.

After working round the end of the great spur whilst following down the crest of a fork, we found Karague separated by a deep valley from the hilly country of Uhaiya, famous for its ivory and coffee productions. On entering the rich plantain gardens of Kisaho, I was informed we must halt there a day for Maula to join us, as he had been detained by Rumanika, who, wishing to give him a present, had summoned Rozaro's sister to his palace for that purpose. She was married to another, and had two children by him, but that did not signify, as it was found in time her husband had committed a fault, on account of which it was thought necessary to confiscate all his property.

At this place all the people were in a constant state of inebriety, drinking pombe all day and all night. I shot a montana antelope, and sent its head and skin back to Grant, accompanied with my daily report to Rumanika.

Maula having joined me, we marched down to near the end of the fork overlooking the plain of Kitangule – the Waganada drums beating, and whistles playing all the way we went along.

We next descended from the Mountains of the Moon, and spanned a long alluvial plain to the settlement of the so-long-heard-of Kitangule, where Rumanika keeps his thousands and thousands of cows. In former days the dense green forests peculiar to the tropics, which grow in swampy places about this plain, were said to have been stocked by vast herds of elephants; but, since the ivory trade had increased, these animals had all been driven off to the hills of Kisiwa and Uhaiya, or into Uddu beyond the river, and all the way down to the N'yanza.

To-day we reached the Kitangule Kagera, or river, which, as I ascertained in the year 1858, falls into the Victoria N'yanza on the west side. Most unfortunately, as we led off to cross it, rain began to pour, so that everybody and everything was thrown into confusion. I could not get a sketch of it, though Grant was more fortunate afterwards; neither could I measure or fathom it; and it was only after a long contest with the superstitious boatmen that they allowed me to cross in their canoe with my shoes on, as they thought the vessel would either upset, or else the river would dry up, in consequence of their Neptune taking offence at me. Once over, I looked down on the noble stream with considerable pride. About eight yards broad, it was sunk down a considerable depth below the surface of the land, like a huge canal, and is so deep, it could not be poled by the canoemen; while it runs at a velocity of from three to four knots an hour.

I say I viewed it with pride, because I had formed my judgment of its being fed from high-seated springs in the Mountains of the Moon solely on scientific geographical reasonings; and, from the bulk of the stream, I also believed those mountains must obtain an altitude of 8,000 feet[1] or more, just as we find they do in Ruanda. I thought then to myself, as I did at Rumanika's, when I first viewed the Mfumbiro cones, and gathered all my distant geographical information there, that these highly saturated Mountains of the Moon give birth to the Congo as well as to the Nile, and also to the Shire branch of the Zambeze.

I came, at the same time, to the conclusion that all our previous information concerning the hydrography of these regions, as well as the Mountains of the Moon, originated with the ancient Hindus, who told it to the priests of the Nile; and that all those busy Egyptian geographers, who disseminated their knowledge with a view to be famous for their long-sightedness, in solving the deep-seated mystery with enshrouded the source of their holy river, were so many hypothetical humbugs. Reasoning thus, the Hindu traders alone, in those days, I believed, had a firm basis to stand upon, from their intercourse with the Abyssinians – through whom they must have heard of the country of Amara, which they applied to the N'yanza – and with the Wanyamuezi or men of the Moon, from whom they heard of the

Tanganyika and Karague mountains. I was all the more impressed with this belief, by knowing that the two church missionaries, Rebmann and Erhardt, without the smallest knowledge of the Hindus' map, constructed a map of their own, deduced from the Zanzibar traders, something on the same scale, by blending the Victoria N'yanza, Tanganyida, and N'yazza into one; whilst to their triuned lake they gave the name Moon, because the men of the Moon happened to live in front of the central lake. And later still, Mr. Leon, another missionary, heard of the N'yanza and the country Amara, near which he heard the Nile made its escape.

Going on with the march we next came to Ndongo, a perfect garden of plantains. The whole country was rich – most surprisingly so.

The same streaky argillaceous sandstones prevailed as in Karague.

There was nothing, in fact, that would not have grown here, if it liked moisture and a temperate heat. It was a perfect paradise for negroes: as fast as they sowed they were sure of a crop without much trouble; though, I must say, they kept their huts and their gardens in excellent order.

As Maula would stop here, I had to halt also. The whole country along the banks of the river, and near some impenetrable forests, was alive with antelopes, principally hartebeests, but I would not fire at them until it was time to return, as the villagers led me to expect buffaloes. The consequence was, as no buffaloes were to be found, I got no sport, though I wounded a hartebeest, and followed him almost into camp, when I gave up the chase to some negroes, and amused myself by writing to Rumanika, to say if Grant did not reach me by a certain date, I would try to navigate the N'yanza, and return to him in boats up the Kitangule river.

We crossed over a low spur of hill extending from the mountainous kingdom of Nkole, on our left, towards the N'yanza. Here I was shown by Nasib a village called Ngandu, which was the farthest trading depot of the Zanzibar ivory-merchants. It was established by Musa Mzuri, by the permission of Rumanika; for, as I shall have presently to mention, Sunna, after annexing this part of Uddu to Uganda, gave Rumanika certain bands of territory in it as a means of security against the possibility of its being wrested out of his hands again by the future kings of Unyoro. Following on Musa's wake, many Arabs also came here to trade; but they were so oppressive to the Waganda that they were recalled by Rumanika, and obliged to locate themselves at Kufro. To the right, at the end of the spur, stretching as far as the eye could reach towards the N'yanza, was a rich, well-wooded, swampy plain, containing large open patches of water, which not many years since, I was assured, were navigable for miles, but now, like the Urigi lake, were gradually drying up. indeed, it appeared to me as if the N'yanza must have once washed the foot of these hills, but had since shrunk away from its original margin.

On arrival at Ngambezi, I was immensely struck with the neatness and good arrangement of the place, as well as its excessive beauty and richness. No part of Bengal or Zanzibar could excel it in either respect; and my men, with one voice, exclaimed, "Ah, what people these Waganda are!" and passed other remarks, which may be abridged as follows: "They build their huts and keep their gardens just as well as we do at Unguja, with screens and enclosures for privacy, a clearance in front of their establishments, and a baraza or reception-hut facing the buildings. Then, too, what a beautiful prospect it has! – rich marshy plains studded with mounds, on each of which grow the umbrella cactus, or some other evergreen tree; and beyond, again, another hill-spur such as the one we have crossed over." One of king Mtesa's uncles, who had not been burnt to death by the order of the late king Sunna on his ascension to the throne, was the proprietor of this place, but unfortunately he was from home. However, his substitute gave me his baraza to live in, and brought many presents of goats, fowls, sweet potatoes, yams, plantains, sugarcane, and Indian corn, and apologised in the end for deficiency in hospitality. I, of course, gave him beads in return.

Continuing over the same kind of ground in the next succeeding spurs of the streaky red-clay sandstone hills, we put up at the residence of Isamgevi, a Mkungu or district officer of Rumanika's. His residence was as well kept as Mtesa's uncle's; but instead of a baraza fronting his house, he had a small enclosure, with three small huts in it, kept apart for devotional purposes, or to propitiate the evil spirits – in short, according to the notions of the place, a church. This officer gave me a cow and some plantains, and I in return gave him a wire and some beads. Many mendicant women, called by some Wichwezi, by others Mabandwa, all wearing the most fantastic dresses of mbugu, covered with beads, shells, and sticks, danced before us, singing a comic song, the chorus of which was a long shrill rolling Coo-roo-coo-roo, coo-roo-coo-roo, delivered as they came to a standstill. Their true functions were just as obscure as the religion of the negroes generally; some called them devil-drivers, other evil-eye averters; but, whatever it was for, they imposed a tax on the people, whose minds being governed by a necessity for making some self-sacrifice to propitiate something, they could not tell what, for their welfare in the world, they always gave them a trifle in the same way as the East Indians do their fakirs.

After crossing another low swampy flat, we reached a much larger group, or rather ramification, of hill-spurs pointing to the N'yanza, called Kisuere, and commanded by M'yombo, Rumanika's frontier officer. Immediately behind this, to the northward, commenced the kingdom of Unyoro; and here it was, they said, Baraka would branch off my line on his way to Kamrasi. Maula's home was one march distant from this, so the scoundrel now left me to enjoy himself there, giving as his pretext for doing so, that Mtesa required him, as soon as I arrived here, to send on a messenger that order might be taken for my proper protection on the line of march; for the Waganda were a turbulent set of people, who could only be kept in order by the executioner; and doubtless many, as was customary on such occasions, would be beheaded, as soon as Mtesa heard of my coming, to put the rest in a fright. I knew this was all humbug, of course, and I told him so; but it was of no use, and I was compelled to halt.

On the 23d another officer, named Maribu, came to me and said, Mtesa, having heard that Grant was left sick behind at Karague, had given him orders to go there and fetch him, whether sick or well, for Mtesa was most anxious to see white men. Hearing this I at once wrote to Grant, begging him to come on if he could do so, and to bring with him all the best of my property, or as much as he could of it, as I now saw there was more cunning humbug than honesty in what Rumanika had told me about the impossibility of our going north from Uganda, as well as in his saying sick men could not go into Uganda, and donkeys without trousers would not be admitted there, because they were considered indecent. If he was not well enough to move, I advised him to wait there until I reached Mtesa's, when I would either go up the lake and Kitangule to fetch him away, or would make the king send boats for him, which I more expressly wished, as it would tend to give us a much better knowledge of the lake.

Maula now came again, after receiving repeated and angry messages, and I forced him to make a move. He led me straight up to his home, a very nice place, in which he gave me a very large, clean, and comfortable hut – had no end of plantains brought for me and my men – and said, "Now you have really entered the kingdom of Uganda, for the future you must buy no more food. At every place that you stop for the day, the officer in charge will bring you plantains, otherwise your men can help themselves in the gardens, for such are the laws of the land when a king's guest travels in it. Any one found selling anything to either yourself or your men would be punished." Accordingly, I stopped the daily issue of beads; but no sooner had I done so, than all my men declared they could not eat plantains. It was all very well, they said, for the Waganda to do so, because they were used to it, but it did not satisfy their hunger.

Maula, all smirks and smiles, on seeing me order the things out for the march, begged I would have patience, and wait till the messenger returned from the king; it would not take more than ten days at the most. Much annoyed at this nonsense, I ordered my tent to be pitched. I refused all Maula's plantains, and gave my men beads to buy grain with; and, finding it necessary to get up some indignation, said I would not stand being chained like a dog; if he would not go on ahead, I should go without him. Maula then said he would go to a friend's and come back again. I said, if he did not, I should go off; and so the conversation ended.

26th. – Drumming, singing, screaming, yelling, and dancing had been going on these last two days and two nights to drive the Phepo or devil out of a village. The whole of the ceremonies were most ludicrous. An old man and woman, smeared with white mud, and holding pots of pombe in their laps, sat in front of a hut, whilst other people kept constantly bringing them baskets full of plantain-squash, and more pots of pombe. In the courtyard fronting them, were hundreds of men and women dressed in smart mbugus – the males wearing for turbans, strings of abrus-seeds wound round their heads, with polished boars' tusks stuck in in a jaunty manner. These were the people who, drunk as fifers, were keeping up such a continual row to frighten the devil away. In the midst of this assembly I now found Kachuchu, Rumanika's representative, who went on ahead from Karague palace to tell Mtesa that I wished to see him. With him, he said, were two other Wakungu of Mtesa's, who had orders to bring on my party and Dr. K'yengo's. Mtesa, he said, was so mad to see us, that the instant he arrived at the palace and told him we wished to visit him, the king caused "fifty big men and four hundred small ones" to be executed, because, he said, his subjects were so bumptious they would not allow any visitors to come near him, else he would have had white men before.

27th. – N'yamgundu, my old friend at Usui, then came to me, and said he was the first man to tell Mtesa of our arrival in Usui, and wish to visit him. The handkerchief I had given Irungu at Usui to present as a letter to Mtesa he had snatched away from him, and given, himself, to his king, who no sooner received it than he bound it round his head, and said, in ecstasies of delight, "Oh, the Mzungu, the Mzungu! He does indeed want to see me." Then giving him four cows as a return letter to take to me, he said, "Hurry off as quickly as possible and bring him here." "The cows," said N'yamgundu, "have gone on to Kisuere by another route, but I will bring them here; and then, as Maula is taking you, I will go and fetch Grant." I then told him not to be in such a hurry. I had turned off Maula for treating me like a dog, and I would not be escorted by him again. He replied that his orders would not be fully accomplished as long as any part of my establishment was behind; so he would, if I wished it, leave part of his "children" to guide me on to Mtesa's, whilst he went to fetch Grant. An officer, I assured him, had just gone on to fetch Grant, so he need not trouble his head on that score; at any rate, he might reverse his plan, and send his children for Grant, whilst he went on with me, by which means he would fully accomplish his mission. Long arguments ensued, and I at length turned the tables by asking who was the greatest – myself or my children; when he said, "As I see you are the greatest,

I will do as you wish; and after fetching the cows from Kisuere, we will march to-morrow at sunrise." The sun rose, but N'yam-gundu did not appear. I was greatly annoyed lest Maula should come and try to drive him away. I waited, restraining my impatience until noon, when, as I could stand it no longer, I ordered Bombay to strike my tent, and commence the march. A scene followed, which brought out my commander-in-chief's temper in a rather surprising shape. "How can we go in?" said Bombay. "Strike the tent," said I. "Who will guide us?" said Bombay. "Strike the tent," I said again. "But Rumanika's men have all gone away, and there is no one to show us the way." "Never mind; obey my orders, and strike the tent." Then, as Bombay would not do it, I commenced myself, assisted by some of my other men, and pulled it down over his head, all the women who were assembled under it, and all the property. On this, Bombay flew into a passion, abusing the men who were helping me, as there were fires and powder-boxes under the tent. I of course had to fly into a passion and abuse Bombay. He, in a still greater rage, said he would pitch into the men, for the whole place would be blown up. "That is no reason why you should abuse my men," I said, "who are better than you by obeying my orders. If I choose to blow up my property, that is my look-out; and if you don't do your duty, I will blow you up also." Foaming and roaring with rage, Bombay said he would not stand being thus insulted. I then gave him a dig on the head with my fist. He squared up, and pouted like an enraged chameleon, looking savagely at me. I gave him another dig, which sent him staggering. He squared again: I gave him another; till at last, as the claret was flowing, he sulked off, and said he would not

337

serve me any more. I then gave Nasib orders to take Bombay's post, and commence the march; but the good old man made Bombay give in, and off we went, amidst crowds of Waganda, who had collected to witness with comedy, and were all digging at one another's heads, showing off in pantomime the strange ways of the white man. N'yamgundu then jointed us, and begged us to halt only one more day, as some of his women were still at Kisuere; but Bombay, showing his nozzle rather flatter than usual, said, "No; I got this on account of your lies. I won't tell Bana any more of your excuses for stopping; you may tell him yourself if you like." N'yamgundu, however, did not think this advisable, and so we went on as we were doing. It was the first and last time I had ever occasion to lose my dignity by striking a blow with my own hands; but I could not help it on this occasion without losing command and respect; for although I often had occasion to award 100 and even 150 lashes to my men for stealing, I could not, for the sake of due subordination, allow any inferior officer to strike Bombay, and therefore had to do the work myself.

Skirting the hills on the left, with a large low plain to the right we soon came on one of those numerous rush-drains that appear to me to be the last waters left of the old bed of the N'yanza. This one in particular was rather large, being 150 yards wide. It was sunk where I crossed it, like a canal, 14 feet below the plain; and what with mire and water combined, so deep, I was obliged to take off my trousers whilst fording it. Once across, we sought for and put up in a village beneath a small hill, from the top of which I saw the Victoria N'yanza for the first time on this march. N'yamgundu delighted me much:

treating me as king, he always fell down on his knees to address me, and made all his "children" look after my comfort in camp.

We marched on again over the same kind of ground, alternately crossing rush-drains of minor importance, though provokingly frequent, and rich gardens, from which, as we passed, all the inhabitants bolted at the sound of our drums, knowing well that they would be seized and punished if found gazing at the king's visitors. Even on our arrival at Ukara not one soul was visible. The huts of the villagers were shown to myself and my men without any ceremony. The Wanyambo escort stole what they liked out of them, and I got into no end of troubles trying to stop the practice; for they said the Waganda served them the same way when they went to Karague, and they had a right to retaliate now. To obviate this distressing sort of plundering, I still served out beads to my men, and so kept them in hand a little; but they were fearfully unruly, and did not like my interference with what by the laws of the country they considered their right.

Here I had to stop a day for some of N'yamgundu's women, who, in my hurry at leaving Maula's, were left behind. A letter from Grant was now brought to me by a very nice-looking young man, who had the skin of a leopard-cat (F. Serval) tied round his neck – a badge which royal personages only were entitled to wear. N'yamgundu seeing this, as he knew the young man was not entitled to wear it, immediately ordered his "children" to wrench it from him. Two ruffianly fellows then seized him by his hands, and twisted his arms round and round until I thought they would come out of their sockets. Without uttering a sound the young man resisted, until N'yamgundu told them to be quiet, for he would hold a court on the subject, and see if the young man could defend himself. The ruffians then sat on the ground, but still holding on to him; whilst N'yamgundu took up a long stick, and breaking it into sundry bits of equal length, placed one by one in front of him, each of which was supposed to represent one number in line of succession to his forefathers. By this it was proved he did not branch in any way from the royal stock. N'yamgundu then turning to the company, said, What would he do now to expiate his folly? If the matter was taken before Mtesa he would lose his head; was it not better he should pay one hundred cows? All agreeing to this, the young man said he would do so, and quietly allowed the skin to be untied and taken off by the ruffians.

Next day, after crossing more of those abominable rush-drains, whilst in sight of the Victoria N'yanza, we ascended the most beautiful hills, covered with verdure of all descriptions. At Meruka, where I put up, there resided some grandees, the chief of whom was the king's aunt. She sent me a goat, a hen, a basket of eggs, and some plantains, in return for which I sent her a wire and some beads. I felt inclined to stop here a month, everything was so very pleasant. The temperature was perfect. The roads, as indeed they were everywhere, were as broad as our coach-roads, cut through the long grasses, straight over the hills and down through the woods in the dells – a strange contrast to the wretched tracks in all the adjacent countries. The huts were kept so clean and so neat, not a fault could be found with them – the gardens the same. Wherever I strolled I saw nothing but richness, and what ought to be wealth. The whole land was a picture of quiescent beauty, with a boundless sea in the background. Looking over the hills, it struck the fancy at once that at one period the whole land must have been at a uniform level with their present tops, but that by the constant denudation it was subjected to by frequent rains, it had been cut down and sloped into those beautiful hills and dales which now so much pleased the eye; for there were none of those quartz dykes I had seen protruding through the same kink of aqueous formations in Usui and Karague; nor were there any other sorts of volcanic disturbance to distort the calm quiet aspect of the scene.

From this, the country being all hill and dale, with miry rush-drains in the bottoms, I walked, carrying my shoes and stockings in my hands, nearly all the way. Rozaro's "children" became more and more troublesome, stealing everything they could lay their hands upon out of the village huts we passed on the way. On arrival at Sangua, I found many of them had been seized by some men who, bolder than the rest, had overtaken them whilst gutting their huts, and made them prisoners, demanding of me two slaves and one load of beads for their restitution. I sent my men back to see what had happened, and ordered them to bring all the men on to me, that I might see fair play. They, however, took the law into their own hands, drove off the Waganda villagers by firing their muskets, and relieved the thieves. A complaint was then laid against Nyamgundu by the chief officer of the village, and I was requested to halt. That I would not do, leaving the matter in the hands of the governor-general, Mr. Pokino, whom I heard we should find at the next station, Masaka.

On arrival there at the government establishment – a large collection of grass huts, separated one from the other within

341

large enclosures, which overspread the whole top of a low hill – I was requested to withdraw and put up in some huts a short distance off, and wait until his excellency, who was from home, could come and see me; which the next day he did, coming in state with a large number of officers, who brought with them a cow, sundry pots of pombe, enormous sticks of sugar-cane, and a large bundle of country coffee. This grows in great profusion all over this land in large bushy trees, the berries sticking on the branches like clusters of hollyberries.

I was then introduced, and told that his excellency was the appointed governor of all the land lying between the Katonga and the Kitangule rivers. After the first formalities were over, the complaint about the officers at Sangua was preferred for decision, on which Pokino at once gave it against the villagers, as they had no right, by the laws of the land, to lay hands on a king's guest. Just then Maula arrived, and began to abuse N'yamgundu. Of course I would not stand this; and, after telling all the facts of the case, I begged Pokino to send Maula away out of my camp. Pokino said he could not do this, as it was by the king's order he was appointed; but he put Maula in the background, laughing at the way he had "let the bird fly out of his hands," and settled that N'yamgundu should be my guide. I then gave him a wire, and he gave me three large sheets of mbugu, which he said I should require, as there were so many water-courses to cross on the road I was going. A second day's halt was necessitated by many of my men catching fever, probably owing to the constant crossing of those abominable rush-drains. There was no want of food here, for I never saw such a profusion of plantains anywhere. They were literally lying in heaps on the ground, though the people were brewing pombe all day, and cooking them for dinner every evening.

After crossing many more hills and miry bottoms, constantly coming in view of the lake, we reached Ugonzi, and after another march of the same description, came to Kituntu, the last officer's residence in Uddu. Formerly it was the property of a Beluch named Eseau, who came to this country with merchandise, trading on account of Said Said, late Sultan of Zanzibar; but having lost it all on his way here, paying mahongo, or taxes, and so forth he feared returning, and instead made great friends with the late king Sunna, who took an especial fancy to him because he had a very large beard, and raised him to the rank of Mkungu. A few years ago, however, Eseau died, and left all his family and property to a slave named Uledi, who now, in consequence, is the border officer.

I became now quite puzzled whilst thinking which was the finest spot I had seen in Uddu, so many were exceedingly beautiful; but I think I gave the preference to this, both for its own immediate neighbourhood and the long range of view it afforded of Uganda proper, the lake, and the large island, or group of islands, called Sese where the king of Uganda keeps one of his fleets of boats.

Some little boys came here who had all their hair shaved off excepting two round tufts on either side of the head. They were the king's pages; and, producing three sticks, said they had brought them to me from their king, who wanted three charms or medicines. Then placing one stick on the ground before me, they said, "This one is a head which, being affected by dreams of a deceased relative, requires relief"; the second symbolised the king's desire for the accomplishment of a phenomenon to which the old phalic worship was devoted; "and this third one," they said, "is a sign that the king wants a charm to keep all his subjects in awe of him." I then promised I would do what I could when I reached the palace, but feared to do anything in the distance. I wished to go on with the march, but was dissuaded by N'yamgundu, who said he had received orders to find me some cows here, as his king was most anxious I should be well fed. Next day, however, we descended into the Katonga valley, where, instead of finding a magnificent broad sheet of water, as I had been led to expect by the Arabs' account of it, I found I had to wade through a succession of rush-drains divided one from the other by islands. It took me two hours, with my clothes tucked up under my arms, to get through them all; and many of them were so matted with weeds, that my feet sank down as though I trod in a bog.

The Waganda all said that at certain times in the year no one could ford these drains, as they all flooded; but, strangely enough, they were always lowest when most rain fell in Uganda. No one, however, could account for this singular fact. No one knew of a lake to supply the waters, nor where they came from. That they flowed into the lake there was no doubt – as I could see by the trickling waters in some few places – and they lay exactly on the equator. Rising out of the valley, I found all the country just as hilly as before, but many of the rush-drains going to northward; and in the dells were such magnificent trees, they quite took me by surprise. Clean-trunked, they towered up just as so many great pillars, and then spread out their high branches like a canopy over us. I thought of the blue gums of Australia, and believed these would beat them. At the village of Mbule we were gracefully received by the local officer, who brought a small present, and assured me that the king was in a nervous state of excitement, always asking after me. Whilst speaking he trembled, and he was so restless he could never sit still.

Up and down we went on again through this wonderful country, surprisingly rich in grass, cultivation, and trees. Watercourses were as frequent as ever, though not quite so troublesome to the traveller, as they were more frequently bridged with poles or palm-tree trunks.

This, the next place we arrived at, was N'yamgundu's own residence, where I stopped a day to try and shoot buffaloes. Maula here had the coolness to tell me he must inspect all the things I had brought for presentation to the king, as he said it was the custom; after which he would hurry on and inform his majesty. Of course I refused, saying it was uncourteous to both the king and myself. Still he persisted, until, finding it hopeless, he spitefully told N'yamgundu to keep me here at least two days. N'yamgundu, however, very prudently told him he should obey his orders, which were to take me on as fast as he could. I then gave N'yamgundu wires and beads for himself and all his family round, which made Maula slink further away from me than ever.

The buffaloes were very numerous in the tall grasses that lined the sides and bottoms of the hills; but although I saw some, I could not get a shot, for the grasses being double the height of myself, afforded them means of dashing out of view as soon as seen, and the rustling noise made whilst I followed them kept them on the alert. At night a hyena came into my hut, and carried off one of my goats that was tied to a log between two of my sleeping men.

During the next march, after passing some of the most beautifully-wooded dells, in which lay small rush-lakes on the right of the road, draining, as I fancied, into the Victoria Lake, I met with a party of the king's gamekeepers, staking their nets all along the side of a hill, hoping to catch antelopes by driving the covers with dogs and men. Farther on, also, I came on a party driving one hundred cows, as a present from Mtesa to Rumanika, which the officers in charge said was their king's return for the favour Rumanika had done him in sending me on to him. It was in this way that great kings sent "letters" to one another.

Next day, after going a short distance, we came on the Mwarango river, a broad rush-drain of three hundred yards' span, two-thirds of which was bridged over. Until now I did not feel sure where the various rush-drains I had been crossing since leaving the Katonga valley all went to, but here my mind was made up, for I found a large volume of water going to the northwards. I took off my clothes at the end of the bridge and jumped into the stream, which I found was twelve yards or so broad, and deeper than my height. I was delighted beyond measure at this very surprising fact, that I was indeed on the northern slopes of the continent, and had, to all appearance, found one of the branches of the Nile's exit from the N'yanza. I drew Bombay's attention to the current; and, collecting all the men of the country, inquired of them where the river sprang from. Some of them said, in the hills to the southward; but most of them said, from the lake. I argued the point with them; for I felt quite sure so large a body of flowing water could not be collected together in any place but the lake. They then all agreed to this view, and further assured me it went to Kamrasi's palace in Unyoro, where it joined the N'yanza, meaning the Nile.

Pushing on again we arrived at N'yama Goma, where I found Irungu – the great ambassador I had first met in Usui, with all his "children" – my enemy Makinga, and Suwarora's deputation with wire – altogether, a collection of one hundred souls. They had been here a month waiting for leave to approach the king's palace. Not a villager was to be seen for miles round; not a plantain remained on the trees, nor was there even a sweet potato to be found in the ground. The whole of the provisions of this beautiful place had been devoured by the king's guests, simply because he had been too proud to see them in a hurry. This was alarming, for I feared I should be served the same trick, especially as all the people said this kind of treatment was a mere matter of custom which those great kings demanded as a respect due to their dignity; and Bombay added, with laughter, they make all manner of fuss to entice one to come when in the distance, but when they have got you in their power they become haughty about it, and think only of how they can best impose on your mind the great consequence which they affect before their own people.

Here I was also brought to a standstill, for N'yamgundu said I must wait for leave to approach the palace. He wished to have a look at the presents I had brought for Mtesa. I declined to gratify it, taking my stand on my dignity; there was no occasion for any distrust on such a trifling matter as that, for I was not a merchant who sought for gain, but had come, at great expense, to see the king of this region. I begged, however, he would go as fast as possible to announce my arrival, explain my motive for coming here, and ask for an early interview, as I had left my brother Grant behind at Karague, and found my position, for want of a friend to talk to, almost intolerable. It was not the custom of my country for great men to consort with servants, and until I saw him, and made friends, I should not be happy. I had a great deal to tell him about, as he was the father of the Nile, which river drained the N'yanza down to my country to the northward. With this message N'yamgundu hurried off as fast as possible.

Next day (15th) I gave each of my men a fez cap, and a piece of red blanket to make up military jackets. I then instructed them how to form a guard of honour when I went to the palace, and taught Bombay the way Nazirs was presented at courts in India. Altogether we made a good show. When this was concluded I went with Nasib up a hill, from which we could see the lake on one side, and on the other a large range of huts said to belong to the king's uncle, the second of the late king Sunna's brothers, who was not burnt to death when he ascended the throne.

I then (16th) very much wished to go and see the escape of the Mwerango river, as I still felt a little sceptical as to its origin, whether or not it came off those smaller lakes I had seen on the road the day before I crossed the river; but no one would listen to my project. They all said I must have the king's sanction first, else people, from not knowing my object, would accuse me of practising witchcraft, and would tell their king so. They still all maintained that the river did come out of the lake, and said, if

I liked to ask the king's leave to visit the spot, then they would go and show it me. I gave way, thinking it prudent to do so, but resolved in my mind I would get Grant to see it in boats on his voyage from Karague. There were not guinea-fowls to be found here, nor a fowl, in any of the huts, so I requested Rozaro to hurry off to Mtesa, and ask him to send me something to eat. He simply laughed at my request, and said I did not know what I was doing. It would be as much as his life was worth to go one yard in advance of this until the king's leave was obtained. I said, rather than be starved to death in this ignominious manner, I would return to Karague; to which he replied, laughing, "Whose leave have you got to do that? Do you suppose you can do as you like in this country?" Next day (17th), in the evening, N'yamgundu returned full of smirks and smiles, dropped on his knees at my feet, and, in company with his "children," set to n'yanzigging, according to the form of that state ceremonial already described.[2] In his excitement he was hardly able to say all he had to communicate. Bit by bit, however, I learned that he first went to the palace, and, finding the king had gone off yachting to the Murchison Creek, he followed him there. The king for a long while would not believe his tale that I had come, but, being assured, he danced with delight, and swore he would not taste food until he had seen me. "Oh," he said, over and over again and again, according to my informer, "can this be true? Can the white man have come all this way to see me? What a strong man he must be too, to come so quickly! Here are seven cows, four of them milch ones, as you say he likes milk, which you will give him; and there are three for yourself for having brought him so quickly. Now, hurry off as fast as you can, and tell him I am more delighted at the prospect of seeing him than he can be to see me. There is no place here fit for his reception. I was on a pilgrimage which would have kept me here seven days longer but as I am so impatient to see him, I will go off to my palace at once, and will send word for him to advance as soon as I arrive there." About noon the succeeding day, some pages ran in to say we were to come along without a moment's delay, as their king had ordered it. He would not taste food until he saw me, so that everybody might know what great respect he felt for me. In the meanwhile, however, he wished for some gunpowder. I packed the pages off as fast as I could with some, and tried myself to follow, but my men were all either sick or out foraging, and therefore we could not get under way until the evening. After going a certain distance, we came on a rush-drain, of much greater breadth even than the Mwerango, called the Moga (or river) Myanza, which was so deep I had to take off my trousers and tuck my clothes under my arms. It flowed into the Mwerango, but with scarcely any current at all. This rush-drain, all the natives assured me, rose in the hills to the southward – not in the lake, as the Mwerango did – and it was never bridged over like that river, because it was always fordable. This account seemed to me reasonable; for though so much broader in its bed than the Mwerango, it had no central, deep-flowing current.

1) In "Blackwood's Magazine" for August 1859.
2) See p. 318.

CHAPTER 11

PALACE, UGANDA

Preparations for the Reception at the Court of Mtesa, King of Uganda – The Ceremonial – African Diplomacy and Dignity – Feats with the Rifle – Cruelty and Wastefulness of Life – The Pages – The Queen-Dowager of Uganda – Her Court Reception – I Negotiate for a Palace – Conversations with the King and Queen – The Queen's Grand Entertainment – Royal Dissipation.

To-day the king sent his pages to announce his intention of holding a levee in my honour. I prepared for my first presentation at court, attired in my best, though in it I cut a poor figure in comparison with the display of the dressy Waganda. They wore neat bark cloaks resembling the best yellow corduroy cloth, crimp and well set, as if stiffened with starch, and over that, as upper-cloaks, a patchwork of small antelope skins, which I observed were sewn together as well as any English glovers could have pieced them; whilst their head-dresses, generally, were abrus turbans, set off with highly-polished boar-tusks, stick-charms, seeds, beads, or shells; and on their necks, arms, and ankles they wore other charms of wood, or small horns stuffed with magic powder, and fastened on by strings generally covered with snake-skin. N'yamgundu and Maula demanded, as their official privilege, a first peep; and this being re-

351

fused, they tried to persuade me that the articles comprising the present required to be covered with chintz, for it was considered indecorous to offer anything to his majesty in a naked state. This little interruption over, the articles enumerated below[1] were conveyed to the palace in solemn procession thus: With N'yamgundu, Maula, the pages, and myself on the flanks, the Union-Jack carried by the kirangozi guide led the way, followed by twelve men as a guard of honour, dressed in red flannel cloaks, and carrying their arms sloped, with fixed bayonets; whilst in their rear were the rest of my men, each carrying some article as a present.

On the march towards the palace, the admiring courtiers, wonder-struck at such an unusual display, exclaimed, in raptures of astonishment, some with both hands at their mouths, and others clasping their heads with their hands, "Irungi! Irungi!" which may be translated "Beautiful! Beautiful!" I thought myself everything was going on as well as could be wished; but before entering the royal enclosures, I found, to my disagreeable surprise, that the men with Suwarora's hongo or offering, which consisted of more than a hundred coils of wire, were ordered to lead the procession, and take precedence of me. There was something specially aggravating in this precedence; for it will be remembered that these very brass wires which they saw, I had myself intended for Mtesa, that they were taken from me by Suwarora as far back as Usui, and it would never do, without remonstrance, to have them boastfully paraded before my eyes in this fashion. My protests, however, had no effect upon the escorting Wakungu. Resolving to make them catch it, I walked along as if ruminating in anger up the broad high road into a cleared square, which divides Mtesa's domain on the south from his Kamraviona's, or commander-in-chief, on the north, and then turned into the court. The palace or entrance quite surprised me by its extraordinary dimensions, and the neatness with which it was kept. The whole brow and sides of the hill on which we stood were covered with gigantic grass huts, thatched as neatly as so many heads dressed by a London barber, and fenced all round with the tall yellow reeds of the common Uganda tiger-grass; whilst within the enclosure, the lines of huts were joined together, or partitioned off into courts, with walls of the same grass. It is here most of Mtesa's three or four hundred women are kept, the rest being quartered chiefly with his mother, known by the title of N'yamasore, or queen-dowager. They stood in little groups at the doors, looking at us, and evidently passing their own remarks, and enjoying their own jokes, on the triumphal procession. At each gate as we passed, officers on duty opened and shut it for us, jingling the big bells which are hung upon them, as they sometimes are at shop-doors, to prevent silent, stealthy entrance.

The first court passed, I was even more surprised to find the unusual ceremonies that awaited me. There courtiers of high dignity stepped forward to greet me, dressed in the most scrupulously neat fashions. Men, women, bulls, dogs, and goats, were led about by strings; cocks and hens were carried in men's arms; and little pages, with rope-turbans, rushed about, conveying messages, as if their lives depended on their swiftness, every one holding his skin-cloak tightly round him lest his naked legs might by accident be shown.

This, then, was the ante-reception court; and I might have taken possession of the hut, in which musicians were playing and singing on large nine-stringed harps, like the Nubian tambira, accompanied by harmonicons. By the chief officers in waiting, however, who thought fit to treat us like Arab merchants, I was requested to sit on the ground outside in the sun with my servants. Now, I had made up my mind never to sit upon the ground as the natives and Arabs are obliged to do, nor to make my obeisance in any other manner than is customary in England, though the Arabs had told me that from fear they had always complied with the manners of the court. I felt that if I did not stand up for my social position at once, I should be treated with contempt during the remainder of my visit, and thus lose the vantage-ground I had assumed of appearing rather as a prince than a trader, for the purpose of better gaining the confidence of the king. To avert over-hastiness, however – for my servants began to be alarmed as I demurred against doing as I was bid – I allowed five minutes to the court to give me a proper reception, saying, if it were not conceded I would then walk away.

Nothing, however, was done. My own men, knowing me, feared for me, as they did not know what a "savage" king would do in case I carried out my threat; whilst the Waganda, lost in amazement at what seemed little less than blasphemy, stood still as posts. The affair ended by my walking straight away home, giving Bombay orders to leave the present on the ground, and to follow me.

Although the king is said to be unapproachable, excepting when he chooses to attend court – a ceremony which rarely happens – intelligence of my hot wrath and hasty departure reached him in an instant. He first, it seems, thought of leaving

A Ugandan chief's house.

his toilet-room to follow me, but, finding I was walking fast, and had gone far, changed his mind, and sent Wakungu running after me. Poor creatures! They caught me up, fell upon their knees, and implored I would return at once, for the king had not tasted food, and would not until he saw me. I felt grieved at their touching appeals; but, as I did not understand all they said, I simply replied by patting my heart and shaking my head, walking if anything all the faster.

On my arrival at my hut, Bombay and others came in, wet through with perspiration, saying the king had heard of all my grievances. Suwarora's hongo was turned out of court, and, if I desired it, I might bring my own chair with me, for he was very anxious to show me great respect – although such a seat was exclusively the attribute of the king, no one else in Uganda daring to sit on an artificial seat.

My point was gained, so I cooled myself with coffee and a pipe, and returned rejoicing in my victory, especially over Suwarora.

After returning to the second tier of huts from which I had retired, everybody appeared to be in a hurried, confused state of excitement, not knowing what to make out of so unprecedented an exhibition of temper. In the most polite manner, the officers in waiting begged me to be seated on my iron stool, which I had brought with me, whilst others hurried in to announce my arrival. But for a few minutes only I was kept in suspense, when a band of music, the musicians wearing on their backs long-haired goat-skins, passed me, dancing as they went along, like bears in a fair, and playing on reed instruments worked over with pretty beads in various patters, from which depended leopard-cat skins – the time being regulated by the beating of long hand-drums.

The mighty king was now reported to be sitting on his throne in the statehut of the third tier. I advanced, hat in hand, with my guard of honour following, formed in "open ranks," who in their turn were followed by the bearers carrying the present. I did not walk straight up to him as if to shake hands, but went outside the ranks of a three-sided square of squatting Wakungu, all inhibited in skins, mostly cow-skins; some few of whom had, in addition, leopard-cat skins girt round the waist, the sign of royal blood. Here I was desired to halt and sit in the glaring sun; so I donned my hat, mounted my umbrella, a phenomenon which set them all a-wondering and laughing, ordered the guard to close ranks, and sat gazing at the novel spectacle! A more theatrical sight I never saw. The king, a good-looking, well-figured, tall young man of twenty-five, was sitting on a red blanket spread upon a square platform of royal grass, encased in tiger-grass reeds, scrupulously well dressed in a new mbugu. The hair of his head was cut short, excepting on the top, where it was combed up into a high ridge, running from stem to stern like a cockscomb. On his neck was a very neat ornament – a large ring, of beautifully-worked small beads, forming elegant patterns by their various colours. On one arm was another bead ornament, prettily devised; and on the other a wooden charm, tied by a string covered with snakeskin. On every finger and every toe, he had alternate brass and copper rings; and above the ankles, halfway up to the calf, a stocking of very pretty beads. Everything was light, neat, and elegant in its way; not a fault could be found with the taste of his "getting up." For a handkerchief he held a well-folded piece of bark, and a piece of gold-embroidered silk, which he constantly employed to hide his large mouth when laughing, or to wipe it after a drink of plantain-wine, of which he took constant and copious draughts from neat little gourd-cups, administered by his ladies-in-waiting, who were at once his sisters and wives. A white dog, spear, shield, and woman – the Uganda cognisance – were by his side, as also a knot of staff officers, with whom he kept up a brisk conversation on one side; and on the other was a band of Wichezi, or lady-sorcerers, such as I have already described.

I was now asked to draw nearer within the hollow square of squatters, where leopard-skins were strewed upon the ground, and a large copper kettledrum, surmounted with brass bells on arching wires, along with two other smaller drums covered with cowrie-shells, and beads of colour worked into patterns, were placed. I now longed to open conversation, but knew not the language, and no one near me dared speak, or even lift his head from fear of being accused of eyeing the women; so the king and myself sat staring at one another for full an hour – I mute, but he pointing and remarking with those around him on the novelty of my guard and general appearance, and even requiring to see my hat lifted, the umbrella shut and opened, and the guards face about and show off their red cloaks – for such wonders had never been seen in Uganda.

Then, finding the day waning, he sent Maula on an embassy to ask me if I had seen him; and on receiving my reply, "Yes, for full one hour," I was glad to find him rise, spear in hand, lead his dog, and walk unceremoniously away through the enclosure into the fourth tier of huts; for this being a pure levee day, no

HM Mtesa, King of Uganda.

business was transacted. The king's gait in retiring was intended to be very majestic, but did not succeed in conveying to me that impression. It was the traditional walk of his race, founded on the step of the lion; but the outward sweep of the legs, intended to represent the stride of the noble beast, appeared to me only to realise a very ludicrous kind of waddle, which made me ask Bombay if anything serious was the matter with the royal person.

I had now to wait for some time, almost as an act of humanity; for I was told the state secret, that the king had retired to break his fast and eat for the first time since hearing of my arrival; but the repast was no sooner over than he prepared for the second act, to show off his splendour, and I was invited in, with all my men, to the exclusion of all his own officers save my two guides. Entering as before, I found him standing on a red blanket, leaning against the right portal of the hut, talking and laughing, handkerchief in hand, to a hundred or more of his admiring wives, who, all squatting on the ground outside, in two groups, were dressed in mew mbugus. My men dared not advance upright, nor look upon the women, but, stooping, with lowered heads and averted eyes, came cringing after me. Unconscious myself, I gave loud and impatient orders to my guard, rebuking them for moving like frightened geese, and, with hat in hand, stood gazing on the fair sex till directed to sit and cap.

Mtesa then inquired what messages were brought from Rumanika; to which Maula, delighted with the favour of speaking to royalty, replied by saying, Rumanika had gained intelligence of Englishmen coming up the Nile to Gani and Kidi. The king acknowledged the truthfulness of their story, saying he had heard the same himself; and both Wakungu, as is the custom in Uganda, thanked their lord in a very enthusiastic manner, kneeling on the ground – for no one can stand in the presence of his majesty – in an attitude of prayer, and throwing out their hands as they repeated the words N'yanzig, N'yanzig, ai N'yanzig Mkahma wangi, etc., etc., for a considerable time; when, thinking they had done enough of this, and heated with the exertion, they threw themselves flat upon their stomachs, and, floundering about like fish on land, repeated the same words over again and again, and rose doing the same, with their faces covered with earth; for majesty in Uganda is never satisfied till subjects have grovelled before it like the most abject worms. This conversation over, after gazing at me, and chatting with his women for a considerable time, the second scene ended. The third scene was more easily arranged, for the day was fast declining. He simply moved his train of women to another hut, where, after seating himself upon his throne, with his women around him, he invited me to approach the nearest limits of propriety, and to sit as before. Again he asked me if I had seen him – evidently desirous of indulging in his regal pride; so I made the most of the opportunity thus afforded me of opening a conversation by telling him of those grand reports I had formerly heard about him, which induced me to come all his way to see him, and the trouble it had cost me to reach the object of my desire; at the same time taking a gold ring from off my finger, and presenting it to him, I said, "This is a small token of friendship; if you will inspect it, it is made after the fashion of a dog-collar, and, being the king of metals, gold, is in every respect appropriate to your illustrious race." He said, in return, "If friendship is your desire, what would you say if I showed you a road by which you might reach your home in one month?" Now everything had to be told to Bombay, then to Nasib, my Kiganda interpreter, and then to either Maula or N'yamgundu, before it was delivered to the king, for it was considered indecorous to transmit any message to his majesty excepting through the medium of one of his officers. Hence I could not get an answer put in; for as all Waganda are rapid and impetuous in their conversation, the king, probably forgetting he had put a question, hastily changed the conversation and said, "What guns have you got? Let me see the one you shoot with." I wished still to answer the first question first, as I knew he referred to the direct line to Zanzibar across the Masai, and was anxious, without delay, to open the subject of Petherick and Grant; but no one dared to deliver my statement. Much disappointed, I then said, "I had brought the best shooting-gun in the world – Whitworth's rifle – which I begged he would accept, with a few other trifles; and, with his permission, I would lay them upon a carpet at his feet, as is the custom of my country when visiting sultans." He assented, sent all his women away, and had an mbugu spread for the purpose, on which Bombay, obeying my order, first spread a red blanket, and then opened each article one after the other, when Nasib, according to the usage already mentioned, smoothed them down with his dirty hands, or rubbed them against his sooty face, and handed them to the king to show there was no poison or witchcraft in them. Mtesa appeared quite confused with the various wonders as he handled them, made silly remarks, and pondered over them like a perfect child, until it was quite dark. Torches were then lit, and guns, pistols, powder, boxes, tools, beads –

the whole collection, in short – were tossed together topsy-turvy, bundled into mbugs, and carried away by the pages. Mtesa now said, "It is late, and time to break up; what provisions would you wish to have?" I said, "A little of everything, but no one thing constantly." "And would you like to see me to-morrow?" "Yes, every day." "Then you can't to-morrow, for I have business; but the next day come if you like. You can now go away, and here are six pots of plantain-wine for you; my men will search for food to-morrow."

21st. – In the morning, whilst it rained, some pages drove in twenty cows and ten goats, with a polite metaphorical message from their king, to the effect that I had pleased him much, and he hoped I would accept these few "chickens" until he could send more – when both Maula and N'yamgundu, charmed with their success in having brought a welcome guest to Uganda, never ceased showering eulogiums on me for my fortune in having gained the countenance of their king. The rain falling was considered at court a good omen, and everybody declared the king mad with delight. Wishing to have a talk with him about Petherick and Grant, I at once started off the Wakungu to thank him for the present, and to beg pardon for my apparent rudeness of yesterday, at the same time requesting I might have an early interview with his majesty, as I had much of importance to communicate; but the solemn court formalities which these African kings affect as much as Oriental emperors, precluded my message from reaching the king. I heard, however, that he had spent the day receiving Suwarora's hongo of wire, and that the officer who brought them was made to sit in an empty court, whilst the king sat behind a screen, never deigning to show his majestic person. I was told, too, that he opened conversation by demanding to know how it happened that Suwarora became possessed of the wires, for they were made by the white men to be given to himself, and Suwarora must therefore have robbed me of them; and it was by such practices he, Mtesa, never could see any visitors. The officer's reply was, Suwarora would not show the white men any respect, because they were wizards would did not sleep in houses at night, but flew up to the tops of hills, and practised sorcery of every abominable kind. The king to this retorted, in a truly African fashion, "That's a lie; I can see no harm in this white man; and if he had been a bad man, Rumanika would not have sent him on to me." At night, when in bed, the king sent his pages to say, if I desired his friendship I would lend him one musket to make up six with what I had given him, for he intended visiting his relations the following morning. I sent three, feeling that nothing would be lost by being "open-handed."

22d. – To-day the king went the round of his relations, showing the beautiful things given him by the white man – a clear proof that he was much favoured by the "spirits," for neither his father nor any of his forefathers had been so recognised and distinguished by any "sign" as a rightful inheritor to the Uganda throne: an anti-Christian interpretation of omens, as rife in these dark regions now as it was in the time of King Nebuchadnezzar. At midnight the three muskets were returned, and I was so pleased with the young king's promptitude and honesty, I begged he would accept them.

23d. – At noon Mtesa sent his pages to invite me to his palace. I went, with my guard of honour and my stool, but found I had to sit waiting in an ante-hut three hours with his commander-in-chief and other high officers before he was ready to see me. During this time Wasoga minstrels, playing on tambira, and accompanied by boys playing on a harmonicon, kept us amused; and a small page, with a large bundle of grass, came to me and said, "The king hopes you won't be offended if required to sit on it before him; for no person in Uganda, however high in office, is ever allowed to sit upon anything raised above the ground, nor can anybody but himself sit upon such grass as this; it is all that his throne is made of. The first day he only allowed you to sit on your stool to appease your wrath." On consenting to do in "Rome as the Romans do," when my position was so handsomely acknowledged, I was called in, and found the court sitting much as it was on the first day's interview, only that the number of squatting Wakungu was much diminished; and the king, instead of wearing his ten brass and copper rings, had my gold one on his third finger. This day, however, was cut out for business, as, in addition to the assemblage of officers, there were women, cows, goats, fowls, confiscations, baskets of fish, baskets of small antelopes, porcupines, and curious rats caught by his gamekeepers, bundles of mbugu, etc., etc., made by his linen-drapers, coloured earths and sticks by his magician, all ready for presentation; but, as rain fell, the court broke up, and I had nothing for it but to walk about under my umbrella, indulging in angry reflections against the haughty king for not inviting me into his hut.

When the rain had ceased, and we were again called in, he was found sitting in state as before, but this time with the head of a black bull placed before him, one horn of which, knocked off, was placed alongside, whilst four living cows walked about the court.

I was now requested to shoot the four cows as quickly as possible; but having no bullets for my gun, I borrowed the revolving pistol I had given him, and shot all four in a second of time; but as the last one, only wounded, turned sharply upon me, I gave him the fifth and settled him. Great applause followed this wonderful feat, and the cows were given to my men. The king now loaded one of the carbines I had given him with his own hands, and giving it full-cock to a page, told him to go out and shoot a man in the outer court; which was no sooner accomplished than the little urchin returned to announce his success, with a look of glee such as one would see in the face of a boy who had robbed a bird's nest, caught a trout, or done any other boyish trick. The king said to him, "And did you do it well?" "Oh, yes, capitally." He spoke the truth, no doubt, for he dared not have trifled with the king; but the affair created hardly any interest. I never heard, and there appeared no curiosity to know, what individual human being the urchin had deprived of life.

The Wakungu were not dismissed, and I asked to draw near, when the king showed me a book I had given to Rumanika, and begged for the inspiring medicine which he had before applied for through the mystic stick. The day was now gone, so torches were lit, and we were ordered to go, though as yet I had not been able to speak one word I wished to impart about Petherick and Grant; for my interpreters were so afraid of the king they dared not open their mouths until they were spoken to. The king was now rising to go, when, in great fear and anxiety that the day would be lost, I said, in Kisuahili, "I wish you would send a letter by post to Grant, and also send a boat up the Kitangule, as far as Rumanika's palace, for him, for he is totally unable to walk." I thus attracted his notice, though he did not understand one word I uttered. The result was, that he waited for the interpretation, and replied that a post would be no use, for no one would be responsible for the safe delivery of the message; he would send N'yamgundu to fetch him, but he thought Rumanika would not consent to his sending boats up the Kitangule as far as the Little Windermere; and then, turning round with true Mganda impetuosity, he walked away without taking a word from me in exchange.

24th. – Early this morning the pages came to say Mtesa desired I would send him three of my Wanguaga to shoot cows before him. This was just what I wanted. It had struck me that personal conferences with me so roused the excitable king, that there was no bringing plain matters of business home to him; so, detaching seven men with Bombay, I told him, before shooting, to be sure and elicit the matter I wanted – which was, to excite the king's cupidity by telling him I had a boat full of stores with two white men at Gani, whom I wished to call to me if he would furnish some guides to accompany my men; and further, as Grant could not walk, I wished boats sent for him, at least as far as the ferry on the Kitangule, to which place Rumanika, at any rate, would slip him down in canoes. At once, on arriving, Mtesa admitted the men, and ordered them to shoot at some cows; but Bombay, obeying my orders to first have his talk out, said, No – before he could shoot he must obey master and deliver his message; which no sooner was told than the king, in a hurry, excited by the prospects of sport, impatiently said, "Very good; I will send men either by water or overland through Kidi,[2] just as your master likes; only some of his men had better go with mine: but now shoot cows, shoot cows; for I want to see how the Waguana shoot." They shot seven, and all were given to them when they were dismissed. In the evening the pages came to ask me if I would like to shoot kites in the palace with their king; but I declined shooting anything less than elephants, rhinoceros, or buffaloes; and even for these I would not go out unless the king went with me – a dodge I conceived would tend more than any other to bring us together, and so break through those ceremonial restraints of the court, which at present were stopping all pans of progression.

25th. – The king invited me to shoot with him – really buffaloes – close to the palace; but as the pages had been sent off in a hurry, without being fully instructed, I declined, on the plea that I had always been gulled and kept waiting or treated with incivility, for hours before I obtained an interview; and as I did not wish to have any more ruptures in the palace, I proposed Bombay should go to make proper arrangements for my reception on the morrow – as anyhow, at present I felt indisposed. The pages dreaded their master's wrath, departed for a while, and then sent another lad to tell me he was sorry to hear I felt unwell, but he hoped I would come if only for a minute, bringing my medicines with me, for he himself felt pain. That this second message was a forged one I had no doubt, for the boys had not been long enough gone; still, I packed up my medicines and went, leaving the onus, should any accident happen, upon the mischievous story-bearers.

As I anticipated, on arrival at the palace I found the king was not ready to receive me, and the pages desired me to sit with the officers in waiting until he might appear. I found it necessary to fly at once into a rage, called the pages a set of deceiving young blackguards, turned upon my heel, and walked straight back through the courts, intending to leave the palace. Everybody was alarmed; information of my retreat at once reached the king, and he sent his Wakungu to prevent my egress. These officers passed me, as I was walking hurriedly along under my umbrella, in the last court, and shut the entrance-gate in front of me. This was too much, so I stamped, and, pointing my finger, swore in every language I knew, that if they did not open the gate again, as they had shut it at once, and that, too, before my face, I would never leave the spot I stood upon alive. Terror-stricken, the Wakungu fell on their knees before me, doing as they were bid; and, to please them, I returned at once, and went up to the king, who, now sitting on his throne, asked the officers how they had managed to entice me back; to which they all replied in a breath, n'yanzigging heartily, "Oh, we were so afraid – he was so terrible! But he turned at once as soon as we opened the gate." "How? What gate? Tell us all about it." And when the whole story was fully narrated, the matter was thought a good joke. After pausing a little, I asked the king what ailed him, for I was sorry to hear he had been sick; but instead of replying, he shook his head, as much as to say, I had put a very uncouth question to his majesty – and ordered some men to shoot cows.

Instead of admiring this childish pastime, which in Uganda is considered royal sport, I rather looked disdainful, until, apparently disappointed at my indifference, he asked what the box I had brought contained. On being told it was the medicine he desired, he asked me to draw near, and sent his courtiers away.

When only the interpreters and one confidential officer were left, besides myself, he wished to know if I could apply the medicine without its touching the afflicted part. To give him confidence in my surgical skill, I moved my finger, and asked him if he knew what gave it action; and on his replying in the negative, I have him an anatomical lecture, which so pleased him, he at once consented to be operated on, and I applied a blister accordingly. The whole operation was rather ridiculous; for the blister, after being applied, had to be rubbed in turn on the hands and faces of both Bombay and Nasib, to show there was no evil spirit in the "doctor." Now, thought I to myself, is the right time for business; for I had the king all to myself, then considered a most fortunate occurrence in Uganda, where every man courts the favour of a word with his king, and adores him as a deity, and he in turn makes himself as distance as he can, to give greater effect to his exalted position. The matter, however, was merely deferred: for I no sooner told him my plans for communicating quickly with Petherick and Grant, than, after saying he desired their coming even more than myself, he promised to arrange everything on the morrow.

26th. – In the morning, as agreed, I called on the king, and found the blister had drawn nicely; so I let off the water, which Bombay called the malady, and so delighted the king amazingly. A basket of fruit, like Indian loquots, was then ordered in, and we ate them together, holding a discussion about Grant and Petherick, which ended by the king promising to send an officer by water to Kitangule, and another with two of my men, via Usoga and Kidi, to Gani; but as it was necessary my men should go in disguise, I asked the king to send me four mbugu and two spears; when, with the liberality of a great king, he sent me twenty sheets of the former, four spears, and a load of sun-dried fish strung on a stick in shape of a shield.

27th. – At last something was done. One Uganda officer and one Kidi guide were sent to my hut by the king, as agreed upon yesterday, when I detached Mabruki and Bilal from my men, gave them letters and maps addressed to Petherick; and giving the officers a load of Mtende to pay their hotel bills on the way, I gave them, at the same time, strict orders to keep by the Nile; then, having dismissed them, I called on the king to make arrangements for Grant, and to complain that my residence in Uganda was anything but cheerful, as my hut was a mile from the palace, in an unhealthy place, where he kept his Arab visitors. It did not become my dignity to live in houses appropriated to persons in the rank of servants, which I considered the ivory merchants to be; and as I had come only to see him and the high officers of Uganda, not seeking for ivory or slaves, I begged he would change my place of residence to the west end, when I also trusted his officers would not be ashamed to visit me, as appeared to be the case at present. Silence being the provoking resort of the king, when he did not know exactly what to say, he made no answer to my appeal, but instead, he began a discourse on geography, and then desired me to call upon his mother, N'yamasore, at her palace Masorisori, vulgarly called Soli Soli, for she also required medicine; and, moreover, I was cautioned that for the future the Uganda court etiquette required I should attend on the king two days in succession, and every third day on his mother the queen-dowager, as such were their respective rights.

Till now, owing to the strict laws of the country, I had not been able to call upon anybody but the king himself. I had not been able to send presents or bribes to any one, nor had any one, except the cockaded pages, by the king's order, visited me; neither was anybody permitted to sell me provisions, so that my men had to feed themselves by taking anything they chose from certain gardens pointed out by the king's officers, or by seizing pombe or plantains which they might find Waganda carrying towards the palace. This non-interventive order was part of the royal policy, in order that the king might have the full fleecing of his visitors.

To call upon the queen-mother respectfully, as it was the opening visit, I too, besides the medicine-chest, a present of eight brass and copper wire, thirty blue-egg beads, one bundle of diminutive beads, and sixteen cubits of chintz, a small guard, and my throne of royal grass. The palace to be visited lay half a mile beyond the king's, but the highroad to it was forbidden me, as it is considered uncourteous to pass the king's gate without going in. So after winding through back-gardens, the slums of Bandowaroga, I struck upon the highroad close to her majesty's, where everything looked like the royal palace on a miniature scale. A large cleared space divided the queen's residence from her Kamraviona's. The outer enclosures and courts were fenced with tiger-grass; and the huts, though neither so numerous nor so large, were constructed after the same fashion as the king's. Guards also kept the doors, on which large bells were hung to give alarm, and officers in waiting watched the throne-rooms. All the huts were full of women, save those kept as waiting-rooms; where drums and harmonicons were played for amusement. On first entering, I was required to sit in a waiting-hut till my arrival was announced; but that did not take long, as the queen was prepared to receive me; and being of a more affable disposition than her son, she held rather a levee of amusement than a stiff court of show. I entered the throne-hut as the gate of that court was thrown open, with my hat off, but umbrella held over my head, and walked straight towards her till ordered to sit upon my bundle of grass.

Her majesty – fat, fair, and forty-five – was sitting, plainly garbed in mbugu, upon a carpet spread upon the ground within a curtain of mbugu, her elbow resting on a pillow of the same bark material; the only ornaments on her person being an abrus necklace, and a piece of mbugu tied round her head, whilst a folding looking-glass, much the worse for wear, stood open by her side. An iron rod like a spit, with a cup on the top, charged with magic powder, and other magic wands, were placed before the entrance; and within the room, four Mabandwa sorceresses or devil-drivers, fantastically dressed, as before described, and a mass of other women, formed the company. For a short while we sat at a distance, exchanging inquiring glances at one another, when the women were dismissed, and a band of music, with a court full of Wakungu, was ordered in to change the scene. I also got orders to draw near and sit fronting her within the hut. Pombe, the best in Uganda, was then drunk by the queen, and handed to me and to all the high officers about her, when she smoked her pipe, and bade me smoke mine. The musicians, dressed in long-haired Usoga goat-skins, were now ordered to strike up, which they did, with their bodies swaying or dancing like bears in a fair. Different drums were then beat, and I was asked if I could distinguish their different tones.

The queen, full of mirth, now suddenly rose, leaving me sitting, whilst she went to another hut, changed her mbugu for a deole, and came back again for us to admire her, which was no sooner done to her heart's content, than a second time, by her order, the court was cleared, and, when only three or four confidential Wakungu were left, she took up a small faggot of well-trimmed sticks, and, selecting three, told me she had three complains. "This stick," she says, "represents my stomach, which gives me much uneasiness; this second stick my liver, which causes shooting pains all over my body; and this third one my heart, for I get constant dreams at night about Sunna, my late husband, and they are not pleasant." The dreams and sleeplessness I told her was a common widow's complaint, and could only be cured by her majesty making up her mind to marry a second time; but before I could advise for the bodily complaints, it would be necessary for me to see her tongue, feel her pulse, and perhaps, also, her sides. Hearing this, the Wakungu said, "Oh, that can never be allowed without the sanction of the king"; but the queen, rising in her seat, expressed her scorn at the idea to taking advice from a mere stripling, and submitted herself for examination.

I then took out two pills, the powder of which was tasted by the Wakungu to prove that there was no devilry in "the doctor," and gave orders for them to be eaten at night, restricting her pombe and food until I saw her again. My game was now advancing, for I found through her I should get the key to an influence that might bear on the king, and was much pleased to hear her express herself delighted with me for everything I had done except stopping her grog, which, naturally enough in this great pombe-drinking country, she said would be a very trying abstinence.

The doctoring over, her majesty expressed herself ready to inspect the honorarium I had brought for her, and the articles were no sooner presented by Bombay and Nasib, with the usual formalities of stroking to insure their purity, than she, boiling with pleasure, showed them all to her officers, who declared, with a voice of most exquisite triumph, that she was indeed the most favoured of queens. Then, in excellent good taste, after saying that nobody had ever given her such treasures, she gave me, in return, a beautifully-worked pombe sucking-pipe, which was acknowledged by every one to be the greatest honour she could pay me.

Not satisfied with this, she made me select, though against my desire, a number of sambo, called here gundu, rings of giraffe hair wound round with thin iron or copper wire, and worn as anklets; and crowned with all sundry pots of pombe, a cow, and a bundle of dried fish, of the description given in the woodcut, called by my men Samaki Kambari. This business over, she begged me to show her my picture-books, and was so amused with them that she ordered her sorceresses and all the other women in again to inspect them with her. Then began a warm and complimentary conversation, which ended by an inspection of my rings and al the contents of my pockets, as well as of my watch, which she called Lubari – a term equivalent to

375

a place of worship, the object of worship itself, or the iron horn or magic pan. Still she said I had not yet satisfied her; I must return again two days hence, for she like me much – excessively – she could not say how much; but now the day was gone, I might go. With this queer kind of adieu she rose and walked away, leaving me with my servants to carry the royal present home.

28th. – My whole thoughts were now occupied in devising some scheme to obtain a hut in the palace, not only the better to maintain my dignity, and so gain superior influence in the court, but also that I might have a better insight into the manners and customs of these strange people. I was not sorry to find the king attempting to draw me to court, daily to sit in attendance on him as his officers were obliged to do all day long, in order that he might always have a full court or escort whenever by chance he might emerge from his palace, for it gave me an opening for asserting my proper position.

Instead, therefore, of going at the call of his pages this morning I sent Bombay with some men to say that although I was desirous of seeing him daily, I could not so expose myself to the sun. In all other countries I received, as my right, a palace to live in when I called on the king of my country, and unless he gave one now I should feel slighted; moreover, I should like a hut in the same enclosure as himself, when I could sit and converse with him constantly, and teach him the use of the things I had given him. By Bombay's account, the king was much struck with the force of my humble request, and replied that he should like to have Bana, meaning myself, ever by his side, but his huts were all full of women, and therefore it could not be managed;

if, however, Bana would but have patience for a while, a hut should be built for him in the environs, which would be a mark of distinction he had never paid to any visitor before. Then changing the subject by inspecting my men, he fell so much in love with their little red "fez" caps, that he sent off his pages to beg me for a specimen, and, on finding them sent by the boys, he remarked, with warm approbation, how generous I was in supplying his wishes, and then, turning to Bombay, wished to know what sort of return-presents would please me best. Bombay, already primed, instantly said, "Oh, Bana, being a great man in his own country, and not thirsting for gain in ivory or slaves, would only accept such things as a spear, shield, or drum, which he could take to his own country as a specimen of the manufactures of Uganda, and a pleasing recollection of his visit to the king." "Ah," says Mtesa, "if that is all he wants, then indeed will I satisfy him, for I will give him the two spears with which I took all this country, and, when engaged in so doing, pierced three men with one stab.

"But, for the present, is it true what I have heard, that Bana would like to go out with me shooting?" "Oh yes, he is a most wonderful sportsman – shoots elephants and buffaloes, and birds on the wing. He would like to go out on a shooting excursion and teach you the way." Then turning the subject, in the highest good-humour the king made centurions of N'yamgundu and Maula, my two Wakungu, for their good service, he said, in bringing him such a valuable guest. This delighted them so much that as soon as they could they came back to my camp, threw themselves at my feet, and n'yanzigging incessantly, narrated their fortunes, and begged, as a great man, I would lend them some cows to present to the king as an acknowledgement for the favour he had shown them. The cows, I then told them, had come from the king, and could not go back again, for it was not the habit of white men to part with their presents; but as I felt their promotion redounded on myself, and was certainly the highest compliment their king could have paid me, I would give them each a wire to make their salaam good.

This was enough; both officers got drunk, and, beating their drums, serenaded the camp until the evening set in, when, to my utter surprise, an elderly Mganda woman was brought into camp with the commander-in-chief's metaphorical compliments, hoping I would accept her "to carry my water"; with this trifling addition, that in case I did not think her pretty enough, he hoped I would not hesitate to select which I liked from ten others, of "all colours," Wahuma included, who, for that purpose, were then waiting in his palace.

Unprepared for this social addition in my camp, I must now confess I felt in a fix, knowing full well that nothing so offends as rejecting an offer at once, so I kept her for the time being, intending in the morning to send her back with a string of blue beads on her neck; but during the night she relieved me of my anxieties by running away, which Bombay said was no wonder, for she had obviously been seized as part of some confiscated estate, and without doubt knew where to find some of her friends.

To-day, for the first time since I have been here, I received a quantity of plantains. This was in consequence of my complaining that the king's orders to my men to feed themselves at others' expense was virtually making them a pack of thieves.

1st. – I received a letter from Grant, dated 10th February, reporting Baraka's departure for Unyoro on the 30th January, escorted by Kamrasi's men on their return, and a large party of Rumanika's bearing presents as a letter from their king; whilst Grant himself hoped to leave Karague before the end of the month. I then sent Bombay to see the queen, to ask after her health, beg for a hut in the palace enclosures, and say I should have gone myself, only I feared her gate might be shut, and I cannot go backwards and forwards so far in the sun without a horse or an elephant to ride upon. She begged I would come next morning. A wonderful report came that the king put two tops of powder into his Whitworth rifle to shoot a cow, and the bullet not only passed through the cow, but through the court fence, then through the centre of a woman, and, after passing the outer fence, flew whizzing along no one knew where.

2d. – Calling on the queen early, she admitted me at once, scolding me severely for not having come or sent my men to see her after she had taken the pills. She said they did her no good, and prevailed on me to give her another prescription. Then sending her servant for a bag full of drinking-gourds, she made me select six of the best, and begged for my watch. That, of course, I could not part with; but I took the opportunity of telling her I did not like my residence; it was not only far away from everybody, but it was unworthy of my dignity. I came to Uganda to see the king and queen, because the Arabs said they were always treated with great respect; but now I could perceive those Arabs did not know what true respect means. Being poor men, they thought much of a cow or goat given gratis, and were content to live in any hovels. Such, I must inform her, was not my case. I could neither sit in the sun nor live in a poor man's hut. When I rose to leave for breakfast, she requested me to stop, but I declined, and walked away. I saw, however, there was something wrong; for Maula, always ordered to be in attendance when anybody visits, was retained by her order to answer why I would not stay with her longer. If I wanted food or pombe, there was plenty of it in her palace, and her cooks were the cleverest in the world; she hoped I would return to see her in the morning.

3d. – Our cross purposes seemed to increase; for, while I could not get a satisfactory interview, the king sent for N'yamgundu to ascertain why I had given him good guns and many pretty things which he did not know the use of, and yet I would not visit him to explain their several uses. N'yamgundu told him I lived too far off, and wanted a palace. After this I walked off to see N'yamasore, taking my blankets, a pillow, and some cooking-pots to make a day of it, and try to win the affections of the queen with sixteen cubits bindera, three pints peke, and three pints mtende beads, which, as Waganda are all fond of figurative language, I called a trifle for her servants.

I was shown in at once, and found her majesty sitting on an Indian carpet, dressed in a red linen wrapper with a gold border, and a box, in shape of a lady's work-box, prettily coloured in divers patters with minute beads, by her side. Her councillors were in attendance; and in the yard a band of music, with many minor Wakungu squatting in a semicircle, completed her levee. Maula on my behalf opened conversation, in allusion to her yesterday's question, by saying I had applied to Mtesa for a palace, that I might be near enough both their majesties to pay them constant visits. She replied, in a good hearty manner, that indeed was a very proper request, which showed my good sense, and ought to have been complied with at once; but Mtesa was only a Kijana or stripling, and as she influenced all the government of the country, she would have it carried into effect. Compliments were now passed, my presents given and approved of; and the queen, thinking I must be hungry, for she wanted to eat herself, requested me to refresh myself in another hut. I complied, spread my bedding, and ordered in my breakfast; but as the hut was full of men, I suspended a Scotch plain, and quite eclipsed her mbugu curtain.

Reports of this magnificence at once flew to the queen, who sent to know how many more blankets I had in my possession, and whether, if she asked for one, she would get it. She also desired to see my spoons, fork, and pipe – an English meerschaum, mounted with silver; so, after breakfast, I returned to see her, showed her the spoons and forks, and smoked my pipe, but told her I had no blankets left but what formed my bed. She appeared very happy and very well, did not say another word about the blankets, but ordered a pipe for herself, and sat chatting, laughing, and smoking in concert with me.

I told her I had visited all the four quarters of the globe, and had seen all colours of people, but wondered where she got her pipe from, for it was much after the Rumish (Turkish) fashion, with a long stick. Greatly tickled at the flattery, she said, "We hear men like yourself come to Amara from the other side, and drive cattle away." "The Gallas, or Abyssinians, who are tall and fair, like Rumanika," I said, "might do so, for they live not far off on the other side of Amara, but we never fight for such paltry objects. If cows fall into our hands when fighting, we allow our soldiers to eat them, while we take the government of the country into our hands." She then said, "We hear you don't like the Unyamuezi route, we will open the Ukori one for you." "Thank your majesty," said I, in a figurative kind of speech to please Waganda ears; and turning the advantage of the project on her side, "You have indeed hit the right nail on the head. I do not like the Unyamuezi route, as you may imagine when I tell you I have lost so much property there by mere robbery of the people and their kings. The Waganda do not see me in a true light; but if they have patience for a year or two, until the Ukori road is open, and trade between our respective countries shall commence, they will then see the fruits of my advent; so much so, that every Mganda will say the first Uganda year dates from the arrival of the first Mzundu (white) visitor. As one coffee-seed sown brings forth fruit in plenty, so my coming here may be considered." All appreciated this speech, saying, "The white man, he even speaks beautifully! beautifully! beautifully! beautifully!" and, putting their hands to their mouths, they looked askance at me, nodding their admiring approval.

The queen and her ministers then plunged into pombe and became uproarious, laughing with all their might and main. Small bugu cups were not enough to keep up the excitement of the time, so a large wooden trough was placed before the queen and filled with liquor. If any was spilt, the Wakungu instantly fought over it, dabbing their noses on the ground, or grabbing it with their hands, that not one atom of the queen's favour might be lost; for everything must be adored that comes from royalty, whether by design or accident. The queen put her head to the trough and drank like a pig from it, and was followed by her ministers. The band, by order, then struck up a tune called the Milele, playing on a dozen reeds, ornamented with beads and cow-tips, and five drums, of various tones and sizes, keeping time. The musicians dancing with zest, were led by four bandmasters, also dancing, but with their backs turned to the company to show off their long, shaggy, goat-skin jackets, sometimes upright, at other times bending and on their heels, like the hornpipe-dancers or western countries.

It was a merry scene, but soon became tiresome; when Bombay, by way of flattery, and wishing to see what the queen's wardrobe embraced, told her, Any woman, however ugly, would assume a goodly appearance if prettily dressed; upon which her gracious majesty immediately rose, retired to her toilet-hut, and soon returned attired in a common check cloth, and abrus tiara, a bead necklace, and with a folding looking-glass, when she sat, as before, and was handed a blown-glass cup of pombe, with a cork floating on the liquor, and a napkin mbugu covering the top, by a naked virgin. For her kind condescension in assuming plain raiment, everybody, of course, n'yanzigged. Next she ordered her slave girls to bring a large number of sambo (anklets), and begged me to select the best, for she liked me much. In vain I tried to refuse them: she had given more than enough for a keepsake before, and I was not hungry for property; still I had to choose some, or I would give offence. She then gave me a basket of tobacco, and a nest of hen eggs for her "son's" breakfast. When this was over, the Mukonderi, another dancing-tune, with instruments something like clarionets, was ordered; but it had scarcely been struck up, before a drenching rain, with strong wind, set in and spoilt the music, though not the playing – for none dared stop without an order; and the queen, instead of taking pity, laughed most boisterously over the exercise of her savage power as the unfortunate musicians were nearly beaten down by the violence of the weather.

When the rain ceased, her majesty retired a second time to her toilet-hut, and changed her dress for a puce-coloured wrapper, when I, ashamed of having robbed her of so many sambo, asked her if she would allow me to present her with a little English "wool" to hang up instead of her mbugu curtain on cold days like this.

Of course she could not decline, and a large double scarlet blanket was placed before her. "Oh, wonder of wonders!" exclaimed all the spectators, holding their mouths in both hands at a time – such a "pattern" had never been seen here before. It stretched across the hut, was higher than the men could reach – indeed it was a perfect marvel; and the man must be a good one who brought such a treasure as this to Uddu. "And why not say Uganda?" I asked. "Because all this country is called Uddu. Uganda is personified by Mtesa; and no one can say he has seen Uganda until he has been presented to the king." As I had them all in a good humour now, I complained I did not see enough of the Waganda – and as every one dressed so remarkably well, I could not discern the big men from the small; could she not issue some order by which they might call on me, as they did not dare do so without instruction, and then I, in turn, would call on them? Hearing this, she introduced me to her prime minister, chancellor of exchequer, women-keepers, hangmen, and cooks, as the first nobles in the land, that I might recognise them again if I met them on the road. All n'yanzigged for this great condescension, and said they were delighted with their guest; then producing a strip of common joho to compare it with my blanket, they asked if I could recognise it. Of course, said I, it is made in my country, of the same material, only of coarser quality, and everything of the same sort is made in Uzungu. Then, indeed, said the whole company, in one voice, we do like you, and your cloth too – but you most. I modestly bowed my head, and said their friendship was my chief desire.

This speech also created great hilarity; the queen and councillors all became uproarious. The queen began to sing, and the councillors to join in chorus; then all sang and all drank, and drank and sang, till, in their heated excitement, they turned the palace into a pandemonium; still there was not noise enough, so the band and drums were called again, and tomfool – for Uganda, like the old European monarchies, always keeps a jester – was made to sing in the gruff, hoarse, unnatural voice which he ever affects to maintain his character, and furnished with pombe when his throat was dry.

Now all of a sudden, as if a devil had taken possession of the company, the prime minister with all the courtiers jumped upon their legs, seized their sticks, for nobody can carry a spear when visiting, swore the queen had lost her heart to me, and running into the yard, returned, charging and jabbering at the queen; retreated and returned again, as if they were going to put an end to her for the guilt of loving me, but really to show their devotion and true love to her. The queen professed to take this ceremony with calm indifference, but her face showed that she enjoyed it. I was not getting very tired of sitting on my low stool, and begged for leave to depart, but N'yamasore would not hear of it; she loved me a great deal too much to let me go away at this time of day, and forthwith ordered in more pombe. The same roystering scene was repeated; cups were too small, so the trough was employed; and the queen graced it by drinking, pig-fashion, first, and then handing it round to the company.

Now, hoping to produce gravity and then to slip away, I asked if my medicines had given her any relief, that I might give her more to strengthen her. She said she could not answer that question just yet; for though the medicine had moved her copiously, as yet she had seen no snake depart from her. I told her I would give her some strengthening medicine in the morning: for the present, however, I would take my leave, as the day was far gone, and the distance home very great; but though I dragged my body away, my heart would still remain here, for I loved her much.

This announcement took all by surprise; they looked at me and then at her, and looked again and laughed, whilst I rose, waved my hat, and said, "Kua heri, Bibi" (good-bye, madam). On reaching home I found Maribu, a Mkungu, with a gang of men sent by Mtesa to fetch Grant from Kitangule by water. He would not take any of my men with him to fetch the kit from Karague, as Mtesa, he said, had given him orders to find all the means of transport; so I gave him a letter to Grant, and told him to look sharp, else Grant would have passed the Kitangule before he arrived there. "Never mind," says Maribu, "I shall walk to the mouth of the Katonga, boat it to Sese island, where Mtesa keeps all his large vessels, and I shall be at Kitangule in a very short time."

Speke and Grant at an audience granted by the queen mother.

4th. – I sent Bombay off to administer quinine to the queen; but the king's pages, who watched him making for her gateway, hurried up to him, and turned him back by force. He pleaded earnestly that I would flog him if he disobeyed my orders, but they would take all the responsibility – the king had ordered it; and then they, forging a lie, bade him run back as fast as he could, saying I wanted to see the king, but could not till his return. In this way poor Bombay returned to me half-drowned in perspiration. Just then another page hurried in with orders to bring me to the palace at once, for I had not been there these four days; and while I was preparing to express the proper amount of indignation at this unceremonious message, the last impudent page began rolling like a pig upon my mbugued or carpeted floor, till I stormed and swore I would turn him out unless he chose to behave more respectfully before my majesty, for I was no peddling merchant, as he had been accustomed to see, and would not stand it; moreover, I would not leave my hut at the summons of the king or anybody else, until I chose to do so.

This expression of becoming wrath brought every one to a sense of his duty; and I then told them all I was excessively angry with Mtesa for turning back my messenger; nobody had ever dared do such a thing before, and I would never forgive the king until my medicines had been given to the queen. As for my going to the palace, it was out of the question, as I had been repeatedly before told the king, unless it pleased him to give me a fitting residence near himself. In order now that full weight should be given to my expressions, I sent Bombay with the quinine to the king, in company with the boys, to give an account of all that had happened; and further, to say I felt exceedingly distressed I could not go to see him constantly – that I was ashamed of my domicile – the sun was hot to walk in; and when I went to the palace, his officers in waiting always kept me waiting like a servant – a matter hurtful to my honour and dignity. It now rested with himself to remove these obstacles. Everybody concerned in this matter left for the palace but Maula, who said he must stop in camp to look after Bana. Bombay no sooner arrived in the palace, and saw the king upon his throne, than Mtesa asked him why he came? "By the instructions of Bana," was his reply, "for Bana cannot walk in the sun; no white man of the sultan's breed can do so." Hearing this, the king rose in a huff, without deigning to reply, and busied himself in another court. Bombay, still sitting, waited for hours till quite tired, when he sent a boy in to say he had not delivered half my message; he had brought medicine for the queen, and as yet he had no reply for Bana. Either with haughty indifference, or else with injured pride at his not being able to command me at his pleasure, the king sent word, if medicine is brought for the queen, then let it be taken to her; and so Bombay walked off to the queen's palace. Arrived there, he sent in to say he had brought medicine, and waited without a reply till nightfall, when, tired of his charge, he gave the quinine into N'yamgundu's hands for delivery, and returned h home. Soon after, however, N'yamgundu also returned to say the queen would not take the dose to-day, but hoped I would administer it personally in the morning.

Whilst all this vexations business had been going on in court – evidently dictated by extreme jealousy because I showed, as they all thought, a preference for the queen – Maula, more than tipsy, brought a Mkungu of some standing at court before me, contrary to all law – for as yet no Mganda, save the king's pages, had ever dared enter even the precincts of my camp. With a scowling, determined, hang-dog-looking countenance, he walked impudently into my hut, and taking down the pombe-suckers the queen had given me, showed them with many queer gesticulations, intended to insinuate there was something between the queen and me. Among his jokes were, that I must never drink pombe excepting with these sticks; if I wanted any when I leave Uganda, to show my friends, she would give me twenty more sticks of that sort if I liked them; and, turning from verbal to practical jocularity, the dirty fellow took my common sucker out of the pot, inserted one of the queen's, and sucked at it himself, when I snatched and threw it away.

Maula's friend, who, I imagined, was a spy, then asked me whom I liked most – the mother or the son; but, without waiting to hear me, Maula hastily said, "The mother, the mother of course! He does not care for Mtesa, and won't go to see him." The friend coaxingly responded, "Oh no; he likes Mtesa, and will go and see him too; won't you?" I declined, however, to answer from fear of mistake, as both interpreters were away. Still the two went on talking to themselves, Maula swearing that I loved the mother most, whilst the friend said, No, he loves the son, and asking me with anxious looks, till they found I was not to be caught by chaff, and then, both tired, walked away – the friend advising me, next time I went to court, to put on an Arab's gown, as trousers are indecent in the estimation of every Mganda.

5th. – Alarmed at having got involved in something that looked like court intrigues, I called up N'yamgundu; told him all that happened yesterday, both at the two courts and with Maula at home; and begged him to apply to the king for a meeting of five elders, that a proper understanding might be arrived at; but instead of doing as I desired, he got into a terrible fright, calling Maula, and told me if I pressed the matter in this way men would lose their lives. Meanwhile the cunning blackguard Maula begged for pardon; said I quite misunderstood his meaning; all he had said was that I was very fortunate, being in such favour at court, for the king and queen both equally loved me.

N'yamgundu now got orders to go to Karague overland for Dr. K'yengo; but, dreading to tell me of it, as I had been so kind to him, he forged a falsehood, said he had leave to visit his home for six days, and begged for a wire to sacrifice to his church. I gave him what he wanted, and away he went. I then heard his servants had received orders to go overland for Grant and K'yengo; so I wrote another note to Grant, telling him to come sharp, and bring all the property by boat that he could carry, leaving what he could not behind in charge of Rumanika.

At noon, the plaguy little imps of pages hurried in to order the attendance of all my men fully armed before the king, as he wished to seize some refractory officer. I declined this abuse of my arms, and said I should first go and speak to the king on the subject myself, ordering the men on no account to go on such an errand; and saying this, I proceeded towards the palace, leaving instructions for those men who were not ready to follow. As the court messengers, however, objected to our going in detachments, I told Bombay to wait for the rest, and hurry on to overtake me. Whilst lingering on the way, every minute expecting to see my men, the Wazinza, who had also received orders to seize the same officer, passed me, going to the place of attack, and, at the same time, I heard my men firing in a direction exactly opposite to the palace. I now saw I had been duped, and returned to my hut to see the issue. The boys had deceived us all. Bombay, tricked on the plea of their taking him by a short cut to the palace, suddenly found himself with all the men opposite the fenced gardens that had to be taken – the establishment of the recusant officer – and the boys, knowing how eager all blacks are to loot, said, "Now, then, at the houses; seize all you can, sparing nothing – men, women, or children, mbugus or cowries, all alike – for it is the order of the king"; and in an instant my men surrounded the place, fired their guns, and rushed upon the inmates. One was speared forcing his way through the fence, but the rest were taken and brought triumphantly into my camp. It formed a strange sight in the establishment of an English gentleman, to see my men flushed with the excitement of their spoils, staggering under loads of mbugu, or leading children, mothers, goats, and dogs off in triumph to their respective huts.

Bombay alone, of all my men, obeyed my orders, touching nothing; and when remonstrated with for having lead the men, he said he could not help it – the boys had deceived him in the same way as they had tricked me.

It was now necessary that I should take some critical step in African diplomacy; so, after ordering all the seizures to be given up to Maula on behalf of the king, and threatening to discharge any of my men who dared retain one item of the prop-

392

erty, I shut the door of my hut to do penance for two days, giving orders that nobody but my cook Ilmas, not even Bombay, should come near me; for the king had caused my men to sin – had disgraced their red cloth – and had inflicted on me a greater insult than I could bear. I was ashamed to show my face. Just as the door was closed, other pages from the king brought the Whitworth rifle to be cleaned, and demanded an admittance; but no one dared approach me, and they went on their way again.

6th. – I still continued to do penance. Bombay, by my orders, issued from within, prepared for a visit to the king, to tell him all that had happened yesterday, and also to ascertain if the orders for sending my men on a plundering mission had really emanated from himself, when the bothering pages came again, bringing a gun and knife to be mended. My door was found shut, so they went to Bombay, asked him to do it, and told him the king desired to know if I would go shooting with him in the morning. The reply was, "No; Bana is praying to-day that Mtesa's sins might be forgiven him for having committed such an injury to him, sending his soldiers on a mission that did not become them, and without his sanction too. He is very angry about it, and wished to know if it was done by the king's orders." The boys said, "Nothing can be done without the king's orders." After further discussion, Bombay intimated that I wished the king to send me a party of five elderly officers to counsel with, and set all disagreeables to rights, or I would not go to the palace again; but the boys said there were no elderly gentlemen at court, only boys such as themselves. Bombay now wished to go with them before the king, to explain matters to him, and to give him all the red cloths of my men, which I took from them, because they defiled their uniform when plundering women and children; but the boys said the king was unapproachable just them, being engaged shooting cows before his women. He then wished the boys to carry the cloth; but they declined, saying it was contrary to orders for anybody to handle cloth, and they could not do it.

1) 1 block-tin box, 4 rich silk cloths, 1 rifle (Whitworth's), 1 gold chronometer, 1 revolver pistol, 3 rifled carbines, 3 sword-bayonets, 1 box ammunition, 1 box bullets, 1 box gun-caps, 1 telescope, 1 iron chair, 10 bundles best beads, 1 set of table-knives, spoons, and forks.

2) The straight road down the Nile through Unyoro no one dares allude to at this time, as the two kings were always fighting.

CHAPTER 12

PALACE, UGANDA – CONTINUED

Continued Diplomatic Difficulties – Negro Chaffing – The King in a New Costume – Adjutant and Heron Shooting at Court – My Residence Changed – Scenes at Court – The Kamraviona, or Commander-in-Chief – Quarrels – Confidential Communications with the King – Court Executions and Executioners – Another Day with the Queen.

7th. – The farce continued, and how to manage these haughty capricious blacks puzzled my brains considerably; but I felt that if I did not stand up now, no one would ever be treated better hereafter. I sent Nasib to the queen, to explain why I had not been to see her. I desired to do so, because I admired her wisdom; but before I went I must first see the king, to provide against any insult being offered to me, such as befell Bombay when I sent him with medicine. Having despatched him, I repaired again to the palace. In the antechamber I found a number of Wakungu, as usual, lounging about on the ground, smoking, chatting, and drinking pombe, whilst Wasoga amused them singing and playing on lap-harps, and little boys kept time on the harmonicon.

These Wakungu are naturally patient attendants, being well trained to the duty; but their very lives depend upon their presenting themselves at court a certain number of months every year, no matter from what distant part of the country they have to come. If they failed, their estates would be confiscated, and their lives taken unless they could escape. I found a messenger who consented to tell the king of my desire to see him. He returned to say that the king was sleeping – a palpable falsehood. In a huff, I walked home to breakfast, leaving my attendants, Maula and Uledi, behind to make explanations. They saw the king, who simply asked, "Where is Bana?" And on being told that I came, but went off again, he said, as I was informed, "That is a lie, for had he come here to see me he would not have returned"; then rising, he walked away and left the men to follow me.

I continued ruminating on these absurd entanglements, and the best way of dealing with them, when lo! to perplex me still more, in ran a bevy of the royal pages to ask for mtende beads – a whole sack of them; for the king wished to go with his women on a pilgrimage to the N'yanza. Thinking myself very lucky to buy the king's ear so cheaply, I sent Maula as before, adding that I considered my luck very bad, as nobody here knew my position in society, else they would not treat me as they did. My proper sphere was the palace, and unless I got a hut there, I wished to leave the country. My first desire had always been to see the king; and if he went to the N'yanza, I trusted he would allow me to go there also. The boys replied, "How can you go with his women? No one ever is permitted to see them." "Well," said I, "if I cannot go to the N'yanza with him" (thinking only of the great lake, whereas they probably meant a pond in the palace enclosures, where Mtesa constantly frolics with his women), "I wish to go to Usoga and Amara, as far as the Masai; for I have no companions here but crows and vultures." They promised to take the message, but its delivery was quite another thing; for no one can speak at this court till he is spoken to, and a word put in out of season is a life lost.

On Maula's return, I was told the king would not believe so generous a man as Bana could have sent him so few beads; he believed most of my store must have been stolen on the road, and would ask me about that to-morrow. He intimated that for the future I must fire a gun at the waiting-hut whenever I entered the palace, so that he might hear of my arrival, for he had been up that morning, and would have been glad to see me, only the boys, from fear of entering his cabinet, had forged a lie, and deprived him of any interview with me, which he had long wished to get. This ready cordiality was as perplexing as all the rest. Could it be possible, I thought, I had been fighting with a phantom all this while, and yet the king had not been able to perceive it? At all events, now, as the key to his door had been given, I would make good use of it and watch the result. Meanwhile Nasib returned from the queen-dowager's palace without having seen her majesty, though he had waited there patiently the whole day long, for she was engaged in festivities, incessantly drumming and playing, in consequence of the birth of twins (Mabassa), which had just taken place in her palace; but he was advised to return on the morrow.

8th. – After breakfast I walked to the palace, thinking I had gained all I wanted; entered, and fired guns, expecting an instant admittance; but, as usual, I was required to sit and wait; the king was expected immediately. All the Wagungu talked in whispers, and nothing was heard but the never-ceasing harps and harmonicons. In a little while I felt tired of the monotony, and wished to hang up a curtain, that I might lie down in privacy and sleep till the king was ready; but the officers in waiting forbade this, as contrary to law, and left me the only alternative of walking up and down the court to kill time, spreading my umbrella against the powerful rays of the sun. A very little of that made me fidgety and impetuous, which the Waganda noticed, and, from fear of the consequences, they began to close the gate to prevent my walking away. I flew out on them, told Bombay to notice the disrespect, and shamed them into opening it again. The king immediately, on hearing of this, sent me pombe to keep me quiet; but as I would not touch it, saying I was sick at heart, another page rushed out to say the king was ready to receive me; and, opening a side gate leading into a small open court without a hut in it, there, to be sure, was his majesty, sitting on an Arab's donkey run, propped against one page, and encompassed by four others.

On confronting him, he motioned me to sit, which I did upon my bundle of grass, and, finding it warm, asked leave to open my umbrella. He was much struck at the facility with which I could make shade, but wondered still more at my requiring it. I explained to him that my skin was white because I lived in a colder country than his, and therefore was much more sensitive to the heat of the sun than his black skin; adding, at the same time, if it gave no offence, I would prefer sitting in the shade of the court fence. He had no objection, and opened conversation by asking who it was that gave me such offence in taking my guard from me to seize his Wakungu. The boy who had provoked me was then dragged in, tied by his neck and hands, when the king asked him by whose orders he had acted in such a manner, knowing that I objected to it, and wished to speak to him on the subject first. The poor boy, in a dreadful fright, said he had acted under the instructions of the Kamraviona: there was no harm done, for Bana's men were not hurt. "Well, then," said the king, "if they were not injured, and you only did as you were ordered, no fault rests with you; but begone out of my sight, for I cannot bear to see you, and the Kamraviona shall be taught a lesson not to meddle with my guests again until I give him authority to do so." I now hoped, as I had got the king all by himself, and apparently in a good humour with me, that I might give him a wholesome lesson on the manners and customs of the English nation, to show how much I felt the slights I had received since my residence in Uganda; but he never lost his dignity and fussiness as an Uganda king. My words must pass through his Mkungu, as well as my interpreter's, before they reached him; and, as he had no patience, everything was lost till he suddenly asked Maula, pretending not to know, where my hut was; why everybody said I lived so far away; and when told, he said, "Oh! that is very far, he must come nearer." Still I could not say a word, his fussiness and self-importance overcoming his inquisitiveness.

Rain now fell, and the king retired by one gate, whilst I was shown out of another, until the shower was over. As soon as the sky was clear again, we returned to the little court, and this time became more confidential, as he asked many questions about England – such as, Whether the Queen knew anything about medicines? Whether she kept a number of women as he did?

and what her palace was like? – which gave me an opportunity of saying I would like to see his ships, for I heard they were very numerous – and also his menagerie, said to be full of wonderful animals. He said the vessels were far off, but he would send for them; and although he once kept a large number of animals, he killed them all in practising with his guns. The Whitworth rifle was then brought in for me to take to pieces and teach him the use of; and then the chronometer. He then inquired if I would like to go shooting? I said, "Yes, if he would accompany me – not otherwise." "Hippopotami?" "Yes; there is great fun in that, for they knock the boats over when they charge from below." "Can you swim?" "Yes." "So can I. And would you like to shoot buffalo?" "Yes, if you will go." "At night, then, I will send my keepers to look out for them. Here is a leopard-car, with white behind its ears, and a Ndezi porcupine of the short-quilled kind, which my people eat with great relish; and if you are fond of animals, I will give you any number of specimens, for my keepers net and bring in live animals of every kind daily; for the present, you can take this basket of porcupines home for your dinner." My men n'yanzigged – the king walked away, giving orders for another officer to follow up the first who went to Ukori, and bring Petherick quickly – and I went home.

This was to be a day of varied success. When I arrived at my hut I found a messenger sent by the queen, with a present of a goat, called "fowls for Bana, my son," and a load of plantains, called potatoes, waiting for me; so I gave the bearer fundo of mtende beads, and told again the reasons why I had not been able to call upon the queen, but I hoped to do so shortly, as the king had promised me a house near at hand. I doubt, however, whether one word of my message ever reached her. That she wanted me at her palace was evident by the present, though she was either too proud or too cautious to say so.

At night I overheard a chat between Sangizo, a Myamuezi, and Ntalo, a freed man of Zanzibar, very characteristic of their way of chaffing. Sangizo opened the battle by saying, "Ntalo, who are you?" N. "A Mguana" (freed man). S. "A Mguana, indeed! Then where is your mother?" N. "She died at Anguja." S. "Your mother died at Anguja! Then where is your father?" N. "He died at Anguja likewise." S. "Well, that is strange; and where are your brothers and sister?" N. "They all died at Anguja." S. (then changing the word Anguja for Anguza, says to Ntalo) "I think you said your mother and father both died at Anguza, did you not?" N. "Yes, at Anguza." S. "Then you had two mothers and two fathers – one set died at Anguja, and the other set at Anguza; you are a humbug; I don't believe you; you are no Mguana, but a slave who has been snatched from his family, and does not know where any of his family are. Ah! Ah! Ah!" And all the men of the camp laugh together at the wretched Ntalo's defeat; but Ntalo won't be done, so retorts by saying, "Sangizo, you may laugh at me because I am an orphan, but what are you? You are a savage – a Mshezi; you come from the Mashenzi, and you wear skins, not cloths, as men do; so hold your impudent tongue" – and the camp pealed with merry boisterous laughter again.

9th. – Early in the morning, and whilst I was in bed, the king sent his pages to request me to visit his royal mother, with some specific for the itch, with which her majesty was then afflicted. I said I could not go so far in the sun; I would wait till I received the promised palace near her. In the meanwhile I prepared to call on him. I observed, in fact, that I was an object of jealousy between the two courts, and that, if I acted skilfully and decidedly, I might become master of the situation, and secure my darling object of a passage northwards. The boys returned, bringing a pistol to be cleaned, and a message to say it was no use my thinking of calling on the king – that I must go to the queen immediately, for she was very ill. So far the queen won the day, but I did not obtain my new residence, which I considered the first step to accomplishing the greater object; I therefore put the iron farther in the fire by saying I was no man's slave, and I should not go until I got a house in the palace – Bombay could teach the boys the way to clean the pistol. The perk monkeys, however, turned up their noses at such menial service, and Uledi was instructed in their stead.

10th. – To surprise the queen, and try another dodge, I called on her with all my dining things and bedding, to make a day of it, and sleep the night. She admitted me at once, when I gave her quinine, on the proviso that I should stop there all day and night to repeat the dose, and tell her the reason why I did not come before. She affected great anger at Mtesa having interfered with my servants when coming to see her – sympathised with me on the distance I had to travel – ordered a hut to be cleared for me ere night – told me to eat my breakfast in the next court – and, rising abruptly, walked away. At noon we heard the king approaching with his drums and rattle-traps, but I still waited on till 5 P.M., when, on summons, I repaired to the throne-hut. Here I heard, in an adjoining court, the boisterous, explosive laughs of both mother and son – royal shouts loud enough to be heard a mile off, and inform the community that their sovereigns were pleased to indulge in hilarity. Immediately afterwards, the gate between us being thrown open, the king, like a very child, stood before us, dressed for the first time, in public, in what Europeans would call clothes. For a cap he wore a Muscat alfia, on his neck a silk Arab turban, fastened with a ring. Then for a coat he had an Indian kizbow, and for trousers a yellow woollen doti; whilst in his hand, in imitation of myself, he kept running his ramrod backwards and forwards through his fingers. As I advanced and doffed my hat, the king, smiling, entered the court, followed by a budding damsel dressed in red bindera, who carried the chair I had presented to him, and two new spears.

He now took his seat for the first time upon the chair, for I had told him, at my last interview, that all kings were expected to bring out some new fashion, or else the world would never make progress; and I was directed to sit before him on my grass throne. Talking, though I longed to enter into conversation, was out of the question; for no one dared speak for me, and I could not talk myself; so we sat and grinned, till in a few minutes the queen, full of smirks and smiles, joined us, and sat on a mbugu. I offered the medicine-chest as a seat, but she dared not take it; in fact, by the constitution of Uganda, no one, however high in rank, not even his mother, can sit before the king. After sundry jokes, whilst we were all bursting with laughter at the theatrical phenomenon, the Wakungu who were present, some twenty in number, threw themselves in line upon their bellies, and wriggling like fish, n'yanzigged, n'goned, and demaned, and uttered other wonderful words of rejoining – as, for instance, "Hai Minange! Hai Mkama wangi!" (O my chief! O my king!) – whilst they continued floundering, kicking about their legs, rubbing their faces, and patting their hands upon the ground, as if the king had performed some act of extraordinary munificence by showing himself to them in that strange and new position – a thing quite enough to date a new Uganda era from.

The king, without deigning to look upon his grovelling subjects, said, "Now, mother, take your medicine"; for he had been called solemnly to witness the medical treatment she was undergoing at my hands. When she had swallowed her quinine with a wry face, two very black virgins appeared on the stage holding up the double red blanket I had given the queen; for nothing, however trifling, can be kept secret from the king. The whole court was in raptures. The king signified his approval by holding his mouth, putting his head on one side, and looking askance at it. The queen looked at me, then at the blanket and her son in turn; whilst my men hung down their heads, fearful lest they should be accused of looking at the ladies of the court; and the Wakungu n'yanzigged again, as if they could not contain the gratification they felt at the favour shown them. Nobody had ever brought such wonderful things to Uganda before, and all loved Bana.

Till now I had expected to vent my wrath on both together for all past grievances, but this childish, merry, homely scene – the mother holding up her pride, her son, before the state officers – melted my heart at once. I laughed as well as they did, and said it pleased me excessively to see them both so happy together. It was well the king had broken through the old-fashioned laws of Uganda, by sitting on an iron chair, and adopting European dresses; for now he was opening a road to cement his own dominions with my country. I should know what things to send that would please him. The king listened, but without replying; and said, at the conclusion, "It is late, now let us move"; and walked away, preserving famously the lion's gait. The mother also vanished, and I was led away to a hut outside, prepared for my night's residence. It was a small, newly-built hut, just large enough for my bed, with a corner for one servant; so I turned all my men away, save one – ate my dinner, and hoped to have a quiet cool night of it, when suddenly Maula flounced in with all his boys, lighting a fire, and they spread their mbugus for the night. In vain I pleaded I could not stand the suffocation of so many men, especially of Waganda, who eat raw plantains; and unless they turned out, I should do so, to benefit by the pure air. Maula said he had the queen's orders to sleep with Bana, and sleep there he would; so rather than kick him out, which I felt inclined to do, I smoked my pipe and drank pombe all night, turning the people out and myself in, in the morning, to prepare for a small house-fight with the queen.

11th. – Early in the morning, as I expected, she demanded my immediate attendance; and so the little diplomatic affair I had anticipated came on. I began the affair by intimating that I am in bed, and have not breakfasted. So at 10 A.M. another messenger arrives, to say her majesty is much surprised at my not coming. What can such conduct mean, when she arranged everything so nicely for me after my own desire, that she might drink her medicine properly? Still I am not up; but nobody will let me rest for fear of the queen; so, to while away the time, I order Bombay to call upon her, give the quinine, and tell her all that has happened; at which she flies into a towering rage, says she will never touch medicine administered by any other hands but mine, and will not believe in one word Bombay says, either about Maula or the hut; for Maula, whose duty necessarily obliged him to take my servants before her majesty, had primed her with a lot of falsehoods on the subject; and she had a fondness for Maula, because he was a clever humbug and exceeding rogue – and sent Bombay back to fetch me, for nobody had ever dared disobey her mandates before.

It had now turned noon, and being ready for the visit, I went to see the queen. Determined to have her turn, she kept me waiting for a long time before she would show herself; and at last, when she came, she flounced up to her curtain, lay down in a huff, and vented her wrath, holding her head very high, and wishing to know how I could expect officers, with large establishments, to be turned out of their homes merely to give me room for one night; I ought to have been content with my fare; it was no fault of Maula's. I tried to explain through Nasib, but she called Nasib a liar, and listened to Maula who told the lies; then asked for her medicine; drank it, saying it was a small dose; and walked off in ill humour as she had come. I now made up my mind to sit till 3 P.M., hoping to see the queen again, whilst talking with some Kidi officers, who, contrary to the general law of the country, indulged me with some discourses on geography, from which I gathered, though their stories were rather confused, that beyond the Asua river, in the Galla country, there was another lake which was navigated by the inhabitants in very large vessels; and somewhere in the same neighbourhood there was an exceedingly high mountain covered with yellow dust, which the natives collected, etc., etc.

Time was drawing on, and as the queen would not appear of her own accord, I sent to request a friendly conversation with her before I left, endeavouring, as well as I could, to persuade her that the want of cordiality between us was owing to the mistakes of interpreters, who had not conveyed to her my profound sentiments of devotion. This brought her gracious corpulence out all smirks and smiles, preceded by a basket of potatoes for "Bana, my son." I began conversation with a speech of courtesy, explaining how I had left my brother Grant and my great friend Rumanika at Karague – hastening, in compliance with the invitation of the king, to visit him and herself, with the full hope of making friends in Uganda; but now I had come, I was greatly disappointed; for I neither saw half enough of their majesties, nor did any of their officers ever call upon me to converse and pass away the dreary hours. All seemed highly pleased, and complimented my speech; while the queen, turning to her officers, said, "If that is the case, I will send these men to you"; whereupon the officers, highly delighted at the prospect of coming to see me, and its consequence a present, n'yanzigged until I thought their hands would drop off. Then her majesty to my thorough annoyance, and before I had finished half I had to say, rose from her seat, and, showing her broad stern to the company, walked straight away. The officers then drew near me, and begged I would sleep there another night; but as they had nothing better to offer than the hut of last night, I declined and went my way, begging them to call and make friends with me.

12th. – Immediately after breakfast the king sent his pages in a great hurry to say he was waiting on the hill for me, and begged I would bring all my guns immediately. I prepared, thinking, naturally enough, that some buffaloes had been marked down; for the boys, as usual, were perfectly ignorant of his designs. To my surprise, however, when I mounted the hill half-way to the palace, I found the king standing, dressed in a rich filagreed waistcoat, trimmed with gold embroidery, tweedling the loading-rod in his fingers, and an alfia cap on his head, whilst his pages held his chair and guns, and a number of officers, with dogs and goats for offerings, squatted before him.

When I arrived, hat in hand, he smiled, examined my firearms, and proceeded for sport, leading the way to a high tree, on which some adjutant birds were nesting, and numerous vultures resting.

This was the sport; Bana must shoot a nundo (adjutant) for the king's gratification. I begged him to take a shot himself, as I really could not demean myself by firing at birds sitting on a tree; but it was all of no use – no one could shoot as I could, and they must be shot. I proposed frightening them out with stones, but no stone could reach so high; so, to cut the matter short, I killed an adjutant on the nest, and, as the vultures flew away, brought one down on the wing, which fell in a garden enclosure.

The Waganda were for a minute all spell-bound with astonishment, when the king jumped frantically in the air, clapping his hands above his head, and singing out, "Woh, woh, woh! What wonders! Oh, Bana, Bana! What miracles he performs!" – and all the Wakungu followed in chorus. "Now load, Bana –

load, and let us see you do it," cried the excited king; but before I was half loaded, he said, "Come along, come along, and let us see the bird." Then directing the officers which way to go – for, by the etiquette of the court of Uganda, every one must precede the king – he sent them through a court where his women, afraid of the gun, had been concealed. Here the rush onward was stopped by newly made fences, but the king roared to the officers to knock them down. This was no sooner said than done, by the attendants in a body shoving on and trampling them under, as an elephant would crush small trees to keep his course. So pushing, floundering through plaintain and shrub, pell-mell one upon the other, that the king's pace might not be checked, or any one come in for a royal kick or blow, they came upon the prostrate bird. "Woh, woh, woh!" cried the king again, "there he is, sure enough; come here, women – come and look what wonders!" And all the women, in the highest excitement, "woh-wohed" as loud as any of the men. But that was not enough. "Come along, Bana," said the king, "we must have some more sport"; and, saying this he directed the way towards the queen's palace, the attendants leading, followed by the pages, then the king, next myself – for I never would walk before him – and finally the women, some forty or fifty, who constantly attended him.

To make the most of the king's good-humour, while I wanted to screen myself from the blazing sun, I asked him if he would like to enjoy the pleasures of an umbrella; and before he had time to answer, held mine over him as we walked side by side. The Wakungu were astonished, and the women prattled in great delight; whilst the king, hardly able to control himself, sidled and spoke to his flatterers as if he were doubly created monarch of all he surveyed. He then, growing more familiar, said, "Now, Bana, do tell me – did you not shoot that bird with something more than common ammunition? I am sure you did, now; there was magic in it." And all I said to the contrary would not convince him. "But we will see again." "At buffaloes?" I said. "No, the buffaloes are too far off now; we will wait to go after then until I have given you a hut close by." Presently, as some herons were flying overhead, he said, "Now, shoot, shoot!" and I brought a couple down right and left. He stared, and everybody stared, believing me to be a magician, when the king said he would like to have pictures of the birds drawn and hung up in the palace; "but let us go and shoot some more, for it is truly wonderful." Similar results followed, for the herons were continually whirling round, as they had their nests upon a neighbouring tree; and then the king ordered his pages to carry all the birds, save the vulture – which, for some reason, they did not touch – and show them to the queen.

He then gave the order to move on, and we all repaired to the palace. Arrived at the usual throne-room, he took his seat, dismissed the party of wives who had been following him, as well as the Wakungu, received pombe from his female evil-eye averters, and ordered me, with my men, to sit in the sun facing him, till I complained of the heat, and was allowed to sit by his side. Kites, crows, and sparrows were flying about in all directions, and as they came within shot, nothing would satisfy the excited boy-king but I must shoot them, and his pages take them to the queen, till my ammunition was totally expended. He then wanted me to send for more shot; and as I told him he must wait for more until my brothers come, he contented himself with taking two or three sample grains and ordering his iron-smiths to make some like them.

Cows were now driven in for me to kill two with one bullet; but as the off one jumped away when the gun fired, the bullet passed through the near one, then through all the courts and fences, and away no one knew where. The king was delighted, and said he must keep the rifle to look at for the night. I now asked permission to speak with him on some important matters, when he sent his women away and listened. I said I felt anxious about the road on which Mabruki was travelling, to which I added that I had ordered him to tell Petherick to come here or else to send property to the value of one thousand dollars; and I felt anxious because some of the queen's officers felt doubtful about Waganda being able to penetrate Kidi. He said I need not concern myself on that score; he was much more anxious for the white men to come here than even I was, and he would not send my men into any danger; but it was highly improper for any of his people to speak about such subjects. Then, assembling the women again, he asked me to load Whitworth for him, when he shot the remaining cow, holding the rifle in both hands close to his thigh. The feat, of course, brought forth great and uproarious congratulations from his women. The day thus ended, and I was dismissed.

13th. – Mabriki and Bilal come into camp: they returned last night; but the Waganda escort, afraid of my obtaining information of them before the king received it, kept them concealed. They had been defeated in Usoga, two marches each of Kira, at the residence of Nagozigombi, Mtesa's border officer, who gave

them two bullocks, but advised their returning at once to inform the king that the independent Wasoga had been fighting
with his dependent Wasoga subjects for some time, and the battle would not be over for two months or more, unless he sent
an army to their assistance.

I now sent Bombay to the king to request an interview, as I
had much of importance to tell him; but the could not be seen,
as he was deep in the interior of the palace enjoying the society
of his wives. The Kamraviona, however, was found there waiting, as usual, on the mere chance of his majesty taking it into
his head to come out. He asked Bombay if it was true the
woman he gave me ran away; and when Bombay told him, he
said, "Oh, he should have chained her for two or three days, until she became accustomed to her residence; for women often
take fright and run away in that way, believing strangers to be
cannibals." But Bombay replied, "She was not good enough for
Bana; he let her go off like a dog; he wants a young and beautiful Mhuma, or none at all." "Ah, well, then, if he is so particular, he must wait a bit, for we have none on hand. What I gave
him is the sort of creature we give all our guests." A Msoga was
sent by the king to take the dead adjutant of yesterday out of
the nest – for all Wasoga are expert climbers, which is not the
case with the Waganda; but the man was attacked half-way up
the tree by a swarm of bees, and driven down again.

14th. – After all the vexatious haggling for a house, I gained
my object to-day by a judicious piece of bribery which I had intended to accomplish whenever I could. I now succeeded in
sending – for I could not, under the jealous eyes in Uganda, get
it done earlier – a present of fifteen pints mixed beads, twenty

blue eggs, and five copper bracelets, to the commander-in-chief, as a mark of friendship. At the same time I hinted that I should like him to use his influence in obtaining for me a near and respectable residence, where I hoped he, as well as all the Waganda nobility, would call upon me; for my life in Uganda was utterly miserable, being shut up like a hermit by myself every day. The result was, that a number of huts in a large plantain garden were at once assigned to me, on the face of a hill, immediately overlooking and close to the main road. It was considered the "West End." It had never before been occupied by any visitors excepting Wahinda ambassadors; and being near, and in full view of the palace, was pleasant and advantageous, as I could both hear the constant music, and see the throngs of people ever wending their way to and from the royal abodes. I lost no time in moving all my property, turning out the original occupants – in selecting the best hut for myself, giving the rest to my three officers – and ordering my men to build barracks for themselves, in street form, from my hut to the main road. There was one thing only left to be done; the sanitary orders of Uganda required every man to build himself a house of parliament, such being the neat and cleanly nature of the Waganda – a pattern to all other negro tribes.

15th. – As nobody could obtain an interview with the king yesterday, I went to the palace to-day, and fired three shots – a signal which was at once answered from within by a double discharge of a gun I had just lent him on his returning my rifle. In a little while, as soon as he had time to dress, the king, walking like a lion, sallied forth, leading his white dog, and beckoned me to follow him to the state hut, the court of which was filled with squatting men as usual, well dressed, and keeping perfect order. He planted himself on his throne, and begged me to sit by his side. Then took place the usual scene of a court levee, as described in Chapter 10, with the specialty, in this instance, that the son of the chief executioner – one of the highest officers of state – was led off for execution, for some omission or informality in his n'yanzigs, or salutes.

At this levee sundry Wakungu of rank complained that the Wanyambo plundered their houses at night, and rough-handled their women, without any respect for their greatness, and, when caught, said they were Bana's men. Bombay, who was present, heard the complaint, and declared these were Suwarora's men, who made use of the proximity of my camp to cover their own transgressions. Then Suwarora's deputation, who were also present, cringed forward, n'yanzigging like Waganda, and denied the accusation, when the king gave all warning that he would find out the truth by placing guards on the look-out at night.

Till this time the king had not heard one word about the defeat of the party sent for Petherick. His kingdom might have been lost, and he would have been no wiser; when the officer who led Mabruki came forward and told him all that had happened, stating, in addition to what I heard before, that they took eighty men with them, and went into battle three times successfully. Dismissing business, however, the king turned to me, and said he never saw anything so wonderful as my shooting in his life; he was sure it was done by magic, as my gun never missed, and he wished I would instruct him in the art. When I denied there was any art in shooting, further than holding the gun straight, he shook his head, and getting me to load his revolving pistol for him, he fired all five barrels into two cows before the multitude. He then thought of adjutant-shooting with ball, left the court sitting, desired me to follow him, and leading the way, went into the interior of the palace, where only a few select officers were permitted to follow us. The birds were wild, and as nothing was done, I instructed him in the way to fire from his shoulder, placing the gun in position. He was shy at first, and all the people laughed at my handling royalty like a schoolboy; but he soon took to it very good-naturedly, when I gave him my silk necktie and gold crest-ring, explaining their value, which he could not comprehend, and telling him we gentlemen prided ourselves on never wearing brass or copper.

He now begged hard for shot; but I told him again his only chance of getting any lay in opening the road onwards; it was on this account, I said, I had come to see him to-day. He answered, "I am going to send an army to Usoga to force the way from where your men were turned back." But this, I said, would not do for me, as I saw his people travelled like geese, not knowing the direction of Gani, or where they were going to when sent. I proposed that if he would call all his travelling men of experience together, I would explain matters to them by a map I had brought; for I should never be content till I saw Petherick.

The map was then produced. He seemed to comprehend it immediately, and assembled the desired Wakungu; but, to my mortification, he kept all the conversation to himself, Waganda fashion; spoke a lot of nonsense; and then asked his men what they thought had better be done. The sages replied, "Oh, make friends, and do the matter gently." But the king proudly raised his head, laughed them to scorn, and said, "Make friends with men who have crossed their spears with us already! Nonsense! they would only laugh at us; the Uganda spear alone shall do it." Hearing this bravado, the Kamraviona, the pages, and the elders, all rose to a man, with their sticks, and came charging at their king, swearing they would carry out his wished with their lives. The meeting now broke up in the usual unsatisfactory, unfinished manner, by the king rising and walking away, whilst I returned with the Kamraviona, who begged for ten more blue eggs in addition to my present to make a full necklace, and told my men to call upon him in the morning, when he would give me anything I wished to eat. Bombay was then ordered to describe what sort of food I lived on usually; when, Mganda fashion, he broke a stick into ten bits, each representing a differing article, and said, "Bana eat mixed food always"; and explained that stick No. 1 represented beef; No. 2, mutton; No. 3, fowl; No. 4, eggs; No. 5, fish; No. 6, potatoes; No. 7, plantains; No. 8, pombe; No. 9, butter; No. 10, flour.

16th. – To-day the king was amusing himself among his women again, and not to be seen. I sent Bombay with ten blue eggs as a present for the Kamraviona, intimating my desire to call upon him. He sent me a goat and ten fowls' eggs, saying he was not visible to strangers on business to-day. I inferred that he required the king's permission to receive me. This double failure was a more serious affair then a mere slight; for my cows were eaten up, and my men clamouring incessantly for food; and though they might by orders help themselves "ku n'yanga-nia" – by seizing – from the Waganda, it hurt my feelings so much to witness this, that I tried from the first to dispense with it, telling the king I had always flogged my men for stealing, and now he turned them into a pack of thieves. I urged that he should either allow me to purchase rations, or else feed them from the palace as Rumanika did; but he always turned a deaf ear, or said that what Sunna his father had introduced it ill became him to subvert; and unless my men helped themselves they would die of starvation.

On the present emergency I resolved to call upon the queen. On reaching the palace, I sent an officer in to announce my arrival, and sat waiting for the reply fully half an hour, smoking my pipe, and listening to her in the adjoining court, where music was playing, and her voice occasionally rent the air with merry boisterous laughing.

The messenger returned to say no one could approach her sanctuary or disturb her pleasure at this hour; I must wait and bide my time, as the Uganda officers do. Whew! Here was another diplomatic crisis, which had to be dealt with in the usual way. "I bide my time!" I said, rising in a towering passion, and thrashing the air with my ramrod walking-stick, before all the visiting Wakungu, "when the queen has assured me her door would always be open to me! I shall leave this court at once, and I solemnly swear I shall never set foot in it again, unless some apology be made for treating me like a dog." Then, returning home, I tied up all the presents her majesty had given me in a bundle, and calling Maula and my men together, told them to take them where they came from; for it ill became me to keep tokens of friendship when no friendship existed between us. I came to make friends with the queen, not to trade or take things from her – and so forth. The blackguard Maula, laughing, said, "Bana does not know what he is doing; it is a heinous offence in Uganda sending presents back; nobody for their lives dare do so to the queen; her wrath would know no bounds. She will say, 'I took a few trifles from Bana as specimens of his country, but they shall all go back, and the things the king has received shall go back also, for we are all of one family'; and then won't Bana be very sorry? Moreover, Wakungu will be killed by dozens, and lamentations will reign throughout the court to propitiate the devils who brought such disasters on them." Bombay, also in a fright, said, "Pray don't do so; you don't know these savages as we do; there is no knowing what will happen; it may defeat our journey altogether. Further, we have had no food these four days, because row succeeds row. If we steal, you flog us; and if we ask the Waganda for food, they beat us. We don't know what to do." I was imperative, however, and said, "Maula must take back these things in the morning, or stand the consequences." In fact, I found that, like the organ-grinders in London, to get myself moved on I must make myself troublesome.

17th. – The queen's presents were taken back by Maula and Nasib, whilst I went to see the Kamraviona. Even this gentleman kept me waiting for some time to show his own importance, and then admitted me into one of his interior courts, where I found him sitting on the ground with several elders; whilst Wasoga minstrels played on their lap-harps, and sang songs in praise of their king, and the noble stranger who wore fine clothes and eclipsed all previous visitors. At first, on my approach, the haughty young chief, very handsome, and twenty years of age, did not raise his head; then he begged me to be seated, and even enquired after my health, in a listless, conde-scending kind of manner, as if the exertion of talking was too much for his constitution or his rank; but he soon gave up this nonsense as I began to talk, inquired, amongst other things, why I did not see the Waganda at my house, when I said I should so much like to make acquaintance with them, and begged to be introduced to the company who were present.

I was now enabled to enlarge the list of topics on which it is prohibited to the Waganda to speak or act under pain of death. No one even dare ever talk about the royal pedigree of the coun-tries that have been conquered, or even of any neighbouring countries; no one dare visit the king's guests, or be visited by them, without leave, else the king, fearing sharers in his plun-der, would say, What are you plucking our goose for? Neither can any one cast his eye for a moment on the women of the palace, whether out walking or at home, lest he should be ac-cused of amorous intentions. Beads and brass wire, exchanged for ivory or slaves, are the only articles of foreign manufacture any Mganda can hold in his possession. Should anything else be seen in his house – for instance, cloth – his property would be confiscated and his life taken.

I was now introduced to the company present, of whom one Mgema, an elderly gentleman of great dignity, had the honour to carry Sunna the late king; Mpungu, who cooked for Sunna, also ranks high in court; then Usungu and Kunza, executioners, rank very high, enjoying the greatest confidence with the king; and, finally, Jumba and Natigo, who traced their pedigree to the age of the first Uganda king. As I took down a note of their sev-eral names, each seemed delighted at finding his name written down by me; and Kunza, the executioner, begged as a great favour that I would plead to the king to spare his son's life, who, as I have mentioned, was ordered out to execution on the last levee day. At first I thought it necessary, for the sake of maintaining my dignity, to raise objections, and said it would ill become one of my rank to make any request that might possibly be rejected; but as the Kamraviona assured me there would be no chance of failure, and everybody else agreed with him, I said it would give me intense satisfaction to serve him; and the old man squeezed my hand as if overpowered with joy.

This meeting, as might be imagined, was a very dull one, because the company, being tongue-tied as regards everything of external interest, occupied themselves solely on matters of home business, or indulged their busy tongues, Waganda fashion, in gross flattery of their "illustrious visitor." In imitation of the king, the Kamraviona now went from one hut to another, requesting us to follow that we might see all his greatness, and then took me alone into a separate court, to show me his women, some five-and-twenty of the ugliest in Uganda. This, he added, was a mark of respect he had never conferred on any person before; but, fearing lest I should misunderstand his meaning and covet any of them, he said, "Mind they are only to be looked at." As we retired to the other visitors, the Kamraviona, in return for some courteous remarks of mine, said all the Waganda were immensely pleased with my having come to visit them; and as he heard my country is governed by a woman, what would I say if he made the Waganda dethrone her, and create me king instead? Without specially replying, I showed him a map, marking off the comparative sizes of British and Waganda possessions, and shut him up. The great Kamraviona, or commander-in-chief, with all his wives, has no children, and was eager to know if my skill could avail to remove this cloud in his fortunes. He generously gave me a goat and eggs, telling my men they might help themselves to plantains from any gardens they liked beyond certain limits, provided they did not enter houses or take anything else. He then said he was tired and walked away without another word.

On returning home I found Nasib and Maula waiting for me, with all the articles that had been returned to the queen very neatly tied together. They had seen her majesty, who, on receiving my message, pretended excessive anger with her doorkeeper for not announcing my arrival yesterday – flogged him severely – inspected all the things returned – folded them up again very neatly with her own hands – said she felt much hurt at the mistake which had arisen, and hoped I would forgive and forget it, as her doors would always be open to me.

I now had a laugh at my friends Maula and Bombay for their misgivings of yesterday, telling them I knew more of human nature than they did; but they shook their heads, and said it was all very well Bana having done it, but if Arabs or any other person had tried the same trick, it would have been another affair. "Just so," said I; "but then, don't you see, I know my value here, which makes all the difference you speak of."

18th. – Whilst walking towards the palace to pay the king a friendly visit, I met two of my men speared on the head, and streaming with blood; they had been trying to help themselves to plantains carried on the heads of Waganda; but the latter proving too strong, my people seized a boy and woman from their party as witnesses, according to Uganda law, and ran away with them, tied hand and neck together. With this addition to my attendance I first called in at the Kamraviona's for justice; but as he was too proud to appear at once, I went on to the king's, fired three shots as usual, and obtained admittance at once, when I found him standing in a yard dressed in cloth, with his iron chair behind him, and my double-gun loaded with half charges of powder and a few grains of iron shot, looking eagerly about for kites to fly over. His quick eye, however, readily detected my wounded men and prisoners, as also some Wazinza prisoners led in by Waganda police, who had been taken in the act of entering Waganda houses and assailing their women. Thus my men were cleared of a false stigma; and the king, whilst praising them, ordered all the Wazinza to leave his dominions on the morrow.

The other case was easily settled by my wounded men receiving orders to keep their prisoners till claimed, when, should any people come forward, they would be punished, otherwise their loss in human stock would be enough. The Wanguana had done quite right to seize on the highway, else they would have starved; such was the old law, and such is the present one. It was no use our applying for a change of system. At this stage of the business, the birds he was watching having appeared, the king, in a great state of excitement, said, "Shoot that kite," and then "Shoot that other"; but the charges were too light; and the birds flew away, kicking with their claws as if merely stung a little.

Whilst this was going on, the Kamraviona, taking advantage of my having opened the door with the gun, walked in to make his salutations. A blacksmith produced two very handsome spears, and a fisherman a basket of fish, from which two fish were taken out and given to me. The king then sat on his iron chair, and I on a wooden box which I had contrived to stuff with the royal grass he gave me, and so made a complete miniature imitation of his throne. The folly in now allowing me to sit upon my portable iron stool, as an ingenious device for carrying out my determination to sit before him like an Englishman. I wished to be communicative, and, giving him a purse of money, told him the use and value of the several coins; but he paid little regard to them, and soon put them down. The small-talk of Uganda had much more attractions to his mind than the wonders of the outer world, and he kept it up with his Kamraviona until rain fell and dispersed the company.

19th. – As the queen, to avoid future difficulties, desired my officers to acquaint her beforehand whenever I wished to call upon her, I sent Nasib early to say I would call in the afternoon; but he had to wait till the evening before he could deliver the message, though she had been drumming and playing all the day. She then complained against my men for robbing her gardeners on the highway, wished to know why I didn't call upon her oftener, appointed the following morning for an interview, and begged I would bring her some liver medicines, as she suffered from constant twinges in her right side, sealing her "letter" with a present of a nest of eggs and one fowl.

Whilst Nasib was away, I went to the Kamraviona to treat him as I had the king. He appeared a little more affable to-day, yet still delighted in nothing but what was frivolous. My beard, for instance, engrossed the major part of the conversation; all the Waganda would come out in future with hairy faces; but when I told them that, to produce such a growth, they must wash their faces with milk, and allow a cat to lick it off, they turned up their noses in utter contempt.

20th. – I became dead tired of living all alone, with nothing else to occupy my time save making these notes every day in my office letter-book, as my store of stationery was left at Karague. I had no chance of seeing any visitors, save the tiresome pages, who asked me to give or to do something for the king every day; and my prospect was cheerless, as I had been flatly refused a visit to Usoga until Grant should come. For want of better amusement, I made a page of Lugoi, a sharp little lad, son of the late Beluch, but adopted by Uledi, and treated him as a son, which he declared he wished to be, for he liked me better than Uledi as a father. He said he disliked Uganda, where people's lives are taken like those of fowls; and wished to live at the coast, the only place he ever heard of, where all the Wanguana come from – great swells in Lugoi's estimation. Now, with Lugoi dressed in a new white pillow-case, with holes trimmed with black tape for his head and arms to go through, a dagger tied with red bindera round his waist, and a square of red blanket rolled on his shoulder as a napkin, for my gun to rest on, or in place of a goat-skin run when he wished to sit down, I walked off to inquire how the Kamraviona was, and took my pictures with me.

Lugoi's dress, however, absorbed all their thoughts, and he was made to take it off and put it on again as often as any fresh visitor came to call. Hardly a word was said about anything else; even the pictures, which generally are in such demand, attracted but little notice. I asked the Kamraviona to allow me to draw his pet dog; when the king's sister Miengo came in and sat down, laughing and joking with me immoderately.

At first there was a demur about my drawing the dog – whether from fear of bewitching the animal or not, I cannot say; but instead of producing the pet – a beautifully-formed cream-coloured dog – a common black one was brought in, which I tied in front of Miengo, and then drew both woman and dog together. After this unlawful act was discovered, of drawing the king's sister without his consent, the whole company roared with laughter, and pretended nervous excitement lest I should book them likewise. One of my men, Sangoro, did not return to camp last night from foraging; and as my men suspect the Waganda must have murdered him, I told the Kamraviona, requesting him to find out; but he coolly said, "Look for him yourselves two days more, for Wanguana often make friends with our people, and so slip away from their masters; but as they are also often murdered, provided you cannot find him in that time, we will have the Mganga out."

21st. – Last night I was turned out of my bed by a terrible hue and cry from the quarter allotted to Rozaro and his Wanyambo companions; for the Waganda had threatened to demolish my men, one by one, for seizing their pombe and plaintains, though done according to the orders of the king; and now, finding the Wanyambo nearest to the road, they set on them by moonlight, with spear and club, maltreating them severely, till, with reinforcements, the Wanyambo gained the ascendancy, seized two spears and one shield as a trophy, and drove their enemies off. In the morning, I sent the Wakungu off with the trophies to the king, again complaining that he had turned my men into a pack of highwaymen, and, as I foresaw, had thus created enmity between the Waganda and them, much to my annoyance. I therefore begged he would institute some means to prevent any further occurrence of such scenes, otherwise I would use firearms in self-defence.

Whilst these men were on this mission, I went on a like errand to the queen, taking my page Lugoi with the liver medicine. The first object of remark was Lugoi, as indeed it was everywhere; for, as I walked along, crowds ran after the little phenomenon. Then came the liver questions; and, finally what I wanted – her complaint against my men for robbing on the road, as it gave me the opportunity of telling her the king was doing what I had been trying to undo with my stick ever since I left the coast; and I begged she would use influence to correct these disagreeables. She told me for the future to send my men to her palace for food, and rob no more; in the meanwhile, here were some plantains for them. She then rose and walked away, leaving me extremely disappointed that I could not make some more tangible arrangement with her – such as, if my men came and found the gate shut, what were they to do then? There were forty-five of them; how much would she allow; etc. etc. But this was a true specimen of the method of transacting business among the royal family of Uganda. They gave orders without knowing how they are to be carried out, and treat all practical arrangements as trifling details not worth attending to.

After this unsatisfactory interview, I repaired to the king's, knowing the power of my gun to obtain an interview, whilst doubting the ability of the Wakungu to gain an audience for me.

Such was the case. These men had been sitting all day without seeing the king, and three shots opened his gate immediately to me. He was sitting on the iron chair in the shade of the court, attended by some eighty women, tweedling the loading rod in his fingers; but as my rod appeared a better one than his, they were exchanged. I then gave him a tortoise-shell comb to comb his hair straight with, as he invariably remarked on the beautiful manner in which I dressed my hair, making my uncap to show it to his women, and afterwards asked my men to bring on the affair of last night. They feared, they said, to speak on such subjects whilst the women were present. I begged for a private audience; still they would not speak until encouraged and urged beyond all patience. I said, in Kisuahili, "Kbakka" (king), "my men are afraid to tell you what I want to say"; when Maula, taking advantage of my having engaged his attention, though the king did not understand one word I said, said of himself, by way of currying favour, "I saw a wonderful gun in Rumankika's hands, with six barrells; not a short one like your fiver" (meaning the revolving pistol) "but a long one, as long as my arm." "Indeed," says the king, "we must have that." A page was then sent for by Maula, who, giving him a bit of stick representing the gun required, told him to fetch it immediately.

The king then said to me, "What is powder made of?" I began with sulphur (kibriti), intending to explain everything; but the word kibriti was enough for him, and a second stick was sent for kibriti, the bearer being told to hurry for his life and fetch it. The king now ordered some high officers who were in waiting to approach. They come, almost crouching to their knees, with eyes averted from the women, and n'yanzigged for the favour of being called, till they streamed with perspiration. Four young women, virgins, the daughters of these high officers, nicely dressed, were shown in as brides, and ordered to sit with the other women. A gamekeeper brought in baskets small antelopes, called mpeo – with straight horns resembling those of the saltiana, but with coats like the hog-deer of India – intended for the royal kitchen. Elderly gentlemen led in goats as commutation for offences, and went through the ceremonies due for the favour of being relieved of so much property. Ten cows were then driven in, plundered from Unyoro, and outside, the voices of the brave army who captured them were heard n'yanzigging vehemently. Lastly, some beautifully made shields were presented, and, because extolled, n'yanzigged over; when the king rose abruptly and walked straight away, leaving my fools of men no better off for food, no reparation for their broken heads, than if I had never gone there.

22d. – I called on the queen to inquire after her health, and to know how my men were to be fed; but, without giving me time to speak, she flew at me again about my men plundering. The old story was repeated; I had forty-five hungry men, who must have food, and unless either she or the king would make some proper provision for them, I could not help it. Again she promised to feed them, but she objected to them bearing swords, "for of what use are swords? If the Waganda don't like the Wanguana, can swords prevail in our country?" And, saying this, she walked away. I thought to myself that she must have directed the attack upon my camp last night and is angry at the Wanguana swords driving her men away. At 3 P.M. I visited the king, to have a private chat, and state my grievances; but the three shots fired brought him out to levee, when animals and sundry other things were presented; and appointments of Wakungu were made for the late gallant services of some of the men in plundering Unyoro.

The old executioner, Kunza, being present, I asked the king to pardon his son. Surprised, at first Mtesa said, "Can it be possible Bana has asked for this?" And when assured, in great glee he ordered the lad's release, amidst shouts of laughter from everybody but the agitated father, who n'yanzigged, cried, and fell at my feet, making a host of powerful signs as a token of his gratitude; for his heart was too full of emotion to give utterance to his feelings. The king them, in high good-humour, said, "You have called on me many times without broaching the subject of Usoga, and perhaps you may fancy we are not exerting ourselves in the matter; but my army is only now returning from war" (meaning plundering in Unyoro), "and I am collecting another one, which will open Usoga effectually." Before I could say anything, the king started up in his usual manner, inviting a select few to follow him to another court, when my medicine-chest was inspected, and I was asked to operate for fistula on one of the royal executioners. I had no opportunity of incurring this responsibility; for while professing to prepare for the operation, the king went off in a fling.

When I got home I found Sangoro, whom we thought lost or murdered, quietly ensconced in camp. He had been foraging by himself a long way from camp, in a neighbourhood where many of the king's women are kept; and it being forbidden ground, he was taken up by the keepers, placed in the stocks, and fed, until to-day, when he extricated his legs by means of his sword, and ran away. My ever-grumbling men mobbed me again, clamouring for food, saying, as they eyed my goats, I lived at ease and overlooked their wants. In vain I told them they had fared more abundantly than I had since we entered Uganda; whilst I spared my goats to have a little flesh of their cows as rapidly as possible, selling the skins for pombe, which I seldom tasted; they robbed me as long as I had cloth or beads, and now they had all become as fat as hogs by lifting food off the Waganda lands.

As I could not quiet them, I directed that, early next morning, Maula should go to the king and Nasib to the queen, while I proposed going to Kamraviona's to work them all three about this affair of food.

23d. – According to the plan of last night, I called early on the Kamraviona. He promised me assistance, but with an air which seemed to say, What are the sufferings of other men to me? So I went home to breakfast, doubting if anything ever would be done. As Kaggo, however, the second officer of importance, had expressed a wish to see me, I sent Bombay to him for food, and waited the upshot. Presently the king sent to say he wished to see me with my compass; for the blackguard Maula had told him I possessed a wonderful instrument, by looking at which I could find my way all over the world. I went as requested, and found the king sitting outside the palace on my chair dressed in cloths, with my silk neckerchief and crest-ring, playing his flute in concert with his brothers, some thirty-odd young men and boys, one half of them manacled, the other half free, with an officer watching over them to see that they committed no intrigues.

We then both sat side by side in the shade of the courtwalls, conversed and had music by turns; for the king had invited his brothers here to please me, the first step towards winning the coveted compass. My hair must now be shown and admired, then my shoes taken off and inspected, and my trousers tucked up to show that I am white all over. Just at this time Bombay, who had been in great request, came before us laden with plantains. This was most opportune; for the king asked what he had been about, and then the true state of the case as regards my difficulties in obtaining food were, I fancy, for the first time, made known to him. In a great fit of indignation he said, "I once killed a hundred Wakungu in a single day, and now, if they won't feed my guests, I will kill a hundred more; for I know the physic for bumptiousness." Then, sending his brothers away, he asked me to follow him into the back part of the palace, as he loved me so much he must show me everything. We walked along under the umbrella, first looking down one street of huts, then up another, and, finally, passing the sleeping-chamber, stopped at one adjoining it. "That hut," said the king, "is the one I sleep in; no one of my wives dare venture within it unless I call her." He let me feel immediately that for the distinction conferred on me in showing me this sacred hut a return was expected. Could I after that refuse him such a mere trifle as a compass? I told him he might as well put my eyes out and ask me to walk home, as take away that little instrument, which could be of no use to him, as he could not read or understand it. But this only excited his cupidity; he watched it twirling round and pointing to the north, and looked and begged again, until, tired of his importunities, I told him I must wait until the Usoga road was open before I could part with it, and then the compass would be nothing to what I would give him. Hearing this, "That is all on my shoulders; as sure as I live it shall be done; for that country has no king, and I have long been desirous of taking it." I declined, however, to give him the instrument on the security of his promise, and he went to breakfast.

I walked off to Usungu to see what I could do for him in his misery. I found that he had a complication of evils entirely beyond my healing power, and among them inveterate forms of the diseases which are generally associated with civilisation and its social evils. I could do nothing to cure him, but promised to do whatever was in my power to alleviate his sufferings.

24th. – Before breakfast I called on poor Usungu, prescribing hot coffee to be drunk with milk every morning, which astonished him not a little, as the negroes only use coffee for chewing. He gave my men pombe and plantains. On my return I met a page sent to invite me to the palace. I found the king sitting with a number of women. He was dressed in European clothes, part of them being a pair of trousers he begged for yesterday, that he might appear like Bana. This was his first appearance in trousers, and his whole attire, contrasting strangely with his native habiliments, was in his opinion very becoming, though to me a little ridiculous; for the legs of the trousers, as well as the sleeves of the waistcoat, were much too short, so that his black feet and hands stuck out at the extremities as an organ-player's monkey's do, whilst the cockscomb on his head prevented a fez cap, which was part of his special costume for the occasion, from sitting properly. This display over, the women were sent away, and I saw shown into a court, where a large number of

Women of HM Mtesa's palace being led to execution.

plantains were placed in a line upon the ground for my men to take away, and we were promised the same treat every day. From this we proceeded to another court, where we sat in the shade together, when the women returned again, but were all dumb, because my interpreters dared not for their lives say anything, even on my account, to the king's women. Getting tired, I took out my sketch-book and drew Lubuga, the pet, which amused the king immensely as he recognised her cockscomb.

Then twenty naked virgins, the daughters of Wakungu, all smeared and shining with grease, each holding a small square of mbugu for a fig-leaf, marched in a line before us, as a fresh addition to the harem, whilst the happy fathers floundered n'yanzigging on the ground, delighted to find their darlings appreciated by the king. Seeing this done in such a quiet mild way before all my men, who dared not lift their heads to see it, made me burst into a roar of laughter, and the king, catching the infection from me, laughed as well: but the laughing did not end there – for the pages, for once giving way to nature, kept bursting – my men chuckled in sudden gusts – while even the women, holding their mouths for fear of detection, responded – and we all laughed together. Then a sedate old dame rose from the squatting mass, ordered the virgins to right-about, and marched them off, showing their still more naked reverses. I now obtained permission for the Wakungu to call upon me, and fancied I only required my interpreters to speak out like men when I had anything to say, to make my residence in Uganda both amusing and instructive; but though the king, carried off by the prevailing good-humour of the scene we had both witnessed, supported me, I found that he had counter-ordered what he had said as soon as I had gone, and, in fact, no Mkungu ever dared come near me.

25th. – To-day I visited Usungu again, and found him better. He gave pombe and plantains for my people, but would not talk to me, though I told him he had permission to call on me.

I have now been for some time within the court precincts, and have consequently had an opportunity of witnessing court customs. Among these, nearly every day since I have changed my residence, incredible as it may appear to be, I have seen one, two, or three of the wretched palace women led away to execution, tied by the hand, and dragged along by one of the body-guard, crying out, as she went to premature death, "Hai Minange!" (O my lord!) "Kbakka!" (My king!) "Hai N'yawo!" (My mother!) at the top of her voice, in the utmost despair and lamentation; and yet there was not a soul who dared lift hand to save any of them, though many might be heard privately commenting on their beauty.

26th. – To-day, to amuse the king, I drew a picture of himself holding a levee, and proceeded to visit him. On the way I found the highroad thronged with cattle captured in Unyoro; and on arrival at the ante-chamber, amongst the officers in waiting, Masimbi (Mr. Cowries or Shells), the queen's uncle, and Congow, a young general, who once led an army into Unyoro, past Kamrasi's palace. They said they had obtained leave for me to visit them, and were eagerly looking out for the happy event. At once, on firing, I was admitted to the king's favourite place, which, now that the king had a movable chair to sit upon, was the shade of the court screen. We had a chat; the picture was shown to the women; the king would like to have some more, and gave me leave to draw in the palace any time I liked. At the same time he asked for my paint-box, merely to look at it. Though I repeatedly dunned him for it, I could never get it back from him until I was preparing to leave Uganda.

27th. – After breakfast I started on a visit to Congow; but finding he had gone to the king as usual, called at Masimbi's and he being absent also, I took advantage of my proximity to the queen's palace to call on her majesty. For hours I was kept waiting; firstly, because she was at breakfast; secondly, because she was "putting on medicine"; and, thirdly, because the sun was too powerful for her complexion; when I became tired of her nonsense, and said, "If she does not wish to see me, she had better say so at once, else I shall walk away; for the last time I came I saw her but for a minute, when she rudely turned her back upon me, and left me sitting by myself." I was told not to be in a hurry – she would see me in the evening. This promise might probably be fulfilled six blessed hours from the time when it was made; but I thought to myself, every place in Uganda is alike when there is no company at home, and so I resolved to sit the time out, like Patience on a monument, hoping something funny might turn up after all.

At last her majesty stumps out, squats behind my red blanket, which is converted into a permanent screen, and says hastily, or rather testily, "Can't Bana perceive the angry state of the weather? Clouds flying about, and the wind blowing half a gale? Whenever that is the case, I cannot venture out." Taking her lie without an answer, I said, I had now been fifty days or so doing nothing in Uganda – not one single visitor of my own rank ever came near me, and I could not associated with people far below her condition and mine – in fact, all I had to amuse me at home now was watching a hen lay her eggs upon my spare bed. Her majesty became genial, as she had been before, and promised to provide me with suitable society. I then told her I had desired my officers several times to ask the king how marriages were conducted in this country, as they appeared so different from ours, but they always said they dared not put such a question to him, and now I hoped she would explain it to me. To tell her I could not get anything from the king, I knew would be the surest way of eliciting what I wanted from her, because of the jealousy between the two courts; and in this instance it was fully proved, for she brightened up at once, and, when I got her to understand something of what I meant by a marriage ceremony, in high good humour entered on a long explanation, to the following effect: There are no such things as marriages in Uganda; there are no ceremonies attached to it. If any Mkungu possessed of a pretty daughter committed an offence, he might give her to the king as a peace-offering; if any neighbouring king had a pretty daughter, and the king of Uganda wanted her, she might be demanded as a fitting tribute. The Wakungu in Uganda are supplied with women by the king, according to their merits, from seizures in battle abroad, or seizures from refractory officers at home. The women are not regarded as property according to the Wanyamuezi practice, though many exchange their daughters; and some women, for misdemeanours, are sold into slavery; whilst others are flogged, or are degraded to do all the menial services of the house.

The Wakungu then changed the subject by asking, if I married a black woman, would there be any offspring, and what would be their colour? The company now became jovial, when the queen improved it by making a significant gesture, and with roars of laughter asking me if I would like to be her son-in-law, for she had some beautiful daughters, either of the Wahuma, or Waganda breed. Rather staggered at first by this awful proposal, I consulted Bombay what I should do with one if I got her. He, looking more to number one than my convenience, said, "By all means accept the offer, for if YOU don't like her, WE should, and it would be a good means of getting her out of this land of death, for all black people love Zanzibar." The rest need not be told; as a matter of course I had to appear very much gratified, and as the bowl went round, all became uproarious. I must wait a day or two, however, that a proper selection might be made; and when the marriage came off, I was to chain the fair one two or three days, until she became used to me, else, from mere fright, she might run away.

To keep up the spirits of the queen, though her frequent potions of pombe had wellnigh done enough, I admired her neck-ring, composed of copper wire, with a running inlaid twist of iron, and asked her why she wore such a wreath of vine-leaves, as I had often seen on some of the Wakungu. On this she produced a number of rings similar to the one she wore, and taking off her own, placed it round my neck. Then, pointing to her wreath, she said, "This is the badge of a kidnapper's office – whoever wears it, catches little children." I inferred that its possession, as an insignia of royalty, conferred on the bearer the power of seizure, as the great seal in this country confers power on public officers.

The queen's dinner was now announced; and, desiring me to

remain where I was for a short time, she went to it. She sent me several dishes (plantain-leaves), with well-cooked beef and mutton, and a variety of vegetables, from her table, as well as a number of round moist napkins, made in the shape of wafers, from the freshly-drawn plantain fibres, to wash the hands and face with. There was no doubt now about her culinary accomplishments. I told her so when she returned, and that I enjoyed her parties all the more because they ended with a dinner. "More pombe, more pombe," cried the queen, full of mirth and glee, helping everybody round in turn, and shouting and laughing at their Kiganda witticisms – making, though I knew not a word said, an amusing scene to behold – till the sun sank; and her majesty remarking it, turned to her court and said, "If I get up, will Bana also rise, and not accuse me of deserting him?" With this speech a general rising took place, and, watching the queen's retiring, I stood with my hat in hand, whilst all the Wakungu fell upon their knees, and then all separated.

28th. – I went to the palace, and found, as usual, a large levee waiting the king's pleasure to appear; amongst whom were the Kamraviona, Masimbi, and the king's sister Miengo. I fired my gun, and admitted at once, but none of the others could follow me save Miengo. The king, sitting on the chair with his women by his side, ordered twelve cloths, the presents of former Arab visitors, to be brought before him; and all of these I was desired to turn into European garments, like my own coats, trousers, and waistcoats. It was no use saying I had no tailors – the thing must be done somehow; for he admired my costume exceedingly, and wished to imitate it now he had cloth enough for ever to dispense with the mbugu.

As I had often begged the king to induce his men, who are all wonderfully clever artisans, to imitate the chair and other things I gave him, I now told him if he would order some of his sempsters, who are far cleverer with the needle than my men, to my camp, I would cut up some old clothes, and so teach them how to work. This was agreed to, and five cows were offered as a reward; but as his men never came, mine had to do the job.

Maula then engaged the king's attention for fully an hour, relating what wonderful things Bana kept in his house, if his majesty would only deign to see them; and for this humbug got rewarded by a present of three women. Just at this juncture an adjutant flew overhead, and, by way of fun, I presented my gun, when the excited king, like a boy from school, jumped up, forgetting his company, and cried, "Come, Bana, and shoot the nundo; I know where he has gone – follow me." And away we went, first through one court, then through another, till we found the nundo perched on a tree, looking like a sedate old gentleman with a bald head, and very sharp, long nose. Politeness lost the bird; for whilst I wished the king to shoot, he wished me to do so, from fear of missing it himself. He did not care about vultures – he could practise at them at any time; but he wanted a nundo above all things. The bird, however, took the hint, and flew away.

CHAPTER 13

PALACE, UGANDA – CONTINUED

A Visit to a Distinguished Statesman – A Visit from the King – Royal Sport – The Queen's Present of Wives – The Court Beauties and Their Reverses – Judicial Procedure in Uganda – Buffalo-Hunting – A Musical Party – My Medical Practice – A Royal Excursion on the N'yanza – The Canoes of Uganda – A Regatta – Rifle Practice – Domestic Difficulties – Interference of a Magician – The King's Brothers.

29th. – According to appointment I went early this morning to visit Congow. He kept me some time waiting in his outer hut, and then called me in to where I found him sitting with his women – a large group, by no means pretty. His huts are numerous, the gardens and courts all very neat and well kept. He was much delighted with my coming, produced pombe, and asked me what I thought of his women, stripping them to the waist. He assured me that he had thus paid me such a compliment as nobody else had ever obtained, since the Waganda are very jealous of one another – so much so, that any one would be killed if found starring upon a woman even in the highways. I asked him what use he had for so many women? To which he replied, "None whatever; the king gives them to us to keep up our rank, sometimes as many as one hundred together, and we either turn them into wives, or make servants of them, as we please." Just then I heard that Mkuenda, the queen's woman-keeper, was outside waiting for me, but dared not come in, because Congow's women were all out; so I asked leave to go home to breakfast, much to the surprise of Congow, who thought I was his guest for the whole day. It is considered very indecorous in Uganda to call upon two persons in one day, though even the king or the queen should be one of them. Then, as there was no help for it – Congow could not detain me when hungry – he showed me a little boy, the only child he had, and said, with much fatherly pride, "Both the king and queen have called on me to see this fine little fellow"; and we parted to meet again some other day. Outside his gate I found Mkuenda, who said the queen had sent him to invite "her son" to bring her some stomach medicine in the morning, and come to have a chat with her. With Mkuenda I walked home; but he was so awed by the splendour of my hut, with its few blankets and bit of chintz, that he would not even sit upon a cow-skin, but asked if any Waganda dared venture in there. He was either too dazzled or too timid to answer any questions, and in a few minutes walked away again.

After this, I had scarcely swallowed by breakfast before I received a summons from the king to meet him out shooting, with all the Wanguana armed, and my guns; and going towards the palace, found him with a large staff, pages and officers as well as women, in a plantain garden, looking eagerly out for birds, whilst his band was playing. In addition to his English dress, he wore a turban, and pretended that the glare of the sun was distressing his eyes – for, in fact, he wanted me to give him a wideawake like my own. Then, as if a sudden freak had seized him, though I knew it was on account of Maula's having excited his curiosity, he said, "Where does Bana live? Lead away." Bounding and scrambling, the Wakungu, the women and all, went pell-mell through everything towards my hut. If the Kamraviona or any of the boys could not move fast enough, on account of the crops on the fields, they were piked in the back till half knocked over; but, instead of minding, they trotted on, n'yanzigging as if honoured by a kingly poke, though treated like so many dogs.

Arrived at the hut, the king took off his turban as I took off my hat, and seated himself on my stool; whilst the Kamraviona, with much difficulty, was induced to sit upon a cowskin, and the women at first were ordered to squat outside. Everything that struck the eye was much admired and begged for, though nothing so much as my wideawake and mosquito-curtains; then, as the women were allowed to have a peep in and see Bana in his den, I gave them two sacks of beads, to make the visit profitable, the only alternative left me from being forced into inhospitality, for no one would drink from my cup. Moreover, a present was demanded by the laws of the country.

The king, excitedly impatient, now led the way again, shooting hurry-scurry through my men's lines, which were much commented on as being different from Waganda hutting, on to the tall tree with the adjutant's nest. One young bird was still living in it. There was no shot, so bullets must be fired; and the cunning king, wishing to show off, desired me to fire simultaneously with himself. We fired, but my bullet struck the bough the nest was resting on; we fired again, and the bullet passed through the nest without touching the bird. I then asked the king to allow me to try his Whitworth, to which a little bit of stick, as a charm to secure a correct aim, had been tied below the trigger-guard. This time I broke the bird's leg, and knocked him half out of the nest; so, running up to the king, I pointed to the charm, saying, That has done it – hoping to laugh him out of the folly; but he took my joke in earnest, and he turned to his men, commenting on the potency of the charm. Whilst thus engaged, I took another rifle and brought the bird down altogether. "Woh, woh, woh!" shouted the king; "Bana, Mzungu, Mzungu!" he repeated, leaping and clapping his hands, as he ran full speed to the prostrate bird, whilst the drums beat, and the Wakungu followed him: "Now, is not this a wonder? But we must go and shoot another." "Where?" I said; "we may walk a long way without finding, if we have nothing but our eyes to see with. Just send for your telescope, and then I will show you how to look for birds." Surprised at this announcement, the king sent his pages flying for the instrument, and when it came I instructed him how to use it; when he could see with it, and understand its powers, his astonishment knew no bounds; and, turning to his Wakungu, he said, laughing, "Now I do see the use of this thing I have been shutting up in the palace. On that distant tree I can see three vultures. To its right there is a hut, with a woman sitting inside the portal, and many goats are feeding all about the palace, just as large and distinct as if I was close by them." The day was now far spent, and all proceeded towards the palace.

On the way a mistletoe was pointed out as a rain-producing tree, probably because, on a former occasion, I had advised the king to grow groves of coffee-trees about his palace to improve its appearance, and supply the court with wholesome food – at the same time informing him that trees increase the falls of rain in a country, though very high ones would be dangerous, because they attract lightning. Next the guns must be fired off; and, as it would be a pity to waste lead, the king, amidst thunders of applause, shot five cows, presenting his gun from the shoulder.

So ended the day's work in the field, but not at home; for I had hardly arrived there before the pages hurried in to beg for powder and shot, then caps, then cloth, and, everything else failing, a load of beads. Such are the persecutions of this negro land – the host every day must beg something in the most shameless manner from his guest, on the mere chance of gaining something gratis, though I generally gave the king some trifle when he least expected it, and made an excuse that he must wait for the arrival of fresh stores from Gani when he asked.

30th. – To fulfil my engagement with the queen, I walked off to her palace with stomach medicine, thinking we were now such warm friends, all pride and distant ceremonies would be dispensed with; but, on the contrary, I was kept waiting for hours till I sent in word to say, if she did not want medicine, I wished to go home, for I was tired of Uganda and everything belonging to it. This message brought her to her gate, where she stood laughing till the Wahuma girls she had promised me, one of twelve and the other a little older, were brought in and made to squat in front of us. The elder, who was in the prime of youth and beauty, very large of limb, dark in colour, cried considerably; whilst the younger one, though very fair, had a snubby nose and everted lips, and laughed as if she thought the change in her destiny very good fun. I had now to make my selection, and took the smaller one, promising her to Bombay as soon as we arrived on the coast, where, he said, she would be considered a Hubshi or Abyssinian. But when the queen saw what I had done, she gave me the other as well, saying the little one was too young to go alone, and, if separated, she would take fright and run away. Then with a gracious bow I walked of with my two fine specimens of natural history, though I would rather have had princes, that I might have taken them home to be instructed in England; but the queen, as soon as we had cleared the palace, sent word to say she must have another parting look at her son with his wives. Still laughing, she said, "That will do; you look beautiful; now go away home"; and off we trotted, the elder sobbing bitterly, the younger laughing.

As soon as we reached home, my first inquiry was concerning their histories, of which they appeared to know but very little. The elder, whom I named Meri (plantains), was obtained by Sunna, the late king, as a wife, from Nkole; and though she was a mere Kahala, or girl, when the old king died, he was so attached to her he gave her twenty cows, in order that she might fatten up on milk after her native fashion; but on Sunna's death, when the establishment of women was divided, Meri fell to N'yamasore's (the queen's) lot. The lesser one, who still retains the name of Kahala, said she was seized in Unyoro by the Waganda, who took her to N'yamasore, but what became of her father and mother she could not say.

It was now dinner-time, and as the usual sweet potatoes and goat's flesh were put upon my box-table, I asked them to dine with me, and we became great friends, for they were assured they would finally get good houses and gardens at Zanzibar; but nothing would induce either of them to touch food that had been cooked with butter. A dish of plantains and goat-flesh was then prepared; but though Kahala wished to eat it, Meri rejected the goat's flesh, and would not allow Kahala to taste it either; and thus began a series of domestic difficulties. On inquiring how I could best deal with my difficult charge, I was told the Wahuma pride was so great, and their tempers so strong, they were more difficult to break in than a phunda, or donkey, though when once tamed, they became the best of wives.

31st. – I wished to call upon the queen and thank her for her charming present, but my hungry men drove me to the king's palace in search of food. The gun firing brought Mtesa out, prepared for a shooting trip, with his Wakungu leading, the pages carrying his rifle and ammunition, and a train of women behind. The first thing seen outside the palace gate was a herd of cows, from which four were selected and shot at fifty paces by the king, firing from his shoulder, amidst thunders of applause and hand-shakings of the elders. I never saw them dare touch the king's hand before. Then Mtesa, turning kindly to me, said, "Pray take a shot"; but I waived the offer off, saying he could kill better himself. Ambitious of a cut above cows, the king tried his hand at some herons perched on a tree, and, after five or six attempts, hit one in the eye. Hardly able to believe in his own skill, he stood petrified at first, and then ran madly to the fallen bird, crying, "Woh, woh, woh! Can this be? Is it true? Woh, woh!" He jumped in the air, and all his men and women shouted in concert with him. Then he rushes at me, takes both my hands – shakes, shakes – woh, woh! – then runs to his women, then to his men; shakes them all, woh-wohing, but yet not shaking or wohing half enough for his satisfaction, for he is mad with joy at his own exploit.

The bird is then sent immediately to his mother, whilst he retires to his palace, woh-wohing, and taking "ten to the dozen" all the way and boasting of his prowess. "Now, Bana, tell me – do you not think, if two such shots as you and I were opposed to an elephant, would he have any chance before us? I know I can shoot – I am certain of it now. You have often asked me to go hippopotamus-shooting with you, but I staved it off until I learnt the way to shoot. Now, however, I can shoot – and that remarkably well too, I flatter myself. I will have at them, and both of us will go on the lake together." The palace was now reached; musicians were ordered to play before the king, and Wakungu appointments were made to celebrate the feats of the day. Then the royal cutler brought in dinner-knives made of iron, inlaid with squares of copper and brass, and goats and vegetables were presented as usual, when by torchlight we were dismissed, my men taking with them as many plantains as they could carry.

1st. – I stayed at home all this day, because the king and queen had set it apart for looking at and arranging their horns – mapembe, or fetishes, as the learned call such things – to see that there are no imperfections in the Uganga. This was something like an inquiry into the ecclesiastical condition of the country, while, at the same time, it was a religious ceremony, and, as such, was appropriate to the first day after the new moon appears. This being the third moon by account, in pursuance of ancient customs, all the people about court, including the king, shaved their heads – the king, however, retaining his cockscomb, the pages their double cockades, and the other officers their single cockades on the back of the head, or either side, according to the official rank of each. My men were occupied making trousers for the king all day; whilst the pages, and those sent to learn the art of tailoring, instead of doing their duty, kept continually begging for something to present the king.

2d. – The queen now taking a sporting fit into her head, sent for me early in the morning, with all my men, armed, to shoot a crested crane in her palace; but though we were there as required, we were kept waiting till late in the afternoon, when, instead of talking about shooting, as her Wakungu had forbidden her doing it, she asked after her two daughters – whether they had run away, or if they liked their new abode? I replied I was sorry circumstances did not permit my coming to thank her sooner, for I felt grateful beyond measure to her for having charmed my house with such beautiful society. I did not follow her advice to chain either of them with iron, for I found cords of love, the only instrument white men know the use of, quite strong enough. Fascinated with this speech, she said she would give me another of a middle age between the two, expecting, as I thought, that she would thus induce me to visit her more frequently than I did her son; but, though I thanked her, it frightened me from visiting her for ages after.

She then said, with glowing pride, casting a sneer on the king's hospitality, "In the days of yore, Sunna, whenever visitors came to see him, immediately presented them with women, and, secondly, with food; for he was very particular in looking after his guests' welfare, which is not exactly what you find the case now, I presume." The rest of the business of the day consisted in applications for medicine and medical treatment, which it was difficult satisfactorily to meet.

3d. – To-day Katumba, the king's head page, was sent to me with deoles to be made into trousers and waistcoats, and a large sixty-dollar silk I had given him to cover the chair with. The king likes rich colours, and I was solemnly informed that he will never wear anything but clothes like Bana.

4th. – By invitation I went to the palace at noon, with guns, and found the king holding a levee, the first since the new moon, with all heads shaved in the manner I have mentioned. Soon rising, he showed the way through the palace to a pond, which is described as his bathing N'yanza, his women attending, and pages leading the way with his guns. From this we passed on to a jungle lying between the palace hill and another situated at the northern end of the lake, where wild buffaloes frequently lie concealed in the huge papyrus rushes of a miry drain; but as none could be seen at that moment, we returned again to the palace. He showed me large mounds of earth, in the shape of cocked hats, which are private observatories, from which the surrounding country can be seen. By the side of these observatories are huts, smaller than the ordinary ones used for residing in, where the king, after the exertion of "looking out," takes his repose. Here he ordered fruit to be brought – the Matunguru, a crimson pod filled with acid seeds, which has only been observed growing by the rivers or waters of Uganda – and Kasori, a sort of liquorice-root. He then commenced eating with us, and begging again, unsuccessfully, for my compass. I tried again to make him see the absurdity of tying a charm on Whitworth's ri-

450

fle, but without the least effect. In fact he mistook all my answers for admiration, and asked me, in the simplest manner possible, if I would like to possess a charm; and even when I said "No, I should be afraid of provoking Lubari's" (God's) "anger if I did so," he only wondered at my obstinacy, so thoroughly was he wedded to his belief. He then called for his wideawake, and walked with us into another quarter of his palace, when he entered a dressing-hut, followed by a number of full-grown, stark-naked women, his valets; at the same time ordering a large body of women to sit on one side the entrance, whilst I, with Bombay, were directed to sit on the other, waiting till he was ready to hold another levee. From this, we repaired to the great throne-hut, where all his Wakungu at once formed court, and business was commenced. Amongst other things, an officer, by name Mbogo, or the Buffalo, who had been sent on a wild-goose chase to look after Mr. Petherick, described a journey he had made, following down the morning sun. After he had passed the limits of plantain-eating men, he came upon men who lived upon meat alone, who never wore mbugus, but either cloth or skins, and instead of the spear they used the double-edged sime. He called the people Wasewe, and their chief Kisawa; but the company pronounced them to be Masawa (Masai).

After this, about eighty men were marched into the court, with their faces blackened, and strips of plantain-bark tied on their heads, each holding up a stick in his hand in place of a spear, under the regulation that no person is permitted to carry weapons of any sort in the palace. They were led by an officer, who, standing like a captain before his company, ordered them to jump and praise the king, acting the part of fugleman himself. Then said the king, turning to me, "Did I not tell you I had sent many men to fight? These are some of my army returned; the rest are coming, and will eventually, when all are collected, go in a body to fight in Usoga." Goats and other peace-offerings were then presented; and, finally a large body of officers came in with an old man, with his two ears shorn off for having been too handsome in his youth, and a young woman who, after four days' search, had been discovered in his house. They were brought for judgment before the king.

Nothing was listened to but the plaintiff's statement, who said he had lost the woman four days, and, after considerable search, had found her concealed by the old man, who was indeed old enough to be her grandfather. From all appearances one would have said the wretched girl had run away from the plaintiff's house in consequence of ill treatment, and had harboured herself on this decrepid old man without asking his leave; but their voices in defence were never heard, for the king instantly sentenced both to death, to prevent the occurrence of such impropriety again; and, to make the example more severe, decreed that their lives should not be taken at once, but, being fed to preserve life as long as possible, they were to be dismembered bit by bit, as rations for the vultures, every day, until life was extinct. The dismayed criminals, struggling to be heard, in utter despair, were dragged away boisterously in the most barbarous manner, to the drowning music of the milele and drums.

The king, in total unconcern about the tragedy he had thus enacted, immediately on their departure said, "Now, then, for shooting, Bana; let us look at your gun." It happened to be

loaded, but fortunately only with powder, to fire my announcement at the palace; for he instantly placed caps on the nipples,
and let off one barrel by accident, the contents of which stuck
in the thatch. This created a momentary alarm, for it was supposed the thatch had taken fire; but it was no sooner sup-
pressed than the childish king, still sitting on his throne, to astonish his officers still more, levelled the gun from his shoulder,
fired the contents of the second barrel into the faces of his
squatting Wakungu, and then laughed at his own trick. In the
meanwhile cows were driven in, which the king ordered his
Wakungu to shoot with carbines; and as they missed them, he
showed them the way to shoot with the Whitworth, never missing. The company now broke up, but I still clung to the king,
begging him to allow me to purchase food with beads, as I
wanted it, for my establishment was always more or less in a
starving state; but he only said, "Let us know what you want
and you shall always have it"; which, in Uganda, I knew from
experience only meant, Don't bother me any more, but give me
your spare money, and help yourself from my spacious gardens
– Uganda is before you.

5th – To-day the king went on a visit with his mother, and
therefore neither of them could be seen by visitors. I took a
stroll towards the N'yanza, passing through the plantain-groves
occupied by the king's women, where my man Sangoro had
been twice taken up by the Mgemma and put in the stocks. The
plantain gardens were beautifully kept by numerous women,
who all ran away from fright at seeing me, save one who, taken
by surprise, threw herself flat on the ground, rolled herself up
in her mbugu, and, kicking with her naked heels, roared mur-

der and help, until I poked her up, and reproached her for her folly. This little incident made my fairies bolder, and, sidling up to me one by one, they sat in a knot with me upon the ground; then clasping their heads with their hands, they woh-wohed in admiration of the white man; they never in all their lives saw anything so wonderful; his wife and children must be like him; what would not Sunna have given for such a treat? – but it was destined to Mtesa's lot. What is the interpretation of this sign, if it does not point to the favour in which Mtesa is upheld by the spirits? I wished to go, but no: "Stop a little more," they said, all in a breath, or rather out of breath in their excitement; "remove the hat and show the hair; take off the shoes and tuck up the trousers; what on earth is kept in the pockets? Oh, wonder of wonders! – and the iron!" As I put the watch close to the ear of one of them, "Tick, tick, ticks – woh, woh, woh" – everybody must hear it; and then the works had to be seen. "Oh, fearful!" said one, "hide your faces: it is the Lubari. Shut it up, Bana, shut it up; we have seen enough; but you will come again and bring us beads." So ended the day's work.

6th. – To-day I sent Bombay to the palace for food. Though rain fell in torrents, he found the king holding a levee, giving appointments, plantations, and women, according to merit, to his officers. As one officer, to whom only one woman was given, asked for more, the king called him an ingrate, and ordered him to be cut to pieces on the spot; and the sentence was, as Bombay told me, carried into effect – not with knives, for they are prohibited, but with strips of sharp-edged grass, after the executioners had first dislocated his neck by a blow delivered behind the head, with a sharp, heavy-headed club.

No food, however, was given to my men, though the king, anticipating Bombay's coming, sent me one load of tobacco, one of butter, and one of coffee. My residence in Uganda became much more merry now, for all the women of the camp came daily to call on my two little girls; during which time they smoked my tobacco, chewed my coffee, drank my pombe, and used to amuse me with queer stories of their native land. Rozaro's sister also came, and proposed to marry me, for Maula, she said, was a brutal man; he killed one of his women because he did not like her, and now he had clipped one of this poor creature's ears off for trying to run away from him; and when abused for his brutality, he only replied, "It was no fault of his, as the king set the example in the country." In the evening I took a walk with Kahala, dressed in a red scarf, and in company with Lugoi, to show my children off in the gardens to my fair friends of yesterday. Everybody was surprised. The Mgemma begged us to sit with him and drink pombe, which he generously supplied to our heart's content; wondered at the beauty of Kahala, wished I would give him a wife like her, and lamented that the king would not allow his to wear such pretty clothes. We passed on a little farther, and were invited to sit with another man, Lukanikka, to drink pombe and chew coffee – which we did as before, meeting with the same remarks; for all Waganda, instructed by the court, know the art of flattery better than any people in the world, even including the French.

7th. – In the morning, whilst it rained hard, the king sent to say that he had started buffalo-shooting, and expected me to join him. After walking a mile beyond the palace, we found him in a plantain garden, dressed in imitation of myself, wideawake and all, the perfect picture of a snob. He sent me a pot of pombe, which I sent home to the women, and walked off for the shooting-ground, two miles further on, the band playing in the front, followed by some hundred Wakungu – then the pages, then the king, next myself, and finally the women – the best in front, the worst bringing up the rear, with the king's spears and shield, as also pots of pombe, a luxury the king never moves without. It was easy to see there would be no sport, still more useless of offer any remarks, therefore all did as they were bid. The broad road, like all in Uganda, went straight over hill and dale, the heights covered with high grass or plantain groves, and the valleys with dense masses of magnificent forest-trees surrounding swamps covered with tall rushes half bridged. Proceeding on, as we came to the first water, I commenced flirtations with Mtesa's women, much to the surprise of the king and every one. The bridge was broken, as a matter of course; and the logs which composed it, lying concealed beneath the water, were toed successively by the leading men, that those who followed should not be tripped up by them. This favour the king did for me, and I in return for the women behind; they had never been favoured in their lives with such gallantry, and therefore could not refrain from laughing, which attracted the king's notice and set everybody in a giggle; for till now no mortal man had ever dared communicate with his women.

Shortly after this we left the highway, and, turning westwards, passed through a dense jungle towards the eastern shores of the Murchison Creek, cut by runnels and rivulets, where on one occasion I offered, by dumb signs to carry the fair ones pick-a-back over, and after crossing a second myself by a floating log, offered my hand. The leading wife first fears to take it, then grows bold and accepts it; when the prime beauty, Lubuga, following in her wake, and anxious to feel, I fancy, what the white man is like, with an imploring face holds out both her hands in such a captivating manner, that though I feared to draw attention by waiting any longer, I could not resist compliance. The king noticed it; but instead of upbraiding me, passed it off as a joke, and running up to the Kamraviona, gave him a poke in the ribs, and whispered what he had seen, as if it had been a secret. "Woh, woh!" says the Kamraviona, "what wonders will happen next?" We were now on the buffalo ground; but nothing could be seen save some old footprints of buffaloes, and a pitfall made for catching them. By this time the king was tired; and as he saw me searching for a log to sit upon, he made one of his pages kneel upon all fours and sat upon his back, acting the monkey in aping myself; for otherwise he would have sat on a mbugu, in his customary manner, spread on the ground. We returned, pushing along, up one way, then another, without a word, in thorough confusion, for the king delights in boyish tricks, which he has learned to play successfully. Leaving the road and plunging into thickets of tall grass, the band and Wakungu must run for their lives, to maintain the order of march, by heading him at some distant point of exit from the jungle; whilst the Kamraviona, leading the pages and my men, must push head first, like a herd of buffaloes, through the sharp-cutting grass, at a sufficient rate to prevent the royal walk from being impeded; and the poor women, ready to sink with exhaustion, can only be kept in their places by fear of losing their lives.

We had been out the whole day; still he did not tire of these tricks, and played them incessantly till near sundown, when we entered the palace. Then the women and Wakungu separating from us, we – that is, the king, the Kamraviona, pages, and myself – sat down to a warm feast of sweet potatoes and plantains, ending with pombe and fruit, whilst moist circular napkins, made in the shape of magnificent wafers out of plantain fibre, acted at once both the part of water and towel. This over, as the guns had to be emptied, and it was thought sinful to waste the bullets, four cows were ordered in and shot by the king. Thus ended the day, my men receiving one of the cows.

8th. – As Mtesa was tired with his yesterday's work, and would not see anybody, I took Lugoi and Kahala, with a bundle of beads, to give a return to the Mgemma for his late treat of pombe. His household men and women were immensely delighted with us, but more so, they said, for the honour of the visit. They gave us more pombe, and introduced us to one of N'yamasore's numerous sisters, who was equally charmed with myself and my children. The Mgemma did not know how he could treat us properly, he said, for he was only a poor man; but he would order some fowls, that I might carry them away. When I refused this offer, because we came to see him, and not to rob him, he thought it the most beautiful language, and said he would bring them to the house himself. I added, I hoped he would do so in company with his wife, which he promised, though he never dared fulfil the promise; and, on our leaving, set all his servants to escort us beyond the premises. In the evening, as the king's musicians passed the camp, I ordered them in to play the milele, and give my men and children a treat of dancing. The performers received a bundle of beads and went away happy.

9th. – I called on Congow, but found him absent, waiting on the king, as usual; and the king sent for my big rifle to shoot birds with.

10th. – In consequence of my having explained to the king the effect of the process of distilling, and the way of doing it, he sent a number of earthen pots and bugus of pombe that I might produce some spirits for him; but as the pots sent were not made after the proper fashion, I called at the palace and waited all day in the hope of seeing him. No one, however, dared enter his cabinet, where he had been practising "Uganga" all day, and so the pombe turned sour and useless. Such are the ways of Uganda all over.

11th. – The king was out shooting; and as nothing else could be done, I invited Uledi's pretty wife Guriku to eat a mutton breakfast, and teach my child Meri not to be so proud. In this we were successful; but whether her head had been turned, as Bombay thought, or what else, we know not; but she would neither walk, nor talk, nor do anything but lie at full length all day long, smoking and lounging in thorough indolence.

12th. – I distilled some fresh pombe for the king; and taking it to him in the afternoon, fired guns to announce arrival. He was not visible, while fearful shrieks were heard from within, and presently a beautiful woman, one of the king's sisters, with cockscomb erect, was dragged out to execution, bewailing and calling on her king, the Kamraviona, and Mzungu, by turns, to save her life. Would to God I could have done it! But I did not know her crime, if crime she had committed, and therefore had to hold my tongue, whilst the Kamraviona, and other Wakun-gu present, looked on with utter unconcern, not daring to make the slightest remark. It happened that Irungu was present in the ante-chamber at this time; and as Maula came with my party, they had a fight in respect to their merits for having brought welcome guests to their king. Mtesa, it was argued, had given N'yamgundu more women and men than he did to Maula, be-cause he was the first to bring intelligence of our coming, as well as that of K'yengo, and Suworora's hongo to his king; whilst, finally, he superseded Maula by taking me out of his charge, and had done a further good service by sending men on to Karague to fetch both Grant and K'yengo.

Maula, although he had received the second reward, had lit-erally done nothing, whilst Irungu had been years absent at Usui, and finally had brought a valuable hongo, yet he got less than Maula. This, Irungu said, was an injustice he would not stand; N'yamgundu fairly earned his reward, but Maula must have been tricking to get more than himself. He would get a suitable offering of wire, and lay his complaint in court the first opportunity. "Pooh, pooh! Nonsense!" says Maula, laughing; "I will give him more wires than you, and then let us see who will win the king's ear." Upon this the two great children began col-lecting wire and quarrelling until the sun went down, and I went home. I did not return to a quiet dinner, as I had hoped, but to meet the summons of the king. Thinking it policy to obey, I found him waiting my coming in the palace. He made apologies for not answering my gun, and tasted some spirits re-sembling toddy, which I had succeeded in distilling. He im-bibed it with great surprise; it was wonderful tipple; he must have some more; and, for the purpose of brewing better, would send the barrel of an old Brown Bess musket, as well as more pombe and wood in the morning.

13th. – As nothing was done all day, I took the usual promenade in the Seraglio Park, and was accosted by a very pretty little woman, Kariana, wife of Dumba, who, very neatly dressed, was returning from a visit. At first she came trotting after me, then timidly paused, then advanced, and, as I approached, stood spellbound at my remarkable appearance. At last recovering herself, she woh-wohed with all the coquetry of a Mganda woman, and a flirtation followed; she must see my hair, my watch, the contents of my pockets – everything; but that was not enough. I waved adieu, but still she followed. I offered my arm, showing her how to take it in European fashion, and we walked along to the surprise of everybody, as if we had been in Hyde Park rather than in Central Africa, flirting and coquetting all the way. I was surprised that no one came to prevent her forwardness; but not till I almost reached home did any one appear; and then, with great scolding, she was ordered to return – not, however, without her begging I would call in and see her on some future occasion, when she would like to give me some pombe.

14th. – As conflicting reports came about Grant, the king very courteously, at my request, forwarded letters to him. I passed the day in distilling pombe, and the evening in calling on Mrs. Dumba, with Meri, Kahala, Lugoi, and a troop of Wanyamuezi women. She was very agreeable; but as her husband was attending the palace, could not give pombe, and instead gave my female escort sundry baskets of plaintains and potatoes, signifying a dinner, and walked half-way home, flirting with me as before.

15th – I called on the king with all the spirits I had made, as well as the saccharine residue. We found him holding a levee, and receiving his offerings of a batch of girls, cows, goats, and other things of an ordinary nature. One of the goats presented gave me an opportunity of hearing one of the strangest stories I had yet heard in this strange country: it was a fine for attempted regicide, which happened yesterday, when a boy, finding the king alone, which is very unusual, walked up to him and threatened to kill him, because, he said, he took the lives of men unjustly. The king explained by description and pantomime how the affair passed. When the youth attacked him he had in his hand the revolving pistol I had given him, and showed us, holding the pistol to his cheek, how he had presented the muzzle to the boy, which, though it was unloaded, so frightened him that he ran away. All the courtiers n'yanzigged vigorously for the condescension of the king in telling the story. There must have been some special reason why, in a court where trifling breaches of etiquette were punished with a cruel death, so grave a crime should have been so leniently dealt with; but I could not get at the bottom of the affair. The culprit, a good-looking young fellow of sixteen or seventeen, who brought in the goat, made his n'yanzigs, stroked the goat and his own face with his hands, n'yanzigged again with prostrations, and retired.

After this scene, officers announced the startling fact that two white men had been seen at Kamrasi's, one with a beard like myself, the other smooth-faced. I jumped at this news, and said, "Of course, they are there; do let me send a letter to them." I believed it to be Petherick and a companion whom I knew he was to bring with him. The king, however, damped my ardour by saying the information was not perfect, and we must wait until certain Wakungu, whom he sent to search in Unyoro, returned.

16th. – The regions about the palace were all in a state of commotion to-day, men and women running for their lives in all directions, followed by Wakungu and their retainers. The cause of all this commotion was a royal order to seize sundry refractory Wakungu, with their property, wives, concubines – if such a distinction can be made in this country – and families all together. At the palace Mtesa had a musical party, playing the flute occasionally himself. After this he called me aside, and said, "Now, Bana, I wish you would instruct me, as you have often proposed doing, for I wish to learn everything, though I have little opportunity for doing so." Not knowing what was uppermost in his mind, I begged him to put whatever questions he liked, and he should be answered seriatim – hoping to find him inquisitive on foreign matters; but nothing was more foreign to his mind: none of his countrymen ever seemed to think beyond the sphere of Uganda.

The whole conversation turned on medicines, or the cause and effects of diseases. Cholera, for instance, very much affected the land at certain seasons, creating much mortality, and vanishing again as mysteriously as it came. What brought this scourge? And what would cure it? Supposing a man had a headache, what should he take for it? Or a leg ache, or a stomach-ache, or itch; in fact, going the rounds of every disease he knew, until, exhausting the ordinary complaints, he went into particulars in which he was personally much interested; but I was unfortunately unable to prescribe medicines which produce the physical phenomenon next to his heart.

17th. – I called upon the king by appointment, and found a large court, where the Wakungu caught yesterday, and sentenced to execution, received their reprieve on paying fines of cattle and young damsels – their daughters. A variety of charms, amongst which were some bits of stick strung on leather and covered with serpent-skin, were presented and approved of. Kaggao, a large district officer, considered the second in rank here, received permission for me to call upon him with my medicines. I pressed the king again to send men with mine to Kamrasi's to call Petherick. At first he objected that they would be killed, but finally he yielded, and appointed Budja, his Unyoro ambassador, for the service. Then, breaking up the court, he retired with a select party of Wakungu, headed by the Kamraviona, and opened a conversation on the subject which is ever uppermost with the king and his courtiers.

18th. – To-day I visited Kaggao with my medicine-chest. He had a local disease, which he said came to him by magic, though a different cause was sufficiently obvious, and wanted medicine such as I gave Mkuenda, who reported that I gave him a most wonderful draught. Unfortunately I had nothing suitable to give my new patient, but cautioned him to have a care lest contagion should run throughout his immense establishment, and explained the whole of the circumstances to him. Still he was not satisfied; he would give me slaves, cows, or ivory, if I would only cure him. He was a very great man, as I could see, with numerous houses, numerous wives, and plenty of everything, so that it was ill-becoming of him to be without his usual habits. Rejecting his munificent offers, I gave him a cooling dose of calomel and jalap, which he drank like pombe, and pronounced beautiful – holding up his hands, and repeating the words "Beautiful, beautiful! They are all beautiful together! There is Bana beautiful! His box is beautiful! And his medicine beautiful!" – and, saying this, led us in to see his women, who at my request were grouped in war apparel – viz., a dirk fastened to the waist by many strings of coloured beads. There were from fifty to sixty women present, all very lady-like, but none of them pretty. Kaggao then informed me the king had told all his Wakungu he would keep me as his guest four months longer to see if Petherick came; and should he not by that time, he would give me an estate, stocked with men, women, and cattle, in perpetuity, so that, if I ever wished to leave Uganda, I should always have something to come back to; so I might now know what my fate was to be. Before leaving, Kaggao presented us with two cows and ten baskets of potatoes.

19th. – I sent a return present of two wires and twelve fundo of beads of sorts to Kaggao, and heard that the king had gone to show himself off to his mother dressed Bana fashion. In the evening Katunzi, N'yamasore's brother, just returned from the Unyoro plunder, called on me whilst I was at dinner. Not knowing who he was, and surprised at such audacity in Uganda, for he was the first officer who ever ventured to come near me in this manner, I offered him a knife and fork, and a share in the repast, which rather abashed him; for, taking it as a rebuff, he apologised immediately for the liberty he had taken, contrary to the etiquette of Uganda society, in coming to a house when the master was at dinner; and he would have left again had I not pressed him to remain. Katunzi then told me the whole army had returned from Unyoro, with immense numbers of cows, women, and children, but not men, for those who did not run away were killed fighting. He offered me a present of a woman, and pressed me to call on him.

20th. – Still I found that the king would not send his Wakungu for the Unyoro expedition, so I called on him about it. Fortunately he asked me to speak a sentence in English, that he might hear how it sounds; and this gave me an opportunity of saying, if he had kept his promise by sending Budja to me, I should have despatched letters to Petherick. This was no sooner interpreted than he said, if I would send my men to him with letters in the morning he would forward them on, accompanied with an army. On my asking if the army was intended to fight, he replied, in short, "First to feel the way." On hearing this, I strongly advised him, if he wished the road to be kept permanently open, to try conciliation with Kamrasi, and send him some trifling present.

Now were brought in some thirty-odd women for punishment and execution, which the king, who of late had been trying to learn Kisuahili, in order that we might be able to converse together, asked me, in that language, if I would like to have some of these women; and if so, how many? On my replying "One," he begged me to have my choice, and a very pretty one was selected. God only knows what became of the rest; but the one I selected, on reaching home, I gave to Ilmas, my valet, for a wife. He and all the other household servants were much delighted with this charming acquisition; but the poor girl, from the time she had been selected, had flattered herself she was to be Bana's wife, and became immensely indignant at the supposed transfer, though from the first I had intended her for Ilmas, not only to favour him for his past good services, but as an example to my other men, as I had promised to give them all, provided they behaved well upon the journey, a "free-man's garden," with one wife each and a purse of money, to begin a new life upon, as soon as they reached Zanzibar. The temper of Meri and Kahala was shown in a very forcible manner: they wanted this maid as an addition to my family, called her into the hut and chatted till midnight, instructing her not to wed with Ilmas; and then, instead of turning into bed as usual, they all three slept upon the ground. My patience could stand this phase of henpecking no longer, so I called in Manamaka, the head Myamuezi woman, whom I had selected for their governess, and directed her to assist Ilmas, and put them to bed "bundling."

21st. – In the morning, before I had time to write letters, the king invited me to join him at some new tank he was making between his palace and the residence of his brothers. I found him sitting with his brothers, all playing in concert on flutes. I asked him, in Kisuahili, if he knew where Grant was? On replying in the negative, I proposed sending a letter, which he approved of; and Budja was again ordered to go with an army for Petherick.

22d. – Mabruki and Bilal, with Budja, started to meet Petherick, and three more men, with another letter to Grant. I called on the king, who appointed the 24th instant for an excursion of three days' hippopotamus-shooting on the N'yanza.

23d. – To-day occurred a brilliant instance of the capricious restlessness and self-willedness of this despotic king. At noon, pages hurried in to say that he had started for the N'yanza, and wished me to follow him without delay. N'yanza, as I have mentioned, merely means a piece of water, whether a pond, river, or lake; and as no one knew which N'yanza he meant, or what project was on foot, I started off in a hurry, leaving everything behind, and walked rapidly through gardens, over hills, and across rushy swamps, down the west flank of the Murchison Creek, till 3 P.M., when I found the king dressed in red, with his Wakungu in front and women behind, travelling along in the confused manner of a pack of hounds, occasionally firing his rifle that I might know his whereabouts. He had just, it seems, mingled a little business with pleasure; for noticing, as he passed, a woman tied by the hands to be punished for some offence, the nature of which I did not learn, he took the executioner's duty on himself, fired at her, and killed her outright.

On this occasion, to test all his followers, and prove their readiness to serve him, he had started on a sudden freak for the three days' excursion on the lake one day before the appointed time, expecting everybody to fall into place by magic, without the smallest regard to each one's property, feelings, or comfort.

The home must be forsaken without a last adieu, the dinner untasted, and no provision made for the coming night, in order that his impetuous majesty should not suffer one moment's disappointment. The result was natural; many who would have come were nowhere to be found; my guns, bed, bedding, and note-books, as well as cooking utensils, were all left behind, and, though sent for, did not arrive till the following day.

On arriving at the mooring station, not one boat was to be found, nor did any arrive until after dark, when, on the beating

The soldiers of Mtesa's guard preparing the mess rations.

of drums and firing of guns, some fifty large ones appeared. They were all painted with red clay, and averaged from ten to thirty paddles, with long prows standing out like the neck of a syphon or swan, decorated on the head with the horns of the Nsunnu (lencotis) antelope, between which was stuck upright a tuft of feathers exactly like a grenadier's plume. These arrived to convey us across the mouth of a deep rushy swamp to the royal yachting establishment, the Cowes of Uganda, distant five hours' travelling from the palace. We reached the Cowes by torchlight at 9 P.M., when the king had a picnic dinner with me, turned in with his women in great comfort, and sent me off to a dreary hut, where I had to sleep upon a grass-strew floor. I was surprised we had to walk so far, when, by appearance, we might have boated it from the head of the creek all the way down; but, on inquiry, was informed of the swampy nature of the ground at the head of the creek precluded any approach to the clear water there, and hence the long overland journey, which, though fatiguing to the unfortunate women, who had to trot the whole way behind Mtesa's four-mile-an-hour strides, was very amusing. The whole of the scenery – hill, dale, and lake – was extremely beautiful. The Wanguana in my escort compared the view to their own beautiful Poani (coast); but in my opinion it far surpassed anything I ever saw, either from the sea or upon the coast of Zanzibar.

The king rose betimes in the morning and called me, unwashed and very uncomfortable, to picnic with him, during the collection of the boats. The breakfast, eaten in the open court, consisted of sundry baskets of roast-beef and plantain-squash, folded in plantain-leaves. He sometimes ate with a copper knife and picker, not forked – but more usually like a dog, with both hands. The bits too tough for his mastication he would take from his mouth and give as a treat to the pages, who n'yanzigged, and swallowed them with much seeming relish. Whatever remained over was then divided by the boys, and the baskets taken to t he cooks. Pombe served as tea, coffee, and beer for the king; but his guests might think themselves very lucky if they ever got a drop of it.

Now for the lake. Everybody in a hurry falls into his place the best way he can – Wakungu leading, and women behind. They rattle along, through plantains and shrubs, under large trees, seven, eight, and nine feet in diameter, till the beautiful waters are reached – a picture of the Rio scenery, barring that of the higher mountains in the background of that lovely place, which are here represented by the most beautiful little hills. A band of fifteen drums of all sizes, called the *Mazaguzo*, playing with the regularity of a lot of factory engines at work, announced the king's arrival, and brought all the boats to the shore – but not as in England, where Jack, with all the consequence of a lord at home, invites the ladies to be seated, and enjoys the sight of so many pretty faces. Here every poor fellow, with his apprehensions written in his face, leaps over the gunwale into the water – ducking his head for fear of being accused of gazing on the fair sex, which is death – and bides patiently his time. They were dressed in plantain leaves, looking like grotesque Neptunes. The king, in his red coat and wideawake, conducted the arrangements, ordering all to their proper places – the women, in certain boats, the Wakungu and Wanguana in others, whilst I sat in the same boat with him at his feet, three women hold-

471

ing mbugus of pombe behind. The king's Kisuahali now came into play, and he was prompt in carrying out the directions he got from myself to approach the hippopotami. But the waters were too large and the animals too shy, so we toiled all the day without any effect, going only once ashore to picnic; not for the women to eat – for they, poor things, got nothing – but the king, myself, the pages, and the principal Wakungu. As a wind-up to the day's amusement, the king led the band of drums, changed the men according to their powers, put them into concert pitch, and readily detected every slight irregularity, showing himself a thorough musician.

This day requires no remark, everything done being the counterpart of yesterday, excepting that the king, growing bolder with me in consequence of our talking together, became more playful and familiar – amusing himself, for instance, sometimes by catching hold of my beard as the rolling of the boat unsteadied him.

We started early in the usual manner; but after working up and down the creek, inspecting the inlets for hippopotami, and tiring from want of sport, the king changed his tactics, and, paddling and steering himself with a pair of new white paddles, finally directing the boats to an island occupied by the Mgussa, or Neptune of the N'yanza, not in person – for Mgussa is a spirit – but by his familiar or deputy, the great medium who communicates the secrets of the deep to the king of Uganda. In another sense, he might be said to be the presiding priest of the source of the mighty Nile, and as such was, of course, an interesting person for me to meet. The first operation on shore was picnicking, when many large bugus of pombe were brought for the king; next, the whole party took a walk, winking through the trees, and picking fruit, enjoying themselves amazingly, till, by some unlucky chance, one of the royal wives, a most charming creature, and truly one of the best of the lot, plucked a fruit and offered it to the king, thinking, doubtless, to please him greatly; but he, like a madman, flew into a towering passion, said it was the first time a woman ever had the impudence to offer him anything, and ordered the pages to seize, bind, and lead her off to execution.

These words were no sooner uttered by the king than the whole bevy of pages slipped their cord turbans from their heads, and rushed, like a pack of cupid beagles upon the fairy queen, who, indignant at the little urchins daring to touch her majesty, remonstrated with the king, and tried to beat them off like flies, but was soon captured, overcome, and dragged away, crying, in the names of the Kamraviona and Mzungu (myself), for help and protection; whilst Lubuga, the pet sister, and all the other women, clasped the king by his legs, and, kneeling, implored forgiveness for their sister. The more they craved for mercy, the more brutal he became, till at last he took a heavy stick and began to belabour the poor victim on the head.

Hitherto I had been extremely careful not to interfere with any of the king's acts of arbitrary cruelty, knowing that such interference, at an early stage, would produce more harm than good. This last act of barbarism, however, was too much for my English blood to stand; and as I heard my name, Mzungu, imploringly pronounced, I rushed at the king, and, staying his uplifted arm, demanded from him the woman's life. Of course I ran imminent risk of losing my own in thus thwarting the capricious tyrant; but his caprice proved the friend of both. The novelty of interference even made him smile, and the woman was instantly released.

Proceeding on through the trees of this beautiful island, we next turned into the hut of the Mgussa's familiar, which at the farther end was decorated with many mystic symbols amongst others a paddle, the badge of his high office – and for some time we sat chatting, when pombe was brought, and the spiritual medium arrived. He was dressed Wichwezi fashion, with a little white goat-skin apron, adorned with numerous charms, and used a paddle for a mace or walking stick. He was not an old man, though he affected to be so – walking very slowly and deliberately, coughing asthmatically, glimmering with his eyes, and mumbling like a witch. With much affected difficulty he sat at the end of the hut beside the symbols alluded to, and continued his coughing full half an hour, when his wife came in in the same manner, without saying a word, and assumed the same affected style. The king jokingly looked at me and laughed, and then at these strange creatures, by turn, as much as to say, What do you think of them? But no voice was heard save that of the old wife, who croaked like a frog for water, and, when some was brought, croaked again because it was not the purest of the lake's produce – had the first cup changed, wetted her lips with the second, and hobbled away in the same manner as she came.

At this juncture the Mgussa's familiar motioned the Kamraviona and several officers to draw around him, when, in a very low tone, he gave them all the orders of the deep, and walked away. His revelations seemed unpropitious, for we immediately repaired to our boats and returned to our quarters. Here we no sooner arrived than a host of Wakungu, lately returned from the Unyoro war, came to pay their respects to the king: they had returned six days or more, but etiquette had forbidden their approaching majesty sooner. Their successes had been great, their losses, nil, for not one man had lost his life fighting. To these men the king narrated all the adventures of the day; dwelling more particularly on my defending his wife's life, whom he had destined for execution. This was highly approved of by all; and they unanimously said Bana knew what he was about, because he dispenses justice like a king in his own country.

Early in the morning a great hue and cry was made because the Wanguana had been seen bathing in the N'yanza naked, without the slightest regard to decency. We went boating as usual all day long, sometimes after hippopotami, at others racing up and down the lake, the king and Wakungu paddling and steering by turns, the only break to this fatigue being when we went ashore to picnic, or the king took a turn at the drums. During the evening some of the principal Wakungu were collected to listen to an intellectual discourse on the peculiarities of the different women in the royal establishment, and the king in good-honour described the benefits he had derived from this pleasant tour on the water.

Whilst I was preparing my Massey's log to show the use of it to the king, he went off boating without me; and as the few remaining boats would not take me off because they had received no orders to do so, I fired guns, but, getting no reply, went into the country hoping to find game; but, disappointed in that also, I spent the first half of the day with a hospitable old lady, who treated us to the last drop of pombe in her house – for the king's servants had robbed her of nearly everything – smoked her pipe with me, and chatted incessantly on the honour paid her by the white king's visit, as well as of the horrors of Uganda punishment, when my servants told her I saved the life of one queen. Returning homewards, the afternoon was spent at a hospitable officer's, who would not allow us to depart until my men were all fuddled with pombe, and the evening setting in warned us to wend our way. On arrival at camp, the king, quite shocked with himself for having deserted me, asked me if I did not hear his guns fire. He had sent twenty officers to scour the country, looking for me everywhere. He had been on the lake the whole day himself, and was now amusing his officers with a little archery practice, even using the bow himself, and making them shoot by turns. A lucky shot brought forth immense applause, all jumping and n'yanzigging with delight, whether it was done by their own bows or the king's.

A shield was the mark, stuck up at only thirty paces; still they were such bad shots that they hardly ever hit it. Now tired of this slow sport, and to show his superior prowess, the king ordered sixteen shields to be placed before him, one in front of the other, and with one shot from Whitworth pierced the whole of them, the bullet passing through the bosses of nearly every one. "Ah!" says the king, strutting about with gigantic strides, and brandishing the rifle over his head before all his men, "what is the use of spears and bows? I shall never fight with anything but guns in the future." These Wakungu, having only just then returned from plundering Unyoro, had never before seen their

476

king in a chair, or anybody sitting, as I was, by his side; and it being foreign to their notions, as well as, perhaps, unpleasant to their feelings, to find a stranger sitting higher than themselves, they complained against this outrage to custom, and induced the king to order my dethronement. The result was, as my iron stool was objectionable, I stood for a moment to see that I thoroughly understood their meaning; and then showing them my back, walked straightway home to make a grass throne, and dodge them that way.

There was nothing for dinner last night, nothing again this morning, yet no one would go in to report this fact, as rain was falling, and the king was shut up with his women. Presently the thought struck me that the rifle, which was always infallible in gaining me admittance at the palace, might be of the same service now. I therefore shot a dove close to the royal abode, and, as I expected, roused the king at once, who sent his pages to know what the firing was about. When told the truth – that I had been trying to shoot a dish of doves for breakfast, as I could get neither meat nor drink from his kitchen – the head boy, rather guessing than understanding what was told him, distorted my message, and said to the king, as I could not obtain a regular supply of food from his house, I did not wish to accept anything further at his hands, but intended foraging for the future in the jungles. The king, as might be imagined, did not believe the boy's story, and sent other pages to ascertain the truth of the case, bidding them listen well, and beware of what they were about. This second lot of boys conveyed the story rightly, when the king sent me a cow. As I afterwards heard, he cut off the ears of the unfortunate little mischief-maker for not making a proper use of those organs; and then, as the lad was the son of one of his own officers he was sent home to have the sores healed. After breakfast the king called me to go boating, when I used my grass throne, to the annoyance of the attendants. This induced the king to say before them, laughing, "Bana, you see, is not to be done; he is accustomed to sit before kings, and sit he will." Then by way of a change, he ordered all the drums to embark and play upon the waters; whilst he and his attendants paddled and steered by turns, first up the creek, and then down nearly to the broad waters of the lake.

There was a passage this way, it was said, leading up to Usoga, but very circuitous, on account of reefs or shoals, and on the way the Kitiri island was passed; but no other Kitiri was known to the Waganda, though boats went sometimes coasting down the western side of the lake to Ukerewe. The largest island on the lake is the Sese,[1] off the mouth of the Katonga river, where another of the high priests of the Neptune of the N'yanza resides. The king's largest vessels are kept there, and it is famous for its supply of mbugu barks. We next went on shore to picnic, when a young hippopotamus, speared by harpoon, one pig, and a pongo or bush-boc, were presented to the king. I now advised boat-racing, which was duly ordered, and afforded much amusement as the whole fifty boats formed in line, and paddle furiously to the beat of drum to the goal which I indicated.

The day was done. In great glee the king, ever much attached to the blackguard Maula, in consequence of his amusing stories, appointed him to the office of seizer, or chief kidnapper of Wakungu; observing that, after the return of so many officers from war, much business in that line would naturally have to be

478

done, and there was none so trustworthy now at court to carry out the king's orders. All now went to the camp; but what was my astonishment on reaching the hut to find every servant gone, along with the pots, pans, meat, everything; and all in consequence of the king's having taken the drums on board, which, being unusual, was regarded as one of his delusive tricks, and a sign of immediate departure. He had told no one he was going to the N'yanza, and now it was thought he would return in the same way. I fired for my supper, but fired in vain. Boys came out, by the king's order to inquire what I wanted, but left again without doing anything further.

At my request the king sent off boats to inquire after the one that left, or was supposed to have left, for Grant on the 3d of March, and he then ordered the return home, much to my delight; for, beautiful as the N'yanza was, the want of consideration for other people's comfort, the tiring, incessant boating, all day long and every day, in the sun, as well as the king's hurry-scurry about everything he undertook to do, without the smallest forethought, preparation, or warning, made me dream of my children, and look forward with pleasure to rejoining them. Strange as it may appear to Englishmen, I had a sort of paternal love for those little blackamoors as if they had been my offspring; and I enjoyed the simple stories that their sable visitors told me every day they came over to smoke their pipes, which they did with the utmost familiarity, helping themselves from my stores just as they liked.

Without any breakfast, we returned by the same route by which we had come, at four miles an hour, till half the way was cleared, when the king said, laughing, "Bana, are you hungry?"

– a ridiculous question after twenty-four hours of starvation, which he knew full well – and led the way into a plantain-grove, where the first hut that was found was turned inside out for the king's accommodation, and picnic was prepared. As, however, he ordered my portion to be given outside with the pages', and allowed neither pombe or water, I gave him the slip, and walked hurriedly home, where I found Kahala smirking, and apparently glad to see us, but Meri shamming ill in bed, whilst Manamaka, the governess, was full of smiles and conversation. She declared Meri had neither tasted food or slept since my departure, but had been retching all the time. Dreadfully concerned at the doleful story I immediately thought of giving relief with medicines, but neither pulse, tongue, nor anything else indicated the slightest disorder; and to add to these troubles, Ilmas's woman had tried during my absence to hang herself, because she would not serve as servant but wished to be my wife; and Bombay's wife, after taking a doze of quinine, was delivered of a still-born child.

1st. – I visited the king, at his request, with the medicine-chest. He had caught a cold. He showed me several of his women grievously affected with boils, and expected me to cure them at once. I then went home, and found twenty men who had passed Grant, coming on a stretcher from Karague, without any of the rear property. Meri, still persistent, rejected strengthening medicines, but said, in a confidential manner, if I would give her a goat to sacrifice to the Uganga she would recover in no time. There was something in her manner when she said this that I did not like – it looked suspicious; and I contented myself by saying, "No, I am a wiser doctor than any in these lands;

if anybody could cure you, that person is myself: and further, if I gave you a goat to sacrifice, God would be angry with both of us for our superstitious credulity; you must therefore say no more about it."

2d. – The whole country around the palace was in a state of commotion to-day, from Maula and his children hunting down those officers who had returned from the war, yet had not paid their respects to the king at the N'yanza, because they thought they would not be justified in calling on him so quickly after their arrival. Maula's house, in consequence of this, was full of beef and pombe; whilst, in his courtyard, men, women, and children, with feet in stocks, very like the old parish stocks in England, waited his pleasure, to see what demands he would make upon them as the price of their release. After anxiously watching, I found out that Meri was angry with me for not allowing Ilmas's woman to live in my house; and, to conquer my resolution against it – although I ordered it with a view to please Ilmas, for he was desperately in love with her – she made herself sick by putting her finger down her throat. I scolded her for her obstinacy. She said she was ill – it was not feigned; and if I would give her a goat to sacrifice she would be well at once; for she had looked into the magic horn already, and discovered that if I have her a goat for that purpose it would prove that I loved her, and her health would be restored to her at once. Hallo! Here was a transformation from the paternal position into that of a henpecked husband! Somebody, I smelt at once, had been tampering with my household whilst I was away. I commenced investigations, and after a while found out that Rozaro's sister had brought a magician belonging to her family into the hut during my absence, who had put Meri up to this trick of extorting a goat from me, in order that he might benefit by it himself, for the magician eats the sacrifice, and keeps the skin.

I immediately ordered him to be seized and bound to the flag-staff, whilst Maula, Uledi, Rozaro, and Bombay were summoned to witness the process of investigation. Rozaro flew into a passion, and tried to release the magician as soon as he saw him, affecting intense indignation that I should take the law into my own hands when one of Rumanika's subjects was accused; but only lost his dignity still more on being told he had acknowledged his inability to control his men so often when they had misbehaved, that I scorned to ask his assistance any longer. He took huff at this, and, as he could not help himself, walked away, leaving us to do as we liked. The charge was fully proved. The impudent magician, without leave, and contrary to all the usages of the country, had entered and set my house against itself during my absence, and had schemed to rob me of a goat. I therefore sentenced him to fifty lashes – twenty-five for the injury he had inflicted on my by working up a rebellion in my house, and the remaining twenty-five for attempting larceny – saying, as he had wanted my goat and its skin, so now in return I wanted his skin. These words were no sooner pronounced than the wretched Meri cried out against it, saying all the fault was hers: "Let the stick skin my back, but spare my doctor; it would kill me to see him touched." This appeal let me see that there was something in the whole matter too deep and intricate to be remedied by my skill. I therefore dismissed her on the spot, and gave her, as a sister and free woman, to Uledi and his pretty Mhmula wife, giving Bombay orders to carry the sentences into execution. After walking about till after dark, on returning to the empty house, I had some misgivings as to the apparent cruelty of abandoning one so helpless to the uncertainties of this wicked world. Ilmas's woman also ran away, doubtless at the instigation of Rozaro's sister, for she had been denied any further access to the house as being at the bottom of all this mischief.

3d. – I was haunted all night by my fancied cruelty, and in the morning sent its victim, after Uganda fashion, some symbolical presents, including a goat, in token of esteem; a black blanket, as a sign of mourning; a bundle of gundu anklets; and a packet of tobacco, in proof of my forgiveness.

---

1) Some say a group of forty islands compose Sese.

CHAPTER 14

PALACE, UGANDA – CONTINUED

Reception of a Victorious Army at Court – Royal Sport – A Review of the Troops – Negotiations for the Opening of the Road Along the Nile – Grant's Return – Pillagings – Court Marriages – The King's Brothers – Divinations and Sacrifices – The Road Granted At Last – The Preparations for Continuing the Expedition – The Departure.

I now received a letter from Grant to say he was coming by boat from Kitangule, and at once went to the palace to give the welcome news to the king. The road to the palace I found thronged with people; and in the square outside the entrance there squatted a multitude of attendants, headed by the king, sitting on a cloth, dressed in his national costume, with two spears and a shield by his side. On his right hand the pages sat waiting for orders, while on his left there was a small squatting cluster of women, headed by Wichwezis, or attendant sorceresses, offering pombe. In front of the king, in form of a hollow square, many ranks deep, sat the victorious officers, lately returned from the war, variously dressed; the nobles distinguished by their leopard-cat skins and dirks, the commoners by coloured mbugu and cow or antelope skin cloaks; but all their faces and arms were painted red, black, or smoke-colour. Within the square of men, immediately fronting the king, the war-arms of Uganda were arranged in three ranks; the great war-drum, covered with a leopard-skin, and standing on a large car-peting of them, was placed in advance; behind this, propped or hung on a rack of iron, were a variety of the implements of war in common use, offensive and defensive, as spears – of which two were of copper, the rest iron – and shields of wood and leather; whilst in the last row or lot were arranged systematical-ly, with great taste and powerful effect, the supernatural arms, the god of Uganda, consisting of charms of various descriptions and in great numbers. Outside the square again, in a line with the king, were the household arms, a very handsome copper kettledrum, of French manufacture, surmounted on the outer edge with pretty little brass bells depending from swan-neck-shaped copper wire, two new spears, a painted leather shield, and magic wands of various devices, deposited on a carpet of leopard-skins – the whole scene giving the effect of true bar-barous royalty in its uttermost magnificence.

Approaching, as usual, to take my seat beside the king, some slight sensation was perceptible, and I was directed to sit be-yond the women. The whole ceremonies of this grand assem-blage were now obvious. Each regimental commandant in turn narrated the whole services of his party, distinguishing those subs who executed his orders well and successfully from those who either deserted before the enemy or feared to follow up their success. The king listened attentively, making, let us sup-pose, very shrewd remarks concerning them; when to the wor-thy he awarded pombe, helped with gourd-cups from large earthen jars, which has n'yanzigged for vehemently; and to the unworthy execution. When the fatal sentence was pronounced,

Pombe trough at the Ugandan court.

a terrible bustle ensued, the convict wrestling and defying, whilst the other men seized, pulled and tore the struggling wretch from the crowd, bound him hands and head together, and led or rather tumbled him away.

After a while, and when all business was over, the king begged me to follow him into the palace. He asked again for stimulants – a matter ever uppermost in his mind – and would not be convinced that such things can do him no possible good, but would in the end be deleterious. Grant's letter was then read to him before his women, and I asked for the dismissal of all the Wanyambo, for they had not only destroyed my peace and home, but were always getting me into disrepute by plundering the Waganda in the highways. No answer was given to this; and on walking home, I found one of the king's women at my hut, imploring protection against the Wanyambo, who had robbed and bruised her so often, she could not stand such abuse any longer.

4th. – I sent Maula, early in the morning, with the plundered woman, and desired him to request that the Wanyambo might be dismissed. He returned, saying he delivered my message, but no reply was given. I then searched for the king, and found him at his brothers' suite of huts playing the flute before them. On taking my seat, he proudly pointed to two vultures which he had shot with bullet, saying to his brothers, "There, do you see these birds? Bana shoots with shot, but I kill with bullets." To try him, I then asked for leave to go to Usoga, as Grant was so far off; but he said, "No, wait until he comes, and you shall both go together then; you fancy he is far off, but I know better. One of my men saw him coming along carried on a stretcher." I said,

"No; that must be a mistake, for he told me by letter he would come by water." Heavy rain now set in, and we got under cover; but the brothers never moved, some even sitting in the streaming gutter, and n'yanzigging whenever noticed. The eldest brother offered me his cup of pombe, thinking I would not drink it; but when he saw its contents vanishing fast, he cried "lekerow!" (hold fast!) and as I pretended not to understand him, continuing to drink, he rudely snatched the cup from my lips. Alternate concerts with the brothers, and conversation about hunting, in consequence of a bump caused by a fall with steeple-chasing, which as discovered on my forehead, ended this day's entertainment.

5th. – As all the Wanguana went foraging, I was compelled to stop at home. The king, however, sent an officer for Grant, because I would not believe in his statement yesterday that he was coming by land; and I also sent a lot of men with a litter to help him on, and bring me an answer.

6th. – I went to the palace at the king's command. He kept us waiting an hour, and then passing out by a side gate, beckoned us to follow. He was dressed in European clothes, with his guns and tin box of clothes leading the way. His first question was, "Well, Bana, where are your guns? For I have called you to go shooting." "The pages never said anything about shooting, and therefore the guns were left behind." Totally unconcerned, the king walked on to his brothers, headed by a band and attendants, who were much lauded for being ready at a moment's notice. A grand flute concert was then played, one of the younger brothers keeping time with a long hand-drum; then the band played; and dancing and duets and singing followed.

After the usual presentations, fines, and n'yanziggings, I asked for leave to go and meet Grant by water, but was hastily told that two boats had been sent for him when we returned from the N'yanza, and that two runners, just returned from Karague, said he was on the way not far off. The child-king then changed his dress for another suit of clothes for his brothers to admire, and I retired, much annoyed, as he would neither give pombe for myself, nor plantains for my men: and I was further annoyed on my arrival at home, to find the Wanguana mobbing my hut and clamouring for food, and calling for an order to plunder if I did not give them beads, which, as the stock had run short, I could only do by their returning to Karague for the beads stored there; and, even if they were obtained, it was questionable if the king would revoke his order prohibiting the sale of provisions to us.

7th. – To-day I called at the queen's, but had to wait five hours in company with some attendants, to whom she sent pombe occasionally; but after waiting for her nearly all day, they were dismissed, because excess of business prevented her seeing them, though I was desired to remain. I asked these attendants to sell me food for beads, but they declared they could not without obtaining permission. In the evening the queen stumped out of her chambers and walked to the other end of her palace, where the head or queen of the Wichwezi women lived, to whom everybody paid the profoundest respect. On the way I joined her, she saying, in a state of high anger, "You won't call on me, now I have given you such a charming damsel: you have quite forgotten us in your love of home." Of course Meri's misdemeanour had to be explained, when she said, "As that is

490

the case, I will give you another; but you must take Meri out of the country, else she will bring trouble on us; for, you know, I never gave girls who lived in the palace to any one in my life before, because they would tell domestic affairs not proper for common people to know." I then said my reason for not seeing her before was, that the four times I had sent messengers to make an appointment for the following day, they had been repulsed from her doors. This she would not believe, but called me a story-teller in very coarse language, until the men who had been sent were pointed out to her, and they corroborated me.

The Wichwezi queen met her majesty with her head held very high, and instead of permitting me to sit on my box of grass, threw out a bundle of grass for that purpose. All conversation was kept between the two queens; but her Wichwezi majesty had a platter of clay-stone brought, which she ate with great relish, making a noise of satisfaction like a happy guinea-pig. She threw me a bit, which to the surprise of everybody, I caught and threw it into my mouth, thinking it was some confection; but the harsh taste soon made me spit it out again, to the amusement of the company. On returning home I found the king had requested me to call on him as soon as possible with the medicine-chest.

8th. – Without a morsel to eat for dinner last night, or anything this morning, we proceeded early to the palace, in great expectation that the medicines in request would bring us something; but after waiting all day till 4 P.M., as the king did not appear, leaving Bombay behind, I walked away to shoot a guinea-fowl within earshot of the palace. The scheme was successful, for the report of the gun which killed the bird reached the king's ear, and induced him to say that if Bana was present he would be glad to see him. This gave Bombay an opportunity of telling all the facts of the case; which were no sooner heard than the king gave his starving guests a number of plantains, and vanished at once, taking my page Lugoi with him, to instruct him in Kisuahili (Zanzibar language).

9th. – As the fruit of last night's scheme, the king sent us four goats and two cows. In great good-humour I now called on him, and found him walking about the palace environs with a carbine, looking eagerly for sport, whilst his pages dragged about five half-dead vultures tied in a bundle by their legs to a string.

"These birds," said he, tossing his head proudly, "were all shot flying, with iron slugs, as the boys will tell you. I like the carbine very well, but you must give me a double smooth gun." This I promised to give when Grant arrived, for his good-nature in sending so many officers to fetch him.

We next tried for guinea-fowl, as I tell him they are the game the English delight in; but the day was far spent, and none could be found. A boy then in attendance was pointed out, as having seen Grant in Uddu ten days ago. If the statement were true, he must have crossed the Katonga. But though told with great apparent circumspection, I did not credit it, because my men sent on the 15th ultimo for a letter to ascertain his whereabouts had not returned, and they certainly would have done so had he been so near. To make sure, the king then proposed sending the boy again with some of my men; but this I objected to as useless, considering the boy had spoken falsely. Hearing this, the king looked at the boy and then at the women in turn, to ascertain what they thought of my opinion, whereupon the boy cried. Late in the evening the sly little girl Kahala changed her cloth wrapper for a mbugu, and slipped quietly away. I did not suspect her intention, because of late she had appeared much more than ordinary happy, behaving to me in every respect like a dutiful child to a parent. A search was made, and guns fired, in the hopes of frightening her back again, but without effect.

10th. – I had promised that this morning I would teach the king the art of guinea-fowl shooting, and when I reached the palace at 6 A.M., I found him already on the ground. He listened to the tale of the missing girl, and sent orders for her apprehension at once; then proceeding with the gun, fired eight shots successively at guinea-birds sitting on trees, but missed them all. After this, as the birds were scared away, and both iron shot and bullets were expended, he took us to his dressing-hut, went inside himself, attended by full-grown naked women, and ordered a breakfast of pork, beef, fish, and plantains to be served me outside on the left of the entrance; whilst a large batch of his women sat on the right side, silently coquetting, and amusing themselves by mimicking the white man eating. Poor little Lugoi joined in the repast, and said he longed to return to my hut, for he was half starved here, and no one took any notice of him; but he was destined to be a royal page, for the king would not part with him. A cold fit then seized me, and as I asked for leave to go, the king gave orders for one of his wives to be flogged. The reason for this act of brutality I did not discover; but the moment the order was issued, the victim begged the pages to do it quickly, that the king's wrath might be appeased; and in an instant I saw a dozen boys tear their cord-turbans from their heads pull her roughly into the middle of the court, and belabour her with sticks, whilst she lay floundering about, screeching to me for protection. All I did was to turn my head away and walk rapidly out of sight, thinking it better not to interfere again with the discipline of the palace; indeed, I thought it not improbable that the king did these things sometimes merely that his guests might see his savage power. On reaching home I found Kahala standing like a culprit before my door. She would not admit, what I suspected, that Meri had induced her to run away; but said she was very happy in my house until yester-evening, when Rozaro's sister told her she was very stupid living with the Mzungu all alone, and told her to run away; which she did, taking the direction of N'yamasore's, until some officers finding her, and noticing beads on her neck, and her hair cut, according to the common court fashion, in slopes from a point in the forehead to the breadth of her ears, suspected her to be one of the king's women, and kept her in confinement all night, till Mtesa's men came this morning and brought her back again. As a punishment, I ordered her to live with Bombay; but my house was so dull again from want of some one to eat dinner with me, that I remitted the punishment, to her great delight.

11th. – To-day I received letters from Grant, dated 22d., 25th, 28th April and 2d May. They were brought by my three men, with Karague pease, flour, and ammunition. He was at Maula's house, which proved the king's boy to be correct; for the convoy, afraid of encountering the voyage on the lake, had deceived my companion and brought him on by land, like true negroes.

12th. – I sent the three men who had returned from Grant to lay a complaint against the convoy, who had tricked him out of a pleasant voyage, and myself out of the long-wished-for survey of the lake. They carried at the same time a present of a canister of shot from me to the king. Delighted with this unexpected prize, he immediately shot fifteen birds flying, and ordered the men to acquaint me with his prowess.

13th. – To-day the king sent me four cows and a load of butter as a return-present for the shot, and allowed one of his officers, at my solicitation, to go with ten of my men to help Grant on. He also sent a message that he had just shot thirteen birds flying.

14th. – Mabuki and Bilal returned with Budja and his ten children from Unyoro, attended by a deputation of four men sent by Kamrasi, who were headed by Kidgwiga. Mtesa, it now transpired, had followed my advice of making friendship with Kamrasi by sending two brass wires as a hongo instead of an army, and Kamrasi in return, sent him two elephant-tusks. Kidgwiga said Petherick's party was not in Unyoro – they had never reached there, but were lying at anchor off Gani. Two white men only had been seen – one, they said, a hairy man, the other smooth-faced; they were as anxiously inquiring after us as we were after them: they sat on chairs, dressed like myself, and had guns and everything precisely like those in my hut. On one occasion they sent up a necklace of beads to Kamrasi, and he, in return, gave them a number of women and tusks. If I wished to go that way, Kamrasi would forward me on to their position in boats; for the land route, leading through Kidi, was a jungle of ten days, tenanted by a savage set of people, who hunt everybody, and seize everything they see.

This tract is sometimes, however, traversed by the Wanyoro and Gani people, who are traders in cows and tippet monkey-skins, stealthily travelling at night; but they seldom attempt it from fear of being murdered. Baraka and Uledi, sent from Karague on the 30th January, had been at Kamrasi's palace upwards of a month, applying for the road to Gani, and as they could not get that, wished to come with Mabruki to me; but this Kamrasi also refused, on the plea that, as they had come from Karague, so they must return there. Kamrasi had heard of my shooting with Mtesa, as also of the attempt made by Mabruki and Uledi to reach Gani via Usoga. He had received my present of beads from Baraka, and, in addition, took Uledi's sword, saying, "If you do not wish to part with it, you must remain a prisoner in my country all your life, for you have not paid your footing." Mabruki then told me he was kept waiting at a village, one hour's walk from Kamrasi's palace, five days before they were allowed to approach his majesty; but when they were seen, and the presents exchanged, they were ordered to pack off the following morning, as Kamrasi said the Waganda were a set of plundering blackguards.

This information, to say the least of it, was very embarrassing – a mixture of good and bad. Petherick, I now felt certain, was on the look-out for us; but his men had reached Kamrasi's, and returned again before Baraka's arrival. Baraka was not allowed to go on to him and acquaint him of our proximity, and the Waganda were so much disliked in Unyoro, that there seemed no hopes of our ever being able to communicate by letter. To add to my embarrassments, Grant had not been able to survey the lake from Kitangule, nor had Usoga and the eastern side of the lake been seen.

15th. – I was still laid up with the cold fit of the 10th, which turned into a low kind of fever. I sent Bombay to the king to tell him the news, and ask him what he thought of doing next. He replied that he would push for Gani direct; and sent back a pot of pombe for the sick man.

16th. – The king to-day inquired after my health, and, strange to say, did not accompany his message with a begging request.

17th. – My respite, however, was not long. At the earliest possible hour in the morning the king sent begging for things one hundred times refused, supposing, apparently, that I had some little reserve store which I wished to conceal from him.

18th and 19th. – I sent Bombay to the palace to beg for pombe, as it was the only thing I had an appetite for, but the king would see no person but myself. He had broken his rifle washing-rod, and this must be mended, the pages who brought it saying that no one dared take it back to him until it was repaired. A guinea-fowl was sent after dark for me to see, as a proof that the king was a sportsman complete.

20th. – The king going out shooting borrowed my powder-horn. The Wanguana mobbed the hut and bullied me for food, merely because they did not like the trouble of helping themselves from the king's garden, though they knew I had purchased their privilege to do so at the price of a gold chronometer and the best guns England could produce.

21st. – I now, for the first time, saw the way in which the king collected his army together. The highroads were all thronged with Waganda warriors, painted in divers colours, with plantain-leaf bands round their heads, scanty goat-skin fastened to their loins, and spears and shield in their hands, singing the tambure or march, ending with a repetition of the word Mkavia, or Monarch. They surpassed in number, according to Bombay, the troops and ragamuffins enlisted by Sultain Majid when Sayyid Sweni threatened to attack Zanzibar; in fact, he never saw such a large army collected anywhere.

Bombay, on going to the palace, hoping to obtain plantains for the men, found the king holding a levee, for the purpose of despatching this said army somewhere, but where no one would pronounce. The king, then, observing my men who had gone to Unyoro together with Kamrasi's, questioned them on their mission; and when told that no white men were there, he waxed wrathful, and said it was a falsehood, for his men had seen them, and could not be mistaken. Kamrasi, he said, must have hidden them somewhere, fearful of the number of guns which now surrounded him; and, for the same reason, he told lies, yes, lies – but no man living shall dare tell himself lies; and now, as he could not obtain his object by fair means, he would use arms and force it out. Then, turning to Bombay, he said, "What does your master think of this business?" upon which Bombay replied, according to his instructions, "Bana wishes nothing done until Grant arrives, when all will go together." On this the king turned his back and walked away.

22d. – Kitunzi called on me early, because he heard I was sick. I asked him why the Waganda objected to my sitting on a chair; but, to avoid the inconvenience of answering a trouble-some question, without replying, he walked off, saying he heard a noise in the neighbourhood of the palace which must be caused by the king ordering some persons to be seized, and his presence was so necessary he could not wait another moment. My men went for plantains to the palace and for pombe on my behalf; but the king, instead of giving them anything, took two fez caps off their heads, keeping them to himself, and ordered them to tell Bana all his beer was done.

23d. – Kidgwiga called on me to say Kamrasi so very much wanted the white men at Gani to visit him, he had sent a hon-go of thirty tusks to the chief of that country in hopes that it would insure their coming to see him. He also felt sure if I went there his king would treat me with the greatest respect. This af-forded an opportunity for putting in a word of reconciliation. I said that it was at my request that Mtesa sent Kamrasi a present; and so now, if Kamrasi made friends with the Waganda, there would be no difficulty about the matter.

24th. – The army still thronged the highways, some going, others coming, like a swarm of ants, the whole day long. Kidg-wiga paid another visit, and I went to the palace without my gun, wishing the king to fancy all my powder was done, as he had nearly consumed all my store; but the consequence was that, after waiting the whole day, I never saw him at all. In the evening pages informed me that Grant had arrived at N'yama Goma, one march distant.

25th. – I prepared twenty men, with a quarter of mutton for Grant to help him on the way, but they could not go without a native officer, lest they should be seized, and no officer would

lead the way. The king came shooting close to my hut and ordered me out. I found him marching Rozaro about in custody
with four other Wanyambo, who, detected plundering by Kitunzi, had set upon and beaten him severely. The king, pointing
them out to me, said, he did not like the system of plundering,
and wished to know if it was the practice in Karague. Of course
I took the opportunity to renew my protest against the plundering system; but the king, changing the subject, told me the
Wazungu were at Gani inquiring after us, and wishing to come
here. To this I proposed fetching them myself in boats, but he
objected, saying he would send men first, for they were not farther off to the northward than the place he sent boats to, to
bring Grant. He said he did not like Unyoro, because Kamrasi
hides himself like a Neptune in the Nile, whenever his men go
on a visit there, and instead of treating his guests with respect,
he keeps them beyond the river. For this reason he had himself
determined on adopting the passage by Kidi.

I was anxious, of course, to go on with the subject thus unexpectedly opened, but, as ill-luck would have it, an adjutant
was espied sitting on a tree, when a terrible fuss and excitement
ensued. The women were ordered one way and the attendants
another, whilst I had to load the gun on the best way I could
with the last charge and a half left in the king's pouch. Ten
grains were all he would have allowed himself, reserving the
residue, without reflecting that a large bird required much shot;
and he was shocked to find me lavishly use the whole, and still
say it was not enough.

The bird was then at a great height, so that the first shot
merely tickled him, and drove him to another tree. "Woh!

Woh!" cried the king, "I am sure he is hit; look there, look there"; and away he rushed after the bird; down with one fence, then with another, in the utmost confusion, everybody trying to keep his proper place, till at last the tree to which the bird had flown was reached, and then, with the last charge of shot, the king killed his first nundo. The bird, however, did not fall, but lay like a spread eagle in the upper branches. Wasoga were called to climb the tree and pull it down; whilst the king, in ecstasies of joy and excitement, rushed up and down the potato-field like a mad bull, jumping and plunging, waving and brandishing the gun above his head; whilst the drums beat, the attendants all woh-wohed, and the women, joining with their lord, rushed about lullalooing and dancing like insane creatures. Then began congratulations and hand-shakings, and, finally, the inspection of the bird, which, by this time, the Wasoga had thrown down. Oh! Oh! what a wonder! Its wings outspread reached further than the height of a man; we must go and show it to the brothers. Even that was not enough – we must show it to the mother; and away we all rattled as fast as our legs could carry us.

Arrived at the queen's palace, out of respect to his mother, the king changed his European clothes for a white kid-skin wrapper, and then walked in to see her, leaving us waiting outside. By this time Colonel Congow, in his full-dress uniform, had arrived in the square outside, with his regiment drawn up in review order. The king, hearing the announcement, at once came out with spears and shield, preceded by the bird, and took post, standing armed, by the entrance, encircled by his staff, all squatting, when the adjutant was placed in the middle of the company. Before us was a large open square, with the huts of the queen's Kamraviona or commander-in-chief beyond. The battalion, consisting of what might be termed three companies, each containing 200 men, being drawn up on the left extremity of the parade-ground, received orders to march past in single file from the right of companies, at a long trot, and re-form again at the other end of the square.

Nothing conceivable could be more wild or fantastic than the sight which ensued – the men all nearly naked, with goat or cat skins depending from their girdles, and smeared with war colours according to the taste of each individual; one-half of the body red or black, the other blue, not in regular order – as, for instance, one stocking would be red, the other black, whilst the breeches above would be the opposite colours, and so with the sleeves and waistcoat. Every man carried the same arms – two spears and one shield – held as if approaching an enemy, and they thus moved in three lines of single rank and file, at fifteen to twenty paces asunder, with the same high action and elongated step, the ground leg only being bent, to give their strides the greater force. After the men had all started, the captains of companies followed, even more fantastically dressed; and last of all came the great Colonel Congow, a perfect Robinson Crusoe, with his long white-haired goat-skins, a fiddle-shaped leather shield, tufted with white hair at all six extremities, bands of long hair tied below the knees, and a magnificent helmet, covered with rich beads of every colour, in excellent taste, surmounted with a plume of crimson feathers, from the centre of which rose a bent stem, tufted with goat-hair. Next they charged in companies to and fro; and, finally, the senior officers came charging at their king, making violent professions of faith and honesty, for which they were applauded. The parade then broke up, and all went home.

26th. – One of king Mtesa's officers now consenting to go to N'yama Goma with some of my men, I sent Grant a quarter of goat. The reply brought to me was, that he was very thankful for it; that he cooked it and ate it on the spot; and begged I would see the king, to get him released from that starving place. Rozaro was given over to the custody of Kitunzi for punishment. At the same time, the queen, having heard of the outrages committed against her brother and women, commanded that neither my men nor any of Rozaro's should get any more food at the palace; for as we all came to Uganda in one body, so all alike were, by her logic, answerable for the offence. I called at the palace for explanation but could not obtain admittance because I would not fire the gun.

27th. – The king sent to say he wanted medicine to propitiate lightning. I called and described the effects of a lightning-rod, and tried to enter into the Unyoro business, wishing to go there at once myself. He objected, because he had not seen Grant, but appointed an officer to go through Unyoro on to Gani, and begged I would also send men with letters. Our talk was agreeably interrupted by guns in the distance announcing Grant's arrival, and I took my leave to welcome my friend. How we enjoyed ourselves after so much anxiety and want of one another's company, I need not describe. For my part, I was only too rejoiced to see Grant could limp about a bit, and was able to laugh over the picturesque and amusing account he gave me of his own rough travels.

28th. – The king in the morning sent Budja, his ambassador, with Kamrasi's Kidgwiga, over to me for my men and letters, to go to Kamrasi's again and ask for the road to Gani. I wished to speak to the king first, but they said they had no orders to stop for that, and walked straight away. I sent the king a present of a double-barrelled gun and ammunition, and received in answer a request that both Grant and myself would attend a levee, which he was to hold in state, accompanied by his bodyguard, as when I was first presented to him. In the afternoon we proceeded to court accordingly, but found it scantily attended; and after the first sitting, which was speedily over, retired to another court, and saw the women. Of this dumb show the king soon got tired; he therefore called for his iron chair, and entered into conversation, at first about the ever-engrossing subject of stimulants, till we changed it by asking him how he liked the gun? He pronounced it a famous weapon, which he would use intensely. We then began to talk in a general way about Suwarora and Rumanika, as well as the road through Unyamuezi, which we hoped would soon cease to exist, and be superseded by one through Unyoro.

It will be kept in view that the hanging about at this court, and all the perplexing and irritating negotiations here described, had always one end in view – that of reaching the Nile where it pours out of the N'yanza, as I was long certain that it did. Without the consent and even the aid of this capricious barbarian I was now talking to, such a project was hopeless. I naturally seized every opportunity for putting in a word in the direction of my great object, and here seemed to be an opportunity. We now ventured on a plump application for boats that we might feel our way to Gani by water, supposing the lake and river to be navigable all the way; and begged Kitunzi might be appointed to accompany us, in order that whatever was done might be done all with good effect in opening up a new line of commerce, by which articles of European manufacture might find a permanent route to Uganda. It was "no go," however. The appeal, though listened to, and commented on, showing that it was well understood, got no direct reply. It was not my policy to make our object appear too important to ourselves, so I had to appear tolerably indifferent, and took the opportunity to ask for my paint-box, which he had borrowed for a day and had kept in his possession for months. I got no answer to that request either, but was immediately dunned for the compass, which had been promised on Grant's arrival. Now, with a promise that the compass would be sent him in the morning, he said he would see what pombe his women could spare us; and, bidding good evening, walked away.

29th. – I sent Bombay with the compass, much to the delight of the king, who no sooner saw it than he jumped and woh-wohed with intense excitement at the treasure he had gained, said it was the greatest present Bana had ever given him, for it was the thing by which he found out all the roads and countries – it was, in fact, half his knowledge; and the parting with it showed plainly that Bana entertained an everlasting friendship for him. The king then called Maula, and said, "Maula, indeed you have spoken the truth; there is nothing like this instrument," etc., etc., repeating what he had already told Bombay. In the evening, the king, accompanied by all his brothers, with iron chair and box, came to visit us, and inspected all

Grant's recently brought pictures of the natives, with great acclamation. We did not give him anything this time, but, instead, dunned him for the paint-box, and afterwards took a walk to my observatory hill, where I acted as guide. On the summit of this hill the king instructed his brothers on the extent of his dominions; and as I asked where Lubari or God resides, he pointed to the skies.

30th. – The king at last sent the paint-box, with some birds of his own shooting, which he wished painted. He also wanted himself drawn, and all Grant's pictures copied. Then, to wind up these mild requests, a demand was made for more powder, and that all our guns be sent to the palace for inspection.

31st. – I drew a large white and black hornbill and a green pigeon sent by himself; but he was not satisfied; he sent more birds, and wanted to see my shoes. The pages who came with the second message, however, proving impertinent, got a book flung at their heads, and a warning to be off, as I intended to see the king myself, and ask for food to keep my ever-complaining Wanguana quiet. Proceeding to the palace, as I found Mtesa had gone out shooting, I called on the Kamraviona, complained that my camp was starving, and as I had nothing left to give the king said I wished to leave the country. Ashamed of its being supposed that his king would not give me any food because I had no more presents to give him, the Kamraviona, from his own stores, gave me a goat and pombe, and said he would speak to the king on the subject.

1st. – I drew for the king a picture of a guinea-fowl which he shot in the early morning, and proceeded on a visit with Grant to the queen's, accompanied only by seven men, as the rest preferred foraging for themselves, to the chance of picking up a few plantains at her majesty's. After an hour's waiting, the queen received us with smiles, and gave pombe and plantains to her new visitor, stating pointedly she had none for me. There was deep Uganda policy in this: it was for the purpose of treating Grant as a separate, independent person, and so obtaining a fresh hongo or tax. Laughing at the trick, I thanked her for the beer, taking it personally on my household, and told her when my property arrived from Karague, she should have a few more things as I promised her; but the men sent had neither brought my brother in a vessel, as they were ordered, not did they bring my property from Karague.

Still the queen was not content: she certainly expected something from Grant, if it was ever so little, for she was entitled to it, and would not listen to our being one house. Turning the subject, to put in a word for my great object, I asked her to use her influence in opening the road to Gani, as, after all, that was the best way to get new things into Uganda. Cunning as a fox, the queen agreed to this project, provided Grant remained behind, for she had not seen enough of him yet, and she would speak to her son about the matter in the morning.

This was really the first gleam of hope, and I set to putting our future operations into a shape that might lead to practical results without alarming our capricious host. I thought that whilst I could be employed in inspecting the river, and in feeling the route by water to Gani, Grant could return to Karague by water, bringing up our rear traps, and, in navigating the lake, obtain the information he had been frustrated in getting by the machinations of his attendant Maribu. It was agreed to, and all seemed well; for there was much left to be done in Uganda and Usoga, if we could only make sure of communicating once with Petherick. Before going home we had some more polite conversation, during which the queen played with a toy in the shape of a cocoa du mer, studded all over with cowries: this was a sort of doll, or symbol of a baby and her dandling it was held to indicate that she would ever remain a widow. In the evening the king returned all our rifles and guns, with a request for one of them; as also for the iron chair he sat upon when calling on us, an iron bedstead, and the Union Jack, for he did not honour us with a visit for nothing; and the head page was sent to witness the transfer of the goods, and see there was no humbug about it. It was absolutely necessary to get into a rage, and tell the head page we did not come to Uganda to be swindled in that manner, and he might tell the king I would not part with one of them.

2d. – K'yengo, who came with Grant, now tried to obtain an interview with the king, but could not get admission. I had some further trouble about the disposal of the child Meri, who said she never before had lived in a poor man's house since she was born. I thought to content her by offering to marry her to one of Rumanika's sons, a prince of her own breed, but she would not listen to the proposal.

3d. – For days past, streams of men have been carrying faggots of firewood, clean-cut timber, into the palaces of the king, queen, and the Kamraviona; and to-day, on calling on the king, I found him engaged having these faggots removed by Colonel Mkavia's regiment from one court into another, this being his way of ascertaining their quantity, instead of counting them.

About 1,600 men were engaged on this service, when the king, standing on a carpet in front of the middle hut of the first court, with two spears in his hand and his dog by his side, surrounded by his brothers and a large staff of officers, gave orders for the regiment to run to and fro in column, that he might see them well; then turning to his staff, ordered them to run up and down the regiment, and see what they thought of it. This ridiculous order set them all flying, and soon they returned, charging at the king with their sticks, dancing and jabbering that their numbers were many, he was the greatest king on earth, and their lives and services were his for ever. The regiment now received orders to put down their faggots, and, taking up their own sticks in imitation of spears, followed the antics of their officers in charging and vociferating. Next, Mkavia presented five hairy Usoga goats, n'yanzigging and performing the other appropriate ceremonies. On asking the king if he had any knowledge of the extent of his army, he merely said, "How can I, when these you see are a portion of them just ordered here to carry wood?" The regiment was now dismissed; but the officers were invited to follow the king into another court, when he complimented them on assembling so many men; they, instead of leaving well alone, foolishly replied they were sorry they were not more numerous, as some of the men lived so far away they shirked the summons; Maula, then, ever forward in mischief, put a cap on it by saying, if he could only impress upon the Waganda to listen to his orders, there would never be a deficiency. Upon which the king said, "If they fail to obey you, they disobey me; for I have appointed you as my orderly, and thereby you personify the orders of the king." Up jumped Maula in a moment as soon as these words were uttered, charging with his stick, then floundering and n'yanzigging as if he had been signally rewarded. I expected some piece of cruel mischief to come of all this, but the king, in his usual capricious way, suddenly rising, walked off to a third court, followed only by a select few.

Here, turning to me, he said, "Bana, I love you, because you have come so far to see me, and have taught me so many things since you have been here." Rising, with my hand to my heart, and gracefully bowing at this strange announcement – for at that moment I was full of hunger and wrath – I intimated I was much flattered at hearing it, but as my house was in a state of starvation, I trusted he would consider it. "What!" said he, "do you want goats?" "Yes, very much." The pages then received orders to furnish me with ten that moment, as the king's farmyard was empty, and he would reimburse them as soon as more confiscations took place. But this, I said, was not enough; the Wanguana wanted plantains, for they had received none these fifteen days. "What!" said the king, turning to his pages again, "have you given these men no plantains, as I ordered? Go and fetch them this moment, and pombe too, for Bana." The subject then turned on the plan I had formed of going to Gani by water, and of sending Grant to Karague by the lake; but the king's mind was fully occupied with the compass I had given him.

He required me to explain its use, and then broke up the meeting.

4th. – Viarungi, an officer sent by Rumanika to escort Grant to Uganda, as well as to apply to king Mtesa for a force to fight his brother Rogero, called on me with Rozaro, and said he had received instructions from his king to apply to me for forty cows and two slave-boys, because the Arabs who pass through his country to Uganda always make him a present of that sort after receiving them from Mtesa. After telling him we English never give the presents they have received away to any one, and never make slaves, but free them, I laid a complaint against Rozaro for having brought much trouble and disgrace upon my camp, as well as much trouble on myself, and begged that he might be removed from my camp. Rozaro then attempted to excuse himself, but without success, and said he had already detached his residence from my camp, and taken up a separate residence with Viarungi, his superior officer.

I called on the king in the afternoon, and found the pages had already issued plantains for my men and pombe for myself. The king addressed me with great cordiality, and asked if I wished to go to Gani. I answered him with all promptitude – Yes, at once, with some of his officers competent to judge of the value of all I point out to them for future purposes in keeping the road permanently open. His provoking capriciousness, however, again broke in, and he put me off till his messengers should return from Unyoro. I told him his men had gone in vain, for Budja left without my letter or my men; and further, that the river route is the only one that will ever be of advantage to Uganda, and the sooner it was opened up the better. I entreated him to listen to my advice, and send some of my men to Kamrasi direct, to acquaint him with my intention to go down the river in boats to him; but I could get no answer to this. Bombay then asked for cows for the Wanguana, getting laughed at for his audacity, and the king broke up the court and walked away.

5th. – I started on a visit to the queen, but half-way met Congow, who informed me he had just escorted her majesty from his house, where she was visiting, to her palace. By way of a joke and feeler, I took it in my head to try, by taking a harmless rise out of Congow, whether the Nile is understood by the natives to be navigable near its exit from the N'yanza. I told him he had been appointed by the king to escort us down the river to Gani. He took the affair very seriously, delivering himself to the following purport: "Well, then, my days are numbered; for if I refuse compliance I shall lose my head; and if I attempt to pass Kamrasi's, which is on the river, I shall lose my life; for I am a marked man there, having once led an army past his palace and back again. It would be no use calling it a peaceful mission, as you propose; for the Wanyoro distrust the Waganda to such an extent, they would fly to arms at once." Proceeding to the queen's palace, we met Murondo, who had once travelled to the Masai frontier. He said it would take a month to go in boats from Kira, the most easterly district in Uganda, to Masai, where there is another N'yanza, joined by a strait to the big N'yanza, which king Mtesa's boats frequent for salt; but the same distance could be accomplished in four days overland, and three days afterwards by boat. The queen, after keeping us all day waiting, sent three bunches of plantains and a pot of pombe, with a message that she was too tired to receive visitors, and hoped we would call another day.

6th. – I met Pokino, the governor-general of Uddu, in the morning's walk, who came here at the same time as Grant to visit the king, and was invited into his house to drink pombe. His badge of office is an iron hatchet, inlaid with copper and han-

512

dled with ivory. He wished to give us a cow, but put it off for another day, and was surprised we dared venture into his premises without permission from the king. After this, we called at the palace, just as the king was returning from a walk with his brothers. He saw us, and sent for Bana. We entered, and presented him with some pictures, which he greatly admired, looked at close and far, showed to the brothers, and inspected again. Pokino at this time came in with a number of well-made shields, and presented them grovelling and n'yanzigging; but though the governor of an important province, who had not been seen by the king for years, he was taken no more notice of than any common Mkungu. A plan of the lake and Nile, which I brought with me to explain our projects for reaching Karague and Gani, engaged the king's attention for a while; but still he would not agree to let anything be done until the messenger returned from Unyoro. Finding him inflexible, I proposed sending a letter, arranging that his men should be under the guidance of my men after they pass Unyoro on the way to Gani; and this was acceded to, provided I should write a letter to Petherick by the morrow. I then tried to teach the king the use of the compass. To make a stand for it, I turned a drum on its head, when all the courtiers flew at me as if to prevent an outrage, and the king laughed. I found that, as the instrument was supposed to be a magic charm of very wonderful powers, my meddling with it and treating it as an ordinary movable was considered a kind of sacrilege.

7th. – I wrote a letter to Petherick, but the promised Wakungu never came for it. As K'yengo was ordered to attend court with Rumanika's hongo, consisting of a few wires, small beads, and a cloth I gave him, as well as a trifle from Nnanji, I sent Bombay, in place of going myself, to remind the king of his promises for the Wakungu to Gani, as well as for boats to Karague, but a grunt was the only reply which my messenger said he obtained.

8th. – Calling at the palace, I found the king issuing for a walk, and joined him, when he suddenly turned round in the rudest manner, re-entered his palace, and left me to go home without speaking a word. The capricious creature then reissued, and, finding me gone, inquired after me, presuming I ought to have waited for him.

9th. – During the night, when sleeping profoundly, some person stealthily entered my hut and ran off with a box of bullets towards the palace, but on the way dropped his burden. Maula, on the way home, happening to see it, and knowing it to be mine, brought it back again. I stayed at home, not feeling well.

10th. – K'yengo paid his hongo in wire to the king, and received a return of six cows. Still at home, an invalid, I received a visit from Meri, who seemed to have quite recovered herself. Speaking of her present quarters, she said she loved Uledi's wife very much, thinking birds of a feather ought to live together. She helped herself to a quarter of mutton, and said she would come again.

11th. – To-day Viarungi, finding Rozaro's men had stolen thirty cows, twelve slaves, and a load of mbugu from the Waganda, laid hands on them himself for Rumanika, instead of giving them to King Mtesa. Such are the daily incidents among our neighbours.

12th. – At night a box of ammunition and a bag of shot, which were placed out as a reserve present for the king, to be given on our departure, were stolen, obviously by the king's boys, and most likely by the king's orders; for he is the only person who could have made any use of them, and his boys alone know the way into the hut; besides which, the previous box of bullets was found on the direct road to the palace, while it was well known that no one dared to touch an article of European manufacture without the consent of the king.

13th. – I sent a message to the king about the theft, requiring him, if an honest man, to set his detectives to work, and ferret it out; his boys, at the same time, to show our suspicions, were peremptorily forbidden ever to enter the hut again. Twice the king sent down a hasty message to say he was collecting all his men to make a search, and, if they do not succeed, the Mganga would be sent; but nothing was done. The Kamraviona was sharply rebuked by the king for allowing K'yengo to visit him before permission was given, and thus defrauding the royal exchequer of many pretty things, which were brought for majesty alone. At night the rascally boys returned again to plunder, but Kahala, more wakeful than myself, heard them trying to untie the door-handle, and frightened them away in endeavouring to awaken me.

14th and 15th. – Grant, doing duty for me, tried a day's penance at the palace, but though he sat all day in the antechamber, and musicians were ordered into the presence, nobody called for him.

K'yengo was sent with all his men on a Wakungu-seizing expedition – a good job for him, as it was his perquisite to receive the major part of the plunder himself.

16th. – I sent Kahala out of the house, giving her finally over to Bombay as a wife, because she preferred playing with dirty little children to behaving like a young lady, and had caught the itch.

This was much against her wish, and the child vowed she would not leave me until force compelled her; but I had really no other way of dealing with the remnant of the awkward burden which the queen's generosity had thrown on me. K'yengo went to the palace with fifty prisoners; but as the king had taken his women to the small pond, where he has recently placed a tub canoe for purposes of amusement, they did no business.

17th. – I took a first convalescent walk. The king, who was out shooting all day, begged for powder in the evening. Uledi returned from his expedition against a recusant officer at Kituntu, bringing with him a spoil of ten women. It appeared that the officer himself had bolted from his landed possessions, and as they belonged to "the church," or were in some way or other sacred from civil execution, they could not be touched, so that Uledi lost an estate which the king had promised him. We heard that Ilmas, wife of Majanja, who, as I already mentioned, had achieved an illustrious position by services at the birth of the king, had been sent to visit the late king Sunna's tomb, whence, after observing certain trees which were planted, and divining by mystic arts what the future state of Uganda required, she would return at a specific time, to order the king at the time of his coronation either to take the field with an army, to make a pilgrimage, or to live a life of ease at home; whichever of these courses the influence of the ordeal at the grave might prompt her to order, must be complied with by the king.

18th. – I called at the palace with Grant, taking with us some pictures of soldiers, horses, elephants, etc. We found the guard fighting over their beef and plantain dinner. Bombay remarked that this daily feeding on beef would be the lot of the Wanguana if they had no religious scruples about the throat-cutting of animals for food. This, I told him, was all their own fault, for they have really no religion or opinions of their own; and had they been brought up in England instead of Africa, it would have been all the other way with them as a matter of course; but Bombay replied, "We could no more throw off the Mussulman faith than you could yours." A man with a maniacal voice sang and whistled by turns. Katumba, the officer of the guards, saw our pictures, and being a favourite, acquainted the king, which gained us an admittance.

We found his majesty sitting on the ground, within a hut, behind a portal, encompassed by his women, and took our seats outside.

At first all was silence, till one told the king we had some wonderful pictures to show him; in an instant he grew lively, crying out, "Oh, let us see them!" and they were shown, Bombay explaining. Three of the king's wives then came in, and offered him their two virgin sisters, n'yanzigging incessantly, and beseeching their acceptance, as by that means they themselves would become doubly related to him. Nothing, however, seemed to be done to promote the union, until one old lady, sitting by the king's side, who was evidently learned in the etiquette and traditions of the court, said, "Wait and see if he embraces, otherwise you may know he is not pleased." At this announcement the girls received a hint to pass on, and the king commenced bestowing on them a series of huggings, first sitting on the lap of one, whom he clasped to his bosom, crossing his neck with hers to the right, then to the left, and, having finished with her, took post in the second one's lap, then on that of the third, performing on each of them the same evolutions. He then retired to his original position, and the marriage ceremony was supposed to be concluded, and the settlements adjusted, when all went on as before.

The pictures were again looked at, and again admired, when we asked for a private interview on business, and drew the king outside. I then begged he would allow me, whilst his men were absent at Unyoro, to go to the Masai country, and see the Salt Lake at the north-east corner of the N'yanza, and to lend me some of his boats for Grant to fetch powder and beads from Karague. This important arrangement being conceded by the king more promptly than we expected, a cow, plantains, and pombe were requested; but the cow only was given, though our men were said to be feeding on grass. Taking the king, as it appeared, in a good humour, to show him the abuses arising from the system of allowing his guests to help themselves by force upon the highways, I reported the late seizures made of thirty cows and twelve slaves by the Wanyambo; but, though surprised to hear the news, he merely remarked that there were indeed a great number of visitors in Uganda. During this one day we heard the sad voice of no less than four women, dragged from the palace to the slaughter-house.

19th. – To follow up our success in the marching question and keep the king to his promise, I called at his palace, but found he had gone out shooting. To push my object further, I then marched off to the queen's to bid her good-bye, as if we were certain to leave the next day; but as no one would dare to approach her cabinet to apprise her of our arrival, we returned home tired and annoyed.

20th. – The king sent for us at noon; but when we reached the palace we found he had started on a shooting tour; so, to make the best of our time, we called again upon the queen for the same purpose as yesterday, as also to get my books of birds and animals, which, taken merely to look at for a day or so, had been kept for months. After hours of waiting, her majesty appeared standing in an open gateway; beckoned us to advance, and offered pombe; then, as two or three drops of rain fell, she said she could not stand the violence of the weather, and forthwith retired without one word being obtained. An officer, however, venturing in for the books, at length I got them.

21st. – To-day I went to the palace, but found no one; the king was out shooting again.

22d. – We resolved to-day to try on a new political influence at the court. Grant had taken to the court of Karague a jumping-jack, to amuse the young princes; but it had a higher destiny, for it so fascinated the king Rumanika himself that he would not part with it – unless, indeed, Grant would make him a big one out of a tree which was handed to him for the purpose. We resolved to try the influence of such a toy on king Mtesa, and brought with us, in addition, a mask and some pictures. But although the king took a visiting card, the gate was never opened to us. Finding this, and the day closing, we deposited the mask and pictures on a throne, and walked away. We found that we had thus committed a serious breach of state etiquette; for the guard, as soon as they saw what we had done, seized the Wanguana for our offences in defiling the royal seat, and would have bound them, had they not offered to return the articles to us.

23d. – Early in the morning, hearing the royal procession marching off on a shooting excursion, we sent Bombay running after it with the mask and pictures, to aquaint the king with our desire to see him, and explain that we had been four days successively foiled in attempts to find him in his palace, our object being an eager wish to come to some speedy understanding about the appointed journeys to the Salt Lake and Karague. The toys produced the desired effect; for the king stopped and played with them, making Bombay and the pages don the masks by turns. He appointed the morrow for an interview, at the same time excusing himself for not having seen us yesterday on the plea of illness. In the evening Kahala absconded with another little girl of the camp in an opposite direction from the one she took last time; but as both of them wandered about not knowing where to go to, and as they omitted to take off all their finery, they were soon recognised as in some way connected with my party, taken up, and brought into camp, where they were well laughed at for their folly, and laughed in turn at the absurdity of their futile venture.

24th. – Hoping to keep the king to his promise, I went to the palace early, but found he had already gone to see his brothers, so followed him down, and found him engaged playing on a harmonicon with them. Surprised at my intrusion, he first asked how I managed to find him out; then went on playing for a while; but suddenly stopping to talk with me, he gave me an opportunity of telling him I wished to send Grant off to Karague, and start myself for Usoga and the Salt Lake in the morning. "What! Going away?" said the king, as if he had never heard a word about it before; and then, after talking the whole subject over again, especially dwelling on the quantity of powder I had in store at Karague, he promised to send the necessary officers for escorting us on our respective journeys in the morning.

The brothers' wives then wished to see me, and came before us, when I had to take off my hat and shoes as usual, my ready compliance inducing the princes to pass various compliments of my person and disposition. The brothers then showed me a stool made of wood after the fashion of our sketching-stool, and a gun-cover of leather, made by themselves, of as good workmanship as is to be found in India. The king then rose, followed by his brothers, and we all walked off to the pond. The effect of stimulants was mooted, as well as other physiological phenomena, when a second move took us to the palace by torchlight, and the king showed a number of new huts just finished and beautifully made. Finally, he settled down to a musical concert, in which he took the lead himself. At eight o'clock, being tired and hungry, I reminded the king of his promises, and he appointed the morning to call on him for the Wakungu, and took leave.

25th. – Makinga, hearing of the intended march through Usoga, was pleased to say he would like to join my camp and spend his time in buying slaves and ivory there. I went to the palace for the promised escort, but was no sooner announced by the pages than the king walked off into the interior of his harem, and left me no alternative but to try my luck with the Kamraviona, who, equally proud with his master, would not answer my call – and so another day was lost.

26th. – This morning we had the assuring intelligence from Kaddu that he had received orders to hold himself in readiness for a voyage to Karague in twenty boats with Grant, but the date of departure was not fixed. The passage was expected to be rough, as the water off the mouth of the Kitangule Kagera (river) always runs high, so that no boats can go there except at night, when the winds of day subside, and are replaced by the calms of night. I called at the palace, but saw nothing of the king, though the court was full of officials; and there were no less than 150 women, besides girls, goats, and various other things, seizures from refractory state officers, who, it was said, had been too proud to present themselves at court for a period exceeding propriety.

All these creatures, I was assured, would afterwards be given away as return-presents for the hongos or presents received from the king's visitors. No wonder the tribes of Africa are mixed breeds. Amongst the officers in waiting was my friend Budja, the ambassador that had been sent to Unyoro with Kidgwiga, Kamrasi's deputy. He had returned three days before, but had not yet seen the king. As might have been expected, he said he had been anything but welcomed in Unyoro. Kamrasi, after keeping him half-starved and in suspense eight days, sent a message – for he would not see him – that he did not desire any communication with blackguard Waganda thieves, and therefore advised him, if he valued his life, to return by the road by which he came as speedily as possible. Turning to Congow, I playfully told him that, as the road through Unyoro was closed, he would have to go with me through Usoga and Kidi; but the gallant colonel merely shuddered, and said that would be a terrible undertaking.

27th. – The king would not show, for some reason or other, and we still feared to fire guns lest he should think our store of powder inexhaustible, and so keep us here until he had extorted the last of it. I found that the Waganda have the same absurd notion here as the Wanyambo have in Karague, of Kamrasi's supernatural power in being able to divide the waters of the Nile in the same manner as Moses did the Red Sea.

28th. – The king sent a messenger-boy to inform us that he had just heard from Unyoro that the white men were still at Gani inquiring after us; but nothing was said of Budja's defeat. I sent Bombay immediately off to tell him we had changed our plans, and now simply required a large escort to accompany us through Usoga and Kidi to Gani, as further delay in communicating with Petherick might frustrate all chance of opening the Nile trade with Uganda. He answered that he would assemble all his officers in the morning to consult with them on the subject, when he hoped we would attend, as he wished to further our views. A herd of cows, about eighty in number, were driven in from Unyoro, showing that the silly king was actually robbing Kamrasi at the same time that he was trying to treat with him. K'yengo informed us that the king, considering the surprising events which had lately occurred at his court, being very anxious to pry into the future, had resolved to take a very strong measure for accomplishing that end. This was the sacrifice of a child by cooking, as described in the introduction – a ceremony which it fell to K'yengo to carry out.

29th. – To have two strings to my bow, and press our departure as hotly as possible, I sent first Frij off with Nasib to the queen, conveying, as a parting present, a block-tin brush-box, a watch without a key, two sixpenny pocket-handker-chiefs, and a white towel, with an intimation that we were going, as the king had expressed his desire of sending us to Gani. Her majesty accepted the present, finding fault with the watch for not ticking like the king's, and would not believe her son Mtesa had been so hasty in giving us leave to depart, as she had not been consulted on the subject yet. Setting off to attend the king at his appointed time, I found the Kamraviona already there, with a large court attendance, patiently awaiting his majesty's advent. As we were all waiting on, I took a rise out of the Kamraviona by telling him I wanted a thousand men to march with me through Kidi to Gani. Surprised at the extent of my requisition, he wished to know if my purpose was fighting. I made him a present of the great principle that power commands respect, and it was to prevent any chance of fighting that we required so formidable an escort. His reply was that he would tell the king; and he immediately rose and walked away home.

K'yengo and the representatives of Usui and Karague now arrived by order of the king to bid farewell, and received the slaves and cattle lately captured. As I was very hungry, I set off home to breakfast. Just as I had gone, the provoking king inquired after me, and so brought me back again, though I never saw him the whole day. K'yengo, however, was very communicative. He said he was present when Sunna, with all the forces he could muster, tried to take the very countries I now proposed to travel through; but, though in person exciting his army to victory, he could make nothing of it. He advised my returning to Karague, when Rumanika would give me an escort through Nkole to Unyoro; but finding that did not suit my views, as I swore I would never retrace one step, he proposed my going by boat to Unyoro, following down the Nile.

This, of course, was exactly what I wanted; but how could king Mtesa, after the rebuff he had received from Kamrasi be induced to consent to it? My intention, I said, was to try the king on the Usoga and Kidi route first, then on the Masai route to Zanzibar, affecting perfect indifference about Kamrasi; and all those failing – which, of course, they would – I would ask for Unyoro as a last and only resource. Still I could not see the king to open my heart to him, and therefore felt quite nonplussed. "Oh," says K'yengo, "the reason why you do not see him is merely because he is ashamed to show his face, having made so many fair promises to you which he knows he can never carry out: bide your time, and all will be well." At 4 P.M., as no hope of seeing the king was left, all retired.

30th. – Unexpectedly, and for reasons only known to himself, the king sent us a cow and load of butter, which had been asked for many days ago. The new moon seen last night kept the king engaged at home, paying his devotions with his magic horns or fetishes in the manner already described. The spirit of this religion – if such it can be called – is not so much adoration of a Being supreme and beneficent, as a tax to certain malignant furies – a propitiation, in fact, to prevent them bringing evil on the land, and to insure a fruitful harvest. It was rather ominous that hail fell with violence, and lightning burnt down one of the palace huts, while the king was in the midst of his propitiatory devotions.

1st. – As Bombay was ordered to the palace to instruct the king in the art of casting bullets, I primed him well to plead for the road, and he reported to me the results, thus: First, he asked one thousand men to go through Kidi. This the king said was impracticable, as the Waganda had tried it so often before without success. Then, as that could not be managed, what would the king devise himself? Bana only proposed the Usoga and Kidi route, because he thought it would be to the advantage of Uganda. "Oh," says the king, cunningly, "if Bana merely wishes to see Usoga, he can do so, and I will send a suitable escort, but no more." To this Bombay replied, "Bana never could return; he would sooner do anything than return – even penetrate the Masai to Zanzibar, or go through Unyoro"; to which the king, ashamed of his impotence, hung down his head and walked away.

In the meanwhile, and whilst this was going on at the king's palace, I went with Grant, by appointment, to see the queen. As usual, she kept us waiting some time, then appeared sitting by an open gate, and invited us, together with many Wakungu and Wasumbua to approach. Very lavish with stale sour pombe, she gave us all some, saving the Wasumbua, whom she addressed very angrily, asking what they wanted, as they have been months in the country. These poor creatures, in a desponding mood, defended themselves by saying, which was quite true, that they had left their homes in Sorombo to visit her, and to trade. They had, since their arrival in the country, been daily in attendance at her palace, but never had the good fortune to see her excepting on such lucky occasions as brought the Wazungu (white men) here, when she opened her gates to them, but otherwise kept them shut. The queen retorted, "And what have you brought me, pray? Where is it? Until I touch it you will neither see me nor obtain permission to trade. Uganda is no place for idle vagabonds." We then asked for a private interview, when, a few drops of rain falling, the queen walked away, and we had orders to wait a little. During this time two boys were birched by the queen's orders, and an officer was sent out to inquire why the watch he had given her did not go. This was easily explained. It had no key; and, never losing sight of the main object, we took advantage of the opportunity to add, that if she did not approve of it, we could easily exchange it for another on arrival at Gani, provided she would send an officer with us.

The queen, squatting within her hut, now ordered both Grant and myself to sit outside and receive a present of five eggs and one cock each, saying coaxingly, "These are for my children." Then taking out the presents, she learned the way of wearing her watch with a tape guard round her neck, reposing the instrument in her bare bosom, and of opening and shutting it, which so pleased her, that she declared it quite satisfactory. The key was quite a minor consideration, for she could show it to her attendants just as well without one. The towel and handkerchiefs were also very beautiful, but what use could they be put to? "Oh, your majesty, to wipe the mouth after drinking pombe." "Of course," is the reply, "excellent; I won't use a mbugu napkin any more, but have one of these placed on my cup when it is brought to drink, and wipe my mouth with it afterwards. But what does Bana want?" "The road to Gani," says

Bombay for me. "The king won't see him when he goes to the palace, so now he comes here, trusting your superior influence and good-nature will be more practicable." "Oh!" says her majesty, "Bana does not know the facts of the case. My son has tried all the roads without success, and now he is ashamed to meet Bana face to face." "Then what is to be done, your majesty?" "Bana must go back to Karague and wait for a year, until my son is crowned, when he will make friends with the surrounding chiefs, and the roads will be opened." "But Bana says he will not retrace one step; he would sooner lose his life." "Oh, that's nonsense! He must not be headstrong; but before anything more can be said, I will send a message to my son, and Bana can then go with Kaddu, K'yengo, and Viarungi, and tell all they have to say to Mtesa to-morrow, and the following day return to me, when everything will be concluded." We all now left but Kaddu and some of the queen's officers, who waited for the message to her son about us. To judge from Kaddu, it must have been very different from what she led us to expect, as, on joining us, he said there was not the smallest chance of our getting the road we required, for the queen was so decided about it no further argument would be listened to.

2d. – Three goats were stolen, and suspicion falling on the king's cooks, who are expert foragers, we sent to the Kamraviona, and asked him to order out the Mganga; but his only reply was, that he often loses goats in the same way. He sent us one of his own for present purposes, and gave thirty baskets of potatoes to my men. As the king held a court, and broke it up before 8 A.M., and no one would go there for fear of his not appearing again, I waited, till the evening for Bombay, Kaddu,

K'yengo, and Viarungi, when, finding them drunk, I went by myself, fired a gun, and was admitted to where the king was hunting guinea-fowl. On seeing me, he took me affectionately by the hand, and, as we walked along together, he asked me what I wanted, showed me the house which was burnt down, and promised to settle the road question in the morning.

3d. – With Kaddu, K'yengo, and Viarungi all in attendance, we went to the palace, where there was a large assemblage prepared for a levee, and fired a gun, which brought the king out in state. The Sakibobo, or provincial governor, arrived with a body of soldiers armed with sticks, made a speech, and danced at the head of his men, all pointing sticks upwards, and singing fidelity to their king.

The king then turned to me, and said, "I have come out to listen to your request of last night. What is it you do want?" I said, "To open the country to the north, that an uninterrupted line of commerce might exist between England and this country by means of the Nile. I might go round by Nkole" (K'yengo looked daggers at me); "but that is out of the way, and not suitable to the purpose." The queen's deputation was now ordered to draw near, and questioned in a whisper. As K'yengo was supposed to know all about me, and spoke fluently both in Kiganda and Kisuahili, he had to speak first; but K'yengo, to everybody's surprise, said, "One white man wishes to go to Kamrasi's, whilst the other wishes to return through Unyamuezi." This announcement made the king reflect; for he had been privately primed by his mother's attendants, that we both wished to go to Gani, and therefore shrewdly inquired if Rumanika knew we wished to visit Kamrasi, and whether he was aware we should attempt the passage north from Uganda. "Oh yes! Of course Bana wrote to Bana Mdogo" (the little master) "as soon as he arrived in Uganda and told him and Rumanika all about it." "Wrote! What does that mean?" And I was called upon to explain. Mtesa, then seeing a flaw in K'yengo's statements, called him a story-teller; ordered him and his party away, and bade me draw near.

The moment of triumph had come at last, and suddenly the road was granted! The king presently let us see the motive by which he had been influenced. He said he did not like having to send to Rumanika for everything: he wanted his visitors to come to him direct; moreover, Rumanika had sent him a message to the effect that we were not to be shown anything out of Uganda, and when we had done with it, were to be returned to him. Rumanika, indeed! Who cared about Rumanika? Was not Mtesa the king of the country, to do as he liked? And we all laughed. Then the king, swelling with pride, asked me whom I liked best – Rumanika or himself – an awkward question, which I disposed of by saying I liked Rumanika very much because he spoke well, and was very communicative; but I also liked Mtesa, because his habits were much like my own – fond of shooting and roaming about; whilst he had learned so many things from my teaching, I must ever feel a yearning towards him.

With much satisfaction I felt that my business was now done; for Budja was appointed to escort us to Unyoro, and Jumba to prepare us boats, that we might go all the way to Kamrasi's by water.

Viarungi made a petition, on Rumanika's behalf, for an army

of Waganda to go to Karague, and fight the refractory brother, Rogero; but this was refused, on the plea that the whole army was out fighting at the present moment. The court then broke up and we went home.

To keep the king up to the mark, and seal our passage, in the evening I took a Lancaster rifle, with ammunition, and the iron chair he formerly asked for, as a parting present, to the palace, but did not find him, as he had gone out shooting with his brothers.

4th. – Grant and I now called together on the king to present the rifle, chair, and ammunition, as we could not thank him in words sufficiently for the favour he had done us in granting the road through Unyoro. I said the parting gift was not half as much as I should like to have been able to give; but we hoped, on reaching Gani, to send Petherick up to him with everything that he could desire. We regretted we had no more powder or shot, as what was intended, and actually placed out expressly to be presented on this occasion, was stolen. The king looked hard at his head page, who was once sent to get these very things now given, and then turning the subject adroitly, asked me how many cows and women I would like, holding his hand up with spread fingers, and desiring me to count by hundreds; but the reply was, Five cows and goats would be enough, for we wished to travel lightly in boats, starting from the Murchison Creek. Women were declined on such grounds as would seem rational to him. But if the king would clothe my naked men with one mbugu (bark cloth) each, and give a small tusk each to nine Wanyamuezi porters, who desired to return to their home, the obligation would be great.

Everything was granted without the slightest hesitation; and then the king, turning to me, said, "Well, Bana, so you really wish to go?" "Yes, for I have not seen my home for four years and upwards" – reckoning five months to the year, Uganda fashion. "And you can give no stimulants?" "No." "Then you will send me some from Gani – brandy if you like; it makes people sleep sound, and gives them strength." Next we went to the queen to bid her farewell, but did not see her.

On returning home I found half my men in a state of mutiny. They had been on their own account to beg for the women and cows which had been refused, saying, If Bana does not want them we do, for we have been starved here ever since we came, and when we go for food get broken heads; we will not serve with Bana any longer; but as he goes north, we will return to Karague and Unyanyembe.

Bombay, however, told them they never had fed so well in all their lives as they had in Uganda, counting from fifty to sixty cows killed, and pombe and plantains every day, whenever they took the trouble to forage; and for their broken heads they invariably received a compensation in women; so that Bana had reason to regret every day spent in asking for food for them at the palace – a favour which none but his men received, but which they had not, as they might have done, turned to good effect by changing the system of plundering for food in Uganda.

5th. – By the king's order we attended at the palace early. The gun obtained us all a speedy admittance, when the king opened conversation by saying, "Well, Bana, so you really are going?" "Yes; I have enjoyed your hospitality for a long time, and now wish to return to my home." "What provision do you want?" I said, Five cows and five goats, as we shan't be long in Uganda; and it is not the custom of our country, when we go visiting, to carry anything away with us. The king then said, "Well, I wish to give you much, but you won't have it"; when Budja spoke out, saying, "Bana does not know the country he had to travel through; there is nothing but jungle and famine on the way, and he must have cows"; on which the king ordered us sixty cows, fourteen goats, ten loads of butter, a load of coffee and tobacco, one hundred sheets of mbugu, as clothes for my men, at a suggestion of Bombay's, as all my cloth had been expended even before I left Karague.

This magnificent order created a pause, which K'yengo took advantage of by producing a little bundle of peculiarly-shaped sticks and a lump of earth – all of which have their own particular magical powers, as K'yengo described to the king's satisfaction. After this, Viarungi pleaded the cause of my mutinous followers, till I shook my finger angrily at him before the king, rebuked him for intermeddling in other people's affairs, and told my own story, which gained the sympathy of the king, and induced him to say, "Supposing they desert Bana, what road do they expect to get?" Maula was now appointed to go with Rozaro to Karague for the powder and other things promised yesterday, whilst Viarungi and all his party, though exceedingly anxious to get away, had orders to remain here prisoners as a surety for the things arriving. Further, Kaddu and two other Wakungu received orders to go to Usui with two tusks of ivory to purchase gunpowder, caps, and flints, failing which they would proceed to Unyanyembe, and even to Zanzibar, for the king must not be disappointed, and failure would cost them their lives.

Not another word was said, and away the two parties went, with no more arrangement than a set of geese – Maula without a letter, and Kaddu without any provision for the way, as if all the world belonged to Mtesa, and he could help himself from any man's garden that he liked, no matter where he was. In the evening my men made a humble petition for their discharge, even if I did not pay them, producing a hundred reasons for wishing to leave me, but none which would stand a moment's argument: the fact was, they were afraid of the road to Unyoro, thinking I had not sufficient ammunition.

6th. – I visited the king, and asked leave for boats to go at once; but the fleet admiral put a veto on this by making out that dangerous shallows exist between the Murchison Creek and the Kira district station, so that the boats of one place never visit the other; and further, if we went to Kira, we should find impracticable cataracts to the Urondogani boat-station; our better plan would therefore be, to deposit our property at the Urondogani station, and walk by land up the river, if a sight of the falls at the mouth of the lake was of such material consequence to us.

Of course this man carried everything his own way, for there was nobody able to contradict him, and we could not afford time to visit Usoga first, lest by the delay we might lose an opportunity of communicating with Petherick. Grant now took a portrait of Mtesa by royal permission, the king sitting as quietly as his impatient nature would permit. Then at home the Wanyamuezi porters received their tusks of ivory, weighing from 16 to 50 lb.each, and took a note besides on Rumanika each for twenty fundo of beads, barring one Bogue man, who, having lent a cloth to the expedition some months previously, thought it would not be paid him, and therefore seized a sword as security; the consequence was, his tusk was seized until the sword was returned, and he was dismissed minus his beads, for having so misconducted himself. The impudent fellow then said, "It will be well for Bana if he succeeds in getting the road through Unyoro; for, should he fail, I will stand in his path at Bogue." Kitunzi offered an ivory for beads, and when told we were not merchants, and advised to try K'yengo, he said he dared not even approach K'yengo's camp lest people should tell the king of it, and accuse him of seeking for magical powers against his sovereign. Old Nasib begged for his discharge. It was granted, and he took a $50 letter on the coast, and a letter of emancipation for himself and family, besides an order, written in Kisuahili, for ten fundo of beads on Rumanika, which made him very happy.

In the evening we called again at the palace with pictures of the things the king required from Rumanika, and a letter informing Rumanika what we wished done with them, in order that there might be no mistake, requesting the king to forward them after Mula.

Just then Kaddu's men returned to say they wanted provisions for the way, as the Wazinza, hearing of their mission, asked them if they knew what they were about, going to a strange country without any means of paying their way. But the king instead of listening to reason, impetuously said, "If you do not pack off at once, and bring me the things I want, every man of you shall lose his head; and as for the Wazinza, for interfering with my orders, they shall be kept here prisoners until you return." On the way home, one of the king's favourite women overtook us, walking, with her hands clasped at the back of her head, to execution, crying, "N'uawo!" in the most pitiful manner. A man was preceding her, but did not touch her; for she loved to obey the orders of her king voluntarily, and in consequence of previous attachment, was permitted, as a mark of distinction, to walk free. Wondrous world! It was not ten minutes since we parted from the king, yet he had found time to transact this bloody piece of business.

7th. – Early in the morning the king bade us come to him to say farewell. Wishing to leave behind a favourable impression, I instantly complied. On the breast of my coat I suspended the necklace the queen had given me, as well as his knife, and my medals. I talked with him in as friendly and flattering a manner as I could, dwelling on his shooting, the pleasant cruising on the lake, and our sundry picnics, as well as the grand prospect there was now of opening the country to trade, by which his guns, the best in the world, would be fed with powder – and other small matters of a like nature – to which he replied with great feeling and good taste. We then all rose with an English bow, placing the hand on the heart whilst saying adieu; and there was a complete uniformity in the ceremonial, for whatever I did, Mtesa, in an instant, mimicked with the instinct of a monkey.

We had, however, scarcely quitted the palace gate before the king issued himself, with his attendants and his brothers leading, and women bringing up the rear; here K'yengo and all the Wazinza joined in the procession with ourselves, they kneeling and clapping their hands after the fashion of their own country. Budja just then made me feel very anxious, by pointing out the position of Urondogani, as I thought, too far north. I called the king's attention to it, and in a moment he said he would speak to Budja in such a manner that would leave no doubts in my mind, for he liked me much, and desired to please me in all things. As the procession now drew to our camp, and Mtesa expressed a wish to have a final look at my men, I ordered them to turn out with their arms and n'yanzig for the many favours they had received. Mtesa, much pleased, complimented them on their goodly appearance, remarking that with such a force I would have no difficulty in reaching Gani, and exhorted them to follow me through fire and water; then exchanging adieus again he walked ahead in gigantic strides up the hill, the pretty favourite of his harem, Lubuga – beckoning and waving with her little hands, and crying, "Bana! Bana!" – trotting after him conspicuous amongst the rest, though all showed a little feeling at the severance. We saw them no more.

CHAPTER 15

MARCH DOWN
THE NORTHERN
SLOPES OF AFRICA

Kari – Tragic Incident There – Renewals of Troubles – Quarrels with the Natives – Reach the Nile – Description of the Scene There – Sport – Church Estate – Ascend the River to the Junction with the Lake – Ripon Falls – General Account of the Source of the Nile – Descend Again to Urondogani – The Truculent Sakibobo.

7th to 11th. – With Budja appointed as the general director, a lieutenant of the Sakibobo's to furnish us with sixty cows in his division at the first halting-place, and Kasoro (Mr. Cat), a lieutenant of Jumba's, to provide the boats at Urondogani, we started at 1 P.M., on the journey northwards. The Wanguana still grumbled, swearing they would carry no loads, as they got no rations, and threatening to shoot us if we pressed them, forgetting that their food had been paid for to the king in rifles, chronometers, and other articles, costing about $2,000, and, what was more to the point, that all the ammunition was in our hands. A judicious threat of the stick, however, put things right, and on we marched five successive days to Kari – as the place was afterwards named, in consequence of the tragedy mentioned below – the whole distance accomplished being thirty miles from the capital, through a fine hilly country, with jungles and rich cultivation alternating. The second march, after crossing the Katawana river with its many branches flowing north-east into the huge rush-drain of Luajerri, carried us beyond the influence of the higher hills, and away from the huge grasses which characterise the southern boundary of Uganda bordering on the lake.

Each day's march to Kari was directed much in the same manner.

After a certain number of hours' travelling, Budja appointed some village of residence for the night, avoiding those which belonged to the queen, lest any rows should take place in them, which would create disagreeable consequences with the king, and preferring those the heads of which had been lately seized by the orders of the king. Nevertheless, wherever we went, all the villagers forsook their homes, and left their houses, property, and gardens an easy prey to the thieving propensities of the escort. To put a stop to this vile practice was now beyond my power; the king allowed it, and his men were the first in every house, taking goats, fowls, skins, mbugus, cowries, beads, drums, spears, tobacco, pombe – in short, everything they could lay their hands on – in the most ruthless manner. It was a perfect marauding campaign for them all, and all alike were soon laden with as much as they could carry.

A halt of some days had become necessary at Kari to collect the cows given by the king; and, as it is one of the most extensive pasture-grounds, I strolled with my rifle (11th) to see what new animals could be found; but no sooner did I wound a zebra than messengers came running after me to say Kari, one of my men, had been murdered by the villagers three miles off; and such was the fact. He, with others of my men, had been induced to go plundering, with a few boys of the Waganda escort, to a certain village of potters, as pots were required by Budja for making plantain-wine, the first thing ever thought of when a camp is formed. On nearing the place, however, the women of the village, who were the only people visible, instead of running away, as our braves expected, commenced hullalooing, and brought out their husbands. Flight was now the only thought of our men, and all would have escaped had Kari not been slow and his musket empty. The potters overtook him, and, as he pointed his gun, which they considered a magic-horn, they speared him to death, and then fled at once. Our survivors were not long in bringing the news into camp, when a party went out, and in the evening brought in the man's corpse and everything belonging to him, for nothing had been taken.

12th. – To enable me at my leisure to trace up the Nile to its exit from the lake, and then go on with the journey as quickly as possible, I wished the cattle to be collected and taken by Budja and some of my men with the heavy baggage overland to Kamrasi's.

Another reason for doing so was, that I thought it advisable Kamrasi should be forewarned that we were coming by the water route, lest we should be suspected and stopped as spies by his officers on the river, or regarded as enemies, which would provoke a fight.

Budja, however, objected to move until a report of Kari's murder had been forwarded to the king, lest the people, getting bumptious, should try the same trick again; and Kasoro said he would not go up the river, as he had received no orders to do so.

In this fix I ordered a march back to the palace, mentioning the king's last words, and should have gone, had not Budja ordered Kasoro to go with me. A page then arrived from the king to ask after Bana's health, carrying the Whitworth rifle as his master's card, and begging for a heavy double-barrelled gun to be sent him from Gani.

I called this lad to witness the agreement I had made with Budja, and told him, if Kasoro satisfied me, I would return by him, in addition to the heavy gun, a Massey's patent log. I had taken it for the navigation of the lake, and it was now of no further use to me, but, being an instrument of complicated structure, it would be a valuable addition to the king's museum of magic charms. I added I should like the king to send me the robes of honour and spears he had once promised me, in order that I might, on reaching England, be able to show my countrymen a specimen of the manufactures of his country. The men who were with Kari were now sent to the palace, under accusation of having led him into ambush, and a complaint was made against the villagers, which we waited the reply to. As Budja forbade it, no men would follow me out shooting, saying the villagers were out surrounding our camp, and threatening destruction on any one who dared show his face; for this was not the highroad to Uganda, and therefore no one had a right to turn them out of their houses and pillage their gardens.

13th. – Budja lost two cows given to his party last night, and seeing ours securely tied by their legs to trees, asked by what spells we had secured them; and would not believe our assurance that the ropes that bound them were all the medicines we knew of. One of the Queen's sisters, hearing of Kari's murder, came on a visit to condole with us, bringing a pot of pombe, for which she received some beads. On being asked how many sisters the queen had, for we could not help suspecting some imposition, she replied she was the only one, till assured ten other ladies had presented themselves as the queen's sisters before, when she changed her tone, and said, "That is true, I am not the only one; but if I had told you the truth I might have lost my head." This was a significant expression of the danger to telling court secrets.

I suspected that there must be a considerable quantity of game in this district, as stake-nets and other traps were found in all the huts, as well as numbers of small antelope hoofs spitted on pipe-sticks – an ornament which is counted the special badge of the sportsman in this part of Africa. Despite, therefore, of the warnings of Budja, I strolled again with my rifle, and saw pallah, small plovers, and green antelopes with straight horns, called mpeo, the skin of which makes a favourite apron for the Mabandwa.

14th. – I met to-day a Mhuma cowherd in my strolls with the rifle, and asked him if he knew where the game lay. The unmannerly creature, standing among a thousand of the sleekest cattle, gruffishly replied, "What can I know of any other animals than cows?" and went on with his work, as if nothing in the world could interest him but his cattle-tending. I shot a doe, leucotis, called here nsunnu, the first one seen upon the journey.

15th. – In the morning, when our men went for water to the springs, some Waganda in ambush threw a spear at them, and this time caught a Tartar, for the "horns," as they called their guns, were loaded, and two of them received shot-wounds. In the evening, whilst we were returning from shooting, a party of Waganda, also lying in the bush, called out to know what we were about; saying, "Is it not enough that you have turned us out of our homes and plantations, leaving us to live like animals in the wilderness?" And when told we were only searching for sport, would not believe that our motive was any other than hostility to themselves.

At night one of Budja's men returned from the palace, to say the king was highly pleased with the measures adopted by his Wakungu, in prosecution of Kari's affair. He hoped now as we had cows to eat, there would be no necessity for wandering for food, but all would keep together "in one garden." At present no notice would be taken of the murderers, as all the culprits would have fled far away in their fright to escape chastisement. But when a little time had elapsed, and all would appear to have been forgotten, officers would be sent and the miscreants apprehended, for it was impossible to suppose anybody could be ignorant of the white men being the guests of the king, considering they had lived at the palace for so long. The king took this opportunity again to remind me that he wanted a heavy solid double gun, such as would last him all his life; and intimated that in a few days the arms and robes of honour were to be sent.

16th. – Most of the cows for ourselves and the guides – for the king gave them also a present, ten each – were driven into camp. We also got 50 lb. of butter, the remainder to be picked up on the way. I strolled with the gun, and shot two zebras, to be sent to the king, as, by the constitution of Uganda, he alone can keep their royal skins.

17th. – We had to halt again, as the guides had lost most of their cows, so I strolled with my rifle and shot a ndjezza doe, the first I had ever seen. It is a brown animal, a little smaller than leucotis, and frequents much the same kind of ground.

18th. – We had still to wait another day for Budja's cows, when, as it appeared all-important to communicate quickly with Petherick, and as Grant's leg was considered too weak for travelling fast, we took counsel together, and altered our plans. I arranged that Grant should go to Kamrasi's direct with the property, cattle, and women, taking my letters and a map for immediate despatch to Petherick at Gani, whilst I should go up the river to its source or exit from the lake, and come down again navigating as far as practicable.

At night the Waganda startled us by setting fire to the huts our men were sleeping in, but providentially did more damage to themselves than to us, for one sword only was buried in the fire, whilst their own huts, intended to be vacated in the morning, were burnt to the ground. To fortify ourselves against another invasion, we cut down all their plaintains to make a boma or fence.

We started all together on our respective journeys; but, after the third mile, Grant turned west, to join the highroad to Kamrasi's, whilst I went east for Urondogani, crossing the Luajerri, a huge rush-drain three miles broad, fordable nearly to the right bank, where we had to ferry in boats, and the cows to be swum over with men holding on to their tails. It was larger than the Katonga, and more tedious to cross, for it took no less than four hours mosquitoes in myriads biting our bare backs and legs all the while. The Luajerri is said to rise in the lake and fall into the Nile, due south of our crossing-point. On the right bank wild buffalo are described to be as numerous as cows, but we did not see any, though the country is covered with a most inviting jungle for sport, which intermediate lays of fine grazing grass. Such is the nature of the country all the way to Urondogani, except in some favoured spots, kept as tidily as in any part of Uganda, where plantains grow in the utmost luxuriance. From want of guides, and misguided by the exclusive ill-natured Wahuma who were here in great numbers tending their king's cattle, we lost our way continually, so that we did not reach the boat-station until the morning of the 21st.

Here at last I stood on the brink of the Nile; most beautiful was the scene, nothing could surpass it! It was the very perfection of the kind of effect aimed at in a highly kept park; with a magnificent stream from 600 to 700 yards wide, dotted with islets and rocks, the former occupied by fishermen's huts, the latter by sterns and crocodiles basking in the sun – flowing between the fine high grassy banks, with rich trees and plantains in the background, where herds of the nsunnu and hartebeest could be seen grazing, while the hippopotami were snorting in the water, and florikan and guinea-fowl rising at our feet. Unfortunately, the chief district officer, Mlondo, was from home, but we took possession of his huts – clean, extensive, and tidily kept – facing the river, and felt as if a residence here would do one good. Delays and subterfuges, however, soon came to damp our spirits. The acting officer was sent for, and asked for the boats; they were all scattered, and could not be collected for a day or two; but, even if they were at hand, no boat ever went up or down the river. The chief was away and would be sent for, as the king often changed his orders, and, after all, might not mean what had been said. The district belonged to the Sakibobo, and no representative of his had come here.

These excuses, of course, would not satisfy us. The boats must be collected, seven, if there are not ten, for we must try them, and come to some understanding about them, before we march up stream, when, if the officer values his life, he will let us have them, and acknowledge Karoso as the king's representative, otherwise a complaint will be sent to the palace, for we won't stand trifling.

We were now confronting Usoga, a country which may be said to be the very counterpart of Uganda in its richness and beauty. Here the people use such huge iron-headed spears with short handles, that, on seeing one to-day, my people remarked that they were better fitted for digging potatoes than piercing men. Elephants, as we had seen by their devastations during the last two marches, were very numerous in this neighbourhood. Till lately, a party from Unyoro, ivory-hunting, had driven them away. Lions were also described as very numerous and destructive to human life. Antelopes were common in the jungle, and the hippopotami, though frequenters of the plantain-garden and constantly heard, were seldom seen on land in consequence of their unsteady habits.

The king's page again came, begging I would not forget the gun and stimulants, and bringing with him the things I asked for – two spears, one shield, one dirk, two leopard-cat skins, and two sheets of small antelope skins. I told my men they ought to shave their heads and bathe in the holy river, the cradle of Moses – the waters of which, sweetened with sugar, men carry all the way from Egypt to Mecca, and sell to the pilgrims. But Bombay, who is a philosopher of the Epicurean school, said, "We don't look on those things in the same fanciful manner that you do; we are contented with all the common-places of life, and look for nothing beyond the present. If things don't go well, it is God's will; and if they do go well, that is His will also."

22d. – The acting chief brought a present of one cow, one goat, and pombe, with a mob of his courtiers to pay his respects. He promised that the seven boats, which are all the station he could muster, would be ready next day, and in the meanwhile a number of men would conduct me to the shooting-ground. He asked to be shown the books of birds and animals, and no sooner saw some specimens of Wolf's handiwork, than, in utter surprise, he exclaimed, "I know how these are done; a bird was caught and stamped upon the paper," using action to his words, and showing what he meant, while all his followers n'yanzigged for the favour of the exhibition.

In the evening I strolled in the antelope parks, enjoying the scenery and sport excessively. A noble buck nsunnu, standing by himself, was the first thing seen on this side, though a herd of hertebeests were grazing on the Usoga banks. One bullet rolled my fine friend over, but the rabble looking on no sooner saw the hit than they rushed upon him and drove him off, for he was only wounded. A chase ensued, and he was tracked by his blood when a pongo (bush box) was started and divided the party. It also brought me to another single buck nsunnu, which was floored at once, and left to be carried home by some of my men in company with Waganda, whilst I went on, shot a third nsunnu buck, and tracked him by his blood till dark, for the bullet had pierced his lungs and passed out on the other side. Failing to find him on the way home, I shot, besides florikan and guinea-chicks, a wonderful goatsucker, remarkable for the exceeding length of some of its feathers floating out far beyond the rest in both wings.[1] Returning home, I found the men who had charge of the dead buck all in a state of excitement; they no sooner removed his carcass, than two lions came out of the jungle and lapped his blood. All the Waganda ran away at once; but my braves feared my answer more than the lions, and came off safely with the buck on their shoulders.

23d. – Three boats arrived, like those used on the Murchison Creek, and when I demanded the rest, as well as a decisive answer about going to Kamrasi's, the acting Mkungu said he was afraid accidents might happen, and he would not take me. Nothing would frighten this pig-headed creature into compliance, though I told him I had arranged with the king to make the Nile the channel of communication with England. I therefore applied to him for guides to conduct me up the river, and ordered Bombay and Kasoro to obtain fresh orders from the king, as all future Wazungu, coming to Uganda to visit or trade, would prefer the passage by the river. I shot another buck in the evening, as the Waganda love their skins, and also a load of guinea-fowl – three, four, and five at a shot – as Kasoro and his boys prefer them to anything.

24th. – The acting officer absconded, but another man came in his place, and offered to take us on the way up the river to-morrow, humbugging Kasoro into the belief that his road to the palace would branch off from the first state, though in reality it was here. The Mkungu's women brought pombe, and spent the day gazing at us, till, in the evening, when I took up my rifle, one ran after Bana to see him shoot, and followed like a man; but the only sport she got was on an ant-hill, where she fixed herself some time, popping into her mouth and devouring the white ants as fast as they emanated from their cells – for, disdaining does, I missed the only pongo buck I got a shot at in my anxiety to show the fair one what she came for.

Reports came to-day of new cruelties at the palace. Kasoro improved on their off-hand manslaughter by saying that two Kamravionas and two Sakibobos, as well as all the old Wakungu of Sunna's time, had been executed by the orders of king Mtesa. He told us, moreover, that if Mtesa ever has a dream that his father directs him to kill anybody as being dangerous to his person, the order is religiously kept. I wished to send a message to Mtesa by an officer who is starting at once to pay his respects at court; but although he received it, and promised to deliver it, Kasoro laughed at me for expecting that one word of it would ever reach the king; for, however, appropriate or important the matter might be, it was more than anybody dare do to tell the king, as it would be an infringement of the rule that no one is to speak to him unless in answer to a question. My second buck of the first day was brought in by the natives, but they would not allow it to approach the hut until it had been skinned; and I found their reason to be a superstition that otherwise no others would ever be killed by the inmates of that establishment.

I marched up the left bank of the Nile at a considerable distance from the water, to the Isamba rapids, passing through rich jungle and plantain-gardens. Nango, an old friend, and district officer of the place, first refreshed us with a dish of plantain-squash and dried fish, with pombe. He told us he is often threatened by elephants, but he sedulously keeps them off with charms; for if they ever tasted a plantain they would never leave the garden until they had cleared it out. He then took us to see the nearest falls of the Nile – extremely beautiful, but very confined. The water ran deep between its banks, which were covered with fine grass, soft cloudy acacias, and festoons of lilac convolvuli; whilst here and there, where the land had slipped above the rapids, bared places of red earth could be seen, like that of Devonshire; there, too, the waters, impeded by a natural dam, looked like a huge mill-pond, sullen and dark, in which two crocodiles, laving about, were looking out for prey. From the high banks we looked down upon a line of sloping wooded islets lying across the stream, which divide its waters, and, by interrupting them, cause at once both dam and rapids. The whole was more fairy-like, wild, and romantic than – I must confess that my thoughts took that shape – anything I ever saw outside of a theatre. It was exactly the sort of place, in fact, where, bridged across from one side-slip to the other, on a moonlight night, brigands would assemble to enact some dreadful tragedy. Even the Wanguana seemed spellbound at the novel beauty of the sight, and no one thought of moving till hunger warned us night was setting in, and we had better look out for lodgings.

Start again, and after drinking pombe with Nango, when we heard that three Wakungu had been seized at Kari, in consequence of the murder, the march was commenced, but soon after stopped by the mischievous machinations of our guide, who pretended it was too late in the day to cross the jungles on ahead, either by the road to the source or the palace, and therefore would not move till the morning; then, leaving us, on the pretext of business, he vanished, and was never seen again. A small black fly, with thick shoulders and bullet-head, infests the place, and torments the naked arms and legs of the people with its sharp stings to an extent that must render life miserable to them.

After a long struggling march, plodding through huge grasses and jungle, we reached a district which I cannot otherwise describe than by calling it a "Church Estate." It is dedicated in some mysterious manner to Lubari (Almighty), and although the king appeared to have authority over some of the inhabitants of it, yet others had apparently a sacred character, exempting them from the civil power, and he had no right to dispose of the land itself. In this territory there are small villages only at every fifth mile, for there is no road, and the lands run high again, whilst, from want of a guide, we often lost the track. It now transpired that Budja, when he told at the palace that there was no road down the banks of the Nile, did so in consequence of his fear that if he sent my whole party here

Antelopes in a swamp.

they would rob these church lands, and so bring him into a scrape with the wizards or ecclesiastical authorities. Had my party not been under control, we could not have put up here; but on my being answerable that no thefts should take place, the people kindly consented to provide us with board and lodgings, and we found them very obliging. One elderly man, half-witted – they said the king had driven his senses from him by seizing his house and family – came at once on hearing of our arrival, laughing and singing in a loose jaunty maniacal manner, carrying odd sticks, shells, and a bundle of mbugu rags, which he deposited before me, dancing and singing again, then retreating and bringing some more, with a few plantains from a garden, when I was to eat, as kings lived up-on flesh, and "poor Tom" wanted some, for he lived with lions and elephants in a hovel beyond the gardens, and his belly was empty. He was precisely a black specimen of the English parish idiot.

At last, with a good push for it, crossing hills and threading huge grasses, as well as extensive village plantations lately dev-astated by elephants – they had eaten all that was eatable, and what would not serve for food they had destroyed with their trunks, not one plantain or one hut being left entire – we ar-rived at the extreme end of the journey, the farthest point ever visited by the expedition on the same parallel of latitude as king Mtesa's palace, and just forty miles east of it.

We were well rewarded; for the "stones," as the Waganda call the falls, was by far the most interesting sight I had seen in Africa. Everybody ran to see them at once, though the march had been long and fatiguing, and even my sketch-block was called into play. Though beautiful, the scene was not exactly what I expected; for the broad surface of the lake was shut out from view by a spur of hill, and the falls, about 12 feet deep, and 400 to 500 feet broad, were broken by rocks. Still it was a sight that attracted one to it for hours – the roar of the waters, the thousands of passenger-fish, leaping at the falls with all their might; the Wasoga and Waganda fisherman coming out in boats and taking post on all the rocks with rod and hook, hippopotami and crocodiles lying sleepily on the water, the ferry at work above the falls, and cattle driven down to drink at the margin of the lake – made, in all, with the pretty nature of the country – small hills, grassy-topped, with trees in the folds, and gardens on the lower slopes – as interesting a picture as one could wish to see.

The expedition had now performed its functions. I saw that old father Nile without any doubt rises in the Victoria N'yanza, and, as I had foretold, that lake is the great source of the holy river which cradled the first expounder of our religious belief.

I mourned, however, when I thought how much I had lost by the delays in the journey having deprived me of the pleasure of going to look at the north-east corner of the N'yanza to see what connection there was, by the strait so often spoken of, with it and the other lake where the Waganda went to get their salt, and from which another river flowed to the north, making "Usoga an island."

But I felt I ought to be content with what I had been spared to accomplish; for I had seen full half of the lake, and had information given me of the other half, by means of which I knew all about the lake, as far, at least, as the chief objects of geographical importance were concerned.

Let us now sum up the whole and see what it is worth. Comparative information assured me that there was as much water on the eastern side of the lake as there is on the western – if anything, rather more. The most remote waters, or top head of the Nile, is the southern end of the lake, situated close on the third degree of south latitude, which gives to the Nile the surprising length, in direct measurement, rolling over thirty-four degrees of latitude, of above 2,300 miles, or more than one-eleventh of the circumference of our globe. Now from this southern point, round by the west, to where the great Nile stream issues, there is only one feeder of any importance, and that is the Kitangule river; whilst from the southernmost point, round by the east, to the strait, there are no rivers at all of any importance; for the travelled Arabs one and all aver, that from the west of the snow-clad Kilimandjaro to the lake where it is cut by the second degree, and also the first degree of south latitude, there are salt lakes and salt plains, and the country is hilly, not unlike Unyamuezi; but they said there were no great rivers, and the country was so scantily watered, having only occasional runnels and rivulets, that they always had to make long marches in order to find water when they went on their trading journeys: and further, those Arabs who crossed the strait when they reached Usoga, as mentioned before, during the late interregnum, crossed no river either.

There remains to be disposed of the "salt lake," which I believe is not a salt, but a fresh-water lake; and my reasons are, as before stated, that the natives call all lakes salt, if they find salt beds or salt islands in such places. Dr. Krapf, when he obtained a sight of the Kenia mountain, heard from the natives there that there was a salt lake to its northward, and he also heard that a river ran from Kenia towards the Nile. If his information was true on this latter point, then, without doubt, there must exist some connection between his river and the salt lake I have heard of, and this in all probability would also establish a connection between my salt lake and his salt lake which he heard was called Baringo.[2] In no view that can be taken of it, however, does this unsettled matter touch the established fact that the head of the Nile is in 3° south latitude, where in the year 1858, I discovered the head of the Victoria N'yanza to be.

I now christened the "stones" Ripon Falls, after the nobleman who presided over the Royal Geographical Society when my expedition was got up; and the arm of water from which the Nile issued, Napoleon Channel, in token of respect to the French Geographical Society, for the honour they had done me, just before leaving England, in presenting me with their gold medal for the discovery of the Victoria N'yanza. One thing seemed at first perplexing – the volume of water in the Kitangule looked as large as that of the Nile; but then the one was a slow river and the other swift, and on this account I could form no adequate judgment of their relative values.

Not satisfied with my first sketch of the falls, I could not resist sketching them again; and then, as the cloudy state of the weather prevented my observing for latitude, and the officer of the place said a magnificent view of the lake could be obtained from the hill alluded to as intercepting the view from the falls, we proposed going there; but Kasoro, who had been indulged with nsunnu antelope skins, and with guinea-fowl for dinner, resisted this, on the plea that I never should be satisfied. There were orders given only to see the "stones," and if he took me to one hill I should wish to see another and another, and so on. It made me laugh, for that had been my nature all my life; but, vexed at heart, and wishing to trick the young tyrant, I asked for boats to shoot hippopotami, in the hope of reaching the hills to picnic; but boating had never been ordered, and he would not listen to it. "Then bring fish," I said, that I might draw them: no, that was not ordered. "Then go you to the palace, and leave me to go to Urondogani to-morrow, after I have taken a latitude"; but the wilful creature would not go until he saw me under way. And as nobody would do anything for me without Kasoro's orders, I amused the people by firing at the ferry-boat upon the Usoga side, which they defied me to hit, the distance being 500 yards; but nevertheless a bullet went through her, and was afterwards brought by the Wasoga nicely folded up in a piece of mbugu. Bombay then shot a sleeping crocodile with his carbine, whilst I spent the day out watching the falls.

This day also I spent watching the fish flying at the falls, and felt as if I only wanted a wife and family, garden and yacht, rifle and rod, to make me happy here for life, so charming was the place. What a place, I thought to myself, this would be for missionaries! They never could fear starvation, the land is so rich; and, if farming were introduced by them, they might have hundreds of pupils. I need say no more.

In addition to the rod-and-line fishing, a number of men, armed with long heavy poles with two iron spikes, tied prong-fashion to one end, rushed to a place over a break in the falls, which tired fish seemed to use as a baiting-room, dashed in their forks, holding on by the shaft, and sent men down to disengaged the pined fish and relieve their spears. The shot they made in this manner is a blind one – only on the chance of fish being there – and therefore always doubtful in its result.

Church Estate again. As the clouds and Kasoro's wilfulness were still against me, and the weather did not give hopes of a change, I sacrificed the taking of the latitude to gain time. I sent Bombay with Kasoro to the palace, asking for the Sakibobo himself to be sent with an order for five boats, five cows, and five goats, and also for a general order to go where I like, and do what I like, and have fish supplied me; "for, though I know the king likes me, his officers do not"; and then on separating I retraced my steps to the Church Estate.

1st. – To-day, after marching an hour, as there was now no need for hurrying, and a fine pongo buck, the Ngubbi of Uganda, offered a tempting shot, I proposed to shoot it for the men, and breakfast in a neighbouring village. This being agreed to, the animal was despatched, and we no sooner entered the village than we heard that nsamma, a magnificent description of antelope, abound in the long grasses close by, and that a rogue elephant frequents the plantains every night. This tempting news created a halt. In the evening I killed a nsamma doe, an animal very much like the Kobus Ellipsiprymnus, but without the lunated mark over the rump; and at night, about 1 A.M., turned out to shoot an elephant, which we distinctly heard feasting on plantains; but rain was falling, and the night so dark, he was left till the morning.

2d. – I followed up the elephant some way, till a pongo offering an irresistible shot I sent a bullet through him, but he was lost after hours' tracking in the interminable large grasses. An enormous snake, with fearful mouth and fangs, was speared by the men. In the evening I wounded a buck nsamma, which, after tracking till dark, was left to stiffen ere the following morning; and just after this on the way home, we heard the rogue elephant crunching the branches not far off from the track; but as no one would dare follow me against the monster at this late hour, he was reluctantly left to do more injury to the gardens.

3d. – After a warm search in the morning we found the nsamma buck lying in some water; the men tried to spear him, but he stood at bay, and took another bullet. This was all we wanted, affording one good specimen; so, after breakfast, we marched to Kirindi, where the villagers, hearing of the sport we had had, and excited with the hopes of getting flesh, begged us to halt a day.

4th. – Not crediting the stories told by the people about the sport here, we packed to leave, but were no sooner ready than several men ran hastily in to say some fine bucks were waiting to be shot close by. This was too powerful a temptation to be withstood, so, shouldering the rifle, and followed by half the village, if not more, women included, we went to the place, but, instead of finding a buck – for the men had stretched a point to keep me at their village – we found a herd of does, and shot one at the people's urgent request.

We reached this in one stretch, and put up in our old quarters, where the women of Mlondo provided pombe, plantains, and potatoes, as before, with occasional fish, and we lived very happily till the 10th, shooting buck, guinea-fowl, and florikan, when, Bombay and Kasoro arriving, my work began again. These two worthies reached the palace, after crossing twelve considerable streams, of which one was the Luajerri, rising in the lake. The evening of the next day after leaving me at Kira, they obtained an interview with the king immediately; for the thought flashed across his mind that Bombay had come to report our death, the Waganda having been too much for the party. He was speedily undeceived by the announcement that nothing was the matter, excepting the inability to procure boats, because the officers at Urondogani denied all authority but the Sakibobo's, and no one would show Bana anything, however trifling, without an express order for it.

Irate at this announcement, the king ordered the Sakibobo, who happened to be present, to be seized and bound at once, and said warmly, "Pray, who is the king, that the Sakibobo's orders should be preferred to mine?" And then turning to the Sakibobo himself, asked what he would pay to be released? The Sakibobo, alive to his danger, replied at once, and without the slightest hesitation, Eighty cows, eighty goats, eighty slaves, eighty mbugu, eighty butter, eighty coffee, eighty tobacco, eighty jowari, and eighty of all the produce of Uganda. He was then released. Bombay said Bana wished the Sakibobo to come to Urondogani, and gave him a start with five boats, five cows, and five goats; to which the king replied, "Bana shall have all he wants, nothing shall be denied him, not even fish; but it is not necessary to send the Sakibobo, as boys carry all my orders to kings as well as subjects. Kasoro will return again with you, fully instructed in everything, and, moreover, both he and Budja will follow Bana to Gani." Four days, however, my men were kept at the palace ere the king gave them the cattle and leave to join me, accompanied with one more officer, who had orders to find the boats at once, see us off, and report the circumstance at court. Just as at the last interview, the king had four women, lately seized and condemned to execution, squatting in his court. He wished to send them to Bana, and when Bombay demurred, saying he had no authority to take women in that way, the king gave him one, and asked him if he would like to see some sport, as he would have the remaining women cut to pieces before him. Bombay, by his own account, behaved with great propriety, saying Bana never wished to see sport of that cruel kind, and it would ill become him to see sights which his master had not. Viarungi sent me some tobacco, with kind regards, and said he and the Wazina had just obtained leave to return to their homes, K'yengo alone, of all the guests, remaining behind as a hostage until Mtesa's powder-seeking Wakungu returned. Finally, the little boy Lugoi had been sent to his home. Such was the tenor of Bombay's report.

11th. – The officer sent to procure boats, impudently saying there were none, was put in the stocks by Kasoro, whilst other men went to Kirindi for sailors, and down the stream for boats. On hearing the king's order that I was to be supplied with fish, the fishermen ran away, and pombe was no longer brewed for fear of Kasoro.

12th. – To-day we slaughtered and cooked two cows for the journey–– the remaining three and one goat having been lost in the Luajerri – and gave the women of the place beads in return for their hospitality. They are nearly all Wanyoro, having been captured in that country by king Mtesa and given to Mlondo. They said their teeth were extracted, four to six lower incisors, when they were young, because no Myoro would allow a person to drink from his cup unless he conformed to that custom. The same law exists in Usoga.

---

1) Named by Dr. P. L. Sclater, Cosmetornis Spekii. The seventh pen feathers are double the length of the ordinaries, the eighth double that of the seventh, and the ninth 20 inches long. Bombay says the same bird is found in Uhiyow.

2) It is questionable whether or not this word is a corruption of Bahr (sea of) Ingo.

CHAPTER 16

BAHR EL ABIAD

First Voyage on the Nile – The Starting – Description of the River and the Country – Meet a Hostile Vessel – A Naval Engagement – Difficulties and Dangers – Judicial Procedure – Messages from the King of Uganda – His Efforts to Get Us Back – Desertion – The Wanyoro Troops – Kamrasi – Elephant-Stalking – Diabolical Possessions.

In five boats of five planks each, tied together and caulked with mbugu rags, I started with twelve Wanguana, Kasoro and his page-followers, and a small crew, to reach Kamrasi's palace in Unyoro – goats, dogs, and kit, besides grain and dried meat, filling up the complement – but how many days it would take nobody knew.

Paddles propelled these vessels, but the lazy crew were slow in the use of them, indulging sometimes in racing spurts, then composedly resting on their paddles whilst the gentle current drifted us along. The river, very unlike what it was from the Ripon Falls downward, bore at once the character of river and lake – clear in the centre, but fringed in most places with tall rush, above which the green banks sloped back like park lands. It was all very pretty and very interesting, and would have continued so, had not Kasoro disgraced the Union Jack, turning it to piratical purposes in less than one hour.

A party of Wanyoro, in twelve or fifteen canoes, made of single tree trunks, had come up the river to trade with the Wasoga, and having stored their vessels with mbugu, dried fish, plantains cooked and raw, pombe, and other things, were taking their last meal on shore before they returned to their homes. Kasoro seeing this, and bent on a boyish spree, quite forgetting we were bound for the very ports they were bound for, ordered our sailors to drive in amongst them, landed himself, and sent the Wanyoro flying before I knew what game was up, and then set to pillaging and feasting on the property of those very men whom it was our interest to propitiate, as we expected them shortly to be our hosts.

The ground we were on belonged to king Mtesa, being a dependency of Uganda, and it struck me as singular that Wanyoro should be found here; but I no sooner discovered the truth than I made our boatmen disgorge everything they had taken, called back the Wanyoro to take care of their things, and extracted a promise from Kasoro that he would not practise such wicked tricks again, otherwise we could not travel together. Getting to boat again, after a very little paddling we pulled in to shore, on the Uganda side, to stop for the night, and thus allowed the injured Wanyoro to go down the river before us. I was much annoyed by this interruption, but no argument would prevail on Kasoro to go on. This was the last village on the Uganda frontier, and before we could go any farther on boats it would be necessary to ask leave of Kamrasi's frontier officer, N'yamyonjo, to enter Unyoro. The Wanguana demanded ammunition in the most imperious manner, whilst I, in the same tone, refused to issue any lest a row should take place and they then would desert,

Ripon Falls – The Nile's exit from Lake Victoria Nyanza.

alluding to their dastardly desertion in Msalala, when Grant was attacked. If a fight should take place, I said they must flock to me at once, and ammunition, which was always ready, would be served out to them. They laughed at this, and asked, Who would stop with me when the fight began? This was making a jest of what I was most afraid of – that they would all run away.

I held a levee to decide on the best manner of proceeding. The Waganda wanted us to stop for the day and feel the way gently, arguing that etiquette demands it. Then, trying to terrify me, they said, N'yamyonjo had a hundred boats, and would drive us back to a certainty if we tried to force past them, if he were not first spoken with, as the Waganda had often tried the passage and been repulsed. On the other hand, I argued that Grant must have arrived long ago at Kamrasi's, and removed all these difficulties for us; but, I said, if they would send men, let Bombay start at once by land, and we will follow in boats, after giving him time to say we are coming. This point gained after a hot debate, Bombay started at 10 A.M., and we not till 5 P.M., it being but one hour's journey by water. The frontier line was soon crossed; and then both sides of the river, Usoga as well as Unyoro, belong to Kamrasi.

I flattered myself all my walking this journey was over, and there was nothing left but to float quietly down the Nile, for Kidgwiga had promised boats, on Kamrasi's account, from Unyoro to Gani, where Petherick's vessels were said to be stationed; but this hope shared the fate of so many others in Africa. In a little while an enormous canoe, full of well-dressed and well-armed men, was seen approaching us. We worked on, and found they turned, as if afraid. Our men paddled faster, they did the same, the pages keeping time playfully by beat of drum, until at last it became an exciting chase, won by the Wanyoro by their superior numbers. The sun was now setting as we approached N'yamyongo's. On a rock by the river stood a number of armed men, jumping, jabbering, and thrusting with their spears, just as the Waganda do. I thought, indeed, they were Waganda doing this to welcome us; but a glance at Kasoro's glassy eyes told me such was not the case, but, on the contrary, their language and gestures were threats, defying us to land.

The bank of the river, as we advanced, then rose higher, and was crowned with huts and plantations, before which stood groups and lines of men, all fully armed. Further, at this juncture, the canoe we had chased turned broadside on us, and joined in the threatening demonstrations of the people on shore. I could not believe them to be serious – thought they had mistaken us – and stood up in the boat to show myself, hat in hand. I said I was an Englishman going to Kamrasi's, and did all I could, but without creating the slightest impression. They had heard a drum beat, they said, and that was a signal of war, so war it should be; and Kamrasi's drums rattled up both sides the river, preparing everybody to arm. This was serious. Further, a second canoe full of armed men issued out from the rushes behind us, as if with a view to cut off our retreat, and the one in front advanced upon us, hemming us in. To retreat together seemed our only chance, but it was getting dark, and my boats were badly manned. I gave the order to close together and retire, offering ammunition as an incentive, and all came to me but one boat, which seemed so paralysed with fright, it kept spinning round and round like a crippled duck.

The Wanyoro, as they saw us retreating, were now heard to say, "They are women, they are running, let us at them"; whilst I kept roaring to my men, "Keep together – come for powder"; and myself loaded with small shot, which even made Kasoro laugh and inquire if it was intended for the Wanyoro. "Yes, to shoot them like guinea-fowl"; and he laughed again. But confound my men! They would not keep together, and retreat with me. One of those served with ammunition went as hard as he could go up stream to be out of harm's way, and another preferred hugging the dark shade of the rushes to keeping the clear open, which I desired for the benefit of our guns. It was not getting painfully dark, and the Wanyoro were stealing on us, as we could hear, though nothing could be seen. Presently the shade-seeking boat was attacked, spears were thrown, fortunately into the river instead of into our men, and grappling-hooks were used to link the boats together. My men cried, "Help, Bana! They are killing us"; whilst I roared to my crew, "Go in, go in, and the victory will be ours"; but not a soul would – they were spell-bound to the place; we might have been cut up in detail, it was all the same to those cowardly Waganda, whose only action consisted in crying, "N'yawo! n'yawo!" – mother, mother, help us! Three shots from the hooked boat now finished the action. The Wanyoro had caught a Tartar. Two of their men fell – one killed, one wounded. They were heard saying their opponents were not Waganda, it were better to leave them alone; and retreated, leaving us, totally uninjured, a clear passage up the river. But where was Bombay all this while! He did not return till after us, and then, in considerable excitement, he told his tale. He reached N'yamyongo's village before noon, asked for the officer, but was desired to wait in a hut until the chief should arrive, as he had gone out on business; the villagers inquired, however, why we had robbed the Wanyoro yesterday, for they had laid a complaint against us. Bombay replied it was no fault of Bana's, he did everything he could to prevent it, and returned all that the boatmen took.

These men then departed, and did not return until evening, when they asked Bombay, impudently, why he was sitting there, as he had received no invitation to spend the night; and unless he walked off soon they would set fire to his hut. Bombay, without the smallest intention of moving, said he had orders to see N'yamyonjo, and until he did so he would not budge. "Well," said the people, "you have got your warning, now look out for yourselves"; and Bombay, with his Waganda escort, was left again. Drums then began to beat, and men to hurry to and fro with spears and shields, until at last our guns were heard, and, guessing the cause, Bombay with his Waganda escort rushed out of the hut into the jungle, and, without daring to venture on the beaten track, through thorns and thicket worked his way back to me, lame, and scratched all over with thorns.

Crowds of Waganda, all armed as if for war, came to congratulate us in the morning, jumping, jabbering, and shaking their spears at us, denoting a victory gained – for we had shot Wanyoro and no harm had befallen us. "But the road," I cried, "has that been gained? I am not going to show my back. We must go again, for there is some mistake; Grant is with Kamrasi, and N'yamyongo cannot stop us. If you won't go in boats, let us go by land to N'yamyongo's, and the boats will follow after." Not a soul, however, would stir. N'yamyongo was described as an independent chief, who listened to Kamrasi only when he liked. He did not like strange eyes to see his secret lodges on the N'yanza; and if he did not wish us to go down the river, Kamrasi's orders would go for nothing. His men had now been shot; to go within his reach would be certain death. Argument was useless, boating slow, to send messages worse; so I gave in, turned my back on the Nile, and the following day (16th) came on the Luajerri.

Here, to my intense surprise, I heard that Grant's camp was not far off, on its return from Kamrasi's. I could not, rather would not, believe it, suspicious as it now appeared after my reverse.

The men, however, were positive, and advised my going to king Mtesa's – a ridiculous proposition, at once rejected; for I had yet to receive Kamrasi's answer to our Queen, about opening a trade with England. I must ascertain why he despised Englishmen without speaking with them, and I could not believe Kamrasi would prove less avaricious than either Rumanika or Mtesa, especially as Rumanika had made himself responsible for our actions. We slept that night near Kari, the Waganda eating two goats which had been drowned in the Luajerri; and the messenger-page, having been a third time to the palace and back again, called to ask after our welfare, on behalf of his king, and remind us about the gun and brandy promised.

17th and 18th. – The two following days were spent wandering about without guides, trying to keep the track Grant had taken after leaving us, crossing at first a line of small hills, then traversing grass and jungle, like the dak of India. Plantain-gardens were frequently met, and the people seemed very hospitably inclined, though they complained sadly of the pages rudely rushing into every hut, seizing everything they could lay their hands on, and even eating the food which they had just prepared for their own dinners, saying, in a mournful manner, "If it were not out of respect for you we should fight those little rascals, for it is not the king's guest nor his men who do us injury, but the king's own servants, without leave or licence." I observed that special bomas or fences were erected to protect these villages against the incursions of lions. Buffaloes were about, but the villagers cautioned us not to shoot them, holding them as sacred animals; and, to judge from the appearance of the country, wild animals should abound, were it not for the fact that every Mganda seems by instinct to be a sportsman.

At last, after numerous and various reports about Grant, we heard his drums last night, but we arrived this morning just in time to be too late. He was on his march back to the capital of Uganda, as the people had told us, and passed through N'yakinyama just before I reached it. What had really happened I knew not, and was puzzled to think. To insist on a treaty, demanding an answer, to the Queen, seemed the only chance left; so I wrote to Grant to let me know all about it, and waited the result. He very obligingly came himself, said he left Unyoro after stopping there an age asking for the road without effect, and left by the orders of Kamrasi, thinking obedience the better policy to obtain our ends. Two great objections had been raised against us; one was that we were reported to be cannibals, and the other that our advancing by two roads at once was suspicious, the more especially so as the Waganda were his enemies; had we come from Rumanika direct, there would have been no objection to us.

When all was duly considered, it appeared evident to me that the great king of Unyoro, "the father of all the kings," was merely a nervous, fidgety creature, half afraid of us because we were attempting his country by the unusual mode of taking two routes at once, but wholly so of the Waganda, who had never ceased plundering his country for years. As it appeared that he would have accepted us had we come by the friendly route of Kisuere, a further parley was absolutely necessary, and the more especially so, as now we were all together and in Uganda, which, in consequence, must relieve him from the fear of our harbouring evil designs against him. No one present, however, could be prevailed on to go to him in the capacity of ambassador, as the frontier officer had warned the Wageni or guests that, if they ever attempted to cross the border again, he was bound in duty, agreeably to the orders of his king, to expel them by force; therefore, should the Wageni attempt it after this warning, their first appearance would be considered a casus belli; and so the matter rested for the day.

To make the best of a bad bargain, and as N'yakinyama was "eaten up," we repaired to Grant's camp to consult with Budja; but Budja was found firm and inflexible against sending men up to Unyoro.

His pride had been injured by the rebuffs we had sustained. He would wait here three or four days as I proposed, to see what fortune sent us, if I would not be convinced that Kamrasi wished to reject us, and he would communicate with his king in the meantime, but nothing more. Here was altogether a staggerer: I would stop for three or four days, but if Kamrasi would not have us by that time, what was to be done? Would it be prudent to try Kisuere now Baraka had been refused the Gani route? Or would it not be better still for me to sell Kamrasi altogether, by offering Mtesa five hundred loads of ammunition, cloth and beads, if he would give us a thousand Waganda as a force to pass through the Masai to Zanzibar, this property to be sent back by the escort from the coast? Kamrasi would no doubt catch it if we took this course, but it was expensive.

Thus were we ruminating, when lo, to our delight, as if they had been listening to us, up came Kidgwiga, my old friend, who, at Mtesa'a place, had said Kamrasi would be very glad to see me, and Vittagura, Kamrasi's commander-in-chief, to say their king was very anxious to see us, and the Waganda might come or not as they liked. Until now, the deputation said, Kamrasi had doubted Budja's word about our friendly intentions, but since he saw us withdrawing from his country, those doubts were removed. The N'yamswenge, they said – meaning, I thought, Petherick – was still at Gani; no English or others on the Nile ever expressed a wish to enter Unyoro, otherwise they might have done so; and Baraka had left for Karague, carrying off an ivory as a present from Kamrasi.

21st. – I ordered the march to Unyoro; Budja, however, kept brooding over the message sent to the Waganda, to the effect that they might come or not as they liked, and considering us with himself to have all been treated "like dogs," begged me to give him my opinion as to what course he had better pursue; for he must, in the first instance, report the whole circumstances to the king, and could not march at once. This was a blight on our prospects, and appeared very vexatious, in the event of Budja waiting for an answer, which, considering Mtesa had ordered his Wakungu to accompany us all the way to Gani, might stop our march altogether.

I therefore argued that Kamrasi's treatment of us was easily accounted for: he heard of us coming by two routes from an enemy's country, and was naturally suspicious of us; that had now been changed by our withdrawing, and he invited us to him. Without doubt, his commander-in-chief was never very far away, and followed on our heels. Such precaution was only natural and reasonable on Kamrasi's part, and what had been done need not alarm any one. "If you do your duty properly, you will take us at once into Unyoro, make your charge over to these men, and return or not as you like; for in doing so you will have fulfilled both Mtesa's, and Kamrasi's orders at once." "Very good," says Budja, "let it be so; for there is great wisdom in your words: but I must first send to my king, for the Waganda villagers have struck two of your men with weapons" (this had happened just before my arrival here), "and this is a most heinous offence in Uganda, which cannot be overlooked. Had it been done with a common stick, it could have been overlooked; but the use of weapons is an offence, and both parties must go before the king." This, of course, was objected to on the plea that it was my own affair. I was king of the Wanguana, and might choose to dispense with the attendance. The matter was compromised, however, on the condition that Budja should march across the border to-morrow, and wait for the return of these men and for further orders on the Unyoro side.

The bait took. Budja lost sight of the necessity there was for his going to Gani to bring back a gun, ammunition, and some medicine – that is to say, brandy – for his king; and sent his men off with mine to tell Mtesa all our adventures – our double repulse, the intention to wait on the Unyoro side for further orders, and the account of some Waganda having wounded my men. I added my excuses for Kamrasi, and laid a complaint against Mtesa's officers for having defrauded us out of ten cows, five goats, six butter, and sixty mbugu. It was not that we required these things, but I knew that the king had ordered them to be given to us, and I thought it right we should show that his officers, if they professed to obey his orders, had peculated. After these men had started, some friends of the villager who had been apprehended on the charge of assailing my men, came and offered Budja five cows to overlook the charge; and Budja, though he could not overlook it when I pleaded for the man, asked me to recall my men. Discovering that the culprit was a queen's man, and that the affair would cause bad blood at court should the king order the man's life to be taken, I tried to do so, but things had gone too far.

Again the expedition marched on in the right direction. We reached the last village on the Uganda frontier, and there spent the night. Here Grant shot a nsunnu buck. The Wanguana mutinied for ammunition, and would not lift a load until they got it, saying, "Unyoro is a dangerous country," though they had been there before without any more than they now had in pouch. The fact was, my men, in consequence of the late issues on the river, happened to have more than Grant's men, and every man must have alike. The ringleader, unfortunately for himself, had lately fired at a dead lion, to astonish the Unyoro, and his chum had fired a salute, which was contrary to orders; for ammunition was at a low ebb, and I had done everything in my power to nurse it. Therefore, as a warning to the others, the guns of these two were confiscated, and a caution given that any gun in future let off, either by design or accident, would be taken.

To-day I felt very thankful to get across the much-vexed boundary-line, and enter Unyoro, guided by Kamrasi's deputation of officers, and so shake off the apprehensions which had teased us for so many days. This first march was a picture of all the country to its capital: an interminable forest of small trees, bush, and tall grass, with scanty villages, low huts, and dirty-looking people clad in skins; the plantain, sweet potato, sesamum, and ulezi (millet) forming the chief edibles, besides goats and fowls; whilst the cows, which are reported to be numerous, being kept, as everywhere else where pasture-lands are good, by the wandering, unsociable Wahuma are seldom seen. No hills, except a few scattered cones, disturb the level surface of the land, and no pretty views ever cheer the eye. Uganda is now entirely left behind; we shall not see its like again; for the further one leaves the equator, and the rain-attracting influences of the Mountains of the Moon, vegetation decreases proportionately with the distance.

Fortunately the frontier-village could not feed so large a party as ours, and therefore we were compelled to move farther on, to our great delight, through the same style of forest acacia, cactus, and tall grass, to Kidgwiga's gardens, where we no sooner arrived than Mtesa's messenger-page, with a party of fifty Waganda, dropped in, in the most unexpected manner, to inquire after "his royal master's friend, Bana." The king had heard of the fight upon the river, and thought the Wanguana must be very good shots. He still trusted we would not forget the gun and ammunition, but, above all, the load of stimulants, for he desired that above all things on earth. This was the fourth message to remind us of these important matters which we had received since leaving his gracious presence, and each time brought by the same page. While the purpose of the boy's coming with so many men was not distinctly known, the whole village and camp were in a state of great agitation, Budja fearing lest the king had some fault to find with his work, and the Wanyoro deeming it a menace of war, whilst I was afraid they might take fright and stop our progress.

But all went well in the end; Massey's log, which I have mentioned as a present I intended for Mtesa, was packed up, and the page departed with it. Some of Rumanika's men, who came into Unyoro with Baraka, with four of K'yengo's, were sent to call us by Kamrasi. Through Rumanika's men it transpired that he had stood security for our actions, else, with the many evil reports of our being cannibals and such-like, which had preceded our coming here, we never should have gained admittance to the country. The Wanyoro, who are as squalid-looking as the Wanyamuezi, and almost as badly dressed, now came about us to hawk ivory ornaments, brass and copper twisted wristlets, tobacco, and salt, which they exchanged for cowries, with which they purchase cows from the Waganda. As in Uganda, all the villagers forsook their huts as soon as they heard the Wageni (guests) were coming; and no one paid the least attention to the traveller, save the few head-men attached to the escort, or some professional traders.

25th to 28th. – I had no sooner ordered the march than Vittagura counter-ordered it, and held a levee to ascertain, as he said, if the Waganda were to go back; for though Kamrasi wished to see us, he did not want the Waganda. It was Kamrasi's orders that Budja should tell this to his "child the Mkavia," meaning Mtesa; for when the Waganda came the first time to see him, three of his family died; and when they came the second time, three more died; and as this rate of mortality was quite unusual in his family circle, he could only attribute it to foul magic. The presence of people who brought such results was of course by no means desirable. This neat message elicited with a declaration of the necessity of Budja's going to Gani with us, and a response from the commander-in-chief, probably to terrify the Waganda, that although Gani was only nine days' journey distant from Kamrasi's palace, the Gani people were such barbarians, they would call a straight-haired man a magician, and any person who tied his mbugu in a knot upon his shoulder, or had a full set of teeth as the Waganda have, would be surely killed by them. Finally, we must wait two days, to see if Kamrasi would see us or not. Such was Unyoro diplomacy.

An announcement of a different kind immediately followed. The king had heard that I gave a cow to Vittagura and Kidgwiga when they first came to me in Uganda, and wished the Wanyamuezi to ascertain if this was true. Of course, I said they were my guests in Uganda, and if they had been wise they would have eaten their cow on the spot; what was that to Kamrasi? It was a pity he did not treat us as well who have come into his country at his own invitation, instead of keeping us starving in this gloomy wilderness, without a drop of pombe to cheer the day – why could not he let us go on? He wanted first to hear if the big Mzungu, meaning myself, had really come yet. All fudge! Three days were spent in simply waiting for return messages on both sides, and more might have been lost in the same way, only we amused Vittagura and gave him confidence by showing our pictures, looking-glass, scissors, knives, etc., when he promised a march in the morning, leaving a man behind to bring on the Wanguana sent to Mtesa's, it being the only alternative which would please Budja; for he said there was no security for life in Unyoro, where every Mkungu calls himself the biggest man, and no true hospitality is to be found.

The next two days took us through Chagamoyo to Kiratosi, by the aid of the compass; for the route Kamrasi's men took differed from the one which Budja knew, and he declared the Wanyoro were leading us into a trap, and would not be convinced we were going on all right till I pulled out the compass and confirmed the Wanyoro. We were anything but welcomed at Kiratosi, the people asking by what bad luck we had come there to eat up their crops; but in a little while they flocked to our doors and admired our traps, remarking that they believed each iron box contained a couple of white dwarfs, which we carry on our shoulders, sitting straddle-legs, back to back, and they fly off to eat people whenever they get the order. One of these visitors happened to be the sister of one of my men, named Baruti, who no sooner recognised her brother, than, without saying a word, she clasped her head with her hands, and ran off, crying, to tell her husband what she had seen. A spy of Kamrasi dropped the report that the Wanguana were returning from Mtesa's, and hurried on to tell the king.

31st. – Some Waganda hurrying in, confirmed the report of last night, and said the Wanguana, footsore, had been left at the

Uganda frontier, expecting us to return, as Mtesa, at the same time that he approved highly of my having sent men back to inform him of Kamrasi's conduct, begged we would instantly return, even if found within one march of Kamrasi's, for he had much of importance to tell his friend Bana. The message continued to this effect: I need be under no apprehensions about the road to the coast, for he would give me as many men as I liked; and, fearing I might be short of powder, he had sent some with the Wanguana. Both Wanguana were by the king given women for their services, and an old tin cartridge-box represented Mtesa's card, it being an article of European manufacture, which, if found in the possession of any Mganda, would be certain death to him. Finally, all the houses and plantains where my men were wounded had been confiscated.

When this message was fully delivered, Budja said we must return without a day's delay. I, on the contrary, called up Kidgwiga. I did not like my men having been kept prisoners in Uganda, and pronounced in public that I would not return. It would be an insult to Kamrasi my doing so, for I was now in his "house" at his own invitation. I wished Bombay would go with him (Kidgwiga) at once to his king, to say I had hoped, when I sent Budja with Mabruki, in the first instance, conveying a friendly present from Mtesa, which was done at my instigation, and I found Kamrasi acknowledged it by a return-present, that there would be no more fighting between them. I said I had left England to visit these countries for the purpose of opening up a trade, and I had no orders to fight my way except with the force of friendship. That Rumanika had accepted my views Kamrasi must be fully aware by Baraka's having visited him; and that

Mtesa did the same must also be evident, else he would never have ordered his men to accompany me to Gani; and I now fondly trusted that these Waganda would be allowed to go with me, when, by the influence of trade, all animosity would cease, and friendly relations be restored between the two countries.

This speech was hardly pronounced when Kajunju, a fine athletic man, dropped suddenly in, nodded a friendly recognition to Budja, and wished to know what the Waganda meant by taking us back, for the king had heard of their intention last night; and when told by Budja his story, and by Kidgwiga mine, he vanished like a shadow. Budja, now turning to me, said, "If you won't go back, I shall; for the orders of Mtesa must always be obeyed, else lives will be lost; and I shall tell him that you, since leaving his country, and getting your road, have quite forgotten him." "If you give such a message as that," I said, "you will tell a falsehood. Mtesa has no right to order me out of another man's house, to be an enemy with one whose friendship I desire. I am not only in honour bound to speak with Kamrasi, but I am also bound to carry out the orders of my country just as much as you are yours; moreover, I have invited Petherick to come to Kamrasi's by a letter from Karague, and it would be ill-becoming in me to desert him in the hands of an enemy, as he would then certainly find Kamrasi to be if I went back now." Budja then tried the coaxing dodge, saying, "There is much reason in your words, but I am sorry you do not listen to the king, for he loves you as a brother. Did you not go about like two brothers – walking, talking, shooting, and even eating together? It was the remark of all the Waganda, and the king will be so vexed when he finds you have thrown him over. I did not tell you before, but the king says, 'How can I answer Rumanika if Kamrasi injures Bana? Had I known Kamrasi was such a savage, I would not have let Bana go there; and I should now have sent a forge to take him away, only that some accident might arise from it by Kamrasi's taking fright; the road even to Gani shall be got by force if necessary.'" Then, finding me still persistent, Budja turned again and threatened us with the king's power, saying, "If you choose to disobey, we will see whether you ever get the road to Gani or not; for Kamrasi is at war on all sides with his brothers, and Mtesa will ally himself with them at any moment that he wishes, and where will you be then?" Saying this, Budja walked off, muttering that our being here would much embarrass Mtesa's actions; whilst my Wanguana, who had been attentively listening, like timid hares, made up their minds to leave me, and tried, through Bombay, to obtain a final interview with me, saying they knew Mtesa's power, and disobedience to him would only end in taking away all chance of escape. In reply, I said I would not listen to them, as I had seen enough of them to know it was no use speaking to a pack of unreasonable cowards, having tried it so often before; but I sent a message requesting them, if they did desert me at last, to leave my guns; and, further, added an intimation that, as soon as they reached the coast, they would be put into prison for three years. The scoundrels insolently said "tuende setu" (let's be off), rushed to the Waganda drums, and beat the march.

1st. – Early in the morning, as Budja drummed the home march, I called him up, gave him a glass rain-gauge as a letter for Mtesa, and instructed him to say I would send a man to Mtesa as soon as I had seen Kamrasi about opening the road; that I trusted he would take all the guns from the deserters and keep them for me, but the men themselves I wished transported to an island on the N'yanza, for I could never allow such scoundrels again to enter my camp. It was the effect of desertions like these that prevented any white men visiting these countries. This said, the Waganda all left us, taking with them twenty-eight Wanguana, armed with twenty-two carbines. Amongst them was the wretched governess, Manamaka, who had always thought me a wonderful magician, because I possessed, in her belief, an extraordinary power in inclining all the black kings' hearts to me, and induced them to give the roads no one before of my colour had ever attempted to use.

With a following reduced to twenty men, armed with fourteen carbines, I now wished to start for Kamrasi's, but had not even sufficient force to lift the loads. A little while elapsed, and a party of fifty Wanyoro rushed wildly into camp, with their spears uplifted, and looked for the Waganda, but found them gone.

The athletic Kajunju, it transpired, had returned to Kamrasi's, told him our story, and received orders to snatch us away from the Waganda by force, for the great Mkamma, or king, was most anxious to see his white visitors; such men had never entered Unyoro before, and neither his father nor his father's fathers had ever been treated with such a visitation; therefore he had sent on these fifty men to fall by surprise on the Waganda, and secure us. But again, in a little while, about 10 A.M., Kajunju, in the same wild manner, at the head of 150 warriors, with the soldier's badge – a piece of mbugu or plantain-leaf tied round their heads, and a leather sheath on their spear-heads, tufted with cow's-tail – rushed in exultingly, having found, to their delight, that there was no one left to fight with, and that they had gained an easy victory. They were certainly a wild set of ragamuffins – as different as possible from the smart, well-dressed, quick-of-speech Waganda as could be, and anything but prepossessing to our eyes. However, they had done their work, and I offered them a cow, wishing to have it shot before them; but the chief men, probably wishing the whole animal to themselves, took it alive, saying the men were all the king's servants, and therefore could not touch a morsel.

Kamrasi expected us to advance next day, when some men would go on ahead to announce our arrival, and bring a letter which was brought with beads by Gani before Baraka's arrival here. It was shown to Baraka in the hope that we would come by the Karague route, but not to Mabruki, because he came from Uganda. Kidgwiga informed us that Kamrasi never retaliated on Mtesa when he lifted Unyoro cows, though the Waganda keep their cattle on the border – which simply meant that he had not the power of doing so. The twenty remaining Wanguana, conversing over the sudden scheme of the deserters, proposed, on one side, sending for them, as, had they seen the Wanyoro arrive, they would have changed their minds; but the other side said, "What! those brutes who said we should all die here if we stayed, and yet dared not face the danger with us, should we now give them a helping hand? Never! We told them we would share our fate with Bana, and share it we will, for God rules everything: every man must die when his time comes." We marched for the first time without music, as the drum is never allowed to be beaten in Unyoro except when the necessities of war demand it, or for a dance. Wanyamuezi and Wanyoro, in addition to our own twenty men, carried the luggage, though no one carried more than the smallest article he could find. It was a pattern Unyoro march, of only two hours' duration. On arrival at the end we heard that elephants had been seen close by. Grant and I then prepared our guns, and found a herd of about a hundred feeding on a plain of long grass, dotted here and there by small mounds crowned with shrub. The animals appeared to be all females, much smaller than the Indian breed; yet though ten were fired at, none were killed, and only one made an attempt to charge. I was with the little twin Manua at the time, when, stealing along under cover of the high grass, I got close to the batch and fired at the larges, which sent her round roaring. The whole of them then, greatly alarmed, packed together and began sniffing the air with their uplifted trunks, till, ascertaining by the smell of the powder that their enemy was in front of them, they rolled up their trunks and came close to the spot where I was lying under a mound. My scent then striking across them, they pulled up short, lifted their heads high, and looked down sideways on us. This was a bad job. I could not get a proper front shot at the boss of any of them, and if I had waited an instant we should both have been picked up or trodden to death; so I let fly at their temples, and instead of killing, sent the whole of them rushing away at a much faster pace than they came. After this I gave up, because I never could separate the ones I had wounded from the rest, and thought it cruel to go on damaging more. Thinking over it afterwards, I came to the conclusion I ought to have put in more powder; for I had, owing to their inferior size to the Indian ones, rather despised them, and fired at them with the same charge and in the same manner as I always did at rhinoceros.

Though puzzled at the strange sound of the rifle, the elephants seldom ran far, packed in herd, and began to graze again. Frij, who was always ready at spinning a yarn, told us with much gravity that two of my men, Uledi and Wadi Hamadi, deserters, were possessed of devils (Phepo) at Zanzibar. Uledi, not wishing to be plagued by his Satanic majesty's angels on the march, sacrificed a cow and fed the poor, according to the great Phepo's orders, and had been exempted from it; but Wadi Hamadi, who preferred taking his chance, had been visited several times: once at Usui, when he was told the journey would be prosperous, only the devil wanted one man's life, and one man would fall sick; which proved true, for Hassani was murdered, and Grant fell sick in Karague. The second time Wadi Hamadi saw the devil in Karague, and was told one man's life would be required in Uganda, and such also was the case by Kari's murder; and a third time, in Unyoro, he was possessed, when it was said that the journey would be prosperous but protracted.

3d. – Though we stormed every day at being so shamefully neglected and kept in the jungles, we could not get on, nor find out the truth of our position. I asked if Kamrasi was afraid of us, and looking into his magic horn; and was answered, "No; he is very anxious to see you, or he would not have sent six of his highest officers to look after you, and prevent the unruly peasantry from molesting you." "Then by whose orders are we kept here?" "By Kamrasi's." "Why does Kamrasi keep us here?" "He thinks you are not so near, and men have gone to tell him."

"How did we come here from the last ground?" "By Kamrasi's orders; for nothing can be done excepting by his orders." "Then he must know we are here?" "He may not have seen the men we sent to him; for unless he shows in public no one can see him." The whole affair gave us such an opinion of Kamrasi as induced us to think it would have served him right had we joined Mtesa and given him a thrashing. This, I said, was put in our power by an alliance with his refractory brothers; but Kidgwiga only laughed and said, "Nonsense! Kamrasi is the chief of all the countries round here – Usoga, Kidi, Chopi, Gani, Ulega, everywhere; he has only to hold up his hand and thousands would come to his assistance." Kwibeya, the officer of the place, presented us with five fowls on the part of the king, and some baskets of potatoes.

4th. – We halted again, it was said, in order that Kwibeya might give us all the king had desired him to present. I sent Bombay off with a message to Kamrasi explaining everything, and begging for an early interview, as I had much of importance to communicate, and wished, of all things, to see the letter he had from Gani, as it must have come from our dear friends at home. Seven goats, flour, and plantains, were now brought to us; and as Kidgwiga begged for the flour without success, he flew into a fit of high indignation because these things were given and received without his having first been consulted. He was the big man and appointed go-between, and no one could dispute it. This was rather startling news to us, for Vittagura said he was commander-in-chief; Kajunju thought himself biggest, so did Kwibeya, and even Dr. K'yengo's men justified Budja's speech.

5th and 6th. – Still another halt, with all sorts of excuses. Frij, it appeared, dreamt last night that the king of Uganda came to fight us for not complying with his orders, and that all my men ran away except Uledi and himself. This, according to the interpretation of the coast, would turn out the reverse, otherwise his head must be wrong, and, according to local science, should be set right again by actual cautery of the temples; and as Grant dreamt a letter came from Gani which I opened and ran away with, he thought it would turn out no letter at all, and therefore Kamrasi had been humbugging us. We heard that Bombay had shot a cow before Kamrasi and would not be allowed to return until he had eaten it.

At last we made a move, but only of two hours' duration, through the usual forest, in which elephants walked about as if it were their park. We hoped at starting to reach the palace, but found we must stop here until the king should send for us. We were informed that doubtless he was looking into his Uganga, or magic horn, to discover what he had to expect from us; and he seemed as yet to have found no ground for being afraid of us. Moreover, it is his custom to keep visitors waiting on him in this way, for is he not the king of kings, the king of Kittara, which includes all the countries surrounding Unyoro?

CHAPTER 17

UNYORO

Invitation to the Palace At Last – Journey to It – Bombay's Visit to King Kamrasi – Our Reputation as Cannibals – Reception at Court – Acting the Physician Again – Royal Mendicancy.

We halted again, but in the evening one of Dr. K'yengo's men came to invite us to the palace. He explained that Kamrasi was in a great rage because we only received seven goats instead of thirty, the number he had ordered Kwibeya to give us, besides pombe and plantains without limitation. I complained that Bombay had been shown more respect than myself, obtaining an immediate admittance to the king's presence. To this he gave two ready answers – that every distinction shown my subordinate was a distinction to myself, and that we must not expect court etiquette from savages.

9th. – We set off for the palace. This last march differed but little from the others. Putting Dr. K'yengo's men in front, and going on despite all entreaties to stop, we passed the last bit of jungle, sighted the Kidi hills, and, in a sea of swampy grass, at last we stood in front of and overlooked the great king's palace, situated N. lat. 1° 37' 43", and E. long. 32° 19' 49", on a low tongue of land between the Kafu and Nile rivers. It was a dumpy, large hut, surrounded by a host of smaller ones, and the worst royal residence we had seen since leaving Uzinza. Here Kajunju, coming from behind, overtook us, and breathless with running, in the most excited manner, abused Dr. K'yengo's men for leading us on, and ordered us to stop until he saw the king, and ascertained the place his majesty wished us to reside in. Recollecting Mtesa's words that Kamrasi placed his guest on the N'yanza, I declined going to any place but the palace, which I maintained was my right, and waited for the issue, when Kajunju returned with pombe, and showed us to a small, dirty set of huts beyond the Kafu river – the trunk of the Mwerango and N'yanza branches which we crossed in Uganda – and trusted this would do for the present, as better quarters in the palace would be looked for on the morrow. This was a bad beginning, and caused a few of the usual anathemas in which our countrymen give vent to their irritation.

Two loads of flowers, neatly packed in long strips of rushpith, were sent for us "to consume at once," as more would be given on the morrow. To keep us amused, Kidgwiga informed us that Kamrasi and Mtesa – in fact, all the Wahuma – came originally from a stock of the same tribe dwelling beyond Kidi. All bury their dead in the same way, under ground; but the kings are toasted first for months till they are like sun-dried meat, when the lower jaw is cut out and preserved, covered with beads. The royal tombs are put under the charge of special officers, who occupy huts erected over them. The umbilical cords are preserved from birth, and, at death, those of men are placed within the door-frame, whilst those of women are buried without – this last act corresponding, according to Bombay, with the custom of the Wahiyow. On the death of any of the great officers of state, the finger-bones and hair are also preserved; or if they have died shaven, as sometimes occurs, a bit of their mbugu dress will be preserved in place of the hair. Their families guard their tombs.

The story we heard at Karague, about dogs with horns in Unyoro, was confirmed by Kidgwiga, who positively assured us that he once saw one in the possession of an official person, but it died. The horn then was stuffed with magic powder, and, whenever an army was ordered for war, it was placed on the war-track for the soldiers to step over, in the same way as a child is sacrificed to insure victory in Unyomuezi. Of the Karague story, according to which all the Kidi people sleep in trees, Kidgwiga gave me a modified version. He said the bachelors alone do so, whilst the married folk dwell in houses. As most of these stories have some foundation in fact, we presumed that the people of Kidi sometimes mount a tree to sleep at night when travelling through their forests, where lions are plentiful – but not otherwise.

10th. – I sent Kidgwiga with my compliments to the king, and a request that his majesty would change my residence, which was so filthy that I found it necessary to pitch a tent, and also that he would favour me with an interview after breakfast. The return was a present of twenty cows, ten cocks, two bales of flour, and two pots of pombe, to be equally divided between Grant and myself, as Kamrasi recognised in us two distinct camps, because we approached his country by two different routes – a smart method for expecting two presents from us, which did not succeed, as I thanked for all, Grant being "my son" on this occasion. The king also sent his excuses, and begged pardon for what happened to us on entering his country, saying it could not have taken place had we come from Rumanika direct. His fear of the Waganda gave rise to it, and he trusted we would forget and forgive. To-morrow our residence should be changed, and an interview follow, for he desired being friends with us just as much as we did with him.

At last Bombay came back. He reported that he had not been allowed to leave the palace earlier, though he pleaded hard that I expected his return; and the only excuse he could extract from the king was, that we were coming in charge of many Wakungu, and he had found it necessary to retard our approach in consequence of the famine at Chaguzi. His palace proper was not here, but three marches westward: he had come here and pitched a camp to watch his brothers, who were at war with him. Bombay, doing his best to escape, or to hurry my march, replied that he was very anxious on our account, because the Waganda wished to snatch us away.

It was no doubt this hint that brought the messenger to our relief yesterday; and otherwise we might have been kept in the jungle longer. When told by Bombay of our treatment on the Nile, the king first said he did not think we wished to see him, else we would have come direct from Rumanika; but when asked if Baraka's coming with Rumanika's officers was not sufficient to satisfy him on this point, he hung down his head, and evaded the question, saying he had been the making of Mtesa of Uganda; but he had turned out a bad fellow, and now robbed him right and left.[1] The Gani letter, supposed to be from Petherick, was now asked for, and a suggestion made about opening a trade with Gani, but all with the provoking result we had been so well accustomed to. No letter like that referred to had ever been received, so that Frij's interpretation about Grant's letter-dream was right; and if we wished to go to Gani, the king would send men travelling by night, for his brothers at war with him lay upon the road. As to the Uganda question, and my desiring him to make friends with Mtesa, in hopes that the influence of trade would prevent any plundering in future, he merely tossed his head. He often said he did not know what to think about his guests, now he had got them; to which Bombay, in rather successful imitation of what he had heard me say on like occasions, replied, "If you do not like them after you have seen them, cut their heads off, for they are all in your hands."

11th. – With great apparent politeness Kamrasi sent in the morning to inquire how we had slept. He had "heard our cry" – an expression of regal condescension – and begged we would not be alarmed, for next morning he would see us, and after the meeting change our residence, when, should we not approve of wading to his palace, he would bridge all the swamps leading up to it; but for the present he wanted two rounds of ball-cartridge – one to fire before his women, and the other before his officers and a large number of Kidi men who were there on a visit. To please this childish king, Bombay was sent with two other of my men, and no sooner arrived than a cow was placed before them to be shot. Bombay, however, thinking easy compliance would only lead to continued demands on our short store of powder, said he had no order to shoot cows, and declined. A strong debated ensued, which Bombay, by his own account, turned to advantage, by saying, "What use is there in shooting cows? We have lots of meat; what we want is flour to eat with it." To which the great king retorted, "If you have not got flour, that is not my fault, for I ordered your master to come slowly, and to bring provisions along with him." Then getting impatient, as all his visitors wanted sport, he ordered the cow out again, and insisted on my men shooting at it, saying at the same time to his Kidi visitors, boastfully, "Now I will show you what devils these Wanguana are: with firearms they can kill a cow with one bullet; and as they are going to Gani, I advise you not to meddle with them." The Kidi visitors said, "Nonsense; we don't believe in their power, but we will see." Irate at his defeat, Bombay gave orders to the men to fire over the cow, and told Kamrasi why he had done so – Bana would be angry with him. "Well," said the king of kings, "if that is true, go back to your master, tell him you have disappointed me before these men, and obtain permission to shoot the cow in the morning; after which, should you succeed, your master can come after break- fast to see me – but for the present, take him this pot of pombe."

12th. – To back Bombay in what he had said, I gave him two more cartridges to shoot the cow with, and orders as well to keep Kamrasi to his word about the oft-promised interview and change of residence. He gave me the following account on his return: Upwards of a thousand spectators were present when he killed the cow, putting both bullets into her, and all in a voice, as soon as they saw the effect of the shot, shouted in amazement; the Kidi visitors, all terror-stricken, crying out, as they clasped their breasts, "Oh, great king, do allow us to return to our coun- try, for you have indeed got a new specimen of man with you, and we are greatly afraid!" – a lot of humbug and affectation to flatter the king, which pleased him greatly. It was not sufficient, however, to make him forget his regal pride; for though Bombay pleaded hard for our going to see him, and for a change of residence, the immovable king, to maintain the imperial state he had assumed as "king of kings," only said, "What difference does it make whether your master sees me to-day or to-morrow? If he wants to communicate about the road to Gani, his property at Karague, or the guns at Uganda, he can do so as well through the medium of my officers as with me direct, and I will send men whenever he wishes to do so. Perhaps you don't know, but I expect men from Gani every day, who took a present of slaves, ivory and monkey-skins to the foreigners residing there, who, in the first instance sent me a necklace of beads [showing them] by some men who wore clothes. They said white men were coming from Karague, and requested the beads might be shown them should they do so. They left this two moons before Baraka arrived here, and I told them the white men would not come here, as I heard they had gone to Uganda." Bombay then, finding the king very communicative, went at him for his inhospitality towards us, his turning us back from his country twice, and now, after inviting us, treating us as Suwarora did. On this he gave, by Bombay's account, the following curious reason for his conduct: "You don't understand the matter. At the time the white men were living in Uganda, many of the people who had seen them there came and described them as such monsters, they ate up mountains and drank the N'yanza dry; and although they fed on both beef and mutton, they were not satisfied until they got a dish of the 'tender parts' of human beings three times a-day. Now, I was extremely anxious to see men of such wonderful natures. I could have stood their mountain-eating and N'yanzi-drinking capacities, but on no consideration would I submit to sacrifice my subjects to their appetites, and for this reason I first sent to turn them back; but afterwards, on hearing from Dr. K'yengo's men that, although the white men had travelled all through their country, and brought all the pretty and wonderful things of the world there, they had never heard such monstrous imputations cast upon them, I sent a second time to call them on: these are the facts of the case. Now, with regard to your accusation of my treating them badly, it is all their own fault. I ordered them to advance slowly and pick up food by the way, as there is a famine here; but they, instead, hurried on against my wishes. That they want to see and give me presents you have told me repeatedly – so do I them; for I want them to teach me the way to shoot, and when that is accomplished, I will take them to an island near Kidi, where there are some men [his refractory brothers] whom I wish to frighten away with guns; but still there is no hurry – they can come when I choose to call them, and not before." Bombay to this said, "I cannot deliver such a message to Bana; I have told so many falsehoods about your saying you will have an interview to-morrow, I shall only catch a flogging"; and forthwith departed.

13th. – More disgusted with Kamrasi than ever, I called Kidgwiga up, and told him I was led to expect from Rumanika that I should find his king a good and reasonable man, which I believed, considering it was said by an unprejudiced person. Mtesa, on the contrary, told me Kamrasi treated all his guests with disrespect, sending them to the farther side of the N'yanzi. I now found his enemy more truthful than his friend, and wished him to be told so. "For the future, I should never," I said, "mention his name again, but wait until his fear of me had vanished; for he quite forgot his true dignity as a host and king in his surprise and fear, merely because we were in a hurry and desired to see him." He was reported to-day, by the way, to be drunk.

As nothing could be done yesterday, in consequence of the king being in his cups, the Wakungu conveyed my message to-day, but with the usual effect, till a diplomatic idea struck me, and I sent another messenger to say, if our residence was not changed at once, both Grant and myself had made up our minds to cut off our hair and blacken our faces, so that the king of all kings should have no more cause to fear us. Ignoring his claims to imperial rank, I maintained that his reason for ill-treating us must be fear – it could be nothing else. This message acted like magic; for he fully believed we would do as we said, and disappoint him altogether of the strange sight of us as pure white men. The reply was, Kamrasi would not have us disfigured in this way for all the world; men were appointed to convey our traps to the west end at once; and Kidgwiga, Vittagura, and Kajunju rushed over to give us the news in all hast lest we should execute our threat, and they were glad to find us with our faces unchanged. I now gave one cow to the head of Dr. K'yengo's party, and one to the head of Rumanika's men, because I saw it was through their instrumentality we gained admittance in the country; and we changed residence to the west end of Chaguzi, and found there comfortable huts close to the Kafu, which ran immediately between us and the palace.

Still our position in Unyoro was not a pleasant one. In a long field of grass, as high as the neck, and half under water, so that no walks could be taken, we had nothing to see but Kamrasi's miserable huts and a few distant conical hills, of which one Udongo, we conceive, represents the Padongo of Brun-Bollet, placed by him in 1° south latitude, and 35° east longitude. We were scarcely inside our new dwelling when Kamrasi sent a cheer of two pots pombe, five fowls, and two bunches of plantains, hoping we were now satisfied with his favour; but he damped the whole in a moment again, by asking for a many-bladed knife which his officers had seen in Grant's possession. I took what he sent, from fear of giving offence, but replied that I was surprised the great king should wish to see my property before seeing myself, and although I attached no more value to my property than he did to his, I could not demean myself by sending him trifles in that way. However, should he, after hearing my sentiments, still persist in asking for the knife to be sent by the hands of a black man, I would pack it up with all the things I had brought for him, and send them by a black man, judging that he liked black men more than white.

Dr. K'yengo's men then informed us they had been twice sent with an army of Wanyoro to attack the king's brothers, on a river-island north of this about three days' journey, but each time it ended in nothing. You fancy yourself, they said, in a magnificent army, but the enemy no sooner turn out than the cowardly Wanyoro fly, and sacrifice their ally as soon as not into the hands of the opponents. They said Kamrasi would not expect us to attack them with our guns. Rionga was the head of the rebels; there were formerly five, but now only two of the brothers remained.

15th. – Kamrasi, after inquiring after our health, and how we had slept, through a large deputation of head men, alluded to the knife question of yesterday, thinking it very strange that after giving me such nice food I should deny him the gratification of simply looking at a knife; he did not intend to keep it if it was not brought for him, but merely to look at and return it. To my reply of yesterday I added, I had been led, before entering Unyoro, to regard Kamrasi as the king of all kings – the greatest king that ever was, and one worthy to be my father; but now, as he expected me to amuse him with toys, he had lowered himself in my estimation to the position of being my child. To this the sages said, "Bana speaks beautifully, feelingly, and moderately. Of course he is displeased at seeing his property preferred before himself; all the right is on his side: we will now return and see what can be done – though none but white men in their greatest dare send such messages to our king." Dr. K'yengo's men were now attacked by Kidgwiga for having taken a cow from me yesterday, and told they should not eat it, because both they and myself were the king's guests, and it ill became one to eat that which was given as a dinner for the other. Fortunately, foreseeing this kind of policy, as Kamrasi had been watching our actions, I invariably gave in presents those cows which came with us from Uganda, and therefore defied any one to meddle with them. This elicited the true facts of the case. Dr. K'yengo's men had been sent out to our camp to observe if anybody received presents from us, as Kamrasi feared his subjects would have the fleecing of us before his turn came; and these men had reported the two cows given by me as mentioned above. Kamrasi no sooner heard of this than he took the cows and kept them himself. In their justification, Dr. K'yengo's men said that had they not been in the country before us, Kamrasi would not have had such guests at all; for when he asked them if the Waganda reports about our cannibalism and other monstrosities were true, their head man denied it all, offered to stand security for our actions, and told the king if he found us cannibals he might make a Mohammedan of him, and sealed the statement with his oath by throwing down his shield and bow and walking over them. To this Kamrasi was said to have replied, "I will accept your statements, but you must remain with me until they come." Kajunju came with orders to say Kamrasi would seize anybody found staring at us. I requested a definite answer would be given as regards Kamrasi's seeing us. Dr. K'yengo's men then said they were kept a week waiting before they could obtain an interview, whilst Kajunju excused his king by saying, "At present the court is full of Kidi, Chopi, Gani, and other visitors, who he does not wish should see you, as some may be enemies in disguise. They are all now taking presents of cows from Kamrasi, and going to their homes, and, as soon as they are disposed of, your turn will come."

16th. – We kept quiet all day, to see what effect that would have upon the king. Kidgwiga told us that, when he was a lad, Kamrasi sent him with a large party of Wanyoro to visit a king who lived close to a high mountain, two months' journey distant, to the east or south-east of this, and beg for a magic horn, as that king's doctor was peculiarly famed for his skill as a magician. The party carried with them 600 majembe (iron spades), two of which expended daily paid for their board and lodgings on the way. The horn applied for was sent by a special messenger to Kamrasi, who, in return, sent one of his horns; from which date, the two kings, whenever one of them wishes to communicate with the other, sends, on the messenger's neck, the horn that had been given him, which both serves for credentials and security, as no one dare touch a Mbakka with one of these horns upon his neck.

A common source of conversation among our men now was the desertion of their comrades, all fancying how bitterly they would repent it when they heard how we had succeeded, eating beef every day; and Uledi now, in a joking manner, abused Mektub for having urged him to desert. He would not leave Bana, and if he had not stopped, Mektub would have gone, for they both served one master at Zanzibar, and therefore were like brothers; whilst Mektub, laughing over the matter as if it were a good joke, said, "I packed up my things to go, it is true; but I reflected if I got back to the coast Said Majid would only make a slave of me again." M'yinzuggi, the head of Rumanika's party, gave me to-day a tippet monkey-skin in return for the cow I had given him on the 14th. These men, taking their natures from their king Rumanika, are by far the most gentle, polite, and attentive of any black men we have travelled amongst.

17th. – Tired and out of patience with our prison – a river of crocodiles on one side, and swamps in every other direction, while we could not go out shooting without a specific order from the king – I sent Kidgwiga and Kajunju to inform Kamrasi that we could bear this life no longer. As he did not wish to see white men, our residing here could be of no earthly use. I hoped he would accept our present from Bombay, and give us leave to depart for Gani. The Wakungu, who thought, as well as ourselves, that we were in nothing better than a prison, hurried off with the message, and soon returned with a message from their king that he was busily engaged decorating his palace to give us a triumphant reception; for he was anxious to pay us more respect than anybody who had ever visited him before. We should have seen him yesterday, only that it rained; and, as a precaution against our meeting being broken up, a shed was being built. He could not hear of our leaving the country without seeing him.

18th. – At last we were summoned to attend the king's levee; but the suspicious creature wished his officers to inspect the things we had brought for him before we went there. Here was another hitch. I could not submit to such disrespectful suspicions, but if he wished Bombay to convey my present to him, I saw no harm in the proposition. The king waived the point, and we all started, carrying as a present the things enumerated in the note.[2] The Union Jack led the way. At the ferry three shots were fired, when, stepping into two large canoes, we all went across the Kafu together, and found, to our surprise, a small hut built for the reception, low down on the opposite bank, where no strange eyes could see us.

Within this, sitting on a low wooden stool placed upon a double matting of skins – cows' below and leopards' above – on an elevated platform of grass, was the great king Kamrasi, looking, enshrouded in his mbugu dress, for all the world like a pope in state – calm and actionless. One bracelet of fine-twisted brass wire adorned his left wrist, and his hair, half an inch long, was worked up into small peppercorn-like knobs by rubbing the hand circularly over the crown of the head. His eyes were long, face narrow, and nose prominent, after the true fashion of his breed; and though a finely-made man, considerably above six feet high, he was not so large as Rumanika. A cow-skin, stretched out and fastened to the roof, acted as a canopy to prevent dust falling, and a curtain of mbugu concealed the lower parts of the hut, in front of which, on both sides of the king, sat about a dozen head men.

This was all. We entered and took seats on our own iron stools, whilst Bombay placed all the presents upon the ground before the throne. As no greetings were exchanged, and all at first remained as silent as death, I commenced, after asking about his health, by saying I had journeyed six long years (by the African computation of five months in the year) for the pleasure of this meeting, coming by Karague instead of by the Nile, because the "Wanya Beri" (Bari people at Gondokoro) had defeated the projects of all former attempts made by white men to reach Unyoro. The purpose of my coming was to ascertain whether his majesty would like to trade with our country, exchanging ivory for articles of European manufacture; as, should he do so, merchants would come here in the same way as they went from Zanzibar to Karague. Rumanika and Mtesa were both anxious for trade, and I felt sorry he would not listen to my advice and make friend with Mtesa; for unless the influence of trade was brought in to check the Waganda from pillaging the country, nothing would do so.

Kamrasi, in a very quiet, mild manner, instead of answering the questions, told us of the absurd stories which he had heard from the Waganda, said he did not believe them, else his rivers, deprived of their fountains, would have run dry; and he thought, if we did eat hills and the tender parts of mankind, we should have had enough to satisfy our appetites before we

605

reached Unyoro. Now, however, he was glad to see that, although our hair was straight and our faces white, we still possessed hands and feel like other men.

The present was then opened, and everything in turn placed upon the red blanket. The goggles created some mirth; so did the scissors, as Bombay, to show their use, clipped his beard, and the lucifers were considered a wonder; but the king scarcely moved or uttered any remarks till all was over, when, at the instigation of the courtiers, my chronometer was asked for and shown. This wonderful instrument, said the officers (mistaking it for my compass), was the magic horn by which the white men found their way everywhere. Kamrasi said he must have it, for, besides it, the gun was the only thing new to him. The chronometer, however, I said, was the only one left, and could not possibly be parted with; though, if Kamrasi liked to send men to Gani, a new one could be obtained for him.

Then, changing the subject, much to my relief, Kamrasi asked Bombay, "Who governs England?" "A woman." "Has she any children?" "Yes," said Bombay, with ready impudence; "these are two of them" (pointing to Grant and myself). That settled, Kamrasi wished to know if we had any specked cows, or cows of any peculiar colour, and would we like to change four large cows for four small ones, as he coveted some of ours. This was a staggerer. We had totally failed, then, in conveying to this stupid king the impression that we were not mere traders, ready to bargain with him. We would present him with cows if we had such as he wanted, but we could not bargain. The meeting then broke up in the same chilling manner as it began, and we returned as we came, but no sooner reached home than four pots of pombe were sent us, with a hope that we had arrived all safely. The present gave great satisfaction. The Wanguana accused Frij of having "unclean hands," because the beef had not lasted so long as it should do – it being a notable fact in Mussulman creed, that unless the man's hands are pure who cuts the throat of an animal, its flesh will not last fresh half the ordinary time.

19th. – As the presents given yesterday occupied the king's mind too much for other business, I now sent to offer him one-third of the guns left in Uganda, provided he would send some messengers with one of my men to ask Mtesa for them, and also the same proportion of the sixty loads of property left in charge of Rumanika at Karague, if he would send the requisite number of porters for its removal. But of all things, I said, I most wished to send a letter to Petherick at Gani, to apprise him of our whereabouts, for he must have been four years waiting our arrival there, and by the same opportunity I would get a watch for the king. He sent us to-day two pots of pombe, one sack of salt, and what might be called a screw of butter, with an assurance that the half of everything that came to his house – and everything was brought from great distances in boats – he would give me; but for the present the only thing he was in need of was some medicine or stimulants. Further, I need be under no apprehension if I did not find men at once to go on the three respective journeys; it should be all done in good time, for he loved me much, and desired to show us so much respect that his name should be celebrated for it in songs of praise until he was bowed down by years, and even after death it should be remembered.

I ascertained then that the salt, which was very white and pure, came from an island on the Little Luta Nzige, about sixty miles west from the Chaguzi palace, where the lake is said to be forty or fifty miles wide. It is the same piece of water we heard of in Karague as the Little Luta Nzige, beyond Utumbi; and the same story of Unyoro being an island circumscribed by it and the Victoria N'yanza connected by the Nile, is related here, showing that both the Karague and Unyoro people, as indeed all negroes and Arabs, have the common defect in their language, of using the same word for a peninsula and an island. The Waijasi – of whom we saw a specimen in the shape of an old woman, with her upper lip edged with a row of small holes, at Karague – occupy a large island on this lake named Gasi, and sometimes come to visit Kamrasi. Ugungu, a dependency of Kamrasi's, occupies this side, the lake, and on the opposite side is Ulegga; beyond which, in about 2° N. lat. And 28° E. long., is the country of Namachi; and further west still about 2°, the Wilyanwantu, or cannibals, who, according to the report both here and at Karague, "bury cows but eat men." These distant people pay their homage to Kamrasi, though they have six degrees of longitude to travel over. They are, I believe, a portion of the N'yam N'yams – another name for cannibal – whose country Petherick said he entered in 1857-58. Among the other wild legends about this people, it was said that the Wilyanwantu, in making brotherhood, exchanged their blood by drinking at one another's veins; and, in lieu of butter with their porridge, they smear it with the fat of fried human flesh.

20th. – I had intended for to-day an expedition to the lake; but Kamrasi, harbouring a wicked design that we should help in an attack on his brothers, said there was plenty of time to think of that; we would only find that all the waters united go to Gani, and he wished us to be his guests for three or four months at least. Fifty Gani men had just arrived to inform him that Rionga had lately sent ten slaves and ten ivory tusks to Petherick's post, to purchase a gun; but the answer was, that a thousand times as much would not purchase a weapon that might be used against us; for our arrival with Kamrasi had been heard of, and nothing would be done to jeopardise our road.

To talk over this matter, the king invited us to meet him. We went as before, minus the flag and firing, and met a similar reception. The Gani news was talked over, and we proposed sending Bombay with a letter at once. I could get no answer; so, to pass the time, we wished to know from the king's own lips if he had prevented Baraka from going to Gani, as he had carried orders from Rumanika as well as from myself to visit Kamrasi, to give him fifty egg-beads, seventy necklaces of mtende, and seventy necklaces of kutuamnazi beads, and then to pass on to Gani and give its chief fifty egg-beads and forty necklaces of ku-tuamnazi. Kamrasi replied, "I did not allow him to go, because I heard you had gone to Uganda"; and Dr. K'yengo's men happening to be present, added, "Baraka used up all the beads save forty which he gave to Kamrasi, living upon goats all the way; and when he left, took back a tusk of ivory." This little controversy was amusing, but did not suit Kamrasi, who had his eye on a certain valuable possession of mine. He made his approach towards it by degrees, beginning with a truly royal speech thus: "I am the king of all these countries, even including Uganda and Kidi – though the Kidi people are such savages they obey no man's orders – and you are great men also, sitting on chairs before kings; it therefore ill becomes us to talk of such trifles as beads, especially as I know if you ever return this way I shall get more from you." "Begging your majesty's pardon," I said, "the mention of beads only fell in the way of our talk like stones in a walk; our motive being to get at the truth of what Baraka did and said here, as his conduct in returning after receiving strict orders from Rumanika and ourselves to open the road, is a perfect enigma to us. We could not have entered Unyoro at all excepting through Uganda, and we could not have put foot in Uganda without visiting its king." Without deigning to answer, Kamrasi, in the metaphorical language of a black man, said, "It would be unbecoming of me to keep secrets from you, and therefore I will tell you at once; I am sadly afflicted with a disorder which you alone can cure." "What is it, your majesty? I can see nothing in your face; it may perhaps require a private inspection." "My heart," he said, "is troubled, because you will not give me your magic horn – the thing, I mean, in your pocket, which you pulled out one day when Budja and Vittagura were discussing the way; and you no sooner looked at it than you said, 'That is the way to the palace.'" So! the sly fellow has been angling for the chronometer all this time, and I can get nothing out of him until he has got it – the road to the lake, the road to Gani, everything seemed risked on his getting my watch – a chronometer worth $50, which would be spoilt in his hands in one day. To undeceive him, and tell him it was the compass which I looked at and not the watch, I knew would only end with my losing that instrument as well; so I told him it was not my guide, but a time-keeper, made for the purpose of knowing what time to eat my dinner by. It was the only chronometer I had with me; and I begged he would have patience until Bombay returned from Gani with another, when he should have the option to taking this or the new one. "No; I must have the one in your pocket; pull it out and show it." This was done, and I placed it on the ground, saying, "The instrument is yours, but I must keep it until another one comes." "No; I must have it now, and will send it you three times every day to look at." The watch went, gold chain and all, without any blessings following it; and the horrid king asked if I could make up another magic horn, for he hoped he had deprived us of the power of travelling, and plumed himself on the notion that the glory of opening the road would devolve upon himself. When I told him that to purchase another would cost five hundred cows, the whole party were more confirmed than ever as to its magical powers; for who in his sense would give five hundred cows for the mere gratification of seeing at what time his dinner should be eaten? Thus ended the second meeting. Kamrasi now said the Gani men would feast on beef to-morrow, and the next day be ready to start with my men for Petherick's camp. He then accompanies us to the boats, spear in hand, and saw us cross the water. Long tail-hairs of the giraffe surrounded his neck, on which little balls and other ornaments of minute beads, after the Uganda fashion, were worked. In the evening four pots of pombe and a pack of flour were brought, together with the chronometer, which was sent to be wound up – damaged of course – the seconds-hand had been dislodged.

21st. – I heard from Kidgwiga that some of those Gani men now ordered to go with Bombay had actually been visiting here when the latter shot his first cow at the palace, but had gone to their homes to give information of us, and had returned again. Eager to get on with my journey, and see European faces again, I besought the king to let us depart, as our work was all finished here, since he had assured us he would like to trade with England. The N'yanswenge – meaning Petherick's party – who have hitherto been afraid to come here, would do so now, when they had seen us pass safely down, and could receive my guns and property left to come from Uganda and Karague, which we ourselves could not wait for. Kamrasi, thinking me angry for his having taken the watch so rudely out of my pocket, took fright at the message, sent some of his attendants quickly back to me, requesting me to keep the instrument until another arrived, and begged I would never say I wished to leave his house again.

22d. – Kamrasi sent to say Bombay was not to start to-day, but to-morrow, so we put the screw on again, and said we must go at once; if he would give us guides to Gani, we would return him his twenty cows and seven goats with pleasure. I let him understand we suspected he was keeping us here to fight his brothers, and told him he must at once know we would never lift hand against them. It was contrary to the laws of our land. "I have got no orders to enter into black men's quarrels, and my mother" (the Queen), "whom I see every night in my sleep calling me home, would be very angry if she heard of it. Rumanika once asked me to fight his brothers Rogero and M'yongo, but my only reply to all had been the same – I have no orders to fight with, only to make friends of, the great kings of Africa." The game seemed now to be won. At once Kamrasi ordered Bombay to prepare for the journey. Five Wanyoro, five Chopi men, and five Gani men, were to escort him. There was no objection to his carrying arms. The moment he returned, which ought to be in little more than a fortnight, we would all go together. An earnest request was at the same time made that I would not bully him in the mean time with any more applications to depart. So Bombay and Mabruki, carrying there muskets, and a map and letter for Petherick, departed.

23d and 24th. – Kamrasi, presuming he had gained favour in our eyes, sent, begging to know how we had slept, and said he would like us to inform him what part of his journey Bombay had this morning reached – a fact which he had no doubt must be divinable through the medium of our books. The reply was, that Bombay's luck was so good we had no doubt regarding his success; but now he had gone, and our days here were numbered, we should like to see the palace, his fat wives and children, as well as the Wanyoro's dances, and all the gaiety of the place. We did not think our reception-hut by the river sufficiently dignified, and our residence here was altogether like that of prisoners – seeing no one, knowing no one. In answer to this, Kamrasi sent one pot of pombe and five fowls, begging we would not be alarmed; we should see everything in good time, if we would but have patience, for he considered us very great men, as he was a great man himself, and we had come at his invitation. He must request, in the mean time, that we would send no more messages by his officers, as such messages are never conveyed properly. At present there was a great deal of business in the palace.

We asked for some butter, but could get none, as all the milk in the palace was consumed by the wives and children, drinking all day long, to make themselves immovably fat.

25th. – In the morning, the commander-in-chief wished us to cast a horoscope, and see where Bombay was, and if he were getting on well. That being negatived, he told us to put our hut in order, as Kamrasi was coming to see us. Accordingly we made everything as smart as possible, hanging the room round with maps, horns, and skins of animals, and places a large box covered with a red blanket, as a throne for the king to set upon. As he advanced, my men, forming a guard of honour fired three shots immediately on his setting foot upon our side the river; whilst Frij, with his boatswain's whistle, piped the 'Rogue's March,' to prepare us for his majesty's approach. We saluted him, hat in hand, and, leading the way, showed him in. He was pleased to be complimentary, remarking, what Waseja (fine men) we were, and took his seat. We sat on smaller boxes, to appear humble, whilst his escort of black "swells" filled the doorway, squatting on the ground, so as to stop the light and interfere with our decorations.

After the first salutations, the king remarked the head of a nsamma buck, and handled it; then noticed my mosquito-curtains hanging over the bed, and begged for them. He was told they could not be given until Bombay returned, as the mosquitoes would eat us up. "But there were two," said the escort, "for we have seen one in the other hut." That was true; but were there not two white men? However, if the king wanted gauze, here was a smart gauze veil – and the veil vanished at once. The iron camp-bed was next inspected, and admired; then the sextant, which was coveted and begged for, but without success, much to the astonishment of the king, as his attendants had led him to expect he would get anything he asked for. Then the thermometers were wanted and refused; also table-knives, spoons, forks, and even cooking-pots, for we had no others, and could not part with them. The books of birds and animals had next to be seen, and being admired were coveted, the king offering one of the books I first gave him in exchange for one of these. In fact, he wanted to fleece us of everything; so, to shut him up, I said I would not part with one bird for one hundred tusks of ivory; they were all the collections I had made in Africa, and if I parted with them my journey would go for nothing; but if he wanted a few drawings of birds I would do some for him – at present I wished to speak to him. "Well, what is it? We are all attention." "I wish to know positively if you would like English traders to come here regularly, as the Arabs do to trade at Karague? And if so, would you give me a pembe (magic horn) as a warrant, that everybody may know Kamrasi, king of Unyoro, desires it?" Kamrasi replied, "I like your proposition very much; you shall have the horn you ask for, either large or small, just as you please; and after you have gone, should we hear any English are at Gani wishing to come here, as my brothers are in the way we will advance with spears whilst they approach with guns, and between us both, my brothers must fly – for I myself will head the expedition. But now you have had your say I will have mine if you will listen." "All right, your majesty; what is it?" "I am constantly stricken with fever and pains, for which I know no remedy but cautery; my children die young; my family is not large enough to uphold my dignity and station in life; in fact, I am infirm and want stimulants, and I wish you to prescribe for me, which considering you have found your way to this, where nobody came before, must be easy to you." Two pills and a draught for the morning were given as a preliminary measure, argument being of no avail; and to our delight the king said it was time to go.

We jumped off our seats to show him the way, hoping our persecutions were over; but still he sat, and sat, until at length, finding we did not take the hint to give him a parting present, he said, "I never visited any big man's house without taking home some trifle to show my wife and children." "Indeed, great king! Then you did not come to visit us, but to beg, eh? You shall have nothing, positively nothing; for we will not have it said the king did not come to see us, but to beg." Kamrasi's face changed colour; he angrily said, "Irokh togend" (let us rise and go), and forthwith walked straight out of the hut. Frij piped, but no guns fired; and as he asked the reason why he was told it would be offensive to say we were glad he was going. The king was evidently not pleased for no pombe came to-day.

1) This obviously was an allusion to the way in which the first king of Uganda was countenanced by the great king of Kittara, according to the tradition given in Chapter 9.

2) 1 double rifle, 1 block-tin box, 1 red blanket, 1 brown do., 10 copper wire, 4 socks full of different-coloured minute beads, 2 socks full of blue and white pigeon eggs, 1 Rodgers's pen-knife, 2 books, 1 elastic circle, 1 red handkerchief, 1 bag gun-caps, 1 pair scissors, 1 pomatum-pot, 1 quart bottle, 1 powder flask, 7 lb. powder, 1 dressing-case, 1 blacking-box, 1 brass lock and key, 4 brass handles, 8 brass sockets, 7 chintz, 7 binders, 1 red bag, 1 pair glass spectacles, 1 lucifer-box.

CHAPTER 18

UNYORO – CONTINUED

The Ceremonies of the New Moon – Kamrasi's Rule and Discipline – An Embassy from Uganda, and Its Results – The Rebellious Brothers – An African Sorcerer and His Incantations – The Kamraviona of Unyoro – Burial Customs – Ethiopian Legends – Complicated Diplomacy for Our Detention – Proposal to Send Princes to England – We Get Away.

26th. – We found that the palace was shut up in consequence of the new moon, seen for the first time last evening; and incessant drumming was the order of the day. Still, private interviews might be granted, and I sent to inquire after the state of the king's health. The reply was, that the medicine had not taken, and the king was very angry because nothing was given him when he took the trouble to call on us. He never called at a big man's house and left it mwiko (empty-handed) before; if there was nothing else to dispose of, could Bana not have given him a bag of beads? To save us from this kind of incessant annoyance, I now thought it would be our best policy to mount the high horse and bully him. Accordingly, we tied up a bag of the commonest mixed beads, added the king's chronometer, and sent them to Kamrasi with a violent message that we were thoroughly disgusted with all that had happened; the beads were for the poor beggar who came to our house yesterday, not to see us, but to beg; and as we did not desire the acquaintance of beggars, we had made up our minds never to call again, nor receive any more bread or wine from the king.

This appeared to be a hit. Kamrasi, evidently taken aback, said, if he thought he should have offended us by begging, he would not have begged. He was not a poor man, for he had many cows, but he was a beggar, of course, when beads were in the question; and, having unwittingly offended, as he desired our friendship, he trusted his offence would be forgiven. On opening the chronometer, he again wrenched back the seconds-hand, and sent it for repair, together with two pots of pombe as a peace-offering. Frij, who accompanied the deputation, overheard the counsellors tell their king that the Waganda were on their way back to Unyoro to snatch us away; on hearing which the king asked his men if they would ever permit it; and, handling his spear as if for battle, said at the same time he would lose his own head before they should touch his guests. Then, turning to Frij, he said, "What would you do if they came? – Go back with them?" To which Frij said, "No, never, when Gani is so near; they might cut our heads off, but that is all they could do." The watch being by this time repaired, it gave me the opportunity of sending Kidgwiga back to the palace to say we trusted Kamrasi would allow Budja to come here, if only with one woman to carry his pombe, else Mtesa would take offence, form an alliance with Rionga, and surround the place with warriors, for it was not becoming in great kings to treat civil messengers like dogs.

The reply to this was, that Kamrasi was very much pleased with my fatherly wisdom and advice, and would act up to it, allowing Budja only to approach with one woman; we need, however, be under no apprehensions, for Kamrasi's power was infinite; the Gani road should be opened even at the spear's point; he had been beating the big drum in honour of us the whole day; he would not allow any beggars to come and see us, for he wanted us all to himself, and for this reason had ordered a fence to be built all round our house; but he had got no present from Grant yet, though all he wanted was his mosquito-curtains, whilst he wished my picture-books to show his women, and be returned. We sent a picture of Mtesa as a gift, the two books to look at and an acknowledgement that the mosquito-curtains were his, only he must have patience until Bombay arrived; but his proposition about the fence we rejected with scorn. The king had been raising an army to fight Rionga – the true reason, we suspect, for the beating of the drums.

27th and 28th. – There was drumming and music all day and night, and the army was being increased to a thousand men, but we poor prisoners could see nothing of it. Frij was therefore sent to inspect the armament and brings us all the news. Some of N'yamyonjo's men, seeing mine armed with carbines, became very inquisitive about them, and asked if they were the instruments which shot at their men on the Nile – one in the arm, who died; the other on the top of the shoulder, who was recovering. The drums were kept in private rooms, to which a select few only were admitted. Kamrasi conducts all business himself, awarding punishments and seeing them carried out. The most severe instrument of chastisement is a knob-stick, sharpened at the back, like that used in Uganda, for breaking a man's neck before he is thrown into the N'yanza; but this severity is seldom resorted to, Kamrasi being of a mild disposition compared with Mtesa, whom he invariably alludes to when ordering men to be flogged, telling them that were they in Uganda, their heads would suffer instead of their backs. In the day's work at the palace, army collecting, ten officers were bound because they failed to bring a sufficient number of fighting men, but were afterwards released on their promising to bring more.

Nothing could be more filthy than the state of the palace and all the lanes leading up to it: it was well, perhaps, that we were never expected to go there, for without stilts and respirators it would have been impracticable, such is the dirty nature of the people. The king's cows, even, are kept in the palace enclosure, the calves actually entering the hut, where, like a farmer, Kamrasi walks amongst them up to his ankles in filth, and, inspecting them, issues his orders concerning them. What has to be selected for his guests he singles out himself.

Dr. K'yengo's men, who had been sent three times into action against the refractory brothers, asked leave to return to Karague; but the king, who did not fear for their lives when his work was to be done, would not give them leave, lest accident should befall them on the way. We found no prejudice against eating butter amongst these Wahuma, for they not only sold us some, but mixed it with porridge and ate it themselves.

29th. – The king has appointed a special officer to keep our table supplied with sweet potatoes, and sent us a pot of pombe, with his excuses for not seeing us, as business was so pressing, and would continue to be so until the army marched. Budja and Kasoro were again reported to be near with a force of fifty Waganda, prepared to snatch us away; and the king, fearing the consequences, had sent to inform Budja, that if he dared attempt to approach, he would slip us off in boats to Gani, and then fight it out with the Waganda; for his guests, since they had been handed over to him, had been treated with every possible respect.

To keep Kamrasi to his promise, as we particularly wished to hear the Uganda news, Frij was sent to inform him on my behalf that Mtesa only wished to make friends with all the great kings surrounding his country before his coronation took place, when his brothers would be burnt, and he would cease to take advice from his mother. To treat his messengers disrespectfully could do no good, and might provoke a war, when we should see my deserters joined with the Waganda really coming in force against us; whereas, if we saw Budja, we could satisfy him, and Mtesa too, and obviate any such calamity. The reply was, that Kamrasi would arrange for our having a meeting with Budja alone if we wished it; he did not fear my deserters siding with king Mtesa, but he detested the Waganda, and could not bear to see them in his country.

30th. – At breakfast-time we heard that my old friend Kasoro had come to our camp without permission, to the surprise of everybody, attended by all his boys, leaving Budja and his children, on account of sickness, at the camp assigned to the Waganda, five miles off. Kasoro wished to speak to us, and we invited him into the hut; but the interview could not be permitted until Kamrasi's wishes on the subject had been ascertained. In a little while the Kamraviona, having seen Kamrasi, said we might converse with one another whilst his officers were present listening, and sent a cow as a present for the Waganda. Kasoro with his children now came before us in their usual merry manner and, after saluting, told us how the deserters, on reaching Uganda, begged for leave to proceed to Karague; but Mtesa, who would only allow two of them to approach him, abused them, saying, "Did I not command you to take Bana to Gani at all risks? If there was no road by land, you were to go by water; or, if that failed, to go under-ground, or in the air above, and if he died, you were to die with him: what, then, do you mean by deserting him and flying here? You shall not move a yard from this until I receive a messenger from him to hear what he has got to say on the matter." Mtesa would not take their arms, even at the desire of Budja, on my behalf; for as no messenger on my behalf came to him, he would not believe what Budja said, and feared to touch any of our property. The chief item of court news was, that Mtesa had shot a buffalo which was attacking him behind the palace, and made his Wakungu carry the animal bodily, whilst life was in it, into his court. The ammunition I wrote for to Rumanika had been brought by Maula.

As Kasoro still remained silent with regard to Mtesa's message, I told him we shot two of N'yamyonjo's men on our retreat up the Nile, and that Kamrasi turned us back because some miscreant Waganda had forged lies and told him we were terrible monsters, who ate hills and human flesh, and drank up all the water of the lake. He laughed, but still was silent; so I said, "What message have you brought from Mtesa?" To which, in a timid, modest kind of manner, he said, "Bana knows – what more need I say? Has he forgotten Mtesa, who loves him so?" I said, "No, indeed, I have not forgotten Mtesa; and, moreover, as I expected you back again, I have sent Bombay to bring the stimulants and all the things I promised Mtesa from Gani; in two or three days he will return." "No," said Kasoro, "that is not it; we must go to Gani with you; for Mtesa says he loves you so much he will never allow you to part from his hand until his servants have seen you safely at your homes." I replied, "If Mtesa wishes you to see my vessels and all the wonders they contain, as far as I am concerned you may do so, and I shall be only too happy to show you a little English hospitality; but the road is in Kamrasi's hands, and his wishes must now be heard." The commander-in-chief, now content with all he had heard, went to Kamrasi to receive his orders, whilst I gave Kasoro a feast of porridge and salt, with pombe to wash it down, and a cow to take home with him; for the poor creatures said they were all starving as the Wanyoro would not allow them to take a single plantain from the field until Kamrasi's permission had been given.

Kamrasi's reply now arrived; it was to the following effect: "Tell my children, the Waganda, they were never turned out of Unyoro by my orders: if they wish to go to Gani, they can do so; but, first of all, they must return to Mtesa, and ask him to deliver up all of Bana's men." I answered, "No; if any one of those scoundrels who has deserted me ever dares show his face to me again, I will shoot him like a dog. Moreover, I want Mtesa to take their guns from them, and, without taking life, to transport them all to an island on the N'yanza, where they can spend their days in growing plantains; for it is such men who prevent our travelling in the country and visiting kings." Kasoro on this said, "Mtesa will do so in a minute if you send a servant to him, but he won't if we only say you wish it." The commander-in-chief then added, as to Kasoro's wish to accompany me,

"If Mtesa will send another time one of his people whose life he wishes sacrificed on the journey, or tells, Here is a man whom I wish you to send to Gani at all hazards, and without responsibility for his life on our part, we will be very glad to send him; but as we are at war with the Gani people continually, there will be no security for a Mganda's life there." To this I added, "Now, Kasoro, you see how it is; Kamrasi does not wish you to do to Gani, so if you take my advice you will return to Mtesa. Give this tin cartridge-box, which first came from him, back to him again, to show him you have seen me, and say, This is Bana's letter; he wishes you to transport the deserters and seize their guns. The guns, of course, I shall want again at some other time, when I will send one of my English children to visit him; for now Kamrasi has opened his country to us, and given us leave to come and purchase ivory, I never shall be very far away." I gave them three pills for Budja, blistered two of the pages, and started the whole merrily off, Kasoro asking me to send Mtesa some pretty things from England such as he never saw.

1st. – Kamrasi sent his commander-in-chief to inquire after my health, and to say Budja had left in fear and trembling lest Mtesa should cut all their heads off for failing in the mission; but he had sent Kidgwiga's brother with a pot of pombe to escort the Waganda beyond his frontier, and cheer them on the way; for the tin cartridge-box, he thought, would save their lives by satisfying Mtesa they had seen me. The commander-in-chief then told me Kamrasi did not wish them to accompany me through Kidi for the Kidi people don't like the Waganda, and, discovering their nationality by the fullness of their teeth, would bring trouble on us whilst trying to kill them.

I *The blue expanse of Lake Victoria borders on Tanzania, Uganda, and Kenya.*

II-III *The Blue Nile breaks into a series of cascades and cataracts at the Tis-Esat Falls, in Ethiopia.*

III bottom *The Ugandan stretch of the Victoria Nile is very fast flowing, and numerous animals inhabit its banks.*
(all © Marcello Bertinetti/Archivio White Star)

III

IV-V *Lake Victoria covers an area of 26,828 square miles, making it the second-largest freshwater lake in the world.*

V bottom *The enormous Nile crocodile has inhabited the Earth for over 200 million years.*
(all © Marcello Bertinetti/Archivio White Star)

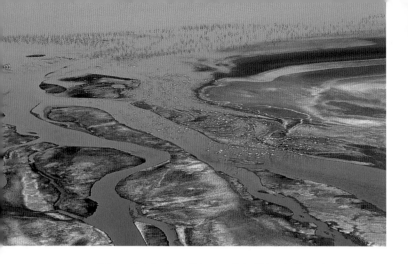

VI top *Pink flamingos flying over Lake Natron in Tanzania.*

VI bottom *The Nile hurls itself over the spectacular Murchison Falls
into Lake Albert, in Uganda.*

VII top *Uganda has extensive virgin forests, like that of Jinja.*

VII bottom *Tea pickers at work in a Ugandan plantation.*

VIII *Crocodiles are widespread on Rubondo Island, in Lake Victoria, Tanzania.*
(all © Marcello Bertinetti/Archivio White Star)

I said I thanked Kamrasi for his having treated the Waganda with such marked respect, in allowing them to see me, and sending them back with an escort; but I thought it would have been better if he had spoken the truth plainly out, for then I could have told them I feared to have them in company with me. In return for my civilities, the king then send one of his chopi officers to see me, who went four stages with Bombay, and he also sent some rich beads which he wished me to look at. They were nicely kept in a neat though very large casing of rush pith, and were those sent as a letter from Gani, to inform him that we were expected to come via Karague. After this, to keep us in good-humour, Kamrasi sent to inform us that some Gani men, twenty-five in number, had just arrived, and had given him a lion-skin, several tippet monkey-skins, and some giraffe hair, as well as a stick of copper or brass wire. Bombay was met by them on the confines of Gani.

2d. – The king sent me a pot of pombe to-day, inquiring after my health, and saying he would like to take the medicine I gave him if I would send Frij over to administer it, but he would be ashamed to swallow pills before me. Hitherto he had not been able to take the medicine from press of business in collecting an army to fight his brothers; but as his troops would all leave for war to-day, he expected to have leisure.

In plying the Kamraviona to try if we could get rid of the annoying restraints which made our residence here a sort of imprisonment, I discovered that the whole affair was not one of blunder or accident, but that we actually were prisoners thus be design. It appeared that Kamrasi's brothers, when they heard we were coming into Unyoro, murmured, and said to the king,

"Why are you bringing such guests amongst us, who will practise all kinds of diabolical sorcery, and bring evil on us?" To
which Kamrasi replied, "I have invited them to come, and they
shall come; and if they bring evil with them, let that all fall on
my shoulders, for you shall not see them." He then built a
palaver-house on the banks of the Kafu to receive us in privately; and when we were to go to Gani, it was his intention to
slip us off privately down the Kafu. The brothers were so thoroughly frightened, that when Kamrasi opened his chronometer
before them to show them the works in motion, they turned
their heads away. The large block-tin box I gave Kamrasi, as
part of his hongo, was, I heard, called Mzungu, or the white
man, by him.

In the evening the beads recently brought from Gani were
sent for my inspection, with an intimation that Kamrasi highly
approved of them, and would like me to give him a few like
them. Some of Kamrasi's spies, whom he had sent to the refractory allies of Rionga his brother, returned bringing a spear and
some grass from the thatch of the hut of a Chopi chief. The removal of the grass was a piece of state policy. It was stolen by
Kamrasi's orders, in order that he might spread a charm on the
Chopi people, and gain such an influence over them that their
spears could not prevail against the Wanyoro; but it was
thought we might possess some still superior magic powder, as
we had come from such a long distance, and Kamrasi would
prefer to have ours.

These Chopi people were leagued with the brothers, and
thus kept the highroad to Gani, though the other half of Chopi
remained loyal; and though Kamrasi continually sent armies

against the refractory half which aided his brothers, they never retaliated by attacking this place.

We found, by the way, that certain drumming and harmonious accompaniments which we had been accustomed to hear all day and night were to continue for four moons, in celebration of twins born to Kamrasi since we came here.

3d. – Kamrasi's political department was active again to-day. Some Gani officials arrived to inform him that there were two white men in the vessel spoken of as at Gani; a second vessel was coming in there, and several others were on their way. A carnelian was shown me which the Gani people gave to Kamrasi many years ago. Kamrasi expressed a wish that I would exchange magic powders with him. He had a very large variety, and would load a horn for me with all those I desired most. He wanted also medicines for longevity and perpetual strength. Those I had given him had, he said, deprived him of strength, and he felt much reduced by their effects. He would like me to go with him and attack the island his three brothers, Rionga, Wahitu, and Pohuka, are in possession of. When I said I never fought with black men, he wished to know if I would not shoot them if they attacked me. My reply was, alluding to our fight in the river, "How did N'yamyonjo's men fare?" I found that Kamrasi had thirty brothers and as many sisters.

4th. – I gave Kamrasi a bottle of quinine, which we call "strong back," and asked him in return for a horn containing all the powders necessary to give me the gift of tongues, so that I should be able to converse with any black men whom I might meet with. We heard that Kamrasi has called all his Gani guests to play before him, and a double shot from his Blissett rifle announced to our ears that he in turn was amusing them. This was the first time the gun had been discharged since he received it, and, fearing to fire it himself, he called one of my men to do it for him.

5th. – At 9 A.M., the time for measuring the fall of rain for the last twenty-four hours, we found the rain-gauge and the bottle had been removed, so we sent Kidgwiga to inform the king we wished his magicians to come at once and institute a search for it. Kidgwiga immediately returned with the necessary adept, an old man, nearly blind, dressed in strips of old leather fastened to the waist, and carrying in one hand a cow's horn primed with magic powder, carefully covered on the mouth with leather, from which dangled an iron bell. The old creature jingled the bell, entered our hut, squatted on his hams, looked first at one, then at the other – inquired what the missing things were like, grunted, moved his skinny arm round his head, as if desirous of catching air from all four sides of the hut, then dashed the accumulated air on the head of his horn, smelt it to see if all was going right, jingled the bell again close to his ear, and grunted his satisfaction; the missing articles must be found.

To carry out the incantation more effectually, however, all my men were sent for to sit in the open before the hut, when the old doctor rose, shaking the horn and tinkling the bell close to his ear. He then, confronting one of the men, dashed the horn forward as if intending to strike him on the face, then smelt the head, then dashed at another, and so on, till he became satisfied that my men were not the thieves. He then walked into Grant's hut, inspected that, and finally went to the place where the bottle had been kept. There he walked about the grass with his arm up, and jingling the bell to his ear, first on one side, then on the other, till the track of a hyena gave him the clue, and in two or three more steps he found it. A hyena had carried it into the grass and dropped it. Bravo, for the infallible horn! And well done the king for his honesty in sending it! So I gave the king the bottle and gauge, which delighted him amazingly; and the old doctor who begged for pombe, got a goat for his trouble. My men now, recollecting the powder robbery at Uganda, said king Mtesa would not send his horn when I asked for it, because he was the culprit himself.

6th. – Kidgwiga told us to-day that king Kamrasi's sisters are not allowed to wed; they live and die virgins in his palace. Their only occupation in life consisted of drinking milk, of which each one consumes the produce daily of from ten to twenty cows, and hence they become so inordinately fat that they cannot walk. Should they wish to see a relative, or go outside the hut for any purpose, it requires eight men to lift any of them on a litter. The brothers, too, are not allowed to go out of his reach. This confinement of the palace family is considered a state necessity, as a preventive to civil wars, in the same way as the destruction of the Uganda princes, after a certain season, is thought necessary for the preservation of peace there.

7th. – In the morning the Kamraviona called, on the king's behalf, to inquire after my health, and also to make some important communications. First he was to request a supply of bullets, that the king might fire a salute when Bombay returned from Gani; next, to ask for stimulative medicine, now that he had consumed all I gave him, and gone through the preliminary course; further, to request I would spread a charm over all his subjects, so that their hearts might be inclined towards him, and they would come without calling and bow down at his feet; finally, he wished me to exchange my blood with him, that we might be brothers till death. I sent the bullets, advised him to wait a day or two for the medicine, and said there was only one charm by which he could gain the influence he required over his subjects – this was, knowledge and the power of the pen. Should he desire some of my children (meaning missionaries) to come here and instruct his, the thing would be done; but not in one year, nor even ten, for it takes many years to educate children.

As to exchanging by blood with a black man's, it was a thing quite beyond my comprehension; though Rumanika, I must confess, had asked me to do the same thing. The way the English make lasting friendships is done either by the expressions of their hearts, or by the exchange of some trifles, as keepsakes; and now, as I had given Kamrasi some specimens of English manufacture, he might give me a horn, or anything else he chose, which I could show to my friends, so as to keep him in recollection all my life.

The Kamraviona, before leaving, said, for our information, that a robbery had occurred in the palace last night; for this morning, when Kamrasi went to inspect his Mzungu (the block-tin box), which he had forgotten to lock, he found all his beads had been stolen. After sniffing round among the various wives, he smelt the biggest one to be the culprit, and turned the beads out of her possession. Deputies came in the evening with a pot of pombe and small screw of butter, to tell me some Gani people had just arrived, bringing information that the vessel at

Gani had left to go down the river; but when intelligence reached the vessel of the approach of my men they turned and came back again. Bombay was well feasted on the road by Kamrasi's people, receiving eight cows from one and two cows from another.

8th and 9th. – We had a summons to attend at the Kafu palace with the medicine-chest, a few select persons only to be present. It rained so much on the 8th as to stop the visit, but we went next day. After arriving there, and going through the usual salutations, Kamrasi asked us from what stock of people we came, explaining his meaning by saying, "As we, Rumanika, Mtesa, and the rest of us (enumerating the kings), are Wawitu (or princes), Uwitu (or the country of princes) being to the east." This interesting announcement made me quite forget to answer his question, and induced me to say, "Omwita, indeed, as the ancient names for Mombas, if you came from that place: I know all about your race for two thousand years or more. Omwita, you mean, was the last country you resided in before you came here, but originally you came from Abyssinia, the sultan of which, our great friend, is Sahela Selassie." He pronounced this name laughing, and said, "Formerly our stock was half-white and half-black, with one side of our heads covered with straight hair, and the other side frizzly: you certainly do know everything." The subject then turned upon medicine, and after inspecting the chest, and inquiring into all its contents, it ended by his begging for the half of everything. The mosquito-curtains were again asked for, and refused until I should leave this. As Kamrasi was anxious I should take two of his children to England to be instructed, I agreed to do so, but said I thought

631

it would be better if he invited missionaries to come here and educate all his family. His cattle were much troubled with sickness, dying in great numbers – could I cure them? As he again began to persecute us with begging, wanting knives and forks, etc., I advised his using ivory as money, and purchasing what he wanted from Gani. This brought out the interesting fact, the truth of which we had never reached before, that when Petherick's servant brought him one necklace of beads, and asked after us, he gave in return fourteen ivories, thirteen women, and seven mbugu cloths. One of his men accompanied the visitors back to the boats, and saw Petherick, who took the ivory and rejected the women.

10th. – At 2 P.M. we were called by Kamrasi to visit him at the Kafu palace again, and requested to bring a lot of medicines tied up in various coloured cloths, so that he might know what to select for different ailments. We repaired there as before, putting the medicines into the sextand-stand box, and found him lying at full length on the platform of his throne, with a glass-bead necklace of various colours, and a charm tied on his left arm. Nobody was allowed to be present at our interview. The medicines, four varieties, were weighed out into ten doses each, and their uses and effects explained. He begged for four bottles to put them in, till he was laughed out of it by our saying he required forty bottles; for if the powders were mixed, how could he separate them again? And to keep his mind from the begging tack, which he was getting alarmingly near, I said, "Now I have given you these things because you would insist on having them. I must also tell you they are dangerous in your hands, in consequence of your being ignorant of their properties. If you take my advice you won't meddle with them until the two children you wish educated have learnt the use of them in England; and if I have to take boys from this, I hope they will be of your family." He said, "You speak like a father to us, and we very much approve. Here is a pot of pombe; I did not give you one yesterday."

11th. – To-day, the king having graciously granted permission, we went out shooting, but saw only a few buffalo tracks.

12th. – The Kamraviona was sent to inquire after our health, and to ascertain from me all I knew respecting the origin of Kamrasi's tribe, the distribution of countries, and the seat of the government. I sent the king a diagram, painted in various colours, with full explanations of everything, and asked permission to send two more of my men in search of Bombay, who had now been absent twenty days. The reply was, that if Bombay did not return within four days, Kamrasi would send other men after him on the fifth day; and, in the meantime, he sent one pot of pombe as a token of his kind regard.

13th. – The Kamraviona was sent to inquire after our health, to ask for medicine for himself, and to inquire more into the origin of his race. I, on the other hand, wishing to make myself as disagreeable as possible, in order that Kamrasi might get tired of us, sent Frij to ask for fresh butter, eggs, tobacco, coffee, and fowls, every day, saying, I will pay their price when I reach Gani, for we were suffering from want of proper food. Kamrasi was surprised at this clamour for food, and inquired what we ate at home that we were so different from everybody else.

We heard to-day a strange story, involving the tragic fate of Budja. On coming here, he had been bewitched by Kamrasi's frontier officer, who put the charm into a pot of pombe. From the moment Budja drank it he was seized with sickness, and remained so until he reached the first station in Uganda, when he died. The facts of the bewitchment had been found out by means of the perpetrator's wives, who, from the moment the pombe was drunk, took to precipitate flight, well knowing what effects would follow, and dreading the chastisement Mtesa would bring upon their household. We heard, too, that the deserters had returned to the place they deserted from, with thirty Waganda, and a present of some cows for me.

14th. – Kamrasi sent me four parcels of coffee, very neatly enclosed in rush pith.

15th. – Getting more impatient, and desirous to move on at any sacrifice, I proposed giving up all claims to my muskets, as well as the present of cows from Mtesa, if Kamrasi would give us boats to Gani at once; but the reply was simply, Why be in such a hurry?

16th. – The Kamraviona was sent to us with a load of coffee, which Kamrasi had purchased with cowries, and to inquire how we had slept. Very badly, was the reply, because we knew Bombay would have been back long ago if Kamrasi was not concealing him somewhere, and we did not know what he was doing with deserters and Waganda. Kamrasi then wanted us to paint his mbugu cloths in different patterns and colours; but we sent him instead six packages of red-ink powder, and got abused for sauciness. He then wanted black ink, else how could he put on the red with taste; but we had none to give him. Next, he asked leave for my men to shoot cows, before his Kidi visitors, which they did to his satisfaction, instructing him at the same time to fire powder with his own rifle; when, triumphant with his success, he protested he would never use anything but guns again, and threw away his spear as useless. Bombay, we learned, had reached Gani, and ought to return in eight days.

17th and 18th. – A large party of Chopi people arrived, by Kamrasi's orders, to tell the reason which induced them to apply for guns to the white men at Gani, as it appeared evident they must have wished to fight their king. The Kidi visitors got broken heads for helping themselves from the Wanyoro's fields, and when they cried out against such treatment, were told they should rob the king, if they wished to rob at all.

19th. – Nothing was done because Kamrasi was dismissing his Kidi guests, 200, with presents of cows and women.

20th. – Having asked Kamrasi to return my pictures, he sent the book of birds, but not of animals; and said he could not see us until a new hut was built, because the old one was flooded by the Kafu, which had been rising several days. We must not, he said, talk about Bombay any more, because everybody said he was detained by the N'yanswenge (Petherick's party), and would return here with the new moon. I would not accept the lie, saying, How can my "children" at Gani detain my messengers, when they have received strict orders from me by letter to send an answer quickly? It was all Kamrasi's doing, for he had either hidden Bombay, or ordered his officers to take him slowly, as he did us, stopping four days at each stage.

Frij again told me he was present when Said Said, the Sultan of Zanzibar, sent an army to assist the Wagunya at Amu, on the coast, against the incursions of the Masai. These Amu people have the same Wahuma features as Kamrasi, whom they also resemble both in general physical appearance, and in many of them having circular marks, as if made by cautery, on the forehead and temples. These marks I took not to be tatooing or decorative, but as a cure for disease – cautery being a favourite remedy with both races.

The battle lasted only two days, though the Masai brought a thousand spears against the Arabs' cannon. But this was not the only battle Said Said had to fight on those grounds; for some years previously he had to subdue the Waziwa, who live on very marshy land, into respect for his sovereignty, when the battle lasted years, in consequence of the bad nature of the ground, and the trick the Waziwa had of staking the ground with spikes. The Wasuahili, or coast-people, by his description, are the bastards or mixed breeds who live on the east coast of Africa, extending from the Somali country to Zanzibar. Their language is Kisuahili; but there is no land Usuahili, though people talk of going to the Suahili in the same vague sense as they do of going to the Mashenzi, or amongst the savages. The common story amongst the Wasuahili at Zanzibar, in regard to the government of that island, was, that the Wakhadim, or aborigines of Zanzibar, did not like the oppressions of the Portuguese, and therefore allied themselves to the Arabs of Muscat – even compromising their natural birthright of freedom in government, provided the Arabs, by their superior power, would secure to them perpetual equity, peace and justice. The senior chief, Sheikh Muhadim, was the mediator on their side, and without his sanction no radial changes compromising the welfare of the land could take place; the system of arbitration being, that the governing Arab on the one side, and the deputy of the Wakhadim on the other, should hold conference with a screen placed between them, to obviate all attempts at favour, corruption, or bribery.

The former report of the approach of my men, with as many Waganda and cows for me, turned out partly false, inasmuch as only one of my men was with 102 Waganda, whilst the whole of the deserters were left behind in Uganda with cows; and Kamrasi hearing this, ordered all to go back again until the whole of my men should arrive.

21st. – I was told how a Myoro woman, who bore twins that died, now keeps two small pots in her house, as effigies of the children, into which she milks herself every evening, and will continue to do so five months, fulfilling the time appointed by nature for suckling children, lest the spirits of the dead should persecute her. The twins were not buried, as ordinary people are buried, under ground, but placed in an earthenware pot, such as the Wanyoro use for holding pombe. They were taken to the jungle and placed by a tree, with the pot turned mouth downwards. Manua, one of my men, who is a twin, said, in Nguru, one of the sister provinces to Unyanyembe, twins are ordered to be killed and thrown into water the moment they are born, lest droughts and famines or floods should oppress the land. Should any one attempt to conceal twins, the whole family would be murdered by the chief; but, though a great traveller, this is the only instance of such brutality Manua had ever witnessed in any country.

In the province of Unyanyembe, if a twin or twins die, they are thrown into water for the same reason as in Nguru; but as their numbers increase the size of the family, their birth is hailed with delight. Still there is a source of fear there in connection with twins, as I have seen myself; for when one dies, the mother ties a little gourd to her neck as a proxy, and puts into it a trifle of everything which she gives the living child, lest the jealousy of the dead spirit should torment her. Further, on the death of the child, she smears herself with butter and ashes, and runs frantically about, tearing her hair and bewailing piteously; whilst the men of the place use towards her the foulest language, apparently as if in abuse of her person, but in reality to frighten away the demons who have robbed her nest.

22d. – I sent Frij to Kamrasi to find out what he was doing with the Waganda and my deserters, as I wished to speak with their two head representatives. I also wanted some men to seek for and to fetch Bombay, as I said I believed him to be tied by the leg behind one of the visible hills in Kidi. The reply was, 102 Waganda, with one of my men only, had been stationed at the village my men deserted from since the date (13th) we heard of them last. They had no cows for me, but each of the Waganda bore a log of firewood, which Mtesa had ordered them to carry until they either returned with me or brought back a box of gunpowder, in default of which they were to be all burnt in a heap with the logs they carried. Kamrasi, still acting on his passive policy, would not admit them here, but wished them to return with a message, to the effect that Mtesa had no right to hold me as his guest now I had once gone into another's hands. We were all three kings to do with our subjects as we liked, and for this reason the deserters ought to be sent on here; but if I wished to speak to the Waganda, he would call their officer. There was no fear, he said, about Bombay; he was on his way;

but the men who were escorting him were spinning out the time, stopping at every place, and feasting every day. To-morrow, he added, some more Gani people would arrive here, when we should know more about it. I still advised Kamrasi to give the road to Mtesa provided he gave up plundering the Wanyoro of women and cattle; but if my counsel was listened to, I could get no acknowledgment that it was so.

23d and 24th. – I sent to inquire what news there was of Bombay's coming, and what measures Kamrasi had taken to call the Waganda's chief officer and my deserters here; as also to beg he would send us specimens of all the various tribes that visit him, in order that me might draw them. He sent four loads of dried fish, with a request for my book of birds again, as it contains a portrait of king Mtesa, and proposed seeing us at the newly-constructed Kafu palace to-morrow, when all requests would be attended to. In the meanwhile, we were told that Bombay had been seen on his way returning from Gani; and the Waganda had all run away frightened, because they were told the Kidi and Chopi visitors, who had been calling on Kamrasi lately, were merely the nucleus of an army forming to drive them away, and to subdue Uganda. Mtesa was undergoing the coronation formalities, and for this reason had sent the deserters to Kari's hill, giving them cows and a garden to live on, as no visitors can remain near the court while the solemnities of the coronation were going on. The thirty-odd brothers will be burnt to death, saving two or three, of which one will be sent into this country – as was the case with one of the late king Sunna's brothers, who is still in Unyoro – and the others will remain in the court with Mtesa as playfellows until the king dies, when, like Sunna's two brothers still living in Uganda, one at N'yama Goma and one at Ngambezi, they will be pensioned off. After the coronation is concluded, it is expected Mtesa will go into Kittari, on the west of Uganda, to fight first, and then, turning east, will fight with the Wasoga; but we think if he fights anywhere, it will be with Kamrasi.

25th and 26th. – I sent Frij to the palace to inquire after Bombay, and got the usual reply: "Why is Bana in such a hurry? He is always for doing things quickly. Tell my 'brother' to keep his mind at rest; Bombay is now on the boundary of Gani coming here, and will in due course arrive." Both Rumanika's men and those belonging to Dr. K'yengo asked Kamrasi's leave to return to their homes, but were refused, because the road was unsafe. "Had they not," it was said, "heard of Budja's telling Mtesa that K'yengo's children prevented the white men from returning to Uganda? And since then Mtesa had killed his frontier officer for being chicken-hearted, afraid to carry out his orders, and had appointed another in his stead, giving him strict orders to make prisoners of all foreigners who might pass that way; and, further, when some twenty Wanyoro were going to Karague, they were hunted down by Mtesa's orders, and three of their number killed; for he was determined to cut off all intercourse between this country and Karague. They must therefore wait till the road is safe." Hearing this, Dr. K'yengo's men, who happened to be as well off here as anywhere, accepted the advice; but Rumanika's men said, "We are starving; we have been here too long already doing nothing, and must go, let what will happen to us." Kamrasi said, "What will be the use of your going empty-handed? I cannot send cows and slaves to Rumanika when the road is so unsafe; you must wait a bit." But they still urged as before, and so forced the king reluctantly to acquiesce, but only on the condition that two of their head men should remain behind until some more of Rumanika's men came to fetch them away – in fact, as we had been accredited to him by Rumanika, he wanted to keep some of that king's people as a security until we were out of his hands.

27th. – I sent Frij to the palace to ask once more for leave to visit the Luta Nzige river-lake to the westward, and to request Kamrasi would send men to fetch my property from Karague. He sent four loads of small fish and one pot of pombe, to say he would see me on the morrow, when every arrangement would be made. Late at night orders came announcing that I might write my despatches, as sixty men were ready to start for Karague.

28th. – I sent one of my men with despatches to Kamrasi, who detained him half the day, and then ordered him to call tomorrow. This being the fifteenth or twentieth time Kamrasi had disappointed me, after promising an interview, that we might have a proper understanding about everything, and when no begging on his party was to interrupt our conversation, I sent him a threatening message, to see what effect that would have. The purport of it was, that I was afraid to send men to Karague, now I had seen his disposition to make prisoners of all who visit him. Here had I been kept six weeks waiting for Bombay's return from Gani, where I only permitted him to go because I was told the journey to and fro would only occupy from eight to ten days at most. Then Rumanika's men, who came here with Baraka, though daily crying to get away, were still imprisoned here, without any hope before them. If I sent Msalima, he would be kept ten years on the road. If I went to the lake Luta Nzige, God only knows when he would let me come back; and now, for once and for all, I wished to sacrifice my property, and leave the countries of black kings; for what Kamrasi had done, Mtesa had done likewise, detaining the two men I detached on a friendly mission, which made me fear to send any more and inquire after my guns, lest he should seize them likewise. I would stay no longer among such people.

Kamrasi, in answer, begged I would not be afraid; there was no occasion for alarm; Bombay would be here shortly. I had promised to wait patiently for his return, and as soon as he did return, I would be sent off without one day's delay, for I was not his slave, that he should use violence upon me. Rumanika's men, too, would be allowed to go, only that the road was unsafe, and he feared Rumanika would abuse him if any harm befell them.

29th. – To-day I met Kamrasi at his new reception-palace on this side the Kafu – taking a Bible to explain all I fancied I knew about the origin and present condition of the Wahuma branch of the Ethiopians, beginning with Adam, to show how it was the king had heard by tradition that at one time the people of his race were half white and half black. Then, proceeding with the Flood, I pointed out that the Europeans remained white, retaining Japhet's blood; whilst the Arabs are tawny, after Shem; and the African's black, after Ham. And, finally, to show the greatness of the tribe, I read the 14th chapter of 2d Chronicles, in which it is written how Zerah, the Ethiopian, with a host of a thousand thousand, met the Jew Asa with a large army, in the valley of

Zephathah, near Mareshah; adding to it that again, at a much later date, we find the Ethiopians battling with the Arabs in the Somali country, and with the Arabs and Portuguese at Omwita (Mombas) – in all of which places they have taken possession of certain tracts of land, and left their sons to people it.

To explain the way in which the type or physical features of people undergo great changes by interbreeding, Mtesa was instanced as having lost nearly every feature of his Mhuma blood, but the kings of Uganda having been produced, probably for several generations running, of Waganda mothers. This amused Kamrasi greatly, and induced me to inquire how his purity of blood was maintained – "Was the king of Unyoro chosen, as in Uganda, haphazard by the chief men – or did the eldest son sit by succession on the throne?" The reply was, "The brothers fought for it, and the best man gained the crown." Kamrasi then began counting the leaves of the Bible, an amusement that every negro that gets hold of a book indulges in; and, concluding in his mind that each page or leaf represented one year of time since the beginning of creation, continued his labour till one quarter of the way through the book, and then only shut it up on being told, if he desired to ascertain the number more closely, he had better count the words.

I begged for my picture-books, which were only lent him at his request for a few days; and then began a badgering verbal conflict: he would not return them until I drew others like them; he would not allow me to go to the Little Luta Nzige, west of this, until Bombay returned, when he would send me with an army of spears to lead the way, and my men with their guns behind to protect the rear. This was for the purpose of making us his tools in his conflict with his brothers. I complained that he had, without consulting me, ordered away the men who had been sent, either to fetch me back to Uganda, or else get powder from me, although they had orders to carry out their king's desire, under the threat of being burnt with the fire logs they carried; and all this Kamrasi had professed to do merely out of respect for my dignity, as I was no slave, that Mtesa should order me about. I argued, founding on each particular in succession, that his conduct throughout was most unjustifiable, and anything but friendly. He then produced an officer, who was to escort my man Msalima to Karague, giving him orders to collect the sixty men required on the way; five of Rumanika's men could go with him, but five must stop, until other Karague men came to say the road was safe, when he would send by them the present he had prepared for Rumanika.

Then, turning to us, he said, "Why have you not brought the medicine-chest and the saw? We wish to see everything you have got, though we do not wish to rob you." When these things came for inspection, he coveted the saw, and discovered there were more varieties of medicine in the chest than had been given him. This he was told was not the case, because the papers given him contained mixed medicines – a little being taken from every bottle. "But there are no pills; why won't you give us pills? We have men, women, and children who require pills as well as you do." We were much annoyed by this dogged begging; and as he said, "Well, if you won't give my anything, I will go," we at once rose, hat in hand; when, regretting the hastiness of his speech, he begged us to be seated again, and renewed his demands. We told him the road to Gani was the only condition on which we would part with any more medicine; we had asked leave to go a hundred times, and that was all we now desired. At last he rose and walked off in a huff; but, repenting before he reached home, he sent us a pot of pombe, when, in return, I finished the farce by sending him a box of pills.

30th. – I gave Msalima a letter in the Kisuahili or coast language to convey to Rumanika, ordering all my property to be sent here, his account of the things as they left him to be given to Msalima to convey to the coast, while I sent him one pound of gunpowder as a sort of agency fee. Msalima also took a map of all the countries we had passed, with lunar observations, and a letter to Rigby, by which he, Baraka, and Uledi would be able to draw their pay on arrival.

31st. – I sent Frij with a letter to the king, containing an acknowledgment that, on the arrival of the rear property from Karague, he would be entitled to half of everything, reserving the other half for any person I might in future send to take them from him. He accepted the letter, and put it into his mzungu – the tin box I had given him. He said he would take every care of the kit from the time it arrived, and would not touch his share of it till my deputy arrived. An inhabitant of Chopi reported that he heard Bombay's gun fire the evening before he left home, and was rewarded with the present of a cow.

1st. – I purchased a small kitten, Felis serval, from an Unyoro man, who requested me to give it back to him to eat if it was likely to die, for it is considered very good food in Unyoro.

Bombay at last arrived with Mabruki in high glee, dressed in cotton jumpers and drawers, presents given them by Petherick's outpost. Petherick himself was not there. The journey to and fro was performed in fourteen days' actual travelling, the rest of the time being frittered away by the guides. The jemadar of the guard said he commanded two hundred Turks, and had orders to wait for me, without any limit as to time, until I should arrive, when Petherick's name would be pointed out to me cut on a tree; but as no one in camp could read my letter, they were doubtful whether we were the party they were looking out for.

They were all armed with elephant-guns, and had killed sixteen elephants. Petherick had gone down the river eight days' journey, but was expected to return shortly. Kamrasi would not see Bombay immediately on his return, but sent him some pombe, and desired an interview the following day.

2d. – I sent Bombay with a farewell present to Kamrasi, consisting of one tent, one mosquito-curtain, one roll of bindera or red cotton cloth, one digester pot, one saw, six copper wires, one box of beads, containing six varieties of the best sort, and a request to leave his country. Much pleased with the things, Kamrasi ordered the tent to be pitched before all his court, pointed out to them what clever people the white people are, making iron pots instead of earthen ones. Covetous and never satisfied, however, instead of returning thanks, he said he was sure I must have more beads than those I sent him; and, instead of granting the leave asked for, said he would think about it, and send the Kamraviona in the evening with his answer. This, when it came, was anything but satisfactory; for we were required to stop here until the king should have prepared the people on the road for our coming, so that they might not be surprised, or try to molest us on the way. Kamrasi, however, returned the books of birds and animals, requesting a picture of the king of Uganda to be drawn for him, and gave us one pot of pombe.

3d. – I sent the picture required, and an angry message to Kamrasi for breaking his word, as he promised us we should go without a day's delay; and go we must, for I could neither eat nor sleep from thinking of my home. His only reply to this was, Bana is always in a preposterous hurry. He answered, that for our gratification he had directed a dwarf called Kimenya to be sent to us, and the Kamraviona should follow after. Kimenya, a little old man, less than a yard high, called on us with a walking-stick higher than himself, made his salaam, and sat down very composedly. He then rose and danced, singing without invitation, and following it up with queer antics. Lastly, he performed the tambura, or charging-march, in imitation of Wakugnu, repeating the same words they use, and ending by a demand for simbi, or cowrie-shells, modestly saying, "I am a beggar, and want simbi; if you have not 500 to spare, you must at any rate give me 400." He then narrated his fortune in life. Born in Chopi, he was sent for by Kamrasi, who first gave him two women, who died; then another, who ran away; and, finally, a distorted dwarf like himself, whom he rejected, because he thought the propagation of his pigmy breed would not be advantageous to society. Bombay then marched him back to the palace, with 500 simbi strung in necklaces round his neck. When these two had gone, the Kamraviona arrived with two spears, one load of flour, and a pot of pombe, which he requested me to accept, adding that the spears were given as it was observed I had accepted some from the king of Uganda; a shield was still in reserve for me, and spears would be sent for

Grant. Then with regard to my going, Kamrasi must beg us to have patience until he had sent messengers into Kidi, requesting the natives there not to molest me on the way, for they had threatened they would do so, and if they persisted, he would send us with a force by another route via Ugungu – another attempt to draw us off to fight against his brothers.

I stormed at this announcement as a breach of faith; said I had given the king my only tent, my only digester, my only saw, my only wire, my only mosquito-curtains, and my last of everything, because he had assured me I should have to pay no more chiefs, and he would give me the road at once. If he did not intend now to fulfil his promise, I begged he would take back his spears, for I would only accept them as a farewell present. The Kamraviona finding me rather warm, with the usual pertinacious duplicity of a negro, then said, "Well, let that subject drop, and consider the present Kamrasi promised you when you gave him the Uganga" (meaning the watch); "Kamrasi's horn is not ready yet." This second prevarication completely set my dander up. If I did not believe in his dangers of the way before, it quite settled my opinion of the worth of his words now. I therefore tendered him what might be called the ultimatum to this effect.

There was no sincerity in such haggling; I would not submit to being told lies by kings or anybody else. He must take back the spears, or give us the road to-morrow; and unless the Kamraviona would tell him this and bring me an answer at once, the spears should not remain in my house during the night. Evidently in alarm, the Kamraviona, with Kidgwiga and Frij in company to bear him witness, returned to the palace, telling

Kamrasi that he saw we were in thorough earnest. He extracted a promise that Kamrasi would have a farewell meeting with us either to-morrow or the next day, when we should have a large escort to Petherick's boats, and the men would be able to bring back anything that he wanted; but he could not let us go without a parting interview, such as we had at Uganda with Mtesa.

The deputation, delighted with their success and the manner in which it was effected, hurried back to me at once, and said they were so frightened themselves that they would have skulked away to their homes and not come near me if they could not have arranged matters to my satisfaction. Kamrasi would not believe I had threatened to turn out his spears until Frij testified to their statements; and he then said, "Let Bana keep the spears and drink the pombe, for I would not wish him to be a prisoner against his will." Bombay, after taking back the dwarf, met one of N'yamasore's officers, just arrived from Uganda on some important business, and upbraided Mtesa for not having carried out my instructions. The officer in turn tried to defend Mtesa's conduct by saying he had given the deserters seventy cows and four women, as well as orders to join us quickly; but they had been delayed on the road, because wherever they went they plundered, and no one liked their company. Had we returned to Uganda, Mtesa would have given us the road through Masai, which, in my opinion, is nearer for us than this one.

This officer had been wishing to see us as much as we had been to see him; but Kamrasi would not allow him to get access to us, for fear, it was said, lest the Waganda should know where we were hidden, and enable Mtesa to send an army to come and snatch us away. As the officer said he would deliver any message I might wish to send to Uganda, I folded a visiting-card as a letter to the queen-dowager, intimating that I wished the two men whom I sent back to Mtesa to be forwarded on to Karague; but desired that the remainder, who deserted their master in difficulty, should be placed on an island of the N'yanza to live in exile until some other Englishman should come to release them; that their arms should be taken from them and kept in the palace. I said further, that should Mtesa act up to my desires, I would then know he was my friend, and other white men would not fear to enter Uganda; but if he acted otherwise, they would fear lest he should imprison them, or seize their property of their men. If these deserters escaped punishment, no white men would ever dare trust their lives with such men again. The officer said he should be afraid to deliver such a message to Mtesa direct; but he certainly would tell the queen every word of it, which would be even more efficacious.

4th. – I bullied Kamrasi by telling him we must go with this moon, for the benefit of its light whilst crossing the Kidi wilderness; as if we did not reach the vessels in time for seasonable departure down the Nile, we should have to wait another year for their return from Khartum. "What!" said Kamrasi, "does Bana forget my promised appointment that I would either see him to-day or to-morrow? I cannot do so to-day, and therefore to-morrow we will certainly meet and bid good-bye." The Gani men, who came with Bombay, said they would escort us to their country, although, as a rule, they never cross the Kidi wilderness above once in two years, from fear of the hunting natives, who make gave of everybody and everything they see; in other words, they seize strangers, plunder them, and sell them as slaves. To cross that tract, the dry season is the best, when all the grass is burnt down, or from the middle of December to the end of March. I gave them a cow, and they at once killed it, and, sitting down, commenced eating her flesh raw, out of choice.

5th. – The Kamraviona came to inform us that the king was ready for the great interview, where we could both speak what we had at heart, for as yet he had only heard what our servants had to say; and there was a supplement to the message, of the usual kind, that he would like a present of a pencil. The pencil was sent in the first place, because we did not like talking about trifles when we visited great kings.

The interview followed. It was opened on our side by our saying we had enjoyed his hospitality a great number of days, and wished to go to our homes; should be have any message to send to the great Queen of England, we should be happy to convey it. A long yarn then emanated from the throne. He defended his over-cautiousness when admitting us into Unyoro. It was caused at first by wicked men who did not wish us to visit him; he subsequently saw through their representations, and now was very pleased with us as he found us. Of course he could not tie us down to stopping here against our wish, but, for safety's sake, he would like us to stop a little longer, until he could send messengers ahead, requesting the wild men in Kidi not to molest us. That state trick failing to frighten and stop us, he tried another, by saying, when we departed, he hoped we would leave two men with guns behind, to occupy our present camp, and so delude the people into the belief that merely a party of their followers, and not the white men themselves, had left his house, for the purpose of spreading terror in the minds of the people we might meet, who, not knowing the number of men behind, would naturally conclude there was a large reserve force ready to release us in case of necessity.

This foxy speech was too transparent to require one moment's reflection. In a country where men were property, the fate of one or two left behind was obvious; and had we doubted that his object was to get possession of them, his next words would have sufficiently revealed it. He said, "As you gave men to Mtesa, why would you refuse them to me?" but was checkmated on being told, "Should any of those men who deserted us in this country ever reach their homes, they will all be hung for breaking their allegiance or oath." "Well," says the king, "I have acceded to everything you have to say; and the day after to-morrow, when I shall have had time to collect men to go with you, and selected the two princes you have promised to educate, we will meet again and say good-bye; but you must give me a gun and some more medicine, as well as the powder and ball you promised after reaching the vessels." This was all acquiesced in, and we wished to take his portrait, but he would not have it done on any consideration. The Kamraviona and Kidgwiga followed us home, and told Bombay the king did not wish us to leave till next moon, and then he would like us to fight his brothers on the way. This message, sent in such an underhand manner after the meeting, Bombay failed to deliver, telling them he should be afraid to do so.

6th. – The Kamraviona was sent to us with four loads of fish and a request for ammunition, notwithstanding everything asked for yesterday had been refused until we reached the vessels. "Confound Kamrasi!" was the reply; "does he think we came here to trick kings that he doubts our words? We came to open the road; and, as sure as we wish it, we will send him everything that has been promised. Why should he doubt our word more than anybody else? We are not accustomed to be treated in this manner, and must beg he won't insult us any more. Then about fighting his brothers, we have already given answer that we never fight with black men; and should the king persist in it, we will never take another thing from his hands. The boys shall not go to England, neither will any other white men come this way." The Kamraviona made the following answer: "But there are two more things the king wishes to know about: he has asked the question before, but forgotten the answers. Is there any medicine for women or children which will prevent the offspring from dying shortly after birth? For it is a common infirmity in this country with some women, that all their children die before they are able to walk, whilst others never lose a child. The other matter of inquiry was, What medicine will attach all subjects to their king? For Kamrasi wants some of that most particularly." I answered, "Knowledge of good government, attended with wisdom and justice, is all the medicine we know of; and this his boys can best learn in England, and instruct him in when they return."

7th. – We went to meet Kamrasi at his Kafu palace to bid good-bye.

After all the huckstering and begging with which he had tormented us, the state he chose to assume on this occasion was very ludicrous. He sat with an air of the most solemn dignity, upon his throne of skins, regarding us like mere slaves, and asking what things we intended to send to him. On being told we did not like being repeatedly reminded of our promises, he came down a little from his dignity, saying, "And what answer have you about the business on the island?" – meaning the request to fight his brothers. That, of course, could not be listened to, as it was against the principle of our country. Grant's rings were then espied, and begged for, but without success. We told him it was highly improper to beg for everything he saw, and if he persisted in it, no one would ever dare to come near him again.

Then, to change the subject, we begged K'yengo's men might be allowed to go as far as Gani with us; but no reply was given, until the question was put again, with a request that the reason might be told us for his not wishing it, as we saw great benefit would be derived to Unyoro, as the Wanyamuezi instead of trading merely with Karague and Zanzibar, would bring their ivory through this country and barter it, thus converting Unyoro into a great commercial country; when Kamrasi said, "We don't want any more ivory in Unyoro; for the tusks are already as numerous as grass." Kidgwiga was then appointed to receive all the things we were to send back from Gani; our departure was fixed for the 9th; and the king walked away as coldly as he came, whilst we felt as jolly as birds released from a cage.

Floating islands of grass were seen going down the Kafu, reminding us of the stories told at Kaze by Musa Mzuri, of the violent manner in which, at certain season, the N'yanza was said to rise and rush with such velocity that islands were uprooted and carried away. In the evening a pot of pombe was brought, when the man in charge, half-drunk, amused us with frantic

Elephants in the Bahr-el-Abiad grasslands.

charges, as if he were fighting with his spear; and after settling the supposed enemy, he delighted in tramping him under foot, spearing him repeatedly through and through, then wiping the blade of the spear in the grass, and finally polishing it on this tufty head, when, with a grunt of satisfaction, he shouldered arms and walked away a hero.

8th. – As the king seemed entirely to disregard our comfort on the journey, we made a request for cows, butter, and coffee, in answer to which we only got ten cows, the other things not being procurable without delay. Twenty-four men were appointed us to escort us and bring back our presents from Gani, which were to be – six carbines, with a magazine of ammunition, a large brass or iron water-pot, a hair-brush, lucifers, a dinner-knife, and any other things procurable that had never been seen in Unyoro.

Two orphan boys, seized by the king as slaves, were brought for education in England; but as they were both of the common negro breed, with nothing attractive about them, and such as no one could love but their mothers, we rejected them, fearing lest no English boys would care to play with them, and told Kamrasi that his offspring only could play with our children, and unless I got some princes of that interesting breed, no one would ever undertake to teach children brought from this country. The king was very much disappointed at this announcement; said they were his adopted children, and the only ones he could part with, for his own boys were mere balls of fat, and too small to leave home.

CHAPTER 19

THE MARCH TO MADI

Sail down the Kafu – The Navigable Nile – Fishing and Sporting Population – The Scenery on the River – An Inhospitable Governor – Karuma Falls – Native Superstitions – Thieveries – Hospitable Reception at Koki by Chongi.

After giving Kamrasi a sketching-stool, we dropped down the Kafu two miles in a canoe, in order that the common people might not see us; for the exclusive king would not allow any eyes but his own to be indulged with the extraordinary sight of white men in Unyoro! The palace side of the river, however, as we paddled away, was thronged with anxious spectators amongst whom the most conspicuous was the king's favourite nurse. Dr. K'yengo's men were very anxious to accompany us, even telling the king, if he would allow the road to be opened to their countrymen, all would hongo, or pay customs-duty to him; but the close, narrow-minded king could not be persuaded. Bombay here told us Kamrasi at the last moment wished to give me some women and ivory; and when told we never accepted anything of that sort, wished to give them to my head servants; but this being contrary to standing orders also, he said he would smuggle them down to the boats for Bombay in such a manner that I should not find out.

We were not expected to march again, but being anxious myself to see more of the river, before starting, I obtained leave to go by boat as far as the river was navigable, sending our cattle by land. To this concession was accompanied a request for a few more gun-caps, and liberty was given us to seize any pombe which might be found coming on the river in boats, for the supplies to the palace all come in this manner. We then took boat again, an immense canoe, and, after going a short distance, emerged from the Kafu, and found ourselves on what at first appeared a long lake, averaging from two hundred at first to one thousand yards broad before the day's work was out; but this was the Nile again, navigable in this way from Urondogani.

Both sides were fringed with the huge papyrus rush. The left one was low and swampy, whilst the right one – in which the Kidi people and Wanyoro occasionally hunt – rose from the water in a gently sloping bank, covered with trees and beautiful convolvuli, which hung in festoons. Floating islands, composed of rush, grass, and ferns, were continually in motion, working their way slowly down the stream, and proving to us that the Nile was in full flood. On one occasion we saw hippopotami, which our men said came to the surface because we had domestic fowls on board, supposing them to have an antipathy to that bird. Boats there were, which the sailors gave chase to; but, as they had no liquor, they were allowed to go their way, and the sailors, instead, set to lifting baskets and taking fish from the snares which fisherman, who live in small huts amongst the rushes, had laid for themselves.

After arrival, as we found the boatmen wished to make off, instead of carrying out their king's orders to take us to the wa-

Kidi natives visiting Kamrasi.

terfall, we seized all the paddles, and kept their tongues quiet by giving them a cow to eat. The overland route, by which Kidgwiga and the cattle went, was not so interesting, by all accounts, as the river one; for they walked the whole way through marshy ground, and crossed one drain in boats, where some savages struggled to plunder our men of their goats.

With a great deal of difficulty, and after hours of delay, we managed to get under way with two boats besides the original one; and, after an hour and a half's paddling in the laziest manner possible, the men seized two pots of pombe and pulled in to Koki, guided by a king's messenger, who said this was one of the places appointed by order to pick up recruits for the force which was to take us to Gani. We found, however, nothing but loss and disappointment – one calf stolen, and five goats nearly so.

Fortunately, the thief who attempted to run off with the goats was taken by my men in the act, tied with his hands painfully tight behind his back, and left, with his face painted white, till midnight, when his comrades stole into Bombay's hut and released him. After all these annoyances, the chief officer of the place offered us a present of a goat, but was sent to the right-about in scorn. How could he be countenanced as a friend when the men under him steal from us? The big boat gave us the slip, floating away and leaving its paddles behind. To supply its place, we took six small boats, turning my men into sailors, and going as we liked. The river still continued beautiful; but after paddling three hours we found it bend considerably, and narrow to two hundred yards, the average depth being from two to three fathoms. At the fourth hour, imagining our cattle to be far behind, we pulled in, and walked up a well-cultivated hill to Yaragonjo's, the governor of these parts. The guide, however, on first sighting his thorn-fenced cluster of huts, regarding it apparently with the awe and deference due to a palace, shrank from advancing, and merely pointed, till he was forced on, and in the next minute we found ourselves confronted with the heads of the establishment. The father of the house, surprised at our unexpected manner of entrance – imagining, probably, we were the king's sorcerers, in consequence of our hats, sent to fight "the brothers" – without saying a word, quietly beckoned us to follow him out of the gate by the same way as we came. Preferring, however, to have a little talk where we were, we remained.

The eldest son, a fine young man considerably above six feet high, with large gashes on his body received in war during late skirmishes with the refractory brothers, now came in, did the honours, and, on hearing of the importance of his visitors, directed us to some huts a little distance off, where we could rest for the night, for there was no accommodation for such a large party in the palace. The red hill we were now on, with plantain-gardens, fine huts neatly kept, and dense grasses covering the country, reminded us of our residence in Uganda. The people seemed of a decidedly sporting order, for they kept hippopotamus-harpoons, attached to strong ropes with trimmers of pith wood, in their huts; and, outside, trophies of their toil in the shape of a pile of heads, consisting of those of buffalo and hippopotami. The women, anything but pretty, wore their mbugu cut into two flounces, fastened with a drawing-string round the waist; and, in place of stockings, they bound strings of small iron beads, kept bright and shining, carefully up the leg from the ankle to the bottom of the calf.

Kidgwiga with our cattle arrived in the morning. A bundle of cartridges, stolen from one of the men's pouches, which we knew could only have been done by some comrade, was discovered by stopping the rations of flesh. The guilty person, to save detection, threw it on the road, and allowed some of the natives to pick it up. Strange as it may appear, the only motive for this petty theft was the hope of being able to sell the cartridges for a trifle at Gani. Yaragonjo brought us a present of a goat and plantains. He was sorry he sent us back yesterday from his house; and invited us to change ground to another village close by, where he would make arrangements for our receiving other boats, as the ones we had in possession must go back. Presuming this to be a very fair proposition, and thinking we would only have to walk across an elbow of land where the river bends considerably, we gave him a return-present of beads, and did as we were bid; but, after moving, it was obvious we had been sold. We had lost our former boats, and no others were near us; therefore, feeling angry with Yaragonjo, I walked back to his palace, taking the presented goat with me, as I knew that would touch the savage in the most tender part; then flaring up with the officer for treating the king's orders with contempt, as well as his guests, by sending us into the jungles like a pack of thieves, whose riddance from his presence was obviously his only intent, I gave him his goat again, and said I would have nothing more to say to him, for I should look to the king for redress.

This frightened him to such an extent that he immediately produced another and finer goat, which he begged me to accept, promising to convey all my traps to the next governor's, where there would be no doubt about our getting boats. He did not intend to deceive us, but committed an error in not informing us he had no boats of his own; and, to show his earnestness, accompanied us to the camp. Here I found the missing calf taken at Koki, and a large deputation of natives awaiting our arrival. They told me that the Koki governor had taken such fright in consequence of my anger when I refused his proffered goat, that he had traced the calf back to Kitwara, and now wished to take Kidgwiga a prisoner to Kamrasi's for having seized five cows of his, and a woman from another governor. As yet I had not heard of this piece of rough justice; and, on inquiry, found out that he had been compelled to do as he had done, because those officers, on finding we had gone ahead in boats would not produce the complement of men required of them by the king's orders for escorting us to Gani; but now they sent the men, the woman and cows could not be returned, as they had been sent overland by the ordinary route to the ferry on the Nile.

Of course we would not listen to this reference for justice with Kamrasi, as the woman and cows were still all alive; commended Kidgwiga for carrying out his orders so well, and told the officers they had merited their punishment – as how could the affairs of government be carried on, when subordinate officers refused immediate compliance? The submkungu of Northern Gueni, Kasoro, now proffered a goat and plantains, and everything was settled for the day.

With a full complement of porters, travelling six miles through cultivation and jungle, we reached the headquarters of governor Kaeru, where all the porters threw down their loads and bolted, though we were still two miles from the post. We inquired for the boats at once, but were told they were some distance off, and we must wait here for the night. Four pots of pombe were sent us, and Kaeru thought we would be satisfied and conform. We suspected, however, that there was some trick at the bottom of all; so, refusing the liquor, we said, with proper emphasis, "Unless we are forwarded to the boats at once, and get them on the following morning, we cannot think of receiving presents from any one." This served our purpose, for a fresh set of porters was found like magic, and traps, pombe, and all together, were forwarded to the journey's end – a snug batch of huts imbedded in large plantain cultivation surrounded by jungle, and obviously near the river, as numerous huge harpoons, intended for striking hippopotami, were suspended from the roof. Kaeru here presented us with a goat, and promised the boats in the morning.

After fighting for the boats, we still had to wait the day for Kidgwiga and his men, who said it was all very well our pushing ahead, indifferent as to whether men were enlisted or not, but he had to prepare for the future also, as he could never re-cross the Kidi wilderness by himself; he must have a sufficient number of men to form his escort, and these were now grinding corn for the journey. Numerous visitors called on us here, and consequently our picture-books were in great request. We gave Kaeru some beads.

After walking two miles to the boats, we entered the district of Chopi, subject to Unyoro, and went down the river, keeping the Kikunguru cone in view. On arrival at camp, Viarwanjo, the officer of the district, a very smart fellow, arrived with a large escort of spearmen, presented pombe, ordered fowls to be seized for us, and promised one boat in the morning, for he had no more disposable, and even that one he felt anxious about lest the men on ahead should seize it.

I gave Viarwanjo some beads, and dropped down the river in his only wretched little canoe – he, with Grant and the traps, going overland. I caught a fever, and so spent the night.

Here I halted to please Magamba, the governor, who is a relation of the king. He called in great state, presented a cow and pombe, was much pleased with the picture-books, and wished to feast his eyes on all the wonders in the hut. He was very communicative, also, as far as his limited knowledge permitted. He said the people are only a sub-tribe of the Madi; and the reason why the right bank of the river is preferred to the left for travelling is, that Rionga, who lives down the river, is always on the look-out for Kamrasi's allies, with a view to kill them. Magamba also, on being questioned, told us about Ururi, a province of Unyoro, under the jurisdiction of Kimerziri, a noted governor, who covers his children with bead ornaments, and throws them into the N'yanza, to prove their identity as his own true offspring; for should they sink, it stands to reason some other person must be their father; but should they float, then he recovers them. One of Kamrasi's cousins, Kaoroti, with his chief officer, called on us, presenting five fowls as an honorarium. He had little to say, but begged for medicine, and when given some in a liquid state, said his sub would like some also; then Kidgwiga's wife, who was left behind, must have some; and as pills were given for her, the two men must have dry medicine too, to take home with them. Severe drain as this was on the medicine-chest, Magamba and his wife must have both wet and dry; and even others put in a claim, but were told they were too healthy to require physicking. Many Kidi men, dressed as in the woodcut, crossed the river to visit Kamrasi; they could not, however, pass us without satisfying their curiosity with a look. Usually these men despise clothes, and never deign to put any covering on except out of respect, when visiting Kamrasi. Their "sou'-wester"-shaped wigs are made of other men's hair, as the negro hair will not grow long enough. A message came from Ukero, the governor-general of Chopi, to request we would not go down the river in boats to-morrow, lest the Chopi ferrymen at the falls should take fright at our strange appearance, paddle precipitately across the river, hide their boats, and be seen no more.

We started, leaving all the traps and men to follow, and made this place in a stride, as a whisper warned me that Kamrasi's officers, who are as thick as thieves about here, had made up their minds to keep us each one day at his abode, and show us "hospitality." Such was the case, for they all tried their powers of persuasion, which failing, they took the alternative of making my men all drunk, and sending to camp sundry pots of pombe. The ground on the line of march was highly cultivated, and intersected by a deep ravine of running water, whose sundry branches made the surface very irregular. The sand-paper tree, whose leaves resemble a cat's tongue in roughness, and which is used in Uganda for polishing their clubs and spear-handles, was conspicuous; but at the end of the journey only was there anything of much interest to be seen. There suddenly, in a deep ravine one hundred yards below us, the formerly placid river, up which vessels of moderate size might steam two or three abreast, was now changed into a turbulent torrent. Beyond lay the land of Kidi, a forest of mimosa trees, rising gently away from the water in soft clouds of green. This, the governor of the place, Kija, described as a sporting-field, where elephants, hippopotami, and buffalo are hunted by the occupants of both sides of the river. The elephant is killed with a new kind of spear, with a double-edged blade a yard long, and a handle which, weighted in any way most easy, is pear-shaped.

With these instruments in their hands, some men climb into trees and wait for the herd to pass, whilst others drive them under.

The hippopotami, however, are not hunted, but snared with lunda, the common tripping-trap with spike-drop, which is placed in the runs of this animal, described by every South African traveller, and generally known as far as the Hametic language is spread. The Karuma Falls, if such they may be called, are a mere sluice or rush of water between high syenitic stones, falling in a long slope down a ten-feet drop. There are others of minor importance, and one within ear-sound, down the river, said to be very grand.

The name given to the Karuma Falls arose from the absurd belief that Karuma, the agent or familiar of a certain great spirit, placed the stones that break the waters in the river, and, for so doing, was applauded by his master, who, to reward his services by an appropriate distinction, allowed the stones to be called Karuma. Near this is a tree which contains a spirit whose attributes for gratifying the powers and pleasures of either men or women who summon its influence in the form appropriate to each, appear to be almost identical with that of Mahadeo's Ligna in India.

20th. – We halted for the men to collect and lay in a store of food for the passage of the Kidi wilderness. Presents of fish, caught in baskets, were sent us by Kija. They were not bad eating, though all ground animals of the lowest order. At the Grand Falls below this, Kidgwiga informs us, the king had the heads of one hundred men, prisoners taken in war against Rionga, cut off and thrown into the river.

21st and 22d. – The governor, who would not let us go until we saw him, called on the 22d with a large retinue, attended by a harpist, and bringing a present of one cow, two loads flour, and three pots of pombe. He expected a chair to sit upon, and got a box, as at home he has a throne only a little inferior to Kamrasi's. He was very generous to Bombay on his former journey to Gani; and then said he thought the white men were all flocking this way to retake their lost country; for tradition recorded that the Wahuma were once half-black and half-white, with half the hair straight and the other half curly; and how was this to be accounted for, unless the country formerly belonged to white men with straight hair, but was subsequently taken by black men? We relieved his apprehensions by telling him his ancestors were formerly all white, with straight hair, and lived in a country beyond the salt sea, till they crossed that sea, took possession of Abyssinia, and are now generally known by the name of Hubshies and Gallas; but neither of these names was known to him.

On the east, beyond Kidi, he only knew of one clan of Wahuma, a people who subsist entirely on meat and milk. The sportsmen of this country, like the Wanyamuezi, plant a convolvulus of extraordinary size by the side of their huts, and pile the jaw-bones and horns of their spoils before, as a means of bringing good-luck. This same flower, held in the hand when a man is searching for anything that he has lost, will certainly bring him to the missing treasure. In the evening, Kidgwiga, at the head of his brave army, made one of their theatrical charges on "Bana" with spear and shield, swearing they would never desert him on the march, but would die to a man if it were necessary; and if they deserted him, then might they be deprived of their heads, or of other personal possessions not much less valuable.

Just as we were ready for crossing the river, a line of Kidi men was descried filing through the jungle on the opposite side, making their way for a new-moon visit to Rionga, who occasionally leads them into battle against Ukero. The last time they fought, two men only were killed on Kamrasi's side, whilst nine fell on Rionga's. There was little done besides crossing, for the last cow was brought across as sunset – the ferrying-toll for the whole being one cow, besides a present of beads to the head officer. Kidgwiga's party sacrificed two kids, one on either side the river, flaying them with one long cut each down their breasts and bellies. These animals were then, spread-eagle fashion, laid on their backs upon grass and twigs, to be steeped over by the travellers, that their journey might be prosperous; and the spot selected for the ordeal was chosen in deference to the Mzimu, or spirit – a sort of wizard or ecclesiastical patriarch, whose functions were devoted to the falls.

After a soaking night, we were kept waiting till noon for the forty porters ordered by Kamrasi, to carry our property to the vessels wherever they might be. Only twenty-five men arrived, notwithstanding the wife and one slave belonging to a local officer, who would not supply the men required of him, were seized and confiscated by Ukero, of Wire. We now mustered twenty Wanguana, twenty-five country porters, and thirty-one of Kidgwiga's "children" – making a total, with ourselves, of seventy-eight souls. By a late arrival a message came from Kamrasi. Its import was, that we must defer the march, as it was reported the refractory brother Rionga harboured designs of molesting us on the way, and therefore the king conceived it prudent to clear the road by first fighting him. Without heeding this cunning advice, we made a short march across swamps, and through thick jungle and long grasses, which proved anything but pleasant – wet and labouring hard all the way.

It was a rainy day, and we had still to toil on fighting with the grasses. We marched up the wet margin of swamp all day, crossing the water at a fork near the end. The same jungle prevails on all sides, excluding all view; and the only signs of man's existence in these wilds lay in the meagre path, which is often lost, and an occasional hut or two, the temporary residence of the sporting Kidi people.

After toiling five miles through the same terrible grasses, and crossing swamp after swamp, we were at last rewarded by a striking view. The jungles had thinned; we found ourselves unexpectedly standing on the edge of a plateau, on the west of which, for distance interminable, lay apparently a low flat country of grass, yellowed by the sun, with a few trees or shrubs only thinly scattered over the surface; while, from fifteen to twenty miles in the rear, bearing south by west, stood conspicuously the hill of Kisuga, said to be situated in Chopi, not far from the refractory brothers. But this view was only for the moment; again we dived into the grasses and forced our way along. Presently elephants were seen, also buffalo; and the guide, to make the journey propitious, plucked a twig, denuded it of its leaves and branches, waved it like a wand up the line of march, muttered some unintelligible words to himself, broke it in twain, and threw the separated bits on either side of the path.

Immediately after starting, the guide ran up on an ant-hill and pointed out to us all the glories of the country round. In our rear we could see back upon Wire and the hill of Kisuga; to the west were the same low plains of grass; east and by south, the jungles of Kidi; and to the northward, over downs of grass, the tops of some hills, which marked the neighbouring village of Koki, which we were making for. Its appearance in the distance warned us that we were closing on the habitations of men, and we were told that Bombay had drunk pombe there. Then plunging through grass again over our heads, and crossing constant swamps, we arrived at a stream which drains all these lands to westward, and rested a while that the men might bathe, and also that they might set fire to the grass as a telegraph to the settlement of Koko, to apprise the people of our advance, and be ready with their pombe ere our arrival. Shortly after, towards the close of the day's work, as a solitary buffalo was seen grazing by a brook, I put a bullet through him, and allowed the savages the pleasure of despatching him in their own wild fashion with spears.

It was a sight quite worthy of a little delay. No sooner was it observed that the huge beast could not retire, than, with springing bounds, the men, all spear in hand, as if advancing on an enemy, went top speed at him, over rise and fall alike, till, as they neared the maddened bull, he instinctively advanced to meet his assailants with the best charge his exhausted body could muster up. Wind, however, failed him soon; he knew his disadvantage, and tried to hide by plunging in the water – the worst policy he could have pursued, for the men from the bank above him soon covered him with bristling spears, and gained their victory. Now, what was to be done with this huge carcass? No one could be induced to leave it. A cow was ordered as a bribe on reaching camp; but no, the buffalo was bigger than a cow, and must be quartered on the spot; so, to gain our object, we went ahead and left the rear men to follow, thus saving a cow in rations, for we required to slaughter one every day.

By dint of hard perseverance we accomplished ten miles over the same downs of tall grass with occasional swamps. We saw a herd of hartebeest, and reached at night a place within easy run of Koki in Gani.

The weather had now become fine. At length we reached the habitations of men – a collection of conical huts on the ridge of a small chain of granitic hills lying north-west. As we approached the southern extremity of this chain, knots of naked men, perched like monkeys on the granite blocks were anxiously awaiting our arrival. The guides, following the usages of the country, instead of allowing us to mount the hill and look out for accommodation at once, desired us to halt, and sent on a messenger to inform Chongi, the governor-general, that we were visitors from Kamrasi, who desired he would take care of us and forward us to our brothers. This Mercury brought forth a hearty welcome; for Chongi had been appointed governor by Kamrasi of this district, which appears to have been the extreme northern limit of the originally vast kingdom of Kittara. All the elite of the place, covered with war-paints, and dressed, so far as their nakedness was covered at all, like clowns in a fair, charging down the hill full tilt with their spears, and, after performing their customary evolutions, mingled with our men, and invited us up the hill, where we no sooner arrived than Chongi, a very old man, attended by his familiar, advanced to receive us – one holding a white hen, the other a small gourd of pombe and a little twig.

Chongi gave us all a friendly harangue by way of greeting; and taking the fowl by one leg, swayed it to and fro close to the ground in front of his assembled visitors. After this ceremony had been also repeated by the familiar, Chongi then took the gourd and twig, and sprinkled the contents all over us; retired to the Uganga, or magic house – a very diminutive hut – sprinkled pombe over it; and, finally, spreading a cow-skin under a tree, bade us sit, and gave us a jorum of pombe, making many apologies that he could not show us more hospitality, as famine had reduced his stores. What politeness in the midst of such barbarism!!! Nowhere had we seen such naked creatures, whose sole dress consisted of bead, iron, or brass ornaments, with some feathers or cowrie-beads on the head. Even the women contented themselves with a few fibres hung like tails before and behind. Some of our men who had seen the Watuta in Utambara, declared these savages to resemble them in every particular, save one small specialty in their costume, alluded to in the description of the Zulu Kafir's dress. The hair of the men was dressed in the same fantastic fashion, and the women placed half-gourds over the baby as it rode on its mother's back. They also, like the Kidi people, whom they much fear, carry diminutive stools to sit upon wherever they go.

Their habitat extends from this to the Asua river, whilst the Madi occupy all the country west of this meridian to the Nile, which is far beyond sight. The villages are composed of little conical huts of grass, on a framework of bamboo raised above low mud walls. There are no sultans here of any consequence, each village appointing its own chief. The granitic hills, like those of Unyamuezi, are extremely pretty, and clad with trees, contrasting strangely with the grassy downs of indefinite extend around, which give the place, when compared with the people, the appearance of a paradise within the infernal regions. From the site of Koki we saw the hills behind which, according to Bombay, Petherick was situated with his vessels; and we also saw a nearer hill, behind which his advanced post of elephant-hunters were waiting our arrival.

I tried to ascertain if there were any prefixes, as in the South African dialects, by which one might determine the difference between the people and the country; but I was assured that both here and in the adjacent countries these people saw Chopi, Kidi, Gani, Madi, Bari, alike for person and place, though Jo in their language is the equivalent for Wa in South Africa, and Dano takes the place of Mtu. All the words and system of language were wholly changed – as for example, Poko poko wingi bongo, means "we do not understand"; Mazi, "fire"; Pi, "water"; Pe, "there is none; Bugra, "cow." In sound, the language of these people resembles that of the Tibet Tartars. Chongi considers

Natives of Gueni.

himself the greatest man in the country, and of noble descent, his great-grandfather having been a Mhuma, born at Ururi, in Unyoro, and appointed by the then reigning king to rule over this country, and keep the Kidi people in check.

30th. – We halted at the earnest solicitation of Chongi, as well as of the Chopi porters, who said they required a day to lay in grain, as the Wichwezi, or mendicant sorcerers – for so they thought fit to designate Petherick's elephant-hunters – had eaten up the country all about them, and those who went before with Bombay to visit their camp could get no food.

1st. – We halted again at the request of all parties, and much to the delight of old Chongi, who supplied us with abundant pombe, promised a cow, that we should not be put to any extra expense by stopping, and said that without fail he would furnish us with guides who knew a short cut across country, by which we might reach the Wichwesi camp in one march, instead of going by the circuitous route which Bombay formerly took. The cow, however, never came, as the old man did not intend to give his own, and his officers refused to obey his orders in giving one of theirs.

We left Koki with difficulty, in consequence of the Chopi porters refusing to carry any loads, leaving the burden of lifting them on the country people, as they said, "We have endured all the trouble and hardships of bringing these visitors through the wilderness; and now, as they have visited you, it is your place to help them on." The consequence was, we had to engage fresh porters at every village, each in turn saying he had done all the work which with justice fell to his lot, till at last we arrived at the borders of a jungle, where the men last engaged, feeling tired of their work, pleaded ignorance of the direct road, and turned off to the longer one, where villages and men were in abundance, thus upsetting all our plans, and doubling the actual distance.

To pass the night half-way was now imperative, as we had been the whole day travelling without making good much ground. From the Gani people we had, without any visible change, mingled with the Madi people, who dress in the same naked fashion as their neighbours, and use bows and arrows. Their villages were all surrounded with bomas (fences), and the country in its general aspect resembled that of Northern Unyamuezi. At one place, the good-natured simple people, as soon as we reached their village, spread a skin, deposited a stool upon it, and placed in front two pots of pombe. At the village where we put up, however, the women and children of the head man at first all ran away, and the head man himself was very shy of us, thinking we were some unearthly creatures. He became more reconciled to us, however, when he perceived we fed like rational beings; and, calling his family in by midnight, presented us with pombe, and made many apologies for having allowed us to dine without a drop of his beer, for he was very glad to see us.

CHAPTER 20

MADI

Junction of the Two Hemispheres – The First Contact with Persons Acquainted with European Habits – Interruptions and Plots – The Mysterious Mahamed – Native Revelries – The Plundering and Tyranny of the Turks – The Rascalities of the Ivory Trade – Feeling for the Nile – Taken to See a Mark Left By a European – Buffalo, Eland, and Rhinoceros Stalking – Meet Baker – Petherick's Arrival at Gondokoro.

After receiving more pombe from the chief, and, strange to say, hot water to wash with – for he did not know how else to show hospitality better – we started again in the same straggling manner as yesterday. In two hours we reached the palace of Piejoko, a chief of some pretensions, and were summoned to stop and drink pombe. In my haste to meet Petherick's expedition, I would listen to nothing, but pushed rapidly on, despite all entreaties to stop, both from the chief and from my porters, who, I saw clearly, wished to do me out of another day.

Half of my men, however, did stop there, but with the other half Grant and I went on; and, as the sun was setting, we came in sight of what we thought was Petherick's outpost, N. lat. 3° 10' 33", and E. long. 21° 50' 45". My men, as happy as we were ourselves, now begged I would allow them to fire their guns, and prepare the Turks for our reception. Crack, bang, went their carbines, and in another instant crack, bang, was heard from the northerners' camp, when, like a swarms of bees, every height and other conspicuous place was covered with men. Our hearts leapt with an excitement of joy only known to those who have escaped from long-continued banishment among barbarians, once more to meet with civilised people, and join old friends. Every minute increased this excitement. We saw three large red flags heading a military procession, which marched out of the camp with drums and fifes playing. I halted and allowed them to draw near. When they did so, a very black man, named Mahamed, in full Egyptian regimentals, with a curved sword, ordered his regiment to halt, and threw himself into my arms, endeavouring to hug and kiss me. Rather staggered at this unexpected manifestation of affection, which was like a conjunction of the two hemispheres, I gave him a squeeze in return for his hug, but raised my head above the reach of his lips, and asked who was his master? "Petrik," was the reply. "And where is Petherick now?" "Oh, he is coming." "How is it you have not got English colours, then?" "The colours are Debono's." "Who is Debono?" "The same as Petrik; but come along into my camp, and let us talk it out there"; saying which, Mahamed ordered his regiment (a ragamuffin mixture of Nubians, Egyptians, and slaves of all sorts, about two hundred in number) to rightabout, and we were guided by him, whilst his men kept up an incessant drumming and fifing, presenting arms and firing, until we reached his huts, situated in a village kept exactly in the same order as that of the natives. Mahamed then gave us two beds to sit upon, and ordered his wives to advance on their knees and give us coffee, whilst other men brought pombe, and prepared us a dinner of bread and honey and mutton.

A large shed was cleared for Grant and myself, and all my men were ordered to disperse, and chum in ones and twos with Mahamed's men; for Mahamed said, now we had come there, his work was finished. "If that is the case," I said, "tell us your orders; there must be some letters." He said, "No, I have no letters or written orders; though I have directions to take you to Gondokoro as soon as you come. I am Debono's Vakil, and am glad you are come, for we are all tired of waiting for you. Our business has been to collect ivory whilst waiting for you." I said, "How is it Petherick has not come here to meet me? Is he married?" "Yes, he is married; and both he and his wife ride fore-and-aft on one animal at Khartum." "Well, then, where is the tree you told Bombay you would point out to us with Petherick's name on it?" "Oh, that is on the way to Gondokoro. It was not Petherick who wrote, but some one else, who told me to look out for your coming this way. We don't know his name, but he said if we pointed it out to you, you would know at once."

4th. – After spending the night as Mahamed's guest, I strolled round the place to see what it was like, and found the Turks were all married to the women of the country, whom they had dressed in clothes and beads. Their children were many, with a prospect of more. Temporary marriages, however, were more common than others – as, in addition to their slaves, they hired the daughters of the villagers, who remained with them whilst they were trading here, but went back to their parents when they marched to Gondokoro. They had also many hundreds of cattle, which it was said they had plundered from the natives, and now used for food, or to exchange for ivory, or other purposes. The scenery and situation were perfect for health and beauty. The settlement lay at the foot of small, well-wooded granitic hills, even prettier than the outcrops of Unyamuezi, and was intersected by clear streams.

At noon, all the rear troops arrived with Bombay and Piejoko in person. This good creature had treated Bombay very handsomely on his former journey. He said he felt greatly disappointed at my pushing past him yesterday, as he wished to give me a cow, but still hoped I would go over and make friends with him. I gave him some beads and off he walked. Old Chongi's "children," who had escorted us all the way from Kamrasi's, then took some beads and cast-off clothes for themselves and their father, and left us in good-humour.

This reduced the expedition establishment to my men and Kidgwiga's. With these, now, as there was no letter from Petherick, I ordered a march for the next morning, but at once met with opposition. Mahamed told me that there were no vessels at Gondokoro; we must wait two months, by which time he expected they would arrive there, and some one would come to meet him with beads. I said in answer, that Petherick had promised to have boats there all the year round, so I would not wait. "Then," said Mahamed, "we cannot go with you, for there is a famine at this season at Gondokoro." I said, "Never mind; do you give me an interpreter, and I will go as I am." "No," said Mahamed, "that will not do, as the Bari people are so savage, you could not get through them with so small a force; besides which, just now there is a stream which cannot be crossed for a month or more." Unable to stand Mahamed's shifting devices with equanimity any longer, I accused him of trying to trick me in the same way as all the common savage chiefs had done wherever I went, because they wished me to stop for their own satisfaction, quite disregarding my wishes and interest; so I said I would not stop there any longer, I would raft over the river, and find my way through the Bari, as I had through the rest of the African savages. We talked and talked, but could make nothing of it. I maintained that if he was commissioned to help me, he at least could not refuse to give me a guide and inter-preter; when, if I failed in the direct route, I would try another, but go I must, as I could not hold out any longer, being short of beads and cows. I had just enough, but none to spare. He told me not to think of such a thing, as he would give me all that was needful, both for myself and my men; but if I would have patience, he would collect all his officers, and the next morning would see what their opinions were on the subject.

5th. – I found that every one of Mahamed's men was against our going to Gondokoro. They told me, in fact, with one voice, that it was quite impossible; but they said, if I liked they would furnish me guides to escort me on ten marches to a depot at the further end of the Madi country, and if I chose to wait there un-til they could collect all their ivory tusks together and join us, we would be a united party too formidable to be resisted by the Bari people. This offer of immediate guides I of course accept-ed at once, as to keep on the move was my only desire at that time; for my men were all drunk, and Kidgwiga's were desert-ing. Once more on the way, I did not despair of reaching Gon-dokoro by myself. In the best good-humour now, I showed Mahamed our picture-books: and as he said he always drilled his two hundred men every Friday, I said I would, if he liked, command them myself. This being agreed to, all the men turned out in their best, and, to my surprise, they not only knew the Turkish words of command, but manoeuvred with some show of good training; though, as might have been expected with men of this ragamuffin stamp, all the privates gave orders as well as their captains.

When the review was over, I complimented Mahamed on the efficiency of his corps, and, retiring to my hut, as I thought I had him now in a good-humour, again discussed our plans for going ahead the next day. Scarcely able to look me in the face, the humbugging scoundrel said he could not think of allowing me to go on without him, for if any accident happened he would be blamed for it. At the same time, he could not move for a few days, as he expected a party of men to arrive about the next new moon with ivory. My hurry he thought was uncalled for; for, as I had spent so many days with Kamrasi, why could I not be content to do so with him? I was provoked beyond measure with this, as it upset all my plans. Kidgwiga's men were deserting, and I feared I should not be able to keep my promise to Kamrasi of sending him another white visitor, who would perhaps do what I had left undone, when I did not follow up the connection of the Little Luta Nzige with the Nile. We battled away again, and then Mahamed said there was not one man in his camp who would go with me until their crops were cut and taken in; for whilst residing here they grew grain for their support. We battled again, and Mahamed at last, out of patience himself, said, "Just look here, what a fix I am in," showing me a hut full of ivory. "Who," he said, "is to carry all this until the natives have got in their crops?" This, I said, so far as I was concerned, was all nonsense. I merely had asked him for a guide and interpreter, for go I must. In a huff he then absconded; and my men – those of them who were not too drunk – came and said to me, "For Godsake let us stop here. Mahamed says the road is too dangerous for us to go alone; he has promised to carry all our loads for us if we stop; and all Kamrasi's men are running away, because they are afraid to go on."

6th. – Next morning I called Kidgwiga, and begged him to procure two men as guides and interpreters. He said he could not find any. I then went at Mahamed again, who first said he would give me the two men I wanted, then went off, and sent word to say he would not be visible for three days. This was too much for my patience, so I ordered all my things to be tied up in marching order, and gave out that I should leave and find out the way myself the following morning. Like an evil spirit stirred up, my preparations for going no sooner were heard of than Mahamed appeared again, and after a long and sharp contest in words, he promised us guides if I would consent to write him a note, testifying that my going was against his expressed desire.

This was done; but the next morning (7th), after our things were put out for the march, all Kidgwiga's men bolted, and no guides would take service with us. It was now obvious that, even supposing I succeeded in taking Kidgwiga to Gondokoro, he would not have a sufficient escort to come back with, unless, indeed, it happened that Englishmen might be there who might wish to carry out my investigations by penetrating to the Little Luta Nzige, and to pay a visit to Kamrasi. I therefore called

Kidgwiga, and after explaining these circumstances, advised him to go back to Kamrasi. He was loth to leave, he said, until his commission was fully performed; but as I thought it advisable, he would consent. I then gave him a double gun and ammunition, as well as some very rich beads which I obtained from Mahamed's stores, to take back to Kamrasi, with orders to say that, as soon as I reached Gondokoro or Khartum, I would send another white man to him – not by the way I had come through Kidi, but by the left bank of the Nile: to which Kidgwiga replied, "That will do famously, for Kamrasi will change his residence soon, and come on the Nile this side of Rionga's palace, in order that he may cut in between his brother and the Turks' guns." After this, I gave a lot of rich beads to Kidgwiga for himself, and a lot also for the senior officers at the Chopi and Kamrasi's palaces, and sent the whole set off as happy as birds. When these men were gone, I tried to get up an elephant-shooting excursion due west of this, with a view to see where the Nile was, for I would not believe it was very far off, although no one as yet, since I left Chopi, either would or could tell me where the stream had gone to.

8th. Mahamed professed to be delighted I had made up my mind to such a scheme. He called the heads of the villages to give me all the information I sought for, and went with me to the top of a high rock, from which we could see the hills I first viewed at Chopi, sweeping round from south by east to north, which demarked the line of the Asua river. The Nile at that moment was, I believed, not very far off; yet, do or say what I would, everybody said it was fifteen marches off, and could not be visited under a month.[1] It would be necessary for me to take thirty-six of Mahamed's men, besides all my own, to go there, which, he said, I was welcome to, but I should have to pay them for their services. This was a damper at once.

I knew in my mind all these reports were false, but, rather than be out of the way when the time came for marching, I agreed to wait patiently, write the history of the Wahuma, and make collections, till Mahamed was ready, trusting that I might find some one at Gondokoro who would finish what I had left undone; or else, after arriving there, I might go up the Nile in boats and see for myself. The same evening I was attracted by the sound of drums to a neighbouring village, where, by the moonlight, I found the natives were dancing. A more indecent or savage spectacle I never witnessed. The whole place was alive with naked humanity in a state of constant motion. Drawing near, I found that a number of drums were beaten by men in the centre. Next to them was a deep ring of women, half of whom carried their babies; and outside these again was a still deeper circle of men, some blowing horns, but most holding their spears erect. To the sound of the music both these rings of the opposite sexes kept jumping and sidling round and round the drummers, making the most grotesque and obscene motions to one another.

9th to 14th. – Nothing of material consequence happened until the 14th, when eighty of Rionga's men brought in two slaves and thirty tusks of ivory, as a present to Mahamed. Of course, I knew this was a bribe to induce Mahamed to fight with Rionga against Kamrasi; but, counting that no affair of mine, I tried to induce these men to give me some geographical information of the countries they had just left. Not one of them would come near me, for they knew I was friends with Kamrasi; and Mahamed's men, when they saw mine attempting to converse with them, abused them for "prying into other men's concerns." "These men," they said, "are our friends, and not yours; if we choose to give them presents of cloth and beads, and they give us a return in ivory, what is that to you?" Mysterious Mahamed next came to me, and begged for a blanket, as he said he was going off for a few days to a depot where he had some ivory; and he also wanted to borrow a musket, as one of his had been burnt.

My suspicions and even apprehensions, were now greatly excited. I began to think he had prevailed on me to stop here, that I might hold the place whilst he went to fight Kamrasi with Rionga's men; so I begged him to listen to my advice, and not attempt to cross the Nile, "else," I said, "all his guns would be taken from him, and his passage back cut off." At once he saw the drift of my thought, and said he was not going towards the Nile, but on the contrary, he was going with Rionga's men in the opposite direction, to a place called Paira. "If that is the case," I said, "why do you want a gun?" "Because there are some other matters to settle. I shall not be long away, and my men will take care of you whilst I am gone." I gave him the blanket after this, but was too suspicious of his object to lend him a gun.

15th to 20th. – I saw Mahamed march his regiment out of the place, drums and fifes playing, colours flying, a hundred guns firing, officers riding – some of them on donkeys and others – yes, actually on cows! – whilst a host of the natives, Rionga's men included, carrying spears and bows and arrows, looked little like a peaceful caravan of merchants, but very much resem-

bled a band of marauders. After this I heard they were not going to Rionga himself, but were going to show Rionga's men the
way that they made friends with old Chongi of Koki. In reality,
Chongi had invited Mahamed to fight against an enemy of his,
in whose territories immense stores of ivory were said to be
buried, and the people had an endless number of cattle – for
they lived by plunder, and had lifted most of old Chongi's; and
this was the service on which the expedition had set off.

21st to 31st. – I had constantly wondered, ever since I first
came here, and saw the brutal manner in which the Turks treated the natives, that these Madi people could submit to their
"Egyptian taskmasters," and therefore was not surprised now to
find them pull down their huts and march off with the materi-
als to a distant site. Every day this sort of migration continued,
just as you see in the picture; and nothing more important occurred until Christmas-day, when an armadillo was caught, and
I heard from Mahamed's head wife that the Turks had plundered and burnt down three villages, and in all probability they
would return shortly laden with ivory. This was a true anticipation; for, on the 31st, Mahamed came in with his triumphant
army laden with ivory, and driving in five slave-girls and thirty
head of cattle.

1st to 3d. – I now wished to go on with the journey, as I
could get no true information out of the suspicious blackguards
who called themselves Turks; but Mahamed postponed it until
the 5th, by which time he said he would be able to collect all
the men he wanted to carry his ivory. Rionga's men then departed, and Mahamed showed some signs of getting ready by
ordering one dozen cows to be killed, the flesh of which was to

be divided amongst those villagers who would carry his ivory, and the skins to be cut into thongs for binding the smaller tusks of ivory together in suitable loads.

4th and 5th. – Another specimen of Turkish barbarity came under my notice, in the head man of a village bringing a large tusk of ivory to Mahamed, to ransom his daughter with; for she had been seized as a slave on his last expedition, in common with others who could not run away fast enough to save themselves from the Turks. Fortunately for both, it was thought necessary for the Turks to keep on good terms with the father as an influential man; and therefore, on receiving the tusk, Mahamed gave back the girl, and added a cow to seal their friendship.

6th to 10th. – I saw this land-pirate Mahamed take a blackmail like a negro chief. Some men who had fled from their village when Mahamed's plundering party passed by them the other day, surprised that he did not stop to sack their homes, now brought ten large tusks of ivory to him to express the gratitude they said they felt for his not having molested them. Mahamed, on finding how easy it was to get taxes in this fashion, instead of thanking them, assumed the air of the great potentate, whose clemency was abused, and told the poor creatures that, though they had done well in seeking his friendship, they had not sufficiently considered his dignity, else they would have brought double that number of tusks, for it was impossible he could be satisfied at so low a price. "What," said these poor creatures, "can we do then? for this is all we have got." "Oh," says Mahamed, "if it is all you have got now in store, I will take these few for the present; but when I return from Gondokoro, I expect you will bring me just as many more. Good-bye, and look out for yourselves." Tired beyond all measure with Mahamed's procrastination, as I could not get him to start, I now started myself, much to his disgust, and went ahead again, leaving word that I would wait for him at the next place, provided he did not delay more than one day. The march led us over long rolling downs of grass, where we saw a good many antelopes feeding; and after going ten miles, we came, among other villages, to one named Panyoro, in which we found it convenient to put up. At first all the villagers, thinking us Turks, bolted away with their cattle and what stores they could carry; but, after finding out who we were, they returned again, and gave us a good reception, helping us to rig up a shed with grass, and bringing a cow and some milk for our dinner.

12th. – To-day I went out shooting, but though I saw and fired at a rhinoceros, as well as many varieties of antelopes, I did not succeed in killing one head. All my men were surprised as well as myself; and the villagers who were escorting me in the hope of getting flesh, were so annoyed at their disappointment, they offered to cut my fore-finger with a spear and spit on it for good-luck. Joining in their talk, I told them the powder must be crooked; but, on inspecting my rifle closer, I found that the sights had been knocked on one side a little, and this created a general laugh at all in turn. Going home from the shooting, I found all the villagers bolting again with their cattle and stores, and, on looking towards Faloro, saw a party of Turks coming.

As well as I could I reassured the villagers, and brought them back again, when they said to me, "Oh, what have you done? We were so happy yesterday when we found out who you were, but now we see you have brought those men, all our hearts have sunk again; for they beat us, they make us carry their loads, and they rob us in such a manner, we know not what to do." I told them I would protect them if they would keep quiet; and, when the Turks came, I told them what I had said to the head man. They were the vanguard of Mahamed's party, and said they had orders to march on as far as Apuddo with me, where we must all stop for Mahamed, who, as well as he could, was collecting men. There was a certain tree near Apuddo which was marked by an Englishman two years ago, and this, Mahamed thought, would keep us amused.

The next march brought us to Paira, a collection of villages within sight of the Nile. It was truly ridiculous; here had we been at Faloro so long, and yet could not make out what had become of the Nile. In appearance it was a noble stream, flowing on a flat bed from west to east, and immediately beyond it were the Jbl (hills) Kuku, rising up to a height of 2,000 feet above the river. Still we could not make out all, until the following day, when we made a march parallel to the Nile, and arrived at Jaifi.

This was a collection of huts close to a deep nullah which drains The central portions of Eastern Madi. At this place the Turks killed a crocodile and ate him on the spot, much to the amusement of my men, who immediately shook their heads, laughingly, and said, "Ewa, Allah! Are these men, then, Mussulmans? Savages in our country don't much like a crocodile." After crossing two nullahs, we reached Apuddo, and at once, I went to see the tree said to have been cut by an Englishman some time before. There, sure enough, was a mark, something like the letters M. I., on its bark, but not distinct enough to be

692

ascertained, because the bark had healed up. In describing the individual who had done this, the Turks said he was exactly like myself, for he had a long beard, and a voice even much resembling mine. He came thus far with Mahamed from Gondokoro two years ago, and then returned, because he was alarmed at the accounts the people gave of the countries to the southward, and he did not like the prospect of having to remain a whole rainy season with Mahamed at Faloro. He knew we were endeavouring to come this way, and directed Mahamed to point out his name if we did so.

We took up our quarters in the village as usual, but the Turks remained outside, and carried off all the tops of the villagers' huts to make a camp for themselves. I rebuked them for doing so, but was mildly told they had no huts of their own. They carried no pots either for cooking their dinners, and therefore took from the villagers all that they wanted. It was a fixed custom now, they told us, and there was no use in our trying to struggle against it. If the natives were wise, they would make enough to sell; but as they would not, they must put up with their lot; for the "government" cannot be baulked of its ivory. Truly there seemed to be nothing but misery here; food was so scarce the villagers sought for wild berries and fruits; whilst the Turks helped themselves out of their half-filled bins – a small reserve store to last up to the far-distant harvest. Then, to make matters worse, all the village chiefs were at war with one another.

At night a party of warriors walked round our village, but feared to attack it because we were inside. Next morning the villagers turned out and killed two of the enemy; but the rest, whilst retreating, sang out that they would not attempt to fight until "the guns" were gone – after that, the villagers had better look out for themselves. I now proposed going on if the Apina, or chief of the village, would give me a guide; but he feared to do so lest I should come to grief, and Mahamed would then be down upon him. Struggling was useless, for I had no beads to pay my way with, and my cows were now all finished; so I took the matter quietly, and went out foraging with the rifle.

18th and 19th. – Antelopes were numerous, but so wild I could not get near them. On bending round homewards, however, three buffaloes, feeding in the distance, on the top of a roll of high ground beyond where we stood, were observed by the natives, who had flocked out in the hopes of getting flesh. To stalk them, I went up wind to near where I expected to find them; then bidding the natives lie down, I stole along through the grass until at last I saw three pairs of horns glistening quite close in front of me. Anxious lest they should take sudden fright, I gently raised myself, wishing to fire, but I was quite puzzled; there was no mistake about what they were; still, look from as high as I would, I could not see their bodies. The thought never struck me they were lying down in such open ground in the day-time; so, as I could not go closer without driving them off, I took a shot with my single rifle at where I judged the chest of the nearest one ought to be, and then discovered my error. In an instant all three sprang on their legs and scampered off. I began loading, but before I had half accomplished my object, those three had mingled with the three previously seen grazing, and all six together came charging straight at me. I really thought I should now catch a toss, if I were not trampled to death; but suddenly, as they saw me standing, whether from fear or what else I cannot say, they changed their ferocious-looking design, swerved round, and galloped off as fast as their legs could carry them. This was bad luck; but Grant made up for it the next day by killing a very fine buck nsamma.

20th. – I went again after the herd of six buffaloes, as I thought one was wounded, and after walking up a long sloping hill for three miles towards the east, I found myself at once in view of the Nile on one hand, and the long-heard-of Asua river on the other, backed by hills even higher than the Jbl Kuku. The bed of the Asua seemed very large, but, being far off, was not very distinct, nor did I care to go and see it them; for at that moment, straight in front of me, five buffaloes, five giraffes, two eland and sundry other antelopes, were too strong a temptation.

The place looked like a park, and I began stalking in it, first at the eland, as I wanted to see if they corresponded with those I shot in Usagara; but the gawky giraffes, always in the way, gave the alarm, and drove all but two of the buffaloes away. At these two I now went with my only rifle, leaving the servants and savages behind. They were out in the open grass feeding composedly, so that I stole up to within forty yards of them, and then, in a small naked patch of ground, I waited my opportunity, and put a ball behind the shoulder of the larger one. At the sound of the gun, in an instant both bulls charged, but they pulled up in the same naked ground as myself, sniffing and tossing their horns, while looking out for their antagonist, who, as quick as themselves, had thrown himself flat on the ground.

There we were, like three fools, for twenty minutes or so; one of the buffaloes bleeding at the mouth and with a broken hind-leg, for the bullet had traversed his body, and the other turning round and round looking out for me, while I was anxiously watching him, and by degrees loading my gun. When ready, I tried a shot at the sound one, but the cap snapped and nearly betrayed me, for they both stared at the spot where I lay – the sound one sniffing the air and tossing his horns, but the other bleeding considerably. Some minutes more passed in this manner, when they allowed me to breathe freer by walking away. I followed, of course, but could not get a good chance; so, as the night set in, I let them alone for the time being, to get out the following morning.

21st and 22d. – At the place where I left off, I now sprang a large herd of fifty or more buffaloes, and followed them for a mile, when the wounded one, quite exhausted from the fatigue, pulled up for a charge, and allowed me to knock him over. This was glorious fun for the villagers, who cut him up on the spot and brought him home. Of course, one half the flesh was given to them, in return for which they brought us some small delicacies to show their gratitude; for, as they truly remarked, until we came to their village they never knew what it was to get a present, or any other gift by a good thrashing.

23d. – To-day I tried the ground again, and, whilst walking up the hill, two black rhinoceros came trotting towards us in a very excited manner. I did not wish to fire at them, as what few bullets remained in my store I wished to reserve in better sport, and therefore for the time being, let them alone. Presently, however, they separated; one passed in front of us, stopped to drink in a pool, and then lay down in it. Not heeding him, I walked up the hill, whilst the other rhinoceros, still trotting, suddenly turned round and came to drink within fifty yards of us, obstructing my path; this was too much of a joke; so, to save time, I gave him a bullet, and knocked him over. To my surprise, the natives who were with me would not touch his flesh, though pressed by me to "n'yam n'yam," or to eat. I found that they considered him an unclean beast; so, regretting I had wasted my bullet, I went farther on and startled some buffaloes.

Though I got very near them, however, a small antelope springing up in front of me scared them away, and I could not get a front shot at any of them. Thus the whole day was thrown away, for I had to return empty-handed.

24th to 30th. – Grant and I after this kept our pot boiling by shooting three more antelopes; but nothing of consequence transpired until the 30th, when Bukhet, Mahamed's factotum, arrived with the greater part of the Turk's property. He then confirmed a report we had heard before, that, some days previously, Mahamed had ordered Bukhet to go ahead and join us, which he attempted to do; but, on arrival at Panyoro, his party had a row with the villagers, and lost their property. Bukhet then returned to Mahamed and reported his defeat and losses; upon hearing which, Mahamed at once said to him, "What do you mean by returning to me empty-handed? Go back at once and recover your things else how can I make my report at Gondokoro?" With these peremptory orders Bukhet went back to Panyoro, and commenced to attack it. The contest did not last long; for, after three of Bukhet's men had been wounded, he set fire to the villages, killed fifteen of the natives, and, besides recovering his own lost property, took one hundred cows.

31st. – To-day Mahamed came in, and commenced to arrange for the march onwards. This, however, was no easy matter, for the Turks alone required six hundred porters – half that number to carry their ivory, and the other half to carry their beds and bedding; whilst from fifty to sixty men was the most a village had to spare, and all the village chiefs were at enmity with one another. The plan adopted by Mahamed was, to summon the heads of all the villages to come to him, failing which, he would seize all their belongings. Then, having once got them together, he ordered them all to furnish him with so many porters a-head, saying he demanded it of them, for the "great government's property" could not be left on the ground. Their separate interests must now be sacrificed, and their feuds suspended: and if he heard, on his return again, that one village had taken advantage of the other's weakness caused by their employment in his service, he would then not spare his bullets – so they might look out for themselves.

Some of the Turks, having found ninty-nine eggs in a crocodile's nest, had a grand feast. They gave us two of the eggs, which we ate, but did not like, for they had a highly musky flavour.

1st. – On the 1st of February we went ahead again, with Bukhet and the first half of Mahamed's establishment, as a sufficient number of men could not be collected at once to move all together. In a little while we struck on the Nile, where it was running like a fine Highland stream between the gneiss and mica-schist hills of Kuku, and followed it down to near where the Asua river joined it. For a while we sat here watching the water, which was greatly discoloured, and floating down rushes. The river was not as full as it was when we crossed it at the Karuma Falls, yet, according to Dr. Khoblecher's[2] account, it ought to

The Nile and the Kuku mountains.

have been flooding just at this time: if so, we had beaten the stream. Here we left it again as it arched round by the west, and forded the Asua river, a stiff rocky stream, deep enough to reach the breast when waded, but not very broad. It did not appear to me as if connected with Victoria N'yanza, as the waters were falling, and not much discoloured; whereas judging from the Nile's condition, it ought to have been rising. No vessel ever could have gone up it, and it bore no comparison with the Nile itself. The exaggerated account of its volume, however, given by the expeditionists who were sent up the Nile by Mehemet Ali, did not surprise us, since they had mistaken its position; for we were now 3° 42' north, and therefore had passed their "farthest point" by twenty miles.

In two hours more we reached a settlement called Madi, and found it deserted. Every man and woman had run off into the jungles from fright, and would not come back again. We wished ourselves at the end of the journey; thought anything better than this kind of existence – living entirely at the expense of others; even the fleecings in Usui felt less dispiriting; but it could not be helped, for it must always exist as long as these Turks are allowed to ride rough-shod over the people. The Turks, however, had their losses also; for on the way four Bari men and one Bari slave-girl slipped off with a hundred of their plundered cattle, and neither they nor the cattle could be found again. Mijalwa was here convicted of having stolen the cloth of a Turk whilst living in his hut when he was away at the Paira plundering and got fifty lashes to teach him better behaviour for the future.

A party of fifty men came from Labure, a station on ahead of this, to take service as porters, knowing that at this season the

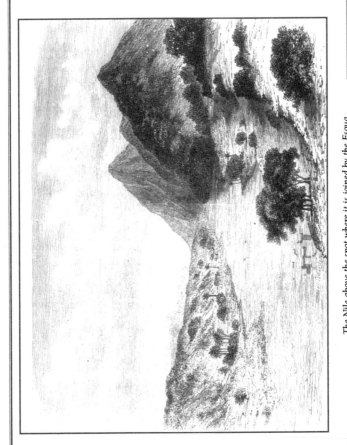

The Nile above the spot where it is joined by the Esoua.

Turks always come with a large herd of plundered cattle, which they call government property, and give in payment to the men who carry their tusks of ivory across the Bari country.

We now marched over a rolling ground, covered in some places with bush-jungle, in others with villages, where there were fine trees, resembling oaks in their outward appearance; and stopping one night at the settlement of Barwudi, arrived at Labure, where we had to halt a day for Mahamed to collect some ivory from a depot he had formed near by. We heard there was another ivory party collecting tusks at Obbo, a settlement in the country of Panuquara, twenty miles east of this.

Next we crossed a nullah draining into the Nile, and, travelling over more rolling ground, flanked on the right by a range of small hills, put up at the Madi frontier station, Mugi, where we had to halt two days to collect a full complement of porters to traverse the Bari country, the people of which are denounced as barbarians by the Turks, because they will not submit to be bullied into carrying their tusks for them. Here we felt an earthquake. The people would not take beads, preferring, they said, to make necklaces and belts out of ostrich-eggs, which they cut into the size of small shirt-buttons, and then drill a hole through their centre to string them together. A passenger told us that three white men had just arrived in vessels at Gondokoro; and the Bari people, hearing of our advance, instead of trying to kill us with spears, had determined to poison all the water in their country. Mahamed now disposed of half of his herd of cows, giving them to the chiefs of the villages in return for porters. These, he said, were all that belonged to the government; for the half of all captures of cows, as well as all slaves, all goats, and sheep, were allowed to the men as part of their pay.

When all was settled we marched, one thousand strong, to Wurungi; and next day, by a double march, arrived at Marson, in the Bari country. I wished still to put up in the native villages, but Mahamed so terrified all my men, by saying these Bari would kill us in the night if we did not all sleep together in one large camp, that we were obliged to submit. The country, still flanked on the right by hills, was undulating and very prettily wooded. Villages were numerous, but as we passed them the inhabitants all fled from us, save a few men, who, bolder than the rest, would stand and look on at us as we marched along. Both night and morning the Turks beat their drums; and whenever they stopped to eat they sacked the villages.

Pushing on by degrees, stopping at noon to eat, we came again in sight of the Nile, and put up at a station called Doro, within a short distance of the well-known hill Rijeb, where Nile voyagers delight in cutting their names. The country continued the same, but the grass was conspicuously becoming shorter and finer every day – so much so, that my men all declared it was a sign of our near approach to England. After we had settled down for the night, and the Turks had finished plundering the nearest villages, we heard two guns fired, and immediately afterwards the whole place was alive with Bari people. Their drums were beaten as a sign that they would attack us, and the war-drums of the villages around responded by beating also. The Turks grew somewhat alarmed at this, and as darkness began to set in, sent out patrols in addition to their nightly watches. The savages next tried to steal in on us, but were soon frightened off by the patrols cocking their guns. Then, seeing themselves defeated in that tactic, they collected in hundreds in front of us, set fire to the grass, and marched up and down, brandishing ignited grass in their hands, howling like demons, and swearing they would annihilate us in the morning.

We slept the night out, nevertheless, and next morning walked in to Gondokoro, N. Lat. 4° 54' 5", and E. long. 31° 46' 9", where Mahamed, after firing a salute, took us in to see a Circassian merchant, named Kurshid Agha. Our first inquiry was, of course, for Petherick. A mysterious silence ensued; we were informed that Mr. Debono was THE man we had to thank for the assistance we had received in coming from Madi; and then in hot haste, after warm exchanges of greeting with Mahamed's friend, who was Debono's agent here, we took leave, to hunt up Petherick. Walking down the bank of the river – where a line of vessels was moored, and on the right hand a few sheds, one-half broken down, with a brick-built house representing the late Austrian Church Mission establishment – we saw hurrying on towards us the form of an Englishman, who, for one moment, we believed was the Simon Pure; but the next moment my old friend Baker, famed for his sports in Ceylon, seized me by the hand. A little boy of his establishment had reported our arrival, and he in an instant came out to welcome us. What joy this was I can hardly tell. We could not talk fast enough, so overwhelmed were we both to meet again. Of course we were his guests in a moment, and learned everything that could be told. I now first heard of the death of H.R.H. the Prince-Consort, which made me reflect on the inspiring words he made use of, in compliment to myself, when I was introduced to him by Sir Roderick

View of Gondokoro.

Murchison, a short while before leaving England. Then there was the terrible war in America, and other events of less startling nature, which came on us all by surprise, as years had now passed since we had received news from the civilised world.

Baker then said he had come up with three vessels – one dyabir and two nuggers – fully equipped with armed men, camels, horses, donkeys, beads, brass wire, and everything necessary for a long journey, expressly to look after us, hoping, as he jokingly said, to find us on the equator in some terrible fix, that he might have the pleasure of helping us out of it. He had heard of Mahamed's party, and was actually waiting for him to come in, that he might have had the use of his return-men to start with comfortably. Three Dutch ladies[3], also, with a view to assist us in the same way as Baker (God bless them), had come here in a steamer, but were driven back to Khartum by sickness. Nobody had even dreamt for a moment it was possible we could come through. An Italian, named Miani, had gone farther up the Nile than any one else; and he, it now transpired, was the man who had cut his name on the tree by Apuddo. But what had become of Petherick? He was actually trading at N'yambara, seventy miles due west of this, though he had, since I left him in England, raised a subscription of $1,000, from those of my friends to whom this Journal is most respectfully dedicated as the smallest return a grateful heart can give for their attempt to succour me, when knowing the fate of the expedition was in great jeopardy.

Instead of coming up the Nile at once, as Petherick might have done – so I was assured – he waited, whilst a vessel was building, until the season had too far advanced to enable him to sail up the river. In short, he lost the north winds at 7° north, and went overland to his trading depot at N'yambara. Previously, however, he had sent some boats up to this, under a Vakil, who had his orders to cross to his trading depot at N'yambara, and to work from his trading station due south, ostensibly with a view to look after me, though contrary to my advice before leaving him in England, in opposition to his own proposed views of assisting me when he applied for help to succour me, and against the strongly-expressed opinions of every European in the same trade as himself; for all alike said they knew he would have gone to Faloro, and pushed south from that place, had his trade on the west of the Nile not attracted him there.

Baker now offered me his boats to go down to Khartum, and asked me if there was anything left undone which it might be of importance for him to go on and complete, by survey or otherwise; for, although he should like to go down the river with us, he did not wish to return home without having done something to recompense him for the trouble and expense he had incurred in getting up his large expedition. Of course I told him how disappointed I had been in not getting a sight of the Little Luta Nzige. I described how we had seen the Nile bending west where we crossed in Chopi, and then, after walking down the chord of an arc described by the river, had found it again in Madi coming from the west, whence to the south, and as far at least as Koshi, it was said to be navigable, probably continuing to be so right into the Little Luta Nzige. Should this be the case, then, by building boats in Madi above the cataracts, a vast region might be thrown open to the improving influences of navigation. Further, I told Baker of my contract with Kamrasi, and of the property I had left behind, with a view to stimulate any enterprising man who might be found at this place to go there, make good my promise, and, if found needful, claim my share of the things, for the better prosecution of his own travels there.

This Baker at once undertook, though he said he did not want my property; and I drew out suggestions for him how to proceed. He then made friends with Mahamed, who promised to help him on to Faloro, and I gave Mahamed and his men three carbines as an honorarium.

I should now have gone down the Nile at once if the moon had been in "distance" for fixing the longitude; but as it was not, I had to remain until the 26th, living with Baker. Kurshid Agha became very great friends with us, and, at once making a present of a turkey, a case of wine, and cigars, said he was only sorry for his own sake that we had found a fellow-countryman, else he would have had the envied honour of claiming us as his guests, and had the pleasure of transporting us in his vessels down to Khartum.

The Rev. Mr. Moorlan, and two other priests of the Austrian Mission, were here on a visit from their station at Kich, to see the old place again before they left for Khartum; for the Austrian Government, discouraged by the failure of so many years, had ordered the recall of the whole of the establishment for these regions. It was no wonder these men were recalled; for, out of twenty missionaries who, during the last thirteen years, had ascended the White river for the purpose of propagating the Gospel, thirteen had died of fever, two of dysentary, and two had retired broken in health, yet not one convert had been made by them.

The fact is, there was no government to control the population or to protect property; boys came to them, looked at their pictures, and even showed a disposition to be instructed, but there it ended; they had no heart to study when no visible returns were to be gained. One day the people would examine the books, at another throw them aside, say their stomachs were empty, and run away to look for food. The Bari people at Gondokoro were described as being more tractable than those of Kich, being of a braver and more noble nature; but they were all half-starved – not because the country was too poor to produce, but because they were too lazy to cultivate. What little corn they grew they consumed before it was fully ripe, and then either sought for fish in the river or fed on tortoises in the interior, as they feared they might never reap what they sowed.

The missionaries never had occasion to complain of these blacks, and to this day they would doubtless have been kindly inclined to Europeans, had the White Nile traders not brought the devil amongst them. Mr. Moorlan remembers the time when they brought food for sale; but now, instead, they turn their backs upon all foreigners, and even abuse the missionaries for having been the precursors of such dire calamities. The shell of the brick church at Gondokoro, and the cross on the top of a native-built hut in Kich, are all that will remain to bear testimony of these Christian exertions to improve the condition of these heathens. Want of employment, I heard was the chief operative cause in killing the poor missionaries; for, with no other resource left them to kill time, they spent their days eating, drinking, smoking, and sleeping, till they broke down their constitutions by living too fast.

Mr. Moorlan became very friendly, and said he was sorry he could not do more for us. His headquarters were at Kich, some way down the river, where, as we passed, he hoped at least he might be able to show us as much attention and hospitality as lay in his power. Mosquitoes were said to be extremely troublesome on the river, and my men begged for some clothes, as Petherick, they said, had a store for me under the charge of his Vakil. The storekeeper was then called, and confirming the story of my men, I begged him to give me what was my own. It then turned out that it was all Petherick's, but he had orders to give me on account anything that I wanted. This being settled, I took ninety-five yards of the commonest stuff as a makeshift for mosquito-curtains for my men, besides four sailor's shirts for my head men.

On the 18th, Kurshid Agha was summoned by the constant fire of musketry, a mile or two down the river, and went off in his vessels to the relief. A party of his had come across from the N'yambara country with ivory, and on the banks of the Nile, a few miles north of this, were engaged fighting with the natives. He arrived just in time to settle the difficulty, and next day came back again, having shot some of the enemy and captured their cows. Petherick, we heard, was in a difficulty of the same kind, upon which I proposed to go down with Baker and Grant to succour him; but he arrived in time, in company with his wife and Dr. James Murie, to save us the trouble, and told me he had brought a number of men with him, carrying ivory, for the purpose now of looking after me on the east bank of the Nile, by following its course up to the south, though he had given up all hope of seeing me, as a report had reached him of the desertion

Mohammed's Turks.

of my porters at Ugogo. He then offered me his dyabir, as well as anything else that I wanted that lay within his power to give. Suffice it to say, I had, through Baker's generosity, at that very moment enough and to spare; but at his urgent request I took a few more yards of cloth for my men, and some cooking fat; and, though I offered to pay for it, he declined to accept any return at my hands.

Though I naturally felt much annoyed at Petherick – for I had hurried away from Uganda, and separated from Grant at Kari, solely to keep faith with him – I did not wish to break friendship, but dined and conversed with him, when it transpired that his Vakil, or agent, who went south from the N'yambara station, came amongst the N'yam N'yam, and heard from them that a large river, four days' journey more to the southward, was flowing from east to west, beyond which lived a tribe of "women," who, when they wanted to marry, mingled with them in the stream and returned; and then, again, beyond this tribe of women there lived another tribe of women and dogs. Now, this may all seem a very strange story to those who do not know the negro's and Arab's modes of expression; but to me it at once came very natural, and, according to my view, could be interpreted thus: The river, running from east to west, according to the native mode of expressing direction, could be nothing but the Little Luta Nzige running the opposite way, according to fact and our mode of expression. The first tribe of women were doubtless the Wanyoro – called women by the naked tribes on this side because they wear bark coverings – an effeminate appendage, in the naked man's estimation; and the second tribe must have been in allusion to the dog-keeping Waganda, who also would be considered women, as they wear bark clothes. In my turn, I told Petherick he had missed a good thing by not going up the river to look for me; for, had he done so, he would not only have had the best ivory-grounds to work upon, but, by building a vessel in Madi above the cataracts, he would have had, in my belief, some hundred miles of navigable water to transport his merchandise. In short, his succouring petition was most admirably framed, had he stuck to it, for the welfare of both of us.[4] We now received our first letters from home, and in one from Sir Roderick Murchison I found the Royal Geographical Society had awarded me their "founder's medal" for the discovery of the Victoria N'yanza in 1858.

1) It will appear shortly that it was actually not more than two marches to the northward of Faloro.

2) Dr. Khoblecher, the founder of the Austrian Church Mission Establishment of Gondokoro, ascertained that the Nile reached its lowest level there in the middle of January.

3) The Baroness Miss A. van Capellan, and Mrs and Miss Tinne.

4) See Petherick's succouring petition, addressed to the Right Hon. Lord Ashburton, President of the Royal Geographical Society, in the Proceedings of that Society, date 10th June 1860.

My journey down to Alexandria was not without adventure, and carried me through scenes which, in other circumstances, it might have been worth while to describe. Thinking, however, that I have already sufficiently trespassed on the patience of the reader, I am unwilling to overload my volume with any matter that does not directly relate to the solution of the great problem which I went to solve. Having now, then, after a period of twenty-eight months, come upon the tracks of European travellers, and met them face to face, I close my Journal, to conclude with a few explanations, for the purpose of comparing the various branches of the Nile with its affluences, so as to show their respective values.

The first affluent, the Bahr el Ghazal, took us by surprise; for instead of finding a huge lake, as described in our maps, at an elbow of the Nile, we found only a small piece of water resembling a duck-pond buried in a sea of rushes. The old Nile swept through it with majestic grace, and carried us next to the Geraffe branch of the Sobat river, the second affluent, which we found flowing into the Nile with a graceful semicircular sweep and good stiff current, apparently deep, but not more than fifty yards broad.

Next in order came the main stream of the Sobat, flowing into the Nile in the same graceful way as the Geraffe, which in breadth it surpassed, but in velocity of current was inferior. The Nile by these additions was greatly increased; still it did not assume that noble appearance which astonished us so much, immediately after the rainy season, when we were navigating it in canoes in Unyoro.

I here took my last lunar observations, and made its mouth N. lat. 9° 20' 48", E. long. 31° 24' 0". The Sobat has a third mouth farther down the Nile, which unfortunately was passed without my knowing it; but as it is so well known to be unimportant, the loss was not great.

Next to be treated of is the famous Blue Nile, which we found a miserable river, even when compared with the Geraffe branch of the Sobat. It is very broad at the mouth, it is true, but so shallow that our vessel with difficulty was able to come up it. It has all the appearance of a mountain stream, subject to great periodical fluctuations. I was never more disappointed that with this river; if the White river was cut off from it, its waters would all be absorbed before they could reach Lower Egypt.

The Atbara river, which is the last affluent, was more like the Blue river than any of the other affluences, being decidedly a mountain stream, which floods in the rains, but runs nearly dry in the dry season.

I had now seen quite enough to satisfy myself that the White river which issues from the N'yanza at the Ripon Falls, is the true or parent Nile; for in every instance of its branching, it carried the palm with it in the distinctest manner, viewed, as all the streams were by me, in the dry season, which is the best time for estimating their relative perennial values.

Since returning to England, Dr. Murie, who was with me at Gondokoro, has also come home; and he, judging from my account of the way in which we got ahead of the flooding of the Nile between the Karuma Falls and Gondokoro, is of opinion that the Little Luta Nzige must be a great backwater to the Nile, which the waters of the Nile must have been occupied in filling during my residence in Madi; and then about the same time that I set out from Madi, the Little Luta Nzige having been surcharged with water, the surplus began its march northwards just about the time when we started in the same direction. For myself, I believe in this opinion, as he no sooner asked me how I could account for the phenomenon I have already mentioned of the river appearing to decrease in bulk as we descended it, than I instinctively advanced his own theory. Moreover, the same hypothesis will answer for the sluggish flooding of the Nile down to Egypt.

I hope the reader who has followed my narrative thus far will be interested in knowing how "my faithful children," for whose services I had no further occasion, and whom I had taken so far from their own country, were disposed of. At Cairo, where we put up in Shepherd's Hotel, I had the whole of them photographed, and indulged them at the public concerts, tableaux vivants, etc. By invitation, we called on the Viceroy at his Rhoda Island palace, and were much gratified with the reception; for, after hearing all our stories with marked intelligence, he most graciously offered to assist me in any other undertaking which would assist to open up and develop the interior of Africa.

I next appointed Bombay captain of the "faithfuls," and gave him three photographs of all the eighteen men and three more of the four women, to give one of each to our Consuls at Suez, Aden, and Zanzibar, by which they might be recognised. I also gave them increased wages, equal to three years' pay each, by orders on Zanzibar, which was one in addition to their time of service; an order for a grand "freeman's garden," to be purchased for them at Zanzibar; and an order that each one should receive ten dollars dowry-money as soon as he could find a wife.

With these letters in their hands, I made arrangements with our Consul, Mr. Drummond Hay, to frank them through Suez, Aden, and the Seychelles to Zanzibar.

Since then, I have heard that Captain Bombay and his party missed the Seychelles, and went on to the Mauritius, where Captain Anson, Inspector-General of Police, kindly took charge of them and made great lions of them. A subscription was raised to give them a purse of money; they were treated with tickets to the "circus," and sent back to the Seychelles, whence they were transported by steamer to Zanzibar, and taken in charge by our lately-appointed Consul, Colonel Playfair, who appears to have taken much interest in them. Further, they volunteered to go with me again, should I attempt to cross Africa from east to west, through the fertile zone.